PLATINUM EDITION

2

Series Director: Diane Larsen-Freeman

GRAMMAR DIMENSIONS

TEACHER'S EDITION

Michelle Sadlier
University of Washington

Heidi Riggenbach
University of Washington

Virginia Samuda
Sonoma State University

Heinle & Heinle
Thomson Learning

Australia • Canada • Denmark • Japan • Mexico • New Zealand
Philippines • Puerto Rico • Singapore • Spain • United Kingdom • United States

Acquisitions Editor: Eric Bredenberg
Senior Developmental Editor: Amy Lawler
Production Editor: Michael Burggren
Senior Marketing Manager: Charlotte Sturdy
Manufacturing Coordinator: Mary Beth Hennebury
Composition/Project Management: The PRD Group, Inc.
Text Design: Sue Gerould, Perspectives
Cover Design: Hannus Design Associates

Heinle & Heinle Publishers
20 Park Plaza
Boston, MA 02116

AUSTRALIA/NEW ZEALAND:
Nelson/Thomson Learning
102 Dodds Street
South Melbourne
Victoria 3205 Australia

CANADA:
Nelson/Thomson Learning
1120 Birchmount Road
Scarborough, Ontario
Canada M1K 5G4

UK/EUROPE/MIDDLE EAST:
Thomson Learning
Berkshire House
168-173 High Holborn
London, WC1V 7AA, United Kingdom

LATIN AMERICA:
Thomson Learning
Seneca, 53
Colonia Polanco
11560 México D.F. México

SPAIN:
Thomson Learning
Calle Magallanes, 25
28015-Madrid
Espana

ASIA (excluding Japan):
Thomson Learning
60 Albert Street #15-01
Albert Complex
Singapore 189969

JAPAN:
Thomson Learning
Palaceside Building, 5F
1-1-1 Hitotsubashi, Chiyoda-ku
Tokyo 100 0003, Japan

ISBN: 0-8384-0275-5

 This book is printed on acid-free recycled paper.

Printed in the United States of America
1 2 3 4 5 6 7 8 9 04 03 02 01 00

Teacher's Edition Contents

Contents

Unit 11   Modals of Necessity and Prohibition   166

Unit 12   Expressing Likes and Dislikes   184

Introduction

A Word from Diane Larsen-Freeman, Series Director

Before *Grammar Dimensions* was published, teachers would always ask me, "What is the role of grammar in a communicative approach?" These teachers recognized the importance of teaching grammar, but they associated grammar with form and communication with meaning, and thus could not see how the two easily fit together. *Grammar Dimensions* was created to help teachers and students appreciate the fact that grammar is not just about form. While grammar does indeed involve form, in order to communicate, language users also need to know the meaning of the forms and when to use them appropriately. In fact, it is sometimes not the form, but the *meaning* or *appropriate use* of a grammatical structure that represents the greatest long-term learning challenge for students. For instance, learning when it is appropriate to use the present perfect tense instead of the past tense, or being able to use two-word or phrasal verbs meaningfully, represent formidable challenges for ESL students.

The three dimensions of form, meaning, and use can be depicted in a pie chart with their interrelationship illustrated by the three arrows:

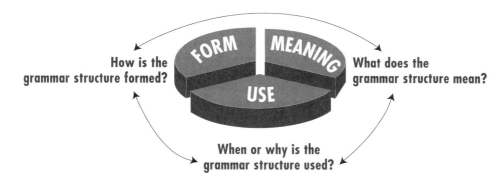

How is the grammar structure formed?

What does the grammar structure mean?

When or why is the grammar structure used?

Helping students learn to use grammatical structures accurately, meaningfully, and appropriately is the fundamental goal of *Grammar Dimensions.* It is consistent with the goal of helping students to communicate meaningfully in English, and one that recognizes the undeniable interdependence of grammar and communication.

Enjoy the Platinum Edition!

To learn more about form, meaning, and use, read *The Grammar Book: An ESL/EFL Teacher's Course,* Second Edition, by Marianne Celce-Murcia and Diane Larsen-Freeman, also from Heinle & Heinle. It helps both prospective and practicing teachers of ESL/EFL enhance their understanding of English grammar, expand their skills in linguistic analysis, and develop a pedagogical approach to teaching English grammar that builds on the three dimensions. ISBN: 0-8384-4725-2.

Welcome to Grammar Dimensions, Platinum Edition!

The most comprehensive communicative grammar series available.

Updated and revised, *Grammar Dimensions, Platinum Edition,* makes teaching grammar easy and more effective than ever. Clear grammar explanations, a wealth of exercises, lively communicative activities, technology resources, and fully annotated Teacher's Editions help both beginning and experienced teachers give their students the practice and skills they need to communicate accurately, meaningfully, and appropriately.

Grammar Dimensions, Platinum Edition is:

Communicative	• Students practice the **form, meaning,** and **use** of each grammar structure. • **Improved! A variety of communicative activities** helps students practice grammar and communication in tandem, eliciting self-expression and personalized practice. • Students learn to communicate accurately, meaningfully, and appropriately.
Comprehensive	• **Improved!** Grammar is presented in **clear charts.** • **A wealth of exercises** helps students practice and master their new language. • **The Workbook** provides extra practice and helps students prepare for the TOEFL® Test. • **Engaging listening activities** on audiocassette further reinforce the target structure. • **New! Enclosed CD-ROM** includes over 500 activities and gives students even more practice in mastering grammar and its use in language. **FREE!**
Clear	• **Improved! Simplified grammar explanations** help both students and teachers easily understand and comprehend each language structure. • **Improved! A fresh new design** makes each activity engaging. • **New! Communicative activities** ("the Purple Pages") are now labeled with the skill being practiced. • **New!** The Teacher's Edition has **page references** for the Student Book and Workbook, minimizing extra preparation time.

User Friendly for Students	• **Contextualized grammar explanations and examples** help students understand the target language. • **New! Goals** at the beginning of each unit focus students' attention on the learning they will do. • **Sample phrases and sentences** model the appropriate use of the structure.
User Friendly for Teachers	• **New!** Teacher's Edition now contains answers, tests, tape script, and complete, **step-by-step teaching suggestions** for every activity. • **New!** "Purple Page" activities are now labeled with the skill. • **Improved! A tight integration** among the Student Book, the Workbook, and the Teacher's Edition make extension activities easy to do.
Flexible	• Instructors can use the units in order or as set by their curriculum. • Exercises can be used in order or as needed by the students. • "Purple Page" activities can be used at the end of the unit or interspersed throughout the unit.
Effective	Students who learn the form, meaning, and use of each grammar structure will be able to communicate more accurately, meaningfully, and appropriately.

Grammar Dimensions, Platinum Edition

In **Grammar Dimensions, Platinum Edition,** students progress from the sentence level to the discourse level, and learn to communicate appropriately at all levels.

Grammar Dimensions Book 1	Grammar Dimensions Book 2	Grammar Dimensions Book 3	Grammar Dimensions Book 4

Sentence level ————————————————→ **Discourse level**

	Grammar Dimensions, Book 1	Grammar Dimensions, Book 2	Grammar Dimensions, Book 3	Grammar Dimensions, Book 4
Level	High beginning	Intermediate	High intermediate	Advanced
Grammar level	Sentence and subsentence level	Sentence and subsentence level	Discourse level	Discourse level
Primary language and communication focus	Semantic notions such as *time* and *place*	Social functions, such as *making requests* and *seeking permission*	Cohesion and coherence at the discourse level	Academic and technical discourse
Major skill focus	Listening and speaking	Listening and speaking	Reading and writing	Reading and writing
Outcome	Students form accurate, meaningful, and appropriate structures at the sentence level.	Students form accurate, meaningful, and appropriate structures at the sentence level.	Students learn how accurate, meaningful, and appropriate grammatical structures contribute to the organization of language above the simple sentence.	Students learn how accurate, meaningful, and appropriate grammatical structures contribute to the organization of language above the simple sentence.

Unit Organization

Used with or without the Workbook and the *Grammar 3D* CD-ROM, ***Grammar Dimensions*** Student Book units are designed to be clear, comprehensive, flexible, and communicative.

Goals	• **Focus students' attention** on the learning they will do in each chapter.
Opening Task	• **Contextualizes** the target grammatical structure. • **Enables teachers to diagnose** their students' performance and identify the aspect of the structure with which their students have the most difficulty. • **Provides a roadmap** for the grammar points students need to work on in that unit.
Focus Boxes	• **Present the form, meaning,** or **use** of a particular grammatical structure. • **Focus students' attention** to a particular feature of the target structure. Each rule or explanation is preceded by examples, so teachers can have students work inductively to try to discover the rule on their own.
Exercises	• Provide a wealth of opportunity to **practice** the form and meaning of the grammar structures. • Help students develop the skill of **"grammaring"**—the ability to use structures accurately, meaningfully, and appropriately. • Are varied, thematically coherent, but purposeful. • Give students many opportunities to personalize and own the language.
Communicative Activities ("The Purple Pages")	• Help students practice **grammar and communication in tandem.** • **Are engaging!** • Encourage students to **use their new language** both inside and outside the classroom. • Provide an opportunity to **practice reading, writing, listening, and speaking skills,** helping students realize the communicative value of the grammar they are learning.

Student Book Supplements

Audiocassettes	• **Provide listening activities for** each unit so students can practice listening to **grammar structures in context.**
Workbooks	• **Provide additional exercises** for each grammar point presented in the student text. • Offer question types found on the **TOEFL®** Test.
CD-ROM	• *Grammar 3D* **provides additional practice** for 34 of the key grammar structures found in the text series. • Offers over **500 activities** for beginning to advanced students. • **Provides an instructional "help page"** that allows students to access grammar explanations at any point. • **Provides feedback** that helps students understand their errors and guides them toward correct answers. • **Free** with each Student Book!
Teacher's Editions	• **Facilitate teaching** by providing in one place notes and examples, answer keys to the Student Book and Workbook, page references to all of the components, the tapescript for the audiocassette activities, and tests with answer keys for each unit. • **Minimize teacher preparation time** by providing step-by-step teaching suggestions for every focus box and activity in the Student Book.

The *Grammar Dimensions, Platinum Edition* Student Books and the additional components help teachers teach and students learn to use English grammar structures in communication accurately, meaningfully, and appropriately.

Acknowledgments

Series Director Acknowledgments

This edition would not have come about if it had not been for the enthusiastic response of teachers and students using the previous editions. I am very grateful for the reception *Grammar Dimensions* has been given.

I am also grateful for all the authors' efforts. To be a teacher, and at the same time a writer, is a difficult balance to achieve . . . so is being an innovative creator of materials, and yet, a team player. They have met these challenges exceedingly well in my opinion. Then, too, the Heinle & Heinle team has been impressive. I am grateful for the leadership exercised by Erik Gundersen, formerly of Heinle & Heinle. I also appreciate all the support from Charlotte Sturdy, Eric Bredenberg, Mike Burggren, Mary Beth Hennebury, and Marianne Bartow. Deserving special mention are Amy Lawler and Nancy Jordan, who never lost the vision while they attended to the detail with good humor and professionalism.

I have also benefited from the counsel of Marianne Celce-Murcia, consultant for the first edition this project, and my friend. Finally, I wish to thank my family members, Elliott, Brent, and Gavin, for not once asking the (negative yes–no) question that must have occurred to them countless times: "Haven't you finished yet?"

Author Acknowledgments

We'd like to give very special thanks to our families, to our friends and above all, to each other, for hanging in through this.

About the Teacher's Edition

The Teacher's Edition includes the following:

- General suggestions for teaching with *Grammar Dimensions Platinum.*
- Detailed teaching suggestions and answer keys for each unit in the Student Book. The following icons appear in this section:

- This icon signals a time when you could present a grammar point on the board.

- The pairwork icon appears when an exercise can be done in pairs.

- The groupwork icon appears when an exercise can be done in a group.

- This icon appears when a corresponding Workbook exercise or exercises can be assigned. The exercise and page number(s) in the Workbook are supplied next to the icon. The answers for the Workbook exercises appear in the Workbook Answer Key section of this Teacher's Edition. The page number for the answers to each exercise appear as part of each Workbook anno.

- This icon and an accompanying anno appear in the "Use Your English" section when there is an audio activity.

- Tests. A 15-minute test is included for each unit. You can administer it after each unit or combine with other units to create longer tests. You are welcome to photocopy the tests for student use. This icon appears when a test can be given.

- Answer key for the tests.
- Answer key for Workbook exercises.
- Tapescripts for the Listening Activities that appear in the "Use Your English" communicative activities section (purple pages) for each unit of the Student Book.

General Teaching Suggestions

OPENING TASK

Our time with our students is very precious. We must seek ways to put it to their best advantage. In order to do this, you need to learn what your students know and don't know how to do. This will allow you to target what you teach to what your students don't know, and therefore, need to learn. This is the major purpose of the opening task. You should be able to obtain invaluable information about your students' learning needs from "reading" (closely observing) your students as they go about doing the task. Each task has been constructed so that students will need to use the target structures in order to complete it.

As the students are focused on completing the task, you are freed to learn as much as you can about your students' learning needs. It will probably be best if after you have introduced the task (making sure students know what they are being asked to do), you have the students carry out as much of the task as they can by themselves. This will allow you to more closely observe your students' performance.

One way of doing this is to circulate in the classroom and "eavesdrop" on small group discussions. Take mental or written notes on your observations. Pay particular attention to how accurate, meaningful, and appropriate your students' use of the target structures is. Hold up the form, meaning, and use pie chart in your mind and see if you can determine where they have been successful, and where they need help. At this point, it is probably better if you refrain from any error correction. The tasks are supposed to encourage students to work meaningfully without concern that they will be interrupted, evaluated, or corrected. The only exception might be the need to remind students to work in English if they are using another language.

Sometimes the tasks involve individual written performances. When this is the case, study carefully what your students write. It, too, can provide valuable clues about what they can and cannot do. In many cases, students will want to hear each other's solutions to the questions or problems posed in the task. This provides yet another excellent opportunity for you to listen to your students and learn what has been easy for them and what has been difficult.

Of course, as with anything, different difficulties are likely to arise for different students. To cope with differing learning needs, you may consider grouping students with similar problems in class and giving each group different exercises to work through and/or different homework assignments. Another possibility is to group students in such a way that students who already know certain aspects of the target structure are grouped with other students who don't. In this way, students can learn from one another as they work through the focus boxes and exercises. If you do group students in this manner, however, it is important that each student be given a role in the group, so that students who are struggling with the content can still be contributing members of the group. For example, give these students the assignment of recording the group's answers, or reporting them to another group or to the whole class.

Obviously, if students demonstrate no ability to use the target structures required in completing the task, you will need to work systematically through the unit. It may be the case, though, that you will discover that students do not need to attend to all the focus boxes or do all the exercises; this makes your teaching more efficient.

Don't hesitate to alter tasks to fit your timetable. For example, have your students do only part of the task, or have them do one of the communicative activities at the end of the unit, if you feel that the opening task would not work as well. Other teachers have found it helpful to have students do the task twice—first for diagnostic purposes and second after students have worked through a unit in order to determine how much they have progressed.

All in all, what we are trying to achieve is an optimal use of the time we have available by identifying teachable moments when the students need to and are ready to learn.

FOCUS BOXES

The focus boxes feature the form, meaning, and use facts concerning the target structure that are appropriate for students at a given level of instruction. By treating one aspect of the structure at a time, followed by exercises providing practice, the focus boxes allow students to develop step-by-step a better understanding of, and an ability to use, the structure accurately, meaningfully, and appropriately.

Use student performance on the opening task as a bridge to the focus boxes. One way to do this is to write students' responses to the task on the blackboard, eliciting or supplying the target structures as they are needed. By going back and pointing out the target structures and asking questions about their form, meaning, or use, you may be able to induce the rules in the focus boxes

(not all at once, of course). At this point, you may want students to consult the relevant focus box in order to confirm the generalizations they have just made. On the other hand, if the students have arrived at the generalizations you feel they need to know, you may simply want to call their attention to the appropriate focus boxes for them to refer to for homework or when needed.

If you prefer a more deductive approach, you could go right to the first or appropriate focus box after the students have completed the task. You could present it orally to students or read it while they listen or read along silently with you. Alternatively, you could have the students read the focus boxes for homework or silently in class. You could help them when they do not understand something. You could check their understanding by asking students to come up with additional examples to supplement the ones in the focus box or asking them to compare how the material in this focus box differs from one earlier in the unit or from those in a related unit that they have completed.

A variation on this is to ask students individually or in pairs to present the information in a focus box to another pair of students, or even to the whole class, adding a few new examples of their own. Teaching something to others is a great way to learn!

Another possible way of teaching the focus boxes is not to present them at all, but rather to assign students the exercises that go along with them. The focus boxes can be used for reference purposes as the students work their way through the exercises. In this way, the material becomes more meaningful to students because they will need to access and understand it in order to do something with it.

EXERCISES

At least one exercise follows each focus box. There is a wide variety of exercises in *Grammar Dimensions*. There are both comprehension and production exercises. Comprehension exercises work on students' awareness and understanding. Production exercises develop students' skill in using the structures.

There are exercises that are consistent with the theme of the task and ones that introduce students to new themes and vocabulary in order to provide variety and to foster students' ability to transfer their learning to new contexts. There are personalized exercises, in which students use their own background knowledge or opinions to answer questions, and ones where students use the information that is supplied in order to complete the exercise.

Then, too, although general directions are provided for each exercise, there is a great deal of flexibility in how the exercises can be handled. Some exercises, such as information gaps, call for pairwork. Others are amenable to many different student configurations: individual, pair, small group, whole class; so you will need to decide what works best for a particular exercise and particular group of students. For instance, some students prefer to work individually at first and then get together with others to go over their answers. The variety of possible student configurations that the exercises permit allows students' differing learning styles to be catered to.

Sometimes you can choose freely whether to have students do an exercise orally or in writing. At other times, an exercise will work better in one modality than another because of the modality in which the structure normally occurs. Some exercises may be done in class, others for homework, and still others skipped all together. Don't forget to consult the Workbook for additional exercises.

There are also many options for how exercise answers can be checked. For example:

1. You can circulate while students are doing an exercise in class and spot-check.
2. You can go over the exercise afterwards as a whole class with each student being called on to supply an answer.
3. Exercises can be done individually and then pairs of students can get together to check their answers with each other. Where a difference of opinion occurs, you (or another pair of students) can act as a referee.
4. Different students, pairs, or groups of students can be assigned different parts of an exercise. For example, the first group does #'s 1–5, the second group does #6–10, etc. The groups post their answers on newsprint or butcher block paper and everyone circulates at the end noting the answers and asking questions.
5. A variation of #4 is to have one student from each group get together and present to the other students the exercise answers that his or her group came up with.
6. You can prepare a handout with the answers, and each student corrects his or her answers individually.
7. You can collect the written work, and make a list of common errors. You can put the errors on an overhead transparency and show it to the students during the next class and have them correct the errors together.

There are both closed and open-ended answers to questions. With closed questions, there is a single right answer. This is the most common type of question in Books 1 and 2. In Books 3 and 4, while closed questions still prevail, sometimes open-ended questions, for which there are no definitive answers, are used. Nuances of the language and contextual differences are such that it is sometimes difficult to say definitively what the single best answer is. The point is that students should understand that they have choices, but they also need to understand the consequences of their choices, i.e., they should be able to explain why they have chosen a particular answer. In many of these cases a "most likely" interpretation (based on English native speaker responses) has been indicated in the answer key, but no feasible opinion offered by your students should be discounted. Giving students an opportunity to defend their answers encourages students to form their own hypotheses about the appropriate use of certain grammar structures and to test these hypotheses through continued observation and analysis.

"USE YOUR ENGLISH" ACTIVITIES

In the "Use Your English" activities section of each unit (the purple pages), students can apply the language discussed in the unit to wider contexts and integrate it with the language they already know. Many activities give students more control over what they want to say or write than the exercises, and offer them more opportunities to express their own points of view across a range of topics. Most of the activities are quite open-ended in that they lend themselves to being done with structures covered in the unit, but they do not absolutely require their use.

The activities section is also designed to give instructors a variety of options. Since time is limited, you probably will not be able to have students do all the activities. You might choose two to do or ask your students to choose ones that they would prefer. Perhaps different groups of students could do different activities and then report on their experience to the whole class. Like the exercises, the activities can be adapted for use with different group configurations and different modalities.

If you are teaching in a program that is skill-based, you might want to collaborate with your colleagues and distribute the activities among yourselves. For example, the writing teacher could assign the activities that involve a written report, the teacher of listening could work on the listening activities during his or her class periods, or the teacher of speaking could work with students on activities where students are supposed to make an oral presentation.

Although the activities are meant to be culminating, it is also possible to intersperse them among the exercises. Sometimes an activity provides a particularly useful follow-up to an exercise. And we have already mentioned that certain activities might work well in place of the recommended opening task. Also, it may be useful to go back to a previous unit and do an activity for review purposes. This is especially useful at the beginning of a new, but related, unit.

The activities are an integral part of each unit because they not only provide students with opportunities to stretch their language use, but as with the opening task, they also provide you with the opportunity to observe your students' language use in action. In this way, activities can be informal holistic assessment measures encouraging students to show you how well they can use the target structures communicatively. Any persistent problems that still exist at this point can be noted for follow-up at a later time when students are more ready to deal with them.

As you can see, *Grammar Dimensions* is meant to provide you with a great deal of flexibility so that you can provide quality instruction appropriate for your class. We encourage you to experiment with different aspects of the material in order to best meet the needs of your unique group of students.

Unit 1

UNIT OVERVIEW

Unit 1 provides practice with the simple present tense and includes an overview of how adverbs of frequency can be included in present tense statements.

UNIT GOALS

Review the goals listed on this page so that students (Ss) understand what they should know by the end of the unit.

OPENING TASK

Note: The **Opening Task** allows Ss to use the target structures and allows teachers to notice what kind of help Ss may need. For a more complete discussion of the Opening Task, see page xxi of this Teacher's Edition.

The purpose of this task is not only to introduce the language focused on in this unit, but also to help you get a feel for the ideas about grammar learning and teaching, some of which may be new to your Ss. You may find it helpful to share something of your own philosophy of grammar teaching and learning.

It is not necessary to deal with accuracy during Steps 1–3, since the purpose of this Opening Task is to focus on meaning, creating a context in which the simple present is likely to be naturally used. This will allow you the opportunity to see if Ss are able to produce the simple present spontaneously, and will allow you to diagnose how much of the unit they will need to work through, and how carefully. The exercises that follow the Opening Task (here Exercises 1 and 2) give Ss the opportunity to return to the Task, to review and revise what they wrote, and to focus on accuracy.

UNIT 1

SIMPLE PRESENT

Habits, Routines, and Facts

UNIT GOALS:
- To know when to use simple present tense
- To form simple present tense correctly
- To understand the meanings of various adverbs of frequency
- To place adverbs of frequency in correct sentence position

▶ OPENING TASK
How Do You Learn Grammar?

STEP 1 Read each statement about learning English grammar. Circle the number that describes you best.

1 = never   2 = rarely   3 = sometimes   4 = often   5 = always

1.	I study grammar books and memorize the rules.	1 2 3 4 5
2.	I read newspapers, watch TV and movies, and listen to songs.	1 2 3 4 5
3.	I use English as much as possible to practice the grammar I know.	1 2 3 4 5
4.	I observe native speakers in different situations and notice what they say and do.	1 2 3 4 5
5.	When I don't know how to say something perfectly, I don't say anything at all.	1 2 3 4 5
6.	I don't worry about making mistakes because I learn from them.	1 2 3 4 5
7.	I learn better when I work in groups with my classmates.	1 2 3 4 5
8.	When a teacher uses words I don't understand, I ask for help.	1 2 3 4 5
9.	When I don't know how to say something, I try to say it another way.	1 2 3 4 5
10.	I think of grammar rules when I speak.	1 2 3 4 5

STEP 2 Compare your answers with another student. Do you like to learn English grammar in the same ways? In what ways are you similar and in what ways are you different? Use the chart below to write down your similarities and differences.

SIMILARITIES	DIFFERENCES

STEP 3 Use the chart to tell the rest of the class how you and your partner learn English grammar.

SETTING UP THE TASK

Model the instructions by reading each statement aloud and checking that Ss understand, explaining vocabulary as necessary. Emphasize that there are no wrong or right answers.

You can also do the questionnaire, based on your own experiences as a language learner.

Step 1

Ss work individually and complete the questionnaire. Ss are bound to finish at different times. Those who finish early can pair up with each other and proceed to Step 2. If Ss do finish at about the same time, you might want to group them according to different educational and cultural backgrounds (if applicable).

Step 2

Ss work in pairs or groups of three to compare their answers and to complete the chart. They can copy this chart into their notebooks if they need more room to write. Encourage them to add anything that they do that isn't on the chart.

Step 3

Bring the class together to share and compare findings.

SUGGESTIONS

1. In a large class, it may be time-consuming and tedious for all pairs to report back. If you circulate and monitor during Step 2, you can call on pairs who have something interesting/ different/ provocative to contribute.
2. Alternatively, kick off Step 3 by sharing your responses to the questionnaire, expanding and elaborating on them with examples from your own experiences as a language learner, and inviting responses from the Ss in light of their experiences.

CLOSING THE TASK

As a wrap-up, you can conduct an informal poll of learning preferences based on the question: *How many people in this room think of grammar rules when they speak?* Answers can be recorded on the board, on poster paper, or on an overhead projector (OHP) transparency.

Note: Answers may vary according to the context in which English is used. (For example, in #10, the response may depend on what type of student is speaking and to whom.) You can draw on this information and link it to what is presented in Focus 1.

FOCUS 1

Note: Focus boxes explain and give examples of each structure. For a more complete discussion of Focus boxes, see page xxii of this Teacher's Edition.

1. Emphasize that simple present verbs are used to talk about habits and everyday routines.

2 Make sure that Ss understand what *habits* and *everyday routines* are. (Note: You might stress that the difference between *habits* and *everyday routines* is not important, but that sometimes people talk about "bad habits," such as smoking.)

3. Give some examples of your own habits and routines and/or ask Ss for examples. If they use phrases rather than full sentences, restate what they say using a full sentence: (Example: Ss say: *exercise, eat breakfast, go to class.* You say: *Oh, first you exercise, then you eat breakfast, then you go to class, right?* AND/OR: *Did everybody understand that? First Kia exercises, then she eats breakfast, then she goes to class.*)

4. Write full sentences on the board, underlining simple present verbs. OR have Ss do this.

Exercise 1

Note: The exercises following each focus box provide meaningful practice with the grammar item presented in that particular box. For a more complete discussion of how to use the Exercises, see page xxiii of this Teacher's Edition.

If you followed the suggestions in this Teacher's Edition for Focus 1, Step 4, this can serve as a natural bridge to Exercise 1.

FOCUS 2

To check Ss' understanding of the different forms of the simple present tense in statements, negatives, questions, and short answers, conduct a brief exercise with contextualized (meaningful) sentences. Ask: *(student's name), what's one thing you do every morning?* (or: *What's one thing that you drink/eat every morning?*) Answer: *I drink tea.* Say (to another student): *What does ( ) do/drink every day?* Answer: *She drinks tea.* Ask (original student): *Do you drink coconut milk/(some other beverage) every day?* Student: *No, I don't drink coconut milk every day. I drink tea.* Ask (another

---

FOCUS **1**

▶ Verbs in the Simple Present Tense

Habits and Routines

EXAMPLES	EXPLANATIONS
(a) I **ask** questions when I **do not understand.**	*Ask, do not understand,* and *uses* are simple present verbs.
(b) Elzbieta **uses** English as much as possible.	Use the simple present to talk about habits (things you do again and again).
(c) Our classes **start** at 9:00 A.M.	Use the simple present to talk about
(d) Daniela **goes** to school five days aweek.	everyday routines (things you do regularly).

EXERCISE 1

Go back to Step 1 of the Opening Task on page 1. Underline all the simple present verbs you can find. Compare your answers with a partner's.

FOCUS **2**

▶ Simple Present Tense

STATEMENT	NEGATIVE	QUESTION	SHORT ANSWER
I You We They } work.	I You We They } do not/don't work.	Yes, { I you we they } work?	Yes, { I you we they } do.
He She It } works.	He She It } does not/doesn't work.	Does { he she it } work?	Yes, { he she it } does.
			No, { I you we they } don't.
			No, { he she it } doesn't.

A N S W E R K E Y

Exercise 1
1. study; memorize... 2. read; watch; listen... 3. use; know... 4. observe; notice; say; do... 5. (don't) know; (don't) say... 6. (don't) worry; help... 7. helps... 8. uses; (don't) understand; ask... 9. (don't) know; try... 10. think; speak

---

EXERCISE 2

Look at what you wrote in Step 2 of the Opening Task on page 1. Underline all the simple present verbs that you used. Did you use them correctly? Check your answers with a partner and then with your teacher.

EXERCISE 3

STEP 1 What are some of the *other* things you do and do not do to learn English grammar? Complete the following, using full sentences.

Some things I do:

1. I _____
2. I _____
3. I _____

Some things I don't do:

1. I _____
2. I _____
3. I _____

STEP 2 Get together with a partner and tell each other about things you do and do not do to learn English grammar. Then, without showing your answers to each other, write about your partner here.

My partner, (name) _____

does several different things to learn English grammar. She or he ____

_____

_____

_____

STEP 3 Now get together with a different partner. Ask each other what you do to learn English grammar (*Do you . . . ?*). Together with your new partner, decide on the three most useful ways to learn English. Share your ideas with the rest of the class. Write them here:

1. We _____
2. We _____
3. We _____

Simple Present: Habits, Routines, and Facts **3**

---

student): *Does ( ) drink coconut milk every day?* and so on to elicit short answers and negatives.

To elicit questions, ask another student to ask the question (this one or another). To elicit plural *they/we*, add another student to original statement: *Who else in this classroom drinks tea everyday? Carlos, do you drink tea everyday?* and so on.

Note: Exercise 3 also goes through this process of checking Ss' understanding of form. Thus it might be more appropriate to move quickly through this focus box if you have the sense that Ss are ready.

Exercise 2

If you still want/need more information about how Ss are, follow the instructions and first have Ss work individually. Circulate, noting which Ss are keeping up (or seem to already know this grammar) and which Ss find this challenging.

This is a good point to think about how you'd like your Ss to pair up. Some teachers find that pairing up weak and strong Ss is beneficial to both. Others like to "match up" Ss according to similar level, and some don't mind pairing up Ss in whatever way is most convenient and efficient—e.g., Ss sitting near each other, Ss who are comfortable with each other, etc.

Exercise 3

Step 2: Besides the suggestions in Exercise 2 for pairing up Ss, you can also let Ss choose based on some other parameter such as "Work with someone on the other side of the room."

This step is designed to focus on third person singular s. To check Ss' answers thoroughly, have them write this step out on a separate sheet of paper and either hand it in as homework or read it aloud (if the class isn't *too* big—otherwise it would be tedious).

SUGGESTION
Step 3

Ss can write their strategies on the board or on poster paper if you think it would be helpful for your class to see these displayed.

EXPANSION

Ask Ss to keep in their notebooks a list of strategies for successful language/grammar learning. As time passes, they might want to add to their repertoire of strategies.

ANSWER KEY

Exercise 2
Answers will vary, depending on what Ss wrote in Step 2 of the Opening Task. It is likely that many of the verbs in Step 1 will be used: study/studies, memorize/memorizes; read/reads, etc. Other possibilities include: like/likes/don't like/doesn't like, prefer/prefers, etc.

Exercise 3
It is impossible to predict answers here, as they will obviously depend on Ss' own experiences.

Use information about Ss' own lives (Exercise 3) or about Ss' grammar learning approaches (Opening Task, Exercises 1 and 2) to expand on this focus box.

SUGGESTION

1. Write the adverbs of frequency on the board as in (a).
2. Expand by explaining and asking about each adverb. Say: *When we use the adverb "always," we are talking about something we do 100% of the time.* Ask: *What is something you always do?/something you do every day/morning/evening/etc.?* Answer: *I always wake up before 8:00 a.m.* Ask: *So is it true that you <u>never</u> wake up after 8:00 a.m.?* Lead further discussion. Then elicit/ask or explain: *We use the adverb "never" when we are talking about something we do 0% of the time.*
3. Go through the other adverbs of frequency, estimating what they mean in terms of % of time.

Note: There are no "set" answers, only approximations. For example, "sometimes" may mean 1 out of 3 times (33%) or it may mean half of the time (50%). Ask Ss for their estimates and see if you agree.

FOCUS **3**

FORM MEANING

Showing How Often Something Happens

Adverbs of Frequency

EXAMPLES	EXPLANATIONS

(a) Kazue **often** uses a dictionary, but Florian **never** uses one.
 	
Most Often (100%)
↑ always
  usually
  often
  sometimes
  seldom
  rarely
  hardly ever
↓ never
Least Often (0%)
	Often and *never* are adverbs of frequency. They show how often something happens.
	
	For more information on adverbs of frequency, see Unit 18, Focus 5.

(b) I **usually** get up early. **(c)** He **never** calls me.	Where to put adverbs of frequency: **before** the main verb (b and c)
(d) She is **always** happy. **(e)** They are **rarely** late.	**after** the verb *be* (d and e)

4 UNIT 1

EXERCISE 4

1

2

3

4

We asked several students to describe their English classes. Read the descriptions on the next page and match each description to a picture. Write the number of the picture beside each description. Compare your answers with a partner's.

This exercise can serve as an "icebreaker" in a multilingual/multicultural classroom, or in a monolingual classroom in a setting foreign to you, the teacher.

SUGGESTIONS

1. In the former situation, allow time for "representatives" of different cultures to describe classroom settings in their own countries (or in countries they know about).

2. In the latter situation—if your Ss are familiar with an educational setting different than that of your "home" culture, allow different Ss the opportunity to tell you about these differences. Then encourage them to ask you questions about the educational setting you are familiar with. If it's relevant, tell them about some of the academic expectations in "your" setting (example: In U.S. classrooms, Ss are expected to participate in discussions and ask questions.)

ANSWER KEY

Exercise 4

A. 2 (or 3)   **B.** 1   **C.** 4 (or 1)   **D.** 3 (or 1)

A We sit in rows and the teacher stands at the front. The teacher explains grammar rules and the students listen and take notes. Students sometimes practice their writing in class.

B Our English classes are always very relaxed. We usually work in pairs or small groups and often play games in class to practice our English. These games are a lot of fun and we sometimes laugh a lot. We don't feel nervous about speaking English when we play games.

C We often work on special projects in our English class. We use computers to find information about a topic or we interview people to see what they think. Then we make a presentation about our topic to the rest of the class.

D The students in my English class are very enthusiastic. Every time the teacher asks a question, everybody wants to answer it. We always raise our hands and hope that the teacher will choose us.

How are the classes in the photographs like (or unlike) classes in your country? First, discuss this question with your partner and then be ready to tell the rest of the class.

EXERCISE 5

STEP 1 Complete the chart about students and teachers in your country and in this country. The first one has been done for you as an example. If you do not have enough room to write your answers on the chart, copy the chart into your notebook.

Exercise 5

You may need to clarify what "my" and "this" mean in foreign language or monolingual settings. One option is to cross out "this country" in the chart on page 7 and substitute it for a country that you or your Ss know about.

	TEACHERS IN MY COUNTRY	STUDENTS IN MY COUNTRY	TEACHERS IN THIS COUNTRY	STUDENTS IN THIS COUNTRY
Usually	stand in front of the class			
Sometimes				
Hardly ever				
Never				

STEP 2 Get together with a student from another country, if possible. Ask him or her questions about teachers and students in his or her country. For example: *Tell me about teachers in your country. Do they usually give a lot of homework? Do they tell jokes in class?*

STEP 3 Look at the information from your chart and from your partner's. Use this information to make as many true sentences as you can. For example: *Students in this country never stand up when the teacher comes into the room.*

EXERCISE 6

STEP 1 Get together with a partner. Quickly look at the occupations in the box below.

OCCUPATIONS

a student	a police officer	a businessperson
secretaries	a flight attendant	a bartender
mechanics	teachers	a nurse
an architect	a bus driver	a waitress

Step 2: If it is not possible for Ss to pair up with people from other countries, have them discuss their own country together.

Exercise 6

Step 1: Preview or follow up this step by reviewing the vocabulary in "Occupations." If you think it would be helpful, elicit definitions rather than providing them yourself. This can also help you get a sense of Ss' vocabulary level and of their ability to describe, define, and guess.

Note: "server" is the nonsexist (new) term for what previously was called waitress (female) or waiter (male).

ANSWER KEY

Exercise 5

Step 3: Answers will vary. Depending on the cultural backgrounds of your Ss, possible answers may include: *Teachers in my country hardly ever talk to students outside of class. Students in my country never ask questions in class. Teachers in this country usually give homework. Students in this country sometimes call their teachers by their first names. Teachers in my country stand in front of the class.*

Step 2: It might be helpful to do item 1 together as a class, perhaps right after you review the meanings of the various "Occupations" in the list in Step 1.

V A R I A T I O N

If you're up to it, and if you're comfortable with competitive activities, try Step 2 as a game: The pair that finishes (correctly!) first, wins. If you do this, you will need to ensure that your Ss all start at the same time and that they understand they are under time pressure, i.e., that it's a game.

Steps 3 and 5: Decide how you want to handle errors in simple present tense. For example, you can give Ss the opportunity to correct themselves, or you can ask other Ss: *Was the sentence accurate? Were there any errors?* A common error at this level is to omit the *s* on third person singular verbs. *She go to town every Saturday.* rather than: *She goes to town.*

STEP 2 Read the job descriptions below. Can you match them with the occupations in the box? Write the occupation on the line next to each description.

1. He wears a uniform and usually travels many miles a day. He serves food and drink, but he hardly ever prepares them himself. _____

2. She works in an office, but she often takes work home with her. She generally earns a high salary, but often feels a lot of stress. She sometimes entertains clients in the evening. _____

3. He usually wears a uniform and always carries a gun. He leads a dangerous life, so his job rarely gets boring. _____

4. He often works at night and meets many different people. He serves drinks and gets tips when people like his service. _____

5. She wears a uniform and drives many miles a day. She never serves food drinks. _____

6. He spends many hours in the classroom and asks questions. He always has a lot of work to do and sometimes writes on the board. _____

7. She often wears a uniform and walks many miles a day. She works very hard and does not earn very much money, although she sometimes gets generous tips. _____

8. They spend a lot of time in the classroom and like to ask questions. They often write on the board. _____

STEP 3 Now write similar descriptions for the jobs in the box that are not described above. What do these workers do?

9. _____
   _____

10. _____
    _____

11. _____
    _____

12. _____
    _____

A N S W E R   K E Y

Exercise 6
Step 2: 1. a flight attendant . . . **2.** a business person . . . **3.** a police officer . . . **4.** a bartender . . . **5.** a bus driver . . . **6.** a student (or teacher) . . . **7.** a server (or waitress) . . . **8.** teachers (or students)
Step 3: Answers will vary. For example: secretaries: They work in offices. They answer telephones, type letters, and make appointments for their bosses. They are usually very organized people. An architect: She plans buildings where people work or live. She is good at math and drawing.
Step 4: #13 and #14 depend on what occupations Ss list.
Step 5: Answers will vary.

STEP 4 On your own, think of two more jobs and write a short job description for each one.

13. _____

_____

14. _____

_____

STEP 5 Get together with another student and read your descriptions to each other. Ask and answer questions until you guess the jobs your partner has described. For example: *Does she or he . . . ? Is he or she a . . . ?*

EXERCISE 7

Sam is looking for a roommate to share his apartment, and Dave is looking for a place to live. They are trying to find out if they will get along as roommates. Complete their conversation, using verbs that fit the meaning of the sentences. Sometimes more than one answer is possible.

Sam: What do you usually do on weekends?

Dave: Well, I usually (1) ____wake up____ early, about 5:30, and then I

(2) _____ by the river for an hour or so before breakfast.

Sam: Yeah? And what (3) _____ you _____ next?

Dave: After breakfast, I (4) _____ a cold shower, and

then I usually (5) _____ my bike or I sometimes

(6) _____ tennis for a couple of hours. What (7) _____

you _____ on Saturday mornings?

Sam: I like to relax on weekends; I (8) _____ home and

(9) _____ the newspaper and (10) _____ TV.

Dave: All weekend?

Sam: No. On Sundays, I often get in my sports car and (11) _____ to the beach.

Dave: Great! I like swimming too. It's a habit that I learned from my

brother. He (12) _____ in the ocean every day of the year, even in the winter.

Simple Present: Habits, Routines, and Facts **9**

STEP 5: VARIATION

Ask Ss to read their descriptions aloud to the rest of the class, rather than to a partner. Have members of the class guess what job is being described.

Exercise 7

SUGGESTIONS

It's fun to do this orally, as a "real," natural-sounding dialogue.

1. If you do this, first give Ss a few minutes to work with a partner, and check to make sure they have answers for each blank. This will allow the reading to move along smoothly so that the class is not waiting for the speakers to search for the answers.
2. Before Ss read, explain to them that for natural "fluent"-sounding speech, they need to link words together smoothly and to use appropriate intonation—falling intonation at the end of a statement, rising intonation at the end of a yes–no question, and louder volume, higher pitch for emphasis (such as Dave's "Great!", just before #12) or for important or surprising information.
3. Because this dialogue is so long, it is appropriate to switch speakers part of the way through—after Dave's #7 question, for example, and at a later point.

ANSWER KEY

Exercise 7

Some answers may vary.

2. walk/run/jog . . .   **3.** do (you) do . . .
4. take . . .   **5.** ride . . .   **6.** play/watch . . .
7. do (you) do . . .   **8.** stay . . .   **9.** read . . .
10. watch . . .   **11.** drive . . .
12. swims/surfs . . .   **13.** swim . . .
14. sit/stay/lie . . .   **15.** meet/call/visit . . .
16. don't go/belong . . .   **17.** dance . . .
18. likes

Sam: Well, I rarely (13) _____ in the ocean. I usually

(14) _____ on the beach and try to get a good sun tan. Then I

(15) _____ some of my friends and we go to a nightclub and dance.

Dave: Don't you ever exercise?

Sam: Well, I (16) (not) _____ to a health club or gym, but every

Saturday night, I go to a disco and I (17) _____ for hours. That's

my idea of exercise.

Dave: Look, here's the phone number of a friend of mine. He

(18) _____ dancing and night clubs, just like you. Why don't you

give him a call and see if he wants to be your roommate?

Talking About Facts

EXAMPLES	EXPLANATION
(a) The sun **rises** in the east and **sets** in the west. (b) Brazilians **speak** Portuguese. (c) Water **boils** at 100° C.	Use the simple present to talk about facts (things that are true).

EXERCISE 8

STEP 1 Match the pictures to the animal names.

horse	elephant	spider	bat
bear	swan	scorpion	antelope

What do you know about these animals? Be ready to tell the rest of the class anything that you know.

---

1. To expand on the examples here, you can ask your Ss similar questions: *What language do Chinese/Mexicans/ Angolans speak?* To Ss who speak more than one language: *What languages do you speak?* Or ask Ss' about facts about their own countries. *What's the capital of _____? What's the weather usually like in _____?* You might want to first model the statements: *Washington, D.C. is the capital of the United States. In the north of the U.S., winters are usually long and cold, but in the south, winters are mild.*

2. After each statement and question, point out the use of the simple present. You can do this by writing each sentence on the board or on an overhead transparency if you access to an overhead projector (OHP). Underline each simple present tense verb. Or have Ss do the writing and the underlining.

Workbook Exs. 1 & 3, p. 1, 3.
Answers: TE p. 486.

Exercise 8

If Ss don't recognize some of the animals, this will be worked out as they go along.

A N S W E R   K E Y

Exercise 8
Step 1: (from left to right)
bat   bear   spider
elephant   swan   horse
antelope   scorpion

SUGGESTION

Regroup after Step 1 and have Ss share information. However, this may make Step 2 *too* easy for some of them!

Step 3: Assign specific pairs to work together, or let Ss choose based on some other parameter such as "Work with a pair on the other side of the room" or "Try to find a pair that you've never worked with yet."

VARIATION
Step 4

Assign this as a short written exercise: 3–5 sentences for each animal. Ss can work together on their "animal of choice," pooling information.

UNIT GOAL REVIEW

Ask Ss to look at the goals on the opening page of the unit again. Help them understand how much they have accomplished in each area. For example, make sentences that contrast different adverbs of frequency (e.g., *never* and *always*) and ask Ss to explain the differences in meaning (Goal #3). This is also an opportunity to ask Ss to identify which areas they would like more practice with and to point out that different verb tenses are covered in other units of this book. You may want to allow plenty of time for the activities and/or for reviewing the relevant focus boxes.

STEP 2 Get together with a partner and draw lines connecting the animals in Column A with appropriate information about them in Column B. Don't worry if you are not sure of all the answers. With your partner, decide what you think is **probably** the best match for each piece of information.

A	B
Horses	live for about two years.
Bats	sometimes go for four days without water.
Scorpions	stay with the same mates all their lives.
Elephants	use their ears to "see."
Swans	have twelve eyes.
Antelopes	sleep during the winter months.
Bears	sleep standing up.
Spiders	run at 70 miles per hour.

STEP 3 Get together with another pair and compare your answers. When you are ready, compare your answers with the rest of the class. As a class, decide on what you think are **probably** the best answers. Then check your answers on page A-14.

STEP 4 Do you know any other unusual facts about these animals or any other animals? Tell the rest of the class about them.

ANSWER KEY

Exercise 8

Step 2 and 3: Horses sleep standing up. Bats use their ears to "see." Scorpions have twelve eyes. Elephants sometimes go for four days without water. Swans stay with the same mates all their lives. Antelopes run at 70 miles per hour. Bears sleep during the winter months. Spiders live for about two years.

Use Your English

ACTIVITY 1: SPEAKING/LISTENING

The purpose of this activity is to prove or disprove the following statements about your classmates. Stand up, walk around the room, and ask your classmates questions to see if the following are true (T) or false (F).

1.	Most of the people in this room do not eat breakfast.	T	F
2.	Women drink more coffee than men.	T	F
3.	Fifty percent of the people in this room watch TV at night.	T	F
4.	Somebody in this room wears contact lenses.	T	F
5.	More than three people read a newspaper in English every day.	T	F
6.	More than 50% of the people in this room drive a car.	T	F
7.	Nobody likes opera.	T	F
8.	More than two people here come to school by bike.	T	F
9.	Everybody gets more than six hours of sleep a night.	T	F
10.	Most of the people in this room have a sister.	T	F

USE YOUR ENGLISH

The activities in the purple pages at the end of the unit contain situations that should naturally elicit the structures covered in the unit. For a more complete discussion of how to use the Use Your English Activities, see page xxiv of this Teacher's Edition.

When Ss are doing these activities in class, you can circulate and listen to see if they are using the structures accurately. Have they achieved the goals presented at the beginning of the unit?

Activity 1

VARIATION

Turn this into a research/interview project by asking research teams of 4 to 6 Ss to find out about a certain population of people. Instead of all the Ss in the room they can find out about: family members, people of a particular age (example: 25 and over/under), Ss in another class (ESL classes might want to combine classes occasionally and work together), all the Ss they know from a particular place/region/ country, people that live together (e.g., a student dormitory), etc. Ss can pool their information and prepare a short written or oral report.

ANSWER KEY

Activity 1

Answers will vary, depending on the class (and the population studied, if the research activity is conducted).

Activity 2

VARIATION

If you are in a monolingual or non-English speaking setting, you can adapt this activity to populations other than Americans. Choose special days/holidays that are relevant for that population.

For situations where there is little or no access to native English speakers, but there are a number of people available who speak English proficiently and/or who have lived in English-speaking countries, Ss can conduct interviews with them.

SUGGESTION

If tape-recording is not possible, be sure to have more than one student conducting the interview. Research teams of two or more people have an advantage since you can allocate responsibilities: one person asks the questions, one person asks for clarification or elaboration if necessary, one person focuses on what specific words are used (in this case, what form of the verb), etc.

ACTIVITY 2: SPEAKING/LISTENING

The purpose of this activity is to find out what North Americans usually do on certain special days.

STEP 1 Form a team with one or two other students and choose one of the special days from the chart below.

STEP 2 Tell the rest of the class which special day your team has chosen. Make sure that there is at least one team for each special day.

STEP 3 With your team, interview three different people (native speakers of English if possible) and find out what usually happens on this special day. Make notes on the chart below or in your notebook. If possible, tape-record your interviews.

STEP 4 After doing your interviews, use your notes to tell the rest of the class what your team found.

ST. PATRICK'S DAY
VALENTINE'S DAY
THANKSGIVING DAY
HALLOWEEN

STEP 5 Listen to your tape-recorded interview or use your notes to identify and write down any sentences that contain the simple present tense or adverbs of frequency.

ACTIVITY 3: LISTENING

STEP 1 Listen to the tape of people describing what they do on certain special days. Which special days do you think each speaker is talking about? Write your answers under "Special Day" in the chart below.

Speaker	Special Day	Verbs in the Simple Present Tense
Speaker 1		
Speaker 2		
Speaker 3		

STEP 2 Listen to the tape again. On the right side of the chart, write down as many examples of verbs in the simple present tense as you can.

Activity 3

Play textbook audio. The tapescript for this listening activity appears on p. 504 of this book.

This is a nice follow-up to Activity 2, since it validates and confirms the "findings" of the interviews conducted on this topic. Ss can copy the chart from Activity 3 into their notebooks if they want more room for notes.

EXPANSION

If Ss in your class have not been exposed to natural native-speaker English, encourage them to talk about their impressions. Ask: *What do you notice about how the speakers said things? Is there anything about the talk that surprised you, or was hard to understand?* (Likely answers: *They speak so quickly. Their words "run together." They always use contractions. Sometimes you can't hear certain syllables or words.*) You can explain that words in "native speaker" or "fluent" English are linked together smoothly, and that reduced forms, contractions and ellipses are common.

ANSWER KEY

Activity 3
Special Days: Speaker 1, St. Patrick's Day; Speaker 2, Thanksgiving; Speaker 3: Halloween. Check the tapescript (on p. 504) for verbs to fill in the chart. Answers may include: I've, don't have to be, wear, like, don't/do, have, is, eat, get, give, do get, sounds, love, dress up, want

Activity 4

If your class is large, consider dividing the class into groups. Let each group stay together through the whole process. If you want, you can regroup and share the results of Step 7.

SUGGESTION

Although some Ss seem overwhelmed at the prospect of memorizing and re-memorizing sentences, they usually get the hang of it after a couple of times. You can allow them to take notes, perhaps just writing down the verb and another word or two that will help them remember. However, one of the best parts of this activity is the final step, when you can all see how "mismatched" the final version is with the original information. This is less likely to happen if they're allowed to take notes.

By the way, it's fun to do this activity along with your Ss.

ACTIVITY 4: SPEAKING/LISTENING/WRITING

STEP 1 Complete the following with information that is true about yourself. Write complete sentences.

Something I usually do in summer	
Something I often do on weekends	
Something I rarely do in this country	
Something I sometimes do on Fridays	

STEP 2 Memorize these four sentences about yourself.

STEP 3 Walk around the room. When your teacher tells you to stop, find the nearest person. Tell the person your four sentences and listen to that person's sentences. Then memorize each other's sentences.

STEP 4 Walk around the room. When your teacher tells you to stop, find a different person. Tell this new person about **the last person you spoke to.** Then listen to that person's sentences. Do not talk about yourself. Memorize what he or she tells you.

STEP 5 Find someone different. Tell him or her the information the last person told you. Listen to the new person's sentences. Memorize what he or she tells you.

STEP 6 Now find someone new. Continue the process for as long as possible. Remember, you always pass along the information the last person tells you. Try to speak to as many different people as possible.

STEP 7 At the end, tell the rest of the class the information you heard from the last person. Is all the information true?

ACTIVITY 5: SPEAKING/LISTENING

STEP 1 Prepare a short talk for your classmates, describing a special day or holiday that people celebrate in your country, city, or region. Talk about what people usually do on this day and how they celebrate. Don't forget to include an introduction to your talk. For example: *I am going to tell you about a very special holiday in my country. The name of the holiday is. . . .* If possible, tape your talk.

STEP 2 After you give your talk, listen to your tape. Did you use any verbs in the simple present tense? Did you use any adverbs of frequency?

ACTIVITY 6: WRITING

STEP 1 Write a description of a typical high school classroom in your country. For example, what does the room look like? Where do the students sit? Where does the teacher sit? Is there any special equipment in the room? What is on the walls? What do teachers and students usually do when they are in the classroom? In your opinion, what are the strengths (best parts) of this kind of classroom and what are the weaknesses (worst parts)?

STEP 2 When you finish, read your work carefully. Did you use any simple present verbs or adverbs of frequency?

Activity 5

Step 1: If you conducted Activity 2 on a population other than Americans (as suggested in this Teacher's Edition), that will link nicely into this activity. Ss can use the information from Activity 2 to supplement their own experience/knowledge of particular days.

VARIATION

If it's not possible to tape record (Steps 1 and 2) Ss giving their talks, assign Ss from the "audience" to be notetakers who focus specifically on simple present tense usage. After each talk, have the listeners/notetakers give feedback to the speaker: They provide examples of speakers' sentences with simple present tense usage, and they point out and/or correct any errors that the speaker made in simple present tense usage.

Activity 6

Assign this as homework or allow enough time for Ss to develop their descriptions (30 minutes minimum).

EXPANSION

Make this into a peer editing activity, in which a student exchanges his/her description with someone else's:

1. Ss read each other's descriptions for content. Are all statements clear? If not, they can ask the writer of the description for clarification or elaboration where necessary.
2. Ss check each other's descriptions for the grammar targeted in this unit. Did they use the simple present tense accurately and appropriately?

The test for this unit can be found on pp. 410–411 of this book. The answers are on TE p. 412.

Unit 2

UNIT OVERVIEW

Unit 2 provides practice with the present progressive, contrasts the present progressive with the simple present, and includes an overview of major verbs not usually used in the progressive.

UNIT GOALS

Review the goals listed on this page so that students (Ss) understand what they should know by the end of the unit.

OPENING TASK

The purpose of this task is to create a context in which Ss will need to use the present progressive to describe actions in progress. The problem-solving format focuses attention on meaning rather than form. This focus allows you to see how far Ss are able to produce the target forms spontaneously.

SUGGESTION

Make an overhead transparency of the incomplete picture on p. 19 to help you focus attention on specific details as necessary.

SETTING UP THE TASK

1. Have Ss look at the picture on p. 19.
2. Explain that the small pictures connect to make one complete picture.
3. Read the instructions for Step 1 aloud with the whole class; check comprehension.

CONDUCTING THE TASK

Step 1

Ss work in pairs or small groups to make guesses and fill in the chart. Circulate and listen in order to get an idea of their current use of the present progressive. Do not correct; accuracy is not important at this stage. Keep a note of some of the different ideas being developed—you can use them later.

SUGGESTION

While Ss are working, draw the chart from Step 1, p. 18 on the board.

Step 2

1. Bring the class together so that Ss can compare their ideas.

UNIT 2

PRESENT PROGRESSIVE AND SIMPLE PRESENT

Actions and States

UNIT GOALS:

- To know when to use present progressive
- To form present progressive correctly
- To choose between simple present and present progressive
- To know which verbs are not usually used in the present progressive

▶ OPENING TASK
What's Happening?

STEP 1 Many parts of the picture on the next page are missing. Get together with a partner and decide what the whole picture is about. For example, where is this? Who are the people? What are they doing? Write your ideas in the chart below.

Where is this?	Who are the people?	What are they doing?

STEP 2 Describe what you think is happening in the picture to the rest of the class. Decide who has the most interesting explanation.

2. Act as secretary and fill in the chart on the board. Write notes under the first two headings but write full sentences in the third column (*What are they doing?*). If Ss make sentences using present progressive, write them without comment. Reframe the incorrect attempts as necessary; for example, if a student says *"A man talking on the phone,"* write the correct version without comment. If some use simple present, write the sentence in the simple present. Reframe inaccurate attempts if necessary. Aim to get five or six examples of the present progressive on the board.

CLOSING THE TASK

Explain that Ss will use their guesses in later activities.

FOCUS 1

This focus box introduces Ss to the concept of using the progressive to describe actions in progress. Further discussion of the form is found in Focus 2.

SUGGESTIONS

1. Provide more examples of actions in progress or ask Ss to provide them, using situations from the classroom: *Leo is looking out of the window. Milan and Kim are writing in their notebooks.* You can also provide examples from Ss' own lives: *Tranh is living with his sister this semester. Prem is looking for a roommate.*

2. Get Ss to identify examples of the present progressive from the Opening Task written on the board. If some verbs are in simple present, invite Ss to make changes as they fit. Help Ss to infer which use of the present progressive this is (action in progress).

Exercise 1

Ss now have a chance to test their ideas from the Opening Task. This activity can be done as a class or in pairs. Answers will vary.

Workbook Ex. 1, p. 7.
Answers: TE p. 486.

▶ Present Progressive: Actions in Progress

EXAMPLES	EXPLANATIONS
(a) Right now, I **am sitting** on the couch and my brothers **are cooking** dinner. **(b)** It **is raining** and Oscar **is waiting** for the bus.	*Am sitting* and *are cooking* are present progressive forms. Use the present progressive to describe an action that is in progress and happening at the time of speaking.
(c) This semester, I **am taking** three math classes. **(d)** Their baby **is waking up** very early these days.	Use the present progressive for an action that is happening **around** the time of speaking, but not happening **exactly** at that time.
At time of speaking: *right now* *at the moment* *today* *at present*	Around time time of speaking: *this year* *this semester* *this week* *these days*	These time expressions are often used with the present progressive.

EXERCISE 1

Read the following statements about the picture in the Opening Task and decide which ones are probably true (T) and which ones are probably false (F).

1. Somebody is eating.   T   F
2. A customer in a restaurant is ordering a meal.   T   F
3. Somebody is playing the piano.   T   F
4. Somebody is reading a newspaper.   T   F
5. Somebody is writing a letter.   T   F
6. Somebody is talking on the telephone.   T   F

Now look at the complete picture on page A-15 at the back of this book. How many of your guesses were correct?

20 | UNIT 2

ANSWER KEY

Exercise 1
1. F   2. F   3. F   4. T   5. T   6. T

Present Progressive

To form the present progressive, use *be* + present participle (*-ing*) of the main verb:

STATEMENT	NEGATIVE	QUESTION	SHORT ANSWER
I am (I'm) working.	I am not (I'm not) working.	Am I working?	Yes, I am. No, I'm not.
You are (you're) working.	You are not (aren't) working.	Are you working?	Yes, you are. No, you aren't. (No, you're not.)
She/He/It is (She's/He's/It's) working.	She/He/It is not (isn't) working.	Is she/he/it working?	Yes, she/he/it is. No, she/he/it isn't. (No, she's/he's/it's not.)
We are (We're) working.	We are not (aren't) working.	Are we working?	Yes, we are. No, we aren't. (No, we're not.)
They are (They're) working	They are not (aren't) working.	Are they working?	Yes, they are. No, they aren't. (No, they're not.)

EXERCISE 2

STEP 1 Study the complete picture on page A-15 for one minute. Close your book and, from memory, write as many sentences as possible to describe what is happening in the picture. Compare your sentences with those of the rest of the class. Who can remember the most?

STEP 2 Look back at the sentences you wrote in Step 1. Did you use the present progressive correctly? If not, go back and rewrite the sentences.

FOCUS 2

Building on Focus 1, Focus 2 illustrates the form of the present progressive.

SUGGESTIONS

1. Briefly read the examples aloud, at normal speed, working across the chart from left to right to give Ss the opportunity to hear how the form sounds (especially the contracted forms). Explain that the chart is for reference, and can be used throughout the unit as necessary.
2. Point out the North American spelling conventions for adding *-ing*:
    write → *writing* (dropping *-e*)
    hit → *hitting* (double consonant in 1-syllable words)
    travel → *traveling* (single consonant in 2-syllable words with <u>first</u> syllable stress)
    rebe → *rebelling* (double consonant in 2-syllable words with <u>second</u> syllable stress)

Exercise 2

This exercise returns to what Ss wrote in the task and focuses on accurate production: oral in Step 1, and written in Step 2.

Workbook Ex. 2, pp. 8–10.
Answers: TE p. 486.

SUGGESTION

If you make a copy of the chart on an overhead transparency, you can add more examples to each explanation by eliciting them from the Ss. For example, for the first simple present explanation (*For an action that happens regularly, again and again*) ask Ss to say some of their habits. Then add the examples to the chart: *Michaela drinks a cup of coffee every morning. Berta goes dancing on Thursdays. Deressa spends a lot of time with his children.*

Grammar Note

Many languages do not have a different form for simple and progressive aspect, so this concept may take some time for Ss to understand and use accurately.

▶ # Simple Present or Present Progressive?

EXAMPLES	EXPLANATIONS	
	Simple Present	Present Progressive
(a) Philippe **watches** six TV programs a day.	For an action that happens regularly, again and again. (See Unit 1.)	
(b) A: Where's Philippe? B: In his room. He's **watching** TV. **(c)** Leanne can't come to the phone right now because she's **taking** a shower.		For an action that is in progress **at** the time of speaking.
(d) Philippe **is watching** more TV than usual these days because he'd rather do that than study for his final exams. **(e)** Audrey **is learning** Greek this semester.		For an action in progress **around** the time of speaking.
(f) Carmina **lives** in Mexico City. **(g)** The sun **rises** in the east. **(h)** Mark always **reads** the sports section of the newspaper first.	For facts, situations, and states that we do not expect to change.	
(i) Angela **is living** with her mother for the time being. (Someday she will move into a house of her own.) **(j)** Matt will start college next year. Until then, he **is working** at Fat Burger.		For situations and actions that are temporary and that we expect to change.

EXERCISE 3

Check (✔) the sentence (*a* or *b*) that is closest in meaning to the first statement(s). Compare your answers with a partner.

1. Kristen's getting really good grades this semester.
   (a) Her grades are always good.
   (b) Her grades are better than they were last semester.

2. Look! Terry's wearing a dress today.
   (a) Terry seldom wears dresses.
   (b) Terry probably wore a dress yesterday, too.

3. Vince and Irene live in New Jersey.
   (a) They expect to move very soon.
   (b) New Jersey is their home.

4. I'm taking the train to work this week.
   (a) I'm sitting on the train right now.
   (b) I don't usually take the train.

5. A: Where's Eddie?
   B: He's asleep on the couch.
   (a) He's sleeping on the couch.
   (b) He sleeps on the couch.

6. A: How's Nina these days?
   B: Busy. She's learning how to dance the tango.
   (a) Nina has a new hobby.
   (b) She's dancing right now.

EXERCISE 4

Complete the following sentences using either the simple present or the present progressive. Use a form of the verb in parentheses. The first one has been done for you.

1. A: Ray! The phone __is ringing__ (ring).
   B: I can't get it. I _____ (wash) my hair.

2. A: Hey, Pam! What a surprise! What _____ you _____ (do) on campus?
   B: I _____ (take) an art class this semester. It's great! I _____ (learn) a lot.

3. A: Please be quiet, we _____ (study) for a test!
   B: What kind of test?
   A: Math. We _____ (have + always) a math test on Mondays.

ANSWER KEY

Exercise 3
1. b 2. a 3. b 4. b 5. a 6. a

Exercise 3

This exercise helps Ss gain skills in talking about meaning, and about how meaning and form are linked. This activity can also be done in larger groups or as a class. Ss answer *Why?* about each of their answers.

Exercise 4

This exercise provides a good opportunity to use contractions in natural contexts—everyday conversational. Ask Ss to look at the example done for them in the text. How can they change the example to be more like spoken English?
is ringing → *'s ringing*

Pronunciation Note

Contracted forms are <u>not</u> bad English, but the normal sound pattern of English. When native speakers talk naturally, the words with *meaning* (such as nouns, adjectives, and main verbs) are emphasized, while the words that express the grammar (auxiliary verbs, articles, and prepositions) are not generally stressed. Therefore, the contraction of the auxiliary verb *be* in the present progressive follows the rules of English pronunciation.

S U G G E S T I O N S

1. Have Ss practice reading the dialogues, being sure to use the contracted form. Model the activity yourself with one student first.
2. Point out that using full forms gives emphasis:
   Q: Katarina says you're not going to work today.
   A: Actually, I <u>am</u> going.
3. After the exercise, elicit or point out how the choice between present progressive and simple present depends on the factors presented in Focus 3—whether the action happens regularly, changes, etc.
4. Return to the pronunciation issue by pointing out that simple present forms aren't reduced, as they are the main verb (not auxiliary).

4. (The phone rings.)

A: Hi, honey. How _____ you _____ (do)?

B: Mom! What a coincidence! I was about to write you a letter.

A: Really? You _____ (write + hardly ever) me letters. Is something wrong?

5. A: What's the matter?

B: It _____ (rain) and I want to go on a picnic today.

A: Why _____ it _____ (rain + always) on the weekends? It _____ (rain + never) during the week.

6. A: Why _____ Brian _____ (wear) a suit today?

B: It's Tuesday. He _____ (go + generally) to lunch with his boss on Tuesdays.

7. A: I just can't go on like this with my roommate.

B: Why? What's wrong?

A: The main problem is that she's a morning person and, as you know, I'm a night person. This means that almost every morning she _____ (get up) before 6:00, _____ (play) really loud music, and _____ (do) aerobics in the living room. She _____ (make) an incredible amount of noise, which _____ (make) me really mad because I usually _____ (get + not) home until after 2:00 A.M. and _____ (like) to sleep late. But these days, thanks to my roommate, I _____ (wake up) at 6:00.

B: Do you want me to talk to her about this? What _____ she _____ (do) at the moment?

A: Thanks for the offer, but she _____ (sleep). She always _____ (go) to bed around 8:00.

EXERCISE 5

Can you translate the following into written English? Write your answers below. After that, underline the verbs in each sentence and write each verb in the appropriate box. The first one has been done for you.

1. 👁 ❤ U. _____I love you._____

2. 👁 CU. _____

3. 👁 H+8 U. _____

4. 👁 H+🖐 U. _____

5. He 🐉 U. _____

6. RU 21 ? _____

7. 👁 CUR YY 4 me! _____

8. 👁 TH+🐝 UR GR+8. _____

You can find the answers to this puzzle on page A-16.

Now underline all the verbs in your sentences and write them in the appropriate boxes below. The first one has been done for you.

Verbs that express emotions and feelings	· Verbs that express senses and perceptions	Verbs that express cognition: knowledge thoughts, and beliefs
love		

Which verb does not fit these categories? _____

This exercise will prepare Ss for the next focus box. Ss might need help "translating" the first one; in this case, demonstrate how to arrive at the answer.

VARIATION

Break the class into teams and do the activity as a competition. Whoever finishes with the most correct answers first is the winner.

Workbook Exs. 3 & 4, pp. 10–11.
Answers: TE p. 487.

ANSWER KEY

Exercise 5
1. I love you . . .   2. I see you . . .
3. I hate you . . .   4. I hear you . . .
5. He knows you . . .   6. Are you 21? . . .
7. I see you are too wise for me.   8. I think you are great.

Emotions and feelings: love, hate . . . *Senses and perceptions:* see, hear . . . *Cognition:* know, think . . . *Verb that does not fit:* be

FOCUS 4

Emphasize that *stative verbs*—verbs that don't normally occur in the progressive—describe "states" (feelings, beliefs, situations) that we don't expect to change. This topic is discussed further in Focus 5.

Grammar Note

There are times when English speakers *do* use these verbs in the progressive. This fact, however, does not contradict the explanation, as the progressive is used to show a change in state:

I'm feeling sick . . . I think I need some air.

-or-

When I first started playing the guitar, I loved it, but lately I'm hating it more and more because it takes too much practice.

The meaning of the above verbs includes a change in state. You may wish to mention this only if Ss bring up questions about it.

Exercise 6

S U G G E S T I O N S

1. Since this passage reads like a report, have Ss practice their pronunciation and presentation skills by reading extended passages (such as paragraphs) aloud to classmates.
2. Make a copy of the passage on an overhead transparency. Review the answers together as a class.

Workbook Ex. 5, p. 11.
Answers: p. TE 487.

Verbs Not Usually Used in the Progressive

EXAMPLES	EXPLANATIONS
(a) He **loves** me, but he **hates** my cat. **(b)** NOT: He is loving me, but he is hating my cat. **(c)** I **know** your sister. **(d)** NOT: I am knowing your sister.	Some verbs are not usually used in the progressive. The reason is that they describe states or situations that we do not expect to change. They do not describe actions.
(e) Hugo **likes** opera, but his girlfriend **prefers** ballet. **(f)** Those flowers **smell** wonderful! **(g)** I **think** the President has some interesting ideas about health care, but many people **believe** he is wrong. **(h)** Please be careful with that vase. It **belongs** to my aunt. **(i)** A: Are you going to buy that radio? B: No, it **costs** too much.	Common nonprogressive (stative) verbs: • Verbs that express feelings and emotions: *love prefer hate like appreciate want dislike* • Verbs that describe the senses: *see hear taste smell* • Verbs that express knowledge, opinions, and beliefs: *think believe know understand* • Verbs that express possession: *have belong own possess* • Other common nonprogressive verbs: *be seem owe exist need appear cost weigh*

EXERCISE 6

Complete the following with the simple present or the present progressive, using the verbs in parentheses.

Today, more and more people (1) _____ (discover) the joys of riding a bicycle. In fact, mountain biking (2) _____ (become) one of America's most popular recreational activities. The bicycle business (3) _____ (grow) fast, and every year it (4) _____ (produce) hundreds of new-model bikes. In general, bike shops (5) _____ (sell) not only bicycles but also a full range of accessories and equipment.

26 | UNIT 2

Paul Brownstein (6) _____ (manage) a popular bike shop in Boston. Many of his customers (7) _____ (be) enthusiastic cyclists, and several of them (8) _____ (own) more than one bicycle. These people usually (9) _____ (ride) several times a week for pleasure, although according to Paul, more and more people these days (10) _____ (ride) their bicycles to work too. They (11) _____ (believe) that bicycles (12) _____ (provide) an alternative to the automobile.

Paul (13) _____ (sell) all kinds of bikes, but these days he (14) _____ (sell) a lot of bicycle clothing as well. In fact, one of his customers regularly (15) _____ (come) into the shop and (16) _____ (buy) clothes, even though she (17) _____ (not + own) a bicycle. She (18) _____ (like) the clothes, but (19) _____ (hate) the sport! Unfortunately, this attitude (20) _____ (not + be) unusual these days, because as everybody (21) _____ (know), some people (22) _____ (think) style and appearance (23) _____ (be) more important than anything else in life.

FOCUS 5

This focus box looks more deeply at the issue of using stative vs. action verbs.

SUGGESTION

Have Ss read this box before you discuss the information in class. Since many languages do not have different forms for states and actions, this information may take time to understand.

States and Actions

EXAMPLES	EXPLANATIONS
(a) I **love** you. (b) I **hate** my job. (c) She **knows** a lot about the history of her country.	Nonprogressive verbs usually describe a state or quality that we do not expect to change. They do not describe actions.

State   Action
(d) I **weigh**   I **am weighing** myself
    120 pounds. (to see if I've gained weight).
(e) Mmm! Dinner I**'m smelling** the milk
    smells great! (to see if it smells fresh).
(f) This soup   He **is tasting** the soup
    tastes good. (to see if it needs salt).
	Some verbs describe both a state **and** an action. If the verb describes a state, use the simple present. If the verb describes an action, use the present progressive.

(g) David **is** very polite. (h) Tanya **is** a little shy.	Do not use *be* in the progressive when it describes a state or quality you do not expect to change.
(i) We **have** two cars. (j) NOT: We are having two cars. (k) We **are having** fun. (l) We always **have fun** on vacation.	Do not use *have* in the progressive to describe possession. However, you can use *have* in the progressive to describe an experience. Use the progressive if the experience is in progress at or around the time of speaking (k). Use the simple present if the experience happens again and again (l). Common expressions using *have* to describe an experience: *have fun* *have a good time* *have problems* *have trouble with* *have difficulty with*
(m) I can't talk to you right now because I **have** a really sore throat. (n) NOT: I am having a sore throat. (o) Sandy **has** a headache and a high fever today; maybe she **has** the flu. (p) NOT: Sandy is having a headache and a high fever today; maybe she is having the flu.	Do not use *have* in the progressive to describe a medical problem or physical discomfort.

28   UNIT 2

EXERCISE 7

Work with a partner or in a small group. You need a die and a small object (like a coin) to represent each person.

STEP 1 Take turns throwing the die. The person who throws the highest number starts.

STEP 2 Put your coins (or objects) on the square marked "Start" on the following page.

STEP 3 Throw the die and move your coin that number of squares.

STEP 4 Complete the sentence in the square on page 30 and say it out loud. If everyone agrees with your answer, you may write it in the square and take another turn. If the class is not sure, the teacher will be the referee. If you make a mistake or do not know the answer, the next person gets a turn. The winner is the first person to reach the final square.

1. To complete this activity, you will need to bring enough dice for small groups to use. Ss can supply their own game piece, as per instructions.
2. After Ss form pairs or small groups, use one group to demonstrate the rules of the game.
3. After the game is completed, review those items that caused disagreement among Ss.

Workbook Exs. 6 & 7, pp. 12–14.
Answers: TE p. 487.

I _____ (love) grammar! **25**	A: The Chef _____ (taste) the food right now. B: Is it good? A: Yes! It _____ (taste) wonderful! **26**	**MISS A TURN** **27**	Did you cut your hand? It _____ (bleed). **28**
She _____ (write) a letter now, but she rarely _____ (write) letters. **24**	**MISS A TURN** **23**	The students _____ (have) some trouble with verbs today. **22**	She _____ (take) three classes this semester, but she usually _____ (take) more. **21**
MISS A TURN **17**	How many pairs of shoes _____ she _____ (own) now? **18**	This suitcase _____ (weigh) too much. I can't carry it. **19**	A: What's wrong? B: I _____ (have) problems with my boyfriend at the moment. **20**
A: Look! There's the President. B: Where? I _____ (not + see) him. **16**	A: _____ you _____ (like) your job? B: No, I _____ (hate) it. **15**	A: _____ you always _____ (take) the bus? B: No, I usually _____ (walk) to work. **14**	A: Where's Tim? B: I _____ (think) he _____ (take) a nap. **13**
A: How are the kids? B: They both _____ (have) sore throats today. **9**	A: Shhh! We _____ (study) for a test. **10**	A: _____ you _____ (like) Mexican food? B: Yes, I _____ (love) it! **11**	A: How's Joe? B: Great. He _____ (have) fun because he _____ (have) a new car. **12**
MISS A TURN **8**	Mmm! Is that a new perfume? You _____ (smell) great. **7**	What _____ you _____ (think) Henry _____ (think) about right now? **6**	People _____ (spend) less money on entertainment these days. **5**
START **1**	Moya always _____ (sit) at the back of the class, but today she _____ (sit) at the front. **2**	Rose _____ (not + know) that it is my birthday today. **3**	**MISS A TURN** **4**

UNIT GOAL REVIEW

Ask Ss to look at the goals on the opening page of the unit again. Help them understand how much they have accomplished in each area.

SUGGESTION

Do a short text analysis. Modify a short newspaper article or book passage that has examples of these structures to make it suitable for your Ss. Make an overhead transparency of the passage, underline the examples, and ask Ss why the author used either the simple or progressive form of each example.

ANSWER KEY

Exercise 7

Note: Board game format; not every number requires an answer.

2. sits; is/'s sitting . . . **3.** does not/doesn't know . . . **5.** are spending . . . **6.** do you think; is/'s thinking . . . **7.** smell . . . **9.** have . . . **10.** are/'re studying . . . **11.** Do you like; love . . . **12.** is/'s having; has . . . **13.** think; is/'s taking . . . **14.** Do you always take; walk . . . **15.** Do you like; hate . . . **16.** do not/don't see . . . **18.** does she own . . . **19.** weighs . . . **20.** am/'m having . . . **21.** is/'s taking; takes . . . **22.** are having . . . **24.** is/'s writing; writes . . . **25.** love . . . **26.** is/'s tasting; tastes . . . **28.** is/'s bleeding

Use Your English

ACTIVITY 1: LISTENING/WRITING

In this activity, you will hear a radio correspondent describing her visit to a country fair. Listen to how she describes what is going on at the fair.

STEP 1 Write down three things that are happening at the fair.

STEP 2 Listen to the tape again. Write down examples of simple present and present progressive verbs in the chart below.

Simple Present	Present Progressive

ACTIVITY 2: WRITING/LISTENING

Go to a crowded place where you can sit, watch, and listen to what is happening around you. Look carefully at everything that is happening. Pretend you are a journalist or radio or television reporter. Describe in writing everything that you see. Do not forget to include everything you hear as well.

Activity 1

Play the textbook audio. The transcript for this listening appears on pp. 504–505 of this book.

If you do not have a copy of the cassette, you can read the tapescript to the class, or have Ss read to each other in pairs.

Activity 2
VARIATION

Bring a video to class. Be sure the scene you show includes a lot of activity (action films and physical comedies like Mr. Bean are good examples). Ss work in pairs, with Student 1 facing the video screen while Student 2 has his/her back to the scene and acts as secretary. Turn the volume all the way down and have Student 1 describe what s/he sees to Student 2. Ss then rewrite the notes together or present them orally to the class.

Activity 3

This activity is best modeled on the board or overhead projector first. Copy or draw the chart, then conduct the activity as a class. Afterwards, Ss can do it in groups.

Do you know how to play tic-tac-toe? In this activity, you will be playing a version of this well-known game. Work with a partner or in teams.

STEP 1   Copy each of the following onto separate cards or different pieces of paper.

she/speak	she/dance (?)*	you/live
we/hear	we/sing	I/see
I/understand	they/work (?)*	
they/eat	he/believe	(?)* = make a question
they/think about	you/write (?)*	

STEP 2   Place the cards face down on the table in front of you.

STEP 3   Player or Team X chooses a square from the box below and picks up a card from the pile. The player must make a meaningful statement that includes the word(s) in the square and the word(s) on the card. If the card has a "?" on it, the player must ask a question. Each statement or question must contain at least four words, not including the words in the square. Use the simple present or present progressive.

STEP 4   If everyone accepts the statement, Player or Team X marks the square with an X.

STEP 5   Player or Team O then chooses a different square and takes a new card. The Player or Team O makes a statement. If the statement is correct, Player or Team O marks the square with an O.

STEP 6   The first person or team to have three Xs or three Os in a straight line wins.

You can play this game again and again by erasing the Xs and Os at the end of each round, or by writing them on small pieces of paper and covering the squares with these. Good luck!

every day	today	usually
this week	occasionally	right now
often	at the moment	sometimes

ACTIVITY 4: SPEAKING/LISTENING/WRITING

STEP 1 Go around the classroom and try to find a different person for each of the situations in the chart below. Write the person's name in the box marked *Name* and add more information in the box marked *Information*. We have given some suggestions here, but you probably have more ideas of your own.

Situation	Name	Information
. . . is reading a book in English		*Title? His/her opinion?*
. . . regularly reads a newspaper from his/her country		*Why?*
. . . has more than $10.00 in cash with him/her right now		*Any coins as well as bills?*
. . . reads more than one book a month (in any language)		*Favorite books?*
. . . is living with an American host family		*Who? Where?*
. . . usually goes to the movies several times a month		*How often? Favorite movie?*
. . . is wearing an article of clothing made in the U.S.A.		*Describe it.*
. . . regularly plays a musical instrument		*What kind? How often?*
. . . is wearing perfume or cologne at the moment		*What kind? Describe it.*
. . . has a pet		*What kind? How old?*

STEP 2 Look at all the information that you collected. Choose three or four of the most interesting or surprising things that you learned about your classmates and write about this information. Remember to include an introduction. For example: *I interviewed some of my classmates and I learned several new things about them. First, I learned that Maria likes to read; in fact, she is reading a book in English that she is enjoying very much. . . .*

Read your report to a partner. Ask your partner to listen first to count the examples of the **simple present** and then listen again, doing the same for the **present progressive**.

Make a copy of the chart on an overhead transparency. Before Ss do the activity on their own, start it together. Direct them to stand up and complete the activity on their own.

Ss can do the writing part of this activity as homework.

The test for this unit can be found on pp. 413–414 of this book. The answers are on p. 415.

Unit 3

UNIT OVERVIEW

Unit 3 provides practice with the future *be going to* and *will*.

UNIT GOALS

Review the goals listed on this page so that students (Ss) understand what they should know by the end of the unit.

OPENING TASK

Note: The Opening Task allows Ss to use the target structures and allows teachers to notice what kind of help they may need. For a more complete discussion of the Opening Task, see page xxi of this Teacher's Edition.

The purpose of this task is to generate talk about the future that naturally uses *be going to* and *will*. It focuses attention on meaning rather than on form, which will allow you to see whether Ss are able to understand and produce *going to* and *will*.

SETTING UP THE TASK

If possible, use real fortune cookies to introduce this task. Otherwise, you will need to explain and/or demonstrate what fortune cookies are, or try making a "model." Ss should work in pairs or small groups to maximize the amount of "talk time."

UNIT 3

TALKING ABOUT THE FUTURE

Be Going To and Will

UNIT GOALS:
- To correctly form statements and questions about the future using *be going to* and *will*
- To know the uses of *be going to* and *will*
- To choose between *be going to* and *will*

▶ OPENING TASK
Fortune Cookie

In North America, Chinese restaurants traditionally give customers a fortune cookie at the end of the meal. This cookie is small and hollow. Inside you find a piece of paper that predicts something about your future.

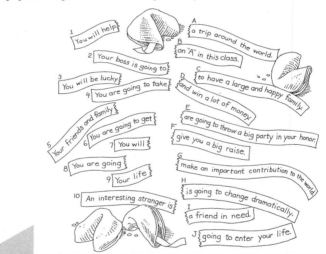

1. You will help
2. Your boss is going to
3. You will be lucky
4. You are going to take
5. Your friends and family
6. You are going to get
7. You will
8. You are going
9. Your life
10. An interesting stranger is

A. a trip around the world.
B. an "A" in this class.
C. to have a large and happy family.
D. and win a lot of money.
E. are going to throw a big party in your honor.
F. give you a big raise.
G. make an important contribution to the world.
H. is going to change dramatically.
I. a friend in need.
J. going to enter your life.

STEP 1   Match the two parts of these fortunes on page 34.

STEP 2   The writer of these fortunes has run out of ideas and needs some help. What kinds of fortunes do **you** like to receive? Write some examples in the spaces below.

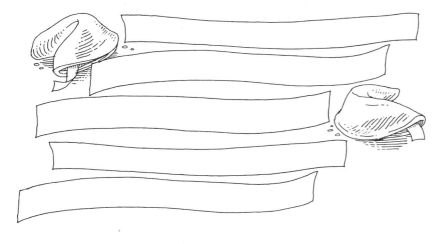

Step 1

Before going on to Step 2, you might want to check the answers for Step 1.

S U G G E S T I O N

A good way to process matching exercises like this is to write the first half of the statement on the board or on an overhead projector (OHP) transparency, and have Ss go to the board (or you can hand around the transparency). They then fill in/write down the second part of the statement.

Step 2

The purpose is to diagnose Ss' current productive use of *will* and *be going* to. If some pairs/groups finish before others, they can get together with other groups/pairs to share the fortunes that they wrote. Finally, bring the whole class together and have Ss share the most interesting/best fortunes. You could write some of these on the board and use them as a bridge to Focus 1.

Exercise 1 returns to the Opening Task and gives Ss the opportunity to revise what they wrote in Step 2, thus focusing on accuracy.

Note: Focus boxes explain and give examples of each structure. For a more complete discussion of focus boxes, see page xxii of this Teacher's Edition.

If you and your Ss wrote sentences on the board in the Opening Task, point to each sentence and ask, *What words or phrases in this sentence talk about the future?* (to elicit *will* and *be going to*).

S U G G E S T I O N

Write on the board alternative sentences that refer to you or the Ss in your class:

    a. *You will all have doctoral degrees. You will all be rich, powerful, famous, or all three.*

    b. *Marisa is going to be living in Egypt.*

    c. *Carlos and Nkonda are going to be living in Asia somewhere.*

Exercise 1

Note: The exercises following each focus box provide meaningful practice with the grammar item presented in that particular box. For a more complete discussion of how to use the exercises, see page xxiii of this Teacher's Edition.

S U G G E S T I O N

If you talked about the answers in the Opening Task, then this can go rather quickly. If you think Ss can use more reading practice, have Ss take turns reading the complete fortunes, concentrating on linking words together smoothly. If they don't need reading practice, skip this and move on to Step 2. Here Ss edit their own fortunes. You can have them check their revisions with a partner.

FOCUS **1**

Talking About the Future with *Will* and Be *Going* To

EXAMPLES	EXPLANATION
(a) An interesting stranger **is going to** enter your life. OR **(b)** An interesting stranger **will** enter your life. **(c)** You **are going to** take a trip around the world. OR **(d)** You **will** take a trip around the world.	Use either *be going to* or *will* to make a prediction or talk about the future

EXERCISE 1

Write the complete predictions about the future from the fortune cookies in the Opening Task on page 34.

  1. _____
  2. _____
  3. _____
  4. _____
  5. _____
  6. _____
  7. _____
  8. _____
  9. _____
10. _____

Look at the fortunes you wrote in Step 2 of the Opening Task. Did you use *will* and *be going to*? If you did not, rewrite the fortunes to include *will* and *be going to*.

A N S W E R   K E Y

Exercise 1
Step 1. 1. You will help a friend in need.
2. Your boss is going to give you a big rais.e
3. You will be lucky and win a lot of money. **4.** You are going to take a trip around the world. **5.** Your friends and family are growing to throw a big party in your honor.
6. You are going to get an "A" in this class.

7. You will make an important contribution to the world. **8.** You are going to have a large and happy family. **9.** Your life is going to change dramatically. **10.** An interesting stranger is going to enter your life.
Step 2. Answers will vary according to Ss' work on the Task.

Will and *Be Going To*

Will does not change to agree with the subject:

STATEMENT	NEGATIVE	QUESTION
I You We They **will leave.** She **'ll** He It	I You We They **will not/won't leave.** She He It	I you we **Will** they leave? she he it

Be going to changes to agree with the subject:

STATEMENT	NEGATIVE	QUESTION
I **am going to leave.** **'m**	I **am not** **'m not going to leave.**	**Am** I going to leave?
She He **is going to leave.** It **'s**	She **is not** He **is't going to leave.** It **'s not**	he **Is** she going to leave? it
You We **are going to leave.** They **'re**	You **are not** We **aren't going to leave.** They **'re not**	you **Are** we going to leave? they

EXERCISE 2

STEP 1 Write predictions about the future for five of your classmates. Be sure to include some predictions that use negative forms. Do not use your classmates' names.

▶ **EXAMPLES:** *He will go to China.*

She will not live at home.

He is going to get an A *in this class.*

1. _____

2. _____

This is a good opportunity to talk about the contractions won't and 'll: (*I'll, You'll,* and so on/upper right of focus box). Ss point out that the words *will not* seem (phonetically) unrelated to the contraction *won't*: "They don't sound the same."

Some might ask why the contraction isn't "willn't". Possible answer: *Good question! That would be logical but languages aren't also clearly logical, although often if you trace a word or phrase back historically, you can understand some of these changes over time. But with will not and won't—and many other cases as well— that's just the way it is!*

When you introduce *going to,* you can mention that the contraction sounds like *gonna* in fast English (or this topic might naturally emerge in the course of doing this unit).

Exercise 2

Tell Ss that these can be real predictions— you really think they will come true—or they can be "highly fictionalized"!

Step 2

SUGGESTION

If you have a large class, have them choose only one of their predictions to read aloud. If one student appears to be getting "picked on," i.e., all the predictions are about him/her, you might want to ask each student to make a prediction about someone who hasn't yet been mentioned.

Feel free to enter into this as well, making predictions about your Ss, or as a "trick"—about yourself (using "she" or "he"). The latter would necessitate your asking yourself a question to find out if this is true, as per instructions!

FOCUS 3

SUGGESTION

Using a book, notebook, or other unbreakable object, demonstrate the difference between "It's gonna fall!" and "It'll fall." With the first, the implication is *right now!* You can exaggerate by expressing "urgency" in your voice and actions (louder volume, a display of nervousness, etc.). With the second, the implication is *if . . . I push it a little farther* (off the edge of a desk)/*move it closer to the edge*. You can contrast this with "It's gonna fall!" with a more calm tone of voice, and a lack of urgency.

Point out that *be going to* is so commonly used that some people wouldn't see the difference in register—how informal or formal it's considered. For example, some would say that it would be appropriate to use "Is the test *going to be* difficult?" in (f), especially considering that classrooms in the U.S. are typically pretty casual and informal.

---

3. _____

4. _____

5. _____

STEP 2 Read each of your predictions aloud. If one of your classmates thinks a prediction is about him or her, invite this person to ask a question to find out if this is true.

▶ **EXAMPLES:** *Will I go to China?*

Yes, you will.

Am I going to get an A?

Yes, you are.

FOCUS **3**

Making Predictions:
Will or Be Going To?

EXAMPLES	EXPLANATIONS
(a) Be careful! That chair **is going to** break. (b) NOT: Be careful! That chair will break! (c) Oh no!! That little boy **is going to** fall off the bridge. (d) NOT: Oh no!! That little boy will fall off the bridge.	It is better to use *be going to* for actions or events that you think will happen very soon or immediately.
(e) *Babysitter to child:* Your mommy's **going to** be very angry about this. (f) *Student to professor:* **Will** the test be difficult? *Professor:* It **will** be tough, but I don't think you **will** have too many problems with it.	When the future event or action will not happen immediately: It is better to use *be going to* in informal situations (relaxed and friendly situations, with family or friends). In informal speech, *going to* is usually pronounced *gonna*. It is better to use *will* in more formal situations.

38 UNIT 3

ANSWER KEY

Exercise 2
Answers will vary according to Ss' predictions about each other.

EXERCISE 3

For each of the following, decide on the best form to use: *be going to* or *will*. In some sentences, it is possible to use both. The first one has been done for you.

1. Quick! Catch the baby! I think he <u>is going to</u> roll off the bed.
2. Excuse me, Mr. President. Do you think unemployment _____ decrease in the foreseeable future?
3. Uh-oh. Look at those clouds. It _____ rain.
4. I predict that you _____ meet a tall, dark, and handsome stranger, and you _____ fall in love and get married.
5. One day we _____ look back at all this and laugh.
6. I don't believe it. Look at Paula! I think she _____ ask that guy to dance with her.
7. A: What do you think about my son's chances of getting into Harvard, Dr. Heath?

   B: I don't think he _____ have any problems at all, Mrs. Lee.
8. Meteorologists predict that the drought _____ end sometime this fall.

FOCUS **4**

Future Plans and Intentions: *Be Going To*

EXAMPLES	EXPLANATION
(a) We**'re going to** spend the month of August in Italy. We bought the tickets last week, and we**'re going to** leave on August 2nd. **(b)** Tasha, age 9: When I grow up, **I'm going to** be the president of the United States.	It is better to use *be going to* to talk about a future plan or intention (something you want to do in the future). This shows that you made the decision to do this **before** speaking.

A N S W E R   K E Y

Exercise 3
2. will   3. is/'s going to   4. will, will (or: are going to, are going to)   5. will/'ll (or: are going to—relaxed situation)   6. is/'s going to   7. will/'ll   8. will

---

Exercise 3
If you still want/need more information about how Ss are doing at this point, follow the instructions and first have them work individually. Circulate, noting which Ss are keeping up (or seem to already know this grammar) and which find this challenging.

S U G G E S T I O N

Since the items here are intended to be spoken statements, it makes sense to regroup and do this exercise aloud as a class, or in groups of 5 to 7 if that's not too chaotic for your particular classroom. If Ss read their sentences with full words rather than contractions, elicit the contractions from them after their first reading or model the way a "fluent" (or native) speaker would say the sentences.

Example: 1. *I think <u>he's gonna</u> roll off the bed.* rather than *I think <u>he is going to</u>.*

FOCUS 4

S U G G E S T I O N S

1. To add to the explanation, point out that using *will* instead of *be going to* sounds like at the moment of speaking you got the idea to do this; you hadn't planned to do this before speaking.
2. Make up a few contrastive sentences with *be going to* and *will*, or ask your Ss to make up sentences in pairs or small groups. It's more meaningful if these sentences are about you, your Ss, or your situation. For example (in a classroom situated in Zimbabwe), contrast: *I'm gonna go to Hwange National Park before I leave Zimbabwe.* with: *I'll go to Hwange National Park before I leave Zimbabwe.*
3. Explain the differences, or elicit them from your Ss. (If they have had exposure to English, they may already have a sense of these differences without knowing it.)

Explanation: *The first sounds like a plan, something you've thought about. Maybe you even have tickets, safari reservations, etc. The second sounds more like a prediction or like you just now got the idea.* This topic also serves as a link to Focus 5.

Exercise 4

The last step (after item 3) asks Ss to talk *about* their choices. If you notice as you are circulating that their explanations are effective—that is, they are convincing each other that their choices are the best choices, then point out to your Ss what they are doing: making grammatical choices and justifying them. Congratulate them. This is a skill that sometimes native speakers haven't developed. Example: Ask a native speaker who hasn't been trained in grammar why you use one word and not another—or one structure and not another, and they will say "it just 'sounds' right." In other words, they don't necessarily know how to explain things in grammatical terms. But your Ss are doing it!

Exercise 5

Ss can do this individually in class or as homework if you want to use class time in more productive ways. In any case, at some point you should have Ss discuss any problems or disagreements. An efficient way to work through this is to first work in pairs or small groups. Then they can summarize their disagreement asking questions and using contrastive examples to explain/defend their point of view. This discussion encourages Ss to take the responsibility for addressing questions that they still have and it provides them practice in talking *about* grammar, which can be useful (to a point) when *learning* grammar.

EXERCISE 4

In this exercise, you need to get information from one of your classmates. Use *be going to* or *will* in your answers, as appropriate.

1. Get together with a partner and find out three things she or he intends to do after class:

   My partner _____

   _____ .

2. Now find out three things she or he does not intend to do after class:

   My partner _____

   _____ .

3. Now make three predictions about your partner's future:

   My partner _____

   _____ .

Finally, look back at what you have written in this exercise. Where did you choose *be going to* and where did you choose *will*? Why did you make these choices?

EXERCISE 5

Read the following carefully and decide if the use of *be going to* or *will* is more appropriate. Check (✔) the sentences you think are acceptable. Correct the sentences you think are unacceptable.

1. A: Do you have any plans for tonight?
   B: Yes. We will go to the baseball game. Do you want to come with us?
2. A: Your nephew is a very talented artist, isn't he?
   B: Yes. We believe he'll be very famous one of these days.
3. A: Who do you think will win the next World Cup?
   B: I think Brazil is going to win next time.
   A: Really?
4. A: Where's Freddie?
   B: He will spend the night at his friend's house.
5. A: Have you heard the news? Heidi's going to get married.
   B: That's great!

ANSWER KEY

Exercise 4
Answers will depend on the Ss' own plans, intentions, or predictions. You might expect answers similar to the following:
1. *My partner is going to go to the library after class.* (plan/intention) 2. *My partner isn't going to do her homework after class.* (plan/intention) 3. *My partner will/is going to have a very successful career* (prediction)

Exercise 5
1. going to go (future plan/intention)
2. acceptable (prediction) 3. acceptable (prediction) 4. *is going to* (future plan/intention) 5. acceptable (future plan/intention)

Two More Uses of *Will*: Making Quick Decisions and Serious Promises

EXAMPLES	EXPLANATIONS
(a) A: I think there's someone at the front door. B: I**'ll** go and check.	Use *will* to show you have decided to do something at that moment. You decide to do this as you speak.
(b) A: Telephone! B: OK. I**'ll** get it.	The contracted *'ll* is usually used in these situations.
(c) A: I need someone to help out at the recycling center. B: Oh, I **will**!	Do not use *'ll* in short answers.
(d) I **will** always love you. **(e)** I**'ll** give you my homework tomorrow, I promise! **(f)** A: Remember, this is top secret. B: I **won't** tell anybody. You can count on me.	Use *will* to make a serious promise.

EXERCISE 6

Complete the following, using *be going to, 'll* or *will* as appropriate.

1. A: What are your plans for the weekend?

B: We _____ take the boat and go fishing.

A: Sounds great. Can I join you?

2. A: Excuse me, but I can't reach those books on the top shelf.

B: Move over. I _____ get them down for you.

3. A: You've bought a lot of groceries today.

B: Yes. I _____ cook dinner for the people who work in my office.

4. A: Here's $20.

B: Thank you. I promise I _____ pay you back next week.

5. A: Oops! I've just spilled my drink all over everything.

B: Don't panic. I _____ get a cloth.

ANSWER KEY

Exercise 6
1. 're/are going to   2. 'll   3. 'm/am going to   4. 'll/will   5. 'll'/will   6. are (you) going to/are going to   7. 'll   8. 'll   9. are (you) going to/'re (you) going to/will /'ll ; 's/is going to/'ll/will

---

The explanation for (a) and (b) might have been touched on in Focus 4 as well, especially if you followed the Focus 4 suggestions in this Teacher's Edition.

SUGGESTION

1. Demonstrate verbally what you *can't* do as in example (c): You can't say, "Oh, I'll!" Point out to Ss that no native speaker would say this. It sounds odd.
2. Emphasize that the context of (d) through (f) can be *very* serious or intimate. Sentence (d), or something similar, is often used in wedding vows, sometimes with the word "promise": example, *I promise (or I vow) that I will love, honor, and respect you."* Sentence (e) would have to involve close friends who can trust each other's word. Sentence (f) is also very serious—top secret, in fact.

Workbook Ex. 3, p. 16.
Answers: TE p. 487.
Workbook Ex. 5, p. 18.
Answers: TE p. 487.

Exercise 6

Since these situations are dialogues, it's fun to do this exercise orally.

SUGGESTIONS

1. Give Ss a few minutes to work with a partner, and check to make sure they have answers for each blank. This will allow the dialogue-reading to move along smoothly so that the class is not waiting for the speakers to search for the answers.
2. Before Ss read, encourage them to use contractions in their answers if appropriate. Even if they're not used to using contractions in their own speech (they certainly don't have to), if they speak with native speakers of English, they will definitely hear them in their speech.

Exercise 7

This might be a good point to see if pairs are "balanced." As you circulate, pay attention to whether both Ss in a pair are talking or not. If not, encourage them to take turns, each giving responses to the items. Sometimes you may have to insist to the "dominant" student: *No, Emmanuel, you answered the last question. It's Miriam's turn for this one.* Or perhaps it's the "quiet" student who needs encouragement or more time. Consider the possibility that some of the contexts or words may be unfamiliar. Ss may need to ask questions first, before they can come up with responses.

    Evaluate how effectively pair work is going in your classes. Are there ways you can make it more effective, such as assigning pairs who you think will be well matched?

---

6. **A:** What (you) _____ wear to Aki's party?

    B: Kuniko and I _____ wear jeans. What about you?

7. **A:** Now, kids, I want you to be very good this afternoon because I'm not feeling well.

    B: It's O.K., Mrs. Swanson. We promise we _____ behave.

8. **A:** What's up?

    B: I'm late for work and my car won't start.

    A: Don't worry. I _____ give you a ride.

9. **A:** What (you) _____ do with your brother when he comes to visit next weekend?

    B: First, Jody and I _____ take him out to brunch down by the beach, and after that Kate _____ show him the sights.

EXERCISE 7

With a partner, look at these situations and decide on ways to respond using *will* or *be going to*.

1. You look out of the window and notice there are a lot of stormy, black clouds in the sky. What do you say?

    _____

    _____

2. Your friend Oscar is interested in music and in physics, but he can't decide which one to major in next year. After a lot of thought and discussion, he has finally decided to major in music. What does he say to his family?

    _____

    _____

3. Your friend is organizing an international potluck. She needs people to bring food from different countries. You want to help. What do you say?

    _____

    _____

4. It's 6:30 A.M. You have to drive to the airport to pick up your uncle at 7:30 A.M., but your car won't start. Your roommate offers to lend you hers, but she needs to have it back by 9:00 A.M. to get to work. What do you tell her?

    _____

    _____

ANSWER KEY

Exercise 7

Answers will vary, depending on Ss' responses. These are possibilities:

1. (It looks like) it's going to rain. 2. (I've decided) I'm going to major in music next year. 3. I'll bring . . . to the potluck (if you think that sounds good). 4. I'll (be sure to) bring the car back by 9:00. 5. (It looks like) your books are going to fall out of your backpack. 6. I'm going to go to class today, so I'll take notes for you (if you'd like). 7. (Watch out! Slow down or) you'll/you're going to hit that little boy! 8. I'm going to go to "Swan Lake". 9. I'll do them later. (I've got to go help my friend.) 10. You will/You're going to.

5. You are standing in line in the campus cafeteria. You notice that the backpack of the student in front of you is open and all her books are about to fall out. What do you tell her?

_____

_____

6. One of your classmates is sick and has to go to the doctor's office. He is very worried about missing his history class. You are also in that class. What can you say to reassure him?

_____

_____

7. Your friend is giving you a ride home. Suddenly you notice a little boy who is about to run into the road. Your friend hasn't seen him. What do you say?

_____

_____

8. Your friend Frank loves ballet. He has just bought the last ticket for a special gala performance of "Swan Lake" next Saturday night. You ask him about his plans for the weekend. What does he say?

_____

_____

9. You have promised to do the dishes and clean up the kitchen after dinner. Just before you get started, you receive an unexpected phone call from a friend whose car has broken down and he urgently needs your help. As you are leaving, your roommate comes into the room and asks, "What about the dishes?" What do you say?

_____

_____

10. Madame Cassandra is a fortune-teller who makes exciting predictions about the future. Your teacher is consulting Madame Cassandra. What does Madame Cassandra tell your teacher?

_____

_____

UNIT GOAL REVIEW

Ask Ss to look at the goals on the opening page of the unit again. Help them understand how much they have accomplished in each area. For example, make sentences that contrast _will_ and _be going to_ and ask Ss to explain the differences in use. This is also an opportunity to ask them to identify which areas they would like more practice with. If you feel that they are still challenged by some of the points in this chapter, allow plenty of time for the activities and/or for reviewing relevant focus boxes and exercises.

USE YOUR ENGLISH

The activities in the purple pages at the end of the unit contain situations that should naturally elicit the structures covered in the unit. For a more complete discussion of how to use the Use Your English Activities, see page xxiv of this Teacher's Edition.

When Ss are doing these activities in class, you can circulate and listen to see how they are using the structures targeted in this unit. Have they achieved the goals presented at the beginning of the unit?

Activity 1

Preview this activity by playing a quick game of Tic Tac Toe with simple Xs and Os on the blackboard. It's best if you can find a student who has played this to volunteer to play it with you. Ask Ss if, as children, they played this game or one similar to it. Then explain that the concept of Tic Tac Toe applies here, since they are trying to answer a line of three squares in any direction—vertically, horizontally, diagonally.

As Ss collect information from each other, circulate, noting any errors in the use of *be going to*. Think about how (and if) you want to address these errors if there are some. For example, do you want read the statements with errors and have the Ss find and correct them? Do you want to review Focus 2?

Use Your English

ACTIVITY 1: SPEAKING/LISTENING/WRITING

The purpose of this activity is to collect as much information as possible about the future plans and intentions of your classmates. Look at the chart below. Complete as many squares as you can by finding the required information. *Maybe* and *I don't know* are not acceptable answers! Write the information in the appropriate square and also the name or names of the people who gave you the information. The first person to get information for three squares in a row in any direction is the winner. Good luck!

Find someone who is going to take the TOEFL soon. When is she or he going to take it?	Find three people who are going to cook dinner tonight. What are they going to cook?	Find two people who are going to go to the library after this class. What are they going to do there?
Find two people who are going to play the same sport this week. What sport are they going to play?	Find someone who is going to move to another city within a year. What city is she or he going to move to?	Find someone who is going to go to the movies today. What movie is she or he going to see?
Find someone who is going to get his or her hair cut in the next two weeks. Where is he or she going to get it cut?	Find two people who are going to watch TV tonight. What are they going to watch?	Find two people who are going to celebrate their birthdays next month. What are their birthdates?

ACTIVITY 2: WRITING/SPEAKING

STEP 1 Write fortune cookie "fortunes" for your teacher and five of your classmates. Write each fortune on a small slip of paper, and give each one to the appropriate person.

STEP 2 The people who receive fortunes will read their fortunes aloud and the rest of the class will decide if they think the fortunes will come true.

ACTIVITY 3: WRITING

What are your predictions for the next ten years? What do you think will happen in the world? What do you think will happen in your country?

STEP 1 Write a brief report on your predictions. Your report should include a short introduction to your topic. It is not necessary to use *will* and *be going to* in every sentence you write!

STEP 2 When you finish writing, read your report carefully and check your use of *will* and *be going to*. Remember, it is often possible to use either one.

We have written the beginning of a report to give you some ideas, but you probably have better ideas of your own.

LIFE IN THE FUTURE

Nobody knows exactly what will happen in the future, but in my opinion, there will be many important changes in the world in the next ten years. Some of them will be good and some of them will be bad. In this short report, I am going to talk about some of my predictions for the future of the world, as well as the future of my country.

First, let me tell you about my predictions for the world. . . .

Activity 2

You might want to add the additional "rule" that if anyone is uncomfortable with his or her fortune, for any reason, they can "pass"— they don't have to read their fortunes aloud to the rest of the class.

EXPANSION

A fun addition to this activity is to get empty fortune cookies (available in some grocery stores) and have Ss insert their own fortunes and deliver the fortune cookie to the intended recipient.

Activity 3
VARIATION

This is a good activity to take outside of the classroom if you have access to native speakers of English or to fluent/proficient speakers of English, some of whom may have lived in English-speaking countries. Ss can work in research teams to find out about what a certain population of people thinks will happen in the future (for example, people of a particular age, e.g., over 60, 20–25; Ss in another class, all the Ss they know from a particular place/region/country, people that live together, etc.). Or they can narrow the topic further: For example, what do they think will happen to the environment, to the warring countries in _____, to women's rights, etc. Research teams then pool their information and write a report, either individually or together as a group.

Activity 4

Play textbook audio. The tapescript for this listening activity appears on p. 505 of this book.

EXPANSION

Take Step 3 further, asking Ss to explain why they think the speaker chose *will* or *be going to*. They can use Focus Boxes 1, 3, 4, and 5 as a resource.

Activity 5

VARIATION

If you are in a monolingual or foreign language (non-English-speaking) setting, you can adapt this activity to populations other than North Americans. Also adapt the instructions in terms of age. If your Ss are interested in what older people or middle-aged people think about their future, they can develop questions that will address these situations instead.

For situations where there is little or no access to native English speakers, but there are a number of people available who speak English proficiently and/or who have lived in English-speaking countries, conduct interviews with them. Alternatively, Ss could conduct interviews in their own languages and then do the other steps in English.

ACTIVITY 4: SPEAKING/ LISTENING

STEP 1 Listen to the tape of three different people talking about their goals and future plans. About how old do you think each speaker is? Take a guess. Take notes on what each speaker says in the chart below.

SPEAKER	AGE	FUTURE PLANS AND GOALS
Speaker 1		
Speaker 2		
Speaker 3		

STEP 2 Think about your own goals and future plans. Are they similar to those of any of the three speakers? Explain to a partner.

STEP 3 Listen to the tape again. Write down all the examples you hear of the future with *will* and *be going to*.

ACTIVITY 5: SPEAKING/ LISTENING

STEP 1 In this activity, you will interview several young North Americans about their goals and future plans. If possible, try to interview at least three young people who are at different stages of their lives: college students, high school students, and children. Find out what they are going to do when they leave school.

STEP 2 Report your findings to the class.

STEP 3 If possible, tape your interviews. Later listen to your tape and take note of the different ways these native speakers talk about the future. Make a list of the most interesting plans and share them with the rest of the class.

ANSWER KEY

Activity 4
Check tapescript for answers (p. 505).

ACTIVITY 6: LISTENING/SPEAKING

In this activity, you will create a chain story about your teacher's next vacation.

STEP 1 Your teacher will start by telling you where he or she is going for his or her next vacation and one thing he or she is going to do:

Teacher: I'm going to Hawaii for my vacation, and I am going to climb a mountain.

STEP 2 The next person repeats the first part and adds another statement about the teacher's vacation until everyone in the room has added to the description.

▶ **EXAMPLE:** *Student 1:* (Teacher's name) is going to Hawaii; he or she is going to climb a mountain; he or she is going to swim in the ocean, too.

Activity 6
SUGGESTION

If you've got a large class, consider starting fresh and/or making up a story about someone else when memories start to fade (somewhere between 10 or 15, maybe more, maybe less!). Or you might consider taking a turn yourself, using first person I, of course, if the story's about you.

The test for this unit can be found on pp. 416–417 of this book. The answers are on p. 418.

TOEFL Test Preparation Exercises for Units 1–3 can be found on pp. 22–25 of the Workbook.
The answers are on p. 488 of this book.

Unit 4

UNIT OVERVIEW

In this unit, students (Ss) are introduced to a variety of question forms, with emphasis on the use of grammatical structures and pronunciation.

UNIT GOALS

If Ss are confused by the term "intonation" when you review these goals, point out that intonation is a pronunciation issue. As many languages have only one intonation pattern for questions, this may be new information.

OPENING TASK

The aim of this task is to use the photograph to illustrate and elicit the form and use of questions. At this level, Ss should already have some familiarity with forming questions.

CONDUCTING THE TASK

Step 1

Have Ss discuss the photograph in pairs or groups. What questions do they think the students in the picture might have for their teacher?

UNIT 4

ASKING QUESTIONS

Yes/No, Wh-, Tag Questions, Choice Questions

UNIT GOALS:

- To know how to form questions (Yes/No, Wh-, choice and tag) and what they mean
- To know the uses of different intonation patterns for various question types

OPENING TASK
Any Questions?

STEP 1

STEP 2 What questions would you like to ask **your** teacher? Work alone or with other students to complete the questions on this page.

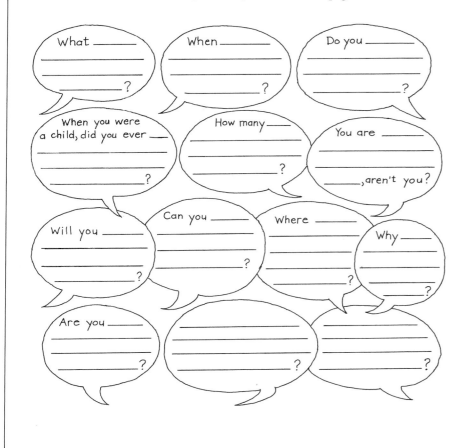

Explain that Ss must use the prompts where indicated, but can use whatever form they like for the last two questions.

COMPLETING THE TASK

1. When Ss are finished, elicit some of their questions, answering them for content, not accuracy.
2. Answers will vary. Use the Answer Key below as a guide.
3. Point out that they will be using these questions in later exercises (1, 2, and 13).

ANSWER KEY

Opening Task

Answers will vary. Examples include (left to right):
1. What will we study next?   **2.** When are we going to study the simple past tense?
3. Do you like your job?   **4.** When you were a child, did you ever travel to another country?   **5.** How many classes do you teach?   **6.** You are going to give us a test, aren't you?   **7.** Will you help me with my pronunciation?   **8.** Can you speak another language?   **9.** Where do you want to travel?   **10.** Why do you like to teach English?   **11.** Are you going to give us homework tonight?

As a review, Focus 1 provides information on form and meaning of questions where the expected answer is *yes* or *no*.

Grammar Note

While the inverted word order of these questions is familiar to those whose languages use the same form, the use of the auxiliary verb *do* with present simple verbs other than *be* sometimes causes confusion. Once Ss recognize that *do* is the simple present auxiliary (or "helping") verb, the subject-auxiliary inversion for *yes/no* questions is regular:

They <u>are</u> Slovak.
→ <u>Are</u> they Slovak?
They (<u>do</u>) speak Slovak.
→ <u>Do</u> they speak Slovak?
They <u>are</u> speaking Slovak.
→ <u>Are</u> they speaking Slovak?
They <u>can</u> speak Slovak.
→ <u>Can</u> they speak Slovak?

If you find some Ss using subject-verb inversion with *have* as the main verb (as with *be*), you can point out that in American English this form is rarely used:
NOT: Have you the time?
→ Do you have the time?
If they have studied British English, they may have encountered this structure.

Pronunciation Notes

1. Many languages use rising intonation for question forms, so this concept is often not a problem. Some languages, however, use a "flatter" tone than English, which may make Ss sound disinterested or bored in English.

2. Using a greater range in rising intonation is especially important when turning statements into questions, as in (u)–(x).

3. You may wish to practice having Ss copy your intonation in reading the example sentences. They can read along with you or repeat after you. This practice can also be done in pairs, with their partners determining if they sound "interested" or not. Ss repeat their sentences until their partner is satisfied.

FOCUS **1**

FORM MEANING

▶ **R**eview of *Yes/No* Questions

EXAMPLES	EXPLANATIONS
(a) *Question*: Are you Brazilian? *Answer*: Yes, I am./No, I'm not. **(b)** *Question*: Do you understand? *Answer*: Yes, I do./No, I don't.	When you ask a *Yes/No* question, you expect the answer *yes* or *no*. *Yes/No* questions end with rising intonation.
subject be **(c)** *Statement*: He is tired. *be subject* Question: **Is** he tired? **(d)** **Are** you ready to go? **(e)** **Am** I too late for dinner? **(f)** **Was** the plane on time? **(g)** **Were** they mad at me?	***Yes/No* questions with *be*:** Invert the subject and the verb (move the verb **in front of** the subject).
subject verb **(h)** *Statement*: They speak Turkish. *do subject base verb* Question: **Do** they **speak** Turkish? **(i)** NOT: Speak they Turkish? **(j)** **Does** the bus **stop** here? **(k)** **Do** you **take** credit cards? **(l)** **Did** the President **know** about this?	***Yes/No* questions with other verbs:** Put the appropriate form of *do* **in front of** the subject. Put the base form of the verb **after** the subject.
subject be verb + -ing **(m)** *Statement*: They are leaving. *be subject verb + -ing* Question: **Are** they **leaving**? **(n)** **Is** your computer **working** today? **(o)** **Are** they **coming** with us? **(p)** **Was** it **raining** there? **(q)** **Were** her parents **visiting**?	***Yes/No* questions with verbs in the progressive:** Invert the subject and *be* (move the *be* verb in front of the subject). For information on *Yes/No* questions with present perfect and past perfect, see Units 13, 14, and 19.

EXAMPLES	EXPLANATIONS
subject modal base verb **(r)** *Statement*: It will rain. *modal subject base verb* *Question*: **Will** it **rain**? **(s)** **Would** you **repeat** that? **(t)** **Can** you **help** me?	**Yes/No questions with modals:** Invert the modal and the subject (put the modal in **front of** the subject).
(u) *Statement*: She asked him out. *Question*: She asked him out? **(v)** You're from England? **(w)** Sasha can come? **(x)** He's 40 years old? Yes, he is.	**Statement form of Yes/No questions:** A statement said with rising intonation is also a type of *Yes/No* question. This type of question is common in informal conversation. When a statement form question is used, the speaker usually expects the listener to agree.

EXERCISE 1

Get together with a partner and make a list of all the *Yes/No* questions you both wanted to ask your teacher in the Opening Task on page 49. Write them here or in a notebook and add three more *Yes/No* questions to ask your teacher. You will have an opportunity to ask these questions later in the unit.

_____

_____

_____

_____

_____

_____

_____

_____

_____

_____

_____

_____

_____

_____

_____

_____

Exercise 1

Note that answers will vary and encourage Ss to help each other correct errors. While they are working, you can circulate around the room to note some of their errors for later discussion.

You can also elicit some of their questions, writing them on the board or overhead projector for class editing.

Workbook Exs. 1–3, pp. 26–28.
Answers: TE p. 488.

This focus box reviews the form and meaning of questions that ask for more information than *yes/no*, usually beginning with *Wh*-words. Further discussion of these question forms is given in Focus 3 and Focus 4.

Pronunciation Notes

Aside from the difference in expected response, the intonation of these questions also differs from those in Focus 1.
While you should avoid discussing this issue at this point, be sure to stress the importance of the use of **falling** intonation, as rising intonation in *Wh*-questions indicates the need for clarification or shows surprise:
What time is it? ↘
(→ general request for information)
What time is it? ↗
(→ checking information or indication of surprise)
The use of falling intonation often takes some practice, as in many languages falling intonation is reserved for statements. The use of rising intonation is discussed in Focus 4.

FOCUS **2**

▶ Review of *Wh*-Questions

EXAMPLES	EXPLANATIONS
(a) Q: What is your name? A: Elena. *Who What When Where* *Why Whose Which How*	A *Wh*-question usually begins with a *Wh*-word and expects the speaker to give information rather than *yes* or *no* in the answer.
(b) Where do you come from? ↘ **(c)** When did you arrive? ↘ **(d)** How many languages do you speak? ↘	*Wh*-questions usually end in falling intonation.
(e) Q: Why are you late? A: Because I missed the bus. *Wh-word be subject* **(f)** **Where is** the restroom? **(g)** **What was** her name? **(h)** **Who are** his friends? **(i)** **What's** the time? **(j)** **Where's** my car?	**_Wh_-questions with _be_:** Choose a *Wh*-word. Invert the subject and the verb. In informal speech, *is* is often contracted to *'s* in *Wh*-questions.
(k) Q: When did she get here? A: Just a few minutes ago. *Wh-word do subject base verb* **(l)** **Who(m) do** you **love**? **(m)** **What does** a judge **do**? **(n)** **Where did** Nicole **live**?	**_Wh_-questions with other verbs:** Choose a *Wh*-word. To form the question, follow the *Wh*-word with a form of *do*.
(o) Q: What time can you leave? A: As soon as this class is over. *Wh-word modal subject base verb* **(p)** **How long can** I **stay**? **(q)** **When will** she **come**?	**_Wh_-questions with modals:** Choose a *Wh*-word. To form a question, put the modal directly after the *Wh*-word and before the subject.

EXERCISE 2

Get together with a partner and write down all the *Wh*-questions that you wanted to ask your teacher in the Opening Task. Write them on a piece of paper and add three more. You will have an opportunity to ask them later in the unit.

EXERCISE 3

Bruno and Ken are friends. Bruno has just introduced Ken to his cousin, Marta. Ken is very interested in getting to know more about her, so now he is asking Bruno all about her.

Get together with a partner and look at the answers that Bruno gave. What questions do you think Ken probably asked? Write them in the appropriate place.

Ken: (1) _____?
Bruno: Yes, I think she does.
Ken: (2) _____?
Bruno: No, she doesn't.
Ken: (3) _____?
Bruno: Usually around midnight.
Ken: (4) _____?
Bruno: Not usually.
Ken: (5) _____?
Bruno: In Buenos Aires.
Ken: (6) _____?
Bruno: Three times a week, I think.
Ken: (7) _____?
Bruno: No, she isn't.
Ken: (8) _____?
Bruno: Yes, I'm pretty sure she was.
Ken: (9) _____?
Bruno: Last year, or maybe the year before. I can't remember exactly.
Ken: (10) _____?
Bruno: I have no idea. You'll have to ask her that question yourself.

Now change partners. Read the questions that you wrote while your new partner reads Bruno's answers. When you finish, change roles to read your partner's dialogue. Compare your questions with a partner's. Does Marta seem like a different person? In what ways?

Exercise 2

As in Exercise 1, answers will vary and Ss should focus on accuracy of form. As you circulate, note errors you hear for later reference.

You can also ask Ss to complete the task on paper to be collected for correction.

Exercise 3

1. Point out that Bruno's short answers contain clues such as auxiliary verbs to give them clues. Model one or two on the board or overhead projector:
   Ken: <u>Is Marta staying long?</u>
   Bruno: *No, unfortunately she isn't.*
   Ken: <u>How old is she?</u>
   Bruno: *Younger than me. I think she's 19.*

2. After Ss have changed partners and practiced their questions, they work with the same or different classmate to discuss the differences in Marta's character. When they are finished, discuss some of their observations as a class, writing down some of the similarities and differences.

Workbook Exs. 4–6, pp. 28–30.
Answers: TE p. 488.

The difference between *Wh-* questions that focus on the subject and object is form.
If the question is about the subject, the *Wh-* word replaces the subject and there is no inversion:
Q: *Who sits next to you?*
A: *Jan sits here.*
When the question is about the object, there is inversion:
Q: *Who are you talking to?* —or—
Q: *To whom are you talking?*
A: *I'm talking to Ali.*
Remind Ss that they will rarely encounter the object form *whom* in spoken English, but that it is used in more formal contexts such as academic writing.

Exercise 4

1. Before Ss start working in pairs, model the first few questions by eliciting them from the class.
2. Note that answers will vary; use the answer key below as a guide. Use the overhead transparency to review some of their options as a class.

S U G G E S T I O N

Make an overhead transparency of the report and question box and fill in the first few items and questions together.

Wh-Questions that Focus on the Subject

EXAMPLES	EXPLANATIONS

(a)   Q: **Who(m)** did you call?
      A: I called Tony.
             object
 (b)   Q: **Who** called you?
      A: Martin called me.
        subject
	This question asks about the object. *Who* is more common in informal speech. *Whom* is very formal.
	 This question asks about the subject.

Wh-word   *Verb*
 (c)   Q: **Who**   lives here?
      A: Shan lives here.
 (d)   Q: **Who** told you?
      A: Herb did.
	For *Wh-*questions about the subject, put the appropriate *Wh-*word in front of the verb. Do not use *do* in the question.

(e)   Q: **What** annoys her?
      A: Everything.
 (f)   Q: **What** music annoys her?
      A: Heavy metal.
 (g)   Q: **What** bands annoy her?
      A: Aerosmith and Megadeth.
	Use *what* to ask a general question about something.
	 Use *what* + a noun when you want a more specific answer. Make the verb singular or plural to agree with the noun.

EXERCISE 4

Get together with another student or someone in your class for this exercise. First read the report below. Next, think of the questions you need to ask your friend in order to complete the report. Write the questions in the "Question Box." Ask your partner all of the questions without showing them to him or her. Finally, use the answers that your friend gives you to complete the report.

Report:

My friend (1) _____ is from (2) _____ and
speaks (3) _____ languages: (4) _____ . S/he was
born in (5) _____ and s/he has (6) _____ brothers
and sisters. Her/his favorite subjects in school were (7) _____ .
S/he is taking this class because (8) _____ . In her free time,
s/he likes to (9) _____ . Her/his favorite (10) _____
is/are (11) _____ . When s/he first came here,
(12) _____ surprised her/him. After s/he finishes school,
s/he hopes to (13) _____ . (14) _____
make(s) her/him happy, but (15) _____ make(s) her/him angry.
Finally, there is one more thing I'd like to tell you about my friend:
(16) _____ .

QUESTION BOX

1	_____ ?	2	_____ ?
3	_____ ?	4	_____ ?
5	_____ ?	6	_____ ?
7	_____ ?	8	_____ ?
9	_____ ?	10	_____ ?
11	_____ ?	12	_____ ?
13	_____ ?	14	_____ ?
15	_____ ?	16	_____ ?

ANSWER KEY

Exercise 4

For 10, 11, and 16, answers will vary. The others will most likely be:
(1) What is your name? **(2)** Where are you from? **(3)** How many languages do you speak? **(4)** What languages do you speak? **(5)** Where were you born? **(6)** How many sisters and brothers do you have? **(7)** What were your favorite subjects in school?

(8) Why are you taking this class? **(9)** What do you like to do in your free time? **(10)** What are your favorite (foods/sports/movies, etc.)? **(12)** What surprised you when you first came here? **(13)** What do you hope to do after you finish school? **(14)** What makes you happy? **(15)** What makes you angry?

Exercise 5

This exercise is similar to Exercise 3, where the answers given offer clues to the form of the question. Answers will vary; use the answer key as a guide.

SUGGESTION

Ss may do the activity in pairs or as written homework. Correct the exercise yourself or have Ss do peer editing in class.

Workbook Exs. 7–9, pp. 30–32.
Answers: TE p. 488.

EXERCISE 5

Chris and Robin have been living together for a long time. Chris wants Robin to help clean the house. Read their conversation below and make a question to go with each of Chris's answers. When you're finished, compare your questions with other students' questions.

1. **Robin:** _____?
   Chris: The closet door is closed because the paint's dry, and so I put everything back in there.

2. **Robin:** _____?
   Chris: The broom is in the closet, along with the mop, and some cleaning supplies.

3. **Robin:** _____?
   Chris: The vacuum cleaner is probably still in the basement where you left it.

4. **Robin:** _____?
   Chris: We need to clean the house because we're having some people over for dinner tonight.

5. **Robin:** _____?
   Chris: Pat, Sam, and their kids are coming, and of course our neighbors, the Smiths.

6. **Robin:** _____?
   Chris: They met them in the Smiths' garden.

7. **Robin:** _____?
   Chris: They met them there yesterday morning when we were gone.

8. **Robin:** _____?
   Chris: The Smiths were planting flowers.

9. **Robin:** _____?
   Chris: Pat and Sam are getting here by car.

10. **Robin:** _____?
    Chris: I told everyone to be here around 7:00. We'd better get busy; we don't have a lot of time to get this place cleaned up.

ANSWER KEY

Exercise 5

1. Why is the closet door closed? **2.** What's in the closet?/Where's the broom?
3. Where's the vacuum cleaner? **4.** Why do we need to clean the house? **5.** Who's coming over for dinner? **6.** Where did Pat and Sam meet the Smiths?/How do Pat and Sam know the Smiths? **7.** When did they meet them there?/When did that happen?
8. What were the Smiths doing in the garden?/What were the Smiths doing when they met Pat and Sam? **9.** How are Pat and Sam getting here? **10.** What time is everyone coming over?

Wh-Questions with Rising Intonation: Checking Information

EXAMPLES	EXPLANATIONS

(a) A: Where are you from? ↘
   B: Vanuatu.
(b) A: **Where** are you from? ↗
   B: Vanuatu. It's in the south Pacific.
(c) A: Michael Jackson was here last night.
   B: **Who** was here last night? ↗
   A: Michael Jackson.
	Most *Wh*-questions end with falling intonation.
	
	A *Wh*-question with rising intonation shows that you are not sure about what you heard or that you want to check that you heard something correctly. The *Wh*-word is also stressed (said strongly).

(d) A: Michael Jackson was here last night. B: **Who?** ↗	Sometimes, just the *Wh*-word (with rising intonation) is used.

EXERCISE 6

Complete the conversation with appropriate *Wh*-questions. For each question, draw an arrow ↗ or ↘ to show if the question ends with falling or rising intonation.

Albert: So, what did you think of the new Eisentraut movie?

Leslie: It was O.K., I guess, but I expected something more from a movie that cost $200 million to make.

Albert: (1) _____?

Leslie: $200 million. Amazing, isn't it? It's hard to imagine that amount of money.

Albert: (2) _____?

Leslie: It's an action movie set in the future, but I thought it was rather slow-moving. In fact, I almost fell asleep a couple of times.

Albert: (3) _____?

Leslie: It's about two hours, maybe a little longer. Luckily the seats were really comfortable.

Albert: (4) _____?

Leslie: At that new movie theater on Fourth Street, across from the parking garage. It only opened a couple of weeks ago, so it's got a state-of-the-art sound system, thick carpets, terrific popcorn. . . .

Albert: (5) _____?

Leslie: Twelve dollars.

Albert: (6) _____?

Leslie: Twelve dollars . . . I'm not kidding! I can't believe I spent twelve bucks on a movie that really wasn't very good.

Here the use of intonation to demonstrate difference in meaning is emphasized. Point out the importance of the proper use of intonation, as misunderstandings can easily occur.

Initial Question:
Q: *Where are you from?* ↘
A: *Seattle.*

Follow-up Question:
Q: *Where?* ↗
A: *Seattle.*
(old information clarified)
-or-
Q: *Where?* ↘
A: *Just northeast of downtown.* (new information)

You can practice first by asking the same initial question (above), using rising intonation for checking their information and falling intonation for further information.

Exercise 6

This activity can be done individually in class or as homework, or as a whole class on an overhead transparency. Point out that repeated information is usually a sign that the questioner is checking information. Answers may vary.

S U G G E S T I O N

Have Ss practice the intonation in pairs. You may find it helpful to have them exaggerate their intonation at first. This is especially helpful when working with Ss who speak languages that have "flatter" intonation than English.

Workbook Ex. 10, p. 32.
Answers: TE p. 488.

A N S W E R   K E Y

Exercise 6
(1) How much did it cost? ↗ **(2)** What's the movie about? ↘ **(3)** How long is it? ↘
(4) Where did you see it?/Where was it playing? ↘ **(5)** How much was the ticket?/How much did it cost? ↘ **(6)** How much? ↗

SUGGESTIONS

1. When introducing the information in this focus box, using an overhead transparency allows you to draw intonation arrows to illustrate the rising and falling pitch of choice questions. In English, choices are indicated by rising pitch until the last item on the list, which is indicated by falling pitch. Ending the final item on a rising pitch often indicates that the listener is able to add more items to the list. For example:
Q: *Do you want Coke ↗ or Sprite↘ ?*
(indicates 2 choices)
A: *Sprite, please.*
-or-
Q: *Do you want Coke ↗, Sprite↘ , juice ↗ . . . ?* (indicates there may be other possibilities)
A: *Actually, I'll just have some water.*

2. Some more examples of short choice questions are:
large or small?, cash, check, or credit card?, debit or credit?, soup or salad?, french fries, rice, or potato?

Exercise 7

Answers will vary. Circulate around the room to provide individual help on pronunciation or content problems.

VARIATION

An alternative to the directions in the book is to conduct a group poll, adapting the questions to suit the character of the group. After the group tallies their answers, they can present them to the class and discuss some of the differences.

FOCUS **5**

▶ Choice Questions

EXAMPLES	EXPLANATIONS
(a) A: Are you **a graduate student or a professor?** B: I'm a graduate student. **(b)** A: Do you live in **a dorm or an apartment?** B: I live off campus, in an apartment.	A choice question has two or more possibilities, or options. The speaker expects you to choose one of these options in your answer. You can add more information in your answer if you want.
(c) Does Tina walk ↗ to school or take ↘ the bus? **(d)** A: Are you from Malaysia or from Indonesia? B: Neither. I'm from Singapore.	Choice questions have a different intonation pattern from *Yes-No* questions. *Yes-No* questions have rising intonation at the end; choice questions have rising intonation in the middle and falling intonation at the end.
(e) A: Would you like coffee or tea? B: I'll have some tea, please.	Choice questions are often used to get information quickly or to make offers (please see Unit 16 for more information on making offers with *Would . . . like*).
(f) A: (Do you want) paper or plastic? B: Paper, please.	In informal conversation, the first part of the question is sometimes dropped. Answers to choice questions are often very short. Adding *please* to your answer makes it more polite.

EXERCISE 7

Thongchai is a new student from Asia. You want to find out some information about him. Complete the following choice questions with options that are similar in meaning and form.

1. Are you from Thailand or _____?

2. Do you speak Chinese or _____?

3. Do you eat noodles or _____ for breakfast?

4. Do you live _____ or _____?

5. Are you going to study _____ or _____?

6. Do you walk to class or _____?

7. Do you like to play tennis or _____?

Practice asking and answering the questions you completed with a partner.

ANSWER KEY

Exercise 7
1. Taiwan   2. Japanese/Thai   3. rice
4. in an apartment/in a house/in a dormitory/ on campus/off campus   5. chemistry/ botany/etc.   6. ride your bike/take the bus/drive   7. volleyball/etc.

EXERCISE 8

Guess where each of the choice questions on the left was probably asked. Choose from the places or situations listed on the right.

Questions	Places/Situations
1. Paper or plastic?	A. a cash register in a department store
2. Would you like cole slaw or french fries with that?	B. a job interview
3. Do you want premium grade or regular?	C. a gas station
4. Will that be cash or charge?	D. a small shop selling hats and T-shirts
5. First class or economy?	E. an airline office
6. Did you say "large" or "extra-large"?	F. a fast-food restaurant
7. Do you prefer mornings or evenings?	G. a check-out counter in a supermarket

Practice asking and answering the questions with a partner. Imagine yourself in each place or situation, and use more than one way of answering.

Exercise 8

This exercise is a helpful activity for contextualizing the places where we are likely to hear choice questions. Ss can also practice asking the questions in sentence or short form. After some practice, they can add some of their own, with their partners guessing in which situations they would hear each question.

ANSWER KEY

Exercise 8
1. G 2. F 3. C 4. A 5. E 6. D
7. B

This focus box introduces tag questions. The intonation of tag questions is discussed in Focus 7.

The key form issues to emphasize in this focus box are:

1. Auxiliary verbs must match in the statement and tag.
2. Statements and tags are rarely both affirmative and are never both negative. Point out sentences (g)–(n) and (o)–(s) to illustrate.

The most important aspect of the meaning of tag questions is that they generally indicate that the speaker is relatively sure that he/she has the correct information and is verifying his or her facts with the listener. Therefore, the answer corresponds with the statement that is being verified. If the speaker is incorrect, we often "soften" our contradiction. For example:

Q: *You're from Kuwait, aren't you?*
A: <u>*Actually*</u>, *I'm from Qatar.*
-or-
A: <u>*Well*</u>, *no, I'm <u>really</u> from Qatar.*

Point out to the Ss that they may have sounded impolite if they had simply answered *no* to the above question.

SUGGESTION

You can further illustrate tag questions and their answers by using examples from the class. For instance:

Q: *Katrin wasn't absent yesterday, was she?*
A: *No, she wasn't.*

Q: *Tomorrow's class meets at 9:00, doesn't it?*
A: *Yes, it does.*

You can also bring up issues from current local or international events.

FOCUS **6**

▶ Tag Questions

EXAMPLES	EXPLANATIONS
statement *tag* **(a)** He is nice, **isn't he**? **(b)** She isn't here, **is she**? **(c)** We're late, **aren't we**? **(d)** They like it, **don't they**? **(e)** NOT: They like it, like they? **(f)** You didn't go, **did you**?	A tag question is a statement, followed by a short question (a tag). Tag questions are often used in conversation. The speaker expects a *Yes* or *No* answer. The verb in the tag agrees with the subject.
statement: *tag:* *affirmative + negative* **(g)** They play tennis, **don't they**? **(h)** The car was hot, **wasn't it**? **(i)** NOT: The car was hot, was not it? **(j)** Our teacher will help, **won't he**? **(k)** She is sleeping, **isn't she**? **(l)** We can wait, **can't we**? **(m)** I am right, **aren't I**? **(n)** NOT: I am right, amn't I?	An affirmative statement has a negative tag. The speaker thinks that the answer will probably be *yes*. The verbs in negative tags are contracted.
statement: *tag:* *negative + affirmative* **(o)** Your friends don't drive, **do they**? **(p)** It wasn't hot, **was it**? **(q)** You won't help, **will you**? **(r)** The baby isn't sleeping, **is she**? **(s)** We can't wait, **can we**?	A negative statement has an affirmative tag. The speaker thinks that the answer will probably be *no*. The verbs in affirmative tags are not contracted.

EXAMPLES	EXPLANATIONS
(t) Q: You're not cold, **are you**? A: No, I'm not. **(u)** NOT: Yes, I'm not. **(v)** Q: You're cold, **aren't you**? **(w)** A: Yes, I am. **(x)** NOT: No, I am.	When you answer a tag question, respond to the statement, not to the tag. If you agree with the statement: Answer *no* to a negative statement. Answer *yes* to an affirmative statement.
(y) Q: She left, **didn't she**? A: (Yes,) she did. OR: Right. OR: I think so. **(z)** Q: They won't call, **will they**? A: (No,) they won't. OR: I doubt it. OR: Probably not. OR: I don't think so. OR: No way.	It's not always necessary to use the words *yes* or *no* in your answers. *No way* is very informal.

EXERCISE 9

Complete the following statements with an appropriate tag.

1. You got there late, _____?
2. Your brother speaks French, _____?
3. It was cold, _____?
4. Teachers give too much homework, _____?
5. The bus isn't coming, _____?
6. Barry doesn't live here anymore, _____?
7. Nurses work very long hours for very little pay, _____?
8. We made a mistake, _____?
9. You didn't tell her, _____?
10. She will do it, _____?
11. I'm late, _____?
12. Your mother is coming too, _____?
13. The car won't start, _____?

Exercise 9

After Ss practice in their books, this activity can be used as a quick drill.
1. Ask Ss to close their books.
2. You supply the statement, calling on Ss to supply the appropriate tag.
3. If they need more practice, Ss can then continue in pairs.

ANSWER KEY

Exercise 9

1. didn't you 2. doesn't he 3. wasn't it
4. don't they 5. is it 6. does he
7. don't they 8. didn't we 9. did you
10. won't she 11. aren't I 12. isn't she
13. will it

Exercise 10

After Ss have filled in the tag questions and put the conversation in order, they can practice the dialogue in pairs.

1. First have them read.
2. The second time, they can use their books, trying to do as much from memory as possible.
3. The third time, ask Ss to close their books and practice the dialog from memory.

VARIATION

Ss can come up with their own conversation, based on this example.

Workbook Ex. 11, p. 33.
Answers: TE p. 488.

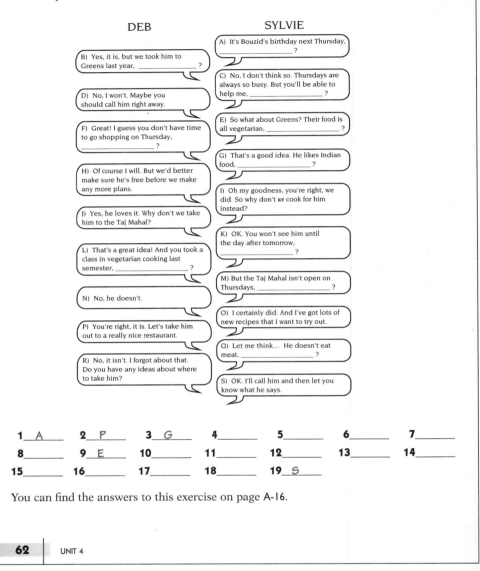

EXERCISE 10

Deb and Sylvie are talking on the phone and making plans for their friend Bouzid's birthday. Work with a partner.

Fill in the blanks with an appropriate tag question and then put the conversation in order. Write the order of the conversation below. We have done some of them for you.

DEB

B) Yes, it is, but we took him to Greens last year, _____?

D) No, I won't. Maybe you should call him right away.

F) Great! I guess you don't have time to go shopping on Thursday, _____?

H) Of course I will. But we'd better make sure he's free before we make any more plans.

J) Yes, he loves it. Why don't we take him to the Taj Mahal?

L) That's a great idea! And you took a class in vegetarian cooking last semester, _____?

N) No, he doesn't.

P) You're right, it is. Let's take him out to a really nice restaurant.

R) No, it isn't. I forgot about that. Do you have any ideas about where to take him?

SYLVIE

A) It's Bouzid's birthday next Thursday, _____?

C) No, I don't think so. Thursdays are always so busy. But you'll be able to help me, _____?

E) So what about Greens? Their food is all vegetarian, _____?

G) That's a good idea. He likes Indian food, _____?

I) Oh my goodness, you're right, we did. So why don't we cook for him instead?

K) OK. You won't see him until the day after tomorrow, _____?

M) But the Taj Mahal isn't open on Thursdays, _____?

O) I certainly did. And I've got lots of new recipes that I want to try out.

Q) Let me think… He doesn't eat meat, _____?

S) OK. I'll call him and then let you know what he says.

1 __A__   2 __P__   3 __G__   4_____   5_____   6_____   7_____
8_____   9 __E__   10_____   11_____   12_____   13_____   14_____
15_____   16_____   17_____   18_____   19 __S__

You can find the answers to this exercise on page A-16.

FOCUS **7**

Tag Question Intonation

EXAMPLES	EXPLANATIONS
(a) Q: His name is Tom, isn't it? ↘ 　　A: Yes, it is. ↘ **(b)** Q: It's not going to rain today, is it? 　　A: No, it isn't. **(c)** Q: His name is Tom, isn't it? ↗ **(d)** Q: It's not going to rain today, is it? ↗	Falling intonation in tag questions shows that the speaker is fairly sure that the information in the statement is true. The speaker is also sure that the listener will agree. A person making an affirmative statement with falling intonation (a) expects the answer *yes*. A person making a negative statement with falling intonation (b) expects the answer *no*. Rising intonation in tag questions shows that the speaker is not sure if the information in the statement is true.

EXERCISE 11

Go back to the conversation in Exercise 10. With a partner, draw arrows ↗ or ↘ to show falling or rising intonation in the tags. One of you will take Sylvie's part and the other will take Deb's. Read the exercise aloud to practice intonation. Finally, get together with another pair and listen to each other's performances.

EXERCISE 12

Your teacher will ask some tag questions. Circle **Y** if you think the expected answer is **yes** and **N** if you think the expected answer is **no**.

1. Y　N　　**4.** Y　N　　**7.** Y　N
2. Y　N　　**5.** Y　N　　**8.** Y　N
3. Y　N　　**6.** Y　N　　**9.** Y　N

FOCUS 7

As with *Wh-* questions, emphasize the importance of intonation in tag questions. Here intonation shows how certain the speaker is of his/her information. Since a person using falling intonation with a tag question expects the listener to agree with his/her statement, the listener should be more careful to "soften" the disagreement (see Focus 6). For example:
Q: *Summers in New Orleans are cold, aren't they?* ↘
A: *Sorry, but I think* summers in New Orleans are really hot!
Depending on the culture(s) you work with, you may need to point out that it <u>is</u> possible to disagree with the speaker, depending on the formality of the situation, and provided that the listener is polite in his/her response.

Exercise 11

Alert Ss to focus mostly on their intonation when practicing this time. Circulate around the room to listen and help Ss who are having trouble emphasizing the difference between rising and falling intonation.

Exercise 12

This exercise focuses on the form of expected answers to tag questions. Read the following questions to the class:
1. He's late, isn't he?
2. You live in Oregon, don't you?
3. You like me, don't you?
4. You're not leaving, are you?
5. Her birthday's in June, isn't it?
6. They won't come, will they?
7. You eat meat, don't you?
8. You don't understand, do you?
9. These are difficult, aren't they?
Answers may vary, depending on your current situation. They can complete the exercise in their books or out loud.

　This exercise provides you with a good opportunity to make sure Ss understand that expected answers agree with the <u>statement</u>, not the tag.

Exercise 13

This exercise can be done as homework or in-class pairwork. You can also make an overhead transparency of the chart to discuss it as a class.

Exercise 14

Exercise 14 gives Ss a chance to be more creative in forming questions than in the previous exercises.

SUGGESTIONS

1. Have Ss review their questions from the Opening Task and edit their own questions.
2. They can then use some of these and/or add new questions.
3. Circulate to help with problems or questions. Since they are coming up with their own ideas, you may need to help with vocabulary.

EXERCISE 13

Read each tag question aloud, using the intonation as marked. For each question, tell whether the speaker expects a certain answer, and if so, what the speaker expects the answer to be, *yes* or *no*. Answer the question the way you think the speaker expects it to be answered.

	(a) Is the speaker fairly sure what the answer will be?	*(b)* If *yes* to (a), answer the question
1. It's going to rain today, isn't it? ↗		
2. You don't know where my umbrella is, do you? ↘		
3. You're driving today, aren't you? ↗		
4. It's not my turn to drive, is it? ↗		
5. You made lunch for me, didn't you? ↘		
6. I didn't forget to thank you, did I? ↗		
7. I'm pretty forgetful, aren't I? ↘		

EXERCISE 14

Your teacher has been nominated for a "Teacher-of-the-Year Award" and will appear at a press conference to answer questions from journalists and reporters. You and your classmates are all newspaper reporters; you need to write a profile of your teacher for your paper and want to get as much information from him or her as possible.

STEP 1 Get together with two or three other students. As a group, choose six questions that you would most like to ask your teacher at the press conference. You can use some of the questions you wrote in Exercise 1, Exercise 2, and the Opening Task if you want to, or you can make completely new questions. Important note:

- Two questions must be *Yes/No* questions.
- Two questions must be *Wh*-questions.
- Two questions must be tag questions.

ANSWER KEY

Exercise 13
1. (a) No   2. (a) Yes   (b) "No, I don't."
3. (a) No   4. (a) No   5. (a) Yes   (b) "Yes, I did."   6. (a) No   7. (a) Yes   (b) "Yes, I'm afraid you are."

Exercise 14
Answers will vary.

STEP 2 When you have decided on your questions, your teacher will hold the press conference, but she or he **will only answer your questions if they are correctly formed and if the intonation is appropriate.** If another group asks a question that your group wanted to ask, you must ask a different question (your teacher will not answer the same question twice). Write your questions **and the answers** below. If possible, tape the "press conference" and listen to the tape to check your intonation and your teacher's answers.

Questions	Answers

UNIT GOAL REVIEW

Ask Ss to look at the goals on the opening page of the unit again. Help them understand how much they have accomplished in each area.

SUGGESTION

Elicit examples of different question forms from Ss, making a 4-column chart on the board or overhead projector of their examples. Using their examples, practice saying some of them with different intonation, asking them what the different intonation patterns in two questions mean.

USE YOUR ENGLISH

These activities are designed to provide more communicative practice of the grammatical structures in this unit. While you can note errors to provide feedback later, the emphasis in these activities is on more natural communication. You may find it helpful to recap and discuss some of the errors you hear at the end of the activity.

Activity 1

This activity is especially helpful in practicing *yes/no* questions. When you are determining what kind of information you put on the pieces of paper, you may want to group the items by type (for example: animals, people, items you find in a kitchen). Be sure to choose items you think your Ss are likely to be familiar with. You can use pictures instead of words. The best way to stick things on Ss' backs is to use self-stick notes or index cards.

Before you have Ss practice as a class, have a student stick an item on your back. You can then model the questions yourself. At the end of the activity, if there are some people left who cannot guess their items, other Ss can give helpful "hints." Conversely, if some Ss guess their items very quickly, give them a second item to guess.

Activity 2

If you have access to the Internet, you can have Ss access a university's website to log on to its student services page. Be sure to find a site that has a list of "FAQs" (Frequently Asked Questions) first. They can write their FAQs from the international student perspective.

Use Your English

ACTIVITY 1: SPEAKING/LISTENING

STEP 1 Your teacher is going to stick a piece of paper on your back and on the backs of your classmates. Get up and walk around the class, looking at what is written on your classmates' backs.

STEP 2 Your job is to guess what is written on your back. You can find this out by asking questions. You can also answer the questions that your classmates ask you about what is written on their backs. For the first five minutes, you can only ask *Yes/No* questions. Refuse to answer any question that is not a *Yes/No* question. When your teacher gives you a signal, you can ask any kind of question that you like. Here are some possible *Yes/No* questions to ask: Is this a person? Is this person male or female? Is this an object? Is it expensive? Is this an animal? Is this food? Here are some possible *Wh*-questions: How big is this? Where was she or he born? What color is this?

ACTIVITY 2: SPEAKING/WRITING

The international student office at your school is preparing a short guide for students who have just arrived in this country. The purpose of this guide is to give new students a clear idea of what to expect when they arrive here. You have been asked to write a chapter called "Most Commonly Asked Questions."

Get together with two or three other students and make a list of all the questions that people in this country usually ask you. Compare your lists with those of other students in the class. Use the information from your classmates to make a list of the questions that people here usually ask international students and that new students should be ready to answer.

ACTIVITY 3: SPEAKING/WRITING

Some of your friends here are thinking of taking a trip. Work in groups with at least one person whose country is not in North America, if possible. Have that person share questions that people in your country usually ask visitors from other countries. Make a list and compare the questions with those of students from different countries and cultures. What differences and similarities do you find?

ACTIVITY 4: WRITING/READING

STEP 1 In this activity you cannot speak, but you can write. Sit down next to a student that you do not know very well. Spend a couple of minutes thinking about some of the things you would like to know about this person. Take a piece of paper and write **one** question for your partner to answer. Pass the question to your partner. Read the question that your partner gives you. Without speaking, write your answer to the question and write another question for your partner to answer. **Do not speak at all**.

STEP 2 Exchange papers with your partner. Read your partner's answer to your question and answer his or her question to you. Continue writing questions and answers to each other until your teacher tells you to stop. Now you can speak!

Optional: With your partner's permission, share some of the information from your silent interview with the rest of the class.

STEP 3 Look back over the questions that you and your partner wrote. Were you able to use any of the kinds of questions discussed in this unit?

Activity 4

VARIATIONS

If you have a class discussion list or your Ss have e-mail accounts, you can do this activity via computer, rather than on paper.

1. If it is done as an in-class activity, you can control the amount of time Ss spend on writing.
2. As a homework assignment, it would be a more free-form activity. Pair Ss ahead of time and allow them time to make an "e-mail appointment" together.

Activity 6

Play textbook audio. Note that the conversation first has only the friend's half of the conversation. The conversation then repeats with the interviewer's questions included. The transcript for this listening appears on pp. 505–506 of this book.

1. The first section of the tapescript has the friend's answers to the questions that are not given. Ss listen and write the questions probably asked by the interviewer.

2. The second section includes the full question and answer exchange. Have Ss listen to the second section to edit their own questions.

3. As a class, discuss some of the questions Ss came up with, noting some of the variations.

ACTIVITY 5: SPEAKING/LISTENING

Your English teacher has just quit her job and is now sunning on a beach in Tahiti. Your class is desperately searching for a new teacher. You have decided to take matters into your own hands and interview teachers yourselves. One of your classmates is an applicant for the position. Ask him or her some questions about his or her experience, interests, and future goals. Listen to your classmate's answers. They may help you ask other questions.

ACTIVITY 6: LISTENING/ WRITING

A friend of yours has applied for a job teaching English in Latvia. She cannot travel to Latvia for a job interview, so the school has to interview her by phone. You are at her house when the school calls. You can hear her half of the conversation (the answers that she gives), but you can't hear the questions that the interviewer asked.

STEP 1   Listen to her half of the conversation on the tape. In the first column, write the questions that you think the interviewer **probably** asked. Then listen to the complete interview to compare your questions with the ones the interviewer **actually** asked. Use the second column to write any questions that are different from the ones in the first column.

1) PROBABLE QUESTIONS	2) ACTUAL QUESTIONS

ANSWER KEY

Activity 6
See tapescript (pp. 505–506) for the actual questions.

ACTIVITY 7: SPEAKING/LISTENING

At school, you have recently lost a very unusual and very valuable piece of jewelry, perhaps a ring or necklace. Now you are sitting in class, and you notice that the person sitting beside you is wearing a ring or necklace just like the one you lost. Of course, you would like to ask the person some questions about it to find out if it might be yours.

You might want to role-play this in teams. One team can serve as coaches for the person who has lost the piece of jewelry. The other team can serve as coaches for the person who is wearing the piece of jewelry.

ACTIVITY 8: SPEAKING/LISTENING/WRITING

With your classmates, brainstorm and write a list of questions that are useful for people learning English, in or outside the classroom setting. Which are the three most useful questions?

To get you started, here are some examples of questions that students have found useful:

• What does _____ mean?

• Can you repeat that, please?

ACTIVITY 9: SPEAKING/LISTENING

Bring in a photograph and give it to your teacher. Each student will look at one photograph for thirty seconds and then give it back to the teacher. Other students will then ask the student questions about the picture he or she studied and try to guess the situation. Try to use all types of questions: *Yes/No*, *Wh-*, statement form, choice, and tag. The person who brought in the picture can then tell the class whether their guesses were correct or not.

Tape yourself as you ask the questions. Afterwards, listen to the tape and check to see if you were able to use the kinds of questions discussed in this unit.

Activity 8
EXPANSIONS

1. Once Ss have come up with their list(s) of useful questions, you can write or print their list on a large piece of paper and post it on the wall in the classroom as a permanent reference.
2. Have Ss start creating their own book of useful expressions. Some teachers prefer to have this kind of notebook as monolingual; others suggest Ss translate the expression into their native languages.

Activity 9

You may prefer to bring in the photographs yourself, especially if your class has been working on a particular theme, such as travel or the environment.

If you don't have access to tape recorders, you can have Ss work in groups and assign a "secretary" to each group who will note down the question types. It may be helpful to provide them with a chart with question types at the top of the columns.

The test for this unit can be found on pp. 419–420 of this book. The answers are on p. 421.

Unit 5

UNIT OVERVIEW

Unit 5 provides practice with modals of probability and possibility: *could, may, might,* and *must.*

UNIT GOALS

Review the goals listed on this page so that students (Ss) understand what they should know by the end of the unit.

OPENING TASK

Note: The Opening Task is intended to focus attention on meaning rather than form, which will allow you to see whether Ss are able to produce the forms spontaneously. For a more complete discussion of the Opening Task, see page xxi of this Teacher's Edition.

The purpose of this task is to generate talk that naturally uses modals *could, may, might,* and *must.*

ⓤ N I T 5

MODALS OF PROBABILITY AND POSSIBILITY

Could, May, Might, Must

UNIT GOALS:

- To use *could, may, might, must,* and *couldn't/can't* to show how certain you are about a present situation
- To correctly form statements and questions to describe probability and possibility in the present and past
- To correctly use the progressive with modals of probability and possibility
- To use *could, may, might, probably, will/be going to, may not,* and *might not* to talk about future probability and possibility

OPENING TASK
Identify the Mystery Person

One evening toward the end of March, a New York taxi driver found that someone had left a briefcase on the back seat of his cab. When he opened it, he found that the briefcase was empty, except for the things you can see on the next page.

STEP 1 With a partner, examine everything on this page carefully. Can you find any clues about the identity of the owner of the briefcase? Use the chart below to write down your ideas and to show how certain you are about them.

GUESSES	HOW CERTAIN ARE YOU?		
	Less than 50% Certain (it's possible)	90% Certain (it's probable)	100% Certain (it's certain)
Name			
Sex			
Age			
Marital Status			
Occupation			
Likes and Interests			
Family and Friends			
Habits			
Recent Activities			
Future Plans			
Anything else?			

MARCH

SUNDAY	MONDAY	TUESDAY	WEDNESDAY	THURSDAY	FRIDAY	SATURDAY
1	2 Board meeting 10:30 send papers to Washington	3 meeting 8 lunch Sally	4 Ash Wednesday NYC EXECUTIVE leave for NYC 7:00	5 MEETING	6 return from NYC meeting 10:30 drinks Bob Theatre 8:30	7 wedding anniversary Dinner 8
8 golf 9:30	9 report on NYC meeting due	10 Sally's Birthday meeting with Vice president 2 p.m. movie 8	11 Paris meeting arrive 14:50	12	13	14 Call Sally
15 Purim	16 Accountant Lunch Robert Haywood Call Paris Office	17 St. Patrick's Day OPERA 9:30	18 Visitors from Tokyo office dinner Japanese restaurant 7 p.m.	19	20 Export meeting	21 Spring begins tennis 2 p.m. Mike Kids home from school
22 golf 9:30	23 Japanese Class	24 Doctor: 8 sales meeting 10:30	25 9:00 Accountant tennis Mike	26 Lunch SALLY	27 Doctor: 9 10:00 sales meeting Japanese Class	28 check passport
29 TOKYO?	30	31				

STEP 2 Now get together with a group and share your ideas about the identity of this mystery person, showing how certain you feel about each one.

SETTING UP THE TASK

1. Talk about things that people usually carry in their purses, wallets, backpacks, or briefcases. For example, hold up your own purse, briefcase, or wallet and invite guesses about what is probably inside. You could also do the same thing with one of your Ss. The idea to establish is that we can often guess something about the owner of the purse, wallet, etc., from its contents.

2. As Ss make guesses about what is in your purse/wallet, you can prepare them for the chart by asking: *Are you certain? Are you really certain? 100 percent certain? Not very certain?* and so on. Don't worry about modal use at this point since the focus here is on preparing Ss for the chart.

CONDUCTING THE TASK

Explain the task situation carefully and go through the chart, checking that Ss understand what they are to do. If they are 100 percent certain that the mystery person is male, they write "male" in the "100%" column. If they are less than 50 percent certain that he or she is 40 years old, they write "40" in the "Less than 50%" column, and so on. They do not need to write full sentences, just the relevant piece of information. Encourage them to examine everything very carefully before completing the chart.

They will get an opportunity later to focus on accuracy, converting the information into full sentences. Exercises 2, 4, 9, and 11 also revisit the task.

There is no right or wrong answer to this task. It all depends on whatever ideas the Ss come up with. For example, some groups have speculated that this is a business executive (male) who was probably involved in a lot of international trade and is now possibly planning on branching out on his own, setting up an import/export business. Others have argued that this is a woman.

REVIEWING THE TASK

Bring the whole class together to share ideas and to establish how certain Ss are about each item on the chart. You can make an overhead transparency of the blank chart or write the headings on the board and fill in the different ideas that Ss contribute. You can then use this as a springboard for the information in Focus 1, by building on Ss' own ideas to weave in or elicit possible modal uses.

Note: Focus boxes explain and give examples of each structure.

1. Copy the arrow onto the blackboard (or on an overhead transparency) labeling the top with "Less Certain" and the bottom as "More Certain," as in the diagram.
2. Use the situations from the "Examples" side, and then write each statement up in the appropriate place along the arrow, as in (a)–(c) and (d)–(f).
3. Point out that there is very little difference in meaning between *could* and *might*, although *may* is a little "stronger." There is, however, a big jump in meaning between all of these and *must*.

SUGGESTION

For further examples, use this situation or make up others. Situation: *He's got a box of matches in his pocket.* Responses: *He could smoke. He might smoke. He may smoke.* Situation (continued): *He smells like an ashtray.* Response: *He must smoke.* Situation: *He's puffing on a cigarette. He always has a cigarette after dinner.* Response: *He definitely smokes!* This can serve as a bridge to Exercise 1, which takes Ss through this same process.

FOCUS **1**

Using *Could, May, Might,* and *Must* to Show How Certain You Are about a Present Situation

EXAMPLES	EXPLANATIONS
Situation: He's got a baseball hat on. ***Less Certain*** ↑ **(a)** He **could** play baseball. | **(b)** He **might** play baseball. ↓ **(c)** He **may** play baseball. ***More Certain*** Situation: She is wearing a white coat. ***Less Certain*** ↑ **(d)** She **could** be a doctor. | **(e)** She **might** be a doctor. ↓ **(f)** She **may** be a doctor. ***More Certain***	*Could, may, might,* and *must* show how certain or not you are about a present situation. **Possible (less than 50% certain)** Use *could, might* or *may* to express possibility (to show that you believe something is possible, but you are not very certain if it is true or not). You are making a guess. *May* shows that you are a little more certain that something is true.
Situation: He's wearing a baseball hat. He's carrying a baseball glove. **(g)** He **must** play baseball. Situation: She is carrying a stethoscope. **(h)** She **must** be a doctor.	**Probable (about 90% certain)** Use *must* to express probability (to show that you believe something is probably true). You are **almost** certain that this is true. You are drawing a conclusion, based on what you know.
Situation: It's the middle of a baseball game. He is throwing a ball to his teammate. **(i)** He **plays** baseball. Situation: She performed surgery on my mother in the hospital and saved her life. **(j)** She **is** a doctor.	**Certain (100% certain)** These are facts. You are completely certain about these situations. Do not use *could, may, might,* or *must.* For information on other ways of using *could, might, may,* and *must,* see Units 10, 11, and 17.

EXERCISE 1

Look at the situations below and complete the sentences to show how certain the speaker is about each one.

Situation	Possible
She always wears a purple hat.	*Less Certain* ↑ 1) She _____ like purple. 2) She _____ like purple. ↓ 3) She _____ like purple. *More Certain*

Situation	Probable
She always wears a purple hat and a purple coat.	4) She _____ like purple.

Situation	Certain
She always wears purple clothes, she drives a purple car and lives in a purple house, surrounded by purple flowers.	5) She _____ purple.

Situation	Possible
He's carrying a French newspaper.	*Less Certain* ↑ 6) He _____ be French. 7) He _____ be French. ↓ 8) He _____ be French. *More Certain*

Situation	Probable
He's carrying a French newspaper and he's speaking French to the people with him.	9) He _____ be French.

Situation	Certain
He's carrying a French newspaper and he's speaking French to the people with him. He was born in France and has a French passport.	10) He _____ French.

Compare your answers with a partner's and then check what you have written with the information in Focus 1.

Modals of Probability and Possibility: Could, May, Might, Must | **73**

ANSWER KEY

Exercise 1

(1) could (2) might (3) may (4) must
(5) likes (6) could (7) might (8) may
(9) must (10) is

The information in the second box (negative statements) may be new for some Ss.

1. To expand on the information there, make up examples or situations that use or elicit *may not, might not, must not, couldn't,* and *can't.*

2. Point out how both words in the modal + negative "pairs"—*must not, might not, may not*—are stressed and not reduced or contracted in speech. Situation: That poor dog (male). His coat is all tangled. Response: *They must not brush him.*

3. Make up examples that elicit or demonstrate the *could-couldn't* and *can-can't* distinction. Situation: *She's sneezing.* Response: *She <u>could</u> be allergic to cats.* Explanation: The speaker isn't certain about this; it's just a guess. OR Another speaker: *No, she <u>can't</u> be allergic to cats. I'm almost certain of this because we were in a pet store together once and she didn't sneeze once. She <u>could</u> be catching a cold.*

Pronunciation Note

Because of the importance of word stress when using these modals, it's helpful for you to model the statements in the examples. Then Ss can repeat each statement, either in chorus or individually. Point out that (k) through (o) are yes-no questions and thus the sentences should end with rising intonation. Model this as well.

▶ **Modals of Probability and Possibility**

EXAMPLES	EXPLANATIONS
subject + modal + verb	**Affirmative Statements**
(a) Jack **could** live here.	Modals come before the base form of the verb.
(b) **NOT:** Jack could lives here.	Modals have only one form. They do not take *s.*
(c) Alex **might** know him.	
(d) **NOT:** Alex mights know him.	
(e) Shirley **may** be at home.	
(f) **NOT:** Shirley maybe at home.	*Maybe* is not a modal.
subject + modal + not + verb	**Negative Statements**
(g) She **must not** like cats.	*May not, might not,* and *must not* are not usually contracted when they express possibility or probability.
(h) Bo **might not** know that.	*Couldn't/can't* shows that you strongly believe that something is impossible. They are usually contracted.
(i) That's impossible! Ron **couldn't** be in Las Vegas. I saw him just a few minutes ago. He **can't** be there.	*Couldn't* therefore expresses very strong certainty. However, *could* expresses very weak certainty; it shows that you are not very certain if something is possible.
(j) I'm not very sure where Sid is. I think he **could** be in Reno.	
modal + subject + verb	**Questions**
(k) **Could** Sid be in Reno?	*May* and *must* are not used in questions about possibility and probability.
(l) **Might** Cathy know about this?	
Question: *Answer:*	**Short Answers**
(m) Does he take the train? I'm not sure. He **might**.	Use the modal by itself in short answers. Use the modal + *be* in short answers to questions with *be.*
(n) Does Sue like Thai food? She **may not**. She doesn't like spicy food very much.	
(o) Is Jay at home? He **might be**. He's not in his office.	

EXERCISE 2

Turn back to the Opening Task on page 71. Make statements about the owner of the briefcase. Use *must, may, could, might, couldn't,* or *can't* to show how certain you feel. Share your opinions with your classmates and be ready to justify them as necessary.

▶ **EXAMPLE:** NAME: *In my opinion, the owner of the briefcase might be called C. Murray because this name is on the boarding pass. However, this boarding pass could belong to somebody else.*

1. SEX: In my opinion, the owner of the briefcase _____ because _____ .

2. OCCUPATION: I believe she or he _____ because _____ .

3. MARITAL STATUS: This person _____ I think this because _____ .

4. LIKES AND INTERESTS: _____ _____ .

5. HABITS: _____ _____ .

6. AGE: _____ _____ .

V A R I A T I O N

If you could use a little movement and activity in the room:

1. Ask Ss to read one statement to a classmate.
2. If the listener is convinced by the statement—the reader's justification makes sense—then the listener says "I am convinced."
3. If the listener is not convinced, he/she says "I am not convinced" and then she reads her/his own statement.
4. Students can move on to their next statements only when someone is convinced; otherwise they must continue to read their original statement until someone is convinced OR they can revise the statement if it is unconvincing.

ANSWER KEY

Exercise 2
Answers will vary depending on the inferences Ss made in the Opening Task.

Exercise 3

Since these are dialogues, it's appropriate to do this exercise orally, with a pair of Ss "performing" or reading a dialogue aloud to the rest of the class. First give Ss a few minutes to work with a partner, and check to make sure they have answers for each blank. This will allow the dialogue-reading to move along smoothly so that the class is not waiting for the speakers to search for the answers.

Before Ss read, encourage them to use contractions in their answers if appropriate, and to try to link together smoothly the words in a sentence.

EXERCISE 3

Add an appropriate short answer to the questions in these conversations.

1. A: Where's Mike? Is he angry?
   B: I don't know. He _____. He didn't say much before he left.
2. A: Does Perry drive to school?
   B: I'm not sure. He _____.
3. A: Does Elka like dogs?
   B: She _____ (not). I know that she doesn't like most animals.
4. A: Do you know if Frankie drinks coffee?
   B: Good question. She _____, but I don't really know.
5. A: Is Connie married?
   B: I think she _____, but nobody seems to know for sure.
6. A: Do you know if Hanh still lives with his parents?
   B: He _____ (not) anymore. I think he was planning on moving out last spring.
7. A: I'm looking for someone to translate this letter into Turkish. Does George speak Turkish?
   B: He _____. He lived there for five years, but I'm not sure how much he remembers.

Modals of Probability and Possibility in the Past

EXAMPLES	EXPLANATIONS
subject + modal + have + past participle **(a)** Vi **may have left.** **(b)** I'm not sure how Liz went home last night; she **could have taken** a cab. **(c)** There's nobody here; everyone **must have gone** out.	**Affirmative Statements** Choose the appropriate modal + *have* + past participle to show how certain you are about something that happened in the past.
subject + modal + not + have + past participle **(d)** I **may not have seen** him. **(e)** Selena **might not have been** in town last week. **(f)** Darius **couldn't have robbed** the store. He was at home with me all evening.	**Negative Statements:** Choose the appropriate modal + *not* + *have* + past participle to show how certain you are that something did **not** happen in the past.
modal + subject + have + past participle? **(g)** **Could** she **have known?** **(h)** **Might** the police **have followed** the stolen car?	**Questions:** Choose the appropriate modal + subject + *have* + past participle to ask about possibility and probability in the past. Remember that *must* and *may* are not usually used in questions about possibility or probability.
(i) Q: Did Jerry talk to Kramer last night? A: I'm not sure. He **may have.** **(j)** Q: Did Bernadette remember to go to the store? A: She **must have.** The refrigerator is full of food.	**Short answers:** Use the appropriate modal + *have* in short answers.
(k) Q: Was Vinny depressed? A: It's hard to say. He **might have been.** **(l)** **NOT:** He might have.	Remember to use the appropriate modal + *have been* in short answers to questions using *be*.

SUGGESTIONS

1. Since there is a lot of information here, it's nice if you can assign this as homework: Ss read over the information and write down examples of their own and any questions they might have. If they find this challenging, slow down your pace and spend a bit of time on each example and explanation.

2. In class, ask individuals to take turns reading the examples (a) through (l). Point out how, although the time frame is different (all of these situations occurred in the past), the meaning of the modal is the same.

3. After each example (from the book or Ss' own), have Ss identify the modal used and explain why they think that modal and not another was used. Answers should be in terms of *how certain* they are.

4. Then ask why *have* + past participle was used. Answers should be along the lines of: *because the situation was in the past.*

Exercise 4

This might be a good point to think about how you want to handle errors. Since Ss are asked to justify their opinions, this keeps the focus on meaning.

SUGGESTIONS

1. If Ss are working in pairs, ask the listener to notice any errors in form, pointing any out to the person who made the statement.
2. If Ss are reading statements aloud to the whole class, open this listening-for-errors exercise up to anybody in the class.
3. You might want to allow Ss who make the error the first opportunity to correct it. Or allow the person who notices the error this opportunity. You might find answers to some of the questions that come up in the later focus boxes in this chapter, so you're at an advantage if you've previewed the chapter.

Exercise 5

Since answers to this exercise can be very original and funny, it calls for Ss volunteering to read their answers aloud. Thus, it's appropriate to allow individual preparation time, either in class or as homework.

VARIATION

Have Ss vote on the best/most convincing/most original/funniest answer for each item.

EXERCISE 4

Turn back to the Opening Task. Make statements showing how certain you are about the person's past activities. Use *must, may, could, might, couldn't,* or *can't* to show how certain you feel. Be ready to share and justify your opinions.

EXERCISE 5

In trying to solve crimes, detectives generally examine evidence carefully and then draw conclusions based on what they observe. Sometimes their conclusions are stronger (or more certain) than at other times, depending on the evidence they have examined. Creative detectives (like Sherlock Holmes) are famous for examining all possibilities in a case. What might Sherlock Holmes conclude about the following people?

▶ **EXAMPLE:** **1.** A woman with a yellow forefinger:

She must be a heavy smoker. OR *She might be a painter, and she might have lost her paintbrush.*

Can you think of any other possibilities? Be ready to share your ideas with your classmates.

2. A very short man with bowlegs: _____

_____

3. A man with a very red nose: _____

_____

4. A woman with rough, hard hands: _____

_____

5. A woman with a fur coat, diamonds, and chauffeur-driven limousine:

_____

_____

6. A man with soft, white hands: _____

_____

7. A man with a lot of tattoos: _____

_____

ANSWER KEY

Exercise 4
Answers are completely dependent on the inferences the Ss make in the Opening Task.

Exercise 5
Answers will vary. The choice of modal depends on the speaker's certainty. Possible answers include:
2. He might be a jockey/He might have been born that way.   3. He might have a cold/be a clown.   4. She could be a construction worker/farmer/gardener/housekeeper. She might wash dishes in a busy restaurant.
5. She might be a movie star/politician.
6. He might be a surgeon/pianist.   7. He might be a gangster/rock star/sailor

FOCUS **4**

Modals of Probability and Possibility with the Progressive

EXAMPLES	EXPLANATIONS
subject + modal + be + verb + -ing **(a)** He **might be sleeping.** **(b)** Q: What's Lisa doing these days? A: I'm really not sure. She **may be working** in Latvia. **(c)** Something smells good! Albert **must be cooking** dinner.	Use modals with the progressive to make a guess or draw a conclusion about something in progress at or around the time of speaking.
(d) You **must know** the Van Billiard family. They live in Amherst. **(e)** **NOT:** You must be knowing the Van Billiard family.	Remember that some verbs cannot be used in the progressive. For more information, see Unit 2.
subject + modal + have been + verb + -ing **(f)** He **may have been sleeping.** **(g)** Mo **must have been working** on his car; his hands are really dirty.	Use this form to make a guess or draw a conclusion about something that was in progress before the time of speaking.

EXERCISE 6

Look back at the situations in Exercise 5. Can you make any statements about the people in these situations using *must, may, might,* or *could* with a progressive form? Use present forms (to talk about what you think they might be doing now) or past forms (to talk about what you think they might have been doing before now). For example: *The woman with a yellow forefinger might be a cook. She might have been cooking curry and she could have been using her finger to taste the food. She might be going home now to take a shower.* You may not be able to use these forms with all of the situations. Compare your ideas with a partner's.

Contrast pairs of example statements or make up your own and ask questions about the differences. Example: 1. What's the difference between (a) *He might be sleeping.* and (similar to) (f) *He might have been sleeping.*? Explanation: In (a), he might be doing this now. In (f) you're talking about the past. 2. What's the difference between (b) *She may be working in Latvia* and (similar to (c) *She must be working in Latvia?* Explanation: In (b) you're not certain; in (c) you're more certain that your guess is true, and so on.

Exercise 6
S U G G E S T I O N

This is a good point to assess what material Ss have learned and what material continues to be challenging. Thus you might want to have Ss work individually on this exercise in class or in pairs, so that you can circulate and make observations. Write down good student examples to share with the class, or tell Ss they are responsible for reading aloud one example each. (You'll have to gauge this to class size, of course.) Also write down common errors and review with the class the relevant focus box points if necessary.

Exercise 6
Answers will vary, depending on what Ss said in Exercise 5.

Exercise 7

This story is open to a range of interpretations and is guaranteed to bring out the "Sherlock Holmes" in every student (if it exists!). The most likely theory:

The victim knew the murderer well (no sign of a forced entry) and may have drunk wine with him or her in her room. The full wine glass suggests that the murderer may have drugged or poisoned the victim by putting something in the wine. The murderer didn't drink from the other glass because he or she knew it was poisoned. The murderer may have long, blond hair and might have worn a shirt of jacket with white buttons. They must have fought or struggled violently at around 11:30 (button, hair, smashed watch). After killing the victim, the murderer might have searched for information or documents in her desk, but he or she must not have found them or might have had to leave before finding what he or she was looking for. The murderer must have left the house by the victim's window. (The doors were locked from the inside.)

Your Ss' theories about why and how the crime occurred might be even more interesting.

Exercise 8
SUGGESTIONS

1. Bring in a newspaper or copy down some real newspaper headlines. Point out how headlines only keep the "essential" words, dropping articles *the* and *a*, *prepositions*, and other "function words" and keeping the "content words"—nouns, verbs, adjectives, adverbs.

Some Ss may feel more comfortable doing this in pairs or small groups, especially if they were "clueless" in the last exercise. Assign one student to be the "recorder" who writes down the headlines and a draft of the report; the other student can be more primary in coming up with ideas; both (or a third student) can be responsible for revising the story and focusing on accurate and appropriate usage.

EXERCISE 7

The police are investigating a murder. What might Sherlock Holmes conclude about the following pieces of evidence? Get together with a partner to come up with a theory. After that, share your conclusions with the rest of the class, using *must, may, could, might,* or *couldn't/can't* to show how certain you feel. Finally, take a vote to decide who has the most interesting theory. How probable do you think this theory is?

> The victim was found in her bedroom on the second floor of her house. The front door and her bedroom door were locked from inside. There were two wine glasses on the table in her room; one was empty, the other was full. There was an ashtray with several cigarette butts in it. The victim had a small white button in her hand and several long, blond hairs. Her watch was found on the floor; it had stopped at 11:30. The drawers of the victim's desk were open, and there were papers all over the floor. Nothing appeared to be missing.

EXERCISE 8

You are a reporter for your local newspaper. The editor has asked you to report on the murder described in Exercise 7. Explain what you think happened and why you believe this to be so. Make a headline for your report. Display your headline and your report so that your classmates can compare the different theories about the murder.

ANSWER KEY

Exercise 8
Answers will vary, depending on Ss' responses in Exercise 7, and / or on new "twists."

▶ # Future Probability and Possibility with Modals

EXAMPLES	EXPLANATIONS
(a) There are a few clouds in the sky; it **could** **might** **may** rain later.	Use *could, might,* or *may* to express future possibility.
(b) Cheer up! She **might** call tomorrow.	
(c) We **may** see them next month.	*May* shows that you are a little more certain that something will happen.
(d) Q: Where's Anna? A: She**'ll probably** get here soon.	Use *will* or *be going to* with *probably* to show that you are almost certain that something will happen in the future. Do not use *must.*
(e) NOT: She must get here soon.	
(f) Q: What's Jim going to do after he graduates next year? A: He**'s probably going to** travel around the world on a motorcycle.	
(g) NOT: He must travel round the world on a motorcycle.	
(h) Look! The sun's coming out. It **may not** rain after all.	Use *may not* or *might not* to show that it is possible that something will **not** happen. Do not use *could not.*
(i) NOT: It could not rain after all.	
(j) Fran **might not** come to the airport with us tomorrow.	
(k) NOT: Fran could not come to the airport with us tomorrow.	

EXERCISE 9

Work with a partner and turn back to the Opening Task. From the evidence given, what can you say about the person's future plans? Use *will/be going to, probably, may, could, must,* or *may not/might not* as necessary. Be prepared to share and justify your answers.

FOCUS 5

1. As with Focus 4, it's helpful to contrast the meaning in pairs of statements (either the examples or ones that you make). Ask questions about the differences. Example: 1. What's the difference between (b) *She might call tomorrow.* and similar to (d) *She'll probably call tomorrow?* Explanation: In (b), you're not sure if she will or won't call. In (d) you're pretty certain that she will call.

2. Also make up examples contrasting future probability/possibility with past and progressive usage (Focus 3 and 4). What's the difference between Focus 3, (c) *He might be cooking dinner.* and similar to (b) *He might cook dinner?* Explanation: In (c) he might be cooking dinner right now; in (b) you're talking about what he might do in the future, and so on.

Workbook Ex. 3, pp. 36–37.
Answers: TE p. 489.
Workbook Ex. 5, pp. 39–40.
Answers: TE p. 489.

Exercise 9

Again, answers are completely dependent on the inferences Ss made in the Opening Task.

SUGGESTIONS

If you choose to have Ss read their statements aloud:

1. concentrate first on meaning, asking questions (you or Ss) if you need clarification.

2. Then focus on accuracy, checking to see if the statements all talk about future plans. Again, you can have Ss be the ones to detect any errors.

3. Ss who make the statements should have an opportunity to defend their answers and to revise their statements if necessary.

Exercise 10

These dialogues are intended to be "performed"/read aloud.

SUGGESTIONS

1. Allow Ss time to find answers for each blank and to rehearse dialogues. For this reason, you might want to assign certain dialogues to certain pairs of Ss: Pair A is assigned 1 and 2, pair B is assigned 3 and 4, etc., depending on class size. This will allow the dialogue-reading to move along smoothly.
2. Encourage Ss to use contractions in their answers if appropriate, to smoothly link together the words in a sentence, and to use falling intonation at the end of a statement, rising intonation at the end of a yes/no question.

EXERCISE 10

Work with a partner and choose the best way to complete each sentence. Discuss the reasons for your choice. Be prepared to share your answers with the rest of the class.

1. A: Where's Rose?
   B: I'm not sure. She _____ in the library.
      is   might be   must be

2. A: My daughter just got a scholarship to Stanford!
   B: You _____ be very proud of her.
      could   must   might

3. A: How does Sheila get to school?
   B: I don't really know. She _____ the bus.
      might take   takes   must take

4. A: It's really cold in here today
   B: Yes. Somebody _____ the window open.
      must leave   might leave   must have left

5. A: I wonder why Zelda always wears gloves.
   B: I don't know. She _____ some kind of allergy.
      may have had   has   may have

6. A: Have you heard the weather forecast?
   B: No, but look at all those dark clouds in the sky. I think it _____ rain.
      could   must   is probably going to

7. A: Did my mother call while I was out?
   B: I'm not sure. She _____ .
      might have   might   did

8. A: Ellen gave a violin recital in front of five hundred people yesterday. It was her first public performance.
   B: Really? She _____ very nervous.
      could have been   must be   must have been

9. A: Are you coming to Jeff's party?
   B: I'm not sure. I _____ go to the coast instead.
      must   will   might

10. A: Can I speak to Professor Carroll?
    B: She's not in her office, and she doesn't have any more classes today, so she _____ home.
       might go   must have gone   will probably go

ANSWER KEY

Exercise 10

1. might be 2. must 3. might take
4. must have left 5. may have 6. is probably going to (preferable to *could* here because "dark clouds" suggests a greater probability of rain) 7. might have 8. must

have been 9. might 10. must have gone
11. must have 12. may have lost
13. could be 14. must be taking
15. may have 16. must be 17. couldn't have 18. might

---

11. A: Jenny's sneezing again.
    B: Yes, she _____ a terrible cold.
       must have   must be having   must have had

12. A: Look, Maynard's sitting outside his own apartment. Isn't that weird?
    B: Not really. He _____ his keys and now he's waiting for his wife to come home.
       may be losing   may have lost   may have been losing

13. A: Is Myrna working in the city today?
    B: She _____ . I'm not sure.
       could   could have   could be

14. A: I can hear the water running in the bathroom.
    B: Yes, Bira _____ another shower.
       must take   must have taken   must be taking

15. A: What's up? You look worried.
    B: I am. My dog's sick. I think he _____ eaten some poison.
       maybe   may have been   may have

16. A: Have you heard? Mel's father died last night.
    B: Poor Mel. He _____ feeling terrible. They were very close.
       must   must be   must have been

17. A: Dean just won a million dollars in the lottery.
    B: He _____ . He never buys lottery tickets.
       must not have   could not   couldn't have

18. A: Does Isaiah still share a house with his sister?
    B: I don't know. He _____ .
       might be   might   might have

EXERCISE 11

Look back at the Opening Task. Who do you think the "Mystery Person" is? What do you think happened to him or her? Complete the following newspaper article with your ideas about what might have happened. Remember to use *must, may, could, might,* or *couldn't/can't* to show how certain you feel.

```
Missing Mystery Person
It has been a week since New York taxi driver Ricardo Oliveiro found
a briefcase on the back seat of his cab. It has been a week
of guessing and speculation: Who is the owner of this briefcase
and where is he or she now? Several different theories have
been proposed, but so far the most interesting is the one which fol-
lows . . . .
```

Exercise 11
V A R I A T I O N

Use this first as a writing exercise (as in instructions) and then as an editing exercise.

1. Ss read over their individually completed newspaper articles, underlining any use of modals + verb, and revising if necessary.
2. Ss exchange papers with a partner, reading over each other's articles first for content/meaning and then for accuracy.
3. Ss ask the writer any questions needed to help clarify meaning. Example: *I didn't understand the statement _____. Can you try to say it in another way so that I understand?* (or "What does _____ mean?")
4. Ss point out any errors; explain their observation and justify their opinion. (It's possible that there is no error, in other words.) While Ss are working, circulate.
5. Go over problematic items and/or good examples when you regroup as a whole class, or ask Ss for these. You might also ask Ss to explain their revisions: What was wrong with the original statement?

UNIT GOAL REVIEW

Ask Ss to look at the goals on the opening page of the unit again. Help them understand how much they have accomplished in each area. This is an opportunity to review some of the meaning/strength distinctions of the different modals and to describe possibility and probability using different time frames. This is also the time to ask Ss to identify which areas they would like more practice with. If you feel that they are still challenged by some of the points in this chapter, allow plenty of time for the activities and/or for reviewing relevant focus boxes and exercises.

A N S W E R   K E Y

Exercise 11
Answers are dependent on the inferences Ss made in the Opening Task.

USE YOUR ENGLISH

The activities in the purple pages at the end of the unit contain situations that should naturally elicit the structures covered in the unit. For a more complete discussion of how to use the Use Your English Activities, see page xxiv of this Teacher's Edition.

When Ss are doing these activities in class, you can circulate and listen to see how they are using the structures targeted in this unit. Do you think they have achieved the goals presented at the beginning of the unit?

Activity 1

It's fun to do this activity "out of the blue," with no warning, before Ss have a chance to look up the answers (on page A-16) or to talk about their ideas with others. You may get some curious answers!

Activity 2

VARIATION

Assign the first step as homework, either to teams or individuals. Sometimes it takes a little time to come up with well-thought-out drawings.

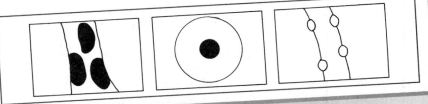

ACTIVITY 1: SPEAKING/LISTENING

Can you guess what these drawings represent? Get together with a partner and see how many different possible interpretations you can come up with for each drawing. Classify your interpretations as "Possible," "Probable," and "Certain." Compare your answers with the rest of the class. (You can find the "official" answers on page A-16.)

ACTIVITY 2: SPEAKING/LISTENING

The purpose of this activity is to confuse your classmates. Form teams and create five different drawings of familiar things seen from an unusual point of view. Exchange papers. Each team receives drawings from another team. As a team, see how many different interpretations you can make for each drawing. Write each beside the appropriate drawing, showing how probable you think your interpretation is.

When you have made your guesses, exchange papers with another team until everyone has had a chance to "interpret" all the drawings. Which team got the most "correct" interpretations? Which team had the most interesting interpretations?

It could be a donut.
It might be a hat from above.
It could be an eyeball.

ACTIVITY 3: SPEAKING/LISTENING

Get together with a partner and examine the photographs below. What's going on? Who are the people? Create a story showing what you think might have happened and what might happen next. You can use the photographs in any order that you like. Compare your story with those of your classmates. In what ways do their interpretations differ from yours?

A

B

C

D

E

SUGGESTIONS

1. Depending on how vivid your Ss' imaginations are, you might want to brainstorm a little together as a group about each picture, or at least identify the things/items in each picture.

2. While Ss are comparing their stories, note which ones are particularly strange, interesting, logical, etc., and ask these Ss to share their stories aloud. You can vote on which stories are the "best" in various categories of your choice (most outlandish, funniest, etc.).

VARIATION

For follow-up accuracy work, tape record Ss as they are presenting their stories. Play the tape and stop it after each statement, checking for accuracy in the use of the appropriate modal and in terms of the time frame.

Activity 4

Ss are especially enthusiastic about this activity if they tape recorded some of their own stories, as suggested in this Teacher's Edition for Activity 3.

VARIATION

If your classroom is in an EFL setting with little access to native speakers, Ss can instead interview other English language learners (other English classes), or people they consider fluent in English, perhaps because they have lived in an English-speaking country, perhaps because they have studied English for a long time.

Activity 5

Play textbook audio. The tapescript for this listening activity appears on p. 506 of this book.

Step 1: Check the tapescripts for answers.
Step 2: Ss can check their sentences with others for accuracy.
Point out that they now have one way of understanding how speakers feel in terms of certainty. The modals they use can show this.
Ask: *What are other ways speakers can let you know how certain they feel?* Likely answers: They use words like *maybe, probably, very*; a person's tone of voice, how loud their voice is, how they emphasize their words (volume, pitch, intonation), and so on.

ACTIVITY 4: SPEAKING/LISTENING

STEP 1 Show the photographs from Activity 3 to a native speaker of English. Ask him or her to tell you what she or he thinks might have happened and what might happen next. Tape the answers he or she gives. Listen to your tape and be ready to tell your classmates what the person says. How many different stories are there? Which one is the most interesting?

STEP 2 Listen to your tape again and write down any sentences with examples of the language from this unit.

ACTIVITY 5: LISTENING

STEP 1 Listen to the tapes of two different people talking about the photographs on page 85. As you listen to their stories, write the letter of each photograph on the chart to show which one comes first, second, and so on.

	SPEAKER 1 Photograph	SPEAKER 2 Photograph
First		
Second		
Third		
Fourth		
Fifth		

Which story is the most interesting, in your opinion?

STEP 2 Listen to the tape again and write down any sentences with *may, might, could,* or *must* that show how certain the speaker feels.

ANSWER KEY

Activity 5
Speaker 1: A, E, B, C, D   **Speaker 2:** A, C, E, B, D

ACTIVITY 6: SPEAKING/LISTENING

In the Opening Task, you looked at the contents of somebody's briefcase and made guesses about his or her identity. The purpose of this activity is to create your own "mystery person." Form groups and collect a number of items that somebody might carry in his or her pockets (tickets, bills, photographs, business cards, etc.). Choose between eight to ten items, put them in a bag, and bring them to class. Exchange bags with another group. With your group, examine the contents of your bag and try to decide on the possible identity of the owner, using the same categories as in the Opening Task. When everyone is ready, share your conclusions with the rest of the class, showing how certain you are. Remember, your classmates might ask you to justify your conclusions, so be ready to justify each one.

ACTIVITY 7: WRITING

Write a profile of the "mystery person" your group presented to the class in Activity 6. Make sure you have an introduction and that you provide evidence to support your conclusions. When you finish writing, read your profile to see how much of the language discussed in this unit you were able to use.

Activity 6

If you have a large class, you might want to form several groups, choose fewer items, and/or have more than one group at a time sharing conclusions.

VARIATION

1. If you feel your Ss need more work on accuracy, have them write down their conclusions in full sentences: *This person might have been meeting someone in hotels. This person must have just had a haircut,* and so on.
2. The group that brought the bag of items cannot respond to the other group's conclusion if their sentence is inaccurate.
3. Keep score if you want, award points for accurate sentences, deducting points for inaccurate sentences, and award points for good conclusions (e.g., well-justified, well-thought-out, very original, etc.).

Activity 7
SUGGESTIONS

1. You can do this activity *along with* Activity 6. When you assign groups to collect their items, have them write their profile at that time. This will ensure that for Activity 6, there is no last-minute adding or deleting conclusions.
2. Do a similar accuracy-based follow-up activity as well. Have individuals rather than the group each write a profile, and do a peer-editing activity, with Ss exchanging papers and focusing on the accuracy of the structures targeted in this unit.

The test for this unit can be found on pp. 422–423 of this book.
The answers are on p. 424.

Unit 6

UNIT OVERVIEW

This unit provides contrasting practice of past progressive with simple past, using the time expressions *when*, *while*, and *as soon as*.

UNIT GOALS

Review the goals listed on this page to see what students (Ss) should be familiar with by the end of this unit.

OPENING TASK

The purpose of this task is to set up a situation in which Ss will naturally use past progressive and simple past structures. In working to solve the mystery, Ss are more likely to focus on communicating than on creating "perfect" sentences; based on their discussion, you can determine where the Ss need the most help.

SETTING UP THE TASK

1. The task illustration is supposed to evoke a *film noir* atmosphere. To provide Ss with background for the task, you could talk with them about some well-known detectives in fiction, film, or TV. Some examples: Sherlock Holmes, Columbo, Miss Marple, Hercule Poirot.
2. Showing pictures may be helpful in eliciting ideas.
3. Provide and elicit key vocabulary, such as:
   murder/murderer/victim/guilty/ innocent/clue/evidence/accuse/ murder weapon/suspicious
4. Looking at the picture, direct Ss to the question, "What probably happened?" Point out that all the clues for solving the murder mystery are in the picture and that the true/false activity will help in finding the solution.

UNIT 6

PAST PROGRESSIVE AND SIMPLE PAST WITH TIME CLAUSES

When, While, and *As Soon As*

UNIT GOALS:

- To choose between past progressive and simple past
- To form past progressive correctly
- To understand the meaning of *when*, *while*, and *as soon as*
- To correctly form clauses with *when*, *while*, and *as soon as*

▶ OPENING TASK
Miami Murder Mystery

Last night Lewis Meyer died at his home in Miami. Phil Fork, a police detective, was the first person to arrive at the house after Mr. Meyer died. This is what he found:

Mr. Meyer's wife, Margo, told Fork: "It was an accident. My husband took a shower at about 10:00 P.M. After his shower, he slipped on a piece of soap and fell down."

Do you believe her?

What probably happened?

Look at the picture and work with a partner. Decide whether the following statements are **probably** true (T) or **probably** false (F). Be ready to share your answers with your classmates and to explain your choices.

1.	Mr. Meyer died after Phil Fork arrived.	T	F
2.	Mr. Meyer died when Phil Fork arrived.	T	F
3.	Mr. Meyer died before Phil Fork arrived.	T	F
4.	Mr. Meyer brushed his teeth before he died.	T	F
5.	Mr. Meyer was brushing his teeth when he died.	T	F
6.	Mr. Meyer was taking a shower when he died.	T	F
7.	Mr. Meyer took a shower before he died.	T	F
8.	Mr. Meyer died when he slipped on a piece of soap.	T	F
9.	Somebody hit Mr. Meyer over the head while he was brushing his teeth.	T	F
10.	The murder weapon is still in the bathroom.	T	F

You are the detective. In your opinion, how did Mr. Meyer die?

With your partner, use the picture and your answers above to try to solve the mystery. Make as many guesses as you like. For example: *We think somebody killed Mr. Meyer while he was brushing his teeth. This is how it happened. . . .* Be ready to share your ideas with the rest of the class. Write your ideas here:

> **What really happened:**

CONDUCTING THE TASK

In order to facilitate more discussion using the target structure, Ss can work in pairs or groups of three to complete the true/false assignment. Alternately, this part of the Opening Task can be completed as a class. If you choose to use pairwork, be sure to review their answers as a class in order to come to a group consensus on which ones are <u>probably</u> true or <u>probably</u> false.

CLOSING THE TASK

In pairs or groups of three, Ss discuss their opinions of how Mr. Meyer died, recording their answers in the box provided. If you run out of time in class, this can be assigned for homework as paragraph writing. Remind them that there is no "correct" answer. A number of different theories generally emerge, and discussion can be heated.

REVIEWING THE TASK

Discuss their theories as a class. Don't worry about accuracy at this point, though you may want to write down some of the mistakes they make in order to focus on those problems later.

ANSWER KEY

Opening Task

1. F **2.** F **3.** T **4.** F **5.** T **6.** F
7. F **8** F **9.** T **10.** T

Solution: Mrs. Meyer killed her husband. She entered the bathroom while he was brushing his teeth, and she hit him over the head with the bathroom scale. Then she turned on the shower and put soap on the floor. How do we know this?

- From the toothbrush: He was brushing his teeth, not walking out of the shower.
- From the soap: It was not possible to slip in this position.
- From the bathroom scale: The scale does not indicate zero.

1. Focus Box 1 provides examples of differences between the use of these structures. Because many languages do not have a different form for progressive and simple usage, pay close attention to the differences illustrated in the examples. Point out how each example illustrates that the simple past focuses more on the *completion* of the event, while the past progressive emphasizes the *continuous nature* of the activity.

2. Extra examples can be taken from class situations (*When I arrived today, Jaro was reading the newspaper and Palo was opening the window to get some fresh air*) or from current local or international events that may be of interest to your class (*Over 300 people were standing outside the building when the incident happened*).

Exercise 1

1. While Ss are following the directions, divide the board into 3 columns and label one column "past progressive", another "simple past", and the last one "both."

2. Elicit some example sentences from Ss, placing their examples into the appropriate column.

3. Rather than correct their errors directly, you could ask the class which sentences are incorrect and how they would correct them.

Workbook Ex. 1, pp. 41–43.
Answers: TE p. 489.

FOCUS **1**

Past Progressive and Simple Past

EXAMPLES	EXPLANATIONS
(a) Phil Fork **arrived** at 10:30. **(b)** Mrs. Meyer **drank** several cups of black coffee.	Use the simple past for an action that started and finished in the past. For a list of irregular past forms, see Appendix 5 on page A-13.
(c) Phil Fork **was eating** dinner at 10:00. **(d)** Mr. Meyer **was brushing** his teeth at 10:00.	*Was eating* and *was brushing* are past progressive. Use the past progressive for an action that was in progress at a specific time in the past.
(e) Mr. Meyer **was brushing** his teeth when the murderer **entered** the room. **(f)** Phil Fork **was eating** dinner when he **heard** about the murder.	Use the past progressive with the simple past to show that one action began first and was still in progress when the second action happened. It is possible that the first action continued after the second action finished.
(g) Mrs. Meyer **was talking** on the phone while her husband **was taking** a shower. **(h)** Phil Fork **was reading** a newspaper while he **was eating** dinner.	Use the past progressive with the past progressive to show two actions in progress at the same time.

EXERCISE 1

Look back at what you wrote in the Opening Task on page 89. Did you use the past progressive and the simple past? If you did, underline all examples of the past progressive, circle all examples of the simple past, and check with your teacher to see if you used them correctly. If you didn't use these forms at all, write three sentences about Mr. Meyer's murder using the past progressive and the simple past. Check with your teacher to see if you used these forms correctly.

FOCUS **2**

Past Progressive

STATEMENT	NEGATIVE	QUESTION
I She } was sleeping. He It	I She } was not sleeping. He (wasn't) It	Was { I she } sleeping? he it
We You } were sleeping. They	We You } was not sleeping. They (weren't)	Were { we you } sleeping? they

EXERCISE 2

Get together with a partner and complete this newspaper report of Mr. Meyer's murder. Use information from the Opening Task on page 88 and your own ideas about what happened to help you.

DAILY NEWS

BATHROOM MURDER

"I am innocent!" says Mrs. Meyer.

Last night police arrested Margo Meyer for the murder of her husband, Lewis. On her way to the police station, Mrs. Meyer told reporters: "I am innocent. I loved my husband very much. I didn't kill him."

According to Mrs. Meyer, on the night of his death, her husband _____

_____when

_____.

However, Detective Phil Fork and his colleagues have a different theory about how Mr. Meyer

died. According to them, _____

_____

_____ while _____

_____.

This focus box illustrates the form of the past progressive, including contractions. Point out some of the American English spelling rules that sometimes cause trouble:
write → writing (dropping -e)
hit → hitting (double consonant in 1-syllable words)
travel → traveling (single consonant in 2-syllable words with <u>first</u> syllable stress)
rebel → rebelling (double consonant in 2-syllable words with <u>second</u> syllable stress)

Exercise 2

Exercise 2 gives Ss a chance to practice both the form and use of past progressive and simple past. To review their answers, you could have each pair compare their answers with another pair and later discuss their disagreements as a class.

SUGGESTION

Make a copy of the exercise on overhead transparency and fill out the news report together, using different pairs' examples. You can correct errors as you write, or point out the errors and ask the class to make corrections.

Workbook Exs. 2 & 3, pp. 43–45.
Answers: TE pp. 489–490.

ANSWER KEY

Exercise 2
Answers will vary. Possibilities;
Mrs. Meyer: was crossing/walking across the bathroom floor **when** *he slipped on a piece of soap/was getting out of the shower* **when** *he*

slipped on a piece of soap/died **when** *he slipped on a piece of soap*
Phil Fork and colleagues: somebody killed him **while** *he was brushing his teeth*

The purpose of this focus box is to introduce the meaning and use of the time expressions *when*, *while*, and *as soon as* (further discussion is provided in Focus 4 on p. 94). Remind Ss of the position choices of these expressions in the sentence. You can use a classroom example to illustrate:

While Jaro was reading the newspaper, Matias was talking with Cindy. OR
*Matias was talking with Cindy **while** Jaro was reading the newspaper.*

***As soon as** I arrived, everybody sat down.* OR
*Everybody sat down **as soon as** I arrived.*

When, While, and As Soon As

EXAMPLES	EXPLANATIONS
(a) **While** Mr. Meyer was getting ready for bed, Mrs. Meyer drank several cups of black coffee. OR (b) Mrs. Meyer drank several cups of black coffee **while** Mr. Meyer was getting ready for bed.	*When, while* and *as soon as* give information about time. You can use them **either** at the beginning of a sentence **or** in the middle. *While* introduces an action in progress. It means "during that time." It is usually used with the past progressive. However, many people now use *when* in place of *while*, especially in conversation.
(c) Mrs. Meyer called the police **when** she found the dead body. OR (d) **When** Mrs. Meyer found her husband's body, she called the police.	*When* introduces a completed action. It is usually used with the simple past. In (c) and (d), *when* introduces the action that happened first: **First** Mrs. Meyer found the body and **then** she called the police.
(e) Mrs. Meyer came to the door **as soon as** Phil Fork arrived. OR (f) **As soon as** Phil Fork arrived, Mrs. Meyer came to the door.	*As soon as* introduces a completed action and means "immediately after."

EXERCISE 3

Make meaningful statements about Mr. Meyer's murder by matching information from A with information from B. The first one has been done for you.

A	**B**
1. Mrs. Meyer called the police	she said that she was innocent.
2. While she was waiting for the police to arrive	Mrs. Meyer took him to the scene of the crime.
3. As soon as Phil Fork heard about the murder	as soon as her husband died.
4. When Fork asked to see the body	while the police were taking her to jail.
5. While Fork was searching the bathroom for clues	while he was brushing his teeth.
6. He saw that Mr. Meyer died	she placed a bar of soap on the bathroom floor.
7. When Fork accused Mrs. Meyer of murder	he rushed to the Meyers' house.
8. A crowd of news reporters tried to interview Mrs. Meyer	he became suspicious of Mrs. Meyer's story.

EXERCISE 4

Look again at the sentences you created in Exercise 3. For each one, underline the part of the sentence that gives information about time. This is the part of the sentence that answers the question "When?" For example: *Mrs. Meyer called the police as soon as her husband died.*

Exercise 3

This exercise uses all three time expressions at different locations in each sentence. Ss will build on this exercise in Exercises 4 and 5.

Exercise 4

Using the sentences from the previous exercise, Ss practice answering the question "When?", underlining the part of the sentence that answers that question. Ss will build on this exercise in Exercise 5

Workbook Ex. 4, p. 46.
Answers: TE p. 490.

ANSWER KEY

Exercises 3 and 4
(Answers to Exercise 4 are underlined)
2. While she was waiting for the police to arrive, she placed a bar of soap on the bathroom floor.   **3.** As soon as Phil Fork heard about the murder, he rushed to the Meyers' house.   **4.** When Fork asked to see the body, Mrs. Meyer took him to the scene of the crime.   **5.** While Fork was searching the bathroom for clues, he became suspicious of Mrs. Meyer's story.   **6.** He saw that Mr. Meyer had died while he was brushing his teeth.   **7.** When Fork accused Mrs. Meyer of murder, she said that she was innocent.   **8.** A crowd of news reporters tried to interview Mrs. Meyer while the police were taking her to jail.

FOCUS 4

This focus box provides further information on the use of the time expressions introduced in Focus 3, concentrating on their form. Ss are introduced to the terms "dependent clause" and "independent/main clause." (The clause led by the time expression "depends" on the main clause to make sense).

1. Be sure Ss understand the difference between these types of clauses.
2. Emphasize the use of the comma in the two forms.

Exercise 5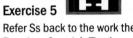

Refer Ss back to the work they completed in Exercises 3 and 4. The Answer Key is located on p. 93.

Workbook Ex. 5, p. 46.
Answers: TE p. 490.
Note: this exercise must be preceded by Exercise 4, p. 93.

FOCUS **4**

Time Clauses with *When, While, As Soon As, Before,* and *After*

EXAMPLES		EXPLANATIONS
Dependent Time Clause	*Main Independent Clause*	A time clause is a **dependent** clause; this means that it is not complete by itself. It needs the rest of the sentence (**the main** or **independent** clause) to complete its meaning.
(a) When Amy returned home,	everyone ran out to greet her.	In order to understand *When Amy returned home,* we need more information.
(b) While my father was cooking dinner, our guests arrived.		A time clause can come at the beginning of a sentence (b) **or** at the end (c). If the time clause comes at the beginning of the sentence, use a comma between the time clause and the main clause.
(c) Our guests arrived while my father was cooking dinner.		

When ~~~~~~~~~~, ~~~~~~~~~~

If the main clause comes at the beginning of the sentence and the time clause comes last, do not use a comma between the two clauses (c).

~~~~~~~~~~when ~~~~~~~~~~

EXERCISE 5

Turn back to the sentences you created in Exercise 3. Write them below and add commas, as necessary.

1. _____ .
2. _____ .
3. _____ .
4. _____ .
5. _____ .
6. _____ .
7. _____ .
8. _____ .

ANSWER KEY

Exercise 5
See Answer Key for Exercises 3 and 4, p. 93, for comma placement.

EXERCISE 6

Check (✔) the sentence—(a) or (b)—closest in meaning to each statement.

1. While Mr. Meyer was brushing his teeth, someone entered the room.
   - (a) Mr. Meyer finished brushing his teeth before someone entered.
   - (b) Mr. Meyer was alone when he started brushing his teeth.

2. When he got Mrs. Meyer's call, Phil Fork left his office and drove to her house.
   - (a) Mrs. Meyer called before Phil Fork left his office.
   - (b) Mrs. Meyer called after Phil Fork left his office.

3. As soon as he got into his car, he took out a cigarette and lit it.
   - (a) He was smoking when he got into the car.
   - (b) He started to smoke after he got into his car.

4. While Fork was driving to the Meyers' house, he was listening to his favorite opera on the radio.
   - (a) He drove his car and listened to the radio at the same time.
   - (b) He turned on the radio when he reached the Meyers' house.

5. When he got there, a number of police officers were searching the house for clues.
   - (a) They started when he got there.
   - (b) They started before he got there.

6. As soon as Fork started to question Mrs. Meyer, she burst into tears.
   - (a) She was crying when he started to question her.
   - (b) She started to cry when he began to question her.

7. Phil Fork carefully reviewed all his notes when he went home.
   - (a) He went home first.
   - (b) He reviewed his notes first.

Exercise 6

This exercise tests Ss' understanding of the time expressions and verb forms used. There is only one correct answer for each statement.

SUGGESTION

Have Ss compare their answers in groups and discuss misunderstandings as a class.

ANSWER KEY

Exercise 6
1. b 2. a 3. b 4. a 5. b 6. b
7. a

Exercise 7

1. The goal of the first part of this activity is to exercise background knowledge on John Lennon through brainstorming. This activity works well in pairs or groups. Don't worry if Ss do not use accurate grammar at this point. Possible answers include:
   He was born in Liverpool, England.
   He was a member of the Beatles.
   His second wife was Japanese.
   He was killed by one of his fans in New York City.
   He believed in peace and love and was against war.
   His sons Julian and Sean are singers.

2. After the brainstorming session, discuss their information as a class, writing some of the facts on the board.

3. The second part of the exercise requires Ss to combine two pieces of information, using *when* and *while* as indicated. Using the information in the chart, Ss fill in the blanks.

S U G G E S T I O N

If you do this activity as a class, copy the exercise on an overhead transparency to fill in Ss' answers.

EXERCISE 7

Work with a partner and write down five things you know about John Lennon.

Here is some more information about John Lennon's life. The wavy line ($\sim\sim\sim$) indicates an action in progress. X indicates a completed action.

1. attend high school $\sim\sim\sim$	2. attend high school
X	X
his mother dies	meet Paul McCartney
3. study at art school $\sim\sim\sim$	4. perform in clubs in Liverpool
X	X
form the Beatles	sign his first recording contract
5. live in London	6. work for peace and write new songs
X	X
fall in love with Yoko Ono	die

7. leave his apartment
X
one of his fans shoots him

Use this information to finish the short biography below. Fill in the blanks, using the simple past or the past progressive. The first one has been done for you as an example.

John Lennon was one of the most famous singer/songwriters of his time. He was born in Liverpool, England, in 1940, but his childhood was not very happy.

(1) _His mother died_ while _he was attending high school_. Life was difficult for John after his mother's death, but after a time things got better. (2) _____ while _____ . Soon Paul introduced him to George Harrison, and they began to play in a band together. After John left high school, he became an art student. (3) While _____ , _____ . After forming the Beatles, John married his first wife, Cynthia, and they had a son, Julian. (4) _____ when _____ . John and the Beatles moved to London and became very famous throughout the world. (5) _____ while _____ . A couple of years later, the Beatles split up. John and Yoko got married and moved to the United States, where their son Sean was born. John (6) _____ when _____ . On December 8, 1980, (7) _____ while _____ . John Lennon died in 1980, but he still has lots of fans all over the world.

ANSWER KEY

Exercise 7

(2) He met Paul McCartney . . . he was attending high school   (3) . . . he was studying at art school, he formed the Beatles.
(4) He was performing in clubs in Liverpool . . . he signed his first recording contract   (5) He fell in love with Yoko Ono . . . he was living in London.
(6) . . . was working for peace and writing new songs . . . he died.   (7) . . . one of his fans shot him . . . he was leaving his apartment.

Exercise 8

The sentences in this exercise build on each other to make a story. Point out that sometimes more than one answer is possible.

UNIT GOAL REVIEW

Ask Ss to look at the goals on the opening page of the unit again. Help them understand how much they have accomplished in each area by eliciting answers from a few examples.

1. Use examples from some of the focus boxes that illustrate the differences between the two structures, asking Ss why they think the writer chose that particular structure there.

2. To test their past progressive form and knowledge of *when*, *while*, and *as soon as*, write a few examples of incorrect use (perhaps taken from errors they have made earlier in the class or homework) on the board. Ask some Ss to correct the errors.

EXERCISE 8

Complete the sentences in the story below using the words in parentheses. Use the simple past or the past progressive.

1. Yesterday morning at 10:00, Marie _____ (go) to see the dentist.

2. While she _____ (wait) for her appointment, her old friend Lin _____ (come) into the dentist's waiting room.

3. Before Marie _____ (get) her new job at the software company, she and Lin _____ (work) together at the bank.

4. When Marie and Lin _____ (see) each other in the waiting room, they _____ (be) surprised and delighted.

5. They _____ (realize) that they had not seen each other for several months.

6. While they _____ (wait) for their appointments, they _____ (talk and laugh) about old times.

7. When it _____ (be) finally time for Marie to see the dentist, they _____ (not + want) to stop talking.

8. Just before Marie _____ (leave) the waiting room, they _____ (make) a date to see each other again.

9. While Marie _____ (leave) the waiting room, Lin _____ (say), "I hope you don't have any cavities!"

ANSWER KEY

Exercise 8
1. went 2. was waiting; came 3. got; worked/were working 4. saw; were 5. realized 6. were waiting; talked and laughed 7. was; did not want 8. left; made 9. was leaving; said

Use Your English

The activities on these "purple pages" at the end of the unit contain situations that should naturally elicit the unit's structures in a more communicative framework. When Ss are doing these activities in class, you can circulate and listen to determine if they have actually achieved the goals on the opening page of the unit.

Activity 1

The goal of this activity is for Ss to combine their information in order to write original sentences to complete Nan Silviera's autobiography.

SUGGESTION

Ss must complete this activity in pairs, since each of them has incomplete information. If you have an odd number of Ss, have some Ss work in groups of three, and assign one student to act as "secretary."

Answers will vary. If you wish to provide feedback to the whole class as a review, select sections of some of the passages that illustrate some typical errors. Put the examples on an overhead transparency and ask Ss to locate and correct the errors in the next class.

ACTIVITY 1: SPEAKING/LISTENING/WRITING

Nan Silviera has just written her first book:

As you can see below, the author's life story on the back of the book is not complete. Work with a partner to finish writing it.

STEP 1 Student A: Turn to page 102. Student B: Turn to page 103.

STEP 2 You both have information about Nan's life, but some of the information is missing. Do not show your pages to each other, but ask each other questions to get information about the parts marked "?".

STEP 3 Write down the information your partner gives you so that when you finish, you will have the complete story.

STEP 4 Use the information from your chart to write about Nan's life. You can use the biography on the back of her book to begin your story.

STEP 5 When you finish writing, check your work to see if you have used time clauses and the past progressive and simple past tenses appropriately.

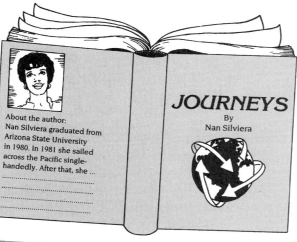

About the author:
Nan Silviera graduated from Arizona State University in 1980. In 1981 she sailed across the Pacific single-handedly. After that, she ...

JOURNEYS
By
Nan Silviera

Activity 2

The chart is intended as a rough guide only and can be modified to fit the needs and personality of your class. Remind Ss that they will need to fill in a time of their own in the last box. Some examples are: *in December 1996; this time three weeks ago; right before class.*

SUGGESTION

To ensure that all Ss are included, write their names on separate slips of paper. Make sure each student's name appears three or four times. Distribute several slips to each student. Ss make guesses about the names they receive. If they receive their own names, they exchange the slip for a different one. (Of course they are free to also make guesses about any other Ss in the class.)

ACTIVITY 2: SPEAKING/LISTENING/WRITING

In this activity, you will be finding information about your classmates' lives by asking what they were doing at the times shown below. In the last box on the chart, add a time of your own choice (for example, on your last birthday, last New Year's Eve, etc.). Do not write information about yourself.

STEP 1 Think about the different students in your class. Can you guess what they were doing at these times? In the box marked *Guesses*, write what **you** think different people were doing at each time.

STEP 2 Go around the room and talk to as many people as possible to find out what they were really doing.

STEP 3 Write this information in the box marked *Facts*.

NOTE: Copy the chart into your notebook if you need more space to write. If your class is very big, you can make guesses about some of your classmates rather than all of them. If you don't want to give information about a certain time, you can say, "I'm sorry but I'd rather not talk about that time." If you can't remember, feel free to invent something.

Times	Guesses	Facts
at 8:30 P.M. last Sunday		
in May 1993		
five years ago		
ten years ago today		
????? (you choose a time)		

STEP 4 When you finish, review the information you collected. Choose the most interesting or surprising facts and make a short report (oral or written). Report on the facts, not on your original guesses. For example:

I recently asked my classmates about certain times in their lives. I was surprised by some of the things they told me. For example, ten years ago, while Sun Wu (she was only eight years old at that time) was going to elementary school, Tranh was working in his father's store. . . .

ACTIVITY 3: SPEAKING/WRITING

STEP 1 Take a large sheet of paper and make a time line for your own life like the one in Activity 1. Bring your time line to class and describe the story of your life to your classmates.

STEP 2 Exchange your time line with a partner. Use his or her time line to write the story of his or her life. How many differences and similarities can you find between your partner's life history and yours?

ACTIVITY 4: SPEAKING/LISTENING/WRITING

The death of President John F. Kennedy in 1963 was an enormous shock to people in the United States and to people all over the world. Many people who were alive at that time can remember exactly what they were doing when they heard the news of Kennedy's assassination.

STEP 1 With a partner, interview one or two people who were alive at that time and find out what they were doing when they heard the news of Kennedy's death. If possible, tape-record your interviews. Before the interview, get together with your partner to make a list of possible questions. You can use the questions below or make other questions of your own, if you prefer.

QUESTIONS:

- What were you doing when you heard the news of President Kennedy's death?
- Where were you living at that time?
- Who were you with?
- What were you doing just before you heard the news of his death?
- What did you do after you heard about it?
- How did you feel?
- Do you remember what you were wearing?
- How old were you? What did you look like at that time?

STEP 2 Share your findings with the rest of the class.

STEP 3 Listen to your tape and write down any sentences with the simple past or the past progressive. Underline any time clauses in these sentences.

Activity 3

Activity 3 allows Ss to share information about themselves while naturally using the structures covered in this unit. Step 2 is especially helpful in practicing the third person–s (i.e., *She **was** living in Sri Lanka when she met her husband*–not- *She ~~were~~ living. . .*).

VARIATION

Have Ss do Step 2 orally as a report to class after the pair discussion.

Activity 4

VARIATIONS

1. Depending on your Ss and the native speakers they have access to, you could substitute someone different. Some possibilities: Princess Diana, John F. Kennedy, Jr., Kurt Cobain, Indira Gandhi, Mother Theresa.
2. Substitute an important international or local event likely to be shared by native speakers in your region. For example: the first moon landing, the Loma Prieta earthquake (San Francisco), or other natural disaster.

Activity 5 🎴

Play textbook audio. The tapescript for this listening appears on p. 506 of this book. Check tapescript for answers.

Step 1 answers:
Speaker 1: England, standing by fish tank
Speaker 2: L.A., ironing
Speaker 3: Phoenix, AZ, working at ad agency

Step 2: Answers may vary. You may wish to discuss their sentences in class to complete each speaker's story (group or whole-class activity).

ACTIVITY 5 : LISTENING 🎴

For this activity, you will hear three people talking about what they were doing when President Kennedy was killed.

STEP 1 Listen to the tape and take notes in the chart below.

Speaker	Place	Activity
Speaker 1		
Speaker 2		
Speaker 3		

STEP 2 Listen to the tape again and write down any sentences with past progressive or simple past.

Activity 1 (from p.99)
Student A

1980 1981 1982 1983 1984 1985 1986 1987 1988 1989 1990 1991 1992 1993 1994 1995 1996

?
Travel in Asia and India
Work in Paris
Study journalism at University of Oregon
?
?

Go to France
Return to USA
Have a baby
Finish book

Graduate from Arizona State University

Begin to write a book

Win Pulitzer Prize for her book

Sail across the Pacific alone

ANSWER KEY

Check tapescript for answers (p. 506).

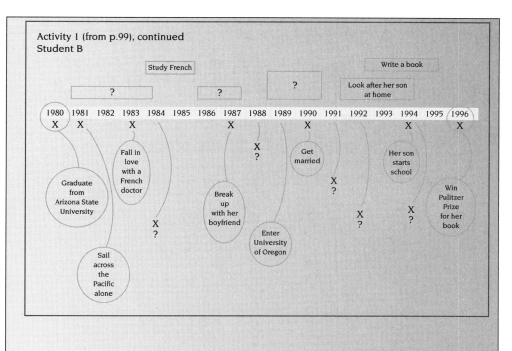

Activity 1 (from p.99), continued
Student B

Study French

Write a book

?

?

?

Look after her son
at home

1980 1981 1982 1983 1984 1985 1986 1987 1988 1989 1990 1991 1992 1993 1994 1995 1996

Graduate from Arizona State University

Fall in love with a French doctor

Sail across the Pacific alone

X ?

Break up with her boyfriend

X ?

Enter University of Oregon

Get married

X ?

X ?

Her son starts school

X ?

X ?

Win Pulitzer Prize for her book

Past Progressive and Simple Past with Time Clauses: When, While, and As Soon As **103**

The test for this unit can be found on pp. 425–426 of this book. The answers are on p. 427.

TOEFL Test Preparation Exercises for Units 4–6 can be found on pp. 48–50 of the Workbook.
The answers are on p. 490 of this book.

Unit 7

UNIT 7

UNIT OVERVIEW

Unit 7 provides practice with comparatives, superlatives, and structures *as . . . as,* and *not as . . . as.*

SIMILARITIES AND DIFFERENCES

Comparatives, Superlatives, As . . . As, Not As . . . As

UNIT GOALS

Review the goals listed on this page to see what students (Ss) should learn by the end of the unit.

UNIT GOALS:

- To know how to use comparatives and superlatives to express differences
- To know the meaning of *as . . . as* and *not as . . . as*
- To know how to form sentences with *as . . . as* and *not as . . . as*
- To use *as . . . as* and *not as . . . as* to make tactful comparisons

OPENING TASK

Note: The purpose of this task is to generate talk about similarities and differences, naturally using comparative structures. The logical problem-solving format focuses attention on meaning rather than form, which will allow you to see whether Ss are able to produce the form spontaneously.

SETTING UP THE TASK

If you decide to have Ss work in pairs or groups, the groups should be small so that each student can talk.

OPENING TASK
Friends

Can you guess the names of the people in this picture? Work by yourself or with a partner and use the information in the chart and the list of clues on the next page to identify each person. Write their names in the correct position on the picture.

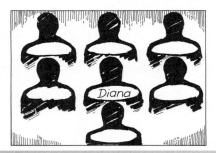

The Left   The Right

Diana

Name	Likes	Age	Hair	Occupation	Eyes	Height
LINDA	football	75	red	doctor	green	5'9 1/2"
BOB	coffee	21	brown	student	blue	5'9 1/2"
SUSAN	music	25	blond	student	green	5'1"
FRANK	cats	43	gray	artist	brown	6'4"
CARLA	food	28	black	singer	blue	5'5"
GEORGE	movies	44	bald	writer	brown	5'10"
DIANA	opera	58	brown	engineer	gray	5'10"

Clues

1. The oldest person is behind the youngest woman.
2. The tallest woman is behind someone who is thirty years younger than she is.
3. The shortest person is in front of someone with green eyes.
4. The tallest man is next to the tallest woman.
5. The 28-year-old singer is not next to anybody.
6. The person who likes coffee is not quite as tall as the person next to him on the right.
7. The man who is on the right of the youngest person is behind the tallest person.
8. The youngest person is as tall as the person next to him on the left.

When you finish, check your answers with the rest of the class to see if you all agree. You can find the solution to the Opening Task on page A-16.

CONDUCTING THE TASK

Draw the chart on the board. It is enough to make lines or spaces (or oval head-shapes) for the seven positions.

While Ss are working, you can circulate and listen in order to get an idea of student's current use of *not as . . . as, as . . . as,* comparative and superlative structures. Note the structures that seem to be problematic (for more than one student there are errors in form).

CLOSING THE TASK

If one group finishes before the rest, disperse the group members among the remaining groups to advise or help.

REVIEWING THE TASK

For each of the seven positions in the Opening Task, you can have a student give one statement that supports their answer. Write these statements on the board, reformulating inaccurate attempts. For example, a student may say: *"The most tallest people are standing next to each other."* Rewrite *"most tallest"* as *"tallest"*.

This focus box explains the difference between comparatives (with –er) and superlatives (with –est). It also gives examples of comparatives and superlatives in different parts of speech. Examples (d) and (e) use irregular forms, rather than –er or –est.

SUGGESTION

Ss can use the phrases from the section, after example (c) to make true statements. For example, *Leah is the youngest student in the class. I am younger than Etsuko.* If you want to concentrate on meaning, you could elicit further examples from Ss, using questions such as: *Who had the biggest breakfast this morning? Who drank the most coffee/tea? Was your breakfast bigger than (student's name)'s? Did you drink more coffee than (student's name)?*
Who traveled the farthest to get to class this morning? Did you travel farther than (student's name)? Who woke up the earliest? Did you wake up earlier/later than (name)?

FOCUS **1**

▶ Expressing Difference: Comparatives and Superlatives

EXAMPLES	EXPLANATIONS
(a) Susan is **the shortest,** and Frank is **the tallest.** *[illustration of seven people standing, labeled Susan ... Frank]*	*The tallest* and *the shortest* are superlatives. Superlatives show extremes of difference among people or things. They show which has the greatest amount of a certain quality in a group of people or things.
(b) George is **taller than** Linda. **(c)** Carla is **shorter than** George. *[illustration of four people standing, labeled Carla Linda George]*	*Taller than* and *shorter than* are comparatives. Comparatives show differences among people or things, but they do not show extremes of difference.
<table><tr><td></td><td>Comparative</td><td>Superlative</td></tr><tr><td>young</td><td>young**er than**</td><td>**the** young**est**</td></tr><tr><td>easy</td><td>eas**ier than**</td><td>**the** eas**iest**</td></tr><tr><td>difficult</td><td>**more** difficult **than**</td><td>**the most** difficult</td></tr><tr><td>carefully fully</td><td>**more** carefully **than**</td><td>**the most** care-</td></tr><tr><td>weigh</td><td>weigh **more than** weigh **less than**</td><td>weigh **the most** weigh **the least**</td></tr><tr><td>money</td><td>**more** money **than** **less** money **than**</td><td>**the most** money **the least** money</td></tr></table>	Comparatives and superlatives can be used with all parts of speech: • adjectives with one syllable • adjectives with one syllable + *-y* • adjectives with two or more syllables • adverbs • verbs • nouns
George is a good singer, but I am not. **(d)** George sings **better than** I do. **(e)** Carla is **the best** singer in the family.	Not all comparative and superlative forms are regular. Examples (d) and (e) use irregular comparative and superlative forms of *good*.

EXERCISE 1

First fill in the blanks with a word or word ending and then use the information from the Opening Task to decide if the statements are true (T) or false (F).

1. The oldest woman is taller _____ the oldest man. T F
2. George is tall _____ than the person beside him. T F
3. Diana is young ____ _____ the man beside her on the right. T F
4. George is tall ____ _____ Frank. T F
5. The singer is several years older _____ the person behind her. T F
6. The doctor is _____ old _____. T F
7. Bob is old ____ _____ the person in front of him. T F
8. The young _____ woman is in front of ____ old _____ woman. T · F
9. Frank is _____ tall _____ man, but he isn't _____ old _____ . T F
10. _____ old _____ man is short _____ _____ the young _____ woman. T F

FOCUS **2**

Similarity and Difference:
As . . . As and
Not As . . . As

EXAMPLES	EXPLANATIONS
Linda is about 5'9". Bob is about 5'9". **(a)** Linda is **as tall as** Bob. OR Bob is **as tall as** Linda. 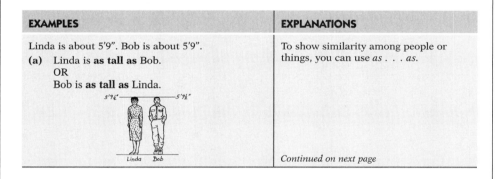	To show similarity among people or things, you can use *as . . . as.* *Continued on next page*

Exercise 1

In order to do this exercise, you will need the information from the Opening Task. The answers here all use regular comparative and superlative forms, not irregular forms or the *as . . . as* structure. The exercise also provides practice with *than*, as in *taller than . . . , younger than . . .*

SUGGESTION

Ask Ss to compare their answers in pairs or groups of three and, when you regroup as a class, to ask you questions about only those answers that they disagree on.

FOCUS 2

1. To make sure Ss understand how to use the *as . . . as* structure, practice using the form with adjectives that describe physical characteristics (see Exercise 2).
2. The information in (b) and (c) might be new for some Ss at this level, so this kind of practice may be helpful. Give additional examples related to your class: *My book is exactly the same as your book.*
3. Emphasize the information in (e)—that these phrases are very informal, and rarely used in formal writing.

ANSWER KEY

Exercise 1
1. than F 2. taller T 3. younger than F
4. taller than F 5. than F 6. the oldest T
7. older than F 8. youngest; the oldest T
9. the tallest; the oldest T 10. The oldest; shorter than the youngest F

EXAMPLES	EXPLANATIONS
(b) George is **exactly as tall as** Diana. OR Diana is **exactly as tall as** George. Diana George	To show that people or things are the same, you can add *exactly*.
George is 5'10". Bob is 5'9 1/2". **(c)** Bob is { **almost** **not quite** **nearly** **as tall as** George. **practically** **just about** } Bob George	To show that people or things are very similar, add: *almost, not quite, nearly, practically,* or *just about*.
George is 5'10". Bob is 5'9 1/2". **(d)** Bob is **not as tall as** George.	To show differences among people or things, you can use *not as . . . as*.
Susan is 5'1". Diana is 5'10". **(e)** **nowhere near** Susan is **not nearly as tall as** Diana. **not anywhere near** Susan Diana	To show a great amount of difference, add: *nowhere near, not nearly,* or *not anywhere near.* *Nowhere near* and *not anywhere near* are only used in very informal conversation with friends.

EXERCISE 2

Get together with another student. Think of all the ways that you are similar and all the ways that you are different. You have five minutes to make as many sentences as you can, using *as . . . as* and *not as . . . as* to show these differences and similarities. Share your sentences with the rest of the class.

EXERCISE 3

Use the information in the Opening Task to write complete sentences about the following people. You can use a comparative, a superlative, *as . . . as* or *not as . . . as* in each sentence. Show the amount of difference or similarity as necessary.

1. Linda/Bob/height
   Linda is as tall as Bob.

2. Susan/Frank/height

3. Linda/Diana/height

4. Linda/Carla/height

5. George/Susan/height and age

6. Bob/George/height

7. Frank/George/age

8. Diana/Linda/age

9. Frank/height

10. Linda/age

11. George/Diana/height

Exercise 2

VARIATION

To make this exercise into a game or competition, give 1 point for each sentence that is correctly formed and factually true. After five minutes, ask each pair of Ss to count the number of sentences they have made. The pair who made the most can share their sentences aloud with the class. The Ss who are listening should determine whether the sentences are correctly formed. If not, they can correct them, and no points are assigned.

Note: If you want to limit the sentences to the structures *as . . . as* and *not as . . . as* (as advised in the instructions), be sure to remind Ss *before* you start. Otherwise, Ss are likely to generate all the different kinds of comparative and superlative structures.

Exercise 3

This exercise can help Ss understand subtle differences in meaning when comparing and contrasting. Remind Ss to use the phrases in Focus 2, boxes (c) and (e) to talk about *amounts* of differences.

ANSWER KEY

Exercise 2

Answers will vary, but will probably include some of the phrases above (Focus 2) if you limit the structures used to *as . . . as* and *not as . . . as*: exactly *as . . . as*, almost/not quite/nearly/ practically/just about as . . . as.

Exercise 3

2. Susan is not as tall as Frank./Susan is shorter than Frank./Frank is taller than Susan. 3. Linda is almost/nearly/not quite/ practically as tall as Diana. 4. Carla is not as tall as Linda./Linda is taller than Carla./ Carla is shorter than Linda. 5. George is (both) older and taller than Susan./Susan is (both) younger and shorter than George. 6. Bob is almost/nearly/not quite/practically as tall as George. 7. Frank is almost/ not quite/nearly/ practically as old as George. 8. Diana is not as old as Linda./Diana is younger than Linda./Linda is older than Diana. 9. Frank is the tallest. 10. Linda is the oldest. 11. George is exactly as tall as Diana./Diana is exactly as tall as George.

FOCUS 3

Point out how versatile the *as . . . as* structure is.

SUGGESTION

Supplement this focus box by providing a description of you compared to a family member or a colleague. For example, *"My sister and I look a lot alike, people tell us, but we're really quite different. I'm not as organized as she is. I'm not as good at keeping track of expenses (as she is), my house isn't as clean (as hers is), my car isn't as new (as hers is) , and my clothes aren't as nice (as hers are)."* Ss may want to note that the second *as* phrase (in parentheses, above) is optional when the context has been established and it is clear *what* is being compared to *what*.

FOCUS **3**

Using *As . . . As* and *Not As . . . As*

EXAMPLES	EXPLANATIONS
	As . . . as and *not as . . . as* can be used with all parts of speech:
(a) Susan is **not as tall as** Carla.	• adjectives
(b) Frank does not work **as quickly as** George.	• adverbs
(c) Linda does not have **as much money as** Diana.	• nouns
(d) Diana does not have **as many friends as** Carla.	
(e) George **works as** much **as** Linda.	• verbs
	In sentences using *as . . . as* or *not as . . . as*, the second *as* can be followed by:
(f) Susan works as hard as **Carla works.**	• clauses
(g) Carla is not as tall as **Linda is.**	
(h) Susan works as hard as **Carla does.**	
(i) Susan works as hard as **Carla.**	• reduced clauses
(j) Carla is not as tall as **her younger sister.**	• noun phrases
(k) Susan works as hard as **I/you/he/she/we/they.**	• subject pronouns
(l) Susan works as hard as he **works.** OR	In sentences where the verb is repeated after the second *as*, you can use a form of *do* instead.
(m) Susan works as hard as he **does.**	
(n) Susan works **as hard as he.** OR	The subject pronoun (*he, she, I, we, you, they*) is very formal.
(o) Susan works **as hard as him.**	The object pronoun (*him, her, me, us, you, them*) is very common in conversation and informal writing.

EXAMPLES	EXPLANATIONS
(p) Susan's hair is not as short as **mine.** **(q)** Susan's hair is as long as **mine.** Susan's Hair — My Hair **(r)** Susan's hair is as long as **me.** Susan's Hair — Me	Remember to use a possessive pronoun where necessary. In examples (q) and (r), both sentences are correct, but there is a big difference in meaning!

EXERCISE 4

Correct the mistakes in the following sentences.

1. All her life, Hester has been lucky than her sister, Miriam.
2. Hester is not intelligent as Miriam but she was always more successful than Miriam in school.
3. For example, Hester's grades were always better than Miriam.
4. Both sisters are pretty, but many people believe that Miriam is prettier that her sister.
5. However, Miriam does not have as many boyfriends than her sister does.
6. They both have excellent jobs, but Miriam thinks her job isn't as interesting as her sister.
7. They both travel as part of their work, but Hester goes to more exciting places than Miriam is.
8. In spite of these differences, Miriam thinks that she is happier that her sister is.
9. However, Hester thinks that good luck is important than good looks and intelligence.

What do **you** think is the most important: good luck, good looks, or intelligence? Why do you think so? Share your ideas with your classmates.

Exercise 4

This exercise can be done in pairs or small groups, and if there are different answers, Ss can explain why their answer is "correct."

VARIATION

Part 2—the discussion about what is most important—can be done as a writing exercise (a short paragraph), which volunteers can read in front of the rest of the class. This can be a good way to generate discussion on the different opinions.

ANSWER KEY

Exercise 4
1. luckier   2. (not) as   3. Miriam's
4. than (not that)   5. as (not than)
6. sister's   7. does (not is)   8. than (not that)   9. more

Exercise 5

This is a highly productive exercise, always much enjoyed by Ss, and is well worth the time it takes to construct the problem. Ss should be encouraged to create people of their own rather than using information based on the people in the Opening Task. Many Ss will choose to write about their classmates or about famous people.

SUGGESTION

The chart is a rough guide only. Ss can copy the chart into their notebooks, making sure that they have enough space for all the people shown in the picture and enough lines for their clues.

VARIATION

If there is not enough time to solve each other's problems, Ss could turn the completed problems in to you, and you can try to solve them for "homework."

EXERCISE 5

Work in a group to create a problem like the one in the Opening Task. First use the picture and blank chart to record your information and then write the clues. Each clue must contain at least one of the following: a comparative; a superlative; *as . . . as; not as . . . as.* Finally, exchange your problem with another group and see if you can solve each other's problems.

NAME	AGE	HEIGHT	OCCUPATION	LIKES

CLUES

_____

_____

_____

_____

_____

FOCUS **4**

Making Tactful Comparisons
with *As . . . As* and *Not As . . . As*

Sometimes it is important to be tactful (more polite and less direct) when you are making comparisons. The adjective you choose can show how tactful your comparison is.

EXAMPLES	EXPLANATIONS
Some adjectives commonly used in making comparisons: Express "MORE": Express "LESS": *tall* — *short* *old* — *young* *large* — *small* *fast* — *slow* **(a)** Linda is **as tall as** Bob.	When you use *as . . . as*, it is more usual to use an adjective that expresses "more." When you use an adjective that expresses "less," you draw special attention to it because it is an unusual use. In (a), the use of *tall* is usual. It does not make us think about **how** tall or **how** short Bob and Linda are, but only that they are the same height.
(b) Linda is **as short as** Bob.	In (b), the use of *short* is unusual. It makes us think that both Bob and Linda are very short.
(c) Patricia is **as old as** Virginia.	In (c), the use of *old* is usual. It shows only that they are the same age.
(d) Patricia is **as young as** Virginia.	In (d), the use of *young* is unusual. It therefore puts special emphasis on *young*.
(e) Bob is **not as tall as** Frank. **(f)** Frank is **not as short as** Bob. Bob Frank	Both (e) and (f) show that Frank is taller than Bob. However, the use of *short* in (f) is unusual, so it draws special attention to the fact that Bob is short. It is more tactful and more polite to choose (e).
(g) Otis is **not quite as smart as** Rocky. **(h)** His latest book is **not quite as good as** his earlier ones.	When you want to be really polite and tactful, you can use *not quite as . . . as*.

To supplement this focus box, it's helpful to give examples of comparisons that can appear impolite: My older sister is *fatter than* my younger sister. Her home is *messier*, and her clothes are *dirtier*. Ask Ss to rephrase these sentences into more polite ones, using *not as . . . as*, and *as . . . as* phrases. Example: My older sister is *not as thin as* my younger sister. Her home is *not as neat*, and her clothes are *not as clean*. This will also help Ss prepare for Exercises 6 and 7.

Workbook Ex. 6, p. 57.
Answers: TE p. 491.

Exercise 6

If you do this exercise in pairs or small groups, it is helpful to regroup as a whole class, having one representative from each group read a rewritten sentence to the class. Those listening can be the judges of whether the rewritten sentences are more tactful or not.

You are working in a company in Spain that does a lot of business with clients from North America. You speak both Spanish and English. Your boss speaks some English, but he often needs help, so he has asked you to assist him at a meeting with some important clients. Your company would very much like to do business with these clients, but there are several problems to discuss because the two companies are very different.

To prepare for the meeting, your boss wrote down some of the differences he wants to discuss. However, because he doesn't speak a lot of English, you feel that some of his statements sound rather direct and will probably offend the clients. You decide to change these statements so that they will be less direct and more tactful. Use the adjectives in parentheses with *not as . . . as*. Add *not quite* if you want to be even more tactful. The first one has been done for you.

1. Your company is smaller than ours. (large)
   <u>Your company is not as large as ours.</u>

2. Your factories are more old-fashioned than ours. (modern)

3. Your workers are lazier than ours. (energetic)

4. Your products are less popular than ours. (well known)

5. Our advertising is more successful than yours. (effective)

6. Your designs are more conservative than ours. (up-to-date)

7. Your production is slower than ours. (fast)

8. The quality of your product line is lower than ours. (high)

9. Your factories are dirtier than ours. (clean)

10. Your factories are more dangerous than ours. (safe)

ANSWER KEY

Exercise 6

2. Your factories are not (quite) as modern as ours. 3. Your workers are not (quite) as energetic as ours. 4. Your products are not (quite) as well known as ours. 5. Your advertising is not (quite) as effective as ours. 6. Your designs are not (quite) as up-to-date as ours. 7. Your production is not (quite) as fast as ours. 8. The quality of your product line is not (quite) as high as ours. 9. Your factories are not (quite) as clean as ours. 10. Your factories are not (quite) as safe as ours.

EXERCISE 7

Omar is president of the International Students' Association at an American college located in a small town in the Midwest. The Chamber of Commerce has asked him to give a speech to local businesses on international students' reactions to life in America. He has made a survey of the international students on campus, and he is using the results of the survey for his speech. Some of the comments are not very complimentary, but he feels the local community should know what international students really think. He therefore decides to edit some of the more direct comments so that they will be informative but not offensive. He is having problems with the following statements.

Can you help him make these statements more tactful and polite?

1. In America, people are less sincere.
   <u>In America, people are not quite as sincere.</u>

2. People in my country are much friendlier and more hospitable.
   _____

3. Americans are often very rude; people in my country are never rude.
   _____

4. The cities here are dirtier and more dangerous than at home.
   _____

5. Americans are lazy compared to people in my country.
   _____

6. American food is tasteless compared to the food in my country.
   _____

7. The nightlife in this town is really boring compared to the nightlife at home.
   _____

8. People here watch too much television. We watch much less TV at home.
   _____

Do you agree or disagree with these comments?

Do you have any comments of your own that Omar could include in his speech? Add them here:

_____

_____

_____

Exercise 7

After Ss work on rewriting these sentences, it is helpful to focus on the questions following the items. Do Ss feel like the rewritten sentences are *really* more tactful and polite, or do some of them still come across as impolite or offensive? Are there ways to make them more polite? For example, would it help to give more background information about the international students' home cultures?

Example: 7. *Because some of us come from places where lots of spices and herbs are used in cooking, some of us feel that American food is not as tasty compared to the food in our own countries.*

UNIT GOAL REVIEW

Ask Ss to look at the goals on the opening page of the unit again. Help them understand how much they have accomplished in each area. You can present the goals as a checklist. For example, can Ss make sentences with each of the different comparative and superlative structures (also see Focus 1, page 106, box #3)? Do they understand the difference in meaning between "*not as tall as*" and "*as short as*" (goal # 4)?

A N S W E R   K E Y

Exercise 7

Some answers will vary.

2. People in America are not (quite) as friendly or as hospitable as people in my country.
3. Americans are not as polite as people in my country.   4. The cities at home are not as dirty or as dangerous as here./The cities here are not quite as clean or as safe as the cities at home.   5. Americans are not (quite) as hardworking as the people in my country.
6. American food is not as spicy as the food in my country.   7. The nightlife at home is not (quite) as boring as the nightlife here./The nightlife here is not as interesting as the nightlife at home.   8. People don't watch as much TV at home.

USE YOUR ENGLISH

The activities in the purple pages at the end of the unit contain situations that should naturally elicit the structures covered in the unit. When Ss are doing these activities in class, you can circulate and listen to see if they are using the structures accurately. Have they achieved the goals presented at the beginning of the unit?

Activity 1

Since this activity asks Ss to write a brief, informative guide for host families, you may need to encourage them to use comparative, superlative or *as . . . as* structures in their descriptions. If this is done orally, in class (i.e., if Ss read their guides aloud), you and other Ss can ask clarification questions, such as: *Do you mean that there aren't as many . . . in* (country being described) *as there are here?*

Activity 2

EXPANSION

You can ask Ss about their own native languages as well. Do they have similar idioms as the ones they have been told about? In other words, are these idioms in English "translatable" to Ss' native languages? In their first languages, are there idioms such as: *as slow as a turtle, as hungry as a horse, as pretty as a picture?*

Use Your English

ACTIVITY 1: WRITING

Write a brief guide for American families who want to become host families for students from other countries. Think about a country you know something about. What should American host families know about the differences between the culture and customs of that country and those of the United States? Be tactful where necessary!

ACTIVITY 2: SPEAKING/LISTENING

There are many common idioms in English that use the construction *as . . . as*.
Here are some common ones:
- as stubborn as a mule
- as happy as a clam
- as strong as an ox

Interview several native speakers of English and ask them to tell you as many of these idioms as they can remember. Then ask them to give you an example of when they might use each idiom.

Idiom	Example of When to Use This Idiom
as _____ as _____	

Choose one of these idioms to explain to your classmates.

ACTIVITY 3: SPEAKING/LISTENING

The purpose of this activity is to think of as many differences as possible between two objects. Your teacher will tell you what you are to compare. Form teams. You have five minutes with your team to make a list of as many differences as possible. After five minutes, the teams take turns sharing their differences. The team with the most differences scores a point. Your teacher will then give you the next two objects to compare. The team with the most points is the winner.

STEP 1 To score a point, your comparison must be meaningful **and** accurate.

STEP 2 You cannot repeat a comparison that another team has already given. However, you **can** express the same idea, using different words. For example:

Team A says: *A Harley Davidson is more expensive than a Honda motorcycle.*

Team B can say: *A Honda isn't as expensive as a Harley Davidson.*

Team C can say: *A Honda is cheaper than a Harley Davidson,* and so on.

If possible, try to tape your team as you play this game. Afterwards listen to the tape and see how many comparative, superlative, and (*not*) *as . . . as* forms you used.

Activity 3

Some ideas for objects to compare are: an apple and an orange, a car and a bicycle, a VW and a Ferrari, a pizza and a hot dog. However, the best comparisons are ones that have some kind of personal relevance to Ss. Examples: two Ss in the class, two celebrities known to all the class, two places known to all the Ss, two different classes they are taking, two books/movies they all know, etc.

VARIATIONS

1. If you are not comfortable using competitive games in your classroom, consider doing this activity in teams but without scoring.
2. You could tape record the statements containing differences, and review them afterwards for accuracy and to see how many varieties of forms were used.

Activity 4

Play textbook audio. The tapescript for this listening activity appears on pp. 506–507 of this book.

You can follow up on Step 2 to see how Ss' own answers compared to what Terry and Robin said. What differences, if any, were there?

Activity 5

EXPANSION

If Ss enjoy this kind of activity, you might ask further related questions: *Did native speakers tend to use different structures than the ones you used* (for example, more *as . . . as* structures, fewer—*er* comparisons)? *Did you notice any errors made by native speakers?*

ACTIVITY 4: LISTENING/SPEAKING

STEP 1 Before you listen to the tape for this activity, get together with a partner. Make a list of all the differences you can think of between a pizza and a hot dog. Write them on the left side of the chart.

What's the Difference Between a Pizza and a Hot Dog?

_____ and I	Terry and Robin
A pizza is more expensive than a hot dog.	

STEP 2 Listen to the tape. You will hear two people, Terry and Robin, comparing a pizza and a hot dog. Add the differences they describe to the right side of the chart. How many differences did you and your partner find? How many did Terry and Robin find?

STEP 3 Now listen to the tape again, and write down any sentences with comparative, superlative, or *(not) as . . . as* forms in them.

ACTIVITY 5: SPEAKING/LISTENING

Choose one set of objects that you compared in Activity 3 (or example, a bicycle and a car). Ask three different native speakers to compare these two objects and tape their replies. Listen to the tape. Did the native speakers make more comparisons than you did? Or did you make more comparisons than them? Compare your findings with those of the rest of the class.

Listen to your tape again and write down any sentences with examples of comparative, superlative, and *(not) as . . . as* forms.

ANSWER KEY

Activity 4
Check tapescript for Terry and Robin's comparisons (pp. 506–507).

ACTIVITY 6: SPEAKING/LISTENING

In North America, it is very common to honor people with special awards for achievements in different fields. For example, the film industry presents Oscars every year for "the best picture," "the best director," and so on. This year, your school has decided to give several special awards to students and teachers for different achievements.

You and your classmates are members of the committee that will decide who should get these awards.

STEP 1 Get together with two or three other students and make a list of awards you would like to give. Decide on who should receive these awards. They don't have to be serious awards. For example, you can give awards for "the best dressed student"; "the most talkative student"; "the most creative dancer"; "the student who is the most likely to become president of his/her country," and so on. You can also give awards to other people on campus or to places that you like in the community ("the teacher who gives the most homework"; "the best hamburger"; "the quietest place to study"; "the best place to meet other students"; "the most romantic place to go on a first date," and so on).

STEP 2 When you are ready, hold your own awards "ceremony" to announce the winners and present your awards.

Tape your group when you present your "awards." Listen to the tape and check to see if you were able to use superlatives correctly.

ACTIVITY 7: WRITING

Your school wants to prepare a short guide for new international students. You have been asked to write a chapter on the best places in town for international students. You can decide on what you want to include in this chapter. Some of the "awards" from Activity 6 may help you here.

Write your chapter for the guide. If you wish, you can include illustrations (photographs, maps, drawings). Share your chapter with the rest of the class.

Activity 6
Ss can talk to native speakers or classmates about the kinds of awards they would like to give others. This can provide your Ss with ideas for the range of possible awards and for the different kinds of awards they may want to give.

Activity 7
You can compile Ss chapters into one chapter and photocopy this for the members of the class.

The test for this unit can be found on pp. 428–429 of this book.
The answers are on p. 430.

Unit 8

UNIT OVERVIEW

Using recipes and cooking as an underlying theme, this unit introduces students (Ss) to the form, meaning, and use of measure words (such as containers, portions, and shapes) and quantifiers (including *all*, *much/many*, and *few/little*).

UNIT GOALS

Draw Ss' attention to the goals by copying them onto the board or overhead projector. You may include some examples of the structures as illustration. For example:

A: *I'd like a piece of pizza, some breadsticks, and a cup of coffee please.*
B: *Would you like parmesan cheese?*
A: *A little.*

OPENING TASK

The purpose of this task is to set a context for measure words, not test a knowledge of cooking. If your Ss have a "mixed" knowledge of cooking, arrange groups so that each includes someone who has an idea about preparing food.

SUGGESTIONS

SETTING UP THE TASK

1. Direct Ss' attention to the photograph. Based on the picture, can they determine what a potluck dinner is? Especially if you are in the U.S., you may find some Ss have already attended a potluck.
2. Run through the initial list of ingredients; pictures or real examples of the items are helpful.

UNIT 8

MEASURE WORDS AND QUANTIFIERS

UNIT GOALS:

- To understand special measure words used with foods
- To correctly use measure words with count and noncount nouns
- To know how to use common quantifiers

OPENING TASK
Getting Ready for a Potluck Dinner

Jim has been invited to a potluck dinner—a meal where each guest brings a dish. The hostess asked him to bring cookies and a salad for six people. Jim wants to make everything himself. He already has these ingredients in his kitchen.

INGREDIENTS

mustard	chocolate chips
sugar	tomatoes
salt	flour
lettuce	olive oil
hard-boiled eggs	butter
cheese	eggs
vinegar	garlic

STEP 1   Help Jim decide which ingredients he can use in each dish. Write each ingredient in a box below.

Salad	Salad Dressing	Chocolate Chip Cookies

STEP 2   How much of each ingredient should Jim use? Write an amount beside each ingredient. Remember, there will be six people at the party.

STEP 3   Are there any **other** ingredients you would include? Add them to the boxes above, with suggested amounts.

CONDUCTING THE TASK

1. Divide the class into groups of 3–4 and go over the three steps of the activity. Remind them that they should use the knowledge they already have, rather than look up information in dictionaries or in the text.
2. You can also break Ss into three groups, with a group focusing on one of the three recipes. If your class is of a lower level or less knowledgeable about cooking, you could focus only on the salad recipe, which is the simplest.
3. Setting a time limit will help keep Ss focused.
4. Circulate around the room to be sure that everyone is involved in the group work. Help out Ss who are less familiar with cooking terminology.

CLOSING THE TASK

Have groups choose a speaker and share their recipes with the class. Members of other groups can discuss how their recipes differ or if they think ingredients have been left out.

REVIEWING THE TASK

To draw their attention to the language being practiced, ask the class to list some of the ways they described the amount of food for each ingredient.

FOCUS 1

Using pictures, this focus box illustrates the meaning of some English measure words used with food. This topic is continued in Focus 2.

SUGGESTIONS

1. Make an overhead transparency of the charts in Focus 1, and underline a few examples of the *a(n) . . . of . . .* structure.

2. Choose some pairs of terms that might be confused (e.g., *bottle & jar, box & carton, slice & piece, tablespoon & teaspoon*). Ask Ss to describe the differences between them. For example, jars and bottles can both be made of glass or plastic, but a bottle has a narrow neck while a glass has a wider neck.

3. See if Ss can add one more food item to each measure word list. For example, a can of . . . (tuna fish, soup), peas, spaghetti, tomato sauce. . . .

4. If Ss are out of their home country, have them describe the differences between the ways food is packaged or prepared in their country and where they are studying. For example, in some countries, milk comes in a bag, bread is only sold in loaves, and recipes are measured in grams and milliliters.

Measure Words with Food

CONTAINERS

Some measure words are **containers** that we can find in a store.

a bottle of (ketchup, soy sauce)

a jar of (peanut butter, mustard)

a box of (crackers, cereal)

a bag of (potato chips, flour)

a carton of (milk, eggs)

a can of (tuna fish, soup)

PORTIONS

Some measure words are **portions.** They describe food items as they are commonly served.

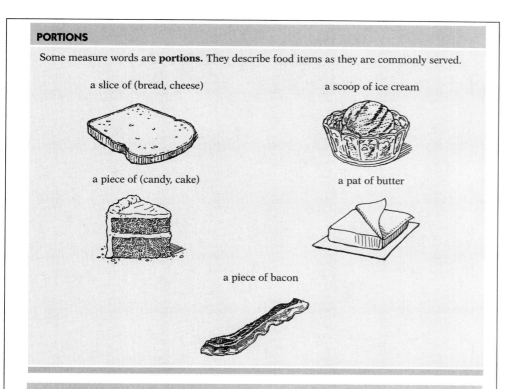

a slice of (bread, cheese)

a scoop of ice cream

a piece of (candy, cake)

a pat of butter

a piece of bacon

MEASUREMENTS

In North America, these **measurements** are common in recipes:

a cup of (rice, water, flour)

a tablespoon of (salt, sugar, water)

a teaspoon of (salt, sugar, water)

a pinch of (pepper, salt)

Measure Words and Quantifiers **123**

Pronunciation Note

The phrase *a(n) . . . of . . .* is usually reduced in everyday conversation:

It's a piece of cake.
(Sounds like:
It's a piece-a cake.)
It's not my cup of tea.
(Sounds like:
It's not my cuppa tea.)

Have Ss practice this reduction by repeating after you the expressions on the charts. You may need to explain that these reductions are not "bad English" but are regular pronunciation patterns (prepositions are generally reduced in spoken English).

Some measure words talk about the **shape** or **appearance** of the food item.

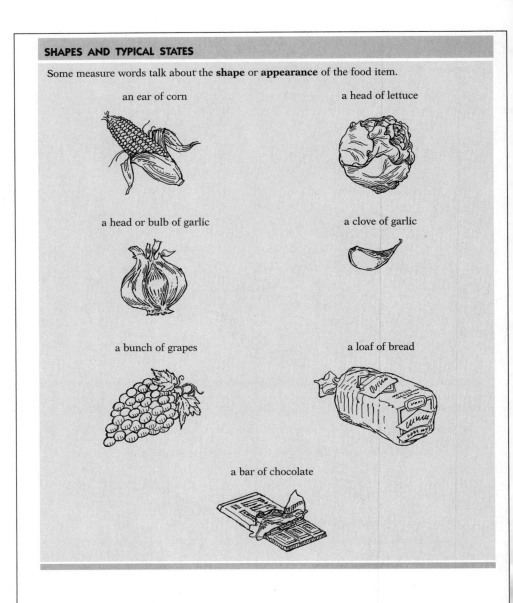

an ear of corn

a head of lettuce

a head or bulb of garlic

a clove of garlic

a bunch of grapes

a loaf of bread

a bar of chocolate

EXERCISE 1

Turn back to the Opening Task on page 121. Look at the ingredients and the amounts. Did you use the right measure words? Make any necessary corrections.

EXERCISE 2

Turn back to the Opening Task and look carefully at the ingredients. Some of these are count nouns (tomatoes) and some are noncount nouns (flour). Write C beside each count noun and NC beside each noncount noun.*

FOCUS **2**

Measure Words with Count and Noncount Nouns

Measure words express specific quantities. They also allow us to make noncount nouns countable.

Three bottles of water

Two scoops of ice cream

Six pounds of coffee

Three cartons of milk

*For more information on count and noncount nouns, see *Grammar Dimensions* Book 1, Unit 4.

Measure Words and Quantifiers | **125**

Most measure expressions follow this pattern.*

A/An/One Two Three	+	Measure Word (Singular/Plural)	+	of	+	Noun (Noncount/Plural)
a		cup		of		milk
a		pound		of		apples
two		cups		of		milk
two		pounds		of		apples

*Exception: specific numbers (including *dozen*):
  a dozen eggs NOT: a dozen of eggs
  ten strawberries NOT: ten of strawberries

Exercise 3

1. Before Ss begin the exercise, quiz them on measure words by copying the picture on an overhead transparency and ask them to name the measure expressions for the items you point to.

EXERCISE 3

These are the recipes that Jim finally used. Complete the missing parts. (The picture may help you.)

Jim's Super Salad

1 large (a) _____ of red lettuce

1 medium-sized (b) _____ of romaine lettuce

1 large cucumber, cut into (c) _____

6 tomatoes, cut into quarters

1/2 (d) _____ of Swiss cheese, cut into small strips

1 (e) _____ cooked chicken, shredded into small pieces

2 hard-boiled eggs, shelled and cut into quarters

    1. Line a large salad bowl with red lettuce leaves.

    2. Tear the romaine lettuce leaves into medium-sized pieces.

    3. Place in the bowl in layers: slices of cucumber and tomato, cheese, lettuce, and chicken.

    4. Add olives and eggs. Cover and refrigerate for one hour. Toss with Jim's Super Salad Dressing just before serving.

Jim's Super Salad Dressing

1 (a) _____ Dijon mustard   1/2 (d) _____ salt

4 (b) _____ red wine vinegar   1/2 (e) _____ pepper

1 (c) _____ sugar   1/2 (f) _____ olive oil

    1. Put the mustard into a bowl. Whisk in vinegar, sugar, salt, and pepper.

    2. Slowly add the oil while continuing to whisk the mixture.

Measure Words and Quantifiers   **127**

2. Have Ss work in pairs to fill in the blanks of the recipes you discussed in the Opening Task. This activity can also be completed as a class by filling in the missing information on an overhead transparency or as a homework assignment.

3. Circulate around the room to help with new vocabulary, paying special attention to people who are less familiar with cooking. Note: review the terminology beforehand to be prepared to describe the difference between such words as *toss*, *whisk*, *cream*, and *sift*.

SUGGESTION

If some Ss finish early, have them write their recipes on the board to provide the class with visual aids as they discuss the differences.

ANSWER KEY

Exercise 3
Jim's Super Salad: (a) head   (b) head
(c) slices   (d) pound   (e) cup of

Jim's Super Salad Dressing: (a) tablespoon of
(b) tablespoons of   (c) tablespoon of
(d) teaspoon of   (e) cup of   (f) cup of

Jim's Granny's Old Time Chocolate Chip Cookies

1/2 (a) _____ butter	1 (e) _____ baking soda
1 (b) _____ brown sugar	1 (f) _____ vanilla extract
3/4 (c) _____ granulated sugar	1 (g) _____ salt
2 eggs	1 1/2 (h) _____ chocolate chips
2 (d) _____ flour	

1. Preheat the oven to 350°F. Grease a cookie sheet.

2. Cream the butter and both the sugars together until light and fluffy. Add the eggs and vanilla and mix well.

3. Sift the flour, baking soda, and salt. Mix thoroughly.

4. Add the chocolate chips.

5. Form into cookies. Place on a cookie tray and put on the middle rack of the oven for 8–10 minutes.

6. Cool for 5 minutes.

7. Enjoy! (This recipe makes about 40 cookies.)

Turn back to the Opening Task on page 121 and look at the ingredients (and the amounts) you suggested for these dishes. How many differences can you find between your suggestions and Jim's recipes? Whose recipe do you think will taste better?

EXERCISE 4

Last week Matthew ate a delicious spaghetti sauce at his friend Nancy's house. He enjoyed it so much that Nancy lent him the recipe so that he could make a copy of it. However, Nancy has obviously used this recipe many times and it is quite difficult to read. Can you help Matthew figure out the recipe? Fill in the missing words below.

> Spaghetti Sauce
>
> (from Nancy's kitchen)
>
> First, cut 3 _____ of bacon into small pieces and cook over a very low heat. Stir in 1/2 _____ of ground meat along with 4 _____ garlic and 2 _____ onion, chopped up very finely. Add 1 _____ salt, a pinch of cayenne pepper, and 2 _____ of fresh herbs. Mix in two 8-ounce _____ tomato sauce. Let it cook on low heat for about 30 minutes. Serve over fresh pasta.

If you were making this recipe yourself, would you change or add anything? Share any changes or additions with your classmates. Try to be as precise as possible.

Exercise 4

Workbook Exs. 3 & 4, pp. 59–60.
Answers: TE p. 491.

ANSWER KEY

Exercise 3
Jim's Granny's Old Time Chocolate Chip Cookies: (a) pound of (b) cup of (c) cup of (d) cups of (e) teaspoon of (f) teaspoon of (g) teaspoon of (h) cups of *Jim's Super Salad:* (a) head (b) head (c) slices (d) pound (e) cup of *Jim's Super Salad Dressing:* (a) tablespoon of (b) tablespoons of (c) tablespoon of (d) teaspoon of (e) cup of

(f) cup of *Jim's Granny's Old Time Chocolate Chip Cookies:* (a) pound of (b) cup of (c) cup of (d) cups of (e) teaspoon of (f) teaspoon of (g) teaspoon of (h) cups of

Exercise 4
slices (of bacon) pound (of ground meat) cloves of (garlic) cups of (onion) teaspoon of (salt) tablespoons (of fresh herbs) cans of (tomato sauce)

FOCUS **3**

▶ Common Quantifiers

AMOUNT	EXAMPLES	EXPLANATIONS
all	**(a)** **All** of the dishes at the potluck were delicious. **(b)** He spends **all** of his money on wine.	Some quantifiers (words that talk about quantity/number or amount) can be used with **both count and noncount nouns.** Use *all* to mean *everything* or *everyone*.
most	**(c)** **Most** of the people in North America take vacations in the summer. **(d)** **Most** of my money has been spent.	*Most* means *almost everyone* or *almost everything*.
many/much	**(e)** We heard that ***many*** people were coming. **(f)** We don't have ***much*** time. **(g)** A: Were ***many*** people hurt? **(h)** B: No, not ***many***.	*Many* is used only with count nouns to talk about a large number. Use *much* with noncount nouns to talk about a large amount. *Many* and *much* are usually used in questions or negative statements.
a lot of/lots of/a great deal of	**(i)** We make ***a lot of*** trips back and forth over the mountains. **(j)** I heard that there was ***lots of*** new snow. **(k)** ***A great deal of*** current information is available on the Internet.	Use *a lot of* or *lots of* with very large numbers or amounts, and with either count or noncount nouns. *Lots of* is used in informal situations. Use *a great deal of* in formal situations, and only with noncount nouns. It means the same as *a lot of* or *lots*.
some	**(l)** We needed ***some*** information about the weather. **(m)** We were glad that we had put ***some*** new snow tires on our car.	*Some* is a smaller amount or quantity than *a lot of/lots of*. *Some* is used with both count and noncount nouns.

SUGGESTION

1. When reviewing the quantifiers in this focus box, make photocopies or an overhead transparency of the chart after you have whited-out the explanations.
2. Have Ss close their books and work in pairs or small groups with this new chart, using the examples to create their own explanations.
3. Talk as a class about their explanations, correcting inaccurate ones and adding important information that has been left out.
4. Direct Ss to return to the chart to take note of which quantifiers take *of* and which do not.
5. Have Ss practice the reduced pronunciation of the expressions with *of* (see Focus 1 Pronunciation Note).

AMOUNT	EXAMPLES	EXPLANATIONS
several	**(n)** We couldn't travel on *several* days last winter because the mountain passes were closed.	*Several* is used only with count nouns. *Several* means more than a small number.
a few/a little	**(o)** In a *few* days, we'll be ready to go. **(p)** There was *a little* snow on the mountains. **(q)** Let's buy *a little* food and *a few* cans of soda.	*A few* means more than two, but not many more. *A few* and *a little* have similar meanings. *A little* is used only with noncount nouns and *a few* is used only with count nouns.
few/little	**(r)** We have *few* friends and *little* money. **(s)** *Few* people know that she has *little* time left.	*Few* and *little* refer to the same amounts or numbers as *a few* and *a little*; however, they have a negative meaning. They mean *almost none*. *Few* is used only with count nouns, *little* only with noncount nouns.
a couple (of)	**(t)** I'd like to get *a couple of* blankets to keep in the car. **(u)** Let's ask *a couple (of)* people to come with us.	*A couple of* means two, but it is sometimes used informally to mean two or more. *A couple of* is used only with count nouns. In informal English, *of* is sometimes omitted.
none/no	**(v)** *None of* the people went to the meeting. **(w)** We heard that there was *no* new snow.	*None* means *not any*, and is used with count nouns. *No* has the same meaning, and is used with noncount nouns.

EXERCISE 5

Find a partner and take turns asking each other questions about your native countries or countries you know about. Use the topics in (A) to ask general questions. In your answers to the questions, give specific examples to explain what you mean. You must use a quantifier (from Focus 3) in your answer. Column (B) gives you ideas for quantifiers you can use in your answers, but you may use others.

▶ **EXAMPLE:**   Q: Is clothing expensive in (Vietnam)?

   A: No, not really. A *lot of* people go to the big cities to buy clothes. There are *lots of* factories in the cities, so you can usually find clothes that are pretty cheap.

(A) TOPIC	(B) QUANTIFIER
1. clothing	some lots of/a lot of
2. tourist attractions	a few a couple of
3. holidays	most some
4. climate	no/none a great deal of
5. fast-food restaurants	some several
6. technology	a few many
7. English speakers	most a lot of
8. entertainment	all much

Exercise 5

This exercise shifts the topic away from the food theme, considering other expressions that take quantifiers. Answers will vary.

1. Review the topics on the list to be sure that Ss are familiar with the vocabulary.
2. After you go over the directions, point out the example. You can also model the activity with a student.

SUGGESTION

Do this exercise as a mixer activity.

1. Direct Ss to stand up and mingle with different classmates as they complete the activity. You can allow them flexibility, or limit the amount of time they can speak to one person to 3 minutes. At the end of each 3-minute period, tell them to find another partner.
2. The object of the activity is to find out as much information about each partner's country as possible while they are covering the topics. Tell them they must cover at least four topics by the time the activity is over.
3. When they finish, have some Ss share their information with the class, correcting only errors in quantifier use.

Exercise 6

This exercise works well as homework or in-class pairwork. When reviewing their answers, be sure to have a copy of the letter on an overhead transparency as a visual aid.

EXPANSIONS

1. Using this letter or bringing in other examples, ask Ss to discuss the differences between writing personal letters in their country and in North America. Are there different ways of beginning and ending the letter? Do English speakers appear to be more or less formal? How can the Ss tell?

2. As a follow-up to this discussion, have Ss write their own letter to a friend following this model. To ensure they practice the structures in this unit, require that they use the same number of quantifiers as in this letter.

Workbook Ex. 5, pp. 60–62.
Answers: TE p. 491.

UNIT GOAL REVIEW

Remind Ss to consider the unit goals on p. 123. Can they find examples of measure words and quantifiers in the photograph? Test their knowledge by writing a list of count and noncount nouns on the board and ask them to give the first quantity or measurement they can think of for each.

EXERCISE 6

Some of the sentences in the following letter have errors with nouns and with quantifiers. Find the errors and correct them. When you have finished, check your answers with another student.

Dear Nell,

I think I'm going to like my new job. So far it's interesting, and I hope that it stays that way! There are several of people who work in the same office with me. At the moment I share a desk with Jessica, who just started a couple week ago, but our office manager just ordered new furnitures so that soon we will each have a desk of our own. There are lot of people in the building who share desks *and* computers, so I feel pretty lucky to have my own to work on.

Every morning Martha, the staff assistant, brings us each a cup of coffee. She already knows that I like sugars in my coffee but no milks. Martha also brings the mails to us, *and* she likes to give us many advice about how to be efficient. Two times a day I get at least fifty letter which I have to respond to, so I do listen to Martha's advices. A few her ideas have really been useful!

Some days I can do most of my business on the computer. Other days I need a little more informations from my customers, so I need to talk to them on the telephone. Every day there are some problem that I cannot handle. If there are only couple of problems, my coworker helps, but on the days when there are lot of problems, we call in Anna, the office supervisor. Already there have been several time when even Anna couldn't handle the problems, and so she has had to call in *her* supervisor.

So you can see that I'm busy, and at this point, I'm *not* bored.

Talk to you soon—

Love,

Elliott

Exercise 6

Error is in parentheses; correction follows.
Paragraph 1: (several of) *several*   (couple week) *couple of weeks*   (furnitures) *furniture*   (lot of) *lots of/a lot of*
Paragraph 2: (sugars) *sugar*   (milks) *milk*   (mails) *mail*   (many advice) *advice/a lot of advice*   (fifty letter) *fifty letters*   (advices) *advice*   (A few) *A few of*

Paragraph 3: (informations) *information*   (some problem) *some problems*   (couple of problems) *a couple of problems*   (lot of problems) *a lot of problems/lots of problems*   (several time) *several times*

Use Your English

ACTIVITY 1: WRITING/SPEAKING

This "recipe" was written by an English teacher:

"Recipe" for the Perfect Student

Ingredients:
1 cup of motivation
1 cup of determination
1/2 cup of patience
1/2 cup of tolerance
1 cup of laughter
1 cup of imagination
1 1/2 cups of willingness to make a guess
1 cup of independence
1 1/2 cups of cooperation with others
1 pinch of fun

Combine ingredients and stir gently to bring out the best flavor.

What do you think the teacher meant by this?

Get together with a partner and create a "recipe" of your own. Here are some ideas, but you probably have plenty of your own:

- Recipe for a long-lasting marriage
- Recipe for the perfect partner
- Recipe for the perfect teacher
- Recipe for the perfect house
- Recipe for the perfect mother/father

Share your recipes with the rest of the class.

USE YOUR ENGLISH

Since the aim of these exercises is to provide practice in fluency, allow the activities to progress without immediate comment on errors.

Activity 1

This activity can be done as homework or in-class writing.

VARIATIONS

1. You can collect all finished recipes and compile them into a creative writing class "cookbook."
2. Have Ss write a recipe of their favorite dishes from their native country/countries (see Activity 4).

Activity 2

Remind Ss to choose someone famous enough to be known by most or all of their classmates. Model the activity first to give them an idea of what is expected.

Activity 3

VARIATION

Put the class into a circle and conduct a chain exercise. The first person starts out with a statement like, "For our weekend trip, we'll need 10 pounds of rice." The second person restates the first part and adds their own item: "For our weekend trip, we'll need 10 pounds of rice and 4 pots." Each person repeats the previous information, adding more items as they go. If Ss are allowed to be creative, they come up with some funny lists that include great examples of the use of quantifiers and terms of measurement.

Activity 4

If there are people who do not feel comfortable cooking, you can have them work in pairs with more experienced cooks. This activity is excellent speaking and listening practice for both the cook and the "assistant."

SUGGESTION

Depending on the culture(s) represented in your class, you may wish to have Ss label their dishes with the ingredients included. Labels will prevent misunderstanding if there are people who do not eat, for example, pork or other meat for religious, cultural, or personal reasons.

ACTIVITY 2: SPEAKING

STEP 1 Work in small groups or with a partner to think of someone famous that everyone in your class knows. Imagine that this person is traveling. What would be in this famous person's suitcase? Make a list of these things, and be sure to include the amounts (*a lot, some, several, a few*).

STEP 2 Then read your list to the other groups in your class, and have them guess who the famous person is. If they can't guess, add more quantifiers in order to make the identity of the famous person clear.

ACTIVITY 3: SPEAKING

Your class is scheduled for a weekend trip in a nearby park. Transportation is provided, and a few small cabins are available. But you will need to decide what food to bring, and also what other things you will need. Here are some ideas: sleeping bags, cooking pots, eating utensils (plates, cups, silverware), firewood (in the winter), sports equipment, depending on the season (fishing poles? swimsuits? skis?).
Work in groups and come up with a list. Be specific about the quantities. Compare lists to make sure you haven't forgotten anything!

ACTIVITY 4: SPEAKING/LISTENING/WRITING

STEP 1 Organize an international potluck. Everyone in the class should prepare a dish, preferably from his or her country. Bring the dish to class to share and enjoy with your classmates, or, if possible, try to arrange your potluck at somebody's house so you can watch each other cook. After the meal, have each person describe their recipes. Tape-record this description.

STEP 2 Listen to the tape and write down these recipes. Collect all the recipes for an international cookbook. Make copies and distribute them to the class.

ACTIVITY 5: LISTENING

Listen to the tape of a person describing a recipe for a traditional North American dish.

STEP 1
1. What dish is the speaker describing?
2. When is this dish usually eaten?
3. What are the important ingredients in the dish?

STEP 2 Listen to the tape again, and this time write down the ingredients and amounts. Work with a partner to make sure that you understand what each ingredient is, and then take turns reading each ingredient and the amount aloud. If you decide to make this dish, it is important that your recipe is accurate!

For each ingredient with a measure word, check to see what kind of measure word is used:

- If it is a **container,** mark it with a C.
- If it is a **portion,** mark it with a P.
- If it is a **shape/typical state,** mark it with a S.
- If it is a **measurement,** mark it with a M.
  - Do you recognize the measurements?
  - Do you know what a teaspoon/tablespoon/cup is?

ACTIVITY 6: SPEAKING/LISTENING

The purpose of this activity is to do some research about various dishes and their recipes. The dishes below are very popular in North America, but different people sometimes have quite different recipes for the same dish. Your goal is to discover some of these variations.

Brownies   Potato Salad   Cheesecake   Cranberry Sauce

Divide into groups and choose **one** of these dishes. (If you prefer, you can select a dish that isn't on this list, preferably one that you don't know how to make.) Interview several different native speakers by asking them to tell you how to make the dish you have chosen. If possible, tape-record your interview. Get together with your group and compare the directions you have gathered. How many differences can you find? Be ready to share your findings with the rest of the class.

Measure Words and Quantifiers | **135**

Play textbook audio. The transcript for this listening exercise appears on p. 507 of this book. Check tapescript for answers.

Activity 6

VARIATION

Conduct a web search for recipes. This provides excellent reading practice, especially with skimming and scanning. Before you choose this option you should be sure that all of the Ss are comfortable working on the Internet; some training may be necessary. You can pair Ss up for this activity, putting less experienced web-users with experts.
and appropriately?

The test for this unit can be found on pp. 431–432 of this book. The answers are on p. 433.

Unit 9

UNIT OVERVIEW

Unit 9 provides practice with words and phrases that show *degree: too, enough* and *very*.

UNIT GOALS

Review the goals listed on this page to see what students (Ss) should learn by the end of the unit.

OPENING TASK

The purpose of this task is to generate talk that will naturally incorporate words and phrases that show *to what degree*: phrases with *very* + adjective, *too* + adjective, and *not* + adjective + *enough*. The task is intended to focus attention on meaning rather than form, which will allow you to see whether Ss are able to produce the forms spontaneously (especially in Steps 3 and 4).

SETTING UP THE TASK

You can bring in some classified ads from your local newspaper and talk about finding a place to rent, asking Ss about their own experiences. Or ask Ss to talk about where they currently live. Go through the Opening Task situation carefully, checking that everyone understand what Maria wants and what she is limited by.

UNIT 9

DEGREE COMPLEMENTS

Too, Enough, and *Very*

UNIT GOALS:

- To understand the meaning of *enough*, *not enough*, and *too*
- To form correct sentences with *enough*, *not enough*, and *too*
- To know how to use *too much*, *too many*, *too little*, and *too few*
- To understand the difference between *too* and *very*

▶ OPENING TASK
Looking for Somewhere to Live

Maria is looking for a place to rent. She is looking for a two-bedroom, unfurnished house or apartment with lots of light and plenty of closet space. She cannot pay more than $900 a month.

STEP 1 When she first looked at the classified ads in the newspaper, she was very confused by some of the strange abbreviations. Can you help her? Get together with a partner and try to guess what these abbreviations mean:

*apt   kit   **BR**   **DR**   sm   lg furn   unfurn*

STEP 2 She read all the ads and decided to go and look at the following places. After she saw each place, she made notes about what she liked and didn't like. Match her notes to the appropriate classified ads.

1

700 SQ FT BASEMENT APT $700.
Newly painted.   Walk to ferry.
Furn/unfur. No pets. Call owner
before 9PM. (718) 441-1320

2

GRAMERCY PARK TOWNHOUSE
"GONE WITH THE WIND" is the only
way to describe this majestic townhouse.
3 BRS. DR. KIT. garden. Call 592-0042

3

PERRY STREET
Historic townhouse. 1 BR:
marble bath: superb kit:
wood floors. $1000. 929-5544

4

GREENWICH VILLAGE
Between Bleeker and McDougal.
Charming 1 BR; new kit & bath.
Very quiet building. $875/mo.
676-4345

5

EAST VILLAGE
Renovated lg 2 BR apt w/new
wood flrs. High ceilings: sunny:
lg windows: lg walk-in closet:
mod kit $990/mo   963-0479

6

GREENWICH ST. 1 BR
Bright: big closets: full bath:
nice kit. Call Tim 985-8246
$900/mo.

7

GREENWICH VILLAGE
W. 11 St. Recent remodel.
2 BR. No elevator. $900.
219-3992

A *beautiful but too BIG!*

B *— not big enough Too quiet?*

C *enough closets — but too small*

D *too many stairs*

E *expensive but otherwise perfect!*

F *— too small — too expensive*

G *— too dark — not enough windows*

STEP 3 Maria lost her notes about the two following ads. What do you think she probably wrote? Write about each one.

MODERN 1 BR APT
LOTS OF STORAGE SPACE
SPECTACULAR VIEWS
$1000

GREAT KIT!! 4 BR basement
apt. 20 minute walk to subway
$795

STEP 4 Look back at all the ads and all Maria's notes. Which place do you think she probably chose? Why?

ANSWER KEY

Opening Task
Step 1: apartment, kitchen, bedroom, dining room, small, large, furnished, unfurnished
Step 2: Answers may vary. Possible answers:

1. G   **2.** A   **3.** F   **4.** B   **5.** E   **6.** C
7. D
Step 3: Answers depend on the Ss.

Step 1: This step helps familiarize Ss with the abbreviations found in classified ads. If you prefer, do Step 1 as a whole class activity before breaking into groups for the remainder.
Step 2: Make sure Ss understand that they have to match the notes with the ad.

Step 3: Answers will depend on your Ss. This is an opportunity to see if they are spontaneously producing the target forms. Don't worry about accuracy here, since Exercise 1 returns to the task and gives Ss the chance to review and revise what they wrote.

Step 4: Maria probably chose 5.

REVIEWING THE TASK

Ask Ss to explain why they chose 5, or if they chose an ad other than 5, why they did so. Write on the board their reasons for choosing their answers; simple phrases are adequate (example: *closets too small, too big, not enough windows, etc.*).

EXPANSION

Give examples about your own living situation. What do you like or dislike about the place where you live? "There's a great view, but *not enough* windows to see the view, and *too many* trees. It's *too dark*. . . ." Then elicit examples from Ss that describe their own living situations: "There are *too many* people living in my house. It's *not big enough* for all of us, and there are*n't enough* closets."

Enough, Not Enough, Too

EXAMPLES	EXPLANATIONS
(a) There are **enough** closets. **(b)** This apartment is big **enough** for both of us.	*Enough* shows something is sufficient. You have as much as you need and you do not need any more. *Enough* usually shows that you are satisfied with the situation.
(c) There are **not enough** windows in this apartment. (I want more windows!) OR: There are**n't enough** windows in this apartment. **(d)** The bedroom is **not** big **enough.** (I want a bigger bedroom!) OR: The bedroom is**n't** big **enough.**	*Not enough* shows that something is insufficient. In your opinion, there should be more. *Not enough* usually shows that you are not satisfied with the situation.
(e) The rent is **too** high. (It is more than I want to pay.) **(f)** The kitchen is **too** small. (I want a bigger one.) **(g)** That coffee is **too** hot. (I can't drink it.) **(h)** He speaks **too** fast. (I can't understand him.) **(i)** She's **too** young to drink. (She has to be 21 to drink alcohol in this state.)	*Too* shows that something is **more** than you want or need OR that it is **less** than you want or need. It depends on the meaning of the word that follows. *Too* usually shows that you are not satisfied with the situation.

Exercise 1

SUGGESTION

Ss can do this exercise individually, or in pairs, discussing any differences in their answers. You might want to circulate to see if there are structures that are problematic for a number of Ss, and then review aloud the relevant rules in Focus 1.

EXERCISE 1

Look back at the notes you wrote in Step 3 of the Opening Task on page 137. Did you use *too, not enough,* or *enough*? If not, rewrite the notes and see if you can use *too, enough,* or *not enough* in them.

In your opinion, what would Maria say about these apartments? Where possible, use *too, enough,* and *not enough*.

1. Tiny but charming studio apartment. Large skylights. Limited storage space.

   _____

   _____

ANSWER KEY

Exercise 1
1. too small, not enough closets   2. too large, too expensive   3. enough closets, big enough, too noisy

2. Gorgeous penthouse apartment. Fabulous views of Central Park. 3 bedrooms, 2 bathrooms. Dining room and roof garden. $1800.

_____

3. Bright two-bedroom apartment. Big closets. Next to fire station. $825.

_____

EXERCISE 2

In this exercise, people are talking about problems that they are having, and their friends are responding by saying what they think caused these problems. For example:

I'm tired all the time.

You don't get enough sleep.

Read the list of problems and the list of causes below. What do you think caused the problems? Work with a partner and match the problems and their causes.

PROBLEMS	CAUSES
1. My feet really hurt.	You don't go to the dentist often enough.
2. I'm broke!	Maybe you shouted too much at the ball game.
3. I failed my math test.	You didn't add enough salt.
4. I've gained a lot of weight recently.	Perhaps your shoes aren't big enough.
5. I never feel hungry at mealtimes.	You spend too much money.
6. I can't sleep at night.	Your stereo is too loud.
7. I have a sore throat.	You don't get enough exercise.
8. This soup is tasteless.	You eat too many snacks.
9. My neighbors are always angry with me.	You drink too much coffee.
10. My teeth hurt.	You didn't study enough.

Degree Complements: Too, Enough, and Very | **139**

Exercise 2

It's fun to do this exercise orally, with one student from a pair stating the problem (have them feel free to read it like a real complaint!) and the other stating the probable cause.

SUGGESTION

If you choose to use the above approach, give Ss a few minutes to work with a partner, and check to make sure they have found the answers. This will allow the reading of the problems and causes to move along smoothly so that the class is not waiting for the pairs to search for the answers.

FOCUS 2

Examples (e) through (h) might be new to some Ss, even those familiar with (a) through (d). It's helpful, therefore, to provide more examples, or have Ss give answers to questions such as these: (e) Are you *old enough* to buy alcohol in the U.S.? (f) Do you know English *well enough* to teach it? (g) Do you *have enough* money to travel around the world for one year? (h) Do you *have enough time to study* English?

Enough, Not Enough, Too

EXAMPLES	EXPLANATIONS
(a) This house is **big enough.** That apartment is **not big enough.** **(b)** Po speaks **clearly enough.** Tan does **not** speak **clearly enough.** **(c)** She **ate enough.** He **did not eat enough.** **(d)** We have **enough money.** They **do not** have **enough money.**	Place *enough* or *not enough*: • after adjectives • after adverbs • after verbs • before nouns
(e) She is **(not) old enough to vote.** **(f)** They studied **hard enough to pass** the test, but they did**n't** study **hard enough to get** a good score. **(g)** We **(don't) earn enough to pay** the rent. **(h)** I (don't) have **enough chocolate to make** a cake.	Notice how *enough* can be used with: • an adjective + an infinitive • an adverb + an infinitive • a verb + an infinitive • a noun + infinitive
(i) She is **too young.** **(j)** They work **too slowly.** **(k)** This tea is **too hot to drink.** **(l)** We worked **too late to go** to the party. **(m)** That book is **too difficult for me to understand.** **(n)** He walked **too fast for the children to keep up.**	Place *too* before adjectives and adverbs. *Too* + adjective or adverb is often followed by an infinitive. *Too* + adjective or adverb is often followed by *for* + noun/pronoun + infinitive.

EXERCISE 3

Complete the following appropriately, using *too*, *enough*, or *not enough*. There are many different ways to make meaningful responses in this exercise. Compare your answers with a partner's and see how many different responses you can make.

1. A: Why are you wearing so many sweaters?
   B: Because this room <u>is too cold/isn't warm enough</u> .

2. A: Does your brother have a car?
   B: No, he's only fourteen! He's _____ .

3. A: Why did they move?
   B: They're expecting a baby, and their old house _____ .

4. A: Would you like some more pie?
   B: No, thanks. It's delicious, but I _____ .

5. A: Can we count on your support in next month's election?
   B: I'm sorry, but I _____ . I won't be eighteen until next year.

6. A: What's wrong?
   B: My jeans _____ . I can't get them on.

7. A: Waiter!
   B: Yes, sir?
   A: We can't eat this. It _____ .

8. A: Let me help you carry that.
   B: Thanks. This suitcase _____ .

S U G G E S T I O N

If you have Ss read their answers aloud, ask the other Ss to listen for accuracy.

1. You can ask if the answer is accurate or inaccurate by taking a show of hands (*How many of you think that answer is OK? How many think that it's not OK?*).

2. If it's inaccurate, give the student who has read the answer the opportunity to correct it. If he/she needs help, ask for a volunteer.

ANSWER KEY

Exercise 3

2. He's not old enough to drive/too young to drive. 3. was too small/wasn't big enough
4. I've had enough/I've eaten too much.

5. I'm not old enough to vote/too young to vote
6. are too tight/are too tight for me to wear
7. is too salty 8. is too heavy for me to carry.

FOCUS 3

SUGGESTION

To supplement this grammar point—which can cause a lot of confusion for Ss—provide them with nouns and ask them to make meaningful sentences using *too much* or *too many*:

- coffee/tea—*You drink too much coffee, in my opinion./I drank too little tea this morning. I can't think straight.*
- milk (in coffee or tea)—*You put too much milk in your coffee. It doesn't taste good that way.*
- time (for friends and family)—*In my opinion, most people in the U.S. have too little time for friends and family.*
- time (for work)—*Americans spend too much time working.*
- exercise
- homework
- social activities

Workbook Ex. 2, pp. 65–67.
Answers: TE p. 491.

Exercise 4
SUGGESTIONS

1. While Ss are working, circulate to see if there are problems and if there are Ss who are doing well and find this exercise easy.
2. When everyone is finished, choose two or three of these latter Ss to read a section of the revised passage aloud to the rest of the class.

FOCUS **3**

Too Much and Too Many; Too Little and Too Few

EXAMPLES	EXPLANATIONS
(a) Walt has **too much money.**	Use *too* + *much* with noncount nouns.
(b) There are **too many students** in this class.	Use *too* + *many* with count nouns. *Too much* and *too many* show that there is more than you want or need. They show that you are not satisfied with the situation.
(c) There's **too little time** to finish this.	Use *too* + *little* with noncount nouns.
(d) The class was canceled because **too few students** enrolled.	Use *too* + *few* **with count nouns.** *Too little* and *too few* show that there is less than you want or need. They show that you are not satisfied with the situation.

EXERCISE 4

Read the following description of a wedding reception where everything went wrong. Underline all the words or phrases that show there was not enough of something. Where possible, replace these with *too little* or *too few* and change the verbs as necessary.

My sister's wedding was a disaster. First of all, she decided to get married very
was too little time to
suddenly, so there wasn't enough time to plan it properly. Nevertheless, about fifty of her friends came to the reception in her studio. Unfortunately, there wasn't enough room for everyone, so it was rather uncomfortable. She only had a few chairs, and our ninety-six-year-old grandmother had to sit on the floor. My father had ordered lots of champagne, but there weren't enough glasses, so some people didn't get very much to drink. In addition, we had several problems with the caterers. There wasn't enough cake for everyone, but there was too much soup! We also had problems with the entertainment. My sister loves Latin music, so she hired a salsa band; however, it was hard to move in such a small space, and my sister got upset when not enough people wanted to dance.

ANSWER KEY

Exercise 4
Expressions of insufficiency underlined; replacement follows.
wasn't enough room   too little room for everyone
only had a few chairs   had too few chairs
weren't enough glasses   were too few glasses
didn't get very much to drink   got too little to drink
wasn't enough cake   was too little cake for everyone
not enough people wanted to dance   too few people wanted to dance

didn't bring enough film   brought too little film
only has about ten wedding photographs   has too few wedding photographs

Note: It's worth pointing out that these changes overload the text with *few* and *much* and that good writing aims at more variety. Ss could work together to redress the balance in this text and see how many ways they can vary the style by using other expressions of insufficiency.

I got into trouble too. I was the official photographer, but I didn't bring enough film with me, so now my sister is mad because she only has about ten wedding photographs—and all of them are pictures of people trying to find a place to sit down!

EXERCISE 5

You and your friends decided to give a big party. You made lots of plans, but unfortunately, everything went wrong and the party was a total disaster. Get together with one or two other students and make a list of all the things that can go wrong at parties. Use this list to make a description of **your** disastrous party, using *too, too much, too many, too little, too few,* or *not enough.* Share your description with the rest of the class and decide who had the "worst" possible party.

FOCUS **4**

*T*oo versus *Very*

EXAMPLES	EXPLANATIONS
(a) This writing is small.	*Very* adds emphasis, but *too* shows that something is more than is necessary or desirable.
(b) This writing is very small.	In (b) the writing is small, but I can read it.
(c) This writing is too small.	In (c) the writing is smaller and I cannot read it.
	In these situations, *too* shows that you are unable to do something, but *very* does not.

EXERCISE 6

Complete the following with *too, too + to,* or *very,* as appropriate.

1. A: Are you really going to buy that motorcycle?
   B: Yes. It's _very_ expensive, but I think I've got enough money in the bank.
2. A: Why aren't you drinking your tea?
   B: I can't. It's _____ hot _____ drink.
3. A: Can I borrow your truck when I move to my new apartment?
   B: Sure.

Degree Complements: Too, Enough, and Very | 143

ANSWER KEY

Exercise 6
2. too hot to   3. too small to carry   4. too
5. very   6. very   7. too busy to call
8. too   9. very   10. too   11. very
12. too

1. If you choose to do this exercise orally, allow Ss a few minutes to practice beforehand and, if possible, to say the sentences from memory, rather than read them word for word.

2. Remind them to speak at a normal pace and to link words together smoothly, using appropriate intonation.

3. You can give examples of what not to do: NOT *Are—you—really—going—to—buy—that—motorcycle?* (each word pronounced separately and distinctly with short pauses in between each word; monotone—flat intonation) BUT *Areyou*really *gonnabuy tha'motorcycle?* (spoken at a normal, somewhat fast pace; words linked together; emphasis on "really"; rising intonation).

   A: Thanks! My car is _____ small _____ carry all my stuff.

4. A: Can you turn your stereo down?
   B: Why?
   A: It's _____ loud! We've been trying to get to sleep for about an hour.

5. A: Do you need some help?
   B: No, thanks. This is _____ heavy, but I think I can manage by myself.

6. A: What do you think of Pat's new boyfriend?
   B: He's _____ quiet, but I like him.

7. A: We haven't heard from you for ages.
   B: I'm sorry. I've been _____ busy _____ call.

8. A: Did you like the movie?
   B: No, it was _____ long.

9. A: Do you want to go home now?
   B: No, not yet. I'm _____ tired, but I think I'll stay a little longer.

10. A: How's the water in the pool?
    B: It's _____ cold! I'm getting out right now.

11. A: Did Brian have fun at the party?
    B: Yes. He seemed to enjoy it _____ much.

12. A: Did Mary decide to rent the apartment?
    B: No, it was _____ small.

EXERCISE 7

Complete the following with *very, too, too + to, enough, not enough,* or *too much/many/little/ few,* as appropriate.

Dear Tom and Wendy,

    I'm writing to answer your questions about life in New York. In fact, this is quite hard to do because my opinions keep changing!

    My apartment is nice, but the rent is (1) _____ very _____ high. Luckily, I earn a good salary and I can afford it. The main problem is that the apartment just is (2) _____ big _____ . I had to sell about half my furniture because I didn't have (3) _____ room for everything. I can't invite people for dinner because the kitchen is (4) _____ small _____ eat in. Luckily, the apartment has lots of windows, so all my plants are getting (5) _____ light. I live (6) _____ close to a subway station; it only takes me a couple of minutes to walk there. However, I never take the subway to work because it's (7) _____ crowded. You wouldn't believe it! There are just (8) _____ people crammed in like sardines, and you can't breathe because there is (9) _____ air. I haven't had the courage to ride my bike yet because there's just (10) _____ traffic. Mostly I walk everywhere, so the good news is that I am getting (11) _____ exercise!

    Despite all this, there are lots of wonderful things about living here. There are (12) _____ museums and art galleries to keep me happy for years! However, at the moment, I have (13) time to enjoy them because my job is driving me crazy. It's impossible to get all the work done because there are (14) _____ projects and (15) _____ good people to work on them. As a result, I am (16) _____ busy to make new friends or meet people. I don't sleep (17) _____ , and so I am always tired. Worst of all, I don't even have (18) _____ time to stay in touch with dear old friends like you! Nevertheless, I'm certain things will get better soon. Why don't you come and visit? That would really cheer me up!

Love,
Mary

Degree Complements: Too, Enough, and Very | **145**

USE YOUR ENGLISH

The activities in the purple pages at the end of the unit contain situations that should naturally elicit the structures covered in the unit. When Ss are doing these activities in class, you can circulate and listen to see if they are using the structures accurately. Have they achieved the goals presented at the beginning of the unit?

Activity 1

VARIATION

This game could be played in teams of four or five, with a large poster-sized version of the tic-tac-toe game (in the book) affixed to the wall.

1. Assign two teams to each poster. Teams can use self-stick notes or pieces of paper with some kind of adhesive backing (such as tape), with X or O marked on each piece of paper.

2. Follow the directions in the book. (If you've done the units in this book in order, then this is not Ss' first experience with tac-tac-toe—see Unit 2, Activity 3 for detailed instructions.)

Use Your English

ACTIVITY 1: SPEAKING

Work with a partner or in teams to play this version of tic-tac-toe.

STEP 1 Decide who will be "X" and who will be "O" and toss a coin to see who will start the game.

STEP 2 For each round of the game, select a different topic from the list below.

STEP 3 Choose the square you want to start with. With your team, agree on a meaningful sentence expressing the idea written in the square and relating to the topic of the round. For example: TOPIC: This classroom. *"This classroom is very small," "There aren't enough chairs in this classroom," "There are too few windows in this classroom,"* and so on.

STEP 4 The first team to get a line is the winner.

TOPICS
1. This campus
2. Television
3. North America
4. This town or city

very	too + to	too
too few	not enough	too much
enough	too many	too little

ACTIVITY 2: SPEAKING/WRITING

STEP 1 Look at the chart below. If you were responsible for making the laws in your community, at what ages would you permit the following activities? Write the ages in the column marked *Ideal Age*.

STEP 2 Go around the room and collect information from your classmates about the ages at which these activities are permitted in the parts of the world (countries, states, provinces) that they know about. You can include information about this country (or state or province) as well. Write this in the last column.

ACTIVITY	IDEAL AGE	REAL AGE / WHERE
drive a car		
drink alcohol		
vote		
join the military		
get married		
own a gun		
leave school		

STEP 3 When you have collected the information, prepare a report (oral or written) on the differences and similarities you found among different parts of the world. Include your own opinions about the ideal ages for these activities and give reasons to support them. Remember to announce the purpose of your report in your introduction and to end with a concluding statement. You can use these headings to organize your information:

Introduction: Purpose of this report
Most interesting similarities among parts of the world:
Most interesting differences among parts of the world:
Your opinions on ideal ages, with reasons to support them:
Brief concluding statement:

Activity 2
Steps 2 and 3

If there is not enough room in the charts for Ss to record their answers, have them record answers in their notebooks.

VARIATION

In monolingual settings, or when it is not practical to go outside of the classroom for interviews, Step 1 could be expanded into a discussion: Ask Ss to interview each other about what they think the ideal age is for the various activities.

EXPANSIONS

Step 3 and 4— An expanded written report, done as homework, is an option here. Or, if you feel Ss need more time to concentrate on writing, make this a two-step process:
1. Ss first turn in rough drafts, which you comment on.
2. Ss revise their drafts accordingly.
3. Record a few of the richer examples of the target structures (see Step 4) and present these to the class on an overhead transparency or on a handout.

If you make a written report, remember to read it through carefully after you finish writing. Check to see if you were able to use any of the language in this unit. If you make an oral report, record your presentation and listen to it later. Write down any sentences that you used containing *too, very, not enough,* or *enough.*

Activity 3
SUGGESTION

A good pre-activity for this is for you or a guest speaker to provide a short lecture on one particular country, covering the points listed under "Issue." Besides providing good listening comprehension practice, the material in the lecture could be used as the basis for comparison from country to country.

Activity 4
SUGGESTION

As with Activity 2, Steps 3 and 4, this can be used as a basis for a two-(or three)-step writing activity--rough draft + revision(s)—if you feel your Ss would benefit from a concentration on writing.

ACTIVITY 3: SPEAKING

The purpose of this activity is to share opinions on different social issues. Work with a partner and look at the issues listed below. For each one, think about what is sufficient (enough), what is insufficient (not enough), and what is excessive (too much) in this country and in other countries you and your partner know about. For example, you might think that public transportation in this country is too expensive and that there is not enough of it, but that public transportation in Egypt is very inexpensive but too slow. Record your opinions in your notebook. Be ready to share your ideas with the rest of the class.

Public Transportation
Health Care
Law and Order
Education
Care of the Elderly

Housing
Employment
Access for Disabled People to Public
Buildings and Transportation

ACTIVITY 4: WRITING

Choose **one** of the social issues you discussed in Activity 3. Review the information you collected on different countries. In your opinion, which country has the best solution? Which country, in your opinion, is the least successful in dealing with this issue? Write a short report, describing the best and worst solutions. Give reasons to support your opinions. Remember to introduce your topic; we have suggested one possibility below, but you can probably think of a better way. When you finish writing, read your report carefully and check to see if you were able to include any of the language discussed in this unit.

In the modern world, many countries are trying to find solutions to the same social issues, and it is interesting to see that different countries and cultures deal with these issues in different ways. In my opinion, some countries have better solutions than others. To illustrate this point, I will talk about
_____ (social issue) and show how
_____ (country) and _____ (country)
both deal with it.

ACTIVITY 5: SPEAKING/LISTENING

STEP 1 Use the information from Activity 3. As a class, choose four topics that interest you. Then, by yourself or with another student, interview a native speaker of English about these topics. Record your interview. Listen to your tape and make a brief summary of the person's opinions. Share your findings with the rest of the class. What similarities and differences did your class find in these interviews?

STEP 2 Listen to your tape again and write down any sentences containing examples of language discussed in this unit.

ACTIVITY 6: LISTENING

STEP 1 Does the world already have too many people? Listen to the tape of two people (a man and a woman) discussing the topic of overpopulation. Write a sentence telling which speaker you agree with and why.

I agree with _____ because _____.

STEP 2 Listen to the tape again. Write down as many phrases containing *too*, *enough*, and *very* as you can.

Degree Complements: Too, Enough, and Very | **149**

Activity 5
EXPANSION

The suggestions for Activity 3—inviting someone to speak about a particular country—can be incorporated into this one. If you are able to tape-record the interview (or lecture, if that is the format used), it is helpful to play it back as a group activity, in order to focus on the use of the structures targeted in this unit: phrases with *very* + adjective, *too* + adjective, and *not* + adjective + *enough*.

Activity 6

Play textbook audio. The tapescript for this listening activity appears on p. 507 of this book.

VARIATIONS

Because of the complexity of the topic, it is useful as a debate topic.
1. Break the class (or let them choose) into three teams: those who agree with the idea that the world is overpopulated, those who disagree, and those who are neutral.
2. While the "pro" and "con" teams prepare, have the "neutral" team develop a checklist that they will use to judge the comments of the teams (example: very/somewhat/not very convincing point; point supported with facts and statistics; etc.). Or, the neutral team could be responsible for deciding what debate rules they will use (amount of time for each main point + response, etc.).

The test for this unit can be found on p. 434 of this book. The answers are on p. 435.

TOEFL Test Preparation Exercises for Units 7–9 can be found on pp. 69–72 of the Workbook.
The answers are on p. 492 of this book.

Unit 10

UNIT OVERVIEW

Unit 10 uses the self-help theme to introduce and practice giving advice and expressing opinions.

UNIT GOALS

While discussing the goals of this unit, find out if students (Ss) have seen these structures before. What situations do they use them in?

OPENING TASK

The self-help context of this unit provides excellent practice for the use of the modals and other structures being practiced in this unit. Find out if your Ss are familiar with the self-help book industry; if they seem unfamiliar, you may need to spend more time setting up the task.

SETTING UP THE TASK

Ask your Ss what they do when they have a problem in their life. Do they ask friends or family for advice? Where else can they go to get advice on how to solve the problem?

SUGGESTIONS

1. Bring a real self-help book or video. Have Ss take a look at your sample and discuss what it is trying to achieve.
2. Have Ss do an Internet search for self-help books or videos. You should prepare by trying the search yourself and giving them hints on key words to use.

CONDUCTING THE TASK

Step 1

1. Review the directions with the class.
2. Have pairs share their ideas with the class. Do all groups have the same ideas?

UNIT 10

GIVING ADVICE AND EXPRESSING OPINIONS

Should, Ought To, Need To, Must, Had Better, Could, and Might

UNIT GOALS:

- To use *must, had better, need to, should, ought to, could, might,* and imperatives to give advice appropriately
- To use *should, ought to,* and *should not* to express opinions

OPENING TASK

How to . . .

In North America, many "self-help" books are published every year. These books give people advice on how to improve their lives.

STEP 1 With a partner, look at the books below. What kinds of advice do you expect to find in each one? Be ready to share your ideas with the rest of the class.

STEP 2   Now read the sample passages from these books and match each one to the book you think it probably comes from.

A

As an important first step, you really ought to eliminate red meat. This may be hard at first, but you will be amazed to find that there are many healthy—and delicious—alternatives.

B

This is never as easy as it sounds, so you should be prepared to put time and effort into it. For example, doing volunteer work is one way to meet people who share your interests, and you may get to know them better as you work on projects together.

C

It's easier than you think. To really make a difference, you should start slowly and establish a routine. Think about one thing that you can easily do (carpool? recycle paper, cans, and glass?) As soon as this becomes a habit, you should start to think about what to do next.

D

You should never settle into a regular, predictable routine. Surprise each other with fun activities, like picnics after work or moonlight barbecues on the beach.

E

You ought to make every effort to motivate yourself to stay on your diet! Buy a dress that is just a little bit too small for you and hang it in your closet. You should look at it every day and dream of the time when it will really fit you.

F

You shouldn't draw attention to yourself. Choose conservative but attractive styles. Navy blue is a good color choice. Remember that you ought to look competent and professional at all times.

STEP 3   With your partner, choose **one** of these self-help books. What advice would **you** give on the topic? Write at least three pieces of advice below:

BOOK:

Three pieces of advice we would give:
1.
2.
3.

A N S W E R   K E Y

Opening Task
A. 3   B. 5   C. 6   D. 1   E. 2   F. 4

Step 2

V A R I A T I O N

Read passages out loud to the class as they read along silently. This approach allows you to control the amount of time they spend on reading, and encourages them to try understanding the passages without relying on their dictionaries for unfamiliar words. Ss can match passages as they listen, or discuss as a class at the end.

Step 3

Point out that Ss will be using their advice in later exercises.

CLOSING THE TASK

Have Ss share their advice with the class. Write some examples on the board. Do not correct form, meaning, or use at this time.

REVIEWING THE TASK

Go back and underline some of the structures Ss used to give advice. Point out that you will be studying these and other ways of giving advice.

All of the focus boxes in this unit build on one another, comparing different forms.

Grammar Note

Be aware that many Ss have been inaccurately taught that modal auxiliaries have a past (would, should, could, might) and present (will, shall, can, may) form and are surprised to see so-called "past" forms used for opinions and advice. If this comes up, point out that these modals can be used to designate past, present, or future meaning and use. The main difference between the two groups is one of "distance"— psychological as well as temporal.

"Distant" modals are often used with present/future meaning when giving advice or opinions because the speaker does not know what the other person will eventually do (psychological distance of reality). For example:
You shouldn't smoke so much.
→ The speaker is giving his/her opinion that it is bad for the listener to smoke.
You shall not smoke so much.
→ The speaker knows that the listener is not going to smoke so much in the future. Perhaps this is an order.

These modals are also used instead of commands to give advice rather than an order (psychological distance of politeness):
You shouldn't smoke so much.
Don't smoke so much.

Workbook Ex. 1, pp. 73–74.
Answers: TE p. 492.

▶ # Giving Advice with *Should, Ought To, Shouldn't*

EXAMPLES	EXPLANATIONS
(a) A: I'm so tired. B: You **should/ought to** get more sleep. **(b)** A: I can't understand my teacher. B: You **ought to/should** talk to her about it.	*Should/should not* and *ought to* are often used to give advice (to tell someone what you think is a good or bad idea for him or her to do). Use *should* or *ought to* to show that you think something is a good idea. *Ought to* is usually pronounced as *oughta* in spoken English.
(c) A: I have a terrible cough. B: You **should not (shouldn't)** smoke so much.	Use *should not (shouldn't)* to show that you think something is a bad idea. *Ought to* is not usually used in negatives or in questions in American English.
(d) Nami works too hard. She **should/ought to** take a vacation. **(e)** **NOT:** She shoulds/oughts to take a vacation.	*Should* and *ought to* are modal auxiliaries. They do not take third person *s*. For more information about the form of modals, see Unit 5.

EXERCISE 1

Look at the advice that you and your partner wrote in the Opening Task on page 151. Did you use *should, ought to, should not?* Check to see if you used them correctly. If you didn't use them at all, rewrite your advice to include them.

Share your advice with the rest of the class. Do not tell your classmates which book you were thinking about when you wrote the advice and see if they can guess correctly.

FOCUS **2**

Using *Need To* and Imperatives to Give Advice

EXAMPLES	EXPLANATIONS
(a) A: My tooth hurts. B: You **need to** see a dentist. (b) A: My tooth hurts. B: You **should/ought to** see a dentist.	*Need to* + base verb can also be used to give advice. It is stronger than *should* or *ought to*. *Need to* is not a modal verb.
(c) A: My tooth hurts. B: **Go** to a dentist. (d) A: I can't sleep. B: **Don't drink** so much coffee! (e) A: I can't sleep. B: You **shouldn't** drink so much coffee.	You can also use an imperative to give advice. An imperative is much stronger and much more direct than *need to*. If you do not know the person you are addressing very well, it is usually better to use *should/shouldn't* or *ought to*.

EXERCISE 2

> ### HEINLE & HEINLE
> *the specialized language publisher*
> A Thomson Learning Company
>
> We are proud to announce an exciting new book, *by* language learners *for* language learners
>
> ### HOW TO BE A BETTER LANGUAGE LEARNER
>
> Language learners from all over the world give you advice
> about ways to learn a second, third, or fourth language.
> This book will change the way you learn languages...

You have been asked to contribute to this exciting new "self-help" book. First, think about your own experience as a language learner. Then, write down at least three important things that you think someone who wants to learn **your** language should or should not do. Get together with a partner and compare your lists. How many similarities and differences can you find in your advice? Share your advice with the rest of the class.

Refer Ss to the difference in strength between these structures and the ones in Focus 1. For your information, see the Grammar Note for Focus 1.

Exercise 2

Ss can write their lists of advice in class or as homework.

In class, have Ss compare their lists.

SUGGESTIONS

1. Have Ss come up to the board and write one suggestion. Point out that they should not repeat a suggestion made by a previous classmate; therefore, they need to read the list carefully before adding to it.
2. When the list is complete, have the class decide which advice is the most important. Do these items use *need to* or *imperatives*?
3. Ask the class if they would modify some of the pieces of advice to make them stronger or weaker.

Workbook Ex. 2, pp. 74–75.
Answers: TE p. 492.

Point out that this distinction is a difference of necessity. *Must* is another way of saying *"It is necessary that . . . ."* Add other examples of times when it is important to express the necessity of a situation: *I really must leave or I'll be late for work and my boss will fire me. You must study hard if you want to get a high score on the TOEFL/Cambridge exam. If she wishes to recover from her illness, she must not overwork herself.*

Exercise 3

While answers may vary, point out that Ss need to have a reason for choosing between the stronger and weaker forms. Some of the differences may depend on the culture(s) in your classroom (for example, wearing a seatbelt or having insurance may not be considered necessary in some cultures). Most likely answers are listed below.

Workbook Ex. 3, p. 75.
Answers: TE p. 492.

Should and *Ought To* versus *Must*

EXAMPLES	EXPLANATIONS
(a) Alma: I can't sleep at night. Bea: You **should** drink a glass of milk before you go to bed.	*Should* and *ought to* shows that something is a good idea. In (a), Bea is giving advice, but Alma is not obliged to follow that advice; she is free to do what she pleases.
(b) Dora: Do I need to get a special visa to visit Taiwan? Wen: Yes, you **must** go to the Taiwanese consulate here and get one before you leave. You **must not** try to enter the country without one.	*Must* is stronger. In (b), it is obligatory for Dora to follow Wen's advice. She is not free to do what she pleases. For more information about this use of *must*, see Unit 11.

EXERCISE 3

Oscar has just bought a used car. Complete the following, using *should, shouldn't, must,* or *must not* as appropriate. Different people may have different opinions about some of these, so be ready to justify your choices.

1. He ＿＿＿＿＿＿ get insurance as soon as possible.
2. He ＿＿＿＿＿＿ take it to a reliable mechanic and have it checked.
3. He ＿＿＿＿＿＿ get it registered.
4. He ＿＿＿＿＿＿ drive it without insurance.
5. He ＿＿＿＿＿＿ drink and drive.
6. He ＿＿＿＿＿＿ wear a seat belt.
7. He ＿＿＿＿＿＿ lock the doors when he parks the car.
8. He ＿＿＿＿＿＿ keep a spare key in a safe place.

ANSWER KEY

Exercise 3
Answers may vary. Probable answers:
1. must 2. should 3. must 4. mustn't/ (shouldn't) 5. mustn't 6. must
7. should 8. should

FOCUS **4**

Should and *Ought To* versus *Had Better*

EXAMPLES	EXPLANATIONS
(a) You **should** go to all your classes every day. **(b)** You **had better** go to all your classes every day.	You can also use *had better* to give advice. *Had better* is much stronger than *should* and *ought to*, but not as strong as *must*. In (a), it is a good idea for you to do this. In (b), if you don't go, something bad will happen.
(c) You **should** see a doctor about that. (It's a good idea.) **(d)** You**'d better** see a doctor about that. (It's urgent.) **(e)** You **must** see a doctor about that. (It's obligatory.)	*Had better* often shows that you think something is urgent. *Had better* is often contracted to *'d better*.
(f) *Teacher to student:* If you want to pass this class, you **had better** finish all your assignments. **(g)** *Student to teacher:* If you come to my country, you **should** visit Kyoto. **(h)** **NOT:** You had better visit Kyoto.	*Had better* is often used in situations where the speaker has more power or authority (for example, boss to employee or teacher to student). In these situations, *had better* sounds like an order or a command. If you want to be sure that you sound polite, use *should* or *ought to*.
(i) You **had better** finish this tomorrow. **(j)** I **had better** leave now. **(k)** He **had better** pay me for this.	*Had better* refers to the present and the future. It does not refer to the past (even though it is formed with *had*).
(l) She**'d better not** tell anyone about this. **(m)** You**'d better not** be late.	Notice how the negative is formed.

Grammar Note

Had better is often used in similar situations with *should, ought to,* and *must,* but tends to emphasize the negative consequences of an action. It is like adding ". . . or else" to the suggestion. This is why it is used with a sense of urgency or authority.

You'd better leave (or else I'm afraid we'll have an argument). You'd better drink your milk (or else you won't grow up strong).

It is not used in the past, because the event has passed and we **know** what the consequences were/are by now.

Exercise 4

S U G G E S T I O N S

1. Have Ss complete the exercise on their own (in class or for homework) and compare answers in a group. Discuss only those examples where Ss disagreed with one another.

2. Copy the exercise on an overhead transparency and do as a class. Ask Ss to give their answers and explain why they chose that form. Have the rest of the class decide if they agree with each S's choice.

Exercise 5

This exercise can be done individually or in pairs.

Workbook Ex. 4, p. 76.
Answers: TE p. 492.

EXERCISE 4

Complete the following with *should, ought to, must,* or *had better,* as necessary.

1. **Inez:** How can I register to take the TOEFL?
   Patsy: First you _____ complete this application form.

2. **Naoko:** I want to get a good score on the TOEFL, but I'm not sure how to do that.
   Kate: I think you _____ take every opportunity to practice your English.

3. **Yu-shan:** I'm sorry I haven't been coming to class recently. My father is in town.
   Advisor: You _____ start attending class regularly if you want to stay in this program.

4. **Herbert:** I think I'm getting the flu.
   Eleanor: You _____ go to bed and drink plenty of orange juice.

5. **Claudia:** I've lost my credit card.
   Rafael: You _____ report it immediately.

6. **Doctor:** You _____ take these pills four times a day. If you forget one, you will feel a lot worse.

7. **Audrey:** I just can't sleep at night.
   Shannon: You _____ try drinking herbal tea just before you go to bed.

8. **Carmen:** I'd love to visit Poland.
   Cherry: Well, first of all you _____ get a special visa.

9. **Debbie:** I've got a sore throat.
   James: You _____ try not to talk too much.

10. **Lois:** You _____ clean up your room. If you don't, there'll be trouble.

EXERCISE 5

Circle your choice in each of the following sentences.

1. You (should not/must not) smoke when you are in a movie theater in the United States.

2. While you are in Los Angeles, you (had better/should) try to visit Disneyland.

3. In the state of Michigan, people under the age of twenty-one (should not/must not) try to purchase alcohol.

156 | UNIT 10

A N S W E R   K E Y

Exercise 4
1. must   2. should/ought to   3. had better
4. should/ought to   5. had better
6. must/had better   7. should/ought to
8. must   9. should   10. had better

Exercise 5
1. must not   2. should   3. must not
4. should   5. had better   6. must
7. had better   8. had better   9. should
10. should

4. People (should/had better) wear helmets when they ride bicycles.

5. Look, the bus is coming! We (should/had better) run if we want to catch it.

6. Everybody who comes into the United States (must/should) show a valid passport or picture ID.

7. I've just spilled coffee on the new rug. I (should/had better) clean it up right away before it stains.

8. Professor Katz gets really angry when students chew gum in class. You (had better/should) get rid of your gum before we get there.

9. Tourists visiting my hometown in the spring (had better/should) bring cameras, as it's very beautiful at that time of year.

10. My brother wants to have more friends. He (must/should) join the tenants' association; maybe he can make some friends there.

FOCUS **5**

Should versus *Could* and *Might*

EXAMPLES	EXPLANATIONS
(a) A: I heard there's a new movie playing in town. B: Yeah, you **should** see that movie. It's great. **(b)** A: I don't know what to do on Friday night. B: You **could** see a movie.	You can also use *could* to give advice. *Could* is not as strong as *should* because it only expresses choices or possibilities. *Could* does not show that the speaker thinks that something is a good idea to do or that it is the right thing to do.
(c) If you want to improve your Spanish, you **could** take classes, you **might** listen to Spanish-speaking stations on the radio, you **could** find a conversation partner, or you **might** take a vacation in Mexico.	We often use *could* or *might* to express many different possibilities, without saying which one we think is best.

Giving Advice and Expressing Opinions: *Should, Ought To, Need To, Must, Had Better, Could,* and *Might* | **157**

FOCUS 5

Grammar Note

Could and might tend to be used to show options, stated or implied. The speaker is giving ideas on the situation, without making a judgment as to whether or not they are wise decisions.

A: I think Martin is really mad at me for what I said.

*B: You **should** call him to apologize. You know how he never forgets these things.*

(B is judging the situation and thinks it is a good idea to call.)

-or-

*B: You **could** call him to apologize. Or you **could** just forget the whole thing. Martin is a pretty forgiving guy.*

(B is giving choices, but doesn't think one idea is better than the other.)

Exercise 6
S U G G E S T I O N S

Step 1
Have Ss complete this step for homework.

Step 2
1. If you have a multinational classroom, have Ss work with people from different cultures. This can lead to interesting discussions as they decide which solution is best.
2. Point out that there is no one correct answer to these situations as they depend on Ss' opinions.
3. As Ss work, circulate to listen to their ideas and help settle disputes. If a group is spending too much time on one decision, suggest they leave that one for the end so that they have time to discuss all eight situations.
4. Compare solutions as a class. Were some decisions more difficult than others? Why?

EXERCISE 6

Your friends always come to you when they have problems because you usually have lots of great ideas about what to do.

STEP 1 For each problem, write down as many possible solutions as you can think of, using *could* and *might*.

STEP 2 Get together with two or three other students and compare your ideas. Decide who has the best solution to each problem and write it down, using *should*.

▶ **EXAMPLE:** Your neighbors play loud rock music all night.
Possibilities: *You could talk with them. You could play very loud opera in the morning when they are still asleep. You might move. You might buy ear plugs. You could call the police.*

In our opinion, the best solution: *You should buy ear plugs.*

1. Your friend's husband snores. Possibilities: _____
_____
In our opinion, the best solution: _____

2. Your friend's father is planning to come and visit for a few days. Unfortunately, he is a heavy smoker and your friend's roommates are nonsmokers who do not permit smoking in the house. Possibilities: _____
_____
In our opinion, the best solution: _____

3. A classmate has just spilled coffee on her favorite white shirt. She doesn't know what to do. Possibilities: _____
In our opinion, the best solution: _____

4. Your friend can't sleep at night. She feels exhausted every morning and doesn't have enough energy to do anything all day. Possibilities: _____
_____
In our opinion, the best solution: _____

5. One of your classmates wants to learn more about American culture and customs and would really like to make friends with some Americans. He doesn't know how to start. You have lots of ideas. Possibilities: _____
_____
In our opinion, the best solution: _____

6. Your partner never has enough money. At the end of the month, he is always broke. He comes to you for some ideas about what to do. Possibilities: _____
_____

In our opinion, the best solution: _____

_____

7. Two of your friends are taking a university class. The professor speaks very fast and they find it hard to follow the lectures. They are afraid that they are going to flunk the class. Possibilities: _____

_____

In our opinion, the best solution: _____

8. Your friend's fiancee has two dogs. She has had these dogs since she was a child and is very attached to them. Unfortunately, your friend is allergic to dogs. He loves his fiancee very much, but the dogs are making him sick. He doesn't want to upset her. Possibilities: _____

_____

In our opinion, the best solution: _____

_____

EXERCISE 7

The following story is a well-known logic problem. Get together with some of your classmates and decide on the best solution.

A woman went shopping. First she bought a large piece of cheese. Then she stopped at a pet store to buy a white mouse for her nephew's birthday. Just as she was leaving the store, she saw an adorable black and white cat. She couldn't leave the store without it, so she bought the cat as well.

Unfortunately, her car is parked a long way from the pet store, and it's only possible for her to carry one thing at a time. What could she do in order to get everything to her car? How many solutions can you find?

She could _____

_____

_____

There are no parking areas near the pet store, so she cannot move her car, and there is nobody around to help her. Unfortunately, cats eat mice and mice eat cheese. This means that if she leaves the cat with the mouse, the cat will eat the mouse, and if she leaves the mouse with the cheese, the mouse will eat the cheese. What should she do? What is the best solution to her problem?

She should _____

_____

_____

You can find the solution to this problem on page A-17.

There are many different versions of this problem. Do you know one? Share it with the rest of the class.

Exercise 7

Many Ss may be familiar with this logic problem. After solving the problem, Ss often like to share other versions that they know about.

Workbook Ex. 5, p. 77.
Answers: TE p. 493.

A N S W E R   K E Y

Exercise 7

First, the woman should take the mouse to the car, leaving the cat with the cheese. Next, she should return and pick up the cat and take it to the car. As soon as she gets to the car with the cat, she should remove the mouse and take it with her, leaving the cat in the car. When she gets back to the shopping area, she should pick up the cheese and leave the mouse. Then she should take the cheese to the car and leave it there with the cat. Finally, she should return to collect the mouse and bring it with her to the car.

Draw Ss' attention to this focus box as a review of the different structures that have been discussed in this unit. You can use an example sentence and discuss the differences between the speaker's judgment when using each different structure. For example:

Before you go to the restaurant, . . .

. . . you **might** *call first . . .*
(=one idea is to call first)

. . . you **could** *call first . . .*
(=one idea is to call first)

. . . you **should** *call first . . .*
(=it's a wise idea to call first)

. . . you **ought** *to call first . . .*
(=it's a wise idea to call first)

. . . you **need** *to call first . . .*
(=it's necessary to call first)

. . . you'd **better** *call first . . .*
(=there are negative consequences if you don't call first)

. . . you **must** *call first . . .*
(=it's absolutely necessary to call first)

. . . to make a reservation.

Exercise 8

S U G G E S T I O N S

1. Read the passage out loud to Ss. Be sure they understand the situation before they write their lists independently.

2. Alternatively, have Ss complete the reading for homework. Remind them that they should only spend 2 minutes writing down solutions to Jennifer's problem.

3. After the exercise is finished, ask if anyone is having difficulties learning English that are similar to those experienced by Jennifer. Are there different suggestions that may apply to their situations?

Workbook Ex. 6, pp. 78–81.
Answers: TE p. 493.

Should and *Ought To* versus *Might, Could, Need To, Had Better,* and *Must*

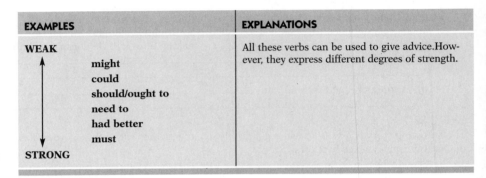

EXAMPLES		EXPLANATIONS
WEAK ↑ ↓ **STRONG**	might could should/ought to need to had better must	All these verbs can be used to give advice. However, they express different degrees of strength.

EXERCISE 8

Read the following situation and follow the instructions given:

Jennifer is an American student. As she is planning to major in international business, she decided that it would be important for her to know how to speak Japanese. She managed to get some money from her father and left for Japan for six months.

She has now been in Tokyo for three months, taking classes in Japanese language and conversation. When she first arrived, she missed home a lot, so she quickly made friends with other Americans she met. Instead of living with a Japanese host family, she decided to move in with two other American women and now she spends all her time with her new friends. She takes Japanese classes every day, but she seldom spends any time with the students who do not speak any English. As a result, she rarely speaks Japanese and has not made much progress in the language. She hasn't learned much about Japanese culture either.

Jennifer is having a great time in Tokyo with her American friends, but now she's in a terrible panic. Her father has just called to tell her that he will be coming to Tokyo on business, and he wants her to help him while he is there. He wants her to help interpret for him, as well as advise him on Japanese culture and customs. She is feeling very anxious about meeting her father. . . .

First, make a list of all the possible solutions to Jennifer's problem that you can think of in two minutes. Then get together with two or three other students and share your solutions. Look at all the possibilities and then select the best three. Be ready to share these with the rest of the class and to justify them as necessary.

160 | UNIT 10

FOCUS 7

Expressing Opinions with *Should, Ought To,* and *Should Not*

EXAMPLES	EXPLANATIONS
(a) Iryna believes that more people **should** drive electric cars. **(b)** In Mune's opinion, couples **ought to** live together for a while before they marry. **(c)** Most of my friends think that we **shouldn't** eat meat.	You can also use *should, ought to,* and *should not* to express your opinions about what you think is right or wrong.

EXERCISE 9

In your opinion, which of the following occupations should receive the highest salaries? Number the occupations in order of the highest to the lowest salaries (Number 1 is the highest salary).

TV news announcer	plumber	politician
firefighter	emergency room doctor	elementary school teacher
professional football player	model	plastic surgeon
member of the clergy	CEO of a large company	police officer
attorney	bus driver	nurse

When you finish, compare your answers with a partner's. Be ready to share and justify your opinions with the rest of the class.

Point out that this meaning is consistent with that expressed in previous focus boxes, as these structures are used to show the speaker's judgment of the situation.

Exercise 9

VARIATIONS

1. Photocopy and cut the chart into individual "job cards." Be sure to make enough copies for each pair to work with.
2. In pairs, Ss arrange the strips of paper in a list, ranking the jobs from highest salary to lowest salary.
3. Have pairs compare their answers with each other, noting similarities and differences.
4. Discuss differences as a class.

UNIT GOAL REVIEW

Ask Ss to look at the goals on the opening page of the unit again. Help them understand how much they have accomplished in each area.
Can Ss explain the difference in strength expressed by these forms?

Workbook Exs. 7–9, pp. 81–83.
Answers: TE p. 493.

USE YOUR ENGLISH

The aim of these activities is to give Ss communicative practice of the structures discussed in this unit. Corrections can be made after the activity has finished. Be sure to focus on repeated errors, rather than "slips of the tongue."

Activity 1
Step 3
SUGGESTION

If you do not have access to recording equipment, assign other Ss to act as secretary, noting sentences where the speaker used those structures.

VARIATION

Add a Step 4 to practice writing by directing Ss to rewrite their presentation, correcting their inaccurate use.

Activity 2
VARIATION

Do this activity as an assignment on an e-mail discussion list. Point out that the language used in e-mail is somewhere between spoken and written English in formality.

1. You can post the initial letter(s) yourself and instruct Ss to provide responses.
2. Ss should each try to come up with a different piece of advice from those previously posted.
3. Allow the discussion to proceed without you, making notes of problems they had using the structures in this unit.
4. After the activity, bring a list of their (anonymous) errors to class and have the class make corrections.

Use Your English

ACTIVITY 1: SPEAKING/ LISTENING

STEP 1 Sometimes, for fun, people give each other advice on the best way to accomplish a negative goal; for example, the best way to lose your job or how to annoy your neighbors. Get together with another student and choose one of the following humorous topics. How many different ideas can you come up with?

- How to get a traffic ticket
- How to get rid of your boyfriend or girlfriend
- How to avoid learning English
- How to get an F in this class
- How to annoy your roommate

STEP 2 With your partner, make a poster presentation on the topic you chose. Take a large poster-sized sheet of paper or card and use it to make a poster that expresses your ideas. You can use graphics, pictures, and diagrams to make your poster informative and eye-catching. Display your poster and use it to explain your ideas to the rest of the class.

STEP 3 Record yourself as you make your poster presentation. Listen to your tape and write down all the sentences where you used *should, shouldn't, ought to, need to, must, had better, might,* or *could.* Did you use them appropriately?

ACTIVITY 2: SPEAKING

Many American newspapers have advice columns. People write to these columns for help with their problems. Three famous ones are "Dear Abby," "Ann Landers," and "Miss Manners." Clip any advice columns you can find in various newspapers and bring them to class. Cut off the answers to the letters and circulate the letters without their replies. In groups, try to come up with helpful advice. Share your responses with the rest of the class. Compare your advice with the advice the professionals gave.

A C T I V I T Y   3 :   W R I T I N G

In groups, write a letter to "Dear Abby," asking for advice on a particular problem. Exchange your problem letter with another group and write solutions to their problem. Share both problem and solution with the rest of the class.

A C T I V I T Y   4 :   W R I T I N G

Write a short report, giving advice to someone who is planning to visit your hometown, your country, or the community where you grew up. Advise him or her on places to visit, clothes to wear, things to bring, things to do, and how to act.

Remember to start your report with an introductory statement. For example: *My hometown/country, (name), is very interesting, and if you follow my advice, I am sure that you will have an enjoyable and rewarding visit. . . .*

When you finish writing, check and see if you have used *should, shouldn't, must, ought to, might, need to, could,* and *had better*. It is not necessary to use one in every sentence, as this would sound very unnatural!

A C T I V I T Y   5 :   S P E A K I N G

Is honesty always the best policy? Should we **always** tell the truth? Think about the following situations. Share your opinions on each one with your classmates. How many people share your point of view? How many have different ideas?

1. You saw your best friend's girlfriend out on a date with someone else. Should you tell your friend what you saw? Why? Why not?

2. A classmate cheated on the last test. Should you tell your teacher? Why? Why not?

3. Your friend has a new haircut. She is really happy with her new "look," but you don't like it at all. In fact, you think it makes her look quite ugly. She asks for your opinion. Should you tell her what you really think? Why? Why not?

4. You catch your eight-year-old son telling a lie. Should you tell him that it is wrong to lie? Why? Why not?

Activity 3

As with Activity 2, this activity can be done via e-mail.

Activity 4
V A R I A T I O N

Increase the formality of this writing exercise by creating a class travel magazine. Because their report is more formal, point out that they should not use contractions or slang in their writing. After their final edit, compile Ss' traveler's advice pieces into a booklet and distribute it to the class.

Activity 5
E X P A N S I O N

As a follow-up activity, if you have a multicultural classroom, discuss what the class thinks about whether honesty really is the best policy. Did they notice different opinions based on culture? Gender? Religion? Be sure to keep the conversation from getting too personal. If the discussion gets too heated, remind Ss that these are opinions and that each individual or group has a right to their ideas.

Activity 6

If you are concerned that these topics may lead to too much controversy, assign this topic as written work.

SUGGESTION

When editing Ss' written work, be sure to include a personal comment on the content of their report. Separate this feedback from your comments on their form, meaning, and use.

ACTIVITY 6: SPEAKING/WRITING

STEP 1 Read the following and circle *should* or *should not* to express the point of view that is closest to your own opinion on the topic.

1. School uniforms should/should not be obligatory.
2. Animals should/should not be used in laboratory experiments.
3. Doctors should/should not reveal the identity of AIDS patients to the patient's employer or school.
4. Mothers should/should not work outside the home when their children are young.
5. A woman should/should not take her husband's family name when she marries.
6. Smoking should/should not be permitted in public places.

STEP 2 Choose the topic that interests you the most and then go around the room until you find one or two other students who share your opinion on that topic. Form a group with these students and brainstorm all the reasons and examples you can think of to support your point of view and then write them down. Choose the strongest ones, with the best examples, and use them to make a short report (oral or written) presenting your opinion. Share your report with the rest of the class and be ready to justify your position as necessary.

STEP 3 If you make a written report, read your report carefully and underline every example you can find of the modal auxiliaries from this unit.

If you choose an oral report, record your report. Listen to your tape and write down every sentence where you use one of the modal auxiliaries from this unit.

ACTIVITY 7: LISTENING

In this activity, you will hear a taped interview on the topic of smoking. Listen to the person's opinion. Does she think smoking should be banned in public places? What other ideas does she express? Check (✔) the statements you think the speaker agrees with.

_____ Smoking should be banned in public places.

_____ People should not be able to buy cigarettes in drug stores and supermarkets.

_____ Parents should not smoke at home in front of children.

_____ Teachers need to teach students about the dangers of smoking.

Listen to the tape again. Write down any sentences that contain examples of the verb forms in this unit.

ACTIVITY 8: SPEAKING/LISTENING

Many people have strong opinions about smoking. Ask five different native speakers of English questions like these: "What's your opinion about smoking in public places?" "Do you think it's a good or bad idea to ban smoking in public places?"

Tape their answers. Listen to your tape and be ready to share the information that you collect with the other people in your class. What do most of the people you interviewed think about this topic?

Listen to your tapes. What are some of the ways people express their opinions? Write down any sentences that contain examples of the verbs from this unit.

Activity 7

Play textbook audio. The tapescript for this listening appears on pp. 507–508 of this book.

Use the tapescript below if you do not have access to a cassette player. Ss can compare answers in groups or as a class.

Activity 8

If your Ss have limited access to native speakers of English, invite people (friends, family, other teachers) who have strong English skills to participate in a panel discussion.

1. Have Ss create and ask their own questions for the panelists.
2. Record the discussion and have the class listen again and take notes of the different ways the speakers expressed their opinions.
3. When reviewing the language, draw a chart on the board with two columns, one for stronger opinions, one for weaker opinions.
4. Elicit from the Ss the different ways people expressed opinions, writing their answers in the appropriate column.

The test for this unit can be found on pp. 437–438 of this book. The answers are on p. 439.

Unit 11

UNIT OVERVIEW

This unit provides practice with modals and phrasal modals of necessity and prohibition: *have to/have got to, do not have to, must/must not,* and *cannot.*

UNIT GOALS

Review the goals listed on this page to see what students (Ss) should learn by the end of this unit.

OPENING TASK

The purpose of this task is to generate talk that will naturally incorporate modals and phrases that express necessity and obligation: *have to/have got to/do not have to/must/must not,* and *cannot.* The task is intended to focus attention on meaning rather than form, which will allow you to see whether Ss are able to produce the forms spontaneously.

SETTING UP THE TASK

All that you need to do to set up this task is to check that everyone understands "U.S. Immigration and Customs." This is usually not a problem, especially if you present it in the context of the task situation, as described in Step 1. If you think it would be helpful to elaborate, you can ask questions like "*What experiences have you had (or have you heard about) with U.S Immigration and Customs?*" and "*Was it easy/difficult to get a visa? In your opinion, is it usually this easy/difficult?*"

U N I T **11**

MODALS OF NECESSITY AND PROHIBITION

Have To/Have Got To, Do Not Have To, Must/Must Not, Cannot

UNIT GOALS:

- To use *must, have to,* and *have got to* to show something is necessary
- To use *must not* and *cannot* to show something is prohibited
- To choose between *have to* and *have got to*
- To use *do not have to* to show something is not necessary
- To use *have to* for *must* in the past

▶ **O P E N I N G   T A S K**
Visiting the United States

STEP 1 A friend of yours from Jamaica is planning a short vacation in California. As he is a Jamaican citizen, he will have to deal with Immigration and Customs when he enters the United States.

He doesn't have much room to pack a lot of things because he's planning to travel with just a backpack. Here are some of the things he is thinking of taking with him:

a passport	a map of the U.S.	an umbrella
a surfboard	fireworks	a business suit
fresh fruit	a laptop computer	hiking boots
an international driver's license	a credit card	
traveler's checks	a tourist visa	
books about Jamaica	California guide books	
a return airline ticket	photographs of his home town	
	many reggae (Jamaican music) tapes and CDs	

STEP 2 Use the boxes below to help him organize the things he wants to take to the United States. Work with a partner and put them in the boxes where you think they belong.

#1 It's necessary and obligatory: You can't enter the United States without this: You must take this with you.	#2 It's prohibited by law: You must not take this into the United States.
#3 It's a good idea to bring this: You should take this with you.	#4 It's O.K. to bring this, but it isn't really necessary: You don't have to take this.

STEP 3 Can you and your partner add any other things to this list? Try to think of at least five more items and put them in the appropriate boxes.

STEP 4 With your partner, write sentences about one or two items in each box, explaining why you think they belong there.

FOCUS **1**

SUGGESTIONS

1. Write down the modals using an arrow showing the different degrees of strength of these modals (see Unit 10, Focus 6, p. 160 as an example). You will need two short lists rather than one, one for "positives"—obligatory actions/ requirements, and one for "negatives"— prohibited actions. *Must/have to/have got to* are very strong modals of necessity and would therefore go on top (of the positive side); *should* is less strong; *can* the weakest. On the negative side, *must not/cannot* are very strong; *don't have to* is weaker and would go on the bottom.

2. Ss might ask about how *need to* and other modals or phrasal modals relate to the modals treated in this unit. The simplest way to treat questions about other modals is to refer Ss to Unit 10. Focus 6, page 160 covers many of the modals Ss might ask about.

Modals of Necessity, Prohibition, and Permission

EXAMPLES	EXPLANATIONS
(a) You **must** have a passport. OR **(b)** You **have to** have a passport. OR **(c)** You **have got to** have a passport.	Use *must, have to,* or *have got to* to show something is necessary and obligatory (something that is strongly required, often by law).
(d) You **must not (mustn't)** bring fresh fruit into the United States. OR **(e)** You **cannot (can't)** bring fresh fruit into the United States.	Use *must not (mustn't)* or *cannot (can't)* to show something is prohibited and absolutely not permitted (often by law). In the past, use *couldn't*. In the future, use *won't be able to*.
(f) You **can** bring a surfboard.	Use *can* to show that something is permitted. In the past, use *could*. In the future, use *will be able to*.
(g) You **should** bring a credit card.	Use *should* to show something is a good idea. For more information about this use of *should* see Unit 10.
(h) You **don't have to** bring a surfboard.	Use *do not (don't) have to* to show something is permitted, but not necessary. You can do this if you want to, but you are not required to.

Exercise 1

This exercise, along with Focus 1, can serve as a bridge to the Opening Task. Ss can work in pairs or small groups and then share one or two sentences aloud with the class. Those listening can check to see that the sentences are correct.

EXERCISE 1

Look back at the sentences you wrote in Step 4 of the Opening Task. Did you use *must, have to, have got to, should, can, can't, mustn't,* and *don't have to* ? If you did, check to see that you used them correctly. If you didn't use them, rewrite the sentences.

▶ **EXAMPLE:** *He must have a valid passport—it is required by law.*

In the rest of this unit, you will have the opportunity to practice all of these in more detail.

168 UNIT 11

ANSWER KEY

Exercise 1
Answers will vary, depending on what Ss wrote in the Opening Task.

Modals and Phrasal Modals:
Must, Have To, and
Have Got To

EXAMPLES	EXPLANATIONS
(a) International students **must** get visas before they enter the United States. **(b)** My Jamaican friend **must** get a tourist visa before he goes to the United States on vacation.	*Must* is a modal and does not change to agree with the subject.
(c) International students **have to** get visas before they enter the United States. **(d)** My Jamaican friend **has to** get a tourist visa before he goes on vacation in the United States.	*Have to* is a phrasal modal. It changes to agree with the subject. *Have to* and *has to* are usually pronounced "hafta" and "hasta" in fast speech and informal conversation.
(e) International students **have got to** get visas before they enter the United States. **(f)** My Jamaican friend **has got to** get a tourist visa before he goes to the United States on vacation.	*Have got to* is a phrasal modal. It changes to agree with the subject. *Have got to* and *has got to* are usually pronounced " 've gotta" and " 's gotta" in fast speech and informal conversation.
(g) **Do** we **have to** go? **Does** she **have to** go too? **(h)** **Have** we **got to** go? **Has** she **got to** go too? **(i)** **Must** we go? **Must** she go too?	Notice how questions with *must, have to,* and *have got to* are formed. Use *do/does* with *have to.* Use *has/have* with *have got to.* Do not use *do/does.* Do not use *do/does* with *must.* However, *must* is rarely used in questions in American English.

Examples (c) through (h) provide good material for listening comprehension practice.

SUGGESTIONS

1. Read these sentences aloud or make up other statements or questions that use *hafta, hasta, 've gotta* and *'s gotta,* the reduced versions of *have to, has to, have got to* and *has got to,* which all naturally occur in informal speech (of most North American dialects). For example: *Do we hafta continue class today? Do you think* (student's name) *hasta study every day?*
2. Ask Ss to write down the full form of the sentence. For example, they would write *"Do we have to"* NOT *"Do we hafta."*

VARIATIONS

1. In groups or as a whole class, have Ss make up sentences and read them aloud while others, including you, transcribe the full form. This allows Ss to practice using reduced forms in their own speech, as well as to listen for and recognize reduced forms in others' speech.
2. Explain that when *have got to* and *has got to* are used in statements, as in examples (e) and (f), sometimes the *has/have* is omitted entirely in informal speech. In other words, rather than hearing *"Students 've gotta get visas.",* they might hear *"Students gotta get visas."*
3. Emphasize that this occurs only in informal settings; Ss would not be likely to hear forms so reduced on the listening comprehension section of the TOEFL Test!

Teacher's Edition: Unit 11 **169**

Exercise 2

The use of *have to* and *have got to* may vary in Ss' answers. It's helpful to explain that there is only a slight difference in meaning between the two phrasal modals (see Focus 3, page 172).

The questions following item 6 are a potentially rich source for an interactive activity in a multicultural, multilingual setting.

VARIATION

Have Ss draw the signs on the board *without* telling others the meaning. Then have others guess the meaning in the form of a statement using *have to, have got to,* or other modals that "fit."

EXERCISE 2

Many road signs are used internationally, but some used in the United States are confusing for tourists from other countries. What do you think the following road signs mean? Complete the sentences, using *have to* and *have got to* in your answers.

1.  In the United States, drivers _____ when they see this sign.

2. Also, when they see this one, they _____ _____

3. This sign tells you that you _____ _____

4. A driver who sees this sign _____ _____

5. Be careful when you see this one. It means that you _____

6. Q: What happens when there are two or three cars waiting at this sign?

A: The car that arrives last _____

_____

How many of these road signs are also found in your country? Are there are any road signs from your country that are not found in North America? Draw the signs and write sentences showing what you have to do when you see them.

EXERCISE 3

Work with a partner and decide which of the following are necessary and obligatory to do if you want to get a driver's license in the United States.

- speak English very well
- know how to drive
- practice before the test
- take an eye test
- take a written test
- have a medical examination
- have a passport or birth certificate as ID

- pass a driving test
- have a high school diploma
- own a car
- study the information booklet from the DMV (Department of Motor Vehicles, the department that issues driver's licenses)
- have an international driver's license

EXERCISE 4

Your friend wants to know what he has to do to get a driver's license. Make statements to explain what it is necessary for him to do if he wants to get a driver's license in the United States; then explain what it is necessary for him to do if he wants to get a driver's license in your country.

Exercise 3
SUGGESTION

If your class is being conducted in the U.S., or if some of your Ss have been to the U.S., this is a good opportunity to share "driver's license stories." For example: *Did you have to take the tests more than once? Did you take driver's education classes, and if so, what was your experience there? Did you or any one you know have a near-accident (or—hopefully not—an actual accident)? Did you or any one you know ever drive illegally (under age)?* Or, if you have a U.S. driver's license and can remember your early driving experiences, tell your class about it.

Exercise 4
EXPANSION

For extra practice with writing, this prompt is suitable for a 2–3 paragraph (or more) comparison-contrast essay. This is also useful if you feel Ss need more practice with the structures covered in Unit 7.

ANSWER KEY

Exercise 3
Answers will vary, depending on Ss' opinions.

Exercise 4
Answers will vary.

SUGGESTIONS

1. Provide a few more examples of the *have to–have got to* distinction. Parent to child: *You have to eat your vegetables.* versus *You have got to eat your vegetables.* Doctor to patient: *You have to watch your weight/salt intake.* versus *You have got to watch your weight/salt intake.*

2. Explain that although some speakers of North American English find little difference in meaning between the two, using *have got to* rather than *have to* expresses urgency, and is perhaps a bit more formal, sometimes reserved for situations of extreme importance and necessity.

3. Again, as with Focus 2, point out that the contraction *'ve* or *'s* with *got to* is sometimes omitted in informal situations. For example, rather than saying "*You've gotta come with me,*" speakers will sometimes say "*You gotta come with me.*"

Workbook Ex. 2, p. 85.
Answers: TE p. 493.
Workbook Ex. 7, p. 90.
Answers: TE p. 494.

FOCUS **3**

Have To versus *Have Got To*

EXAMPLES	EXPLANATIONS
(a) Joe **has to** go on a diet. (b) Joe **has got to** follow a very strict diet because he has a serious heart condition. (If he doesn't follow the diet, he will die.) (c) You **have to** pay your phone bill once a month. (d) You **have got to** pay your phone bill immediately. (If you don't, the phone company will disconnect the phone.)	Both *have to* and *have got to* show that something is necessary and obligatory. However, many people use *have got to* when they want to emphasize that something is **very** important and **very** necessary.
(e) Hey Steve, you**'ve got to (gotta)** see this movie. It's really great.	In very informal conversation among friends, some people use *have got to* to show they think something is a really good thing to do. In (e), Steve's friend is not saying that Steve is obliged to see the movie; she is just strongly advising Steve to see it.

EXERCISE 5

Make a statement for each situation below. Work with a partner and decide which you would use for each one, *have to* or *have got to*.

1. Your sister's four-year-old son takes a nap every day and goes to bed at 8:00 every night. But today he didn't take a nap, and it's now 10:00 P.M.

   She says to her son, "You _____ go to sleep now."

2. The last time your friend went to the dentist was four months ago. He doesn't think he has any problems with his teeth, but he feels he should probably go to the dentist for a checkup.

   He says, "I _____ make an appointment to see the dentist sometime soon."

3. You haven't been reading the assignments for your history class, and you did very badly on the first two quizzes. You are afraid that you'll fail the course.

   You tell your classmate, "I _____ study every day if I don't want to fail my history class."

ANSWER KEY

Exercise 5

Answers may vary, depending on Ss' perceptions of how important and how necessary the actions are. Suggested answers:

1. have got to 2. have to 3. have got to
4. have to 5. have to

4. Your roommate is making dinner. She has just put a loaf of bread in the oven. Suddenly she realizes that she doesn't have an important item that she needs for dessert.

She says, "I _____ go to the store. If I'm not back in ten minutes, can you take the bread out of the oven? It _____ come out at 7:00 or it'll be ruined."

5. You are at a friend's house. You are feeling a little tired and want to go to sleep early.

You say, "I _____ leave now. I'll see you after class tomorrow."

FOCUS **4**

Using *Cannot (Can't)* and *Must Not (Mustn't)* to Show Something Is Prohibited or Not Permitted

EXAMPLES	EXPLANATIONS
(a) You **cannot (can't)** bring fresh fruit into the United States. OR **(b)** You **must not (mustn't)** bring fresh fruit into the United States. **(c)** You **cannot (can't)** smoke in here. OR **(d)** You **must not (mustn't)** smoke in here.	Use *cannot* and *must not* to show that something is completely prohibited or not permitted (often by law). *Cannot* is more common than *must not* in American English. *Cannot* and *must not* are usually contracted to *can't* and *mustn't* in fast speech.
(e) Herbert, you **must not (mustn't)** eat any more of those cookies!	*Must not/mustn't* is also often used as a strong command in situations where you want someone to obey. In (e), eating cookies is not prohibited by law, but the speaker **really** wants Herbert to stop eating them.

Modals of Necessity and Prohibition | **173**

FOCUS 4

Language learners who have had experience with speakers of British English (or dialects other than American English) may note that *must not* seems to be used more frequently than *cannot*.

SUGGESTIONS

1. Explain that the contraction *mustn't* is also used more often in other dialects, in comparison to *can't* in American English, although speakers of English will understand the meaning of both.
2. Emphasize the information in (e)—that is, that for many speakers of English, the use of *must not* may have a slightly stronger sense to it than the use of *cannot*.

Exercise 6

VARIATION

Step 2

Have Ss first display their signs to others in the class and then let other Ss come up with the captions.

Exercise 7

SUGGESTION

Before starting this exercise, you might want to discuss the possible meaning of the word token in this context. To stimulate discussion, ask: *What are the different ways that people can pay for public transportation in the various cities that you/students know? Is there advice about public transportation that you/students would like to give someone who is traveling to a particular city/country?*

EXERCISE 6

STEP 1 Look at the cartoon. Write statements in your notebook, using *cannot* and *must not* to describe each prohibited activity.

STEP 2 With your partner, make signs for your classroom, showing classroom "rules." Write a caption for each sign, using *must, must not,* and *cannot.* For example: *You can't smoke in this room.* Display your signs. Take a vote to see which ones your classmates want to put on your classroom walls.

EXERCISE 7

These photographs were taken in New York City. Photograph A is a sign on a newsstand and Photograph B is a sign in the window of a convenience store. With a partner, try to figure out what the two signs mean. What is the difference between the two photographs? Work with your partner and try to complete the summary below.

PHOTOGRAPH A	**PHOTOGRAPH B**

Reprinted with permission from Mark Chester, *No in America*, Taylor Publishing Co, Dallas (1986).

In Photograph A, you _____

but in Photograph B, you _____

ANSWER KEY

Exercise 6

Answers will vary, but will probably include:

You must not/cannot: walk on the grass; pick the flowers; park here; draw or write on the statue; throw bottles in this bin; let your dog walk here/bring dogs here; smoke in the park; ride a bicycle here; climb the trees.

Exercise 7

In Photograph A, you have to/must buy something to get change, but in Photograph B, you don't have to buy anything to get change.

FOCUS **5**

Must and *Have To* versus *Must Not, Cannot,* and *Do Not Have To*

EXAMPLES	EXPLANATIONS
(a) To enter the United States you **must** have a valid passport. OR **(b)** To enter the United States you **have to** have a valid passport.	**Showing something is necessary and obligatory:** Use either *must* or *have to*. In this situation, they have the same meaning.
(c) You **cannot** bring fireworks into the United States. OR **(d)** You **must not** bring fireworks into the United States. **(e)** **NOT:** You don't have to bring fireworks into the United States.	**Showing something is prohibited:** Use *cannot* or *must not*. Do not use *do not have to*. In negative sentences, they do **not** have the same meaning. In this situation, *must not* means it is prohibited.
(f) You **don't have to** bring a surfboard to California because you can rent one there. **(g)** **NOT:** You must not bring a surfboard to California because you can rent one there. **(h)** There are aren't any classes on Saturdays, so we **don't have to** come to school.	**Showing something is not necessary:** Use *do not have to*. Do not use *cannot* or *must not*. In this situation, *do not have to* means you can do something if you want to, but you are not obliged to do it if you don't want to.

EXERCISE 8
Look back to what you wrote in Exercise 7. Check to see if you used *have to, must,* or *do not have to* correctly. Rewrite your sentences if necessary.

EXERCISE 9
Your teacher wants to visit the country you come from and needs your help. How many different "helpful" statements can you make using *must, have to, have got to, cannot, must not, should, can,* and *do not have to*? For example: You **don't have to** have a tourist visa to visit Spain, but you **must** have a valid passport. All visitors **have to** carry their passports at all times; this is the law.

Modals of Necessity and Prohibition | **175**

ANSWER KEY

Exercise 8
The answers depend on Ss' answers for Exercise 7.

Exercise 9
Answers will vary, depending on Ss' advice and opinions.

FOCUS 5

Emphasize the information in (c) through (h), since the meaning of *don't have to* can be confusing to students.

SUGGESTIONS
Design an activity that allows Ss to make meaningful sentences that display their understanding of the different terms.
1. Choose a topic or have Ss choose a topic about what to do / what not to do when: giving a party, making friends, getting over the flu/a cold, inviting a potential boyfriend/girlfriend/partner out on a date, etc.
2. Write the different modals and phrasal modals from this focus box on index cards: *must, have to, cannot, must not, don't have to*. Make an extra card for *don't have to* to allow extra practice with this (See examples (e) and (g)).
3. Have Ss select a card from the pile and make statements using that modal or phrasal modal.
4. Let other Ss decide whether the statement is "correct." Sometimes this may be a matter of opinion!

VARIATIONS
1. Form teams and assign points to those that come up with statements that everyone agrees with.
2. Vote on who agrees/who doesn't agree, allowing alternate teams the opportunity to revise the initial statement, so that it is more acceptable to more Ss.
3. Award teams points for the funniest, most unusual, most "proper" (formal), etc., advice.

Exercise 8
If Ss did need to rewrite their sentences, ask them to explain why. What was wrong with the original statement? Pay special attention to statements made with *"don't have to,"* checking to see that the meaning is not confused with *cannot* and *must not*.

Exercise 9
EXPANSION
This is an appropriate context for a writing activity, possibly as homework. Ask Ss to write a paragraph or two on the *do's* and *don'ts* when visiting your home country. Remind them that a brief introductory statement or phrase is important in a descriptive paragraph. For example, *"If you want to visit (name of country), there are a few things you need to know . . ."*

Exercise 10

If your class did Exercise 2, you might remind Ss of some of the traffic signs they saw that were different in other countries. Such a reminder can serve as a pre-activity that links previous exercises to Step 3 of this exercise.

EXERCISE 10

The magazine article below is about traffic laws in different European countries.

STEP 1 Before you read the article, look at the following statements. Do you think they are <u>probably</u> true or <u>probably</u> false? Circle T (for true), or F (for false). After you finish reading, look at the statements again and change your answers if necessary.

1. In Germany, you mustn't use bad language or make rude and insulting gestures if you get angry with other drivers. T F
2. You must be careful when you honk your horn in Greece. T F
3. You have to honk your horn when you pass another car in Gibraltar. T F
4. You cannot flash your lights at other drivers in Luxembourg. T F
5. In Scandinavian countries, you cannot drive with your headlights on during the day. T F
6. You have to drive more slowly at night in Austria. T F
7. In Romania, you don't have to keep your car clean. T F

How not to collide with local road laws

If you are planning on driving in Europe, you should know that driving laws and customs vary greatly from country to country.

Be careful not to allow frustration with other drivers to develop into swearing or offensive gestures in Germany: They are illegal. Displays of anger are not welcome in Greece, either. It is unlawful to honk your horn too loudly (although this may surprise many visitors to Athens!). In Gibraltar, using your horn at all is completely prohibited.

In Luxembourg, the law says that drivers have to flash their lights each time they pass another car. In Scandinavian countries, you have to drive with your headlights dimmed during the day, but in Poland, this is obligatory only in winter.

Make sure you fill your tank before you get on the Autobahn in Germany: It is illegal to run out of gas. Speed limits vary too, not just from country to country, but within countries as well. Beware of speed limits that change from one moment to the next. For example, in Austria, speed limits are lower at night and in France, the speed limit on the freeways drops from 130 kmh to 110 kmh when it rains. (And if the French police catch you speeding, you have to pay a massive on-the-spot fine!)

But perhaps the strangest law of all is from Romania, where you must not drive your car if it is dirty.

Adapted from *The European* (Magazine Section), 6/9/95.

ANSWER KEY

Exercise 10

Step 1: Corrected answers, based on the reading:
1. T 2. T 3. T 4. T 5. F 6. T 7. F

STEP 2   Make statements using *must, have to, cannot, mustn't,* or *do not have to* about the following topics from the article.

1.   Driving in Poland during the winter: _____

_____

2.   Driving on the Autobahn in Germany: _____

_____

3.   Driving on the freeways in France: _____

_____

STEP 3   Are there any traffic laws that are sometimes confusing to visitors to the country you come from? Describe them to the rest of your class, using *must, have to, cannot, must not,* and *do not have to* where you can.

SUGGESTIONS
Step 3

1. Depending on the variety of your and your Ss' experience with and knowledge of international traffic laws, this step can be conducted as a whole-class discussion or, if there is less varied experience, as a written exercise.

2. If you feel Ss need more writing practice, assign a 1 or 2 paragraph description of the traffic laws of a country Ss are familiar with. Remind them to use the appropriate modals and phrasal modals covered in this unit.

3. If you feel Ss can benefit from reading and editing practice, use the descriptions Ss have written in a peer editing activity, in which a student exchanges his/her description with someone else's:

   a. Ss read each other's descriptions for content. Are all statements clear? If not, they can ask the writer of the description for clarification where necessary.

   b. Ss check each other's descriptions for the grammar targeted in this unit. Did they use the modals and phrasal modals *must, have to , cannot, mustn't,* or *don't have to* appropriately?

ANSWER KEY

Exercise 10

Step 2: Answers may vary slightly but are likely to be:

1. You must/have to drive with your headlines dimmed during the day.   2. You mustn't/cannot run out of gas.   3. You must/have to reduce your speed when it rains. You cannot/must not drive as fast as the "normal' speed limit when it rains.

Because some of these forms can be troublesome to some Ss, additional experience with error correction is helpful and, in addition, will prepare Ss for doing Exercises 11 and 12.

SUGGESTION

For each example in the focus box, alter the tense of the modal so that it is incorrect, or use a modal that is inappropriate. (Or make sentences of your own). Ss then provide the correct modal/phrasal modal.

Example: (d) *He must to train last night.* Students change it to: *He had to train last night.* Or: (e) *He doesn't have to cross-train last year.* Students change it to: *He didn't have to cross-train last year.*

Talking about the Present, Past, and Future with *Have To* and *Must*

PRESENT	PAST	FUTURE
must	—	must
have to	had to	have to/will have to
do not have to	did not have to	do not have to/will not have to

EXAMPLES	EXPLANATIONS
(a) Olympic athletes **have to** train every day. **(b)** Olympic athletes **must** train every day. **(c)** High school athletes **don't have to** train every day.	Use *must (not)*, *have to*, and *do not have to* to show that something is (or is not) necessary in the present.
(d) He **had to** train hard last night. **(e)** He **didn't have to** cross-train last year.	Notice that there is no past tense form of *must* when it shows necessity. Use *had to* to show that something was necessary in the past.
(f) He **must** start a special diet tomorrow. OR **(g)** He **has to** start a special diet tomorrow. OR **(h)** He **will have to** start a special diet to-morrow. **(i)** He **doesn't have to** start a special diet tomorrow. **(j)** He **will not (won't) have to** start a spe-cial diet tomorrow.	You can use *must*, *have to*, or *will have to* to talk about events that will be necessary in the near future. You can also use negative forms *do not have to* or *will not have to* to talk about the near future.

EXERCISE 11

Maggie and her friend Jan are talking about jobs. Maggie is describing a job she had last summer. Complete their conversation with *have to,* and *do not have to* in the present, past, or future.

Maggie: The worst job I ever had was last summer, when I worked as a waitress in that tourist restaurant down by the aquarium.

Jan: Oh really? What was so terrible about it?

Maggie: For a start, I (1) _____ get up at 5:00 A.M. and, as I didn't have a car then, I (2) _____ walk.

Jan: Why didn't you take the bus?

Maggie: It doesn't start running until 7:00, and I (3) _____ be at the restaurant by 6:30 to set the tables for breakfast.

Jan: That's tough. Did they make you wear a silly uniform or anything?

Maggie: No, thank goodness. We (4) _____ wear any special uniforms, except for hats. We all (5) _____ wear really stupid sailor caps. Mine was too small and it kept falling off.

Jan: So you're probably not planning on working there again next summer.

Maggie: Absolutely not. I'm earning twice as much at my present job, so with a bit of luck, I'll be able to save some money and I (6) _____ work at all next summer.

Jan: That sounds good. What's your present job like?

Maggie: It's much better. I start work at 11:00 A.M.

Jan: So you (7) _____ get up early. What about weekends?

Maggie: I (8) _____ work on weekends, but if I want to make some extra money, I can go in on Saturdays. It's ideal.

Jan: Maybe I should try to get a job there. Our landlord raised the rent last month and I just can't afford to stay there on my present salary.

Exercise 11

It's fun to do this exercise orally, as a "real," natural-sounding dialogue.

SUGGESTIONS

1. If you choose to do this orally, first give Ss a few minutes to work with a partner, and check to make sure they have answers for each blank. This will allow the reading to move along smoothly so that the class is not waiting for the speakers to search for the answers.

2. Because this dialogue is so long, it is appropriate to switch speakers halfway through—right before or after Maggie's line's (4) and (5) in the middle of the page.

ANSWER KEY

Exercise 11

(1) had to   (2) had to   (3) had to
(4) didn't have to   (5) had to   (6) won't
have to   (7) don't have to   (8) don't have to

Exercise 12

As with Exercise 11, these dialogues are also suitable as short mini-dramas.

SUGGESTION

If you have some actors/performers in your class (or even if you think you don't—you may be surprised!):

1. Give them a few minutes to rehearse, so that the dialogue sounds "natural."
2. Before they start, remind them to link words together smoothly, to use reduced forms/contractions (see Focus 2), and to use appropriate intonation—falling intonation at the end of a statement, rising intonation at the end of a yes-no question, and louder volume, higher pitch for important or surprising information (as in Conversation B).
3. Model a dialogue with a student.

UNIT GOAL REVIEW

Ask Ss to look at the goals on the opening page of the unit again. Help them understand how much they have accomplished in each area. For example, make sentences that contrast *have to* and *have got to* (as in Focus 3 and Exercise 5) and have Ss tell you what the difference in meaning is (goal #3). Or ask them to correct ill-formed sentences that confuse *have to/had to/will have to* (see Focus 6), or that use *must* in a past tense context (goal #5).

EXERCISE 12

Read the four conversations below carefully and complete the missing parts with *must, (do not) have to,* or *have got to.*

Conversation A

Ann has just finished talking on the phone with Tom. When she hangs up the phone, her friend Bill wants to know about their conversation.

Bill: You sound worried. Is Tom having problems?

Ann: Tom's landlord sold the apartment house, so Tom (1) _____ find another place to live.

Bill: Oh, that's too bad. When (2) _____ (he) move out of his apartment?

Ann: I think he (3) _____ move out by the end of the month.

Conversation B

Emily, a five-year-old, is playing outside. Her mother, who is watching from the house, suddenly runs out to her. A big car zooms by.

Emily's mother: Emily! You (4) _____ be more careful! Don't cross the street without looking for cars!

Emily: But I didn't see the car!

Emily's mother: You (5) _____ look in both directions before you cross the street.

Conversation C

Outside the classroom, you hear a conversation between your teacher and Wang, one of your classmates.

Your teacher: Wang, I'm afraid this is the last time I'm going to tell you this. You (6) _____ hand in your homework on time.

Wang: I know, I know. But . . .

Your teacher: No more excuses! You really (7) _____ try to keep up with the class if you want to pass.

Conversation D

It's the end of the school year. Ron and Marion have just had their last class.

Ron: Vacation time at last! We (8) _____ come to school for two whole months!

Marion: Not me. My grades were bad, so I (9) _____ go to summer school all summer, without one single day off.

Ron: I know how that feels. I flunked physics two years ago, and I (10)_____ read physics books while my friends were going to the beach every day.

Use Your English

ACTIVITY 1: SPEAKING

In Exercise 6, you saw some examples of signs. The local tourist board has asked you and your classmates to create some signs for tourists visiting the area. Get together with two or three other students and draw at least three signs. For example: *You mustn't feed the ducks. You must have exact change for the bus. You mustn't drink this water.* Draw each sign on a different piece of paper. Do not write anything next to the sign—your classmates must guess what it is. Look at their signs and write down what you think they mean.

ACTIVITY 2: SPEAKING

In this activity, you will be comparing your childhood memories with your classmates'. Think back to when you were a child. Write down five things you had to do then that you do not have to do now. Then write down five things you did not have to do then that you have to do now. Next, compare your list with those of two or three other classmates and be ready to report on your findings to the rest of the class.

YOU		YOUR CLASSMATES	
CHILDHOOD	Now	CHILDHOOD	Now
1	1	1	1
2	2	2	2
3	3	3	3
4	4	4	4
5	5	5	5

USE YOUR ENGLISH

The activities in the purple pages at the end of the unit contain situations that should naturally elicit the structures covered in the unit. When Ss are doing these activities in class, you can circulate and listen to see if they are using the structures accurately. Have they achieved the goals presented at the beginning of the unit?

Activity 1
VARIATION

This activity can be turned into a competitive game, if you are comfortable with that kind of activity. In this case,

1. Have Ss write down what they think the sign means *in silence*.
2. Hold up each sign, having Ss display their written answers. The student who got the most signs "right" (according to the intention of the sign-maker) wins.

Activity 2
EXPANSION

For more writing practice, Ss can use the information they have collected to make a short written report on some of their more interesting findings.

1. Have volunteers read their reports aloud to their class, or you select the reports that will be read.
2. Ss listening to the report can take notes on the things that the writer had to do when he/she was a child that he/she doesn't have to do now, paying particular attention to the use of the phrasal modals *had to, don't have to,* and *didn't have to.*

Activity 3

See ideas for Exercises 3 and 4 from this unit.

Activity 4

Play textbook audio. The tapescript for this listening activity appears on p. 508 of this book.

EXPANSION

If this class is conducted in the U.S. or if there are a number of people who have had long-term experiences in the U.S. available to talk with Ss, expand this activity by having Ss interview these people on the topics *not* discussed in the tape.

1. Ss can conduct their interviews in pairs or small groups, asking the speaker to elaborate about important details.
2. Proceed with Steps 3 and 4 to check to see if their predictions about what a person has to do are correct (Step 3) and if they used modals and phrasal modals expressing necessity and prohibition (Step 4).

ACTIVITY 3: SPEAKING

Do you know how to get a driver's license in any other countries in the world? What do you have to do to get a license there? In what ways is it different here? Talk to your classmates and find out what they know. Be ready to report on your findings.

ACTIVITY 4: SPEAKING/LISTENING

STEP 1 Do you know what a person has to do in order to get any of the following?
- a green card (for permanent residence in the United States)
- a Social Security number
- a marriage license
- a license for a gun
- United States citizenship

With a partner, make a list of what you think a person must or has to do in order to get any of these.

STEP 2 Listen to the tape. You will hear somebody discussing **one** of the above topics. Which topic is the speaker talking about? What does she or he think someone has to do? Make notes on the chart below.

TOPIC	WHAT YOU HAVE TO DO

STEP 3 Now look at the list you and your partner made on the same topic. How many differences and how many similarities can you find?

STEP 4 Listen to the tape again. Write down any sentences containing examples of modals and phrasal modals expressing necessity and prohibition.

Activity 4
Steps 2 and 4: Check tapescript for complete sentences (p. 508).
Step 2:
Topic: Becoming a U.S. citizen
Have to: Be born in this country, get a green card, take a test, go to a ceremony, say the pledge of allegiance

Step 4:
don't have to be from here
don't have to have been born here
have to get a green card
have to take a test
have to go to a special ceremony

ACTIVITY 5: SPEAKING/LISTENING/READING

STEP 1 Choose a topic from Activity 4 that you don't know anything about.

STEP 2 Interview three different native speakers of English and ask them to tell you what they know about the topic. For example, you can ask: What does somebody have to do if they want to get a license for a gun here? Tape-record your interviews. Afterwards, listen to your tape. Did all the people you interviewed tell you the same information? Or did they all tell you different things? Make a list of all the things they told you that a person has to do and share your findings with the rest of your class.

STEP 3 Listen to your tape again, but this time, listen for the language that was used. Write down any sentences containing *must, have to, must not, cannot, do not have to, have got to,* or *should.*

STEP 4 Go to a library and find all the information you can about your topic. Be sure to ask a librarian if you need help locating information. Alternatively, if you have access to a computer and the World Wide Web, you may be able to find all the information there. Take notes on what you read. Are there any differences between the information you found in the library (or on the World Wide Web) and the information that people told you? Make a list of any differences and be ready to share them with the rest of your class.

STEP 5 Write down any examples of the language practiced in this unit that you found in your reading.

ACTIVITY 6: WRITING

A friend of yours is interested in studying at a North American university. Write him or her a letter explaining what he or she will have to do in order to enter a university.

Activity 5

This activity expands on the suggestions for Activity 4 (on the previous page of this teacher's edition). Here, Step 2 asks Ss to interview *three* different speakers; Step 4 asks Ss to elaborate further by conducting library research or research on the Web.

SUGGESTION

If Ss have done all of these activities, then assigning a comparison-contrast essay about the differences they found in their sources of information is appropriate. Or, if you feel Ss would benefit more from presenting this information orally, follow the suggestions in the last part of Step 4.

Activity 6
SUGGESTION

This activity can be conducted as an in-class writing assignment, especially if you are interested in seeing what modals and phrasal modals of necessity and obligation naturally appear. Don't be surprised if few of these structures are used. But if they aren't, you can follow this activity up with a second draft, where Ss re-write their letter, this time incorporating *must, have to, cannot, mustn't,* and *don't have to* whenever appropriate.

It may be helpful for Ss to do these revisions in pairs, since another student may have a "fresh" perspective.

The test for this unit can be found on pp. 440–441 of this book. The answers are on p. 442.

Unit 12

UNIT OVERVIEW

This unit addresses structures used to express likes and dislikes in English, including expressions such as *too, so,* and *(n)either.*

UNIT GOALS

Before you point out the goals of this unit, find examples of each goal as illustration and put these examples up on the board or on an overhead transparency.

OPENING TASK

Returning to the food theme, students (Ss) engage in discussion about their likes and dislikes in an informal activity. Because the goal of the Opening Task is to determine Ss' familiarity with the structures used in this unit, do not correct Ss for inaccuracy; instead, note the language they already seem to be familiar with so that you can focus your later discussions on new information or trouble spots.

SETTING UP THE TASK

To provide background for the task, introduce the topic of food.

SUGGESTION

Do a brainstorming activity, giving the class a minute to write down a list of the foods that they like and a minute to write a list of those that they don't like.

UNIT 12

EXPRESSING LIKES AND DISLIKES

UNIT GOALS:

- To express similarity with *too/either* and *so/neither*
- To express similarity with *so* clauses
- To use short phrases to show agreement and weak agreement
- To express likes and dislikes with gerunds and infinitives

OPENING TASK
What Kind of Food Do You Like?

STEP 1 Work with a partner. One of you is A, the other is B. Talk about food that you like and don't like, and complete the chart together.

STEP 2 In the top left-hand box, write three kinds of food that A and B both like. In the top right-hand box, write three kinds of foods that A does not like, but B does. In the bottom left-hand box, write three kinds of food B doesn't like, but A does. In the last box, write three kinds of food that both A and B do not like.

A

	LIKES	DOESN'T LIKE
B LIKES	(A likes and B likes too.)	(A doesn't like, but B does)
B DOESN'T LIKE	(B doesn't like, but A does).	(B doesn't like, and A doesn't either.)

STEP 3 Share some of these findings with the class. Make statements with *like* and *dislike* (or *don't like*), such as:

I like _____ and _____ does too.
I don't like _____ but _____ does.
I don't like _____ and _____ doesn't either.

CONDUCTING THE TASK

Step 1

Be sure Ss understand the directions for all steps in this task. Remind Ss that this should be a discussion; they shouldn't use their notes while talking with their partner.

Step 2

Draw Ss' attention to the chart. Make an overhead projector transparency for a visual aid, if possible.

Step 3

Ss should use the sentences as a guide only. Encourage them to be creative in their statements.

If you write some of their examples on the board, you can use and/or correct them in Exercises 1 and 2.

CLOSING THE TASK

Point out that Ss will be returning to their statements in later exercises.

FOCUS 1

Point out that to avoid sounding repetitious, the expressions *do too* and *don't either* replace the previous verb phrase. For example:

A: *I love really strong coffee.*
B: *Hey, I do too!*
→ *Do too* replaces *love really strong coffee.*
A: *I don't eat out very often.*
B: *Actually, I don't either. It's too expensive in this city.*
→ *Don't either* replaces *don't eat out very often.*
Focus 2 will build on this information.

Exercise 1

Direct the Ss to return to their statements in the Opening Task.

Return to previous examples on the board or do a few new ones as a class before they complete the exercise in pairs.

Workbook Ex. 1, p. 93.
Answers: TE p. 494.

FOCUS 2

This focus box builds on the information in Focus 1. *So* is used in similar situations as *too, neither* in similar situations as *not either.* Point out the differences in word order.

FOCUS **1**

Expressing Similarity with Too and Either

EXAMPLES	EXPLANATIONS
(a) I like fruit **and** Roberta **does too.**	To avoid repetition in affirmative sentences (sentences without *not*), use *and* (X) *do/does too.*
(b) **NOT:** I like fruit, and Roberta likes fruit.	
(c) Roberta doesn't eat meat and I **don't either.**	To avoid repetition in negative sentences (sentences with *not*), use *and* (X) *do/doesn't either.*
(d) **NOT:** I don't eat meat, and Roberta doesn't eat meat.	

EXERCISE 1

Check the statements you made in the Opening Task on page 185. Did you use *too* and *either* correctly? Did you use *neither* or *so*? If not, rewrite these statements using *too, either, neither,* and *so.*

FOCUS **2**

Expressing Similarity with So and Neither

EXAMPLES	EXPLANATIONS
(a) I like fruit **and so does** Roberta.	Another way to avoid repetition is with *and so do/does* (X) in affirmative sentences, and with *and neither do/does* (X) in negative sentences.
(b) Roberta doesn't eat meat **and neither do I.**	Invert subject and verb after *so* and *neither.*

EXERCISE 2

Now work with a different partner and share the information on your charts in the Opening Task. Use this information to complete the following report. Make sure that your statements are not only grammatical but also true.

My classmates and I have strong opinions about the kinds of food we like and dislike. For example, _____ and so

_____ . _____

and neither _____ . _____

too. _____ either.

We also found other similarities in our taste in food. _____

either. _____ neither

_____ . _____

so _____ . _____

too.

FOCUS **3**

Expressing Similarity with *So*

EXAMPLES	EXPLANATIONS
(a) I speak French and so **does** my mother. **(b)** My mother exercises every day and so **do** I.	Use *do* when you do not want to repeat the verb. Make sure that there is subject/verb agreement: *I do she/he does they/you do*
(c) I **can** speak French and so **can** she. **(d)** I **have** studied it and so **has** she. **(e)** I **am** happy and so **is** she.	Use an auxiliary verb (*can, have, should*) if the first verb uses one. Use *be* if the first verb is *be*.

Exercise 2

Be sure Ss switch partners for this exercise.

SUGGESTIONS

Rather than having Ss complete the exercise in their books, have them work directly on overhead transparencies. This will allow them to receive direct feedback on their accuracy as they present their reports to the class.

1. Make enough overhead transparencies of this exercise so that each pair has one.
2. Give each pair an overhead transparency marker, and have them fill out the report directly onto the transparency.
3. Direct each pair to come up and present their report.
4. Encourage the class to provide correction of errors.

Workbook Ex. 2, pp. 93–94.
Answers: TE p. 494.

FOCUS 3

This focus box returns to the use of *so* in expressing similarity, focusing on the form of the verbs that accompany it.

Grammar Note

Because *do* is the auxiliary verb of all present simple verbs (except *be*), it replaces these verbs in the phrase that replaces the present simple verb phrase:

*I **bike** to work every day and so **does** Leonard.*
*Jaro **writes** music and so **does** Wan.*
*Amanda **travels** a lot and so **do** Seamus and Myshka.*

With all other auxiliaries, the auxiliary is repeated:

*Doug **has** played the guitar all his life and so **has** Johnny.*

*I'**m** going to a show tonight and so **is** Holly.*

*Steve **will** go back to school and so **will** Claire.*

The same is true of *be* as a main verb:

*Heidi and Mike **are** vegetarians and so **is** Catie.*

Workbook Ex. 3, p. 94.
Answers: TE p. 494.

FOCUS 4

You can illustrate these short forms by making statements about your likes and call on Ss who (as you remember from their earlier exercises) share the same taste.

1. Model an example on the board, using the format of the examples in this focus box but substituting actual information from your class.
2. Make a statement that you know one of your Ss would agree with. The S responds with a short answer.
3. Write the exchange on the board, calling on the class to edit as you go.

EXERCISE 3

Match the first half of the sentences in column A with the second half in column B. Draw an arrow to show the connection. The first one has been done for you.

1. She is late
2. We saw it last night
3. They've never eaten there
4. She'll call you tomorrow
5. Barbara was looking sad
6. The children have seen that movie
7. You didn't do the right thing
8. I can't play tennis
9. Her bike wasn't cheap
10. Scott doesn't have any money
11. The secretary speaks Spanish

a. and so have I.
b. and Peter didn't either.
c. and my brother can't either.
d. and so is her boyfriend.
e. and we do too.
f. and her friend was too.
g. and so will I.
h. and neither do we.
i. and we haven't either.
j. and they did too.
k. and neither was her car.

FOCUS **4**

Showing Agreement with Short Phrases

EXAMPLES	EXPLANATIONS
(a) Tina: I love going to movies. Rob: **So do I.** **(b)** Tina: I never go to violent movies. Rob: **Neither do I.** **(c)** Tina: I can't stand watching violence. Rob: **I can't either.** **(d)** Tina: I prefer comedies. Rob: Really? **I do too.**	Short phrases such as *so do I, neither do I, I can't either* and *I do too*, are used to show agreement with somebody else's opinions and ideas. They are very common in informal conversation.

EXERCISE 4

Read the comic strip. Can you find the missing parts of the conversation in the list below? Write the letters in the appropriate cartoon bubble.

1. I'm getting too old for this kind of thing.

2. My back is killing me.

3. I can't keep going for much longer.

4. I'll certainly sleep well tonight.

5. I really don't know why I'm doing this.

6. Actually I think people who run marathons are crazy.

7. I certainly won't do this again.

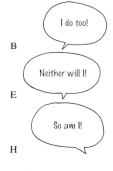

8. Great race! I loved every minute!

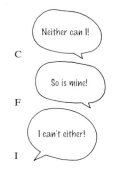

9. I can't wait for the next one.

A. I don't either!

B. I do too!

C. Neither can I!

D. So did I!

E. Neither will I!

F. So is mine!

G. I will too!

H. So am I!

I. I can't either!

Exercise 4

Have Ss do this activity for homework or in-class pairwork.

Make a copy of the comic on an overhead transparency and model the first square of the comic strip.

EXPANSION

Follow up the activity with a discussion on humor. Since different cultures often have conflicting ideas about what is and isn't funny, lead the discussion with specific questions:

Do the Ss think this comic strip funny? What makes it funny? Would people in your Ss' country(s) find this type of humor funny? If not, how could they change this one to make it funnier?

Workbook Ex. 4, p. 95.
Answers: TE p. 494.

ANSWER KEY

Exercise 4

Responses, in the order of the comic strip pictures, are as follows: **1.** So am I!   **2.** So is mine!   **3.** I can't either.   **4.** I will too!   **5.** I don't either!   **6.** I do too!   **7.** Neither will I!   **8.** So did I!   **9.** Neither can I!

FOCUS 5

1. Point out to Ss that they don't always have to agree with the speaker in English (this may need to be emphasized with some cultures in which it is considered impolite not to agree). *Hedges* are ways of avoiding a direct agreement without completely disagreeing. *Kind of* and *sort of* mean "a little bit" or "in a way".

2. Explain that these expressions are less formal than the previously mentioned structures; the result is that they usually are reserved for spoken English and are, therefore, often reduced ("sorta" and "kinda") in pronunciation.

Exercise 5

SUGGESTIONS

1. After Ss complete the dialog, correct the activity as a class, using the exercise on an overhead transparency as a visual aid.

2. Ss practice the corrected dialog in pairs, first using their book and, with some practice, from memory.

3. Ss can then improvise a similar conversation from their own experience, using the one in the book as a model.

FOCUS **5**

▶ **Short Phrases or Hedges**

EXAMPLES	EXPLANATIONS
(a) Sue: I love ballet. What about you? Tien: **Kind of.** (b) Sue: Do you like opera? Tien: **Sort of.** (c) Sue: I hate football. Tien: **So do I.**	If you do not agree strongly with the speaker's opinions, you can use hedges (*sort of, kind of*) in informal conversation. In fast speech, *sort of* sounds like "sorta" and *kind of* sounds like "kinda." Hedges follow a question, while short phrases (*So do* I, I *don't either*) follow a statement.

EXERCISE 5

Claire and Chris have just met at a party and are finding out how much they have in common.

Look at the chart showing their likes and dislikes.

✔✔ = a lot   ✔ = a little

Use the information from the chart to complete the conversation using hedges where appropriate. The first one has been done for you.

	LIKES		DISLIKES
Chris	swimming ✔✔ cats ✔✔ cooking ✔✔	hiking ✔✔ music ✔ Chinese food ✔✔	TV ✔✔ getting up in the morning ✔✔ country music ✔✔
Claire	cats ✔ eating in restaurants ✔✔ Chinese food ✔✔	cooking ✔ music ✔✔ swimming ✔✔ hiking ✔	country music ✔✔ getting out of bed ✔✔ staying home ✔✔ watching TV ✔✔

Chris: Well, let me see . . . what are some of my favorite things? The ocean . . . I love swimming in the ocean.

Claire: (1) ___so do I___. Maybe we should go for a swim sometime.

Chris: Yes, that'd be great! Do you like hiking too?

Claire: (2) _____. In general, I prefer to be active. I mean, I don't like sitting at home and watching TV.

Chris: (3) _____. But I don't like getting up in the morning.

190   UNIT 12

Claire: Well, (4) _____. Most people don't like getting out of bed in the morning! What about music? Do you like music?

Chris: (5) _____. I don't know too much about it, actually.

Claire: Really? I love all kinds of music, except for country. I hate country!

Chris: (6) _____. We certainly agree on that one! What else? I love cooking, do you?

Claire: (7) _____. I really prefer eating out in restaurants, especially in Chinatown. I really love Chinese food.

Chris: (8) _____. I've heard that the new Chinese restaurant on Grant Avenue is supposed to be really good.

Claire: (9) _____. Why don't we give it a try?

Chris: That sounds good. By the way, I have six cats. Do you like cats?

Claire: Well, (10) _____.

Chris: That's O.K.—as long as you don't *hate* them. . . .

EXERCISE 6

One way to meet people is through personal ads in newspapers or magazines. These personal ads appeared in a local newspaper. Read them quickly and then read the statements that follow. Circle T (true) if you think the statement is true and F (false) if you think it is false.

(A) COULD THIS BE YOU?
You are attractive, slim, and athletic. You like dancing, eating candlelit dinners, and walking on the beach by moonlight. Like me, you also enjoy camping and hiking. You love dogs and you don't smoke. If you are the woman of my dreams, send a photo to Box 3092.

(B) BEAUTY & BRAINS
Warm, humorous, well-educated SF loves walking on the beach, dancing, cycling, and hiking. Seeks intelligent life partner with computer interests. P.S.—I'm allergic to cats, dogs, and smoking. Box 875.

(C) I'VE GOT YOU ON MY WAVELENGTH
Athletic, professional, DF, animal lover seeks active man who knows how to treat a lady. Box 4021.

(D) A FEW OF MY FAVORITE THINGS:
Cooking for my friends, cycling, walking on the beach with my dog, wise and witty women. I can't stand: snobs, cheap wine, jogging, people who smoke, women who wear makeup. DM looking for a special woman. Box 49.

1. A likes walking on the beach and so do D and B.   T   F
2. B does not like smokers and neither do A and C.   T   F
3. Cooking for friends is one of B's favorite pastimes.   T   F
4. D does not like women who wear makeup.   T   F
5. D likes dancing, and A does too.   T   F
6. A wants to find someone who likes hiking, and so does D.   T   F
7. Jogging and cycling are two of B's favorite sports.   T   F

Do you think any of these people would make a good couple? If so, why? If not, why not?

Exercise 6

Decide if you want Ss to use dictionaries (monolingual or bilingual) ahead of time. Be prepared to explain the abbreviations:
SF (=single female)
DF (=divorced female)
DM (=divorced male)

This exercise introduces the forms discussed in Focus 6 (p. 192). It is continued in Exercise 7 (p. 192) and can lead to more communicative practice in Activity 6 (p. 195).

SUGGESTIONS

1. If you choose to set the exercise without dictionaries, have them read in pairs so they can help each other with unfamiliar vocabulary.
2. Before they complete the true/false statements, be sure to discuss unfamiliar vocabulary.

Workbook Ex. 5, pp. 95–96.
Answers: TE p. 494.

ANSWER KEY

Exercise 6
1. T   2. F   3. F   4. T   5. F   6. F
7. F

Grammar Note

Gerunds *(singing, running, snowboarding)* and infinitives *(to sing, to run, to snowboard)* are not contrasted in *Grammar Dimensions 2* because the difference in their meaning is not particularly important when expressing likes and dislikes. However, here is some background on these structures:

1. Gerunds and infinitives are nouns that are formed from verbs. They "act" like nouns in the sentence:
   *Karen likes **coffee** in the morning.*
   *Karen likes **dancing** in the evening. -or-*
   *Karen likes **to dance** in the evening.*
2. Gerunds are generally used when talking about *activities*, while infinitives often express *intentions*:
   *If Wan has time, **mountain-biking** is his favorite activity.*
   *Jeff plans **to mountain-bike** with Wan next weekend.*

Exercise 7

Returning to their answers for Exercise 6 (p. 191), Ss focus on the use of gerunds and infinitives in the statements.

Workbook Exs. 6–8, pp. 96–98.
Answers: TE p. 494.

UNIT GOAL REVIEW

Ask Ss to look at the goals on the opening page of the unit again. Help them understand how much they have accomplished in each area.

SUGGESTION

Take an example used previously in class and elicit from Ss the way to rewrite it on the board, using the various forms (*so, too, (n)either*, gerunds and infinitives).

▶ Likes and Dislikes with Gerunds and Infinitives

EXAMPLES	EXPLANATIONS
(a) **Cooking** is my favorite hobby. **(b)** I love **cooking.** Do you? **(c)** My favorite hobby is **cooking.**	*Gerunds* (nouns formed from verb + *-ing*) can be used as: • the subject of a sentence • the object of a sentence • the complement of a sentence (something needed to complete the sentence)
(d) I like **to cook.** **(e)** I don't like **to swim.** **(f)** I hate **to go** to the dentist. **(g)** AWKWARD: **To cook** is my favorite hobby.	*Infinitives* (*to* + verb) are also used in talking about likes and dislikes. In this context, infinitives are usually used as objects of sentences or as complements, but they sound awkward as subjects.
(h) I don't like **swimming.** **(i)** I hate **going** to the dentist	When talking about likes and dislikes, you can usually use infinitives or gerunds. The verbs *hate, like,* and *love* can be followed by either a gerund or an infinitive.

EXERCISE 7

Look back at Exercise 6.

1. Underline all the gerunds.
2. Check (✔) all the gerunds that are subjects and circle the gerunds that are objects or complements.
3. Replace the gerunds with infinitives where possible.
4. Rewrite sentence 2, using a gerund or an infinitive.

Use Your English

ACTIVITY 1 : SPEAKING

The purpose of this activity is to share information with one other person and then to report to the rest of the class on what you find. In sharing information with your partner, try to find out **how many things you have in common.** Some ideas for starting your conversation are given below. When you have nothing more to say on this topic, decide on another one and find out what you have in common on that topic. Use the chart for your notes.

TOPIC	NOTES
family	some ideas: brothers and sisters?/ grandparents alive?/father older than mother?

ACTIVITY 2 : SPEAKING

Form teams. Your job as a team is to find as many similarities as possible among the pairs of things listed below. The team that finds the most similarities is the winner.

1. an apple and an orange
2. learning a foreign language and learning to ride a bike
3. tennis and golf
4. hiking and jogging

USE YOUR ENGLISH

While the intent of these activities is to elicit naturally the structures practiced in this unit, allow Ss to communicate without interruption during these activities.

Activity 1

1. Be sure all Ss are familiar with the term *in common.*
2. Tell Ss to focus more on having a natural conversation than on filling in the chart.
3. They can use their notes from the chart to help in their oral report to the class.

SUGGESTION

As writing and editing practice, have Ss write up their report for homework. Then have the pairs meet together to read and edit their partner's report before handing it in to you.

Activity 2
SUGGESTION

1. Set a time limit ahead of time.
2. Have teams make their lists directly on the board so that the whole class can check and review answers together.

Activity 3

Be sure Ss understand the rules of the game before they begin. Reiterate that each half of the statement goes on a **separate** card.

SUGGESTIONS

1. Have Ss mark "A" or "B" on the backs of the appropriate cards.
2. Circulate around the room to help settle disputes.

ACTIVITY 3 : SPEAKING

Form pairs or groups of three.

STEP 1 Think of fifteen to twenty statements using *so/too/either/neither*. Make sure they are meaningful. Write each statement on two cards, like this:

A	B
My parents live in Paris I don't like broccoli	and so does my sister and they don't either

Therefore, if you have twenty statements, you will have forty cards.

STEP 2 Get together with another pair or threesome. Place all the A cards in one pile and all the B cards in another pile. Shuffle each deck of cards carefully.

STEP 3 Put the A pile face-down on the table. Then distribute the B cards among the players. Do not look at the cards; place them face-down on the table in front of you.

STEP 4 The first player turns the first card from the A pile on the table and puts the first card from his or her B pile beside it. The player must not look at his or her card before putting it down on the table. The object of the game is to create meaningful sentences. If the two cards on the table do not make a meaningful match, the next player puts his or her B card down. The game continues in this way until a meaningful match is created. The first player to spot a match shouts "Match" to stop the game. If the match is acceptable, he or she collects all the B cards on the table. The next A card is then turned over and the game continues.

STEP 5 The player with the most cards at the end is the winner. This game should be played as quickly as possible.

ACTIVITY 4: SPEAKING/LISTENING

STEP 1 Make a chart similar to the one in the Opening Task on page 185 and find out more about your classmates' likes and dislikes. You can ask about movies/movie stars/types of music/singers/musicians/sports/writers/books. Tape-record your conversations or interviews.

STEP 2 Make a report on your findings. Listen to the tape to make sure your report is accurate. For example:

Recently I made a survey of my classmates' likes and dislikes. I asked them their opinions on several different topics and would now like to tell you about some of my findings . . .

STEP 3 Listen to the tape again. Did your classmates use short phrases such as *I do too, so do I, I don't either, neither do I, sort of,* and *kind of*? If not, what did they use instead to agree and disagree with each other?

ACTIVITY 5: LISTENING

Listen to the tape of people talking about what they like and dislike. Number the statements below in the order that you hear them. Mark the first statement as number 1 and so forth.

_____ I do too.

_____ So do I.

_____ I don't either.

_____ Neither do I.

_____ Sort of.

_____ Kind of.

ACTIVITY 6: WRITING

Write a personal ad for yourself like the ones in Exercise 6. Display the ads that the class writes and try to guess who wrote each ad.

Activity 4
VARIATION

Conduct Step 1 of this activity on an e-mail discussion list.

1. Ss post statements about their likes and dislikes. For example:
   Kaori: I like listening to most kinds of music, but I don't like hip-hop.
2. Others respond:
   Mehmet: Wow, Kaori, I don't like hip-hop, either! But I <u>do</u> like rap and funk . . . .
3. Allow the discussion to go without your involvement, but keep track of recurring problems to discuss in class.
4. Follow the other steps, doing them as reading and writing practice.

Activity 5

Play textbook audio. The transcript for this listening appears on p. 508 of this book. Check tapescript for answers.

Activity 6

Refer back to Exercise 6 (p. 191) for examples of personal ads.

SUGGESTIONS

Bring in real personal ads from an English-language newspaper.

1. Choose ones that have language appropriate to the level of your group.
2. Be sure to include an abbreviation key to explain expressions such as SWF (single white female) and ISO (in search of).
3. Have Ss complete the ads using the action jargon of these personal ads.

EXPANSION

When the activity is over, discuss as a class what Ss think makes a good couple.

The test for this unit can be found on pp. 443–444 of this book.
The answers are on p. 445.

TOEFL Test Preparation Exercises for Units 10–12 can be found on pp. 99–101 of the Workbook.
The answers are on p. 495 of this book.

Unit 13

UNIT OVERVIEW

Unit 13 provides practice with the present perfect used with *since* and *for*.

UNIT GOALS

Review the goals listed on this page to see what students (Ss) should be familiar with by the end of the unit.

OPENING TASK

Note: The purpose of this task is to generate talk about different periods in Michael Harris's medical history, naturally using different verb tenses to talk about different time frames. The problem-solving format focuses attention on meaning rather than form, which will allow you to see whether Ss are able to produce the forms spontaneously.

SETTING UP THE TASK

To stimulate discussion and prepare for the task, talk about going to the doctor. What kinds of information do doctors usually ask about? With a bit of luck, this may elicit many of the headings on the chart in Step 1.

UNIT 13

PRESENT PERFECT WITH SINCE AND FOR

UNIT GOALS:

- To use present perfect to show a connection between past and present situations
- To form correct sentences with present perfect
- To know how to use for and since correctly
- To know which verbs not to use with present perfect

OPENING TASK
Medical History

STEP 1 Quickly read the following medical form.

MEDICAL HISTORY
NAME: Michael James Harris
SEX: Male
DATE OF BIRTH: 5/13/56
MARITAL STATUS: Single
HEIGHT: 5 ft 11 in
WEIGHT: 185 lbs
SERIOUS ILLNESS(ES): None
TIME IN HOSPITAL: May 1973. Broke both legs in traffic accident
SMOKING: Stopped 10 years ago
EYESIGHT: Wears glasses for reading; started in 1987
DRINKING: 1 glass of wine with dinner
ALLERGIES: None
PRESENT PROBLEM: Headaches
WHEN PROBLEM STARTED: 2 months ago

STEP 2 Work with a partner and find details from Michael Harris's medical history to complete the following list. Find two things that happened in the past, two things that are true in the present, and two things that started in the past and have continued to the present. (The first one has been done for you.)

PAST

1. _He broke his legs._

2. _____

PRESENT

1. _____

2. _____

FROM PAST TO PRESENT

1. _____

2. _____

CONDUCTING THE TASK

S U G G E S T I O N S

1. Circulate and listen for Ss' current use of the simple past tense (example: he *broke*), the simple present tense (example: he *weighs*), the present perfect with *for* and *since* (example: he *has worn* glasses for reading *since* 1987/*for* 13 years).

2. Note the structures that seem to be problematic—for more than one student there are errors in form.

Step 2

If you feel that one student in the pair is doing most of the work, recommend that Ss take turns filling in the blanks.

REVIEWING THE TASK

Ss will probably have difficulty with the last category: Past to Present.

S U G G E S T I O N

Use this task as a bridge to the information in Focus 1. You can also point out that Exercises 1 to 4 follow up and build on the task and focus attention on accuracy, and more specifically—on using and forming the present perfect accurately.

ANSWER KEY

Opening Task
Answers may vary slightly, depending on what items Ss choose to talk about. They are likely to include the following:
PAST: **2.** He stopped smoking.

PRESENT: **1.** He drinks a glass of wine with dinner. **2.** He weighs 185 pounds.
FROM PAST TO PRESENT: **1.** Glasses **2.** Headaches

SUGGESTION

Ask Ss simple questions related to the examples. *When did you move here, Elanos? How about you, Maria? How long have you lived here?* etc. Have Ss listen to each other's answers for errors. Ask: *Did he/she form the tense correctly?* You can:

1. give the speaker the opportunity to correct himself/herself,
2. write the correct statement on the board or on an overhead transparency, or
3. ask Ss to provide correct/accurate statements for each other, either orally or in writing (on the board or on an overhead transparency).

▶ # Present Perfect: Connecting Past and Present

USE

EXAMPLES	EXPLANATIONS
PAST February: **(a)** I **moved** to New York. (simple past)	Use the simple past for completed actions in the past.
PRESENT September: **(b)** I **live** in New York now. (simple present)	Use the simple present for facts about present situations.
PAST AND PRESENT **(c)** I **have lived** in New York since February. **(d)** I **have lived** in New York for seven months. (present perfect)	Use the present perfect (*have* + past participle) to connect the past and present. One use of the present perfect is to tell us about something that began in the past and continues to the present. (For other uses of the present perfect, see Unit 14.)

EXERCISE 1

Use the information about Michael Harris from the Opening Task on page 197 to complete the doctor's report below. Circle the simple present, simple past, or present perfect.

Report on Michael Harris

Michael Harris spoke with me yesterday about serious headaches. He (1)

(a) has
(b) had   these
(c) has had

headaches for two months. His previous medical history is good. He (2)

(a) doesn't have
(b) didn't have any
(c) hasn't had

serious illnesses. In 1973, he (3)

(a) is
(b) was   in the hospital for three weeks, when he
(c) has been

(4)
(a) breaks
(b) broke   both legs in a car accident. He (5)
(c) has broken

(a) doesn't smoke;
(b) didn't smoke   now; he
(c) hasn't smoked;

(6)
(a) stops
(b) stopped   ten years ago, and he (7)
(c) has stopped

(a) doesn't smoke
(b) didn't smoke   since that time. He
(c) hasn't smoked

(8)
(a) wears
(b) wore   glasses when he reads and he (9)
(c) has worn

(a) wears
(b) wore   them since 1987. He
(c) has worn

(10)
(a) drinks
(b) drank   a little wine with dinner every night.
(c) has drunk

I examined Mr. Harris and did several tests. I asked him to return next week.

It's appropriate to have Ss read their answers aloud if you feel this kind of practice is helpful. In that case:

SUGGESTIONS

1. Specify that Ss read one complete statement rather than one answer (since some statements include two or more multiple-choice items).
2. Or ask Ss to compare their answers in pairs or groups of three and, when you regroup as a class, to raise questions about only those answers that they disagree on.

ANSWER KEY

Exercise 1
1. c **2.** c **3.** b **4.** b **5.** a **6.** b
7. c **8.** a **9.** c **10.** a

SUGGESTIONS

Check to see that Ss can form the present perfect correctly. You can do this by asking real questions that will naturally elicit the use of the different tenses.

1. To elicit the past tense, ask questions about particular events or particular dates, especially those relevant to the Ss in your classroom: *When did you first come to this school? Where were you during the (famous event)/when you first heard about (famous person's death/divorce/marriage)? What did you do on your 20th birthday?* etc.

2. To elicit the present perfect tense, ask *"Have you ever . . ."* or *"How long have you . . ."* questions.

3. For further ideas, and to review the forms of common irregular verbs, see Appendix 5 on page A-12. Examples: *Have you ever drunk herbal tea? How long have you known (student in class)?*

   Another option is to give Ss a few minutes to write their own questions, and then—if you want a lot of movement and activity in the room—ask them as interview questions, or as a "chain": One student asks the next student a question; that student answers it; that student asks the next student a question, etc.

   Think about what you want to do in the case of an error: See Focus 1 on page 198 for suggestions.

Workbook Ex. 3, p. 102.
Answers: TE p. 495.

Exercise 2

SUGGESTIONS

1. If you feel that most of the Ss will be challenged by this exercise (if they had problems with Step 2—Past to Present of the Opening Task), give them a few minutes to work individually or in pairs on the answers, and then review the answers as a whole class.

2. If you feel that most are ready to move ahead quickly, it may be more appropriate to have Ss compare their answers and ask questions about only those answers that they disagree on.

Forming the Present Perfect

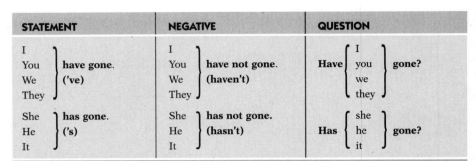

To form the present perfect use *have/has* + past participle.*

STATEMENT	NEGATIVE	QUESTION
I You We They } **have gone.** ('ve)	I You We They } **have not gone.** (haven't)	**Have** { I you we they } **gone?**
She He It } **has gone.** ('s)	She He It } **has not gone.** (hasn't)	**Has** { she he it } **gone?**

*See Appendix 5 on page A-13 for the past participles of some common irregular verbs.

EXERCISE 2

Write the questions that the doctor probably asked Mr. Harris in order to get these responses.

▶ **EXAMPLE:** 1. _Do you drink?_
   Yes, a little. I drink a glass of wine with dinner every night.

2. _____ ?
   Yes, I do. I wear them when I read.

3. _____ ?
   I started wearing them in 1987.

4. _____ ?
   Yes, I've worn them since 1987.

5. _____ ?
   No, I don't smoke now.

6. _____ ?
   I stopped ten years ago.

7. _____ ?
   No, I haven't smoked since that time.

8. _____ ?
   Yes, I have had these headaches for two months.

200 UNIT 13

ANSWER KEY

Exercise 2
2. Do you wear glasses? **3.** When did you start wearing them? **4.** Have you worn them for some time? **5.** Do you smoke? **6.** When did you stop? **7.** Have you smoked since then?/since that time? **8.** Have you had these headaches for some time?

EXERCISE 3

Work with a partner. Ask and answer questions about each other's medical history. Feel free to make up information on the following topics, or use Michael Harris's medical form (on page 197) to answer questions.

serious illnesses	time in hospital
smoking	drinking
eyesight	allergies
present problem	when problem started

EXERCISE 4

Go back to Exercises 1 and 2. Look for the words *for* and *since*. In the boxes below, write down the word or words that directly follow *for* and *since*. The first example is *two months* with *for,* from Exercise 1.

Since	For
	two months

What does this tell you about the use of *since* and *for*? What kinds of words or phrases follow *since* and *for*?

Exercise 3
SUGGESTIONS

1. Circulate while Ss are working to check that they are forming and using the present perfect accurately, and make note of the structure(s) that continue to be challenging for more than one or two Ss.
2. Review Focus 1 and 2 if you feel it would be helpful for Ss to hear the rules stated again.
3. Ask Ss to restate the rules in their own words. Ask, *When do you use the present tense? Can you give me an example? When do you use the present perfect?* etc.
4. Make incorrect questions and statements and ask Ss to restate your sentence correctly.

Exercise 4
SUGGESTION

Elicit Ss' answers and write them on the board or on an overhead transparency with a column for *since* examples and a column for *for* examples. Ss' answers to the last questions in this exercise will serve as a bridge to Focus 3, and, with luck, will resemble the Explanations in Focus 3.

VARIATION

To bridge from the previous exercise, substitute the answers from Exercise 4 to serve as the examples for this focus box. You might also want to have Ss practice answering and asking *"How long have you"* questions if you feel that this would be helpful. (Exercise 5, Exercise 6 and Focus 4 also follow up on this distinction.)

For and Since

EXAMPLES	EXPLANATIONS
(a) **for** two weeks (b) **for** ten years (c) **for** five minutes	*For* is used to show length of time (how long the period of time was).
(d) **since** 1985 (e) **since** my birthday (f) **since** I turned 40 (g) **since** Monday (h) **since** April	*Since* is used to show when a period of time began.

Exercise 5

If you have developed a rapport with your Ss, this is a suitable exercise for a group discussion. It has been our experience that, by this point, Ss have good insights about the differences (and similarities) in meaning in each pair. Thus, this discussion can be confidence-building. If Ss are successful with this exercise, point out to them that they are able to distinguish between subtle nuances in meaning—something most *native speaker* children and a number of adults cannot do.

EXERCISE 5

What difference in meaning (if any) is there in each pair of statements? Discuss with a partner.

1. (a) He lived here for ten years.
   (b) He has lived here for ten years.
2. (It is May. He moved here three months ago.)
   (a) He has lived here for three months.
   (b) He has lived here since February.
3. (a) They have worked for the same company for a long time.
   (b) They worked for the same company for a long time.
4. (They met in 1988.)
   (a) They have known each other for over 10 years.
   (b) They have known each other since 1988.
5. (It is July.)
   (a) Anthony hasn't watched TV for six months.
   (b) Anthony stopped watching TV in January.

ANSWER KEY

Exercise 5
1. (a) He doesn't live here now. (b) He still lives here.   2. No difference.   3. (a) They still work for the same company. (b) They don't still work for the same company.   4. No difference.   5. No difference.

FOCUS **4**

For and Since

EXAMPLES	EXPLANATIONS
(a) She's worked here **(for)** several years. **(b)** **(For)** how long have you lived here? **(c)** **Since** when have you lived here? **(d)** **NOT:** When have you lived here? **(e)** I've lived here **since** January. **(f)** **NOT:** I've lived here January.	The word *for* can be omitted in statements. *For* can also be omitted in questions. *Since* cannot be omitted. *"How long . . ."* is more common than *"Since when . . ."* in questions.

EXERCISE 6

Look at the hotel register below. How many people are staying in the hotel right now? Who has stayed there the longest?

Hotel Beresford Arms

701 Polk Street ▪ San Francisco, CA 94109
(415) 493-0443   Date: 3/11

Guest	Check-in	Check-Out
Mr. Cruise	3/3	
B. Simpson	3/1	
Mr. and Mrs. Kowlowski	3/8	
Mr. and Mrs. Gordon	3/2	3/8
Ms. Chapman	3/2	
Mr. Nixon	3/2	3/5
Maria da Costa	3/6	
Yee Mun Lina	3/4	

Use the information from the register to make statements with the words given below.

1. Mr. and Mrs. Gordon/for

2. Maria da Costa/since

3. Yee Mun Ling/since

4. B. Simpson/for

5. Mr. and Mrs. Kowlowski/for

6. Ms. Chapman/since

7. Mr. Cruise/for

8. Mr. Nixon/for

Present Perfect with Since and For   **203**

SUGGESTIONS

1. For continued practice with *for* and *since,* use the information from Exercise 3, Ss' own medical history (real or fictional), to ask and answer questions.

2. If you used the suggestions provided for Focus 2 and 3 in this Instructor's Manual, you can use that information as well to ask and answer questions using *since* and *for,* or omitting *for.*

3. Or have Ss ask each other questions.

Exercise 6

Check to make sure that Ss can interpret the chart. For example, ask: *When did Mr. Cruise check in?* Answer: *On March 3rd/the third of March.* (You might have to explain that it is the norm in the United States to put the month first, and then the day, while in some countries it is the other way around: 3/1 would be the third of January/January 3rd.) Ask: *When did Mr. Cruise check out?* Answer: *He hasn't checked out yet.*

VARIATIONS

1. If you want more "talk time," have Ss work in pairs or small groups so that each student has the opportunity to give at least two or three answers. You can circulate to check for accuracy.

2. If you feel that it would be beneficial to do this exercise as a whole class—if there seem to be continuing problems using/omitting *since* and *for* correctly, it would be appropriate to do this aloud, item by item.

FOCUS **5**

SUGGESTIONS

Give further examples of verbs that aren't normally used with the present perfect and *for,* using the six verbs in Focus 5. You might want to contrast correct usage with incorrect usage, and ask Ss to tell you what's wrong with your incorrect sentence. For example, why can't you say *"I've begun to study English three years ago."* but you can say *"I began to study English three years ago."*?

Workbook Ex. 7, pp. 107–108.
Answers: TE p. 495.

Exercise 7

This exercise is appropriate for pairs or small groups since it can provide Ss with the opportunity for practice both in using the target structures and in explaining and defending their answers. Circulate while Ss are working to check for accuracy. Note items Ss disagree on (if any), and/or ask Ss to raise questions on those items that they couldn't agree on.

Verbs Not Used with Present Perfect and *For*

EXAMPLES	EXPLANATIONS
(a) Shin **arrived** in the U.S. three years ago.	Some verbs talk about an action that happens all at once, an action that doesn't continue for a period of time.
(b) NOT: Shin has arrived in the U.S. for three years.	
(c) Shin **has lived** in the U.S. for three years.	In (c) we understand that it is the living in the U.S. that continues, not the arriving.
begin arrive meet *end leave stop*	For the same reason, these verbs are not usually used with present perfect and *for.*

EXERCISE 7

Rewrite these sentences using the present perfect and *since* or *for.*

▶ **EXAMPLE:**   Karen wears glasses. She started to wear glasses when she was a child.

Karen has worn glasses since she was a child.

1. He works for the TV station. He started working there eight years ago.
2. They are married. They got married in 1962.
3. She knows how to fix a car. She learned how to do it a long time ago.
4. Tom rides his bike to work. He started to do it when his car broke down.
5. I wanted to go to China several years ago. I still want to go now.
6. My brother started painting when he was in college, and he still paints now.
7. I was afraid of bats when I was a child, and I am afraid of them now.
8. My mother is in France. She went there last week.
9. My sister runs two miles every morning before breakfast. She started to do this when she was fifteen years old.
10. They go to Cape Cod every summer. They started to do this twelve years ago.

ANSWER KEY

Exercise 7
1. He has worked for the TV station for eight years.   2. They have been married since 1962.   3. She has known how to fix a car for a long time.   4. Since his car broke down, Tom has ridden his bike to work.   5. I have wanted to go to China for several years.   6. My brother has painted since he was in college.   7. I have been afraid of bats since I was a child.   8. My mother has been in France since last week.   9. My sister has run two miles every morning since she was 15 years old.   10. They have gone to Cape Cod every summer for 12 years.

EXERCISE 8

Fill in the blanks with *since* or *for* OR the appropriate form of the verb in parentheses.

Leroy and Paula are having a party. Two of their guests, Lee and Bob, have just met.

Lee: (1) <u>Have you known</u> (know) Leroy and Paula (2) _____ a long time?

Bob: I (3) _____ (know) Paula (4) _____ my senior year in college. I first (5) _____ (meet) Leroy at their wedding two years ago. What about you?

Lee: I'm a colleague of Leroy's. We (6) _____ (work) together (7) _____ several years.

Bob: Oh, Leroy (8) _____ (show) me some of your work last week. It's great.

Lee: Thanks. What do you do?

Bob: I (9) _____ (teach) French (10) _____ ten years, but I (11) _____ (quit) a couple of years ago. Now I'm an actor.

Lee: An actor! I thought you looked familiar.

Bob: Well, not really. I (12) _____ (not work) as an actor (13) _____ last October. In fact, last night I (14) _____ (start) to work as a waiter at the Zenon.

Lee: Really? I (15) _____ (eat) there last night. *That's* why you look familiar!

SUGGESTION

If you think it will be helpful for Ss to gain more practice in *talking about* grammar, ask them to explain why they rewrote the statement the way they did: What was wrong with the original statement? Why is the rewritten statement better/correct?

UNIT GOAL REVIEW

Ask Ss to look at the goals on the opening page of the unit again. Help them understand how much they have accomplished in each area.

SUGGESTIONS

1. Present contrasts, and ask Ss to talk about the difference in meaning. (You can use sentences from Exercise 5 or make up some of your own—Goal #3).
2. Or you can create examples of sentences with errors (or take these examples directly from Ss' work in this chapter) and have Ss rework these sentences so that they are correct.

EXERCISE 9

Look for mistakes in the following passage. Correct any mistakes that you find. One has been corrected for you.

1. My sister is very good at languages. She studies
2. Italian at the language institute. She started studying
3. Italian in 1993, so she ~~studies~~ *has studied* Italian several years. When
4. she was a child, she wanted to learn Russian and she still
5. wants to learn it. She has wanted to learn Russian
6. since a long time, but Russian courses are not offered
7. at the language schools near her home. Two years ago
8. she has found out that the local community college offers
9. courses in Chinese, so she started learning Chinese.
10. Unfortunately, she doesn't have a car, so she takes the bus
11. to school since two years.

ANSWER KEY

Exercise 9
Error in parentheses; corrections in italics.
6. (since) *for*   8. (has found out) *found out*
10. (takes) *has taken*   11. (since) *for*   Also
possible: 3. (several years) *for several years*

Use Your English

ACTIVITY 1 : SPEAKING

Work in pairs or groups of three. Complete the following with information about your partner(s). Make a list of appropriate questions and then ask your partner(s) the questions. Here are some sample questions:

How long have you studied English?

How long have you lived in this town?

1. _____ for _____ hours.
2. _____ since _____ .
3. _____ for _____ .
4. _____ for _____ years.
5. _____ since _____ .

USE YOUR ENGLISH

The activities in the purple pages at the end of the unit contain situations which should naturally elicit the structures covered in the unit. When students are doing these activities in class, you can circulate and listen to see if they are using the structures accurately. If not, you may want to spend additional time on the Activities and/or review the relevant Focus Boxes.

Activity 1
VARIATION

Bring in to your class a native speaker visitor, or several, if possible. Have Ss interview these people, and tape record these interviews if people are comfortable with this. You can listen more closely for the use of simple present tense, simple past tense, present perfect, *since* and *for*.

Activity 2

VARIATION

This activity is also fun to do as an interview, with people new to your Ss. In this case, you wouldn't bother with Step 1 guesses (unless you don't mind getting apparently random answers). Instead, Ss' questions would concentrate on getting the facts (Step 2). If there are several people being interviewed, you will also be able to fill in the chart about who has done the various activities the longest.

Activity 3

SUGGESTION

We recommend introducing this activity with a brief discussion of the system in Great Britain, based on the headings in the chart. Or if you are more familiar with another country's system, that would be appropriate.

EXPANSION

If all of your Ss come from the same country, this activity can serve as a useful research project.

1. Ss work in pairs or groups to choose one country and then research the relevant information outside class.
2. In class, they follow the instructions in Step 2, using the "data" they collected.
3. The information that is shared and exchanged can be used as a follow-up written activity.

ACTIVITY 2: SPEAKING/LISTENING

Work with a partner.

STEP 1 Read the statements below and try to match each statement to someone in your class. Write the name in the column marked *Guesses*.

STEP 2 Next, ask your classmates questions using *How long have you . . . ?* in order to find out who has done each thing the longest and shortest amounts of time. Fill in the answers in the column marked *Facts*.

GUESSES	WHO	FACTS
_____	has studied English the longest time?	_____
_____	has been married the longest time?	_____
_____	has owned his or her watch the longest time?	_____
_____	has known how to drive the longest time?	_____
_____	has known how to drive the shortest time?	_____
_____	has had the shoes she or he is wearing today the longest time?	_____
_____	has worn glasses the longest time?	_____
_____	has worn glasses the shortest time?	_____
_____	has had the same hair style the longest time?	_____

ACTIVITY 3: SPEAKING/LISTENING/WRITING

In this activity, you will find out how different countries are governed.

STEP 1 Get together with a group of classmates from different countries, if possible. First use the three charts to note and list information about your own country or another country you are familiar with. We have done some for you, as an example.

STEP 2 When you have all filled in the charts, begin sharing your information. Then use the charts to take more notes on what your classmates tell you. In the first two charts, check (✔) the appropriate box or write in the box marked *other*. In the third chart, write notes.

STEP 3 Be ready to share this information with the rest of the class.

Country	Type of Leadership				
	PRESIDENT	MONARCH*	PRIME MINISTER	MILITARY	OTHER
Great Britain		✔	✔		

*King, queen, emperor, etc.

Country	How Current Leader Came Into Power			
	ELECTION	SUCCESSION*	COUP**	OTHER
Great Britain	✔ (Prime Minister)	✔ (Queen)		

*Succession: the act of a position or title passing from one person to another, usually a relative

**Coup: a sudden or violent seizure of power by a group that has not been elected

Country	What Current Leader Has Done		
	LENGTH OF TIME THE CURRENT LEADER HAS BEEN IN POWER	BEST THING SHE OR HE HAS DONE WHILE IN POWER	WORST THING SHE OR HE HAS DONE WHILE IN POWER***

***Choose to talk about the leader of your country or another one for which you've listed information.

Activity 4

Play textbook audio. The tapescript for this listening activity appears on p. 508 of this book.

VARIATION

Step 2 can first be written, as an individual in-class activity or as homework. For this, Ss will need to take careful notes from the taped job interview. This can be useful practice in writing a persuasive argument (why Ss think the man will or won't get the job) as well as in using the target structures in this unit.

ACTIVITY 4

STEP 1 Listen to the job interview. Match the first part of each sentence in column A with the second part in column B.

1. I've been	a. a lot more than just manage the office.
2. I've done	b. the EDS.
3. I've overhauled	c. new, more efficient software.
4. I've reorganized	d. at the Smithton and Banks firm for seven years now.
5. I've implemented	e. the whole systems management.

STEP 2 Do you think the man will get the job? Why or why not? Discuss with a partner.

STEP 3 Listen to the tape again. This time, listen closely for the questions and statements with the present perfect. For each sentence with the present perfect, complete the following chart.

1. Wendy's questions:	
time expression (*how long*)	subject + verb phrase (*have/has* + verb)

2. Patrick's statements:	
subject + verb phrase (*have/has* + verb)	time expression (*for/since*)

ANSWER KEY

Activity 4
1. d 2. a 3. e 4. b 5. c

ACTIVITY 5: SPEAKING/LISTENING

STEP 1 Find a classmate, a friend, or an acquaintance who is studying the same field as you, or who has or wants a job like yours. Conduct a practice job interview. You can work together to come up with questions, which should include **when** things happened and for **how long:** work experience, job history, and education. Feel free to make up information!

STEP 2 Decide who will be the "employer" (the interviewer) and who will be the "employee" (the interviewee). Take turns if there is time. Tape-record the interviews.

STEP 3 Listen to the recording. Write down all the sentences with the present perfect. In each case, was it used correctly? Were *since* and *for* used correctly? Were there cases where the present perfect should have been used but wasn't?

ACTIVITY 6: WRITING

STEP 1 Choose Activity 3 or Activity 5, whichever was most interesting to you. Write a brief report of two or three paragraphs, summarizing the information that you gathered in that Activity.

STEP 2 Exchange reports with a classmate and check to make sure that the present perfect was used correctly. Were there cases where the present perfect should have been used but wasn't?

Present Perfect with Since and For | **211**

Activity 5
SUGGESTION

A good pre-activity is to talk with people about the information that is usually exchanged in a job interview. If you or your Ss can find someone who has recently been through such an experience, invite them to the class. Ask them what kinds of questions they were asked, what kinds of answers they gave (or would have liked to give!), and what questions they weren't especially prepared for.

Activity 6
SUGGESTION

Step 2: Make sure that when Ss exchange their written reports, they first read the report for general meaning: Can they understand everything? Are there points that need clarification or elaboration? Then continue with Step 2.

The test for this unit can be found on pp. 446–447 of this book.
The answers are on p. 448.

Unit 14

UNIT OVERVIEW

Using a travel and entertainment theme, this unit focuses on the contrast between the present perfect *(have chosen)* and simple past *(chose)*. The meaning and use of *ever, never, already,* and *yet* are also addressed.

UNIT GOALS

While reviewing these goals, try to determine if the students (Ss) are familiar with these grammatical terms (present perfect and simple past) by eliciting some examples from them. For example, you can ask questions such as the following: *How many of you have studied the present perfect before? Can you give me an example? What is the difference between the present perfect and the simple past?*

> Don't correct their errors at this point; just find out what they already know about these linguistic expressions.

OPENING TASK
SETTING UP THE TASK

Direct Ss' attention to the image on this page. Make overhead transparencies of pp. 212 and 213 to use in your review.

SUGGESTION

Get the Ss to start thinking about the travel theme by briefly brainstorming.

1. Before they open their books, tell the Ss they will have 1 minute to determine how many countries are represented in these passport stamps.
2. Have one member of the pair open his/her book to this page while the other takes out a piece of paper.
3. The student with the book must look at the picture and dictate to his/her partner which countries are represented on the page.

UNIT 14

PRESENT PERFECT AND SIMPLE PAST

Ever and *Never, Already* and *Yet*

UNIT GOALS:
- To use present perfect and simple past in the right situations
- To understand the meaning of *ever* and *never* in questions
- To use present perfect questions in the right situations
- To understand the meaning of *already* and *yet*

OPENING TASK
Max's Passport

STEP 1 Work with a partner and look at the stamps on Max's passport to answer these questions:

a) How many different countries has Max visited?

b) When did he visit each one?

STEP 2 Now use Max's passport to complete the following:

Max has visited _____ countries in Asia, Europe,
                    (1)
and North America. He has been to _____ different
                                        (2)
countries in Asia. In 1986, he went to _____ ,
                                             (3)
_____ , and _____ . He has visited
      (4)   (5)
_____ and _____ twice. The first time he
      (6)   (7)
visited Japan was in _____ and the second time was in
                           (8)
_____ . He went to _____ in 1988 and
      (9)   (10)
1995. In 1990, he visited _____ . Max hasn't been to
                                (11)
Europe too ofen; he has been to _____ and
                                      (12)
_____ only once.
      (13)

CONDUCTING THE TASK

Step 1

Start with the lists from the warm-up activity and check that everyone understands the two questions; (a) is trickier than it looks as it is not immediately apparent what the countries are. This exercise is deliberate; it promotes discussion and genuine information exchange. Usually there is at least one person in the class who knows.

Step 2

While Ss complete the text, circulate around the room to listen. Pay special attention to their use of verbs and note errors you hear for later discussion. This can be very helpful when you review Unit Goals at the end of each chapter; you can put some "before and after" examples on the board to show them how much they have learned.

CLOSING THE TASK

SUGGESTION

Have pairs get together in groups of four to compare their answers before discussing as a class.

REVIEWING THE TASK

1. Using the overhead transparencies to label the stamps and fill out the form, find out which ones were difficult to read. Combining the class's efforts, can you label all of the stamps?
2. Returning to the passage in Step 2, ask Ss to point out examples of verbs in the present perfect and simple past. Underline each type with a different colored pen (e.g., green for present perfect, blue for simple past).

ANSWER KEY

Opening Task
1. 9   2. 6   3. Malaysia   4. Indonesia
5. Thailand   6. Japan   7. Singapore

8. 1995   9. 1996   10. Singapore
11. Canada   12. England   13. France

The information in this focus box should be a review of the comparison between these two forms. Note that many languages do not have this distinction; in addition, languages that do make this comparison often use the present perfect differently from English. Elicit some examples from Ss to illustrate each explanation.

Grammar Note

Simple forms are often considered to focus more on the factual nature of the verb; perfect forms tend to be retrospective, connecting a past event to an even later time. In the case of the simple past, the situation is seen as complete; the connection of the event to the present situation is not stated:

*I **lived** in Bratislava for 4 years.* (→ but I don't now)
*Steve **played** hockey when he was a kid.* (→ but he doesn't now)
The present perfect provides more information: a connection between a past event and now:
*I've **lived** in Seattle for 2 years.* (→ I arrived here 2 years ago and still live here now)
*Steve **has played** soccer for a few years.* (→ he started playing soccer at some point in the past and still plays)

FOCUS **1**

Present Perfect versus Simple Past

EXAMPLES	EXPLANATIONS
(a) Last year, she **graduated** from high school.	Use the simple past to talk about something that happened at a **specific time** in the past.
(b) He **lived** in this house from 1980 to 1988.	Use the simple past to show when something happened.
(c) He **has been** to Mexico. **(d)** They **have run** a marathon.	Use the present perfect when you talk about something that happened in the past without mentioning the specific time it happened. The experience is more important than when it happened.
(e) I **have been** to Thailand. I **went** there about ten years ago and **traveled** all over. I **had** a great time. The Thai people **were** open and friendly to tourists.	Use the present perfect to introduce the general idea. Use the simple past to give specific details.

EXERCISE 1

There is a "classic" film festival in town featuring a number of famous American movies at several different movie theaters. Robert loves classic movies, and so he is planning to invite some friends to a movie on Saturday night. Naturally, he wants to suggest a movie that nobody has seen. Use the information below to help him choose.

FILM FESTIVAL

BALBOA
38th & Balboa 555~8184
- HIGH NOON
  4:55 8:30 10:55
- ROMAN HOLIDAY
  6:50 10:25
- PSYCHO
  12:30 4:45 8:40 11:15

CORONET
Geary & Arguelio 555~4400
- ON THE WATERFRONT
  1:20 3:30 5:37 7:30

GALAXY
Van Ness & Sutter 555~8700
- THE GODFATHER
  6:10 8:30 10:55

METRO
Union-Webtser 555~1835
- CASABLANCA
  1:00 3:15 5:30 10:00

REGENCY
Van Ness & Sutter
555~6773
- THE GRADUATE
  4:40 7:40 10:30

Ann has seen the movie at the Coronet.
Patty and Mark went to the Metro last night.
Karen went to the Balboa on Tuesday to see the movie that started at 8:30.
Tom went to the Galaxy last weekend.
Carolyn and Terry have seen the movie at the Regency.
A couple of days ago Robert went to the Balboa and saw the movie that started at 8:40.

1. Which movie should they see?
2. Have **you** seen any of these movies?
3. Find out how many of your classmates have seen these movies.

EXERCISE 2

Use the information from Exercise 1 to make questions that fit with the following answers. The first one has been done for you.

1. _Did Carolyn and Terry go to the movies yesterday?_

   Yes, they did. They went to see *The Graduate* yesterday.

2. _____

   Yes, Tom has seen *The Godfather*.

3. _____

   No, Patty and Mark haven't seen *High Noon*.

Present Perfect and Simple Past: *Ever* and *Never, Already* and *Yet* | **215**

Exercise 1

The problem-solving format of this activity works best in pairs or groups. Aside from question 1 (see answer key below), answers will vary.

SUGGESTION

Have Ss answer question 3 by doing a "Find someone who . . ." competition.
1. Have Ss walk around the room and poll their classmates to find one person who has seen each film.
2. Ss ask, *Have you seen . . . (name of movie)?* Once they have found a person who can answer "yes" to one of the movies, they write their name next to that film and move on to another classmate and ask about another film.
3. Once Ss have found 7 people for the 7 films, they sit down. The first person to sit down is the winner.
4. If no one answers "yes" to some of the films, see who has the most names.

Workbook Ex. 1, pp. 109–110.
Answers: TE p. 495.

Exercise 2

Ss return to the information in Exercise 1. When reviewing the exercise, elicit Ss' questions and write them on the board. Don't correct errors yourself; instead, invite the class to determine if the question is accurate and correct the errors.

---

4. _____

No, she didn't see it last weekend. She saw it on Tuesday.

5. _____

No, they didn't see *Psycho*. They saw *Casablanca*.

6. _____

Yes, he has. He saw it a couple of days ago.

7. _____

No, they haven't seen *Roman Holiday*, but they have seen *The Graduate*.

8. _____

No, he didn't. He saw it last weekend.

Exercise 3

SUGGESTION

1. Have Ss complete this individually in class or as homework.
2. Instruct pairs or small groups to compare their versions of the postcard.
3. Discuss only those points with which groups had disagreements.

Note that because Alice has written this postcard while she is in New York City, the present perfect often makes the most sense. If she were writing after leaving NYC, we would expect all of the verbs to appear in the simple past.

If Ss have questions about the language used in the postcard (e.g., *Having a great time* instead of *I'm having a great time*), point out that postcards are often written informally.

EXERCISE 3

Alice is on vacation in New York City. Complete her postcard home, choosing verbs from the list below (some of the verbs can be used more than once). Use either the simple past or present perfect form of the verb.

try	see	walk	eat
have	go	spend	take

Hi Folks!

Having a great time! I (1)_____ at least 50 miles, but I (2)_____ lots of interesting things. Yesterday I (3)_____ the Staten Island Ferry, and on Thursday I (4)_____ to the top of the Empire State Building. I (5)_____ several shows. Two nights ago I (6)_____ to see "CATS". I (7)_____ great tickets. Wonderful food!!! I (8)_____ some delicious meals. Yesterday I (9)_____ sushi for the first time. See you next week.

Love, Alice

P.S. I (10)_____ lots of money!

The Murphys
1403 Eastwood
Ann Arbor,
MI 48103

ANSWER KEY

Exercise 3

(1) have walked (2) have seen (3) took
(4) went (5) have seen (6) went
(7) had (8) have eaten (9) tried
(10) have spent

FOCUS 2

Ever and *Never* in Questions

EXAMPLES	EXPLANATIONS
(a) A: **Have** you **ever eaten** Mexican food?	Use *ever* in questions with the present perfect to mean "at any time before now."
(b) Yes, I **have eaten** it. **(c)** NOT: Yes, I have **ever** eaten it. **(d)** I **haven't ever eaten** it.	*Ever* is not usually used in affirmative statements (those that mean or use *yes*). *Ever* is used in negative statements.
(e) I **have never eaten** it.	Use *never* with the present perfect to mean "at no time before now."

EXERCISE 4

Read the conversation. Underline and correct any mistakes.

Mick: Have you ever ~~visit~~ ^{visited} Europe?

Dave: Yes. I've been there several times, in fact. Three years ago I've gone to France.

Mick: Really? Where did you go?

Dave: I went to Paris, of course. And then I rode my mountain bike in the Pyrenees. Last year I've ridden my bike in Germany and Switzerland. Have ever you been there?

Mick: I've never been to Germany, but I've ever been to Switzerland.

Dave: When was that?

Mick: I've taken an international business course there about eight years ago.

FOCUS 2

Note the position of *(n)ever* in front of the main (not auxiliary) verb in question and statement forms:
Q: *Has she **ever** <u>tasted</u> Vietnamese food.*
A: *No, I don't think she has **ever** <u>tried</u> it.*

Grammar Note

Many Ss have been taught that *(n)ever* is a "trigger" for the present perfect. While this is generally true for British English, American English allows the use of *(n)ever* with simple past as well:
*<u>Did</u> you **ever** <u>try</u> alligator meat?*
*<u>Have</u> you **ever** <u>tried</u> alligator meat?*
Because both are possible, avoid statements like "always use the present perfect with ever or never."

Exercise 4

Have pairs come to a consensus on errors and corrections. Copy the conversation on an overhead transparency ahead of time; review the exercise as a class.

Workbook Ex. 2, pp. 110–111.
Answers: TE p. 496.

ANSWER KEY

Exercise 4
Errors are underlined; corrections are in italics
2. <u>I've gone</u>; *I went*   3. <u>I've ridden</u>; *I rode*
4. <u>Have ever you been</u>; *Have you ever been*
5. <u>I've ever been</u>; *I've been*   6. <u>I've taken</u>; *I took*

FOCUS 3

This focus box continues with question-forming (see Focus 2).

Grammar Note

Because present perfect is used to ask **if** something has ever happened, it is often used to start conversations. However, once the "if" has been established, the conversation usually shifts to the simple past, to find out more about the situation:

A: Has Amanda ever visited you in Washington?
B: Yeah, she came to visit 5 months ago.
A: Did she come for work or just for fun?
B: Just for fun. We got to see so many concerts while she was here. It was so cool!

This information may help you when you are reviewing the answers for Exercise 5.

Note: You may need to point out that *never* is not commonly used in questions; in rare cases it can be used to express surprise at someone's statement:
A: I don't know anything about computers.
B: Have you never used one before?
The more common reaction would be:
B: Haven't you ever used one before?

Exercise 5

S U G G E S T I O N

Do this activity as a class. Copy this page onto an overhead transparency and invite Ss to volunteer answers. When errors are made, refer Ss back to the explanations in the focus box.

Workbook Ex. 3, pp. 111–112.
Answers: TE p. 496.

▶ **Present Perfect in Questions**

EXAMPLES	EXPLANATIONS
(a) A: **Have** you **ever eaten** frogs' legs? B: No, I haven't. **(b)** A: **Have** you **ever been** to Sub-Saharan Africa? B: Yes, I have.	Use the present perfect with *ever* when you want to know **if** something happened. When you ask these questions, you usually expect the answer to be *Yes, I have* or *No, I haven't.*
(c) A: When **did** you **go** there? B: I went there **last year.**	Use the simple past in questions when you want to know **when** something happened.

EXERCISE 5

Complete the conversations, using the present perfect or the simple past of the verb in parentheses. The first one has been done for you.

1. A: Excuse me, sir, we're doing a survey. Can I ask you a few questions?
   B: Sure, go ahead.
   A: <u>Have you ever used</u> WonderWhite detergent? (you/use/ever)
   B: No, _____ it. (I/try/never)
   A: Why not?
   B: _____ laundry in my life. (I/do/never) My wife always does it.
   A: What about you, sir? _____ your clothes with WonderWhite? (you/wash/ever)
   C: Yes, _____ it. (I/try)
   A: When _____ it for the first time? (you/try)
   C: _____ it for the first time about six months ago. (I/use)

2. A: _____ any books by Latin American writers? (you/read/ever)
   B: Yes, I _____ . I _____ a great novel by a Colombian writer a few years ago. (read)
   A: Which one?
   B: I _____ his name. (forget) He _____ the Nobel Prize several years ago. (win)
   A: Oh, you mean Gabriel Garcia Marquez.

A N S W E R   K E Y

Exercise 5

1. **B** I have/'ve never tried **B** I have/'ve never done **A** Have you ever washed **C** I have/'ve tried **A** did you try **C** I used   2. **A** Have you ever read **B** have; read **B** have/'ve forgotten; won
3. **B** Has he ever been **A** came **B** Has he been **A** he has/'s never been; he has traveled **B** Did you take **A** he has never visited   4. **A** Did you go out **B** We went **A** I have/'ve never been there **B** I have/'ve eaten **A** Have you ever tried **B** We had a

---

3. A: My brother is coming to stay with us for a few days next week. Do you have any ideas about how we can entertain him?

B: _____ here before? (he/be/ever)

A: Yes. He _____ (come) once about three years ago.

B: _____ to Chinatown then? (he/go)

A: No, _____ to Chinatown (he/be/never), but _____ a lot in China and in the Far East. (he/travel)

B: Maybe you'd better not take him to Chinatown then! _____ him to the Greek restaurant when he was here three years ago? (you/take)

A: No, and _____ Greece (he/visit/never).

B: Great! Why don't you take him there?

4. A: _____ last night? (you/go out)

B: Yes. _____ to that new Italian restaurant. (we/go)

A: What's it like? _____ there. (I/be/never)

B: It's O.K., but _____ better Italian food in other restaurants. (I/eat)

A: _____ the one on Main Street? (you/try/ever)

B: Yes. _____ great meal there last weekend. (we/have)

FOCUS **4**

▶ **Already and Yet**

EXAMPLES	EXPLANATIONS
(a) I've **already** eaten. **(b)** I haven't eaten **yet.**	Use *already* to show that an event was completed earlier. Use *yet* when an event has **not** been completed before the time of speaking.
(c) Have you eaten **yet**? **(d)** Have you eaten **already**? OR **(e)** Have you **already** eaten?	*Yet* in questions is more neutral than *already*. The use of *already* in questions shows that the speaker expects that an event has happened before the time of speaking.

Present Perfect and Simple Past: *Ever* and *Never, Already* and *Yet* | **219**

FOCUS 4

1. Be sure to emphasize the different word order with these two expressions.
2. Note that with *yet*, the implication is that the event will be completed at some time in the future:
   Have you seen "Titanic" yet?
   (→ I don't know if you have, but I expect that you will.)
   I haven't done the dishes yet.
   (→ but I'm planning on doing them later.)

SUGGESTION

You can further illustrate the use of *already* and *yet* by taking examples from the Opening Task or from information you've learned about your Ss. For example:
*Max has **already** been to ...,*
But he hasn't been to ... yet.
Q: *Has Jaro's band recorded a CD yet?*
A: *Uh-huh. They've **already** recorded 2, actually.*

Exercise 6

SUGGESTION

Do this as group work and have Ss report findings to the class. Reporting back allows Ss to practice using the third person –s (has), which is often difficult to practice in oral activities.

Exercise 7

As you go over the directions, point out that Ss will find clues to how to form the questions and answers from the context of the other sentences given.

Ss can complete this exercise individually or in pairs.

Workbook Ex. 4, pp. 112–114.
Answers: TE p. 496.

UNIT GOAL REVIEW

Ask Ss to look at the goals on the opening page of the unit again. Help them understand how much they have accomplished in each area.

EXERCISE 6

Get information from your classmates about the following topics and add topics of your own. Use *already, yet, ever,* and *never* when appropriate.

1. study other languages (besides English)
2. receive an F in a class
3. receive an A in a class
4. give a speech
5. be a teacher/teach students
6. feel nervous about speaking another language
7. feel excited about studying/learning
8. earn a Bachelor's degree
9. forget about a test that was scheduled
10. finish studying this chapter
11. master the present perfect tense

EXERCISE 7

Sue and her roommate Betsy are discussing their evening plans. Fill in the missing parts of their conversation. Use *already, yet, ever,* and *never* when appropriate.

Sue: (1) _____ ?

Betsy: No, not yet. But I'm hungry. I didn't eat lunch.

Sue: Well, should we go out to eat? I'd love to try that new Mexican restaurant down the street. (2) _____ ?

Betsy: No, (3) _____ . I was going to go with Deb and Rebecca last week, but at the last minute they changed their minds. (4) _____ out to eat with them? They have a hard time making decisions!

Sue: No, (5) _____ . One time we made plans to, but at the last minute they canceled.

Betsy: I'd rather be invited to their house for dinner, anyway. Deb's a great cook. She went to a chef's school in Paris. (6) _____ ?

Sue: (7) _____ . She makes the best chicken curry. Yum! Which reminds me. . . . You're not the only one that's hungry! Do you need to stop at the cash machine on the way to the restaurant?

Betsy: No, (8) _____ .

Sue: Well, good, let's go then.

ANSWER KEY

Exercise 6
Answers will vary.
Exercise 7
(1) Have you eaten yet? (2) Have you ever eaten/been/gone there? (3) I never have/not yet (4) Have you ever gone (5) I never have (6) Have you ever tried her cooking/eaten a dinner that she cooked (7) Yes, I have (8) I already did/stopped there

Use Your English

ACTIVITY 1: LISTENING/SPEAKING/WRITING

STEP 1 In this activity, you will be finding out about some of the things that your classmates have done. Look at the list below. Move around the class and ask questions to see if you can find anyone who has ever done any of these things.

First you need to find who has had the experience (name); then you need to get specific details about the experience (when) (where) (how/why). Take notes below; it is not necessary to write full sentences at this point. In the box marked ***, you can add an experience of your own if you want to.

Be ready to share your findings with the rest of the class.

HAVE YOU EVER . . . . . ?

Experience	Name	When	Where	How/Why
met a famous person				
climbed a mountain				
seen a shark				
felt really frightened				
flown in a hot-air balloon				
***				

STEP 2 Now use the information you collected to write a report on your findings. Here is one way you can start your report:

A few days ago I interviewed some of my classmates about things they have done before now, and I learned some interesting things about their past experiences. For example, ...

As in previous units, refrain from providing direct feedback on errors during activities, in order to give Ss the full benefit of communicative practice of these structures.

Activity 1
SUGGESTIONS

1. You can use the experiences in the box, or use them as a guide to create your own to match the interests of your class.
2. Have the class create their own experiences around a theme. For example: the law *(gotten a speeding ticket, jay-walked, taken supplies from your workplace)* or the truth *(told someone they looked nice when you thought they looked terrible, lied about their age).*

Activity 2

This can be a good class warm-up activity a few days into the unit as it provides review of the use of present perfect and acts as a "getting-to-know-you" exercise.

Activity 3

1. Be sure everyone knows that they must lie about one of the experiences.
2. Point out that Ss cannot ask the question directly (Have you ever ridden your bicycle from San Francisco to Los Angeles?). To make the activity more difficult, have Ss start by asking yes/no questions only (Do you often travel by boat? -not- How often do you travel by boat?).
3. This activity is a particularly good test of Ss' knowledge of the difference between present perfect and simple past. Note the errors you hear and use them later to review their language use.

ACTIVITY 2: SPEAKING/LISTENING

Move around the class and ask questions to find out if the following statements are true or false. If the statement is true, write T beside it; if it is false, write F.

1. Somebody in this room has appeared on TV. _____
2. Everybody here has eaten tacos. _____
3. At least three people have never ridden a motorcycle. _____
4. Somebody has swum in more than two oceans. _____
5. Several people have seen a ghost. _____
6. At least three people have been to Disneyland. _____
7. Nobody has been to Paris. _____
8. Somebody has run a marathon. _____
9. Half the class has never played soccer. _____
10. Somebody has never driven a car. _____

ACTIVITY 3: SPEAKING/LISTENING

The purpose of this activity is to confuse your classmates. You will tell the class about three things you have done in your life. Two of these things are true, but one is false. Your classmates will try to guess which one is false. For example:

I have ridden a bicycle from San Francisco to Los Angeles.

I have traveled by boat down the Nile.

I have broken my leg twice.

Which statement is false?

In order to decide which one is false, your classmates can ask you questions about the specific details of each experience. For example: "When did you ride your bike to Los Angeles?" "How long did it take?" "Which leg did you break?" and so on. After they have listened to your answers, the class will vote on which experience is false.

Take turns talking about your true and false experiences until everyone has taken part.

ACTIVITY 4: WRITING OR SPEAKING/LISTENING

STEP 1 Write down one of the true stories you told in Activity 3, this time providing lots of details. Read the story aloud and tape-record it.
OR If you want practice in telling the story without writing it down first, take a few minutes to think about the details you want to include. Then tell the story to a classmate and tape-record it.

STEP 2 Listen to your own or each other's tapes for verb tense usage. Was the present perfect used? If it wasn't, were there cases where it **should** have been used? Was the simple past used correctly? Did you use *already, yet, ever*, and *never* appropriately?

ACTIVITY 5: SPEAKING/LISTENING

You have probably had many different experiences since you came to this country, this city, or this school. In this activity you will be finding out the best and worst experiences your classmates have had since they came here. First go around the room and get as much information as you can from at least three different people. Use the chart to take notes on the information your classmates give you.

Name	Length of Stay	Best Experience	Worst Experience

Activity 4
SUGGESTIONS
1. Have Ss conduct the assessment as a peer editing activity. They can provide feedback on either the written or recorded stories.
2. If working with a tape, have Ss critique pronunciation as well as language form and use. They can note problem sounds or unusual intonation patterns, depending on what you have been covering in class.
3. To help them structure their feedback, make a handout of specific points you want them to focus on. For example, list three different features they should focus on: grammar, pronunciation, and content.

Activity 5
This activity can lead to further, written practice in Activity 6 (see below).

Activity 6

Depending on the level of your group, you can use this activity to focus on the use of transition expressions (*however, first of all, on the other hand,* etc.) to create greater cohesion in their articles.

SUGGESTION

1. To find examples of transition expressions in context, have Ss conduct a web search of a news site such as CNN or BBC.
2. Instruct them to find an article, print it out, and underline all of the transition words.
3. Ss can then work in pairs to discuss the difference in meaning and determine why each expression helps readers follow the article more easily.
4. Direct Ss to use some of these expressions in their own articles.

Activity 7

VARIATION

Ss can write their letters to someone they know who speaks English. After they have finished their final drafts, they can send the letter. Giving this activity a realistic end product can increase motivation.

ACTIVITY 6: WRITING

You have been asked to write a short article for your college newspaper on the experiences of international students.

Review the information you collected in Activity 5. Choose the two most interesting or surprising "best" experiences and the two most interesting or surprising "worst" experiences. Organize your article so that you talk first about the bad experiences and then about the good experiences. Start your article with a brief introduction to the topic and to the students you interviewed. For example:

What is it like to be a international student? I will try to answer this question by describing both the good and bad experiences of my classmates. Recently I interviewed four students in my class, and they told me about some of their best and worst experiences since they came here. I would like to share with you some of the things I learned. . . .

ACTIVITY 7: WRITING/READING

Write a letter to a family member or a friend and tell him or her about the best and the worst experiences you have had since you left home. Review your letter for the use of the present perfect. If you feel comfortable sharing your letter with someone, you can review each other's letters. Was the present perfect used? If it wasn't, were there cases where it **should** have been used? Was the simple past used correctly? Did you use *already, yet, ever,* and *never* appropriately?

ACTIVITY 8: LISTENING

Listen to the tape of two people talking about their travels.

STEP 1 Take notes in the chart below, using information from their conversation.

	Speaker 1/the man	Speaker 2/the woman
WHERE? area of the world countries (list them)		
WHEN? what year(s)? length of stay		
HOW? transportation hotels/guesthouses		
WHY? reasons for traveling types of experiences		

STEP 2 Discuss these questions with a partner:

1. How would you describe each speaker's traveling style? In other words, what type of travel do they enjoy? What types of places do they stay in? Do they enjoy being tourists or residents?
2. How does your own style of traveling compare or contrast with these people's?

STEP 3 Now listen to the tape again for the way the speakers used verb tenses. List the phrases from the conversation where the speakers used the present perfect verb form in their questions or answers. Compare your list with your classmates' lists. Did the speakers use *yet, ever,* or *never* with the present perfect?

Present Perfect and Simple Past: *Ever and Never, Already and Yet* **225**

Activity 8

Play textbook audio. The transcript for this listening appears on pp. 508–509 of this book.

SUGGESTION

For **Step 3,** have some Ss write their phrases on the board for the whole class to review together. Use this activity to review the unit goals.

Activity 8
Check transcript for answers (pp. 508–509).

Unit 15

UNIT OVERVIEW

This unit provides practice with the present perfect progressive, and it contrasts the present perfect with the present perfect progressive.

UNIT GOALS

Review the goals listed on this page to see what students (Ss) should be familiar with by the end of this unit.

OPENING TASK

The purpose of this task is to situate Ss in the time frame where the present perfect progressive is naturally used—contexts in which an activity was happening/in progress very recently in the past has an effect or result in the present moment. The task is intended to focus attention on meaning rather than form.

SETTING UP THE TASK

Ss work in groups or pairs to match the statements in Step 1 with an appropriate activity from the list in Step 2. There are more activities than statements to promote a little more discussion.

U N I T 15

PRESENT PERFECT PROGRESSIVE

UNIT GOALS:

- To correctly use present progressive with *just*
- To form present progressive correctly
- To use present progressive to describe unfinished actions and new habits
- To correctly choose between present perfect and present perfect progressive

▶ OPENING TASK
Recent Activities

STEP 1 Read the statements below. Why do you think they were said?

STATEMENT

1. A: Ugh . . . your hands are covered with oil and grease!
    B: Sorry.
2. A: Are you O.K.? Your eyes are all red.
3. A: You look terrible.
    B: I didn't get much sleep last night.
4. A: That's enough for tonight. Give me your car keys.
    B: Why?
    A: I'll take you home. You can't drive like this.
5. A: Why is your hair wet?
6. A: Hey, kids! Stop right there!
    B: What for?
    A: Take your shoes off! I don't want mud all over the carpet.

STEP 2 Now look at the activities in the list. Try to match each of the situations above to an activity below. Write the number of the situation beside the activity.

baking bread	_____	studying for a test	_____
swimming	_____	drinking	_____
chopping onions	_____	fixing a car	_____
eating garlic	_____	watching TV	_____
playing in the yard	_____		

CONDUCTING THE TASK
Step 1
Ss read the statements and try to guess the context, speakers, and setting.

Step 2
Ss match the activities to the statements.

CLOSING THE TASK
Bring the class together to see how much Ss agree/disagree. They should be ready to justify their answers.

REVIEWING THE TASK
You can elicit and/or weave in the fact that the statements refer to something that is apparent in the present and that was caused by something that occurred before the present. This can act as a springboard to Focus 1. Exercise 1 returns to the task by getting Ss to write full sentences.

ANSWER KEY

Opening Task Solution
Answers may vary. Accept anything that can be plausibly justified.

1. fixing a car   2. chopping onions
3. studying for a test   4. drinking
5. swimming   6. playing in the yard

This focus box naturally leads into Exercise 1.

1. Use examples (a) and (b) to introduce this grammar point: (a) explanation—*He's been painting the room so recently that we can still see the effect—His hands still have green paint on them.* (b) *She's been working out so recently that we notice the result—She's very thirsty.*

2. Emphasize the point about *just*, explained in (b).

3. Use the five statements from Exercise 1 and describe them in this way, explaining how/why the activity that was happening in the very recent past has effects that we can see, feel, or notice at the moment of speaking—in the present.

Exercise 1

SUGGESTIONS

1. Focus on meaning in all five statements, explaining how a recent event in progress in the past has an effect or result that is noticeable in the present. (See suggestion in Focus 1, above.) Or, if Ss are up to it, give them a chance to provide the explanation.

2. Check to see that the present perfect progressive has been formed correctly, which will naturally lead you to Focus 2.

3. You can write the accurately formed statements on the board or on an overhead transparency, altering ill-formed statements without saying anything. Or you can move right into the explanation in Focus 2.

Present Perfect Progressive and *Just*: Recent Activities

EXAMPLES	EXPLANATIONS
(a) A: Why are your hands green? B: I **have been painting** my room. *I've been painting my room.*	Use the present perfect progressive to talk about an activity that was happening (in progress) very recently in the past. In (a) the activity is so recent that you can still feel or see the effect or result.
(b) A: How come you're so thirsty? B: I've just been working out.	To emphasize that the activity is recent, use *just*.

EXERCISE 1

Look at the Opening Task on page 227. For statements 1–6, write sentences that give explanations for the situation. The first one has been done for you.

1. She has been fixing a car. _____
2. _____
3. _____
4. _____
5. _____
6. _____

ANSWER KEY

Exercise 1
Answers may vary, depending on Ss' creativity in the Opening Task, but probably include the following: **2.** She has been chopping onions. **3.** She has been studying for a test. **4.** He has been drinking. **5.** She has been swimming. **6.** They have been playing in the yard.

FOCUS **2**

Present Perfect Progressive

Use *has/have* + *been* + verb + *-ing* to form the present perfect progressive.

STATEMENT		NEGATIVE		QUESTION		
I You We They	**have been sleeping.** (**'ve**)	I You We They	**have not been** **sleeping. (haven't)**	Have	I you we they	**been** **sleeping?**
She He It	**has been sleeping.** (**'s**)	She He It	**has not been** **sleeping. (hasn't)**	Has	she he it	**been** **sleeping**

EXERCISE 2

You are riding the subway in a big city, late at night. There are several other people in the same car. You observe them carefully and try to figure out what they have been doing recently. You will probably be able to think of several possibilities for each one.

1. A young man with a black eye and ripped clothing:
   He's been fighting with somebody.

2. Two young men, wearing sweats and carrying tennis racquets:
   _____

3. Two young women with many bags and packages from well-known department stores:
   _____

4. A couple wearing shorts and walking shoes and backpacks. They seem very tired:
   _____

5. A young woman with a bookbag full of chemistry textbooks. She has a book open in her hands and she is asleep:
   _____

6. A woman with red stains on her hands:
   _____

7. A man with white hairs all over his clothes and scratches on his hands:
   _____

Present Perfect Progressive | **229**

FOCUS 2

SUGGESTIONS

1. Revisit Exercise 1, making sure that the statements are correctly formed.
2. Or ask Ss to correct their own statements if the present perfect progressive was not formed correctly.
3. Point out the third person singular distinction: *has*, rather than *have*.
4. Mention that contractions of *have/has* are almost always used in informal speech: *I've been sleeping.* rather than *I have been sleeping.* It is useful for learners to understand that this reduction (reducing the words *have* and *has* to the consonant sounds *'ve* and *'s*) is sometimes troublesome for learners who haven't been exposed to much spoken English and expect to hear every word distinctly enunciated.

Exercise 2

Since answers will vary, a good way to review this exercise is to allow Ss a few minutes to work in pairs and ask for volunteers to provide the answers. Be sure to ask: *Are there any other possible answers?*

ANSWER KEY

Exercise 2
Accept any answers that can be well-justified! Answers are likely to include the following:
2. They have been playing tennis   **3.** They have been shopping   **4.** They have been hiking/walking for a long time.   **5.** She has been doing her homework /studying for a chemistry class.   **6.** She has been eating a hamburger with a lot of ketchup./She has been writing a letter with a red pen.   **7.** He has been playing with a cat/working in a circus or a zoo.

SUGGESTIONS

1. To elicit similar examples from Ss, ask: *Nikko, how long have you been studying English? Michelle, how long have you been speaking English?*
2. If you are aware of any of your Ss' current hobbies or activities, ask questions about these as well: *Maria, how long have you been playing tennis? Tinh, how long have you been studying chemistry?*
3. Draw time lines (as in example (a)) on the board with the information from Ss' answers.
4. Also make statements that are true about your own life: *I've been teaching ESL for 15 years. I've been playing the piano for 20 years.*

Workbook Ex. 4, p. 117.
Answers: TE p. 496.

Exercise 3

Since these are short dialogues, it makes sense to do these orally.

SUGGESTIONS

1. Allow Ss a few minutes to work with a partner, and check to make sure they have answers for each blank, so that the class is not waiting for the speakers to search for the answers during the actual reading of the dialogues.
2. Remind Ss that for natural sounding speech, it's important to link words together smoothly and to use appropriate stress and intonation—falling intonation at the end of a statement, rising intonation at the end of a yes-no question, and louder volume / higher pitch for important or surprising information.
3. If appropriate, after Ss' reading of the dialogues, re-read each statement to demonstrate and then have Ss model *your* reading.

FOCUS **3**

▶ # Perfect Progressive: Unfinished Actions

EXAMPLE	EXPLANATION
(a) He **has been waiting** for twenty minutes. (He's still waiting.) 20 Minutes Ago ——————— Now →	Use the present perfect progressive to describe situations or actions that started in the past and are still going on.

EXERCISE 3

For each conversation, complete the following sentences. The first one has been done for you.

1. **Lee:** What are you doing?
   Mary Lou: I'm waiting to make a phone call. This woman <u>has been talking</u> on the phone for the last twenty minutes. (talk)
2. **Dan:** Haven't you finished writing that book yet?
   Heidi: No, we're still working on it.
   Dan: You _____ it for almost three years! (write)
3. **Steve:** What's up? You look miserable.
   Tom: I am. I want to go for a bike ride, but it _____ since eight o'clock this morning. (rain)
4. **George:** Excuse me, but is this your dog?
   Barbara: Yes. Is there a problem?
   George: I can't get to sleep because that dog _____ for hours! Please keep it under control, or I'll call the police. (bark)
5. **Martin:** Are these your glasses?
   Gin: Yes! Thank you so much. I _____ for them everywhere! (look)

230 | UNIT 15

ANSWER KEY

Exercise 3
2. have been writing 3. has been raining
4. has been barking 5. have been looking
6. have been living 7. have been studying
8. have been trying

---

6. **Sarita:** How are things going in New York?

   Anastasia: We don't live there anymore.

   Sarita: Really?

   Anastasia: Yes. We _____ in Philadelphia since January. (live)

7. **Diane:** Why are Kemal and Cynthia so depressed?

   Marianne: They _____ grammar for ages, but they still don't understand how to use the present perfect progressive. (study)

8. **Pam:** Aren't you ready yet?

   Andrew: No. I've lost my keys and I _____ to find them for the last half hour. (try)

FOCUS **4**

Present Perfect Progressive for New Habits

EXAMPLES	EXPLANATIONS
(a) They**'ve been eating** out a lot recently.	Use the present perfect progressive to talk about a regular habit or activity that is still happening.
(b) He's been exercising a lot **lately**. (c) I've been walking to work **recently**.	Add a time phrase or word to show that the activity started recently.

EXERCISE 4

Pat is talking with her old friend Janet. They have not seen each other for several months, and Janet is surprised by some of the changes in Pat's appearance. Complete their conversation using the verbs from the list below.

happen	sail	cook	do
feel	take	go	study
eat	ride	date	ski
talk	think	see	spend

FOCUS 4

As with Focus 3, ask questions about Ss' own lives and recent habits.

E X P A N S I O N

1. Ask Ss to each write on a piece of paper something they've been doing recently that is still happening. Instruct them *not* to say *"I've been studying English"* but to try to think of something that is new or unusual: *"I've been living with an American family." "I've been going to a lot of Chinese films." "I've been losing things!"*
2. Read each statement and have the other Ss guess who wrote it.
3. If the present perfect progressive is not formed correctly, or if another verb tense is more appropriate, first give Ss the opportunity to find and correct the error.

Workbook Ex. 5, p. 118.
Answers: TE p. 496.

Exercise 4

SUGGESTIONS

If you have Ss read their answers aloud, first allow them a few minutes to work with a partner or individually so that they are not searching for answers *during* the reading and are thus able to focus. While the statement is read, ask the other Ss to listen for accuracy. After the statement:

1. Ask if the answer is accurate or inaccurate by taking a show of hands (*How many of you think that answer is OK? How many think that it's not OK?*).

2. If it's inaccurate, give the student who has read the answer the opportunity to correct it. If he/she needs help, ask for a volunteer.

Because this dialogue is rather long, it is appropriate to switch speakers halfway through—after Pat's line #4—or switch speakers after each full statement (some statements have several blanks—Pat's #7-9, for example).

FOCUS 5

SUGGESTION

1. Read each pair of examples from the focus box and ask, *"Is there a difference in meaning?"* (The only *no* answer is for statements (a)–(b).)

2. Give other examples of this lack of distinction in meaning using the verbs *live* and *study*. Example: *How long have you lived here, Etsuko?* Answer: *I've lived here 3 months.*

3. Ask: *Can you say that in a different way with the same meaning?* Answer: *I've been living here 3 months.*

4. Continue with the other pairs (c)–(h) in the focus box, asking *"Is there a difference in meaning?"*

5. Elaborate on the explanation given in the focus box. Read the explanation, or ask a student to read the explanation. This can serve as a bridge to the next exercise.

Janet: Pat, you look great! You've lost a lot of weight, too.

Pat: Well, I (1) **'ve been riding** my bike to school recently, and I (2) _____ an aerobics class.

Janet: Is that all? No special diets or anything?

Pat: Not really. I (3) _____ (not) to any fast-food restaurants. I (4) _____ at home instead—a lot of fresh vegetables and salads and other healthy stuff like that. It really makes a difference. I (5) _____ much better, with lots more energy.

Janet: Well, you seem to be very busy these days. You're never home when I call. What else (6) _____ you _____ ?

Pat: I (7) _____ somebody special. She's got a boat, so we (8) _____ a lot, and she also has a cabin in the mountains, so we (9) _____ time there, too. And also, we (10) _____ about taking some longer trips together. So it's all pretty exciting. But what about you? What (11) _____ ?

Janet: Nothing. I (12) _____ for my final exams, but when they're over, I'm going to start having fun!

FOCUS **5**

Present Perfect versus Present Perfect Progressive

EXAMPLES	EXPLANATIONS
(a) Jim **has worked** here for ten years. (b) Jim **has been working** here for ten years.	With certain verbs, there is no difference in use between the present perfect and present perfect progressive. Use both to describe something that started in the past and continues to now. These verbs include *work*, *live*, and *study*.

ANSWER KEY

Exercise 4
(2) 've been taking **(3)** haven't been going **(4)** 've been cooking/ eating **(5)** 've been feeling **(6)** have you been doing? **(7)** 've been seeing **(8)** 've been sailing **(9)** 've been spending **(10)** 've been talking/ thinking **(11)** have you been doing **(12)** 've been studying

---

EXAMPLES	EXPLANATIONS
(c) They **have painted** their house. **(d)** They **have been painting** their house. **(e)** Jean **has visited** her grandmother. **(f)** Jean **has been visiting** her grandmother. **(g)** Geraldo **has exercised**. **(h)** Geraldo **has been exercising lately**.	In other cases the present perfect progressive: • shows that the action is incomplete (unfinished). In (c), the painting is complete. In (d), it is not complete (see Focus 3). OR: • emphasizes that the action was in progress recently. (e) tells us that the visit occurred earlier. (f) tells us that the visit occurred recently and perhaps is still in progress (see Focus 1). OR: • talks about a new habit. (g) tells us that Geraldo exercised at some time earlier. (h) suggests that he has started a new habit (see Focus 4).

EXERCISE 5

Read each situation and circle the statement that best describes the situation.

1. Sally ate frogs' legs in September, 1998, and again in December, 1999.
   (a) Sally has eaten frogs' legs.
   (b) Sally has been eating frogs' legs.

2. Bill started reading that book last week and he's not finished yet. He will probably finish it tonight.
   (a) Bill has read that book.
   (b) Bill has been reading that book.

3. I rode a motorcycle once when I was sixteen and once last year.
   (a) I've been riding a motorcycle.
   (b) I've ridden a motorcycle since I was a teenager.
   (c) I've ridden a motorcycle.

4. We first studied English grammar in school, ten years ago. This year we have grammar class for one hour a day, five days a week, and then there's all the homework—sometimes two or three hours every night.
   (a) We've been studying English grammar.
   (b) We've studied English grammar.
   (c) We've been studying English grammar for a long time.
   (d) We've studied English grammar for a long time.

5. My brother just can't quit smoking, even though he knows it's a bad habit. He started smoking when he was seventeen, and now he's almost thirty.
   (a) My brother has smoked.
   (b) My brother has been smoking.
   (c) My brother has been smoking for a long time.
   (d) My brother has smoked for a long time.

Present Perfect Progressive **233**

Exercise 5

This is a suitable exercise for group work or for a group discussion.

VARIATION

Although Ss are asked in this exercise to identify statements similar in meaning, you can also ask them to talk about the *differences* in meaning among the statements in each item. By this point, Ss usually have developed good insights about the differences (and similarities) in meaning among the statements. If they are successful with this exercise, point out to them that takes a good deal of grammar knowledge to be able to distinguish between subtle nuances in meaning.

Exercise 6

SUGGESTIONS

1. Since there's a bit of reading involved in this exercise in order to establish context, it's appropriate to ask Ss to work in small groups or pairs first, so that if you decide to have Ss read the answers aloud, this is done efficiently.
2. Circulate while Ss are working to check for accuracy.
3. Note the items that Ss disagreed on (if any), and/or ask Ss to raise questions on those items that they couldn't agree on.
4. Rather than supplying an explanation yourself of why an answer is correct or incorrect, ask Ss to.
5. If they have difficulty with that, refer them to the explanations in Focus 5.

Exercise 7

Since these are dialogues, it's logical to do this exercise orally.

SUGGESTIONS

1. Rather than doing this as a whole class, however, it may be more appropriate for Ss to work in pairs so as to allow more "talk time" and more opportunities to defend their choices.
2. While Ss are working, circulate to check for accuracy. If you have the sense that most Ss are ready to move ahead, it may not be necessary to go over the exercise item by item, but to raise questions and emphasize points on only those items that are problematic.

EXERCISE 6

What would Doug and Sandy say in each situation below? The words in parentheses will help you, but you will need to add some other words.

1. It's 4:00, and Doug's partner Sandy has been napping since 1:00. Doug is waiting for her to wake up. When she finally does, he says: (I/wait/three hours)

   _____

   _____

2. Sandy has promised to change the oil in Doug's car. While she is sleeping, Doug decides to try to do it himself, but he can't. When Sandy wakes up, he says: (I/try/forty-five minutes)

   _____

   _____

3. Sandy's mother calls to tell her that Sandy's sister has had another baby. Her mother asks, "When are you and Doug going to have kids?" Sandy tells her: (we/discuss/ten years)

   _____

   _____

4. After her nap, Sandy is hungry and she wants Doug to go out with her to eat pizza. Doug doesn't want to go because he bought fresh fish for dinner and wants to try out a new recipe. He tells Sandy, "I don't want to go out because (I/plan/dinner/all day)"

   _____

   _____

EXERCISE 7

Complete the dialogues below, using present perfect progressive, present perfect, or simple past. Be prepared to explain your choice.

Dialogue 1

Keven: What's the matter? You look frustrated.

Tsitsi: I am. I (1) _____ (try) to study all day, but the telephone never stops ringing. People (2) _____ (call) all day about the car.

Keven: That's great. I (3) _____ (hope) to sell that car for six months now. Maybe today's the day!

ANSWER KEY

Exercise 6
1. I've been waiting for you to wake up for three hours.   2. I've been trying to change the oil for forty-five minutes.   3. We've been discussing it for ten years.   4. I've been planning dinner all day.

Exercise 7
(1) have/'ve been trying   (2) have been calling   (3) have/'ve been hoping
(4) Have you been waiting   (5) have you been   (6) have/'ve been standing   (7) has started   (8) started

Dialogue 2

Maria: I'm sorry I'm so late. (4) _____ (you/wait) long?

Alex: Yes, I have! Where (5) _____ (you/be)?

Maria: I really am sorry. My watch is broken, and I didn't know what time it was.

Alex: Why didn't you ask somebody? I (6) _____ (stand) out here in the cold for at least forty minutes.

Maria: Oh, you poor thing! But we'd better hurry to get to the movie the-ater.

Alex: It's too late. The movie (7) _____ (start).

Maria: Really?

Alex: Yes. It (8) _____ (start) twenty minutes ago.

Use Your English

ACTIVITY 1: WRITING

You have just received a letter from the editor of your high school newspaper. She wants to include information about former students in the next edition of the pa-per. Write a letter to the editor, telling her what you have been doing recently. (Do not feel you have to use the present perfect progressive in every sentence! To make this a natural letter, think about all the other tenses you can use as well.)

UNIT GOAL REVIEW

Ask Ss to look at the goals on the opening page of the unit again. Help them understand how much they have accomplished in each area. One way to do this is to present contrasts between the present perfect progressive and the present perfect (Goal #4), and ask Ss to talk about the differences in meaning. (Sentences from Focus 5 and Exercise 5 lend themselves well to this.)

USE YOUR ENGLISH
Activity 1

If you feel Ss need more follow-up in accuracy work, decide how to handle errors in the letters you read. Do you want to simply correct them as you read? Would you prefer that Ss listen for inaccuracies? Or would you like to collect samples of errors and distribute them to Ss (or write on an overhead transparency), allowing them the opportunity for error correction?

VARIATION

After Ss write their letters, read them aloud, anonymously, and have the other Ss guess whose letter it is. If you choose to do this activity in this way, you might want to warn Ss *before* they write their letters so as to not give too much away!

Activity 2

If you think that particular Ss may not be comfortable doing this kind of activity in the classroom, ask each group to choose a volunteer to do the "acting." Rarely, in our experience, have we known an entire class who's hesitant to do such activities; there are also at least a few Ss who are "naturals" at acting and enjoy this.

Activity 3

This is an effective activity for a class lacking energy! Ss almost always participate enthusiastically in this team game. However, if you are the type of teacher who wants order in the classroom, you might think of ways to control or organize how teams will respond. Example: Make rules such as

1. Only one person from each team can respond after a short team conference.
2. Only one team can respond at a time. (You'll have to think of a way to vary this order.)

ACTIVITY 2: SPEAKING

The purpose of this game is to guess recent activities from their current results. Work in teams. Each team should try to think of four different results of recent activities. An example of one of these could be:

Recent Activity	Present Result
You have been exercising	and now you are exhausted.

When everyone is ready, each team takes turns acting out the results of the activities they have chosen. For example, Team A has chosen "being exhausted." Everybody in Team A gets up and acts out being exhausted. The rest of the class tries to guess what Team A has been doing. The first person to guess correctly, "You have been exercising and now you are exhausted," scores a point for his or her team.

ACTIVITY 3: SPEAKING

This is another team game. Each team presents a series of clues, and the rest of the class tries to guess what situation these clues refer to. For example, Team A chooses this situation: A woman has been reading a sad love story. The team tries to think of as many clues as possible that will help the other students guess the situation. When everyone is ready, Team A presents the first clue:

Team A: Her eyes are red.

The other teams make guesses based on this first clue:

Team B: She has been chopping onions.

Team A: No. She feels very sad.

Team C: She's been crying.

Team A: No. She's very romantic.

Team D: She's been fighting with her boyfriend.

Team A: No. She was alone while she was doing this.

Team C: She's been reading a sad love story.

You can choose one of the situations below or you can make up one of your own.

1. She or he has been crying.
2. She or he has been watching old movies.
3. She or he has been working late every night.
4. She or he's been training for the Olympics.
5. She or he has been chopping onions.
6. She or he has been feeling sick.
7. She or he has been gaining weight.

The person who guesses the correct situation scores a point for his or her team.

ACTIVITY 4: LISTENING

Listen to the tape of a conversation between two old friends. These people haven't seen each other for several years, so they have a lot to talk about.

STEP 1 Make a list of the things that each speaker has been doing or has recently done (or the things their family members and friends have done). Compare your list with a classmate's.

Speaker 1/man	Speaker 2/woman

STEP 2 Look at the lists that you and your partner made. Together, write a sentence about each thing on your lists using either the present perfect or the present perfect progressive.

ACTIVITY 5: SPEAKING/LISTENING

STEP 1 Interview a classmate about some of the things that she or he has been doing since coming to this country, this city, or this school that she or he has never done before. Tape-record your interview.

STEP 2 Think about your classmate's experiences. Choose three of them that you think are interesting, unusual, or important to your classmate. Write these down and then give this list to your teacher.

STEP 3 Your teacher will collect all of the lists from the class and then read them aloud. Can you guess who your teacher is talking about? No guesses are allowed if it is about you or the classmate you interviewed!

ACTIVITY 6: LISTENING/WRITING

Listen to the recording of your interview in Activity 5. Write down all the sentences which used the present perfect progressive (if there were any!). In each case, was it used correctly? Were there cases where the present perfect progressive could have been used but wasn't?

Activity 4

Play textbook audio. The tapescript for this listening activity appears on p. 509 of this book.

EXPANSION

To follow up further on Step 2, ask Ss to compare their lists with each other. Were there differences in the statements that they wrote? Discuss any differences as a class, if you feel this would be helpful.

Activity 5

As a pre-activity, ask Ss to think about things they've been doing that are new, unusual, or different from what other Ss have been doing. In other words, they'll need to be more specific (in both their questions and answers) than *"I've been studying English."*

Note: If you did the Variation suggested in Activity 1 of this Instructor's manual, Step 3 here will be redundant.

Activity 6

This is a particularly useful activity if you feel that the present perfect continuous is still a challenge for a number of Ss.

VARIATIONS

1. If you have access to several tape recorders, or to a language lab, it's nice to do this in small groups, or individually, as homework. But if you assign this as homework—if it's not done in the classroom—then you will need to figure out a system for circulating the tapes (assuming that the interviews were not all done on one tape).

2. If you are particularly ambitious, you can dub the separate tapes onto one.

3. You can be selective, choosing only those interviews that have clear examples of the structures you're looking for and speakers who are comprehensible.

The test for this unit can be found on pp. 452–454 of this book.
The answers are on p. 455.

TOEFL Test Preparation Exercises for Units 12–15 can be found on pp. 120–123 of the Workbook.
The answers are on p. 496 of this book.

ANSWER KEY

Activity 4

See tapescript (p. 509). Answers may include: **Man:** Has lived here for 6 years (since 1991), has had two children, has been busy being a dad, has been running a dry cleaning business, wife has been working when she is not busy with the kids. **Woman:** has been here about 5 years, has been working as an editor, has taken sailing lessons, has been mountain climbing; Eddy has been working in a law firm, they have had a child.

Unit 16

UNIT OVERVIEW

Unit 16 addresses the appropriate use of the expression *would you like* as a way to make offers, contrasting it with *do you want*.

UNIT GOALS

When reviewing the goals, you can determine how much students (Ss) may already know by asking them what the difference is between *would you like* and *do you want*. Do not discuss the difference here; at this point you are only reviewing the goals.

OPENING TASK

This **Opening Task** asks Ss to imagine that they are at a noisy party and trying to communicate with someone across the room. Ss often enjoy the opportunity to actually stand up and act out this situation.

SETTING UP THE TASK

To provide them with background, ask Ss to describe what's happening in the picture. By the time you finish this discussion, Ss should have noticed that two friends are trying to talk to each other across the room.

U N I T 16

MAKING OFFERS WITH WOULD YOU LIKE

UNIT GOALS:

- To make offers with *would you like*
- To choose correctly between *would you like* and *do you want*
- To use correct forms when accepting and refusing offers

OPENING TASK
A Noisy Party

Imagine that you are at a party. Your friend is on the other side of the room. You can see each other; but you cannot hear each other because the room is crowded and the music is very loud.

STEP 1 For this activity, work in pairs. Student A: Communicate the problem (listed on the chart below) to Student B **without speaking or writing.** Student B: **Do not** look at the list of problems. Your job is to offer a solution to Student A **without speaking or writing.** You will both need to act out your responses to each other. That is, you will need to use gestures, facial expressions, and other nonverbal ways of communicating.

STEP 2 When you have finished, check the list to see if Student B correctly understood Student A's problems. Then write down an appropriate **offer** using *Would you like . . . ?* on the Solutions side of the chart.

Problems	Solutions
Student A:	
1. You are thirsty.	
2. You have a headache.	
3. You are hot. The room is very stuffy. Your friend is standing by the window.	
4. You are hungry. Your friend is standing by a table with food on it.	
5. You have to sneeze but you don't have a tissue.	
6. You need a light for your cigarette and an ashtray.	
7. You are tired. You want your friend to give you a ride home.	
8. You are bored. The music is playing and you want to dance.	

CONDUCTING THE TASK

Step 1
S U G G E S T I O N
1. Have Ss form two 2 lines, with all the As on one side and all the Bs on the other so that the Ss really have to communicate across the room.
2. Check that Ss understand what they are to do, making it clear that B has to communicate a solution to A's problem.
3. Model the first one: mime that you are thirsty until someone mimes an appropriate "solution" to your problem.

Step 2
Instruct Ss to return to their seats and work together to write their offers. Answers will vary; see possible answers in key below.

CLOSING THE TASK
Discuss which problems were hardest to mime and if they had trouble coming up with solutions.

REVIEWING THE TASK
Have Ss share some of their solutions orally, noting similarities and differences. Point out that they will use their solutions in Exercise 1 (p. 240).

A good way to present this structure is to contrast it with *do you like*. Point out that *do you like* asks about likes and preferences in general, while *would you like* focuses on what the listener wants right now or in the future.

Exercise 1

Direct Ss to work with their partner to edit their solutions from the Opening Task (p. 239). Answers will vary.

Workbook Ex. 1, pp. 124–125.
Answers: TE p. 497.

FOCUS 2

Continuing with the structure addressed in Focus 1, the focus box compares *would you like* with *do you want to* demonstrate the difference in meaning and use. For further discussion of the modal *would*, see Unit 10, Focus 1 Grammar Note. Unit 17 looks at *would* from the point of view of requests.

EXPANSION

Practice the pronunciation of the less formal expression *do you want*:
Do ya wanna cuppa tea?
Does she wanna come over?
Do they wanna leave a little bit earlier?
Point out that this is not bad English, but the normal sound pattern of natural spoken English in less formal situations.

FOCUS **1**

Offers with *Would You Like*

EXAMPLES	EXPLANATIONS
(a) **Would you like** some coffee? (b) **Would you like** some help? (c) **Would you like to** sit down? (d) **Would you like to** use the bathroom?	There are several ways to make offers. Use *Would you like* + noun phrase. Use *Would you like to* + verb phrase.
(e) **Would you like me to** open the window? (f) **Would you like me to** take your coat?	Use *Would you like me to* + verb phrase to make an offer about yourself.
(g) **Would you like** Sally **to** open the window? (h) **Would you like** Auntie Bev **to** help you wash your hands?	Use *Would you like* (person's name) *to* + verb phrase to make an offer about someone else.

EXERCISE 1

Look back at the offers you wrote down in the Opening Task on page 239. Are your offers formed correctly? Change the ones that are not already correct.

FOCUS **2**

Would You Like . . . ?
or *Do You Want . . . ?*

EXAMPLES	EXPLANATIONS
(a) **Would you like** a cup of tea? (b) **Do you want** a cup of tea?	Use *Would you like . . . ?* if you want to be polite. Offers with *Do you want . . . ?* are usually used with close friends and family. Example (a) is more polite or formal than (b).
(c) **Want** me to help you with your bags? (d) **Would you like** me to help you with your bags?	In informal situations *"Do you"* can be omitted from *Do you want . . . ?* Example (c) is less formal than (d).

EXERCISE 2

Your new friend is having her first party in North America. She has invited some of her classmates, her teachers and their partners, and her neighbors, two elderly women. She has asked you to help her because she is nervous and does not know English very well. Change her commands and questions into polite offers, using *Would you like . . . ?* or *Do you want . . . ?*

Make an offer to . . .

1. Come in . . . . everyone
2. Sit down . . . . the neighbors
3. Give me your coat . . . . the teachers and their partners
4. Want a chair? . . . . the classmates
5. Want something to drink?. . . everyone
6. Cream in your coffee? . . . . . . the classmates
7. Want the window open? . . . . the teachers and their partners
8. Give me your cup . . . . the neighbors
I'll get more coffee.

EXERCISE 3

Look at the list below. Choose three things and make offers you hope your class-mates and your teacher will accept. Go around the class and make offers with *Would you like . . . ?* or *Do you want . . . ?* to as many people as possible.

When you respond to an offer: (a) be as polite as possible, and (b) if you must refuse the offer, give a reason for refusing it.

1. borrow a book
2. eat something
3. drink something
4. read a magazine
5. use a Walkman
6. close the window
7. leave the room
8. erase the blackboard
9. _____ (make up your own offer)

Making Offers with Would You Like **241**

Exercise 2

1. Point out that their relationships to the people they are addressing will determine whether it is appropriate to use *would you like* or *do you want* in this activity.
2. Review this activity by putting some Ss' answers on the board and call on the class to determine if the questions are appropriate and the forms are accurate.

Exercise 3

Emphasize the fact that politeness is important in this exercise. Answers will vary.

VARIATION

When Ss respond to offers, have them accept if they think the offer is polite and refuse if they think the offer was not polite enough. Doing the exercise this way illustrates the connections between form, meaning, and use.

Create more examples using your Ss as the "stars" of some realistic situations. For example:

Jorge: *Would you like some more coffee?*
Elda: *No, thanks! I can't have any more caffeine today!*

-or-

Liliana: *Do you guys want to meet later to study?*
Riaz: *Actually, I'm meeting Noom, but thanks anyway.*
Chihiro: *That'd be great for me. Liliana. What time?*

Workbook Exs. 2–4, pp. 125–128.
Answers: TE p. 497.

FOCUS **3**

Accepting and Refusing Offers

EXAMPLES	EXPLANATIONS
(a) A: Would you like something to drink? B: **Yes, please.** **(b)** A: Would you like me to help you? B: Yes, please. **That's very kind of you.** **(c)** A: Do you want the rest of my hamburger? B: **Sure. Thanks.**	**ACCEPTING OFFERS** Use *please* along with yes to politely accept offers. To be **very** polite, use an extra phrase to show that you appreciate the offer. (This is not usually necessary in informal situations.) In informal situations, words such as *sure, yeah,* and *thanks* show that you accept the offer.
(d) A: Would you like some coffee? B: **No, thank you.** OR **No, thanks.** **(e)** A: Would you like some coffee? B: No, thank you. **I've had enough.** **(f)** A: Would you like me to help you? B: No, thanks. **That's nice of you, but I can manage.**	**REFUSING OFFERS** Use *thank you/thanks* with *no* to politely refuse offers. For polite refusals, you can tell why the offer cannot be accepted.

EXERCISE 4

Look at the following responses. What offer was probably made? Write it down in the blank.

1. Offer: _____
   Response: No, thanks. I've had enough.

2. Offer: _____
   Response: Yeah, sure. I haven't eaten a thing all day.

3. Offer: _____
   Response: Oh, no, thank you. I've seen it already.

4. Offer: _____
   Response: No, thanks. I'm warm enough.

5. Offer: _____
   Response: Yeah, it's really heavy. Thanks.

6. Offer: _____
   Response: Thanks, I'd love to. That sounds great.

7. Offer: _____
   Response: Thanks, but I've already got one of my own.

EXERCISE 5

For each of the following situations, write a short dialogue in which one person makes a polite offer (using *Would you like . . .*) and the other person either politely accepts or politely refuses the offer. Then find a partner and read your dialogues aloud, taking parts.

1. The English instructor, at the front of the classroom, is ready to show a video in class today. The switch to turn on the video player is right by Stefan, at the back of the room.

   Stefan says: _____?

   The instructor says: _____.

2. The dinner at Mrs. Zimunga's house is almost finished. Mrs. Zimunga notices that some of the guests ate their dessert—cherry pie—very quickly, and she thinks they might want another piece.

   Mrs. Zimunga says: _____?

   A guest says: _____.

Exercise 4

Copy this exercise onto an overhead transparency. You can fill it out as a class, or have Ss work in pairs and review their answers as a class. Answers will vary.

Exercise 5

1. The first part of this exercise can be completed as homework or individually in class.
2. When Ss have finished working with partners, compare some of their dialogues as a class. Focus their attention on the context as a clue for how polite the requests should be. Remind them that the level of politeness depends on the person to whom the offer is being made, as well as the importance of the offer. It may be necessary to point out that being **too** polite is not always a good thing; with friends, for example, using *do you want* may be more appropriate for showing closeness between them when making small offers:

Amanda: *Wanna come over?*
Misha: *Yeah, great idea! See ya in a minute.*

ANSWER KEY

Exercise 4

1. Would you like some more . . . (coffee) . . . ? 2. Would you like some more . . . (soup/cake) . . . ? 3. Would you like to see . . . (a photograph of something/my new . . .)? 4. Would you like a blanket?/Would you like me to turn up the heat? 5. Would you like me to help you with that?/Would you like me to carry that for you? 6. Would you like to . . . (have lunch sometime?)? 7. Would you like to borrow . . . (my grammar book?)?

Exercise 5

Suggested offers:
1. Would you like me to turn the video on?
2. . . . some more pie? 3. . . . my seat?/. . . to sit here? 4. . . . me to mail these for you? 5. . . . a ride to work?
6. . . . a ride?

3. Alfredo has a seat at the front of the city bus. He notices that an elderly woman has just gotten on, but there are no more seats left.

Alfredo says: _____ ?

The elderly woman says: _____ .

4. As Mary is about to leave for the post office, she sees that there are several envelopes on the desk, stamped and addressed by her roommate Judith.

Mary says: _____ ?

Judith says: _____ .

5. Just as Thomas starts to drive away to work, he sees that his neighbor Rob is walking down the sidewalk to the bus stop. Thomas knows that Rob's office is not far from where he works.

Thomas says: _____ ?

Rob says: _____ .

6. Nyaradzo is jogging in the park, and she is about to cross a road. A stranger is waiting in his car, and he offers her a ride.

The stranger says: _____ ?

Nyaradzo says: _____ .

It's not always necessary to refuse offers **politely!** Check with your classmates to see their answers for Nyaradzo's response in item 6.

UNIT GOAL REVIEW

Ask Ss to look at the goals on the opening page of the unit again. Help them understand how much they have accomplished in each area. Do they think their offers are appropriate to the situation? Would they change any?

Use Your English

ACTIVITY 1: SPEAKING/LISTENING

How do native speakers of English behave at parties? Is their behavior at formal parties different from their behavior at informal parties where the guests are all close friends or relatives?

Use the chart below to interview native speakers (or people who have spent a long time in an English-speaking country). There are blanks at the bottom for other topics you might want to find out about. Tape-record your interview.

What Does the Host Do or Say When He or She...	Formal Parties	Informal Parties
(a) invites the guests to sit down		
(b) offers the guests something to eat		
(c) encourages the guests to eat/drink more		
(d) invites the guests to start some activity (dancing/playing a game)		
(e)		
(f)		

ACTIVITY 2: LISTENING

Listen to the interviews that you and your classmates tape-recorded in Activity 1. Did your classmates get any different information? Add to your chart as necessary.

USE YOUR ENGLISH

Activity 1
VARIATION
If Ss don't have the opportunity to meet native speakers of English in person, you can organize this activity as an e-mail pen-pal questionnaire.

1. Arrange for pen pals ahead of time. Sometimes you can contact Ss of the same age range at a sister school to set up a short- or long-term pen-pal arrangement.
2. Pair your Ss up with people from the other group.
3. Direct Ss to create their own questions, using the chart as a guide.
4. When Ss have finished "interviewing" their pen pal, they can either report back orally or in written form.

Activity 2
If Activity 1 was done as the variation, Activity 2 can be done as a reading exercise, with Ss posting their expressions on an e-mail discussion list. Don't interfere with the flow of the discussion; instead, note some examples to bring to class to illustrate some important examples.

Play textbook audio. The transcript for this listening appears on pp. 509–510 of this book.

Be sure to follow up Activity 3 with a class discussion of some of the language used. Have Ss decide which expressions are most and least formal.

ACTIVITY 3: LISTENING/ WRITING

Listen to the tape of two speakers talking about giving parties.

STEP 1 Listen to the tape of two people talking about giving parties. Write some of the problems the man talks about in the first column below. Write the suggestions the woman makes about each problem in the second column.

Party Problems	Suggestions
1.	
2.	
3.	

STEP 2 Discuss the problems and suggestions with a partner. How did the man respond to the woman's suggestions?

STEP 3 Listen again. What were the exact words the woman suggested using for the three problems you listed in Step 1? Write those words below.

Suggestions:

1. _____

2. _____

3. _____

STEP 4 What might the people at the party say in response to each of these suggestions? List three sentences they might use to accept the offers.

Accepting the Offers:

1. _____

2. _____

3. _____

STEP 5 List three sentences they might use to refuse the offers.

Refusing the Offers:

1. _____

2. _____

3. _____

246 | UNIT 16

ANSWER KEY

Activity 3
Check tapescript for answers (pp. 509–510).

A C T I V I T Y 4 : S P E A K I N G / L I S T E N I N G

STEP 1 How can your classmate help you?

Think of two things that a classmate could do for you that would be helpful. Take two pieces of paper and write down one of those things on each piece. Do not write down your name.

Your teacher will collect the papers.

STEP 2 Your teacher will mix up the papers and give you two papers that other students wrote. (Make sure that you don't get your own!) Your job is to guess who wrote each request for help. Go around the room to find the person. Make an offer to help him or her using *Would you like . . .?* or *Do you want . . .?*

STEP 3 You must accept an offer if it is about the help you requested (the thing you wrote down on your piece of paper). You must refuse all other offers for help, even if they sound good.

A C T I V I T Y 5 : S P E A K I N G / W R I T I N G

STEP 1 Your good friend is at home in bed sick. You want to help out and make your friend feel better. Make a list of things that you might do to help. Then get together with a partner who will play the role of your friend. Make offers using *Would you like . . .?* and *Do you want . . .?* Your "friend" can accept or refuse your offers.

STEP 2 Write down responses to the offers you made in Step 1. If your friend accepted your offer, the response will go in the Accept column. If your friend refused your offer, the response will go in the Refuse column.

For each column, rank these responses in order of politeness. (Which responses seemed most polite? Which seemed least polite?)

Response to your offers	
ACCEPT	REFUSE

Compare your chart to other students' charts

Activity 4

1. You can have Ss write down real requests for help, or have them be more creative and write their "dream" requests. For example:
   Take my TOEFL test for me.
   Give me a million dollars.
   Arrange for me to meet Madonna.
2. Remind them not to write their names on their papers.

Activity 5
E X P A N S I O N

For further discussion of politeness, have Ss consider how they would change their offers if they were speaking with: their grandmother, their younger brother or sister, the President of the United States.

The test for this unit can be found on pp. 456–457.
The answers are on p. 458 of this book.

Unit 17

UNIT OVERVIEW

Unit 17 provides practice with making polite requests, agreeing to and refusing requests, asking for permission, and giving or politely refusing permission. The modals *can, could, will, would,* and *may* are introduced, as they are important elements in performing these functions.

UNIT GOALS

Review the goals listed on this page to see what students (Ss) should be familiar with by the end of this unit.

OPENING TASK

Note: The purpose of this task is to provide a natural context for the use of requests. The problem-solving format focuses attention on meaning rather than form, which will allow you to see whether Ss are able to produce the forms spontaneously.

SETTING UP THE TASK

Carefully explain the task situation here. You could act out what happened—how the coffee got spilled on the note—to show how difficult it is now to read everything clearly.

UNIT 17

REQUESTS AND PERMISSION

Can, Could, Will, Would, **and** *May*

UNIT GOALS:

- To make polite requests
- To politely agree to and refuse requests
- To ask for permission
- To give or politely refuse permission

OPENING TASK
The Messy Note

You are going to take care of a friend's house while she is on vacation. Your friend has left you a note with instructions about what to do while she is gone. Unfortunately, someone has spilled coffee on the note, and now it is difficult to read.

STEP 1 Complete the missing parts of the note so that it makes sense. Example A has been done for you.

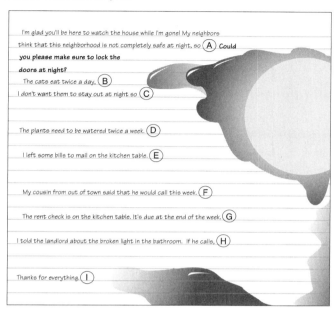

I'm glad you'll be here to watch the house while I'm gone! My neighbors think that this neighborhood is not completely safe at night, so (A) **Could you please make sure to lock the doors at night?**

The cats eat twice a day. (B)

I don't want them to stay out at night so (C)

The plants need to be watered twice a week. (D)

I left some bills to mail on the kitchen table. (E)

My cousin from out of town said that he would call this week. (F)

The rent check is on the kitchen table. It's due at the end of the week. (G)

I told the landlord about the broken light in the bathroom. If he calls, (H)

Thanks for everything. (I)

STEP 2 Now look at the choices for the missing parts of the note above. Write the appropriate number in the spaces on the note.

1. . . . could you ask him to fix it as soon as possible?

2. . . . remember to lock the windows and doors when it gets dark. Thanks.

3. . . . so will you please give them water on Tuesday and Friday?

4. . . . See you next week!

5. . . . Would you mind mailing them for me tomorrow morning?

6. . . . please make sure they come in around 8:00.

7. . . . Would you take a message and tell him I'll be back on the twenty-ninth?

8. . . . so could you feed them in the morning and at night?

9. . . . Please mail it before Friday.

Were your "answers" to the missing parts similar to these?

CONDUCTING THE TASK

Step 1

Ss work in pairs or small groups, reading the note and trying to guess what could go in the missing/illegible parts. They can write the guesses in the spaces on the notes, or on another sheet of paper. It's a good idea to have Ss cover up the actual missing parts listed under Step 2 while they work on Step 1.

SUGGESTION

After this step, it's helpful to bring the class together in order to provide an opportunity for Ss to compare their guesses thus far.

Step 2

Ss read the actual missing parts and decide where they should go in the note.

CLOSING THE TASK

Bring the whole class together to check how much Ss agree.

REVIEWING THE TASK

Weave in or elicit the idea that in each sentence the writer is making a request. As a bridge to Focus 1, you could write on the board or make an overhead transparency of the requests. Underline—or have Ss underline—the parts of the sentence that show that the speaker is making a request.

FOCUS 1

SUGGESTIONS

1. One way to address the grammar point covered here is to read (a) through (f) in order of politeness, asking *Do you see that (a) sounds more polite than (e)?*, etc. Feel free to exaggerate, using your tone of voice to demonstrate distinctions (e.g., (f) in a gruff, flat-toned voice; (b) in a higher pitched, clearly more polite, questioning voice). You could also elicit from Ss (g)—a command: Lend me your notes (the same as (f) but without "*please*").

2. Point out that between some of the questions—(b) as compared to (c), for example—the distinction is very slight, and some native speakers might consider them relatively "equal" in terms of degree of politeness. But the difference between (a) and (e), for example, is noticeable to most native speakers, especially if the *please* in (e) is omitted.

Exercise 1

To give Ss more time to come up with and discuss their answers, it makes sense to do this exercise in small groups or pairs. Ask Ss to defend their answers in terms of the context—how important is it to be polite with those people in that setting. *Why did they choose to make the request in that particular way?*

FOCUS **1**

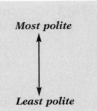

Making Polite Requests

I left my notes at home.
(a)	**Would you mind** lending me your notes?	*Most polite*
(b)	**Would** you (**please**) lend me your notes?	
(c)	**Could** you lend me your notes (**please**)?	
(d)	**Will** you lend me your notes (**please**)?	
(e)	**Can** you (**please**) lend me your notes?	
(f)	**Please** lend me your notes.	*Least polite*

EXERCISE 1

Below are some situations in which requests are commonly made. For each situation, make a polite request.

1. You want to know what time it is. You find someone who is wearing a watch and you say: _____

2. When you pay for your groceries at the supermarket, you remember that you need some change for the telephone. You hand the cashier a dollar and say: _____

3. You have been waiting in line at the bank for fifteen minutes, but you need to get a drink of water. You turn to the friendly-looking person standing behind you in line, and you say: _____

4. You are watching a videotape in class. Your classmate in front of you is in the way. You want him to move his chair. You say: _____

5. Your class has just watched a videotape. It is finished; your classroom is still dark. Your instructor wants the student who is sitting near the light switch to turn on the lights, so she or he says: _____

ANSWER KEY

Exercise 1
Answers will vary.
1. Could you please tell me what time it is?
2. Could I have change for this dollar, please?

3. Would you mind holding my place in line?
4. Could you please move your chair?
5. Would you turn on the light, please?
6. Would you close the door, please?
7. Could you please speak a little more loudly?

6. There is a lot of noise outside your classroom. Your teacher wants the student who is sitting near the door to close it, so she or he says: _____

_____

7. A classmate is giving a presentation, but she is speaking very quietly. You cannot hear her. You say: _____

_____

Politely Refusing Requests

EXAMPLES	EXPLANATIONS
Can you lend me your notes? **(a) I'm sorry,** but I need them to study for the test. OR **(b) I'm afraid that** I didn't take any notes. OR **(c) I'd like to,** but I left mine at home, too.	If you have to refuse a request, it is polite to say **why** you are refusing. Phrases such as *I'm afraid that* or *I'm sorry* help to "soften" the *No*, and make it more polite.

EXERCISE 2

Make requests of all your classmates and find someone who will grant your request (say *yes*) for the following things. For each request, try to find at least one person who will say *yes*. If a classmate says *no*, write down the reason for refusing your request.

REQUEST	REASON FOR SAYING NO
1. lend you some money	
2. buy you a cup of coffee	
3. help you study for a test	
4. give you a ride home after class	
5. teach you how to dance	

Requests and Permission: *Can, Could, Will, Would,* and *May* | **251**

ANSWER KEY

Exercise 2
Since answers are dependent on the reasons that Ss think up, they will vary.

SUGGESTION

1. Contrast these answers with a simple "No." Explain that a lack of elaboration on *why* you are refusing a request is often interpreted as rudeness in most American English-speaking contexts.

2. Ask for comparative examples in other cultures and languages. Is the same action required? In other words, is it acceptable/polite to just say *no* and give no reason for your refusal?

Workbook Ex. 3, p. 132.
Answers: TE p. 498.

Exercise 2
SUGGESTIONS

1. Ss may want to redraw this chart on a larger piece of paper or in their notebooks so that there is more room for notetaking.

2. Some Ss need a little reassurance that it is okay to refuse a request, that there are polite ways to do this, and that the practice they will get in Exercise 2 may be very useful! Remind Ss that it *is* acceptable to refuse requests and, in fact, some native English speakers are irritated if they think that a "yes" is insincere, that the person doesn't actually want to respond positively to a request but feels, for some reason, that he/she must.

EXPANSION

Again, it may be helpful for Ss to give information about their own cultures and languages. Are there situations in the Ss' home cultures where, no matter the circumstance, it is rude to refuse a request?

SUGGESTION

1. Ask Ss if they have heard other positive responses to requests. Then allow them to practice these common responses in Focus 3.
2. It is helpful to model the word *"Yeah"* and have Ss repeat; occasionally there are Ss who have never actually uttered this word themselves (they are likely to say *yes* but not the more informal *yeah*), though they may have heard it.
3. Point out that it's acceptable to just use *"Yes"* or *"Yeah"* rather than following it with *"I can"* and *"I will."*

Exercise 3

VARIATIONS

1. These situations can be performed as role plays, with Ss standing up and speaking "ad lib" or from notes, rather than reading their answers word for word.

To do this exercise efficiently, assign pairs one particular dialogue (one pair is assigned #1, another #2, etc.) so that they are able to focus and practice "their" dialogue. Allow Ss a few minutes to come up with answers and practice.

2. Have the audience "rate" the role play on a 1–5 scale: 5 is appropriate (polite enough but not too polite), 1 is inappropriate (impolite or much too polite, given the circumstances). If there is a lot of variety in the ratings, ask raters to explain and defend their rating, using evidence from the context.

FOCUS **3**

Responding to Requests

EXAMPLES	EXPLANATIONS
Can you lend me your notes? **(a)** I'd be glad to. **(b)** Sure, why not? **(c)** Yeah, no problem. **(d)** Yeah, I guess so.	You can respond to requests with short answers. Examples (b) and (c) are very informal. Example (d) shows that the speaker is uncertain.
Could you loan me five dollars? **(e)** Yes, I can. **(f)** **NOT:** Yes, I could.	*Could* and *would* are **not** used in responses to requests.
Would you go to the store with me? **(g)** Yes, I will. **(h)** **NOT:** Yes, I would.	

EXERCISE 3

Make polite requests for the following situations. Use *can, could, will, would,* or *would you mind* in these requests.

What is the response? How is the request politely accepted or refused?

1. There's a place on your back that suddenly begins to itch. You ask your close friend to scratch it.

   You say: _____ ?

   What does your friend say? _____ .

   But your friend is not quite getting the right place. So you say:

   _____?

ANSWER KEY

Exercise 3

Answers will vary. Possible requests:
1. Can you scratch my back? 2. Would you mind not smoking? 3. Can you move it a little more to the left/right? 4. Would you please take our picture? 5. Would you mind turning down your music?

---

2. You are at a restaurant, and the people at the next table are smoking. You want them to stop, so you say: _____ ?

What do they say? _____ .

3. Your friend is helping you hang a picture on your wall. She is holding it up while you decide where it should go.

You say: _____ ?

What does your friend do or say? _____ .

4. You are visiting a famous tourist site, and a family wants you to take their photograph together.

One of the family members says: _____

_____

What do you do or say? _____

_____

5. You are trying to study for a test, and your neighbors are playing very loud music. You can't concentrate, so you say, _____ ?

Exercise 4

S U G G E S T I O N S

1. This exercise goes quickly if you have a student read each question aloud. You can elicit answers from that student, from the one sitting next to the speaker, or from any one in the class.

2. Point out how these question phrases are reduced in natural, informal speech:
   Do you mind sounds like *D'ya mind*
   Can you sounds like *Can ya*
   Could you sounds like *Could'ja*
   Would you sounds like *Would'ja*

3. Model these questions for Ss and have them imitate your speech. Emphasize that it is not necessary for them to sound like this, but that they are likely to hear native speakers reduce these phrases in this way.

EXERCISE 4

Write the number of the following questions in the appropriate box in the chart below. The first one has been done for you.

Something the Speaker Wants To Do (Request for Permission)	Something the Speaker Wants Somebody Else To Do (General Request)	
1.		

1. Do you mind if I turn on the radio?
2. Can you open the window?
3. May I ask you a question?
4. Could you speak more slowly?
5. Would you mind lending me your dictionary?
6. Can I leave early?
7. Would you tell me the answer?
8. May we swim in your pool?
9. Could you show us how to do it?
10. Could I borrow your knife?
11. Would you mind if I handed in my assignment a day late?

A N S W E R   K E Y

Exercise 4
Request for Permission: 1, 3, 6, 8, 10, 11
General Request: 2, 4, 5, 7, 9

FOCUS **4**

Asking for Permission

(a)	**Would you mind** if I left early?	*Most polite*
(b)	**Do you mind** if I leave early?	
(c)	**May** I leave early?	
(d)	**Could** I leave early?	
(e)	**Can** I leave early?	*Least polite*

EXERCISE 5

For each answer, what was probably the question?

1. Question: _____ ?

Teacher to student: No, I'd like you to hand it in on Friday. I announced the due date two weeks ago, so I'm afraid I won't be able to make any exceptions.

2. Question: _____ ?

Friend to friend: Sure, it is a little cold in here.

3. Question: _____ ?

Lecturer to member of the audience: Sorry, but I'm going to have to ask you to hold your questions until the end of my talk. We'll have 15 minutes for questions.

4. Question: _____ ?

Secretary (on phone): Yes, may I tell him who's calling?

5. Question: _____ ?

Twelve-year-old child (on phone): Yes, may I tell him who's calling?

6. Question: _____ ?

Mother (to child): OK, you can have one more. But only *one*, because we're going to eat soon and I don't want you to spoil your appetite.

7. Question: _____ ?

Hostess to guest: Oh, of course, please help yourself. I'm glad you like them.

8. Question: _____ ?

Customer to salesperson: Yes, I want to look at the sweaters that are on sale. The ones that were advertised in the newspaper?

Requests and Permission: *Can, Could, Will, Would,* and *May* **255**

SUGGESTIONS

1. Point out the similarities between this focus box and Focus 1: that *would you mind* questions are considered most polite; *could* questions somewhere in the middle; and *can* questions least polite.
2. Again, as with Focus 1, explain that the distinctions between (a)–(b) and (c)–(d), for example, aren't particularly "strong," but that the difference between the two extremes (a)–(e) is.

VARIATION

Try eliciting this chart from Ss, rather than presenting it to them first.

1. Ask Ss to make a diagram arrow like the one in Focus 1, with most polite phrases on top and least polite on the bottom.
2. Read (a) through (e) in random order, asking Ss to write the question on the chart in the place they think it should go.
3. Review Focus 4 to see if Ss' guesses/insights were "on" or "off." It has been our experience that they are usually "on."

Workbook Ex. 5, pp. 134–135.
Answers: TE p. 498.

Exercise 5

Since this exercise is "turned around"—Ss supply the question rather than the answer—it might be helpful to do #1 as a group (although there are several exercises like this in previous units).

ANSWER KEY

Exercise 5

Answers will vary. All general requests and requests for permission should include Can . . . ?, Could . . . ?, Will . . . ?, Would . . . ?, May . . . ?, and possibly please or Would you mind . . . ?

1. Would you mind if I handed in my assignment late?   2. May I close the window?   3. Can I ask a question, please?   4. May I speak to . . . ?   5. Can I talk to . . . ?   6. Could I have a cookie?   7. May I have another . . . ?   8. May I help you?

SUGGESTIONS

1. Refer back to Focus 3, pointing out that it's acceptable to just use *"Yes"* or *"Yeah"* for positive responses; it's not always necessary to use the short answers: *"Yes, you can."* or *"Yes, you may."* As with Focus 3, informal responses such as *"Yeah, sure."* and *"No problem."* are also acceptable.

   Learners are sometimes confused by the positive response to *"Would you mind."* since a *"No"* is appropriate (*"No, I wouldn't mind"*).

2. Point out that sometimes an additional phrase is added after the *"No"* for clarification: *"No, that's fine."* Or sometimes *"Okay"* is given as the response rather than *"No."*

3. If this structure appears to be troublesome for Ss, you can supplement this point by having Ss ask and answer *"Would you mind . . . "* questions: *"Would you mind if I borrowed your notes?"* *"Would you mind loaning me your book?"* etc.

Exercise 6

While Ss are working in pairs, circulate and listen, noting questions and responses that strike you as either very good and natural sounding, or as inappropriate. Then tell Ss some of the questions and response you heard, asking them what *their* reactions are.

UNIT GOAL REVIEW

Ask Ss to look at the goals on the opening page of the unit again. Assist them in understanding much they have accomplished in each area. One way is to present the goals as a checklist, having Ss create examples for each.

FOCUS **5**

▶ # Responding to Requests for Permission

EXAMPLES	EXPLANATIONS
Would you mind if I left early?	
(a) No, not at all.	Use short phrases to answer requests for permission. If you refuse a request, it is polite to give the reason.
(b) Sorry, but I need you to stay until 5:00.	
May I leave early?	
(c) Yes, of course.	
(d) Sorry, but I'd rather have you stay until 5:00.	
Could I leave early?	
(e) Yes, you can.	*Could* is not usually used in responses to requests for permission.
(f) **NOT:** Yes, you could.	

EXERCISE 6

For each of the following situations, work with a classmate to make general requests or requests for permission, and then respond to these requests. Decide how polite you need to be in each situation and whether *can, could, will, would, may, would you mind,* or *do you mind* is the most appropriate to use. There is more than one way to ask and answer each question.

1. You are at a friend's house, and you want to use the phone.
2. Your teacher says something, but you do not understand, and you want her to repeat it.
3. Your friend has asked you to pick her up at the airport. You want to know if her flight, #255 from Denver, is on time, so you call the airline.
4. You want to borrow your roommate's car.
5. Your roommate is going to the store, and you remember that you need some film.
6. You are the first one to finish the reading test in class. You want to find out from your teacher if you are allowed to leave the room now.
7. It is very cold in class, and the window is open.
8. You see that your teacher is in her office with the door partly open. You want to go in to talk to her.
9. You are on the phone with the dentist's secretary because you want to change your appointment time.
10. You are at a close friend's house, and you would like a cup of tea.
11. You want to hold your friend's baby.

ANSWER KEY

Exercise 6

Answers will vary. All requests and requests for permission include *Can . . . ? Could . . . ? Will . . . ? Would . . . ? May . . . ?* and possibly *Would you mind . . . ?* Responses can be nonverbal (as in #7—the person simply shuts the window) or they can include short answers such as *Yeah, sure . . .* If requests for permission are refused, they should include a reason and/or *Sorry, but . . .* or another "softening" phrase.

Possible questions are:
1. May I use the phone? **2.** Could you repeat that, please? **3.** Could you please tell me if Flight #255 from Denver is on time? **4.** May I borrow your car? **5.** Would you mind buying me some film? **6.** May I leave the room now? **7.** Can I/Would you shut the window, please? **8.** Can you spare some time to talk with me? **9.** Could I please change my appointment? **10.** Can I have some tea? **11.** May I hold your baby?

Use Your English

ACTIVITY 1: LISTENING/SPEAKING

STEP 1 Go to a restaurant or cafeteria and pay attention to the different kinds of requests that are used. Try to observe five different requests. Take notes on these, using the chart below.

Observation Sheet		
PLACE:		
TIME:		
DAY:		
REQUEST	WHO MADE IT	RESPONSE

STEP 2 Discuss the results of your observations with other classmates. Were their observations similar? What words were used most often in requests: *can, could, will, would,* or *would you mind*?

USE YOUR ENGLISH

Activity 1
SUGGESTIONS

1. Ss may want to redraw these charts on a larger piece of paper so that there is more room for notetaking.

2. If your class hasn't yet done this kind of observation/research activity, it's good to work in teams of two or three, each choosing a different site or a different post at one site (for example, in one cafeteria, Ss go to different places—one near the check stand/cash register, one where the food is served, etc.). This way Ss can check in with each other and give support and suggestions, if they are experiencing problems.

VARIATION

Each research team can present samples of their "data" as a role play. They "perform" for the rest of the class a few of the short interactions that they observed.

Activity 2

SUGGESTION

Remind Ss that their requests should be polite. Or incorporate this reminder into the activity as a "rule": You don't have to respond positively to the request (a "Yes" answer) if you feel that the request was impolite. In this case, the person who made the request must re-phrase it so that it is polite, or make a new request to another person.

Activity 3

VARIATIONS

1. Have Ss "eavesdrop" on telephone conversations that occur in public places, if you feel that this would not be inappropriate (as in crowded areas where you wouldn't be noticed—where it wouldn't offend the speaker, in other words!).

2. If Ss are in a situation where someone they know is about to make a phone call, have them ask her/him if they would mind if they "listened in"—Ss should feel free to tell them the purpose of their research.

ACTIVITY 2: SPEAKING

Play this game in a group of five or six students or with the whole class.

STEP 1 Pick a letter from the alphabet. Ask a classmate to buy you something at the mall that begins with that letter.

STEP 2 Your classmate must think of something to buy that begins with the letter you chose and then he or she must tell you what it is.

STEP 3 Your classmate then chooses another student.

▶ **EXAMPLES:**

Sara: Bruno, would you please buy me something that begins with the letter S?

Bruno: Sure. I'll buy you some stamps. Sue, could you buy me something that begins with the letter M?

Sue: Ok. I'll buy you a magazine. Hartmut, would you mind buying me something that begins with the letter P?

ACTIVITY 3: LISTENING

How do people request permission to speak with someone on the telephone? Are these ways different depending on the situation?

Interview people about what they say in different situations. Some examples are speaking with a doctor, speaking with a teacher, speaking with a close friend, and speaking with a family member.

Setting	Relationship	What They Say

A C T I V I T Y 4 : W R I T I N G

Congratulations! You have just won a certificate for Easy-Does-It Housecleaning Services. This entitles you to four hours of housecleaning service for your home. First make a list of what you want the housecleaner to do in your home (clean the windows, do the laundry, mop the floor, etc.). Then write these requests in a polite note to your housecleaner.

A C T I V I T Y 5 : R E A D I N G / S P E A K I N G

STEP 1 What would you say in each of the situations below? Respond to each situation. Then compare your results with other students' results.

1. You are in the bookstore with a friend, standing in line to buy a textbook you need for class later that day. You realize you have left your wallet at home and you want your friend to lend you twenty dollars to pay for the book.

   You: _____

   _____

   Your friend: Sure. You can pay me back next week.

2. You have just heard about a new teaching assistantship in your field, and you feel that you are qualified. You need to ask your teacher for a letter of recommendation.

   You: _____

   _____

   Your teacher: I'd be happy to. When do you need it?

3. You are visiting a close friend at her house. You realize you are thirsty, but your friend hasn't offered you anything to drink.

   You: _____

   _____

   Your friend: Sure. Help yourself. You know where everything is, right?

Activity 4
S U G G E S T I O N S

1. It might be helpful for Ss to refer back to the Opening Task in order to get a sense of what is meant here by "a polite note."
2. If you think it would be useful, assign this activity as homework. To follow up, you can use examples from Ss' own writing to demonstrate polite (and possibly impolite!) requests.
3. Or show Ss these examples on an overhead transparency or on a handout, and let them judge how appropriate the requests are in terms of politeness.

Activity 5
Step 1

This is an appropriate activity for role plays. Ask volunteers to perform a question and response sequence for the whole class. (If it's possible—and comfortable—tape record these for Activity 6.) For each role play: *How does the "audience" react? Was the request polite enough? If not, what is a better way of making the request?*

A N S W E R K E Y

Activity 5

Step 1: Answers may vary slightly, but all should include a polite request and/or a request for permission.

4. You just made plans to study for a big test with your classmates, but suddenly you realize that you have a doctor's appointment at the same time—at 2:00 tomorrow. You decide that you want to change your doctor's appointment, so you call the doctor's secretary.

You: _____

_____

The secretary: I *think* it's possible. When would you be available?

5. It's time to leave the house to meet your friend for a dinner date. But you can't find your car keys anywhere, and your friend has already left her house to meet you. You want to borrow your roommate's car and look for your car keys later.

You: _____

_____

Your roommate: Yeah, no problem.

6. You are visiting a close friend's mother. She has made peach pie, and you'd love to have a second piece. Your friend has told you that her mother loves to feed people, so you know that it wouldn't be rude to ask for another piece.

You: _____

_____

Your friend's mother: Oh, of course! Let me get it for you.

STEP 2 Ask at least three native speakers of English or people who have spent a long time in an English-speaking country to respond to each situation. Tape-record their answers.

VARIATION
Step 2

If tape-recording is a problem, Ss can do this step in research teams of two or three, and take detailed notes. It's helpful to have more than one student involved, in order to increase the validity of the observation. Compiling notes will help to ensure the accuracy of what was said.

ACTIVITY 6: LISTENING/ WRITING

Now listen to the text tape to hear what other speakers said in response to some of the questions in Activity 5.

STEP 1 Compare the responses of the speakers on the tape with your responses in Activity 5, and also to the responses of the speakers you interviewed. What is your reaction to the speakers' responses? For example, were you surprised at anything they said? Do you consider these polite responses? Do you think any of their requests would be refused?

STEP 2 For each situation, write down the **exact** requests that the speaker made (if there were any). Then rate each request in terms of politeness on a 1 to 5 scale (1 = most polite; 5 = least polite/most informal). Are there any requests that are "off the scale" (not at all polite, or even rude)? Compare your ratings to other classmates' ratings, and discuss your results.

Activity 6

Play textbook audio. The tapescript for this listening activity appears on p. 510 of this book.

SUGGESTION
Step 2

If Activity 5, Steps 1 and 2 were tape recorded, then this activity can be conducted with these as well. Ss write down the exact requests and then rate these on a 1–5 point scale. This is helpful for further listening comprehension practice, since it allows the opportunity for detailed listening. It also helps in "fine tuning" in that Ss can further check their insights about the degree of politeness (or impoliteness) in requests.

✔️

The test for this unit can be found on pp. 459–460 of this book.
The answers are on p. 461.

ANSWER KEY

Activity 6
Step 2
See tapescript (p. 510).
Step 2, exact requests:
Agnes: Please give me some money.
Eliza: Would you be able to lend me some money?

Agnes: Could you please write me a letter of recommendation?
Eliza: Would you be so kind as to write me a letter of recommendation?
Eliza: Could I have a second piece?

Unit 18

UNIT OVERVIEW

In this unit, the structure *used to* is introduced to talk about past facts and habits, contrasting with *still* and *anymore*.

UNIT GOALS

Before beginning the Opening Task, review these goals.

OPENING TASK

The purpose of this activity is to determine how much the students (Ss) already know about this structure. Listen to their language use and make note of errors for later discussion.

SETTING UP THE TASK

If you have a high school yearbook, bring it to class. Since many cultures do not have yearbooks, Ss may want to find out more.

CONDUCTING THE TASK

Step 1

Ss come up with as much information as they can on each person. When groups are finished, they share their information with the class.

VARIATION

Do this activity as a game:
1. Tell Ss that the object of this game is to see which group can label all of the pictures the quickest.
2. Using an overhead transparency of the photos as a visual aid, have groups come to a different section of the board and write a list of these famous people.
3. When each group finishes, they turn around and raise their hands, keeping their list hidden. Note the order in which they finish.
4. Once all have finished, have the Ss return to their seats. Review their lists in the order groups finished. Whichever group was the first to come up with the most complete list wins.
5. Use their list to label the photos on the overhead transparency.

U N I T   18

U SED TO WITH STILL AND ANYMORE

UNIT GOALS:

- To use *used to* to compare past and present situations
- To correctly form statements and questions with *used to*
- To use *still* and *anymore* correctly
- To know the correct sentence positions for adverbs of frequency

OPENING TASK
Famous People Then and Now

STEP 1   Work with several other students. Look at the photographs of these well-known people as they look today. If you are not sure who all these people are or why they are famous, try to find someone in the class who is.

ANSWER KEY

Opening Task Answers
Step 1
Top row (l-r): Meryl Streep Madonna Diana Ross

Bottom row (l-r): Bruce Springsteen Tina Turner Michael Jackson

---

STEP 2 Look below at the photographs of the same people. These photographs all came from their high school yearbooks. Match the old photographs with the current ones.

STEP 3 In your opinion, who has changed a lot? Who hasn't changed much?

▶ **EXAMPLE:** I think Tina Turner has changed a lot.

Why?

Because she used to _____ but now

_____ .

Step 2
In their groups, Ss match these older photos with the more current ones. Review their answers before they move on to Step 3.

Step 3
Groups decide who has changed the most, using the model sentence as a guide. Point out that many answers are possible.

CLOSING THE TASK
Discuss their ideas as a class. Do they have similar ideas?

REVIEWING THE TASK
Review vocabulary which they needed to describe differences in appearance, such as hair styles and color.

EXPANSION
Using your yearbook, have Ss describe how you have changed.

ANSWER KEY

Opening Task Answers
Step 2
Top row (l-r): Tina Turner   Michael Jackson
Diana Ross

Bottom row (l-r): Bruce Springsteen
Meryl Streep   Madonna

Add further examples from ones Ss created
on their own in the Opening Task.

Exercise 1

V A R I A T I O N

Ss can complete this activity on a separate
sheet of paper for homework.
1. To provide feedback to the class,
   combine a list of sentences with errors
   and distribute this list after you have
   discussed Focus 2.
2. Have them work in pairs to correct the
   errors in form and meaning.
3. Discuss their corrections as a class.

Workbook Ex. 1, p. 136.
Answers: TE p. 498.

▶ Comparing Past and Present with *Used To*

EXAMPLES	EXPLANATIONS
(a) Tina Turner **used to** have short, wavy hair (but now she doesn't).	*Used to* can be used to show that something was true in the past, but now it isn't.
(b) Madonna **used to** wear ordinary clothes (but now she doesn't).	*Used to* can also show that something happened regularly (often) in the past, but now it doesn't.

EXERCISE 1

Make statements with *used to* about the changes in Madonna and Bruce
Springsteen. Use the words in parentheses. You can add other ideas of your own,
and you can get information from other students if you need to know more.

1. Madonna
   (a) (go out every night) _She used to go out every night._
   (b) (be a dancer) _____
   (c) (be poor) _____.
   (d) (live in Michigan) _____.
2. Bruce Springsteen
   (a) (have straight hair) _____
   (b) (play football in high school) _____
   (c) (live in New Jersey) _____
   (d) (sing about blue-collar life) _____

Now add statements with *used to* about the other people in the Opening Task.

A N S W E R   K E Y

Exercise 1
1. Madonna didn't use to be a singer; she used
to be a dancer. She used to be poor and she
used to live in Michigan.   2. Bruce
Springsteen used to have straight hair. He used
to play football in high school. In addition, he
used to live in New Jersey and he used to sing
about blue-collar life.

FOCUS **2**

Used To

STATEMENT	NEGATIVE	QUESTION
I You We They } **used to** work	I You We They } did not **use to** work (didn't)	Did { I you we they } **use to** work?
She He It } **used to** work	She He It } did not **use to** work (didn't)	Did { she he it } **use to** work?

FOCUS **3**

Anymore

EXAMPLES	EXPLANATIONS
(a) Madonna used to live in Michigan, but she doesn't live there **anymore**.	Use *anymore* to show a change in a situation or activity.
(b) Madonna used to live in Michigan, but she doesn't **anymore**.	If the second verb phrase has the same verb, you can omit it.
(c) Madonna doesn't live in Michigan **anymore**.	You can use *anymore* without *used to*. In (c) we understand that she used to live there.
(d) We **don't** go there anymore. **(e)** They **never** talk to me anymore. **(f)** **No one** likes him anymore.	Use *anymore* only with a negative.

EXERCISE 2

Interview your classmates about the changes in their lives. Then write short statements about these changes, using *anymore* and *used to*. (The word *but* may be helpful.)

▶ **EXAMPLE:** *Teresita used to live in Guam, but she doesn't anymore. She used to be single, but now she lives with a partner.*

Used To with *Still* and *Anymore* **265**

Sometimes Ss confuse *used to* with *be used to*. If this comes up in class, point out that the structure addressed in this unit is a verb. *Be used to,* on the other hand, is the present form of the verb *be* with the adjective *used +* *to,* meaning "be accustomed to." Point out that *used to* can only occur in the past time, while *be used to* appears in past, present, and future:

*I **used to** live in New Orleans.* (→ past only)
Although it was strange at first . . .
*. . . I **was** soon **used to** living in New Orleans.* (→ past)
*. . . I'm now **used to** living in New Orleans.* (→ present)
*. . . I'll soon **be used to** living in New Orleans.* (→ future)

Workbook Ex. 2, pp. 136–137.
Answers: TE p. 498.

FOCUS 3

While reviewing the information in this focus box, stress the point that *anymore* is not used with <u>positive</u> statements. However, just as with *any,* it can also be used in questions:
A: *Does Sonia live with her parents* ***anymore****?*
B: *Not **anymore**. She's married now.*

Exercise 2

Ss can write their statements in class or for homework.

S U G G E S T I O N

Before they hand in their work to you, have them work in pairs to peer edit. If you give grades, tell them that both the original writer and the editor will be graded on this assignment.

Workbook Ex. 3, pp. 137–138.
Answers: TE p. 498.

Contrast *still* with *anymore* to emphasize the difference in form and use:

A: *Does Sonia **still** live with her parents?*

-or-

A: *Does Sonia live with her parents **anymore**?*

B: *I think she **still** does, but I'm not sure.*

-or-

B: *Not **anymore**. Didn't you know she got married?*

Still can be used in questions, but is not used with <u>negative</u> statements.

Exercise 3

Answers may vary. See possible answers in the key below.

Exercise 4

V A R I A T I O N

1. Have Ss choose two people from the Opening Task, one who has changed very little and one who has changed a lot.
2. Direct them to write a comparison/contrast paragraph.
3. Encourage them to use transitional expressions such as *although, while, on the other hand, in contrast.*

Exercise 5

S U G G E S T I O N S

1. Copy this exercise onto an overhead transparency. Complete the exercise as a class or use the transparency to review their independent work.
2. If you don't have access to overhead projectors, have Ss check their answers with a partner, then discuss problem answers as a class.

FOCUS **4**

▶ *Still*

FORM MEANING

EXAMPLES	EXPLANATIONS
(a) She **still** lives in New Mexico. (She lived in New Mexico fifteen years ago; she lives there now.)	Use *still* to show that something or someone has NOT changed.
(b) He **still** runs five miles a day. (He ran five miles a day in the past; he runs five miles a day now.)	Use *still* to show that an activity or habit has NOT changed.
(c) He **still** lives in New Orleans.	Use *still* before the main verb.
(d) He is **still** crazy after all these years.	Use *still* after the verb *be*.
(e) She can **still** play the piano.	Use *still* after an auxiliary verb such as *can, may, should,* etc.

EXERCISE 3

Write statements using *still* about the people in the Opening Task on page 262 who have not changed very much. The following items will get you started, but you can add ideas of your own. Work with your classmates if you need more information.

1. Meryl Streep
   (a) (long, blond hair) _____.
   (b) (very slim) _____.
2. Bruce Springsteen
   (a) (house in New Jersey) _____.
   (b) (called "The Boss") _____.

EXERCISE 4

Now choose one of the people in the Opening Task, another famous person, or a classmate that you interviewed in Exercise 2. Write a short paragraph showing how that person has or has not changed. Use *still, anymore,* or *used to* in your description.

Share your paragraphs with each other and check to see if *still, anymore,* and *used to* were used appropriately.

EXERCISE 5

Complete the following sentences with *still* or *anymore.*

1. A: Where's Jeff?
   B: He doesn't live here _____.

A N S W E R   K E Y

Exercise 3
1. Meryl Streep still has blond hair and she is still very slim. She still has the same smile. She still looks like she did in high school.
2. Bruce Springsteen still has a house in New Jersey and he is still called "The Boss."

Exercise 5
1. anymore 2. still 3. still 4. anymore
5. still 6. still 7. anymore

---

2. A: Is Gary home yet?

   B: No, he is _____ working.

3. A: Have you finished writing your book?

   B: No, I'm _____ working on it.

4. A: Do you want a cigarette?

   B: No, thanks, I don't smoke _____ .

5. A: Where do you live?

   B: I _____ live at home with my parents.

6. A: Hurry up! We're going to be late!

   B: I'm _____ wrapping the gift.

7. A: How's your grandfather?

   B: He's doing pretty well, even though he can't go out much _____ .

EXERCISE 6

Look at the maps of the island of Madalia. Work with a partner and use the information from the maps to complete the report below. Use *used to, didn't use to, still,* and *anymore* as appropriate. Use the verbs in parentheses. The first one has been done for you as an example.

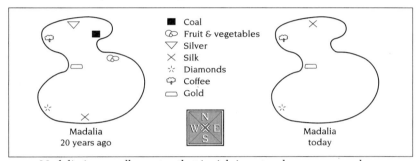

Madalia is a small country that is rich in natural resources, and Madalians have exploited those resources for many years. However, it is possible to note some changes in those resources in the last twenty years. For example, twenty years ago, Madalians (1) ___*used to mine*___ (mine) *coal*_____ in the northeast. In addition, (2) they _____ (grow) _____ in the east. Also, they (3) _____ (mine) _____ , but today, they (4) _____ (not + mine) it _____ . Furthermore, in the past, they (5) _____ (not + produce) _____ in the north; they (6) _____ (produce) it in the _____ .

ANSWER KEY

Exercise 6

Answers will vary.

(2) used to grow fruit and vegetables
(3) used to mine silver in the north   **(4)** do not/don't mine it anymore   **(5)** did not/didn't use to produce silk in the north   **(6)** used to produce it in the south   **(7)** still mine diamonds in the southwest   **(8)** still grow coffee   **(9)** still mine gold

---

Exercise 6 (sidebar)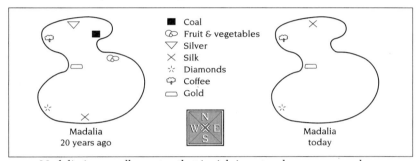

Before they start filling out the form, instruct pairs to discuss the differences they see on the maps first. This will allow them to discuss unfamiliar vocabulary and get an understanding of the map. Circulate around the room to help out during this activity.

SUGGESTIONS

Have pairs get together with other pairs to compare answers before discussing the exercise as a class. Only discuss the ones with which they had problems.

On the other hand, some things have not changed. They

(7) _____ (mine) _____ in the southwest, and

they (8) _____ (grow) _____ in the northwest.

Finally, they (9) _____ (mine) _____ in the west.

EXERCISE 7

The words below tell how often something happens. Arrange these words in a list with **most frequent** at the top and **least frequent** at the bottom. Add any other similar words you can think of and put them in the appropriate place on the list.

often	always	never	seldom
sometimes	hardly ever	usually	rarely

Check your answers with Unit 1, Focus 3.

FOCUS **5**

Adverbs of Frequency

EXAMPLES	EXPLANATIONS
	Adverbs of frequency (***always,*** etc.) can appear in different positions in a sentence:
(a) I **usually** get up at six.	• before the main verb.
(b) They were **rarely** happy.	• after the verb ***be.***
(c) You will **sometimes** hear from them.	• after auxiliary verbs (***will, can, have,*** etc.).
(d) I have **seldom** spoken to her.	
(e) They **never** used to dance.	• before ***used to.***
(f) He **always** used to call her.	

EXERCISE 8

Write a short article for your old high school magazine, reporting on your life and habits and how they have changed (or not) over the years since you left high school. Also describe your present life and habits and compare these with your past.

Try to include the following:

- something you used to do but don't do anymore
- something you used to do and still do
- something you didn't use to do but do now

ANSWER KEY

Exercise 7
always, usually, often, sometimes, seldom,
rarely, hardly ever, never

Exercise 7

Point out that this exercise will prepare them for Focus 5. Answers are on p. 6 of the Ss' book.

Workbook Ex. 4, p. 138.
Answers: TE p. 498.

FOCUS 5

Emphasize the importance of the word order by providing extra examples about your class:
*Roberto **rarely** arrives late to class.*
*Fabiola **always** sits in between Fernando and Satomi.*
*Nabi, Juan and Riho **never** used to eat dinner so early, but now they have to because they live in a dorm.*

Workbook Exs. 5–6, pp. 139–141.
Answers: TE p. 498.

Exercise 8

1. This activity can be done for homework or as timed writing practice in class. Give them 15–30 minutes, depending on the level of your group.
2. Decide ahead of time if you want them to use dictionaries.
3. As they work, circulate around the room to help with vocabulary questions.

- something you never do
- something you seldom do
- something you sometimes do
- something you often do
- something you usually do

Don't forget to include changes (or not) in your physical appearance. We have begun the article for you:

I left high school in _____ (year). As I look back on my life since then, I realize that some things have changed, and some things have stayed the same. Let me start by telling you about some of the changes . . . .

Use Your English

ACTIVITY 1: WRITING

STEP 1 If possible, find an old photograph of yourself (as a baby, a child, or one taken several years ago). If you cannot find a photograph, draw a picture. Attach the photo or picture to a large piece of paper and write several statements about yourself, showing things you used to do and don't do now, things you didn't use to do, and things you still do. Do not write your name on the paper. Your teacher will display all the pictures and descriptions.

STEP 2 Work with a classmate and try to guess the identity of each person. Who in the class has changed the most and who has changed the least?

ACTIVITY 2: WRITING

Think of a place you know well—the place where you were born or where you grew up. Write about the ways it has changed and the ways it has not changed.

UNIT GOAL REVIEW

Ask Ss to look at the goals on the opening page of the unit again. Help them understand how much they have accomplished in each area. Do they have any questions on the form, meaning, or use of these structures?

USE YOUR ENGLISH

While Ss are working on these activities, circulate around the room to listen to their language use. Do they appear to be using these structures accurately? You may wish to review errors you noted at the end of the activity.

Activity 1
VARIATION

Construct this exercise as a matching activity.
1. Ss attach their picture or photo to one piece of paper and write their statements on another piece of paper.
2. Distribute the descriptions to the class, making sure the author does not receive his/her own statements.
3. Put the pictures up around the room.
4. After reading their cards, Ss stand up and find the photograph they think matches the description.
5. Once all cards have been put by a photograph, have Ss come stand by their photos.
6. Determine if the correct matches were made.

Activity 2
SUGGESTION

As a pre-writing activity, have Ss brainstorm their ideas. First have them list places they know well. After they choose one to focus on, have them list ways it has changed and ways it has not changed in two columns on their paper. Emphasize that brainstorming is to help them get ideas on paper—they should not worry about correct grammar, spelling, or even complete sentences at this stage.

Activity 3

If Ss do not have access to a large group of native speakers of English, invite someone who has strong English language skills to class. Ss can interview the guest speaker as a class while you record the discussion.

Activity 5

Play textbook audio. The transcript for this listening appears on pp. 510–511 of this book.

VARIATION

1. Find a segment of a film that has a similar type of dialogue. Remember to keep the segment short so it does not overwhelm Ss.
2. Show the segment 3–4 times: the first time they watch to answer a general comprehension question, the second time they list the changes, and the third time they focus on the actual language used.

Activity 6

SUGGESTION

If this is conducted as an oral report, videotape the speeches. Then review each student's speech with them, providing feedback on presentation skills such as body language, organization, and language use.

ACTIVITY 3: SPEAKING/LISTENING

Interview a senior citizen. Find out about changes in the world or in customs and habits during his or her lifetime. What does she or he think about these changes? Tape-record your interview, and then report on your findings to the class.

ACTIVITY 4: LISTENING

Listen to the tape-recorded interviews from Activity 3. Did the speakers use *used to*, *still*, or *anymore* when talking about changes? If not, what did they use instead?

ACTIVITY 5: LISTENING

Listen to the tape of two senior citizens talking about the changes during their lifetimes.

STEP 1 In your notebook, list each change that they discuss. Count the number of changes on your list and complete this statement:

The senior citizens talked about _____ (number) changes during their lifetimes.

Check with your classmates to see if they agree with your answers.

STEP 2 Listen closely to the **way** the senior citizens talked about changes. Choose five things on your list and answer these questions:

1. Did the speakers use *used to*, *still*, or *anymore* when talking about changes?

2. If not, what did they use instead?

Compare your findings with another student's.

ACTIVITY 6: SPEAKING/WRITING

The women's movement has helped change the lives of many women in different parts of the world. However, some people argue that things have not really changed and many things are still the same for most women. Think about women's lives and roles in your mother's generation and the lives of women today in your country. Make an oral or written report on what has changed and what has stayed the same.

ANSWER KEY

Activity 5
Check tapescript for answers (pp. 510–511).

ACTIVITY 7: SPEAKING

This activity gives you the opportunity to "become" a different person. Choose a new identity for yourself:

What is this person's name, age, sex, profession, habits, occupation, personality, and appearance? How does this new person differ from the "real" you? Create a full description of this person and introduce the "new" you to the class, comparing him or her with the person you used to be. If you want to, make a mask or drawing to represent the "new" you.

▶ **EXAMPLE:** I want to introduce the new me. I used to be a college student, but now I am a secret agent. I never used to leave home, but now I often travel to distant and exotic places. I used to wear practical clothes that I always bought on sale. Now I usually wear black leather jumpsuits, dark glasses, and big hats, but sometimes I wear elegant evening dresses and expensive jewelry. . . .

ACTIVITY 8: SPEAKING/LISTENING/WRITING

Write a profile of one of your classmates.

STEP 1 Interview your partner and find out something that he or she

1. never does
2. seldom does
3. sometimes does
4. often does
5. usually does
6. always does

STEP 2 Write a report of your interview, **without using your classmate's name.** Begin with an introduction: for example, "I am going to tell you some things about one of our classmates." End your report with a question: "Can you guess who this is"?

STEP 3 Read your report out loud, or display it along with all the other reports written by your classmates. Can you identify the people described?

Activity 7
VARIATION

1. Bring in some ads for beauty products or services that use the "before and after" theme. Ss discuss how the people have changed.
2. Tell Ss they will be given a free makeover and can change all the things about their appearance that they want. Have Ss describe their new selves, drawing pictures if they want.

Activity 8
VARIATION

1. Pair Ss up and have them conduct their interviews by e-mail.
2. After their interviews, they can post their reports to the whole class. Of course Ss should not make guesses about their own descriptions!
3. Remember to set a time-limit by which all reports should be identified.

The test for this unit can be found on pp. 462–463 of this book.
The answers are on p. 464.

TOEFL Test Preparation Exercises for Units 16–18 can be found on pp. 142–143 of the Workbook.
The answers are on p. 498 of this book.

Unit 19

UNIT OVERVIEW

Unit 19 provides practice with the past perfect and with words/phrases commonly used with the past perfect: *before, after, by the time,* and *by*. It contrasts the past perfect with the simple past and present perfect.

UNIT GOALS

Review the goals listed on this page so students (Ss) understand what they should learn by the end of the unit.

OPENING TASK

Note: The purpose of this task is to generate talk that will naturally incorporate the past perfect. The task is intended to focus attention on meaning rather than form, which will allow you to see whether Ss are able to produce the forms spontaneously.

SETTING UP THE TASK

In order to do this task, Ss will first need to know how a family tree works and also some of the key vocabulary used in family trees.

1. Look at the family tree in Step 1 and make sure everyone can locate Tom.
2. Briefly elicit/introduce vocabulary for family relationships by asking, for example: *What relationship is Bernard to Tom?* (Answer: *Bernard is Tom's uncle/Tom's father's brother.*) *What relationship is Tom to Catherine Page?* (Answer: *Tom is Catherine's nephew; Catherine is married to Bernard, Tom's father's brother.*) and so on.

CONDUCTING THE TASK

Step 1

Ss can work in pairs to further discuss the relationships in Family Tree A.

UNIT 19

PAST PERFECT

Before and *After*

UNIT GOALS:

- To correctly use past perfect and simple past in a single sentence
- To correctly form past perfect sentences
- To understand the meanings of *before, after, by the time,* and *by*
- To use past perfect and the present perfect in the right situations

OPENING TASK
Family Changes

Family Tree A shows Tom's family when he left home in 1985 to travel around the world.

STEP 1   Work with a partner to study *Family Tree* A. (m) = married

Family Tree A

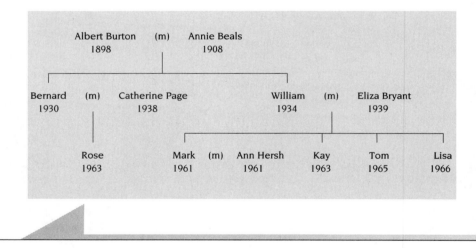

STEP 2 Now look at *Family Tree* B, which shows Tom's family after he returned home from his world travels in 1993.

Family Tree B

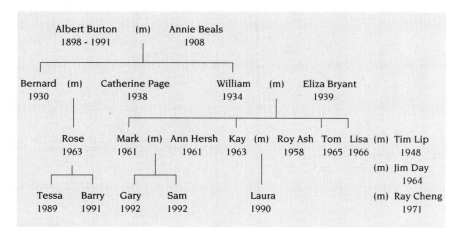

STEP 3 Make at least five statements about changes that had taken place when Tom returned from his travels. Start these statements with:

When Tom returned, ...
OR *Tom returned after. . . .*
OR *By the time Tom returned, ...*

Step 2
Explain that Tom left home to travel overseas and returned eight years later. The family tree in Step 1 shows Tom's family when he left, and in Step 2, when he returned. Ss compare these two charts, discussing the changes in the family trees.

Step 3
Have Ss write five (or more) statements about these changes.

CLOSING THE TASK
After everyone has completed Step 3, bring the class together to see who found the most changes in Tom's family. This is also the point where you would elicit the statements Ss made in Step 3, and an opportunity to see if Ss are spontaneously producing the target forms. Write Ss' statements on the board or on an overhead transparency, reformulating statements where the past perfect was incorrectly formed.

REVIEWING THE TASK
On the basis of Ss' statements in Step 3, move to the information in Focus 1 and 2, as necessary. Exercise 1 then returns to the Opening Task with a focus on accuracy.

SUGGESTIONS

1. Use the statements elicited from Ss in Step 3 of the Opening Task to elaborate on the information presented here. Example: *When Tom returned, his brother Mark and Mark's wife Ann had had two children.* Ask: *Which event happened first?* (Answer: *Tom returned.*) Ask: *Which event happened second?* (Answer: *Mark and Mark's wife Ann had two children.*)
2. Ask similar questions about some or all of Ss' other statements, as you see fit.
3. Be sure to emphasize that when the two events are combined into one sentence, the earliest event uses the past perfect, and the most recent event uses the simple past.
4. Point out that when *have* is the main verb, it becomes *had* in the simple past and *had* + past participle = *had had* in the past perfect. Some Ss may not know that the more formal *"give birth"* or *"bear children"* is rarely used; it's more common to say *"have a baby"* or *"have a child/children."*

FOCUS 2

SUGGESTION

Check to see that Ss can form the past perfect correctly. You can choose a verb and form the different kinds of sentences and short answers, as in Focus 2. Or for more meaningful practice (which Ss will also get throughout this chapter), and to review the forms of common irregular verbs, see Appendix 5 on page A-12. You can ask simple questions using "By the time." Examples: *By the time you came here, had you known (student in class)? By the time you arrived, had you watched any American films?* etc.

Workbook Ex. 3, pp. 146–147.
Answers: TE p. 499.

Past Perfect and Simple Past

EXAMPLE	EXPLANATIONS
(a) When I got there, he **had eaten** all the cookies.  **First,** he ate the cookies; **then,** I got there. (I didn't see him eat the cookies.)	When two events both happened in the past: • use the past perfect for the first (earliest) event. • use the simple past for the second (most recent) event.

FOCUS **2**

Past Perfect

To form the past pefect, use *had*+past participle (*-ed* for regular verbs; see Appendix 5, p. A-13 for forms of irregular verbs).

STATEMENT	NEGATIVE	QUESTION	SHORT ANSWER
I You } **had** arrived We ('**d**) They	I You } **had not** arrived We (**hadn't**) They	**Had** { I you } arrived? we they	Yes, we **had**.
She He } **had** arrived It ('**d**)	She He } **had not** arrived It (**hadn't**)	**Had** { he she } arrived? it	No, she **had not** (**hadn't**).

EXERCISE 1

Look at the family tree in the Opening Task on page 272 to complete the statements. If there is a verb in parentheses, use it; otherwise, use any appropriate verb. Example 1 has been done for you.

1. When he returned home, Tom found that his grandfather (die)
   <u>had died</u> .

2. When Tom returned, he learned that his cousin _____ .

3. Tom arrived home to find that his sister Lisa _____ .

4. When _____, his sister Kay _____ ; in
   addition, she and her husband _____.

5. On his return home, Tom found that his brother and sister-in-
   law _____ .

6. Tom learned that his grandmother had experienced both sorrow and joy.
   On the one hand, she (lose) _____ , but on the other hand,
   she (gain) _____ .

7. Sam and Gary have never met their grandfather, because he _____
   when they _____ .

8. When Tom left home, he didn't have any _____ or nieces;
   when he got home, he had _____ and two _____.

9. By the time Tom got back home, his parents and his aunt and uncle
   (become) _____ .

10. Tom also found that Rose _____ children, but she
    (not) _____ . Lisa, on the other hand, _____ three
    times, but she (not) _____ any children.

SUGGESTION

Since this exercise takes some time—Ss must study the two family trees in the Opening Task—it is not advisable to do this aloud unless there is ample time initially for Ss to complete the exercise. Have Ss work in pairs or small groups.

ANSWER KEY

Exercise 1

2. had had two children   3. had (gotten) married three times/had (gotten) married and divorced three times   4. Tom got/arrived/ returned home; had gotten married; had had a daughter   5. had had twin boys   6. lost her husband; had gained five great-grandchildren
7. had died when they were born
8. nephews; two nieces; three nephews
9. had become grandparents   10. had had; had not/hadn't (gotten) married; had (gotten) married; had not/hadn't had

Exercise 2

During this exercise, Ss sometimes ask about the ordering of events in a sentence. Sample question: *Do we have to put the earliest event first?*

Point out that we understand the order of events because of the verb tense used, not because of the position in the sentences. This grammar point can serve as a bridge into Focus 3 (see comment in **Focus 3**).

EXERCISE 2

In the following pairs of statements, decide which event probably happened first. Write 1 beside the event you think happened first and 2 beside the one you think happened second. Then combine the statements to make one sentence using because. The first one has been done for you.

▶ **EXAMPLE:** My legs ached. 2

I played tennis. 1

My legs ached because I had played tennis.

1. His car broke down.
He took the bus.

_____

2. Charlotte was depressed.
She failed her English exam.

_____

3. Tanya sat in the sun all afternoon.
Her skin was very red.

_____

4. We didn't eat all day.
We were really hungry.

_____

5. Brenda's clothes were too tight.
She didn't exercise for several months.

_____

6. Neville couldn't sleep.
He drank several cups of very strong coffee.

_____

7. We studied hard for three weeks.
We thought the test was easy.

_____

ANSWER KEY

Exercise 2

1. He took the bus because his car had broken down.   2. Charlotte was depressed because she had failed her English exam.   3. Tanya's skin was very red because she had sat in the sun all afternoon.   4. We were really hungry because we hadn't eaten all day.   5. Brenda's clothes were too tight because she hadn't exercised for several months.   6. Neville couldn't sleep because he had drunk several cups of very strong coffee.   7. We thought the test was very easy because we had studied hard for three weeks.

Before, After By *the* Time, By

EXAMPLES		EXPLANATIONS
First Event	Second Event	
(a) She had left	**before** I arrived.	*Before, after,* and *by the time* show the order of events.
(b) She had left	**by the time** I arrived.	
(c) **After** she had left,	I arrived.	You can use the past perfect with *before* and *after*, but it is not necessary. You must use the past perfect in sentences with *by the time*.
(d) She left	**before** I arrived.	
(e) **After** she left,	I arrived.	*By* + a noun phrase can also show order of events.
(f) He had finished all his shopping	**by** Christmas.	

EXERCISE 3

Look at the following sentences; each one uses the past perfect. Check (✔) the sentences where it is necessary to use the past perfect to show the order of events.

1. My sister graduated from college after she had gotten married.
2. I didn't see Brad last night because he had left by the time I got there.
3. After I had finished my work, I took a long, hot bath.
4. Kozue had checked the gas before she started to drive to Houston.
5. By the time the party was over, they had drunk nine bottles of soda.
6. The teacher sent the student home before the class had ended.
7. The store had closed before I got there.
8. We didn't see the movie because it had started before we got to the theater.
9. Cathy never knew her grandparents because they had died before she was born.
10. By noon, when Shirley got to the library, she found that someone had borrowed the book she needed.

Point out that you can shift the two clauses (parts of the sentence) around. Example: *Before I arrived, she had left. By the time I arrived, she had left.* etc.

SUGGESTION

1. Have Ss cover or turn over their books.
2. Read the examples (a)–(f) in random order, some of them as is, some of them with the clauses shifting positions.
3. For each sentence, ask: *Which event happened first? Which event happened second?* Or use sentences from Exercise 1 in this manner.
4. You can mention that the past perfect is not always used by native speakers in informal situations, as is the case with *after* and *before* in this focus box ((d) and (e)). However, be sure to emphasize that formal language tests such as the TOEFL will certainly address this grammar point, and that, therefore, it's important to learn. In addition, the past perfect is naturally used when the order of events is important for the meaning of the sentence.

Workbook Ex. 5, p. 148.
Answers: TE p. 499.

Exercise 3
VARIATION

If this exercise seems to be difficult for your Ss, analyze the sentences in terms of the order of events—which happened first (earliest) and which happened most recently (latest). This will help Ss understand one of the reasons why it's acceptable to omit the past perfect with *after* and *before* sentences—because the order of events in these sentences is clear.

ANSWER KEY

Exercise 3
Sentences with checks: 2, 5, 10

Exercise 4

SUGGESTION

If you feel that most of the Ss in your class are keeping up, for variety you can assign pairs or small groups specific sentences to work on (Group 1 would work on sentences 1–3, Group 2 on sentences 4–6, etc.) Then have a representative from each group read one sentence aloud with the class as a whole, while those listening check to see that the sentence is correct.

FOCUS 4

The exercises following this focus box work further on the present perfect–past perfect distinction. For a review on the use of the present perfect—and how it connects the past to the present, see Units 13 and 14.

SUGGESTION

Give Ss a few more contrasting sentences, as in (a) compared to (b); you can use sentences from Exercise 4 for this. Example: *I had fixed the flat tire and then it broke again.* (two events in the past are contrasting) versus *I've fixed the flat tire and now it's okay.* (event in the past connected to the present).

EXERCISE 4

Rewrite the following sentences. Omit the underlined words and use the word in parentheses. Use the past perfect where necessary.

▶ **EXAMPLE:** First Sue listened to the weather report <u>and then</u> she decided to go for a bike ride. (after)

After Sue listened to the weather report, she decided to go for a bike ride.

OR

After Sue had listened to the weather report, she decided to go for a bike ride.

1. Sue studied several maps, <u>and then</u> she decided on an interesting route for her bike ride. (before)
2. She changed her clothes, <u>and then</u> she checked the tires on her bike. (after)
3. She put fresh water in her water bottle, <u>and next</u> she left home. (before)
4. She rode for several miles, <u>then</u> she came to a very steep hill. (after)
5. She rode to the top of the hill, <u>and then</u> she stopped to drink some water and enjoy the view. (before)
6. She rode for ten more miles, <u>and then</u> she got a flat tire. (after)
7. She fixed the flat tire quickly, <u>and then</u> she continued her ride. (before)
8. It started to rain, <u>and then</u> she decided to go home. (after)
9. She rode 30 miles <u>before</u> she stopped. (by the time)
10. She took a long, hot shower, <u>and finally</u> she ate a huge plate of pasta. (after)

Were there any sentences where you **had to** use the past perfect?

FOCUS **4**

Past Perfect versus Present Perfect

EXAMPLES	EXPLANATIONS
(a) She **was** tired yesterday because she **had taken** a long bike ride.	Use the past perfect to **contrast** two events in the past.
(b) She **is** tired (now) because she **has taken** a long bike ride.	Use the present perfect to **connect** the past with the present.

278   UNIT 19

ANSWER KEY

Exercise 4

1. Sue (had) studied several maps before she decided . . ./Before Sue decided . . . , she (had) studied several maps.   **2.** She checked the tires on her bike after she (had) . . ./ After she (had) changed . . .   **3.** She (had) put fresh water in her bottle before . . ./Before she left home, she (had) put . . .   **4.** She came to a very steep hill after she (had ridden)/rode . . ./After she (had ridden)/rode for several miles, she . . .   **5.** She (had ridden)/rode to the top of the hill before she stopped . . ./Before she stopped to drink

some water and enjoy the view, she (had ridden)/rode . . .   **6.** She got a flat tire after she (had ridden) rode . . ./After she (had ridden) rode for ten more miles, she . . .   **7.** She fixed the flat tire before she . . ./ Before she continued her ride, she . . .   **8.** She decided to go home after it (had) . . ./ After it (had) started to rain, she . . .   **9.** By the time she got home, she had ridden . . ./ She had ridden over 30 miles by the time . . .   **10.** She ate a huge plate of pasta after she (had taken)/took . . ./After she (had taken)/ took a long, hot shower, she ate . . .

EXERCISE 5

Underline the mistakes in the following sentences and correct as necessary.

▶ **EXAMPLE:** I wasn't tired yesterday because I <u>have</u> slept for ten hours the night
before.
had

1. Nigel wasn't hungry last night because he has eaten a large sandwich for lunch.
2. Jan is really confused in class last Tuesday because she hadn't read the assignment.
3. Graham had gone home because he has a terrible headache today.
4. Howard is a lucky man because he had traveled all over the world.
5. Martha went to the hospital after she has broken a leg.
6. Before he has left the house, George locked all the doors and windows.
7. Professor Westerfield always returns our papers after she had graded them.
8. I didn't see you at the airport last night because your plane has left before I got there.
9. Matthew and James were late because they have missed the bus.

EXERCISE 6

In the story below, use the appropriate verb tense (simple past, past progressive, past perfect, present perfect) for the verbs in parentheses.

Some people attend all their high school reunions, but Al (1)
__hasn't gone_____ (go + not) back to his high school since he

(2) _____ (graduate) ten years ago. Five years ago, he

(3) _____ (make) arrangements to go to his five-year high

school reunion, but two days before that reunion he

(4) _____ (break) his leg. He (5) _____ (paint) his

house on a tall ladder when he (6) _____ (lose) his balance. So

he (7) _____ (not + go) to his five-year reunion.

Al (8) _____ (not + visit) his hometown for ten years and

his new wife, Marta, (9) _____ (never + be) there. Al and Marta

(10) _____ (get) married about a year and a half ago and they

(11) _____ (not + be) married long when some of Al's high

school friends (12) _____ (come) to visit them last year. So at

least Marta (13) _____ (meet) a few of Al's old friends, even

though she (14) _____ (not + be) to his hometown.

Past Perfect: Before and After **279**

Exercise 5
SUGGESTION

Because this exercise can be beneficial for Ss in editing their writing, it's a good idea to have them first work individually, and then compare answers with a partner.
1. Circulate while Ss are working individually, and make note of any items that seem to cause problems.
2. Go over these items when you re-group as a whole class, or ask for questions on only those items that Ss disagreed on or had trouble with.
3. Ask Ss to explain their revisions: What was wrong with the original statement?

Exercise 6
SUGGESTION

If this exercise appears to be challenging to Ss, ask them to defend their answers in terms of time frames.

You or a student can write the sentence on the board or on an overhead transparency and then diagram them in terms of:
(1) Did two events happen in the past—one happened first; one happened second? (= past perfect − simple past)
(2) Did the event happen in the past and have an effect on the present? (= present perfect)
(3) Did the event happen at a particular time in the past? (= simple past)
(4) Was the event in progress in the past while another event happened? (= past progressive − simple past)

UNIT GOAL REVIEW

Ask Ss to look at the goals on the opening page of the unit again. Help them understand how much they have accomplished in each area and what goals they may need to continue to work on.

Activity 1

Ss may want to redraw this chart in their notebooks so that there is more room for notetaking.

Use Your English

ACTIVITY 1: SPEAKING/LISTENING WRITING

The purpose of this activity is to compare different events and achievements at different times in our lives. You will need to get information from five of your classmates to complete this activity.

STEP 1 The left-hand column in the chart below shows different ages; your job is to find one interesting or surprising thing each classmate had done by the time he or she reached those ages. If you don't want to talk about your life, feel free to invent things that you had done at those ages. Be ready to report on your findings.

	Name	Name	Name	Name	Name
By the time, she or he was five years old . . .					
By the time she or he was ten years old . . .					
By the time she or he was fifteen years old . . .					
By the time she or he was eighteen years old . . .					
By the time . . .*					
By the time . . .*					

*You choose an age.

STEP 2 Now choose **the three most surprising** pieces of information you found for **each age**.

STEP 3 Present this information as an oral or written report. Be sure to announce your purpose in an introductory sentence and to end with a concluding comment.

For example: *The age of fifteen is very interesting. By the time Roberto, Ali, and Tina were fifteen, they had done quite different things. Roberto had worked in his father's office, Ali had visited ten different countries, and Tina had won several prizes for swimming.*

Step 3

VARIATION

Rather than concentrating on a particular era, have Ss write about a particular person. Collect the reports and read them aloud, not mentioning the person's name: *By the time, X was 15, she/he had traveled to three countries. Before this, X had lived with her/his older sister, since her/his parents' had moved to China for business purposes.* Then have Ss guess who the report is about.

ACTIVITY 2: SPEAKING

STEP 1 Use the information from Activity 1 for a poster presentation. Take a large poster-sized sheet of paper and use this to make a poster that communicates the information you found. You can use graphics, pictures, and diagrams to make your poster interesting and eye-catching.

STEP 2 Display your poster so that your classmates can enjoy it and be ready to answer any questions they might have about it.

ACTIVITY 3: SPEAKING / LISTENING

STEP 1 Find out about someone's family history, preferably someone sixty or older. You can help that person construct a family tree (as in the Opening Task), or you can use a chart like the one below to get information. Tape-record your information-gathering session.

STEP 2 Report your findings to the class, either in a written or an oral report. (Tape-record the report if it's done orally.) Be sure to use the past perfect and *before, after, by,* or *by the time* to contrast past events.

	Births, deaths, marriages, divorces
1980–present	
1960–1980	
1940–1960	
1920–1940	

Activity 2
SUGGESTIONS

1. Bring in a sample of this kind of poster. If you are doing this for the first time, you might want to make one poster together, as a whole class, or keep one of your student's posters (with his/her permission) as a sample for your next class.
2. Although it's nice to have lots of different kinds of materials available for this, a large sheet of paper is really all that's necessary. If Ss seem a little intimidated by such a project, assign them to work in teams (with at least one "artistic type" per team), making this truly collaborative.

Activity 3
VARIATION

This activity is also fun to do as an interview, with people new to your Ss. You or your Ss can invite someone to class to speak about their family history. If there are several older people available (they don't have to be native speakers), then the interview can be conducted in groups.

Activity 4
SUGGESTION

If you have a pool of tapes to select from, from Activity 3, do some pre-listening outside of class. This way you can select one or two tapes where there are a number of examples of past perfect usage. Interestingly, though, many native speakers often use the simple past, with very few cases of past perfect usage.

But it has been our experience that this context—talking about family history—rarely fails: there are at least a *few* cases of the past perfect that are naturally used. If not, concentrate on the last step of this activity: Analyze the oral report or interview for cases where the past perfect or time words *could have been used*, but weren't. Have Ss revise these sentences so that the past perfect and time words *are* used.

Activity 5

Play textbook audio. The tapescript for this listening activity appears on p. 511 of this book.

Step 3:

This step is appropriate for pair or group work, since this kind of collaboration encourages detailed listening. It's helpful to make the tape available to Ss whose answers are different from each other, so they can resolve these differences with "hard" evidence—the audiotaped data.

ACTIVITY 4: LISTENING

Listen to the tapes of your oral reports from Activity 3 or from the actual information-gathering sessions. Was the past perfect used? Were the time words *before, after, by,* or *by the time* used? Were there occasions where the past perfect or time words could have been used, but weren't?

ACTIVITY 5: LISTENING

STEP 1 Listen to the tape of a senior citizen talking about her family history. Each time the speaker talks about an important family event—births, deaths, marriages, divorces—record the date (or the approximate date) on the chart below and write down who the event happened to. The first one is done for you.

Births	Deaths	Marriages	Divorces	Relationship to Speaker
	1940			mother

STEP 2 Work with a classmate to list the speaker's important family events in chronological order.

STEP 3 Listen to the tape for each usage of the past perfect. Write down the sentence. Were the time words *before, after, by* or *by the time* used?

Then complete these sentences.

1. The speaker used the past perfect _____ times.
2. The interviewer used the past perfect _____ times.
3. The time words *before, after, by* or *by the time* were used _____ times altogether (by both speakers).

Do your classmates agree with your answers?

ANSWER KEY

Activity 5/Step 3
Check tapescript for answers (p. 511).

ACTIVITY 6: WRITING/LISTENING

STEP 1 Work in teams. With your team, choose three famous people who are now dead. Make sure that you choose famous people everyone has heard of. For each person, write three statements about what she or he had done before they died.

STEP 2 Team A presents the first statement. The other teams have to try to guess the identity of the person from the statements. Each team can ask two yes/no questions after each statement. (The "trick" is to make your statements difficult, but not impossible!)

▶ **EXAMPLE:** Before he died, he had been a popular president.

People in America had admired him and his wife very much.

He had been born in Massachusetts and was killed in Texas.

(President Kennedy)

ACTIVITY 7: RESEARCH

The purpose of this activity is to compare and contrast important historical events in different countries. You might need to do a bit of research before you do this activity: Look in an encyclopedia or a history textbook to get information about your country or another country you know about.

STEP 1 Copy the chart below into your notebook. Use it to record three events that you think were important in the history of the country you have researched. (The **exact** date is not important, but just mark on the chart approximately when the event happened.)

1300s	1400s	1500s	1600s	1700s	1800s	1900s

STEP 2 Now go around the class comparing your chart with your classmates' charts. Add to your chart significant dates from at least three other students. Try to get information about other countries, if this is possible.

STEP 3 Use the information on your chart to compare and contrast important events in different countries. Present your findings as a written report; don't forget to include an introduction and a conclusion.

STEP 4 Exchange reports with a classmate. Check to see if she/he has chosen the most appropriate tense.

Activity 6

There are usually Ss (or yourself, depending on what setting you're in!) who claim to not know the identity of the person selected. This is the justification for forming two large teams, rather than several smaller teams. Make sure that each team has at least one or two people who can "carry the weight" in this situation. It's been our experience that every classroom has at least a few good game-players or "know-it-alls." (This is meant as a compliment!)

VARIATION

Alternatively, before you do this activity, you can brainstorm a long list of famous people who are now dead. The downside of this is that the game may be too easy!

Activity 7

SUGGESTION

To set this activity in motion, you could model it with events from American history (or the history of a country that you and your Ss are familiar with), emphasizing that exact dates are not necessary. When Ss have completed their original charts, they can compile all their information on one big chart to create a shared point of reference. Ss should redraw this chart so that it is big enough for the information collected.

The test for this unit can be found on pp. 465–466 of this book.
The answers are on p. 467.

Unit 20

UNIT OVERVIEW

Unit 20 looks at the English articles in detail.
The form, meaning and use of *the, a/an,
some,* and Ø (no article) are contrasted.

UNIT GOALS

Draw students' (Ss') attention to the
structures they should be able to use by the
end of this unit.

OPENING TASK

Since Ss are likely to have problems using
articles accurately, it is especially important
to avoid correcting them during the Opening
Task. Remember that the purpose of this task
is to determine how much they already know.

SETTING UP THE TASK

Direct Ss' attention to the photograph of the
house. How does this house differ from
houses they have in their country(s)? Does
this house conform to their idea of "the
perfect house"?

U N I T 20

ARTICLES

The, A/An, Some, and Ø

UNIT GOALS:

- To understand the meaning of the articles *the, a, an,*
  and *some*
- To use articles correctly for first and second
  mentions of an item
- To know which articles to use with singular, plural,
  and noncount nouns
- To understand when to use no article

OPENING TASK
Looking for the Perfect House

STEP 1 Put the following sentences in order so that they make a story. When you have finished, check to see if other students have the story in the same order.

a. _____ Esinam found a real-estate agent to help them.

b. _____ They finally decided to buy the little house and remodel the kitchen.

c. _____ The second place they saw was a pretty brick house by a lake, but the house was too expensive.

d. _____ Finally they saw a little one-bedroom house surrounded by trees at the end of a dead-end street.

e. _____ When I last talked to them, they had finished remodeling the kitchen, and they liked the house a lot.

f. _____ Esinam and Sunita decided to buy a house.

g. _____ The real-estate agent then showed them a house near some apartment buildings, but the house was too big, and the apartment buildings were too ugly.

h. _____ First they looked at a nice house in the suburbs, but there were no trees, and the house was too far away from work.

i. _____ They told the real-estate agent that they wanted to live in a quiet neighborhood. They also said that they preferred small houses.

STEP 2 Number the pictures below so that they match the order of the story.

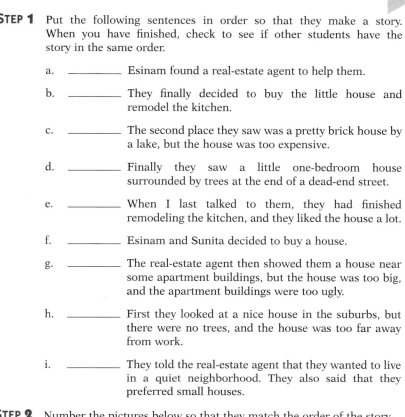

CONDUCTING THE TASK
Step 1
This part of the activity can be done individually or in pairs. Ss will return to this story in Exercise 11 (p. 296).

SUGGESTION
1. Photocopy the statements in Step 1 and cut into strips—make enough copies for the whole class.
2. Give each S or pair one set of statements and ask them to arrange the strips in the correct order.
3. Then have Ss compare their versions of the story.

Step 2
Have Ss continue with Step 2 in the same groupings as in Step 1 (individually or in pairs).

CLOSING THE TASK
Have Ss compare their answers with other Ss or pairs.

REVIEWING THE TASK
Have individual Ss or pairs explain their orders, justifying their answers. As they speak, note some of their errors in using articles. Do not discuss these at the moment, but use the information to help determine where you should spend more time later.

While Ss will have studied articles before, keep in mind that articles are among the most difficult grammatical structures to use accurately.

Grammar Note

Many languages do not have articles and those that do use them differently from English. If Ss are having trouble grasping the basic difference between *the* and *a/an*, you may wish to point out that, historically, *a/an* had the same meaning as *one*, while *the* used to be a different form of *this*. Mentioning this historical distinction often helps Ss grasp the difference between one of a group *(a/an)* and one in particular *(the)*.

Point out that *some* is used instead of *the* or *a/an*:

*I'd like **some** more coffee, please.*
NOT: *I'd like **the some** more coffee, please.*
When *some* is used as a <u>quantity</u>, count nouns must be plural:
*Milo takes **some** vitamins every morning to stay in good health.*
NOT: *Milo takes **some** vitamin every morning to stay in good health.*
Note that this meaning of *some* is different from the one below, which means "unknown":

***Some** friend of yours just stopped by but wouldn't give his name.*
-vs.-
***Some** friends of yours just stopped by but wouldn't give their names.*

In English, singular count nouns must have an article. For a review of the difference between count and noncount nouns, see the Grammar Note for Exercise 2, Unit 8.

FOCUS **1**

Definite and Indefinite Articles:
The, A/An, and Some

EXAMPLES	EXPLANATIONS
(a) Father to son: Where did you park **the** car? 	Use *the* to talk about a specific noun. In (a), the father and son are thinking about the same car—a car that they both can identify.
(b) Which car are they talking about? **The** family car.	With *the,* you can answer the question *Which . . .* ?
(c) Al needs **a** new notebook.	Use *a* or *an* to talk about one of a group of similar things, not about a specific thing. In (c), Al is thinking about notebooks in general. He's not thinking about a specific notebook that he can identify.
(d) What does Al need? **A** new notebook.	With *a/an,* you can answer the question *What . . .* ?
(e) Al needs **a** new computer, new software, and new instructional manuals.	Use *a* or *an* with singular count nouns; use Ø (no article) with noncount nouns or plural count nouns.
(f) Al needs **some** new software and **some** new instruction manuals.	Use *some* to talk about a nonspecific quantity (amount) with plural nouns or noncount nouns.

EXERCISE 1

Fill in the blanks in the story below with *the, a, an, Ø* (no article), or *some*.

1. Sarah wanted to buy _____ doll for her nephew Marty, who was going to turn nine at the end of the month.

2. Marty enjoyed playing with _____ dolls.

3. He had never been very interested in trucks, but he had been playing with _____ dolls since he was two years old.

4. Sarah went to three stores and saw _____ interesting dolls.

5. In the toy store, she finally chose _____ doll.

6. _____ doll that she bought was unusual, Sarah thought.

7. It was wearing _____ baseball player's uniform.

8. _____ uniform had "New York Yankees" written on it.

9. When Sarah gave Marty _____ doll, he was polite but not very impressed.

10. He already had _____ old doll that was similar to Sarah's birthday doll.

11. Sarah realized that she didn't know very much about _____ dolls.

12. She also realized that buying _____ presents for Marty was not an easy task!

Exercise 1

1. Be sure Ss understand the directions before they begin the activity; you may need to explain that Ø = no article.
2. Review answers as a class. Refer Ss back to the relevant point in Focus 1 when errors are made.
3. Ss will refer back to this exercise in Exercise 2 (p. 288) and Exercise 5 (p. 290).

Workbook Ex. 1, p. 150.
Answers: TE p. 500.

FOCUS **2**

▶ ## Using Articles: First and Second Mention

EXAMPLES	EXPLANATIONS
(a) I read **a** great book yesterday. **(b)** Martha just bought **a** new backpack. **(c)** I found **an** old dress of my mother's in the attic.	*A/an* is generally used to talk about a noun for the first time (first mention). Since the noun is introduced for the first time, it is not yet identified as a specific thing.
(d) I found an old dress of my mother's in the attic in the trunk. **The** dress was beautiful, with pearl buttons and lace sleeves.	Use *the* when the noun has been introduced and is now identified (sometimes called "second mention").

Articles: *The, A/An, Some,* and *Ø* | **287**

FOCUS 2

To illustrate the concept of first and second mention, use the example sentences as the start of short dialogues. For example:

A: *I read a great book yesterday.*
B: *Oh yeah, what's* **the** *book called?*
A: *My Year of Meats, by Ruth Ozeki. Have you heard of it?*
B: *Is it* **the** *book that was reviewed on NPR the other day?*
A: *Yeah, that's* **the** *one.*

This concept is further discussed in Focus 8 (p. 295).

Exercise 2

Refer Ss back to Exercise 1 on p. 287

Exercise 3

SUGGESTION

1. Copy the exercise onto an overhead projector transparency so you can make corrections directly in the passage.
2. After Ss complete the activity in pairs or independently, discuss their answers as a class. For each noun phrase, ask the 3 questions in order to come up with the final answer.

Workbook Ex. 2, pp. 151–152.
Answers: TE p. 500.

EXERCISE 2

Now look back at Exercise 1 and tell why you used each article (*a/an, some, the* or Ø). Did you complete the exercise correctly? If not, go back and rewrite the sentences you missed.

EXERCISE 3

Read the following. For each underlined noun phrase, is the article usage correct? If the article usage is not correct, write the correct usage above the underlined words. These questions will help you:

- Is the writer talking about a noun for the first time?
- Is the writer talking about a specific noun?
- Is the writer talking about one of a group of similar things—**not** an identified/specific noun?

Since 1988, a herd of deer has come to Pedro's apple orchard each October
(1)
just after apple harvest. An orchard is bordered by a forest, and Pedro and his
(2)
family are able to watch the herd come out of a forest and walk directly to
(3)   (4)
the nearest apple trees. Within minutes after the deer enter the orchard ,
(5)
the remaining apples are gone, and the deer return to the forest with their
(6)   (7)
cheeks still bulging. Watching the deer has become an annual event for Pedro
(8)
and his family. If Pedro could predict the annual apple-eating feast, he would
(9)
invite his friends and have the deer-watching party .
(10)

Indefinite Articles with Singular, Plural, and Noncount Nouns

EXAMPLES	EXPLANATIONS
(a) I'd like to buy **a** piano and **an** organ.	Use *a* and *an* with singular count nouns.
(b) **a** youngster **(c)** **a** university	Use *a* before consonant sounds and *an* before vowel sounds. It is the **sound,** not the letter, which tells you whether to use *a* or *an*.
(d) **an** energetic woman **(e)** **an** unusual doll	If there is an adjective before the noun, then the first sound of the **adjective** tells you whether to use *a* or *an*, not the first sound of the noun.
(f) I'd like to buy **some** new CDs and tapes, and then I'd like to listen to **music** all day.	Use *some* or Ø (no article) with plural count nouns and noncount nouns.

EXERCISE 4

Fill in the blanks with *a, an,* or Ø (no article).

1. If I won the lottery, first I would buy _____ piece of land in the country.

2. Then I would build _____ unusual house and _____ huge barn.

3. Of course I would build _____ long fence, too.

4. Then I would buy _____ horses, _____ cows, and maybe _____ llama.

5. I would make sure to buy _____ hay for the winter, so that the animals would have plenty to eat.

6. I would probably hire _____ people to take care of the horses.

7. People say that you can't buy _____ happiness, but I think my ranch would certainly make me happy!

Stress the importance of the **sound** in determining whether to use *a* or *an*. Looking at sentences (b) and (c) illustrate the point that *a* comes before a consonant **sound**, as the phonetic transcription demonstrates:
(b) a youngster → [y^g.str]
(c) a university → [yu.nl.vr.sl.ti]
Contrast (c) with:
an uncle → [^g.kl]
Other examples:
a hotel → [ho.tEl]
an hour → [awr]
an honest living → [a.nlst]
The difference between *some* and Ø is discussed further in Focus 4 (p. 290).

Workbook Ex. 3, pp. 152–153.
Answers: TE p. 500.

Note that *some* is used when we want to stress the quantity aspect of the noun phrase; otherwise, it can be omitted:

*She has **some** friends.*
   (but not many)
She has friends.
   (she is not alone in the world)
*I have (**some**) mail for you.*

SUGGESTION

Have Ss practice the pronunciation of *some* as *s'm*. Use the sentences in the examples or create new ones related to classroom experiences.

Exercise 5

1. Refer Ss back to Exercise 1 (p. 287).
2. Have pairs discuss their ideas on when *some* can be used.
3. As a class, review their answers and come to a consensus on when to use *some*.

Workbook Ex. 4, pp. 153–154.
Answers: TE p. 500.

FOCUS **4**

Some Instead of Ø (No Article)

EXAMPLES	EXPLANATIONS
(a) Al needs **some** new clothes. **(b)** I'd like to get **some** tickets to the concert on Friday.	Use *some* with plural count nouns and noncount nouns when you want to talk about quantity (amount).
(c) I'd like to listen to **some** jazz. (I'd like to listen to s'm jazz.) **(d)** Can we get **some** cookies at the bakery? (Can we get s'm cookies at the bakery?)	When *some* is used instead of Ø (no article) in conversation, it is not stressed.
(e) I'd like to listen to (some) jazz. **(f)** Al needs (some) new clothes.	Usually *some* is optional (you **can** use it, but it's not necessary).
(g) Cookies are called biscuits in England. **(h)** Spiders have eight legs.	Do not use *some* when you are talking about **all** members of a group of similar things.

EXERCISE 5

Look at your answers in Exercise 1. Mark with a check (✔) all the answers where Ø (no article) was used with either a plural count noun or a noncount noun. Could you use *some* instead? Explain your answers.

ANSWER KEY

Exercise 5
From Exercise 1:
2. can't use *some* with *dolls* because it is talking about *all* dolls (all members of a group of similar things) **3., 11., 12.** same answer as **2.**

The with Singular, Plural, and Noncount Nouns

EXAMPLES	EXPLANATIONS
(a) *Son to Father:* Where did you put **the** keys? 	Use *the* with all nouns that can be specifically identified: • plural count nouns: In (a) both speakers can identify which specific keys are being talked about.
(b) *Son to Friend:* Turn on **the** light, please.	• singular count nouns: In (b) they can both identify which specific light is being talked about.
(c) *Housemate to Housemate:* I can't find **the** sugar. Where did you put it?	• noncount (mass) nouns: In (c) they can both identify which sugar is being talked about.

EXERCISE 6

Fill in the blanks in the story below with *a/an, some,* or *the.*

1. Last fall Anita worked in _____ apple orchard, picking apples.

2. _____ work was not easy.

3. She had sore muscles _____ first week of work, and every night she slept very soundly.

4. _____ first orchard she worked in was considered small, with only fifty trees.

5. It was owned by _____ old, retired couple, who worked in the orchard as _____ hobby.

6. _____ next orchard Anita worked in was much larger, about twenty acres.

7. In this orchard, _____ trees had yellow apples, which were called "Golden Delicious."

Another way to explain this aspect of using the definite article *the* is that these are shared resources. Outside of the group in which they are speaking, they would need to be identified more clearly. The notion of shared resources explains why we can say *the hospital, the bank, the movies,* even when the exact hospital, bank, or cinema are not being identified. This explanation is related to the point in Focus 7 (p. 293).

Exercise 6

This activity can be done as a class on an overhead transparency, or individually for homework to be later discussed as a class.

Workbook Ex. 5, p. 154.
Answers: TE p. 500.

ANSWER KEY

Exercise 6
1. an   2. The   3. the   4. The   5. an; a
6. The   7. some/the   8. some   9. the;
the; the

8. Every day Anita ate _____ apples for breakfast and for lunch.

9. Even though _____ weather was beautiful, and _____ hard work made her feel very healthy, Anita was relieved when _____ apple-picking season was over.

Now work with a classmate and explain your choices.

The concept of using Ø with general statements is often linked to whether the word is noncount or not. Ss often make the mistake of saying *the nature* or *the sadness* when speaking generally. This is contrasted with specific examples of these noncount nouns, such as:
The nature <u>outside of New York City</u> is actually quite beautiful.
Tell me about **the** time <u>you met your husband for the first time.</u>

FOCUS **6**

Making General Statements with Ø (No Article)

EXAMPLES	EXPLANATIONS
(a) *Al:* I need **new clothes.** 	Use Ø (no) article to make general statements. In (a), Al needs new clothes **in general.** He's not thinking about specific clothes that he and his listener can identify. Use Ø (no) article to talk about plural count nouns that are not specific.
(b) I'd like to get **flowers** for my birthday.	In (b), you can't identify **which** flowers; you and the listener are not thinking about specific flower.
(c) He is hoping to find **love.** **(d)** I like **jazz.**	Use Ø (no article) when you make a general statement using noncount (mass) nouns.
(e) Pencils are made with **lead.** **(f)** **Rice** is eaten in Asia.	Use Ø (no article) when you make a general statement about a whole group or category.
(g) **Medical care** is very expensive in the United States. **(h)** Most people like **vacations.** **(i)** The university offers excellent classes in **art** and **music.**	Statements that use Ø (no article) can usually be paraphrased with *in general.* In (g): *In general,* medical care in the United States is expensive. (There may be some exceptions.)

292 UNIT 20

EXERCISE 7

Circle the errors in article usage in the sentences below. Specifically, should you use *the* or Ø (no article)?

1. The love is a very important thing in our lives.
2. Without the love, we would be lonely and confused.
3. I believe that the money is not as important as love, although some people don't feel this way.
4. If the money is too important, then we become greedy.
5. When we get old, the health becomes as important as love.
6. My grandmother says, "Just wait and see. Work you do and the money you earn are important now, but when you're old . . .
7. . . . love that you feel for your family and friends, health of your loved ones—these are the things that will be most important."

FOCUS **7**

The with Unique/Easily Identified Nouns

EXAMPLES	EXPLANATIONS
(a) In June, **the sun** doesn't set until 9:30.	The definite article *the* is used with nouns that are easily identified. Use *the* with nouns that are **universally** known (everyone in the world can identify it). In (a), everyone knows **which** sun they're talking about, since there's only one.
(b) Mary went to **the coast** on her vacation.	*The* is also used when the noun is **regionally** known (everyone in the region can identify it). In (b), everyone knows **which** coast they're talking about, since there's only one in the region.
(c) Did you feed **the cats**?	We can also use *the* when the noun is **locally** known (everyone in the immediate location can identify it). In (c), everyone in the immediate location knows **which** cats they're talking about, since they live together in the same house.

Articles: *The, A/An, Some,* and *Ø*   **293**

Exercise 7

When reviewing this exercise, refer Ss back to the relevant explanations to help in correcting their errors.

Workbook Ex. 6, p. 155.
Answers: TE p. 500.

FOCUS 7

As in Focus 5 (p. 291), Focus 7 revisits the concept of shared resources, whether at the world, regional, or local level. Use examples from your classroom situation. In your room, you can refer to *the board, the teacher, the room* (there is only one example of these in the context of your class); within the context of the whole school, "your" resources are *a board, a teacher, a room* (because each is one of many).

ANSWER KEY

Exercise 7
1. There should be no article before *love*.
2. No article before *love*.   3. No article before *money*.   4. No article before *money*.
5. No article before *health*.   6. There should be an article before *Work*.   7. There should be an article (the) before both *love* and *health*.

Make sure Ss understand the directions before breaking into pairs. Answers may vary.

SUGGESTION

1. While Ss are working, draw a 3-column chart on the board, labeling columns "where," "who," and "what happened."
2. When reviewing their answers, fill out the chart on the board.

Exercise 9

While Ss may complete this exercise for homework, be sure to review the exercise as a class to ensure that Ss have grasped the concepts of universal, regional, and local knowledge. Point out that knowing the context is the only way to determine which article a person should use.

EXERCISE 8

For sentences 1–10 below, answer these three questions:

(a) Where would you hear this sentence spoken?

(b) Who do you think the speaker is?

(c) What do you think happened or what was the conversation about **before** or **after** the sentence was spoken?

1. Please turn on *the* TV.
2. Could you change *the* channel?
3. We need some more chalk. Would you mind checking *the* blackboard in *the* back?
4. *The* rosebushes are lovely.
5. Could you pass *the* salt, please?
6. Excuse me, where's *the* women's restroom?
7. *The* sky is so blue today. I don't think you'll need *the* umbrella.
8. Have you seen *the* dog?
9. It's so romantic. See how bright *the* moon is?
10. Let's go to *the* mountains for our vacation instead of to *the* beach.

Use your answers to the three questions above to discuss in class why *the* was used in each sentence.

EXERCISE 9

Tell why *the* is used in each of the sentences below. (Some of these you will recognize from Exercise 8.) In the space at the left, write down **where** you think this statement was made. Then, on the right:

- If it is **universally** known, circle **U**.
- If it is **regionally** known, circle **R**.
- If it is **locally** known (because of the immediate location), circle **L**.

Setting

_____	1. Please turn on the TV.	U R L
_____	2. Could you change the channel?	U R L
_____	3. We need some more chalk. Would you mind checking the blackboard in the back?	U R L
_____	4. The rosebushes are lovely	U R L
_____	5. Could you pass the salt, please?	U R L
_____	6. Excuse me, please. Where's the women's restroom?	U R L
_____	7. The sky is so blue today. I don't think you'll need the umbrella.	U R L

ANSWER KEY

Exercise 8
1. (a) In a family's living room. (b) A parent or older sibling speaking to a younger child. (c) **Before**—the listener was near the TV. **After**—he or she turned on the TV. 2. (a) In a family's living room. (b) A parent or older sibling speaking to a younger child. (c) **Before**—the listener was near the TV. **After**—he or she changed the channel. 3. (a) In a classroom. (b) The teacher. (c) **Before**—the teacher ran out of chalk. **After**—a student did what was requested 4. (a) In a garden. (b) A guest/visitor. (c) **Before**—they were taking a tour of the garden.

After—they continued the tour. 5. (a) At dinner. (b) One of the people at the table. (c) **Before**—they were serving themselves. **After**—someone honored the request. 6. (a) In any public place. (b) A woman who needs to use the restroom. (c) **Before**—she was looking for the restroom or for someone to ask. **After**—the person she asked gave her directions. 7. (a) In someone's house. (b) One family member to another (or roommate). (c) **Before**—they were discussing the weather or saying good-bye. **After**—the person said good-bye and left the house (without the umbrella). 8. (a) In

someone's home or outside in the yard. (b) One family member to another (or possibly a neighbor, if she or he doesn't own a dog). (c) **Before**—the person noticed the dog was gone. **After**—the other person answered the question and/or helped look for the dog. 9. (a) Outside (b) Probably two people who are romantically involved, but not necessarily (c) **Before** and **after**—they made small talk and/or kissed 10. (a) Anywhere (b) A family member (c) **Before** and **after**—they were discussing vacation plans and/or talking about mountains, beaches.

	8. Have you seen <u>the</u> dog?	U R L
	9. It's so romantic. See how bright <u>the</u> moon is?	U R L
	10. Let's go to <u>the</u> mountains for our vacation, instead of to <u>the</u> beach.	U R L U R L
	11. *Son:* Hey Dad, can I borrow <u>the</u> car?	U R L
	Dad: Sure, if you can find <u>the</u> keys!	U R L
	12. I like your dress. Did you buy it at <u>the</u> mall?	U R L

FOCUS **8**

▶ **Using *The*: Second Mention, Related Mention, and Certain Adjectives**

EXAMPLES	EXPLANATIONS
(a) She used to have a cat and a dog, but **the** cat died.	Sometimes we use *the* with a noun because the noun has been talked about before (second mention).
(b) Last year I bought a guitar and a banjo. I decided to sell **the** banjo since I rarely play it.	We can identify the cat in (a) and the banjo in (b) because they have been talked about before.
(c) He bought a suit but **the** jacket had a button missing, so he had to return it. **(d)** I had a lock but I lost **the** key for it.	In other situations we can identify a noun because it is *related* to something that has been talked about before (related mention). In (c), we know which jacket they're talking about, since *jacket* is part of *suit*.
(e) She had started to read a book when she noticed that **the** first chapter was missing. **(f)** She's **the** first person I met here and **the** only friend I have. **(g)** That's **the** hardest test I've ever taken. **(h)** You made **the** right choice.	Adjectives or phrases like *last, next, first, only,* and *right*, and superlatives like *best, hardest,* and *happiest* usually use the definite article *the* because they describe something that is "one of a kind." There's only one "first chapter" (in e), only one "first person" (in f), and only one "hardest test" (in g).
(i) It's **the** same old story. **(j)** We are taking **the** same class.	The definite article is always used with the adjective *same*.

Articles: *The, A/An, Some,* and Ø | **295**

FOCUS 8

This focus box continues with the issue raised in Focus 2 (p. 287).

Further illustrate the explanations with examples of local or international interest:
A new movie opened last night and the star came to the premier.
The last time the U.S. president visited our country there was a parade in his honor.
In her opinion, "Built to Spill" is the most popular music group in Seattle.

Exercise 10

In order to get the full benefit of this exercise, Ss should understand the directions before beginning.

Exercise 11

Ss must have completed the Opening Task in order to do this exercise. This activity can be done as written homework.

Exercise 12

SUGGESTION

1. Have Ss look at the photograph on p. 297. Instruct them to make predictions on the topic and events of the story before they read it. Later, find out if any of their predictions were correct.

EXERCISE 10

Decide why *the* is used each time it is underlined. If it is used because it has been talked about before, circle **S** (for **second mention**). If it is used because a **related** noun has been talked about before, circle **R** (for **related mention**).

1. Jerry was late for his appointment, so he went into a telephone booth near the bus stop to make a phone call. It looked like someone was living in <u>the</u> telephone booth.   S R

2. There was a small blanket covering <u>the</u> window of the telephone booth like a curtain.   S R

3. <u>The</u> floor of the telephone booth was swept clean with a broom.   S R

4. <u>The</u> broom was hung on a hook in the corner of the telephone booth.   S R

5. By <u>the</u> telephone, there was a pen and a notepad with a short list of names and telephone numbers.   S R

6. Jerry also noticed that there was a coffee mug and a toothbrush sitting neatly by <u>the</u> telephone directory.   S R

7. <u>The</u> coffee mug looked like it had recently been rinsed. There were still drops of water in it.   S R

8. Jerry had such a strong feeling that he was in someone's living space that he decided to find another place to make <u>the</u> phone call.   S R

EXERCISE 11

Look at the story in the Opening Task on pages 284–285, making sure that it is in the right order. How many times is *the* used? Underline each *the* and explain why it was used.

<u>Reason *the* is used</u>

▶ **EXAMPLE:** i. *the* real-estate agent   *second mention*

EXERCISE 12

Underline each use of *the* in the following story. Then tell why it is used. The possible reasons for the use of *the* with a noun are:

(a) It's universally known.
(b) It's regionally known.
(c) It's locally known—the immediate location makes it clear.
(d) Second mention.
(e) Related mention.
(f) The adjective or phrase makes it "one of a kind."

ANSWER KEY

Exercise 10
1. **S**—because *telephone booth* has been mentioned before.   2. **R**—because a related noun, *telephone booth,* has been mentioned before; *window* is part of the telephone booth.   3. **R**—because a related noun, *telephone booth,* has been mentioned before; all telephone booths have floors.   4. **S**—because *broom* has been mentioned before.   5. **R**—because a related noun, *telephone booth,* has been mentioned before; all telephone booths

have telephones.   6. **R**—because a related noun, *telephone* and *telephone booth,* have been mentioned.   7. **S**—because *coffee mug* has been mentioned before.   8. **S**—because *phone call* has been mentioned before.

Exercise 11
f a i h c g d b e
h. the house—second mention   c. The second place—because of the adjective *second;* the house—second mention   g. the

real estate agent—second mention; the house—second mention; the apartment buildings—second mention   d. the end of a dead-end street—related mention (dead-end streets have an "end") and uniqueness because there is only one end of a dead-end street, which is regionally known   b. the little house—second mention; the kitchen—second mention   e. the kitchen—second mention; the house—second mention

---

296   Grammar Dimensions, Platinum Edition

1   Nobody in eastern Washington, where I live, will forget the summer of
2 1994. My son Robin was only five weeks old when the fire came. Dan, my
3 husband, was a firefighter, and he had been away the whole week working
4 on what the reporters were calling "The Great Fires of 1994."
5   Dan could only come home three times that week, late at night. First he
6 got in the shower and washed off the soot and smoke, and then he looked
7 with wonder at little Robin while telling me the latest fire adventure. Then
8 we watched the fire coverage on the news, but before it was over, Dan was
9 sound asleep. Each morning the alarm went off at 4:00, and Dan was up
10 and out of the door just as the sky was getting light.
11   The fire started burning closer and we were finally forced to evacuate
12 our own home. The smoke was so heavy that we couldn't even see the
13 mountain right across the highway. And the fire seemed to have a mind of
14 its own.

2. Before Ss read, decide if you would like them to use dictionaries or not. If they complete the reading in class, circulate to help with vocabulary questions. Encourage them to consult each other as well.

3. Direct Ss to read the passage before they start, identifying examples of *the*. Have Ss retell the story to be sure they understand it.

4. Review the directions on p. 296 before Ss begin reading. Remind them what these six reasons mean.

5. Ss can work in pairs to identify and explain uses of *the*.

ANSWER KEY

Exercise 12

Answers may vary, since it may be possible to justify the choice of *the* for more than one reason.

line . . . 1 the summer—f
line . . . 2 the fire—b
line . . . 3 the whole week—f
    3 the newspeople—b
    4 The Great Fires—b

6 the shower—c, the soot—c and e
7 the latest fire adventure—f, the fire coverage—c
8 the news—b, the alarm—c
9 the door—c, the sky—a
11 The fire—d
12 The smoke—e
13 the highway—b, the fire—d

Exercise 13

See Exercise 12 for suggestions on how to conduct this exercise. Because of its level of difficulty, setting the exercise for homework would allow Ss time to fully understand the passage before analyzing the article use.

UNIT GOAL REVIEW

Because this is a long chapter, it is especially important to review the goals on p. 284. Use some of the examples you've created to illustrate the goals.

EXERCISE 13

In the following newspaper article, circle each *the* and *a*. Then explain why those articles are used.

Vocabulary:

swath—a wide path
backburn/backfire—a fire started on purpose in order to control the direction that the fire takes next
scorched—burned black
evacuated—forced to leave
take for granted—to treat as fact; to accept without noticing or appreciating

Firefighting Takes a Personal Turn

By Rick Steigmeyer, World staff writer

PESHASTIN, WA- Dan Dittrich wanted to help save the forest and homes on familiar ground. He didn't realize that his toughest rescue mission would be his own home.

A contract logger by trade, Dittrich found a job working on the Tyee Creek Fire near Entiat after its start on July 24. When the Hatchery Creek Fire started getting out of hand, he came down to Leavenworth to help his friends defend their homes. Dittrich built his own house a few years ago on a densely wooded hillside on Mountain Home, above the Blewett Pass Highway.

Later, he went down to the Hatchery Fire base camp at the U.S. Fish Hatchery in Leavenworth to sign up for duty on the main fire.

"While I was at the camp signing in, the Rat Creek Fire took off," said Dittrich at the base camp Monday. Dittrich, smudged, unshaven, and weary after a 16-hour shift, said, "I told them, 'Sorry, I've gotta go protect my own house..'"

Dittrich and friends worked 27 straight hours clearing brush and trees and digging a fireline around his secluded house. The Rat Creek Fire, meanwhile, raged through Icicle Canyon across Wedge Mountain and onto the Leavenworth side of Mountain Home, devouring 14 homes and threatening countless others in the process.

Friends heard about Dittrich's problem and rushed to help him. Fellow firefighter Lance Wyman and later Mike King and Chris Fusare helped cut a swath around the structures. Joseph Roy and Phil and Joan Unterschuetz helped to water everything down and to disconnect the electricity.

"Just as we were finishing, the fire came rushing down over the hill," said Dittrich. "I went running down the hill, lighting fuses for a backfire as I ran. A helicopter above us was yelling out on a loudspeaker 'Negative on that backburn. Negative!' I just kept lighting and running.

Dittrich and friends made it safely to the bottom of the orchard-bordered property and watched the fire as it raced across the hill. The surrounding woods were scorched, but the house was left unharmed.

Dittrich's family had been evacuated soon after the fire started, but he went back to the house to get some sleep on Monday night.

He feels he's earned the right to sleep in his own bed. It's something he's not likely to ever again take for granted.

ANSWER KEY

Exercise 13

Answers may vary, since it may be possible to justify the choice of *the* or *a* for more than one reason.

a personal turn—not specific or identified; first mention
the forest—regionally known
a contract logger—not specific or identified; first mention
a job—not specific or identified; first mention
the Tyee Creek Fire—regionally known
the Hatchery Creek Fire—regionally known

a few years ago—not specific or identified; first mention
a densely wooded hillside—not specific or identified; first mention
the Blewett Pass Highway—regionally known
the Hatchery Fire base camp—regionally known and also related mention (base camp is related to large-scale firefighting efforts)
the U.S. Fish Hatchery—regionally known
the main fire—second mention and also the adjective *main* makes it "one of a kind" (there's only one main fire)

the camp—second mention
The Rat Creek Fire—regionally known
the base camp—second mention
a 16-hour shift—not specific or identified; first mention
a fireline—not specific or identified; first mention
The Rat Creek Fire—second mention and regionally known
the Leavenworth side of Mountain Home—the phrase makes it "one of a kind" (there's only one Leavenworth side)

(continued)

298 Grammar Dimensions, Platinum Edition

Use Your English

While Ss are working on these activities, circulate around the room to listen to their language use. Do they appear to be using these structures accurately? You may wish to review errors you noted at the end of the activity.

ACTIVITY 1: SPEAKING

TIC-TAC-TOE/Arranging Objects

Choose a small common object that can be moved around. It can be something that you are wearing (a ring, a watch) or carrying with you (a pencil, a book). It is all right if some people choose the same object. All of you will give your objects to one student. This student will draw a big tic-tac-toe chart on the blackboard.

Form two teams. Each team will tell the student who has the objects to arrange them according to their directions, one sentence at a time. (For example, "Put a book under the ring. Put the red pencil next to the book.") If the article usage in the sentence is correct (and the person is able to follow the directions), then the team gets to put an X or O in any of the tic-tac-toe squares. If it is not correct, then the team must pass. The first team to get three X's or three O's in a row or diagonally wins the game.

Activity 1

While most Ss will be familiar with this game, they may not know it by the name "tic-tac-toe." Do a quick model of the game as it is usually played before playing this modified game.

VARIATION

Rather than using the board for the tic-tac-toe chart, make a "life-size" chart on paper that can be placed on a desk or the floor. This way the original items can be placed in the chart.

ACTIVITY 2: SPEAKING/LISTENING

Find a photograph or drawing to bring to class. First describe the picture, and then work together to tell the class a story about it. This will be a "chain story." The first person says one thing about the picture, the second person repeats that and adds another sentence, etc., until each student has contributed at least one sentence to the story. Concentrate on using articles correctly.

Activity 2

Arrange the class in a circle to complete this activity. Activity 2 is designed to lead Ss to use the "first mention/second mention" concept in article choice. While they are working do not correct their article use directly; instead, note errors you hear in context and discuss them at the end of the activity.

ACTIVITY 3: WRITING

Now without the help of your classmates, write a short description of the picture that you described in Activity 2. It doesn't have to be exactly the same as the story you made, but again try to use the articles correctly.

Articles: The, A/An, Some, and Ø **299**

ANSWER KEY

Exercise 13 (continued)

the process—related mention (the process of the fire)
a swath—not specific or identified; first mention
the structures—related or second mention (*structures* = another word for *houses*)
the electricity—universally known
the fire—second mention
the hill—related or second mention (*hill* = another word for *mountain* in this context)
a backfire—not specific or identified; first mention

A helicopter—not specific or identified; first mention
a loudspeaker—not specific or identified; first mention
the bottom—regionally known (everyone can identify "which" bottom of the hill) and also related mention (*hills* have bottoms)
the orchard-bordered property—regionally known (everyone can identify "which" orchard-bordered property) and related or second mention (*property* = another word for *land*)
the fire—second mention

the hill—second mention
The surrounding woods—second or related mention (*woods* = another word for *forest*)
the house—second mention
the fire—second mention
the house—second mention
the right to sleep in his own bed—this phrase makes it "one of a kind" (Also could be considered universally known if we believe that all people have this right)

Activity 4

VARIATION

Conduct a poll outside of class.

1. Have Ss work in groups to create questions that will elicit people's opinions on what brings happiness.
2. Use Ss questions to create a class questionnaire. Preferably plan this early enough to allow you to compile and print copies of the questionnaire to give to all class members.
3. Alone or in pairs, Ss ask at least five strangers their questions.
4. After conducting the poll, have Ss compile the results as a class and make generalizations about what makes people happy based on their results.

Activity 5

VARIATION

Have Ss do an Internet news search to gather their headlines.

ACTIVITY 4: SPEAKING/LISTENING/WRITING

Here are some things that people say contribute to their happiness: love, romance, success, wealth/money, fame, popularity, health, religion. Interview three people about what they think is most important for their happiness. (Tape-record people's answers, if possible.) Be sure to get information about the people you are interviewing, such as age group, gender and occupation.

In an oral or written summary, give the results of your interviews and see if there is agreement in people's answers.

ACTIVITY 5: READING

Find at least four headlines in a newspaper. Copy them down or cut them out and bring them to class. Put in articles (*the*, Ø article, *a/an*, or *some*) wherever you think they are appropriate in order to make the headlines into more complete statements. (Note: You might need to add main verbs or auxiliaries too, such as a form of *be* or *do*.)

With the headlines you have chosen, is it possible to use more than one of these articles? If so, does the meaning of the statement change?

▶ **EXAMPLE:** BLIZZARD OF '96 PARALYZES EAST COAST

Adding articles: *The* blizzard of 1996 paralyzes *the* East Coast.

Explanation: *The* is used with *blizzard* because it is a specific blizzard (January 1996) that most North Americans have heard about.

The is used with East Coast because this is from a United States newspaper, so we know *which* East Coast is being talked about.

ACTIVITY 6 : LISTENING

Listen to the tape of two people describing favorite children's toys.

STEP 1 Discuss these questions with a partner.

1. What was the woman's favorite toy when she was young?

2. What was the man's favorite toy when he was young?

STEP 2 Listen to the tape for each mention of (a) the specific toys that the speakers describe, or (b) toys in general. Write down these phrases in the order that you hear them.

Speaker 1/Woman	Speaker 2/Man

STEP 3 Compare your list with a classmate's list. Discuss the reasons for the speakers' choice of articles.

ACTIVITY 7 : SPEAKING/LISTENING

Lots of people like to have nice possessions. What would you like? Describe your "wish list" to someone, and put your choices in order. (Some examples are: land, expensive jewelry, a vacation home, a swimming pool, a sports car, etc.) Tape-record your description.

Listen carefully to your tape. Did you use articles correctly?

ACTIVITY 8 : SPEAKING/LISTENING

Ask a native speaker of English and/or a classmate to describe their house, apartment, or other living space (for example, a dormitory) to someone who has never seen it. Tape-record their descriptions. How many rooms are there? Where are they located? How many doors and windows are there in each room? What kind of furniture is there? Are there curtains, or pictures on the wall?

After you share these descriptions with the rest of the class, listen carefully to the tape for article usage.

Articles: *The, A/An, Some,* and Ø **301**

ANSWER KEY

Activity 6
Check tapescript on p. 511 for answers.

Activity 6

Play textbook audio. The transcript for this listening appears on p. 511 of this book.

Activity 7
VARIATION

Have the class create a class wish list through an e-mail discussion list.

1. After all members of the class make their proposals, compile a list of their ideas and post them again, asking each person to vote on the top three items.

2. Use the results to rank the items on the class wish list.

3. Discuss language issues afterwards in class, bringing examples of errors and calling on Ss to correct the errors.

Activity 8

For writing practice, have Ss write up their report for homework rather than present orally.

The test for this unit can be found on pp. 468–469 of this book.
The answers are on p. 470.

Unit 21

UNIT OVERVIEW

Unit 21 provides practice with articles that occur with names of places and with names of institutions.

UNIT GOALS

Review the goals listed on this page to see what students (Ss) should learn by the end of the unit.

OPENING TASK

Note: The purpose of this task is to generate talk about names of places, not to test geographical knowledge. The quiz format focuses attention on meaning rather than form, which will allow you to see whether Ss are able to produce the forms spontaneously.

SETTING UP THE TASK

Before starting, go over some of the vocabulary that you think your Ss might not know (for example, continent, desert, mountain range, planet).

U N I T 21

ARTICLES WITH NAMES OF PLACES

UNIT GOALS:

* To know how to use articles with names of places
* To know how to use articles with names of institutions

OPENING TASK
Geography Quiz

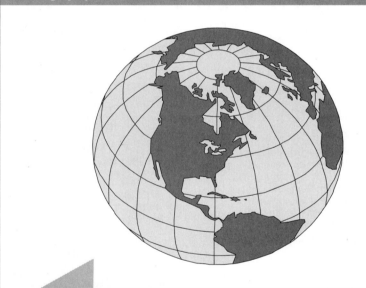

STEP 1 Move around the classroom to collect information to complete the chart below. Write down all the different answers you get in each category.

WHAT IS. . . ?	
the largest continent in the world	
the longest river	
the largest country (in size, not population)	
the biggest island	
the highest mountain range	
the highest mountain	
the biggest desert	
the largest ocean	
the largest lake	
the largest planet	

STEP 2 When you have spoken to five other students, decide on the correct answers. Use a recent edition of an almanac to check your answers.

STEP 3 Take turns making complete statements based on the information in your chart. For example: *The Amazon is* _____.

Step 2: Ss should get together with one or two people they have NOT spoken to yet and compare their answers.

Step 3: Each group can record their answers in full sentence form (*The Amazon is the longest river*) on a large piece of poster paper or newsprint. All the answers can be displayed on the walls and the Ss can walk around to compare answers, noting any differences and noting which answers they think are right.

CLOSING THE TASK

Use the posters as a springboard for Focus 1. Exercise 1 returns to the Opening Task and focuses on accuracy. If there are lots of different answers for the chart in the Opening Task, you can decide here which place names are the right answers or you can wait until Exercise 1 (see answers there), which reviews the chart.

To ensure that Ss understand each point, elicit additional examples for each category. Examples: Question: *Can you give me another example of a continent?*
Possible answers: *Africa, Asia*
Question: *What is the rule for using articles?*
Answer: *Continents use Ø (zero) article.* and so on.

Note: Ss will occasionally come up with examples that don't follow the rules. Point out that these are exceptions (the lower box) and that *most* of the place names do follow these rules for article usage.

FOCUS **1**

Articles with Names of Places

EXAMPLES	EXPLANATIONS
South America Zimbabwe New York First Avenue Interstate 90 Mars Jamaica Mount Shasta Lake Champlain Yosemite National Park	**Use Ø (no article) with names of:** • continents • countries • cities • streets and highways • planets • islands • single mountains • lakes • parks
the Yellow River the Gobi Desert the Arctic Ocean the Caspian Sea the Andes the Hawaiian Islands the Great Lakes the Middle East the Bay of Bengal	**Use *the* with names of:** • rivers • deserts • oceans • seas • mountain ranges • groups of islands • groups of lakes • most regions • when *of* is in the name
 the United States the United Kingdom the Earth or Earth the Sudan or Sudan	Note: These are regular patterns for using articles with place names. You will sometimes find exceptions. For example: • countries that are collections take *the* • certain places sometimes take *the* and sometimes do not

EXERCISE 1

Look at the categories below. For each category (1–10), put the correct answers from the Opening Task in either Column A or B. For example, the largest continent is Asia, which does not use *the*, so this would go in Column B for #1.

Category	(A) Use *the*	(B) Don't Use *the*
1. the largest continent in the world		Asia
2. the longest river		
3. the largest country (in size, not population)		
4. the biggest island		
5. the highest mountain range		
6. the highest mountain		
7. the biggest desert		
8. the largest ocean		
9. the largest lake		
10. the largest planet		

EXERCISE 2

Look at these conversations. Underline all the names of places, names of institutions (such as *the University of Washington*), and names of famous buildings or tourist attractions.

Dialogue 1
A: My brother is a freshman at the University of Washington.
B: Really? I thought he was at Louisiana State.
A: He was. He didn't like the climate in the South, so he decided to move to the Pacific Northwest.

Dialogue 2
A: How long did you stay in Washington, D.C.?
B: Not very long. We had just enough time to see the White House, the Capitol, and the Washington Monument.
A: Did you get to any museum or art galleries?
B: We wanted to go to the Smithsonian and the National Gallery, but we didn't have time.
A: Too bad!

In these examples, when is *the* used and when is it **not** used? List all the examples from the conversations if that is helpful.

Exercise 1

After completing the Opening Task, you probably have some sense of your Ss' knowledge about these geographical place names, or you might have decided to go over the right answers. For some classes, then, this exercise will simply be a matter of filling in the chart: Column A for the place names that use *the*; Column B for the place names that don't use *the* (called "zero article").

VARIATION

If you didn't come up with the right answers in the Opening Task, you can do that before filling in the chart or you can do it while filling in the chart.

Exercise 2

SUGGESTIONS

1. Since the first part is straightforward—identifying and underlining place names—this can be done individually
2. It's nice to pool the information for the next part, so we recommend that Ss work in pairs or small groups and/or that you review this as a whole class.
3. Ask: *When is the used?* Answers: with *"the University of Washington" (Dialogue 1, A)*; with *"the South" and "the Pacific Northwest" (Dialogue 1, last A)* and so on. After each answer, ask: *What kind of place name is it?* Answers: *"the University of Washington" is the name of a university; "the South" and "the Pacific Northwest" are regions.* (See Focus 1; other place names from this exercise are explained in Focus 2.)

Note: This exercise leads naturally to Focus 2. Questions may come up concerning article usage with *University* and *College*. You can answer these by bridging to Exercise 2 (c), (d), and (e).

ANSWER KEY

Exercise 1
(A): 1. the Amazon   **5.** the Himalayas   **7.** the Sahara   **8.** the Pacific Ocean   **(B): 2.** Asia
3. Russia (previously the Soviet Union)
4. Australia (also the name of a country);
Greenland   **6.** Mt. Everest   **9.** Lake Superior
10. Jupiter

Exercise 2
Dialogue 1. A. the University of Washington
B. Louisiana State University   **A.** the South; the Pacific Northwest
Dialogue 2. A. Washington, D.C.   **B.** the White House; the Capitol; the Washington Monument   **B.** the Smithsonian; the National Gallery

Ss can work in pairs to fill in the blanks.

VARIATION

1. If you want to do this exercise as a whole class, for each blank, have your Ss tell you the rule. Example: *Why do answers (1)–(6) use zero article?* Answer: *They are all names of countries, which don't use the/which use zero article.*

2. Depending on your class, some Ss may be familiar with these place names and will be able to fill in the rest of the map without reading the passage. These are the place names that are not marked on the map: the Irrawaddy (River), Rangoon, the Mekong River, and Hkakabo Razi, the mountain. If you or your Ss are not familiar with this part of the world, work through the reading with your class to find the locations of these.

3. Read each sentence, one by one, (or have Ss read) and look at the map to find the places. If they are not marked, fill them in according to the description.

4. If you have a map of this area to bring to class, all the better.

EXERCISE 3

Fill in the blanks with *the* or Ø (no article).

(1) _____ Burma is sandwiched between (2) _____ India and (3) _____ Bangladesh on one side and (4) _____ China, (5) _____ Laos, and (6) _____ Thailand on the other. To the south is (7) _____ Andaman Sea and (8) _____ Bay of Bengal. Burma has several important river systems including (9) _____ Irrawaddy, which runs almost the entire length of the country and enters the sea in a vast delta region southwest of (10) _____ Rangoon, the capital. (11) _____ Mekong River forms the border between Burma and Laos. (12) _____ Himalayas rise in the north of Burma, and (13) _____ Hkakabo Razi, on the border between Burma and Tibet, is the highest mountain in southeast Asia, at 5881 meters (19,297 feet).

Adapted from *Burma, A Travel Survival Kit*, by Tony Wheeler. Lonely Planet Publications, 1982.

Now use the information from this exercise to complete labeling the map.

306 UNIT 21

ANSWER KEY

Exercise 3
1. 0 2. 0 3. 0 4. 0 5. 0 6. 0
7. the 8. the 9. the 10. 0 11. The
12. The 13. 0

FOCUS **2**

▶ **A**rticles with Names of Institutions

EXAMPLES	EXPLANATIONS
(a) Summit Elementary School **(b)** Children's Hospital and Medical Center **(c)** Boston College **(d)** Louisiana State (University) **(e)** the Eiffel Tower **(f)** the University of Northern Iowa	**Use Ø (no article):** • for schools, hospitals, and prisons • when the place name comes **before** *College* or *University* **Use** *the:* • for most tourist attractions • when *University of* comes before the place name

EXERCISE 4

The following conversation is between Sheryl Smith, a real estate agent, and the Joneses, who want to buy a house. Fill in the blanks with *the* or Ø (no article).

Sheryl Smith: I'm sure you'd like the area. It borders (1) _____

Discovery Park, which has free outdoor concerts at (2) _____

Rutherford Concert Hall, and also there's (3) _____

Whitehawk Native American Art Museum, which you've

probably heard of. It's quite well known.

Mike Jones: Yes, yes.

Donna Jones: What about schools?

Sheryl Smith: Well, there's (4) _____ Smith College of

Architecture, of course...

Donna Jones: I mean public schools for our children.

Sheryl Smith: Oh, well, (5) _____ Golden Oaks Elementary

School is only a few blocks away, on (6) _____

First Avenue. And there's a high school about a mile north of

the park.

Mike Jones: (pointing) Aren't those (7) _____ White

Mountains?

Articles with Names of Places | **307**

A N S W E R   K E Y

Exercise 4
1. 0   **2.** 0   **3.** the   **4.** the   **5.** 0   **6.** 0
7. the   **8.** 0   **9.** 0   **10.** The

FOCUS 2

S U G G E S T I O N S

1. If you didn't refer to this focus box in Exercise 2, you can go back over the answers, putting them in the proper categories here: (A) 1 *"The University of Washington" is a place name like (f)—* with *"University of"* before the place name.

2. Or, elicit other examples of place names that your Ss may know, that fit with each example: *(a) names of schools, hospitals, and prisons that your students may know of; (e) names of local tourist attractions or others that your students; may know of;* and so on.

Workbook Ex. 4, pp. 158–159.
Answers: TE p. 500.

Exercise 4

It's fun to do this exercise orally, as a "real," natural-sounding dialogue.

If you choose to do this exercise orally, first give Ss a few minutes to work with a partner, and check to make sure they have answers for each blank. This will allow the reading to move along smoothly so that the class is not waiting for the speakers to search for the answers.

S U G G E S T I O N S

1. Because this dialogue is so long, it is appropriate to switch speakers halfway through—at the end of page 307.
2. Before Ss read, remind them that for natural "fluent"-sounding speech, they need to link words together smoothly and to use appropriate intonation—falling intonation at the end of a statement, rising intonation at the end of a yes-no question, and louder volume, higher pitch for important or surprising information.
3. Demonstrate by reading a sentence or two aloud.

Exercise 5

VARIATION

If you want to make this exercise into a game or competition, form teams and give 1 point for each correct answer. A further variation is to give an extra point for each time a student (or someone from the team) can say *why* their answer is correct. In other words, what is the rule? (You can decide whether or not to have Ss check their answers by looking them up in the focus boxes.)

Sample answers: 1. Hawaii is a state and states (like countries and cities—Focus 1) don't take *the*/use zero article. 2. The Hawaiian Islands is a group of islands and groups of islands use *the* (Focus 1, second box)

Exercise 6

SUGGESTION

Since this is an editing exercise, it's logical to have Ss work on this individually, perhaps as homework. They can check their answers with a partner, or you can conduct this together as a whole class. If there are disagreements, ask the Ss to tell why they chose *the* or Ø article: *What is the rule?* They can refer to focus boxes.

UNIT GOAL REVIEW

Ask Ss to look at the goals on the opening page of the unit again. Assist them in understanding how much they have learned. One way is to present the items in the focus boxes as a checklist, having Ss give examples for each.

Sheryl Smith: Yes. On clear days, you can even see (8) _____ Mt. Wildman, the tallest mountain in the range.

Mike Jones: Oh, yes. I heard about a good fishing spot there, on (9) _____ Blue Lake.

Sheryl Smith: Yes, my husband goes there and to (10) _____ Nooksack River to fish. He could tell you all about it.

Mike Jones: Ms. Smith, I think you might have made a sale today.

EXERCISE 5

Fill in the blanks with *the* or Ø (no article). The first two have been done for you.

1. _Ø_____ Hawaii
2. _the____ Hawaiian Islands
3. _____ Saudi Arabia
4. _____ Harvard University
5. _____ Himalayas
6. _____ Museum of Modern Art
7. _____ First Avenue
8. _____ Mississippi River
9. _____ University of Iowa
10. _____ Turkey
11. _____ United States
12. _____ Pyramids
13. _____ West
14. _____ Africa
15. _____ Lake Wenatchee
16. _____ Saturn

EXERCISE 6

For each underlined place name, check to see if the article is used correctly. If it is wrong, correct it: Add *the* or cross out *the*. The first one has been done for you.

SAN FRANCISCO MUST SEE'S FOR FIRST-TIMERS

Once considered impossible to build, (1) ^*the* Golden Gate Bridge, a 1.7 mile-long single-span suspension bridge, was opened in 1937. A walk across offers a fantastic view of the city, the Marin Headlands, and the East Bay. Experience a taste of (2) the Orient in (3) the Chinatown, the largest Chinese settlement outside (4) the Asia. Originally only sand dunes, (5) the Golden Gate Park owes its existence to Scottish landscape architect John McLaren. In addition to the beauty of its landscape, the park contains: a conservatory modeled after (6) Kew Gardens; (7) Asian Art Museum with its well-known Brundage collection; (8) the Strybing Arboretum with its worldwide plant collection; and (9) California Academy of Sciences, which includes a planetarium and aquarium.

Adapted from *San Francisco TESOL Convention* 1990, Leslie Reichert.

ANSWER KEY

Exercise 5
3. 0   4. 0   5. the   6. the   7. 0
8. the   9. the   10. 0   11. the   12. the
12. the   14. 0   15. 0   16. 0

Exercise 6
2. the   3. 0   4. 0   5. the or 0   6. 0
7. the   8. the or 0   9. the

Use Your English

ACTIVITY 1: SPEAKING/LISTENING

It is often said that Americans do not know very much about world geography, compared to people from other countries. The purpose of this activity is for people who grew up in other countries to conduct a small survey of Americans (or people educated in the United States) to find out to what extent this is true.

Use the information in the Opening Task on page 303 to draw up a chart of your own. Add other items to the chart if you want. Then use this chart to get information from as many Americans as you can—ideally from five different people. Compare the answers you receive with those that your classmates gave you, and share your findings with the rest of the class.

On the basis of the findings from everyone in the class, is it true that Americans know less about world geography than people from other countries? Are there any reasons to explain your results?

ACTIVITY 2: SPEAKING

With the help of your teacher, form teams. Each team will have five minutes to think of as many names of islands, mountains, and lakes as possible. Each name with correct article use will be worth one point. The team that has the most correct names + articles wins.

ACTIVITY 3: WRITING

Think of a city or region you know and like. What places are the "Must See's For First-Timers"? Write a short description of the tourist attractions and special features. If time allows, draw a map giving the relative locations of these places.

USE YOUR ENGLISH

Activity 1
VARIATION

Conduct the information-gathering session with any nationality of people if Americans are not available. Or do a comparative survey:

1. young people compared to older people (You might want to determine the age categories you are interested in beforehand);
2. men compared to women;
3. one nationality compared to another; etc.

Note: Because some of these contrasts may cause friction (for example, the women in your class may end up competing with the men in your class), you will need to think carefully about this beforehand, or let Ss brainstorm on what findings they are interested in. One possibility is to form research teams, with each research team targeting a different "population" (age group, gender, nationality, etc.).

Activity 2
SUGGESTIONS

1. It has been our experience that Ss can think of a great number of place names, so you might want to allow at least 10–15 minutes *after* the initial 5-minute session.
2. If you have a map or globe available for this activity, it's fun to look up the different places, especially if your student population has a lot of variety.

Activity 3
EXPANSION

1. If you feel Ss need more practice with writing and editing, have them exchange their written descriptions with another student, who will

   (a) first read through the paper for general content—Is there anything that he/she can't understand? If so, they can ask the writer for clarification or elaboration.

   (b) edit the description for accuracy in terms of article usage (and other errors, if you choose)—Was *the* or Ø article used correctly?

2. If Ss need more practice with listening, ask them to read their descriptions aloud, with other Ss taking notes on the "Must See's" (also see Exercise 6). When each student has finished reading her/his description, review the place names for accuracy in article usage.

Activity 4

Play textbook audio. The tapescript for this listening activity appears on p. 511 of this book.

If you choose to do this activity as a whole class, check Step 1. 3 with the tape, stopping the tape after each mention of a place name. After each mention, ask why Ø or *the* was used (Step 2): What is the rule?

Activity 5

SUGGESTIONS

1. It's helpful to bring in a sample of this kind of poster. If you are doing this for the first time, you might want to make one poster together, as a whole class, or keep one of your student's posters (with his/her permission, of course) as a sample for your next class. If you want a "professional" poster, a travel agency is a good source for this.

2. Although it's nice to have lots of different kinds of materials available for this, a large sheet of paper, magazines, and/or newspapers (that can be cut up) are all that's necessary. If Ss seem a little intimidated by such a project, assign them to work in teams (with at least one "artistic type" per team), making this truly collaborative.

ACTIVITY 4: LISTENING

STEP 1 Listen to the tape of a person talking about where she lives.

1. Work with a partner. Discuss the place the woman is talking about. Where is it? Why does she like it?

2. Listen again. Circle the names of the places the woman mentions.

—— Leblon Beach

—— Sugar Loaf Mountain

—— City Historic Museum

—— Museum of Brazil

—— North America

—— Santa Marinha Street

—— City Park

—— Ipanema Beach

—— Pacific Ocean

—— South America

—— Rio De Janeiro

3. In front of the names of the places you circled, write the word *the* or leave the space blank. Compare your answers with a classmate's. If you disagree on any answers, look back at Focus 1 and Focus 2 for help in deciding on the correct answer.

STEP 2 Work with a classmate to discuss why Ø (no article) or *the* was used with each place name.

ACTIVITY 5: SPEAKING/WRITING

You have been asked by the local chamber of commerce to design a poster to attract overseas visitors to the region where you are living. Or, if you prefer, you can make a poster about another place you know and like (See Activity 3), especially if there are other students interested in the same place.

Get together with a group of students to brainstorm local areas of interest. Your poster should have pictures and labels about the area and also short written descriptions.

Display and compare your posters.

ANSWER KEY

Activity 4

See tapescript (p. 511).

1. The woman is talking about Rio di Janeiro, in Brazil. See tapescript for reasons why she likes it; there are many, and answers may vary.

2, 3. The places the woman mentions are: Leblon Beach, Sugar Loaf Mountain, *the* City Historic Museum, Santa Marinha Street, City Park, Ipanema Beach, South America, Rio de Janeiro.

ACTIVITY 6: READING

Rita and Ray were planning an overnight backpacking trip into the mountains, so they asked their friend Bill to give them directions to a nice camping spot where he had camped many times. Bill told Ray the directions over the phone. Below are the notes that Ray took:

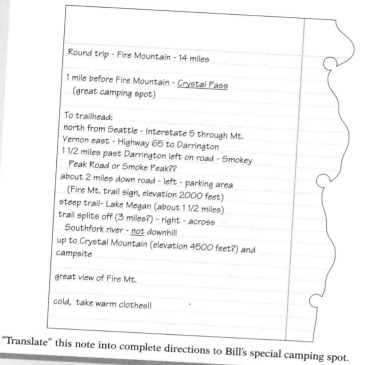

Round trip - Fire Mountain - 14 miles

1 mile before Fire Mountain - <u>Crystal Pass</u>
   (great camping spot)

To trailhead:
north from Seattle - Interstate 5 through Mt.
Vernon east - Highway 65 to Darrington
1 1/2 miles past Darrington left on road - Smokey
   Peak Road or Smoke Peak??
about 2 miles down road - left - parking area
   (Fire Mt. trail sign, elevation 2000 feet)
steep trail- Lake Megan (about 1 1/2 miles)
trail splits off (3 miles?) - right - across
   Southfork river - <u>not</u> downhill
up to Crystal Mountain (elevation 4500 feet?) and
campsite

great view of Fire Mt.

cold, take warm clothes!!

"Translate" this note into complete directions to Bill's special camping spot.

ACTIVITY 7: SPEAKING/LISTENING

The poster that you made in Activity 5 was so successful that you have been asked to talk about the region to a group of tourists and travel guides. Tape-record your short talk. Listen to the tape and check to see if you used *the* and Ø (no article) correctly.

Activity 6
VARIATION

Ask a native speaker to do this activity/"translate" this note into complete oral directions. (Or you can do this.) Tape record this and play it for the class. Discuss any differences in answers or in expected answers—Did the speaker use articles in the way Ss expected them to?

Activity 7
VARIATION

If you feel your Ss need more practice with listening comprehension, get native speakers involved. They can describe a poster that Ss made in Activity 5 if they are familiar with that region, or they can describe any region they know well. Listen to the tape for article usage.

The test for this unit can be found on pp. 471–472 of this book.
The answers are on p. 473.

TOEFL Test Preparation Exercises for Units 19–21 can be found on pp. 160–162 of the Workbook.
The answers are on p. 500 of this book.

Teacher's Edition: Unit 21 **311**

Unit 22

UNIT OVERVIEW

In this unit, students (Ss) look in depth at the passive voice. (*She **was born** on August 23rd/The thief **was** last **seen** on the corner of 12th Avenue and Roy Street/The last room in the hotel **got taken** by the couple right in front of us!*).

UNIT GOALS

Review the unit goals before proceeding to the Opening Task. If Ss are not familiar with the term "agent," you can tell them it's the "doer" of the action (which is not the subject in the passive).

OPENING TASK

Using the theme of resources and industries provides a natural context for the use of the passive. While Ss are doing the Opening Task, listen to their language use to determine their familiarity with this structure.

SETTING UP THE TASK

SUGGESTIONS

1. Make a copy of the map on an overhead transparency.
2. To be sure Ss understand the Opening Task, direct their attention to the map and point out the compass and the list of resources in the "legend."
3. Ask Ss about the resources of their nation(s). Instruct them to compare this island's industries with their country(s) industries.

UNIT 22

THE PASSIVE

UNIT GOALS:

- To know when to use passives
- To correctly form *be* and *get* passives
- To know the difference between the *be* passive and the *get* passive
- To know when to include the agent in the sentence

► OPENING TASK
The Island of Campinilea

You are gathering information for a book on Campinilea, an island located off the coast of Peru. The first chapter will be called "The Products and Natural Resources of Campinilea."

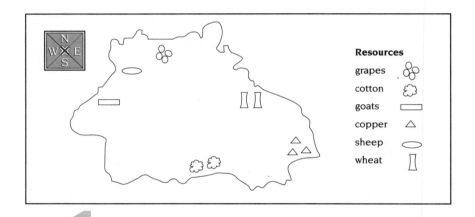

Resources

grapes

cotton

goats

copper

sheep

wheat

STEP **1** Use the information on the map on page 312 to discuss the island's resources.

▶ **EXAMPLE:** Where are grapes cultivated? . . . in the north

Where is cotton grown?

STEP **2** Use the map to match the activities to the appropriate location. The first one has been done for you.

Activities	Locations
cultivate grapes	in the east
raise sheep	in the southeast
grow cotton	in the northwest
grow wheat	in the north
mine copper	in the west
raise goats	in the south

STEP **3** Using the same information, write five sentences about the products and natural resources of Campinilea for the first chapter of your book.

CONDUCTING THE TASK

Steps 1 and 2:
Ask Ss to discuss the location of the resources in pairs or groups, using the example as a guide.

Step 3:
Direct pairs/groups to write at least five sentences about the activities, showing where they take place.

SUGGESTION
Have each group write its sentences on the board, on an overhead transparency, or on a large piece of poster paper.

CLOSING THE TASK
1. Bring the class together to share and compare answers.
2. Point out that Exercises 1–4 (pp. 314–317) build on this task.

ANSWER KEY

Opening Task Answers

grapes in the north   sheep in the northwest
cotton in the south   wheat in the east
copper in the southeast   goats in the west

Use the sentences Ss created in the Opening Task to illustrate the explanations in this focus box that introduces the difference between the active and passive.

Grammar Background

The key difference between these two "voices" is focus. Since the subject is seen as the key noun in the sentence, the passive is used to focus attention on the result or "receiver" of the action by placing it as the subject; the "doer" of the action can be mentioned, but is often not included.

Although they are presented here together, beware of teaching the passive as simply a transformation of the active. There are situations when the passive is far more common or appropriate than the active: *She **was born** in South Africa but is an Australian citizen now.*
(→ NOT: *Her mother **bore** her in South Africa but. . . .*)
[To her boss]: *I'm sorry, but I **was told** there would be no meeting today.*
(→ Having missed the meeting, this person does not want to point out who is to blame, for reasons of kindness or diplomacy.)

Exercise 1

When discussing whether the active or passive sounds better for these sentences, ask Ss to consider whether the product is more important or the producer.
Answers will vary. It is likely that the passive will sound better since it is obvious who is performing the action (farmers, miners, etc.).

Workbook Ex. 1, pp. 163–164.
Answers: Te p. 501.

Passive and Active

EXAMPLES	EXPLANATIONS
(a) Farmers **cultivate** grapes in the north.	Use the active to focus on the person who performs the action.
(b) Grapes **are cultivated** in the north.	Use the passive to focus on the result of the action, not the person who performs it.

EXERCISE 1

Look at each sentence you wrote in Step 3 of the Opening Task on page 313. Did you use the passive or the active? Write each statement both ways.
Which statement sounds better? Why?

FOCUS 2

Forming the *Be* Passive

To form the passive, use the appropriate tense of *be*, followed by the past participle (pp):

EXAMPLES	TENSE	FORM	
(a) Wool **is produced** here.	Simple Present	*am/is/are*	+ pp
(b) Wool **is being produced** here right now.	Present Progressive	*am/is/are being*	+ pp
(c) Wool **was produced** here.	Simple Past	*was/were*	+ pp
(d) Wool **was being produced** here ten years ago.	Past Progressive	*was/were being*	+ pp
(e) Wool **has been produced** here since 1900.	Present Perfect	*have/has been*	+ pp
(f) Wool **had been produced** here when the island was discovered.	Past Perfect	*had been*	+ pp
(g) Wool **will be produced** here next year.	Future (*will*)	*will be*	+ pp
(h) Wool **is going to be produced** here.	Future (*be going to*)	*am/is/are going to be*	+ pp
(i) Wool **will have been produced** here by the year 2010.	Future Perfect	*will have been*	+ pp

EXERCISE 2

The second chapter of the book on Campinilea is called "The People of Campinilea and Their Customs." Look at the following statements about Campinilea; write 1 beside those you think belong to Chapter 1 (Products and Resources) and 2 beside those you think belong to Chapter 2 (People and Customs).

1. In the west, unmarried women leave their family homes at the age of twenty-five and raise goats in the mountains.
2. Miners mined silver throughout the island during the last century.
3. They will plant the first crop of rice in the south next year.
4. In the southeast, fathers take their oldest sons to the copper mines on their twelfth birthday in a special ceremony to teach them the legends and rituals associated with Campinilean copper.
5. Easterners are more traditional than southerners; for example, farmers in the east have harvested wheat in the same way for hundreds of years, while those in the south are constantly exploring new techniques for growing cotton.

The Passive | **315**

FOCUS 2

With Focus Box 2, emphasize that the passive is not a tense, but occurs with almost all tenses. Remind Ss that this form is used to stress the importance of the product or result, not the person doing the production.

Exercise 2

This activity provides an opportunity for Ss working alone or in pairs to consider the appropriateness of using the passive and active voices. In Chapter 1 (Products and Resources), the passive is more likely, while in Chapter 2 (People and Customs), the people—or producers of these products—deserve greater focus and, thus, the active is more appropriate.

A N S W E R   K E Y

Exercise 2
1. 2 **2.** 1 **3.** 1 **4.** 2 **5.** 2 **6.** 1
Yes, because it is not important to know who performed the act (mining, planting, producing).

Rewritten statements: **2.** *Silver has been mined throughout. . . .* **3.** *The first crop of rice will be planted in. . . .* **6.** *Grapes have been produced in . . .*

6. They have produced grapes in Campinilea for only a few years.

Do you think it would be appropriate to use the passive in any of these statements? Why do you think so? Rewrite those statements here:

_____

_____

_____

_____

Exercise 3

SUGGESTION

1. Copy this story on an overhead transparency and do the exercise as a class.
2. When Ss choose passive or active, ask them to explain why they chose it. This will help you explain why they have made errors and reinforce their ability to analyze the situation in order to determine appropriate use.

Workbook Ex. 2, p. 165.
Answers: TE p. 501.

EXERCISE 3

Complete the following, using the verb tense that fits best.

Adventurous tourists are beginning to discover Campinilea, and the island is hard at work getting ready to welcome more visitors. A new airport (1) _____ (build) last year, and at the moment, hotels (2) _____ (construct) along the southern beaches. A new road (3) _____ (finish) next year so visitors will be able to reach the northern region. Five years ago, very little (4) _____ (know) about Campinilea; but last year, three books (5) _____ (write) about the island, and several guide books (6) _____ (publish). At the moment, these books (7) _____ (translate) into different languages. English (8) _____ (teach) in schools so many Campinileans know a little English, but not many other foreign languages (9) _____ (speak).

Tourism has brought many changes to this small island, and people are afraid that it will have a negative effect on the traditional customs and culture of the people. For example, last month in the capital, several young Campinileans (10) _____ (arrest) for being drunk in public, and some tourists (11) _____ (rob) near the beach. However, if you leave the tourist areas and go up to the mountains, you will find that life is still the same as it was hundreds of years ago. For example, since the sixteenth century, the same tribal dances (12) _____ (perform) to celebrate the Campinilean new year, and the same type of food (13) _____ (serve). For centuries, visitors (14) _____ (invite) to join Campinileans in the celebration of festivals, and you will find traditional Campinilean hospitality in these regions has not changed at all.

ANSWER KEY

Exercise 3
(1) was built **(2)** are being constructed
(3) will be finished **(4)** was known
(5) were written **(6)** were published
(7) are being translated **(8)** is (being)
taught **(9)** are spoken **(10)** were arrested **(11)** were robbed **(12)** have been performed **(13)** has been served
(14) have been invited

The Passive

EXAMPLES	EXPLANATIONS
(a) All the cookies **were eaten** last night.	Use the passive when you don't know who performed the action.
(b) Wheat **is grown** in the East.	Use the passive when the person who performed the action is obvious. In example (b), it is obvious that farmers are the people who grow the wheat.
(c) A mistake was **made.**	Use the passive when you don't want to tell who performed the action.
(d) The computer **is protected** from electrical damage by a special grounding plug. **(e)** The proposal **was rejected** by the people of King County in last night's vote.	The passive is more formal than the active. It is more common in writing, especially in scientific and technical reports, and in newspaper articles. It is less common in conversation.

EXERCISE 4

With the growth of tourism, petty crime has unfortunately increased in Campinilea. The Campinilean police are currently investigating a robbery that took place in a hotel room a few nights ago.

Work with a partner. One of you should look at Picture A below; the other should look at Picture B on page A-17. One of you has a picture of the room **before** the robbery, and the other has a picture of the room **after** the robbery. Seven different things were done to the room. **Without looking at your partner's picture,** ask each other questions and find what these seven things were and complete the report below.

ROBBERY AT HOTEL PARAISO

Last night the police were called to investigate a robbery that took place at the Hotel Paraiso. The identity of the thief is still unknown. The police took note of several unusual occurrences. For example,

_____

_____

_____

The public has been asked to contact the police with any information about the identity of the thief. Any information leading to an arrest will be rewarded.

Picture A

FOCUS 3

Here greater attention is given to the use of the passive, which is usually a trickier concept than form and meaning. Use more examples to illustrate the explanations:

(a) *The reason for his disappearance **was** never **discovered.***
 *Karen's purse **was stolen** while she was riding the bus.*

(b) *Many Christians believe the Earth **was created** in seven days.*
 *When he **was arrested**, he used his one phone call to contact his wife.*
 *I can't believe it! **I've been fired**!*

(c) ***I've been informed** that one of you has been stealing from me!*

(d) *The results of this project **will be used** to make important advances in cancer research.*
 *First, the sample **is placed** in a prepared, sanitary container.*
 *At this moment, the president **is being advised** on which action to take.*

Exercise 4

SUGGESTIONS

1. Be sure Ss know they should only look at one of the two pictures.
2. If there is a group of three, two people can look at Picture B and take turns offering information.
3. While Ss are working, circulate around the room and help with verb forms (active or passive).
4. Ss can report back to the class or compile a list of statements about the questions to hand in for correction.

Workbook Ex. 3, p. 166.
Answers: TE p. 501.

Exercise 4

The flowers were moved. The door was opened, and the glass windowpane was broken. The vase was taken. The dresser drawer was opened, and a jewelry box was moved to the top of the dress. Jewelry was stolen from the box. The suitcase was moved and partially unlocked. The telephone was unplugged/disconnected.

FOCUS 4

The meaning and use of the *get*-passive will be addressed in Focus 5 (p. 319). For the meantime, focus on the use of *get* in the tenses illustrated here. Pay special attention to the question and negative forms, which do not follow the same pattern as *be*-passive.

Exercise 5

SUGGESTIONS

1. To ensure that Ss understand what's expected of them, model the first situation.
2. If you have a copy of the exercise on an overhead transparency, you can write the previous event directly onto the line provided. Ss can complete this activity individually or in pairs.

FOCUS **4**

▶ Including the Agent in Passive Sentences

EXAMPLES	EXPLANATIONS
(a) Wheat is grown in the East. **(b)** **NOT:** Wheat is grown in the East by farmers.	In most situations where the passive is used, the *by*-phrase (the agent) is understood and therefore is *not* used.
(c) Wheat is grown in eastern Campinilea. It is planted **by men,** and it is harvested **by women and children.** **(d)** *Hamlet* was written **by William Shakespeare.** **(e)** Several South American countries were liberated **by Simon Bolivar.** **(f)** I can't believe it! This novel was written **by a fourteen-year-old.**	You can include the agent (the person who performs the action) with a *by*-phrase if that information is important. It is important to include the agent: • when new information is added, (Example c, second sentence) • with proper names or famous people (Examples d and e) • when the agent's identity is surprising or unexpected (Example f)

EXERCISE 5

Decide if each italicized phrase (*by* + agent) is necessary in the sentences below. Cross out the *by*-phrases that you think are unnecessary.

Passage 1

Campinilea was described (1) *by Jules Verne* in one of his early novels. It was seen (2) *by people* as an exotic yet stable society. Recently, it was rated (3) *by Travel Magazine* as one of the top ten tourists spots in the world. One of the reasons for the country's popularity is that the products produced (4) *by Campinileans* in Campinilea are excellent.

For example, rugs have been produced (5) *by Campinilean people* for centuries. They are woven (6) *by women from the mountain tribes* and are then transported to the capital (7) *by mule* and are sold in the markets (8) *by relatives of the weavers.*

Another excellent product is the mineral water of Campinilea. In restaurants in the capital city, bottled water is served (9) *by waiters.* It is interesting that this water is rarely drunk (10) *by Campinileans,* but it is much appreciated (11) *by foreign tourists.*

Passage 2

Dear Janette,

I've been working hard this whole week on my book. In some ways, I wish that I hadn't gotten paid an advance (1) *by the publishers,* since now I feel a lot of pressure to finish quickly. I guess that's the purpose of an advance! I really hope, though, that when the book is finally finished (2) *by me,* it will be appreciated (3) *by people.* I am hoping that I can finish soon, because it means that I will soon be paid in full (4) *by the publishers!* Even if it's done soon, the book won't actually be published (5) *by the publishers* until at least six months after the manuscript is received (6) *by them.*

Did I tell you that Scout got hurt (7) *by another dog?* She was playing with Patches, the neighbor's dog, like she always does, and her ear got bitten pretty severely (8) *by Patches.* I had to take her to the vet's and get it stitched up (9) *by the vet.* The vet asked me if Scout got attacked (10) *by Patches,* and I had to explain that no, she and Patches just like to play rough. Luckily, Scout's fine. And of course she and Patches are playing together again, just as hard as ever, so it's clear that their friendship hasn't been damaged (11) *by the experience.* Gotta run! Back to work on the book . . .

Love,

Dean

FOCUS **5**

Forming the *Get*-Passive

To form the *get*-passive, use the appropriate tense of *get,* followed by the past participle (pp):

EXAMPLES		TENSE	FORM	
(a)	Her cookies always **get eaten.**	Present Simple	*get/gets*	+ pp
(b)	Her cookies **are getting eaten.**	Present Progressive	*am/is/are getting*	+ pp
(c)	Her cookies **got eaten.**	Past Simple	*got*	+ pp
(d)	Her cookies **were getting eaten.**	Past Progressive	*was/were getting*	+ pp
(e)	Her cookies **have gotten eaten.**	Present Perfect	*have/has gotten*	+ pp
(f)	Her cookies **had gotten eaten.**	Past Perfect	*had gotten*	+ pp
(g)	Her cookies **will get eaten.**	Future (*will*)	*will get*	+ pp
(h)	Her cookies are **going to get eaten.**	Future (*going to*)	*am/is/are going to get*	+ pp
(i)	Her cookies **will have gotten eaten** by the time we get home.	Future Perfect	*will have gotten*	+ pp

The Passive | **319**

Stress the difference in emphasis between these two passive forms. In particular, note the difference in formality. Note that *get* is almost always associated with informality, whether in passive or in phrasal verbs: *get up* (awaken), *get in* (enter), *get over* (recover), *get into* (become engaged in)

QUESTIONS: Simple present and past:

EXAMPLES	QUESTION FORM
(j) Do her cookies **get eaten**?	*Do/does* + subject + *get* + pp
(k) Did her cookies **get eaten**?	*Did* + subject + *get* + pp

NEGATIVE: Simple present and past:

EXAMPLES	NEGATIVE STATEMENT FORM
(l) Her cookies **do not get eaten**.	subject + *do/does* + *not* + *get* + pp (*don't/doesn't*)
(m) Her cookies **did not get eaten**.	subject + *did not* + *get* + pp (*didn't*)

Exercise 6

Have Ss complete this activity in pairs or individually for homework.

SUGGESTION

When reviewing this exercise, have pairs read out the dialogues. Call on the rest of the class to determine if their choice of active or passive is appropriate.

Workbook Ex. 4, pp. 166–167.
Answers: TE p. 501.

EXERCISE 6

Read the following situations. What do you think probably happened before each one? Match the situation with one of the previous events in the box below.

SITUATION	PREVIOUS EVENT
1. Oh, no! Not my clean white shirt!	_____
2. We're finally able to pay our bills.	_____
3. It's so exciting to see my name in print.	_____
4. I told you not to leave it outside at night!	_____
5. When I came back to the parking lot, I found these dents on the side.	_____
6. They took him straight to the hospital by ambulance.	_____
7. Thank you for all your support. Now that I am mayor, I will work to improve our schools.	_____
8. The packet's empty, and there are only a few crumbs left!	_____

(a) They got paid.	**(b)** His car got hit.
(c) Someone got injured.	**(d)** Some coffee got spilled.
(e) All the cookies got eaten.	**(f)** She got elected.
(g) His book got published.	**(h)** Her bike got stolen.

ANSWER KEY

Exercise 6
1. (d) **2.** (a) **3.** (g) **4.** (h) **5.** (b)
6. (c) **7.** (f) **8.** (e)

EXERCISE 7

Complete the following with the *get*-passive and the appropriate tense.

1. **A:** I think I've prepared too much food for tomorrow's party.
   B: Don't worry. It _____ all _____ (eat).

2. **A:** Where's your car?
   B: It's _____ (fix).

3. **A:** How was your vacation last month?
   B: Terrible. We _____ (rob), and all our traveler's checks _____ (take).

4. **A:** Have you heard? Chuck _____ (invite) to dinner with the President at the White House!
   B: I don't believe it.

5. **A:** Please drive slowly.
   B: Why?
   A: If you don't, we _____ (stop) by the Highway Patrol.

6. **A:** Did you finish your assignments yet?
   B: Yeah. We turned them in, and now they _____ (grade).

7. **A:** Do you know if Sid has moved?
   B: No. Why?
   A: I sent him a letter last week, but it _____ (return) yesterday with no forwarding address.
   B: That's strange.

8. **A:** Al's writing a novel.
   B: Really?
   A: Yes. He hopes it _____ (publish) next year.

9. **A:** Rosa quit her job.
   B: Why?
   A: She _____ (not/pay).

10. **A:** There was a terrible accident here last night.
    B: _____ anyone _____ (arrest)?

Exercise 7

SUGGESTION

1. Have pairs come to a consensus on whether *get* can be used in place of *be*.
2. Pairs should defend their decisions to the class.

Workbook Ex. 5, pp. 167–168.
Answers: TE p. 501.

ANSWER KEY

Exercise 7
1. will; get eaten.   2. getting fixed   3. got robbed; got taken.   4. got invited   5. 'll get
stopped   6. are getting graded   7. got returned   8. will get published   9. didn't get paid   10. Did; get arrested

Note that there is no hard and fast rule about whether to include the agent. However, point out to Ss that if they constantly use the agent—or "doer"—in passive sentences, they will sound unnatural, as the choice of the passive usually means that the agent is less significant than the result or recipient of the action.

   More examples:

(d) *The telephone was invented by Alexander Graham Bell.*

(e) *This school was founded by X.*

(f) *Did you say this test was taken by a beginning-level student? But they got a perfect score!*

Further examples can be taken from classroom situations.

Exercise 8

S U G G E S T I O N

1. Have Ss complete this exercise for homework or independently in class to give them more time to think about the context provided by the passages.
2. Next, direct Ss to compare their answers in pairs, explaining their decisions.
3. Only discuss as a class those points on which pairs could not agree.

FOCUS **6**

▶ Be-Passive versus Get-Passive

EXAMPLES	EXPLANATIONS
(a) They **are married.** (b) They **got married** last year.	In most situations, the *be*-passive emphasizes a continuing state, while the *get*-passive emphasizes a change in the situation.
(c) The answer **was known.** (d) **NOT:** The answer **got known.** (*know* = an unchanging state) (e) She **was wanted** by the police for shoplifting. (f) **NOT:** She **got wanted** by the police for shoplifting.	Because the *get*-passive emphasizes a change in a situation, it is only used with action or process verbs. It cannot be used with stative verbs (verbs that refer to situations, or "states," that do not change). Some common stative verbs: *own like hate see love* *know feel want*
(g) *To a friend:* Have you heard the news? Isao's car **got stolen!** (h) *In a police report:* A white Honda Civic **was stolen** last night.	*Get*-passives are often used in conversation and rarely in writing or formal speaking. *Be*-passives are more formal than *get*-passives.

EXERCISE 8

Where possible, change the underlined verbs to *get*-passives. If it is not possible to use the *get*-passive, explain why.

1. Last week, Marvin had a dinner party. He prepared lots of food, and
   everything was eaten. [*got eaten*]

2. This ring is very valuable because it <u>was owned</u> by Napoleon.

3. We are very sorry that Mr. Gordon is leaving our company—he <u>was liked</u> and respected by us all.

4. What happened to your car?
   It <u>was hit</u> by a truck.

5. Someone broke into her house, but surprisingly, nothing <u>was taken</u>.

ANSWER KEY

Exercise 8
4. got hit   5. got taken   7. will get published   8. got attacked   9. got damaged

6. At the time of his arrest, that man was armed and dangerous, and he <u>was wanted</u> by the police in three different states.

7. We really hope our book <u>will be published</u> some day.

8. I'm sorry I'm late; I had to go to the veterinarian's because my dog <u>was attacked</u> by a cat.

9. Many beautiful houses <u>were</u> badly <u>damaged</u> in last month's earthquake.

10. Marilyn Monroe <u>was admired</u> by many people.

EXERCISE 9

Tabloid newspapers present sensational, but usually untrue, stories. Look at the following tabloid newspaper headlines and in your notebook rewrite each one as a complete sentence. Use a *get*-passive wherever possible; use a *be*-passive where you cannot use a *get*-passive.

1. TEEN EATEN BY GIANT COCKROACHES
2. ELVIS SEEN IN SUPERMARKET LINE
3. VICE-PRESIDENT KIDNAPPED BY SPACE ALIENS
4. BILL AND HILLARY TO DIVORCE?
5. WORLD'S WORST HUSBAND MARRIED 36 TIMES
6. FALSE TEETH STUCK IN MAN'S THROAT FOR SIX MONTHS
7. (Add some that you find) _____
8. _____
9. _____
10. _____

What do you think each headline is about? Why?

The Passive | **323**

Exercise 9
S U G G E S T I O N S

1. Have Ss find their additional headlines on Internet news sites.
2. After the exercise is completed, pairs can compare their headlines for 7–10, guessing what their partners stories are about.

UNIT GOAL REVIEW

Ask Ss to look at the goals on the opening page of the unit again. Help them understand how much they have accomplished in each area.

A N S W E R   K E Y

Exercise 9
1. A teen got eaten by . . .   2. Elvis was seen . . .   3. The vice president got kidnapped . . .   4. Are Bill and Hillary going to get divorced?   5. The world's worst husband got married . . .   6. A man's false teeth got stuck in his throat for . . .

USE YOUR ENGLISH

While Ss are working on these activities, circulate around the room to listen to their language use. Do they appear to be using these structures accurately? You may wish to review errors you noted at the end of the activity.

Activity 1

VARIATION

If Ss have limited access to native speakers of English, organize this activity as an exchange for e-mail pen-pals.

1. Locate a group of English speakers of a similar age to your Ss.
2. Assign Ss to different members of the other group.
3. Ss can then conduct their interview via e-mail.

Activity 2

Review the instructions before arranging the class in a circle to complete this activity. Note that the next person begins with the *get*-passive because they should start their part of the story with that particular event. For example, Student 1 ends with pants, Student 2 starts with pants; Student 2 ends with the dog; Student 3 continues the narrative with more about the dog and continues on to another topic, which he/she introduces in the *get*-passive.

VARIATION

This type of chain story works well via an e-mail discussion list as well.

Use Your English

ACTIVITY 1: READING/SPEAKING/LISTENING

Look at the following tabloid headlines and ask a native speaker of English to explain what she or he thinks the headline means. Tape the conversation and then listen to the recording to see if she or he uses any passive forms in his or her explanations. Share your findings with the rest of the class.

- WOMAN HYPNOTIZED BY ALIENS
- MAN'S LIFE SAVED BY HITCHHIKING GHOST
- SUITCASE DROPPED 5,000 FEET BY AIRLINE
- BIGFOOT FOUND IN NEW YORK CITY
- WOMAN PREGNANT WITH DAUGHTER'S BABY

ACTIVITY 2: SPEAKING/LISTENING

In this activity, you will make a chain story about somebody's bad day—a day when everything went wrong. One student will start the story and will continue until she or he uses a *get*-passive. When she or he uses a *get*-passive, the next person will continue. For example:

Student 1: *Andy had a really bad day. First, he overslept. When he got dressed, he forgot to put his pants on.*

Student 2: *He ran out of the house, but was embarrassed to realize he had forgotten his pants. Before he could get back inside, he got bitten by the neighbor's dog.*

Student 3: *etc.*

ACTIVITY 3: WRITING OR SPEAKING/LISTENING

Have **you** ever had a really bad day? A day when everything went wrong, through no fault of your own? Describe the day, either in an informal letter to a friend, or, if you prefer, out loud to a classmate. If you tell your story rather than write it, tape-record it. Listen to the tape for the use of the passive, especially the *get*-passive.

ACTIVITY 4: LISTENING

Ask someone (a native speaker of English, if possible) to tell you about a really frightening experience she or he has had. Find out what happened, and how it happened. Tape-record the conversation.

Listen to the recording. Was the passive used? If so, was it the *be*-passive or the *get*-passive? Was the agent (the *by*-phrase) used?

ACTIVITY 5: LISTENING

STEP 1 Listen to the tape of two people talking about bad experiences they have had. What experiences did the speakers have? What is similar and different about their experiences?

STEP 2 Listen to the tape again. Write down all the statements which use the passive. For each statement, was the *be*-passive or the *get*-passive used? Was the agent (the *by*-phrase) used?

Activity 3
VARIATION

1. Have Ss work in pairs to mime their worst day, with their partner guessing what the events were.
2. As pairs work, circulate around the room and note examples of the *get*-passive
3. Once the activity is over, note some examples on the board and discuss whether using the *be*-passive would be more or less appropriate.

Activity 5

Play textbook audio. The transcript for this listening appears on pp. 511–512 of this book.

SUGGESTION

Once Ss have written down their passive statements, ask them to consider:
1. why the speaker chose passive and not active voice
2. why an agent was used.

ANSWER KEY

Activity 5
Check tapescript for answers (pp. 511–512).

1. As a warm-up, ask Ss if they know the names of any card games in English. What are their rules?

2. When they finish this activity, find out if this game reminds them of a card game in their culture(s). What is it called? Are there any differences in how it is played?

ACTIVITY 6 : READING

ACHIEVEMENT SNAP

STEP 1 Work in pairs. Try to think of twenty different achievements (discoveries, inventions, or works of art), as well as the name of the person(s) who created them. For example:

The telephone   Alexander Graham Bell

On the next page there are some more ideas to get you going, but you probably have better ideas of your own.

Write each name on an index card and then write each achievement on a **different** index card. You should have a total of forty cards:

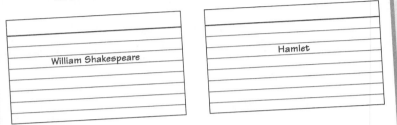

William Shakespeare   Hamlet

Now you are ready to play Achievement Snap.

STEP 2
1. Get together with another pair. Put all your "People Cards" in one deck and all your "Achievement Cards" in another deck. Shuffle each deck carefully.
2. Put the deck of Achievement Cards face-down on a table.
3. Deal the People Cards to the players. Each player should have several cards. Do not look at your cards.
4. The dealer turns over the first Achievement Card and puts down his or her first People Card. The object of the game is to make a correct match between Achievement and Person.

326 UNIT 22

5. Keep taking turns at putting down People Cards until a match is made. The first person to spot a match shouts "Snap" loudly and explains the match: "The telephone was invented by Alexander Graham Bell." If everyone agrees that the match is factually and grammatically correct, the player takes the pile of People Cards on the table.

6. The winner is the person who collects the most People Cards.

(Note: It is possible to continue playing after you lose your People Cards. If you correctly spot a "match," you can collect the cards on the table.)

Some ideas:

Mona Lisa	Leonardo da Vinci
hydrogen bomb	Edward Teller
"Yesterday"	John Lennon and Paul McCartney
Psycho	Alfred Hitchcock
Mount Everest	Tenzing

Remember to use an appropriate verb in matching the person and the achievement. Common verbs include: *compose, write, discover, invent, direct, sing, paint.*

ACTIVITY 7: SPEAKING OR WRITING

Make a presentation (oral or written) about your country or a place that you know well. Describe the resources and products, any changes over time, and any predictions for the future.

ACTIVITY 8: RESEARCH/SPEAKING

Walk around your neighborhood or city. In what ways do you think your neighborhood or city can become a better place to live? What is actually being done to make it a better place to live in?

Report your observation to your classmates: *While I was walking in the neighborhood, I noticed that . . . . (observations) . . . .* Use the passive in your report whenever it is appropriate.

The Passive **327**

Activity 7
EXPANSION

If you have access to video equipment, videotape each Ss' presentation. Later, schedule a one-to-one appointment to watch the tape together, discussing the strengths and areas for improvement.

Activity 8
VARIATION

If Ss are currently living outside of an area that they know well, they can do this as a research project in which they interview people from their new neighborhood, asking them about their observations on changes. When they report back, you may find they naturally use expressions like *I was told that.* . . . Ss may do their interviews in pairs or groups if they feel insecure about interviewing strangers.

The test for this unit can be found on pp. 474–475 of this book.
The answers are on p. 476.

Unit 23

UNIT OVERVIEW

Unit 23 provides practice with phrasal verbs.

UNIT GOALS

Review the goals listed on this page to see what students (Ss) should learn by the end of the unit.

OPENING TASK

Note: The purpose of this task is to generate talk (the cartoon captions) that naturally uses phrasal verbs. It focuses attention on meaning rather than form, which will allow you to see whether Ss are able to understand and produce phrasal verbs spontaneously.

SETTING UP THE TASK

This task is made up of five steps. You may want to have Ss work in pairs or small groups, and bring the class together after each step to check answers.

Explain that the boy in the comic strip really, really hates school.

COMPLETING THE TASK

Step 1

Pairs/groups try to guess what they think the boy is saying in each picture and how he feels. You could bring the class together after a few minutes to briefly share ideas thus far. Pairs/groups then go on to Step 2.

U N I T 23

P HRASAL VERBS

UNIT GOALS:

- To know when to use phrasal verbs
- To know which phrasal verbs take objects and which phrasal verbs do not take objects
- To correctly form sentences containing phrasal verbs and objects
- To know which phrasal verbs are separable and which are inseparable

O PENING TASK
School Days

Calvin and Hobbes was a popular comic strip about a small boy called Calvin, who hates school.

STEP 1 Get together with a partner. Look at the comic strip about Calvin's day at school. How do you think he feels in each picture? What do you think he is saying? Discuss some possibilities with your partner.

CALVIN AND HOBBES/Bill Watterson

1992 © Watterson. Distributed by Universal Press Syndicate.

STEP 2 Look at what Calvin said and match his words with their definitions below:

(a) Confuse things	**(g)** Become awake after being asleep
(b) Make a foolish mistake	**(h)** Rise to a standing position after sitting or lying down
(c) A situation is getting better	
(d) Stop talking (*impolite*)	**(i)** Vomit: food or drink from the stomach comes back out of the mouth
(e) Pay attention	
(f) Make something happen more quickly	

STEP 3 Now match Calvin's words with the pictures in the comic strip. Write his words in the appropriate picture. When you finish, compare your version of the comic strip with the original on page A-18.

STEP 4 Why do you think Calvin uses words like *mix up* and *throw up* instead of *confuse things* and *vomit?*

STEP 5 When you and your classmate were Calvin's age, did you like going to school or did you hate it as much as Calvin does? Ask your classmate to describe a typical day at school when he or she was Calvin's age and make notes on the chart below.

BEFORE GOING TO SCHOOL IN THE MORNING, MY CLASSMATE . . .	AT SCHOOL, MY CLASSMATE . . .	AT SCHOOL, MY CLASSMATE'S TEACHER . . .

ANSWER KEY

Opening Task Solution/Step 2
(a) mix up (b) goof up (c) looking up
(d) shut up (e) listen up (f) hurry up
(g) wake up (h) get up (i) throw up

Opening Task Solution/Step 3
Picture 1. Wake up. Get up. Picture 2. Shut up. Listen up. Picture 3. Throw up Picture 4. Mix up. Goof up. Picture 5. Hurry up. Picture 6. Looking up.

Step 2

When pairs/groups match the words from the comic strip with the "dictionary" definitions, encourage them to guess.

You might want to bring the class together to share and compare answers before going on.

Step 3

You could have pairs/groups compare answers before consulting the solution on page 399.

Step 4

Answers will vary. The purpose of the question is to have Ss think about why one variety of language might be used over another. Ss may come up with responses like: *Calvin's a young boy; the language is more conversational (informal and colloquial); the language shows his emotions; he feels very strongly about all these things.*

Step 5

The purpose of this step is to elicit some language around the context of the task. Don't worry about accuracy or how many (if any) phrasal verbs are used. Exercise 1 returns to this step.

CLOSING THE TASK

You might want to wrap up the task by asking Ss what they notice about everything Calvin says (to elicit the use of *up*) and to use this as a springboard to the information in Focus 1.

Make sure that Ss understand the meaning of the three phrasal verbs presented here. Mime/act out each action if there are any questions, or ask a student to.

There's no need to elaborate further at this point since Exercise 1 and the focus boxes that follow treat each point and return to the task.

Exercise 1

SUGGESTIONS

Ask Ss to tell you the phrasal verbs they used. Write each of these on the board or on an overhead transparency, pointing out the verb and particle in each case (as in Focus 1), or asking Ss to identify these parts.

Step 2

You can circulate to check to see if Ss are "situating" the phrasal verbs accurately in terms of the time frame.

Example: Since they are talking about the past, they might say: *We had to stand up when the teacher entered the classroom.* Or, they might list the things they did: *We stood up when the teacher entered, and then sat down after she/he greeted us.*

If there are mistakes with the past tense, you might want to give examples of different ways to use correct forms.

▶ Phrasal Verbs

EXAMPLES	EXPLANATION
Verb Particle (a) Calvin **gets up** at 7:00. (b) First, he **takes off** his pajamas. (c) Then he **puts on** his jeans.	Phrasal verbs have two parts: a **verb** and a **particle.** Common particles are *off, on, in, out, up.*

EXERCISE 1

STEP 1 With a classmate, look back at what you both wrote in Step 5 of the Opening Task on page 329. Did you use any phrasal verbs? Underline them.

STEP 2 How many **other** phrasal verbs can you think of to describe things you did in school as a child? Write them in the box below and then use each one in a sentence. (Remember that you are talking about the past in these sentences.)

```
stand up




                                                                sit down
```

ANSWER KEY

Exercise 1
Step 1
Answers depend on the sentences that Ss wrote in Step 5 of the opening task.

Step 2
Answers will vary. Some phrasal verbs likely to be used are *stand up, sit down, write down, look up, hand out, fill in, clean up, put down, help out.*

FOCUS **2**

When to Use Phrasal Verbs and How to Learn Them

EXAMPLES	EXPLANATIONS
(a) Look out! There's a car coming! **(b)** The movie starts at 8:00. Please don't **show up** late or we won't get good seats.	Phrasal verbs are very common, especially in informal spoken English. It is often difficult to guess the meaning of a phrasal verb, even when you know the meaning of each part. In some situations, however, the context can help you make a guess. In (a), *look out* means be careful. In (b), *show up* means arrive.
(c) You should **look over** your homework before you give it to the teacher. **(d)** My friend David **looks after** my cats when I go on vacation.	When you use the same verb with a different particle, the meaning usually changes. In (c), *look over* means to check or examine something. In (d), *look after* means to take care of. To remember the meanings of phrasal verbs, learn the two parts together as one vocabulary item, in the same way that you learn new words.

EXERCISE 2

Get together with a classmate and match each verb with a particle from the box below to create a set of phrasal verbs to describe typical school activities. (Notice that some verbs can take different particles to express different meanings.) Check that you understand the meaning of the phrasal verbs you create (your teacher or a good English/English dictionary can help). Remember, in this exercise, we are only thinking about phrasal verbs that are often used to talk about "school."

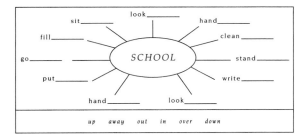

Phrasal Verbs | **331**

A N S W E R   K E Y

Exercise 2
Answers will vary.

FOCUS 2

S U G G E S T I O N S

1. Explain that the meaning of many phrasal verbs is *idiomatic*. As in the explanations, emphasize that a phrasal verb is like any other vocabulary word. It's important to learn the two parts together, since together the two parts form one "word"—one meaning.

2. If your Ss have a lot of exposure to spoken informal English (especially American English), they might be familiar with a number of phrasal verbs. You can elicit phrasal verbs from Ss now or you can wait, since there are plenty introduced in this chapter.

3. If you open your explanations of this focus box to a discussion, you might find these answers to (potential) questions useful: *Like other words, sometimes there is more than one meaning for a phrasal verb.* Or: *Languages are alive and changing. New slang/phrasal verbs are often created. Some of them become popular; others don't.* Also, preview the other focus boxes in this unit, since they can address student questions.

Workbook Ex. 2, p. 170.
Answers: TE p. 501.

Exercise 2
S U G G E S T I O N S

1. Ask Ss to give example sentences for each phrasal verb they come up with. If you or other Ss don't understand the meaning, ask them to explain their answers, either by giving a definition or by miming/acting out the situation.

2. Prepare for this exercise by using each combination of verb and particle, and then eliminating the phrasal verbs that aren't associated with school.
Example: *look up (in the dictionary), look away (not school related—unless the context is plagiarism/cheating), look out (not school related), look in (not school related), look over (an assignment), look down (not school related—unless the context is social status—what higher level Students think of lower level ss, what teachers think of Students,* etc.) and so on with other verbs in the box. Don't be surprised if your Ss can come up with school-related contexts that *do* use the phrasal verbs you eliminated.

Exercise 3

It's fun to do this exercise orally, especially if you are teaching a class where many of the Ss can relate to this teaching method—the context of this exercise.

SUGGESTION

If you want to do this orally, allow Ss a few minutes to work with a partner, and circulate to make sure they have answers for each blank. This will allow the reading to move along smoothly so that the class is not waiting for the speakers to search for the answers. If you do have Ss read aloud, have them read a full sentence (which may contain several blanks) rather than breaking up the sentence.

EXERCISE 3

Use the phrasal verbs from Exercise 2 to complete the text below.

French Lessons

I will never forget my first French lessons many years ago in high school. Our teacher was very strict and rather old-fashioned, even for that time. When she entered the classroom, we all had to (1) stand _____ and say "Bonjour, Madame Morel," and we couldn't (2) sit _____ until she gave us permission. Every class followed exactly the same routine, with absolutely no variation. First, we always had "dictée." The teacher read a passage, sentence by sentence, and we had to (3) write _____ exactly what she said, word for word. We weren't allowed to use dictionaries in class, so we couldn't (4) look _____ the meanings of any words we didn't know. Then, she always gave us precisely five minutes to (5) look _____ our papers to check the spelling and punctuation. This was very important because if we (6) handed _____ work that had more than one mistake in it, we had to stay behind after class. Next, she always (7) handed _____ a list of vocabulary words for us to memorize. Then after exactly ten minutes, she gave us a quiz that always told us to (8) "fill _____ the blanks with the appropriate vocabulary word." Finally, she (9) went _____ the vocabulary words from the previous day's lesson to make sure that we hadn't forgotten them. How I hated French lessons! Even when the bell rang at the end of the day, we couldn't leave until we (10) had cleaned _____ the classroom and (11) put _____ all our books.

ANSWER KEY

Exercise 3

1. up **2.** down **3.** down **4.** up
5. over **6.** in **7.** out **8.** in **9.** over
10. out **11.** away

EXERCISE 4

Use as many of the phrasal verbs from Exercises 1, 2, and 3 as you can to describe any classes you have taken or are taking now. Make a list and then describe the class to a classmate.

FOCUS **3**

Phrasal Verbs that Take Objects

EXAMPLES	EXPLANATIONS
(a) We had to **call off** the meeting because everyone was sick. **(b)** We're trying to sleep. Please **turn down** that radio!	Like other verbs, many phrasal verbs take objects. In (a), the object of the sentence is *the meeting*. In (b), the object of the sentence is *that radio*.

Some common phrasal verbs that take objects:

PHRASAL VERB	EXAMPLE	MEANING*
Call off	We had to **call off** the meeting because everyone was sick.	Cancel
Put off	Let's **put off** our meeting until next week.	Change to a later time or date
Pick up	Please **pick up** your towel! Don't leave it on the bathroom floor.	Lift or take from a particular place
Set up	We need to **set up** a time to discuss this.	Arrange a meeting or appointment
Talk over	It's important for couples to **talk over** their problems and misunderstandings.	Discuss a problem

Exercise 4
VARIATIONS

1. If Ss are in the same classes, ask them to read their descriptions without revealing which class they're talking about. Let other Ss guess.
2. Have Ss tape record their descriptions and then listen to the tape for phrasal verb usage.

FOCUS 3
SUGGESTIONS

1. Discuss each example sentence in the focus box, making sure that Ss understand the meaning of the phrasal verb. For each sentence, ask: *What is the object of the phrasal verb?* Answer: *The meeting* is the object of *call off*. (What did we have to call off? The meeting.) *The meeting* is the object of *put off*. (*What did we have to put off? The meeting.*) and so on.
2. You could go over the phrasal verbs used in the previous exercises and focus boxes. Use each phrasal verb in a sentence (if it's not in a sentence already) and ask: *Does this phrasal verb take an object?* And: *In this sentence, what is the object?*

ANSWER KEY

Exercise 4
Answers will vary.

PHRASAL VERB	EXAMPLE	MEANING*
Throw out	I **threw out** all my old school books and papers when we moved.	Put in the garbage, get rid of
Turn down	We're trying to sleep. Please **turn down** that radio!	Lower the volume of radio, TV, etc.
Turn off	I'll **turn off** the TV as soon as this program ends.	Stop a machine, engine or electrical device
Turn on	She always **turns on** the radio to listen to the news.	Start a machine, engine or electrical device

Some of these phrasal verbs may have different meanings in different situations.

EXERCISE 5

Respond to the following situations using as many of the phrasal verbs discussed so far in this unit as possible. (Some of the language from Unit 10, *Giving Advice and Expressing Opinions,* and Unit 17, *Requests and Permission,* might also help you here.)

1. You are trying to talk on the phone but your roommate is listening to some very loud music. You say:

   Please turn down that radio!!
   _____

2. A friend is applying for a job and has just written a letter of application. He asks you to check the letter for grammatical errors. He says: _____
   _____

3. A family member is sick and you need to leave town for a few days to take care of her. You call a colleague and explain the situation. Then you ask him to telephone your clients and delay all the meetings you had arranged with them until the following week. You say:_____
   _____
   _____

4. It is the first class meeting of the school year. Your new teacher is explaining his policy about grading and homework. He expects students to give him their homework on time. He says: _____
   _____

Exercise 5

SUGGESTIONS

1. To prepare for this activity, ask Ss to keep a vocabulary log—a list (preferably alphabetical) of phrasal verbs they learned in this chapter AND other phrasal verbs they are familiar with. As with any vocabulary list, along with the vocabulary item itself (in this case, the phrasal verb), they should write the meaning and a sample sentence or two that contains the phrasal verb.

2. These situations can be performed orally, with Ss standing up and giving their answers "ad lib" or from notes, rather than reading their answers word for word.

3. To do this exercise efficiently, assign pairs one particular item (one pair is assigned #1, another #2, etc.) so that they are able to focus and practice "their" answer. Allow Ss a few minutes to come up with answers and practice.

ANSWER KEY

Exercise 5

Answers will vary, but possible answers include:
2. Would you mind reading over my letter to see if there are any mistakes? 3. Could you please tell my clients that I need to put off all my meetings and reschedule them next week? 4. I expect you to hand in your homework on time. 5. Can you hand out these fliers to students in the cafeteria? 6. I think you have got to talk this over with *him*.

5. You have helped organize a foreign film festival on campus. You ask some of your classmates to help you distribute fliers about the movies to students in the cafeteria during the lunch break. You say: _____

_____

6. A close friend is having problems with her boyfriend. He leaves his clothes all over the floor, has the TV on constantly, even when he isn't watching anything, and refuses to discuss their relationship. She asks for your advice, so you say: _____

_____

_____

FOCUS **4**

▶ **S**eparating Verbs and Particles

EXAMPLES	EXPLANATIONS
subject *verb* *particle* *object (noun)* **(a)** She **turned** **on** the light. OR *subject* *verb* *object (noun)* *particle* **(b)** She **turned** the light **on.**	Many phrasal verbs are **separable**: When the object is a noun, you can: Put the object **after** the particle. OR Put the object **between** the verb and the particle.
subject *verb* *object (pronoun)* *particle* **(c)** She **turned** **it** **on.** **(d)** NOT: She **turned on** it. **(e)** He **cleaned** it **up.** **(f)** NOT: He **cleaned up** it.	When the object of a separable phrasal verb is a pronoun, you must put the object **between** the verb and the particle.

Phrasal Verbs | **335**

VARIATION
Have the audience develop a rating scale to "rate" the answers. Along with rating the quality of the answer (Was the phrasal verb appropriate in this context, both in terms of meaning and accuracy—the "right" particle, object if necessary, etc.), Ss can also judge how socially appropriate they think the answer is. (Was the answer polite enough?) If there is a lot of variety in the ratings, ask raters to explain and defend their rating, using evidence from the context and from the language used.

FOCUS 4

SUGGESTIONS

1. Discuss the example sentences in the focus box, making sure that Ss understand that although the placement of the full noun phrase object is flexible (Examples (a) and (b)), when the object of the phrasal verb is a pronoun, it must come between the verb and the particle (Examples (c) through (f)).

2. Go over the phrasal verbs used in the previous exercises and focus boxes. Use each *separable* phrasal verb in a sentence (if it's not in a sentence already) and experiment with the placement of the full noun phrase object compared to the pronoun object.
   Example: *We looked up the words in a dictionary. We looked them up.* (Not: *We looked up them.*)
   Note: You might find yourself and Ss also creating sentences like: *We looked the words in the dictionary up.* This can serve as a bridge to Focus 6. (Example: *We looked the words up* sounds acceptable, but *We looked the words in the dictionary up* sounds a little strange, since the object is rather lengthy.)

Workbook Ex. 5, pp. 173–174.
Answers: TE p. 501.

Exercise 6

SUGGESTION

Circulate to listen to the pairs' answers. Note any common errors and review these answers as a whole class. If you think it will be helpful, ask a pair of Ss (or several different pairs) to read their answers aloud to the group, and then discuss only those answers where there are questions or disagreement.

FOCUS 5

SUGGESTION

Emphasize that to learn to *use* a phrasal verb in their speaking and writing, they should know both its meaning *and* its "rules"—whether or not it is separable. If Ss just want to know what a phrasal verb means, when they hear it or read it, the meaning is most important.

EXPANSION

Go over the phrasal verbs used in the previous exercises and focus boxes. Use each *inseparable* phrasal verb in a sentence (if it's not in a sentence already). If Ss have kept a vocabulary log (see Exercise 5 Suggestion), add information if necessary (for example, Ss should note which phrasal verbs are inseparable and separable).

EXERCISE 6

Replace the underlined words with a phrasal verb from the list below. Separate the verb and particle **where possible.**

try on	find out	take off	call up	throw out	set up	take back
	go over	put on	get off	put off		

taking your shoes off

Shirley: Why are you (1) <u>removing</u> your shoes? I thought you were going to go for a walk.

Julia: I decided to (2) <u>wear</u> my boots. It's raining outside.

Shirley: I thought those boots were too small. You said you wanted to (3) <u>return</u> them to the store. Did you (4) <u>discover</u> if they have a larger size?

Julia: I guess I (5) <u>delayed</u> it too long. When I (6) <u>phoned</u> the store, the salesperson said I'd have to wait at least a month for the next delivery, so I decided to keep these after all.

Shirley: That's crazy! Don't wear them if they're too small. Why don't you borrow my hiking boots?

Julia: I thought you (7) <u>put</u> those <u>in the garbage</u> when we moved.

Shirley: No, they're somewhere in my closet if you want to (8) <u>wear</u> them <u>to see if they fit you.</u>

Get together with a classmate. Compare your answers and then read the new dialogue aloud to each other. Change roles and read the dialogue again.

FOCUS **5**

Inseparable Phrasal Verbs

EXAMPLES	EXPLANATIONS
(a) Yesterday I **ran into** my friend Sal. OR **(b)** Yesterday I **ran into** her. **(c)** **NOT:** Yesterday I ran my friend into. **(d)** **NOT:** Yesterday I ran her into.	Not all phrasal verbs can be separated. Some phrasal verbs are **inseparable**: With these verbs you cannot put the object between the verb and the particle, even when the object is a pronoun. It is difficult to guess which phrasal verbs are separable and which are inseparable. It is a good idea to learn if a phrasal verb is separable or inseparable when you learn its meaning. A good dictionary will give you this information.

ANSWER KEY

Exercise 6

2. put my boots on   3. take them back
4. find out   5. put it off   6. called the store
up   7. threw those out   8. try them on

Some common inseparable phrasal verbs:

PHRASAL VERB	EXAMPLE	MEANING*
Come across	You never know what you'll find at a yard sale! Last week, I **came across** a valuable old Beatles record.	Find something or someone
Run into	Colleen was really surprised to **run into** her ex-boyfriend at the super-market.	Meet someone unexpectedly
Get off	Don't **get off** the bus until it stops.	Leave a bus, train, or plane
Get on	You can't **get on** a plane without a boarding pass.	Enter a bus, train, or plane
Go over	Our teacher always **goes over** the main points in a unit before she gives us a test.	Review
Get over	Jeb has gone to bed early because he's still **getting over** the flu.	Recover from an illness

Some of these phrasal verbs may have different meanings in different situations.

EXERCISE 7

Replace the underlined words with phrasal verbs from the list below. Separate the verb and particle where it is possible or necessary.

pass away find out call up cheer up put off run into call on get on

       call Marie up
1. Sally tried to <u>phone</u> Marie yesterday, but Marie's line was busy.
2. So, she decided to <u>visit</u> her <u>at home</u>.
3. Earlier that day, Sally <u>met</u> their friend Ron <u>unexpectedly</u> as he was leaving the apartment building.
4. He was ready to <u>enter</u> the bus to go to his sister's house.
5. He told Sally that his grandfather had <u>died</u> .
6. Of course, Sally was sorry to <u>hear</u> that.
7. She suggested to Marie that the three friends should <u>postpone</u> the dinner party they had been planning.
8. Marie agreed, and she also thought they should do something to <u>make</u> Ron <u>feel</u> <u>happier</u>.

A N S W E R   K E Y

Exercise 7
2. call on her 3. ran into 4. get on
5. passed away 6. find that out 7. put off
8. cheer Ron up

Exercise 8

SUGGESTION

It's best to do the first sample item together as a class.

1. Read the directions for each step and then work that step in the sample. Instruct students: *Look at the first example in Column A, under where it says "Sentence and rewrite".*

2. Point to this place on the page of the student textbook, holding it up for Ss to see. Ask Ss to help each other to find this place if there are problems.

3. Read or have a student read the first sentence: *Please hand in your homework.*

4. Point out the different contexts listed at the top of the page. Ask: *What is the context for this sentence, do you think?/Where do you think this happened?*

   Steps 2 and 3 are straightforward. Follow along with the sample. If Ss find the instructions challenging, go through one or two items together as a class.

   Some of the contexts may stimulate discussion on cultural differences. In other words, what constitutes and requires "politeness" may be different in different regions or countries.

EXERCISE 8

Where do you think the following were **probably** said?

STEP 1 Match the sentences in (A) with a context from the list below. Write the context in (B).

STEP 2 Underline the phrasal verbs. Rewrite each one, moving the particle **if it is possible to do so**.

STEP 3 In (C), write one more sentence, containing a phrasal verb that you might expect to hear in each context.

CONTEXTS:

| In a library | At home | In an office | At school | At a concert |
| On the telephone | In a clothing store | On a bus | At a party | |

A: Sentence and rewrite	B: Context	C: Another sentence same context
Please <u>hand in</u> your homework. (*Also possible:* Hand your homework in.)	At school	Let's <u>go over</u> last week's quiz. (*Cannot separate verb and particle.*)
1) Can I try this on in a larger size?		
2) We'd better sit down. I think they're about to begin playing.		
3) Sorry, but you can't check these out without a current ID.		
4) Turn it up!!!		
5) I want to get off at the next stop.		
6) All international lines are busy. Please hang up and try again later.		
7) Turn on the TV! I don't want to miss the news.		
8) Can we set up a meeting with the board of directors for sometime later in the month?		

ANSWER KEY

Exercise 8
Answers to C will vary.
(1) try on—in a clothing store   **(2)** sit down—at a concert   **(3)** check out—in a library

(4) turn up—at a party   **(5)** get off—on a bus
(6) hang up—on the telephone   **(7)** turn on—at home   **(8)** set up/set a meeting up—in an office

---

FOCUS **6**

When and When Not to Separate Phrasal Verbs

EXAMPLES	EXPLANATIONS
(a) Last week Sharifah organized her closet and **threw out** all her old clothes. OR **(b)** Last week Sharifah organized her closet and **threw** all her old clothes **out**.	You can separate the verb and the particle when the object consists of just a few words.
(c) Last week Sharifah organized her closet and **threw out** all the clothes that were several years old. **(d)** **NOT:** Last week Sharifah organized her closet and **threw** all the clothes that were several years old **out**.	Do not separate the verb and particle when the object is longer than three or four words.

EXERCISE 9

Are the underlined phrasal verbs correct in the following sentences? In sentences where the verb and the particle are incorrectly placed, circle the particle and draw an arrow to show its correct position.

▶ **EXAMPLE:** I have a meeting at 4:00 tomorrow, but I'm trying to put ⌐off (it) until the next day.
    Put it off.   Correct

1. Cherie always <u>shows up</u> for work on time. She has to <u>get on</u> the bus at 7:00 a.m., but yesterday she overslept and didn't <u>get up</u> until 8:00. She was late for work!

2. Last month, Sunny went through her file cabinets and <u>threw</u> all the papers she had been keeping since her time in graduate school <u>out</u>.

3. When Nina <u>ran</u> Tim <u>into</u>, he <u>pointed out</u> that they had not been in touch for over a year. They promised to <u>call</u> each other <u>up</u> more often in the future.

ANSWER KEY

Exercise 9

incorrect placements only   **2.** *threw out* should stay together since the object is too long   **3.** *ran into* should stay together since *run into* is inseparable   **4.** *call back* should be separated—*call her back*—since *her* is a pronoun   **5.** *passed away* should stay together since *pass away* is inseparable. *put off* should stay together since the object is too long.   **6.** *went over* should stay together since *go over* is inseparable

---

SUGGESTIONS

1. To prepare, use the separable phrasal verbs in Focus 3 and 4 (and the exercises in this unit) to make up sentences where the separable phrasal verbs should *not* be separated because of a lengthy object (more than a few words).

2. Alternatively, collect examples of these in Ss' earlier work in this unit, or have Ss make them up. Examples (phrasal verbs from Focus 3, page 333):

call off   She called the meeting for the secretaries and the new employees off. (phrasal verb shouldn't be separated; object too long) Acceptable: *She called the meeting off.*

throw out   Nancy's mother threw all of Nancy's valuable vinyl rock and roll record albums from the 1970s out. (phrasal verb shouldn't be separated; object too long) Acceptable (grammatically, not content-wise!): *Nancy's mother threw all of Nancy's record albums out.*

Exercise 9

This may be another good exercise for individual work, since Ss' pace differs when it comes to learning new vocabulary words (and with phrasal verbs, the other information that goes with them). If you do have Ss work individually on this exercise, or if you assign this as homework, be sure to check to see if there are items where Ss disagreed, or where their answers varied.

SUGGESTION

This might be a point where you could emphasize that the biggest challenge in learning phrasal verbs is, like other vocabulary words, learning their meaning. To encourage Ss, point out how many phrasal verbs they have already learned. If they are keeping a vocabulary log, ask them to count the number of phrasal verbs in their log. Have them give you a few sample sentences, which is evidence that they also know how to use the phrasal verbs accurately (that is, they have demonstrated if it is separable or inseparable, whether it takes an object, etc.).

Exercise 10

If Ss do this exercise individually, have them pool their results and raise questions only on those items they disagree on.

4. When Sandra called, Graham was out. He tried to <u>call back</u> her, but he couldn't get through because the line was busy.

5. Eli's mother <u>passed</u> last year <u>away.</u> Since she died, he has <u>put</u> the decision about what to do with her house in Brooklyn <u>off</u> .

6. When Sally and the other children arrived at camp, the camp counselor <u>went</u> the rules <u>over</u> . The girls had to <u>clean up</u> after breakfast, and the boys had to <u>clean up</u> after lunch.

EXERCISE 10

Go over the sentences you wrote in Exercise 5 on pages 334 and 335. Underline the phrasal verbs you used and separate the particles where you think it is possible.

ANSWER KEY

Exercise 10

These will vary, depending on Ss' sentences in Exercise 5.

Phrasal Verbs that Do Not Take Objects

EXAMPLES	EXPLANATION
(a) My roommate's gone on vacation and I have no idea when he's going to **come back**. **(b)** Cyril waited for his friends for over an hour but they didn't **show up**.	Some phrasal verbs do not take objects. Because they do not take objects, they are inseparable.

Some common phrasal verbs that do not take objects

PHRASAL VERB	EXAMPLE	MEANING*
Break down	My car **broke down**, so I walked.	Stop working (machine, engine etc.)
Catch on	Some fashions **catch on** right away.	Become popular
Come back	Goodbye, please **come back** soon.	Return
Come to	When I **came to,** I was in the hospital.	Regain consciousness
Eat out	Darlene is too busy to cook, so she usually **eats out**.	Eat in a restaurant
Get by	He doesn't earn much, but he seems to **get by**.	Survive satisfactorily, with limited money
Grow up	His mother **grew up** in Vancouver.	Become an adult
Pass out	When Pat broke her leg in a skiing accident, she **passed out**.	Faint, lose consciousness
Show up	It isn't a good idea to **show up** late for a job interview.	Arrive, appear at a place

Some of these phrasal verbs may have different meanings in different situations.

Phrasal Verbs | **341**

FOCUS 7

Ss are likely to come up with more examples that use the main verbs in this focus box (some of which were used earlier in this unit) such as *break up, catch up, pass away, show off.*

S U G G E S T I O N S

1. If examples don't come up spontaneously—and they might not if you are not in an English-speaking situation— then give some examples of your own, making up meaningful sentences.
2. If native English speakers are available, your Ss can elicit phrasal verbs from them, using those listed here in Focus 7 as examples.

Teacher's Edition: Unit 23   **341**

Exercise 11

1. If you have Ss read their answers aloud, first allow them some time to find the answers for all of the items. This way the reading aloud can move ahead smoothly, without pauses to search for answers.

2. If you'd like, after each item, ask the other Ss if they have other comments: *Did they choose another phrasal verb? Are there other ways to say this* (Should the verb + particle be separated/not separated)?

3. After you have gone over this exercise as a class, for additional practice in speaking, you can have one (or more than one) student read an extended piece of this letter aloud. Because this letter is so informal, it can be read in a conversational style. Concentrating on natural, fluent-sounding speech, remind Ss to link words together smoothly and to use appropriate stress and intonation—falling intonation at the end of a statement and louder volume/higher pitch for important or surprising information.

4. If appropriate, re-read each statement to demonstrate and then have Ss model *your* reading/speaking.

EXERCISE 11

Use phrasal verbs to complete the letter from Nancy to her housemate, Mary.

Replace the underlined words with phrasal verbs from the list below. You may need to change the form of the phrasal verb.

If the phrasal verb can or must be separated, put the particle in the appropriate position. (See the example.) You will need to use some of the phrasal verbs more than once; you may not need to use some of them at all.

run into	talk over	turn down	show up
come over	find out	pick up	get off
hang up	come back	grow up	put on
catch on	pass out	eat out	put off

Mary and Nancy have recently moved to a new city and have just bought a house together. Mary is currently overseas on a business trip, so Nancy has written her a letter, telling her all the news.

Dear Mary,

I miss you! Being alone in this new house is a good experience for me, but at the end of the day I wish you were here to (1) <u>discuss</u> talk _____ things *over* with me. I've been very busy painting the kitchen—you won't recognize the place when you (2) <u>return</u> _____ ! However, at the moment it's a terrible mess and there's no way I can cook here yet, so I (3) <u>eat in restaurants</u> _____ every night. You'll be glad to know that there are several excellent Thai restaurants in our neighborhood. It's amazing how Thai food has (4) <u>become popular</u> _____ everywhere in the last few years, isn't it?

Guess what? The other day I (5) <u>met unexpectedly</u> _____ Ruth and Maureen. What a surprise! They 6) <u>were leaving/departing</u> _____ the bus at the bus stop right by our house. It turns out they were on their way to visit Ruth's grandmother, who lives just around the corner. Ruth's son, Sam, was with them. Actually it was a bit embarrassing because I didn't recognize him at first; you really won't believe how much he (7) <u>has matured/become an adult</u> _____ since we last saw him.

I (8) <u>am discovering</u> _____ lots of new things about our neighborhood . . . and our neighbors! We'll have to (9) <u>lower</u>

ANSWER KEY

Exercise 11

2. come back 3. eat out 4. caught on
5. ran into 6. were getting off 7. has grown up 8. finding out 9. turn down/turn the volume down 10. came over
11. talked it over 12. putting on/putting headphones on 13. come back 14. show up

---

_____ the volume on our CD player by 7:30 each night. The neighbors in the green house (10) <u>arrived here/at this place</u> _____, to complain about the noise the other day. They have a three-month-old baby, so they need it to be quiet so the baby can sleep. We (11) <u>discussed</u> _____ it in a very "neighborly" way. I told them, though, that you're a night owl, and that night time is the time you like to listen to music. Loud! We decided you'll have to start (12) <u>wearing</u> _____ headphones!

There's a lot more I could say. I can't wait for you to (13) <u>return</u> _____ This time I promise (14) <u>I'll arrive</u> _____ on time at the airport. See you soon. . . .

Love,

Nancy

EXERCISE 12

STEP 1 Work with a classmate or a small group. Can you fill in the missing words in this word puzzle to create phrasal verbs? Sometimes the missing word is a particle that can combine with all the attached verbs to make different phrasal verbs; other times, the missing word is a verb that can combine with all the attached particles to make different phrasal verbs. (A good English/English dictionary may help you.)

STEP 2 Use each phrasal verb in a sentence, showing that you understand its meaning. State whether the phrasal verb is separable or inseparable.

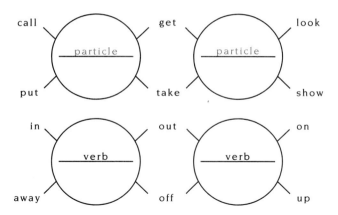

ANSWER KEY

Exercise 12

Step 1: There are different ways to fill in the puzzle.

Upper left: off/up/out   **Lower left:** put/get/take; work/hold/get   **Upper right:** on; up
Lower right: look/put; put/get

Exercise 12

E X P A N S I O N S

Step 1: If there are native speakers available, have Ss consult with them after completing this step. If there are any doubts about whether the phrasal verbs "exist" in English, the native speakers can help with this.

Step 2: This is a good dictionary skills activity, since Ss need to actually use each phrasal verb in a sentence.

V A R I A T I O N

If you want to make this into a competitive activity, have the pair or group that is done first be the "test case." For each phrasal verb, they read one sentence aloud. Ask the rest of the class: 1. *Is this phrasal verb okay in terms of <u>meaning</u>?/Does it make sense in this context?* 2. *Is this phrasal verb okay in terms of <u>grammar</u>?/Is it separated if it should be? Does it stay together if it should stay together?* For each correct answer, award 1 or 2 points. The team or pair that finishes first isn't necessarily the "winner," as they may have made mistakes in their sentences.

UNIT GOAL REVIEW

Ask Ss to look at the goals on the opening page of the unit again. Assist them in understanding how much they have learned. One way is to present a list of phrasal verbs from this unit as a checklist, having Ss check off the phrasal verbs that they can use appropriately and meaningfully in a sentence.

USE YOUR ENGLISH

Activity 1

SUGGESTION

After Step 3, use the same procedure as in Exercise 12 Variation to assess the sentence the team (or player) has made up. It is "impossible" if: *the phrasal verb isn't acceptable in terms of <u>meaning</u>—it doesn't make sense in the context OR the phrasal verb isn't acceptable in terms of <u>grammar</u>—it should be separated but it isn't, or it shouldn't be separated but it is.*

Use Your English

ACTIVITY 1: SPEAKING

You can either play this game with a classmate or in teams. You need a die/dice to play.

STEP 1 Player (or team) 1 throws the die/dice and selects the verb from circle A that corresponds to the number thrown. For example, if she throws 3, then the verb is *turn*.

STEP 2 Player (or team) 2 throws the die/dice again and selects the particle from circle B that corresponds to the number thrown. For example, if she throws 1, the particle is *off*.

STEP 3 The first player (or team) to come up with a sentence containing the verb + particle, scores a point. For example, the player who comes up with a sentence using *turn off* correctly scores the point. If the combination of verb + particle does not create a meaningful phrasal verb, the first player to say "Impossible" scores the point.

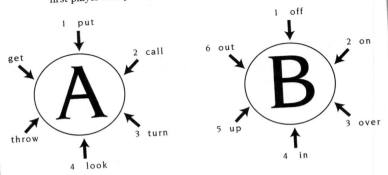

Variation: After you have played this game a few times, get together with some classmates to make your own version. Choose six verbs and six particles. Draw two circles and write the verbs and particles in each circle. Try your game out on your classmates.

If you are playing in a team, you could copy the two circles onto a big piece of paper and stick it on the wall so that everyone can see.

ACTIVITY 2: SPEAKING/LISTENING

STEP 1 Interview three different native speakers of English. Ask them to describe their typical routine every morning, from the moment they wake up until they leave the house to go to work or school. Tape-record their responses.

STEP 2 Listen to what they say. What differences and what similarities do you find? Write down any phrasal verbs that they use. Bring your tape to class and share your findings with your classmates and your teacher.

ACTIVITY 3: LISTENING

Listen to the tape of native speakers of English describing their early morning routines. What differences and similarities do you find among the speakers? Make a list of the phrasal verbs that the speakers used. Compare your list with a classmate's.

Activity 2
SUGGESTIONS

1. If there are difficulties getting access to a tape-recorder, conduct this activity in small "research teams" (of three to five people): one or two people should ask the questions, designing a set of questions beforehand and/or asking the speaker to elaborate whenever more information is needed.
2. The other people in the team should take notes, writing down every phrasal verb used—and if it's unfamiliar—what the context/meaning is. Having more than one student do this helps to ensure that the data is "complete," since one student may catch what another student has missed.

VARIATION

If there isn't a pool of native speakers available in your area, have your Ss interview people who they consider very proficient in English—people who have studied English for many years, for example, or those that have lived in English-speaking countries.

Activity 3

Play textbook audio. The tapescript for this listening activity appears on p. 512 of this book.

SUGGESTION

Ask Ss to compare the phrasal verbs used on the tape with the phrasal verbs speakers used in Activity 2. Or, have them concentrate on more general meaning, if you think this would be helpful. How is the routine of the speakers they interviewed in Activity 2 different than / the same as the speaker on the tape in this Activity?

ANSWER KEY

Activity 3
See tapescript (p. 512) for similarities and differences; answers may vary. Phrasal verbs used include: wake up, turn on, put on, go out, turn up, take off, jump in, put away, turn off, go off, turn over, go back, get out, put off, get up, get on.

Activity 4

VARIATION

After Step 2, it's fun to have Ss perform their dialogues orally, as "real," natural-sounding conversation.

1. If you choose to do this, first give Ss a few minutes to work with a partner. They can find a partner who chose the same context they did in Step 2. Or you can assign partners, and they can decide which of their two dialogues they would like to perform (or they can write a new one together).

2. Have each pair perform their dialogue in front of the class. Besides determining the context (Step 2), the audience can also "rate" the dialogue on whatever basis they choose: the funniest, the most/least polite, the most natural sounding, etc.

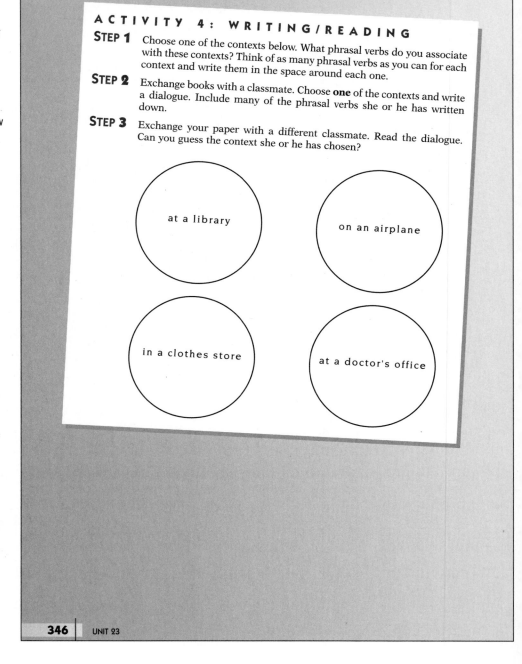

ACTIVITY 4: WRITING/READING

STEP 1 Choose one of the contexts below. What phrasal verbs do you associate with these contexts? Think of as many phrasal verbs as you can for each context and write them in the space around each one.

STEP 2 Exchange books with a classmate. Choose **one** of the contexts and write a dialogue. Include many of the phrasal verbs she or he has written down.

STEP 3 Exchange your paper with a different classmate. Read the dialogue. Can you guess the context she or he has chosen?

at a library

on an airplane

in a clothes store

at a doctor's office

ACTIVITY 5: LISTENING

Your teacher is going to give you a set of instructions. Listen to each instruction; if the instruction contains a phrasal verb, do what your teacher tells you to do. If the instruction does **not** contain a phrasal verb, do nothing. For example, if your teacher says "Stand up," you stand up because *stand up* is a phrasal verb. If your teacher says "Turn to your right," you do nothing at all because *turn* is not a phrasal verb. VARIATION: Anyone who follows a command that does not contain a phrasal verb drops out of the game. The last person to remain in the game is the "winner." After a while, give your teacher a rest and take turns giving the commands to the rest of the class.

ACTIVITY 6: WRITING/READING

The purpose of this activity is to write a set of instructions for somebody who doesn't know how to make a peanut butter and jelly sandwich. First, look at the bag of supplies that your teacher has brought to class. Then, work with your group to write your instructions, trying to use as many phrasal verbs as possible. When you are ready, read the instructions to your teacher, one step at a time, and he or she will try to follow your instructions exactly as you give them.

ACTIVITY 7: WRITING

With a group (or by yourself, if you prefer), think about everything you have done in the last week. Write a letter to your teacher, telling him or her about your week, **trying to use as many phrasal verbs as possible.** Before you hand your letter in, look it over carefully to find out how many phrasal verbs you were able to use. Write the number of phrasal verbs you used at the end of the letter.

Activity 5

Instructions to read to Ss are given below (or make up some of your own). Be sure to mix up the commands with phrasal verbs and those without!

Phrasal verbs: *Stand up. Turn around twice. Turn over that sheet of paper/book. Take off your watch/hat/earring/coat. Clean out/dump out your purse/backpack/ pockets. Write down your name. Hand in your assignment for today/yesterday. Put away your (. . . .). Turn on/off the lights. Talk over this activity with (. . .). and so on.*

Not phrasal verbs: *Say hello to (. . . .). Write your name on the blackboard / that piece of paper. Discuss this activity with (. . . .). Remove your watch/hat/ earring/coat. Shut the door/window. Open the window/door.*

Activity 6

This activity can be very funny if you follow your Ss' instructions to the letter. They are likely to leave out important details. (Example: They may say *Put some peanut butter on the bread* but omit *Put the knife in the peanut butter jar.*)

EXPANSION

If you feel that some of your Ss need extra listening comprehension practice, assign them to be the team that takes notes on what is said: They write down each phrasal verb and/or they write down each step in the process.

Activity 7
VARIATION

Before Ss hand in their written descriptions to you, have them do a peer review, in which they exchange papers with a partner.

1. Make sure that they read the description for general meaning: Can they understand everything? Are there points that need clarification or elaboration?
2. Then have Ss double check each other's papers for the number of phrasal verbs used to see if their counts correspond.
3. Have Ss check to make sure that the phrasal verbs are used appropriately both in terms of meaning and grammar.

The test for this unit can be found on pp. 477–478 of this book.
The answers are on p. 479.

Unit 24

UNIT OVERVIEW

Unit 24 introduces clauses that are used to describe nouns—adjective clauses. In addition, it addresses the difference between past (*bored, tired*) and present (*boring, tiring*) participles when used as adjectives.

UNIT GOALS

In reviewing the unit goals, point out that the structures covered in this chapter will help students (Ss) become more descriptive than only using simple adjectives like *nice, tall, ideal,* and *unusual*.

OPENING TASK

This is another logical problem-solving task, which gives Ss the opportunity to demonstrate their background knowledge on the language being practiced in this unit.

SETTING UP THE TASK
SUGGESTIONS

1. Before they begin planning for the task, have Ss look at the photograph and ask them to decide what relationship the people have to each other. Friends? Roommates? Husband and wife? Brother and sister? What makes them think so?

UNIT 24

ADJECTIVE CLAUSES AND PARTICIPLES AS ADJECTIVES

UNIT GOALS:

- To form correct adjective clauses with *who* and *that* to describe people
- To use adjective clauses with *which* and *that* to describe things
- To understand how to use participles as adjectives
- To know the difference between *-ed* and *-ing* participles

► OPENING TASK
Who Do They Love?

Lee, Tracy, Sid, and Kit are in love. Can you find who belongs together? Get together with a partner to read the clues, complete the chart, and solve the puzzle.

CLUES:

1. Lee loves the person who speaks Swahili.
2. Tracy loves the person who tells amusing stories.
3. The teacher loves the writer.
4. The pilot loves the person who is interested in history.
5. Sid loves the person that plays the piano.
6. The person who tells amusing stories is a pilot.
7. The person that runs three miles a day is a doctor.
8. The person who plays the piano is a teacher.
9. The person who is interested in history is a doctor.
10. The doctor loves the person who tells amusing stories.
11. The person who speaks Swahili is a writer.
12. The pilot loves the person who runs three miles a day.

Information about Lee:	Information about Tracy:
• _____	• _____
• _____	• _____
LEE *loves . . .*	**TRACY** *loves . . .*
• _____	• _____
• _____	• _____
Name:_____	Name:_____

Information about Kit:	Information about Sid:
• _____	• _____
• _____	• _____
KIT *loves . . .*	**SID** *loves . . .*
• _____	• _____
• _____	• _____
Name:_____	Name:_____

(The solution is on page A-18.)

2. Explain that there are four people: Lee, Tracy, Sid, and Kit. The problem is to figure out who loves whom.
3. Quickly read the clues aloud.
4. Model how to complete the chart. Read the first clue and have the Ss look at Lee's box and write: "the person who speaks French" on the line below "LEE loves. . . ."

CONDUCTING THE TASK

1. Put Ss into pairs or groups of three to solve the problem.
2. While they are working, circulate around the room and make sure they understand the task. Also, note problems they have using the structures that will be practiced in this unit.

3. Before Ss finish, draw the chart on the board.

CLOSING THE TASK

Bring the class together and have the Ss tell you where to fill in the information.

REVIEWING THE TASK

Point out the grammatical structures used to describe the people who are loved. If they have a question about who/that plays the piano, note that both of these expressions can refer to people, as they will learn in Focus 1.

Ss will return to the task in Exercise 1 (p. 350).

ANSWER KEY

Opening Task

Information about Lee: plays the piano, is a teacher
LEE loves . . .
the person who speaks French, the writer, Name: SID

Information about Tracy: is interested in history, runs 3 miles a day, is a doctor
TRACY loves . . .
the person who tells amusing stories, the pilot, Name: KIT

Information about Kit: tells amusing stories, is a pilot
KIT loves . . .
the person that/who runs 3 miles a day, the doctor, Name: TRACY

Information about Sid: speaks French, is a writer
SID loves . . .
the person that/who plays the piano, the teacher, Name: LEE

SUGGESTION

1. Introduce this focus box by writing one of the nouns from the chart on the board:

the pilot

2. Ask Ss to come up with ways to describe that noun further. If they can't, start by saying one of your own (e.g. *tall, interesting, proud*), asking Ss where to write the descriptive word (*adjective*):

the _proud_ pilot

3. Point out the adjective clauses in the focus box examples, illustrating with your own example on the board. Explain that adjective clauses also describe the noun. Note that they are placed <u>after</u> the noun because of their length:

the pilot <u>who is proud</u>

4. Ss can be confused about the difference between the main verb of the sentence and the verb in the clause. Pay special attention to the focus box examples (g) and (h). Give them extra examples of difference between subject and object clauses from the class, circling or underlining the main verbs of the sentences:

Subject:
The student that is from Spain <u>can dance</u> flamenco beautifully.
Your classmates who have lived in the U.S. for a short time <u>may be experiencing</u> culture shock.

Object:
Jorge <u>helped</u> the student that sits next to him with her homework.
<u>Do</u> you <u>know</u> anyone who is from Singapore?

Exercise 1

If necessary, further model this exercise with some of the examples from the focus box.

FOCUS **1**

Adjective Clauses: Using *Who* and *That* to Describe People

EXAMPLES	EXPLANATIONS
(a) The person **who speaks Swahili** is a writer. (b) The pilot loves the person **who runs three miles a day.**	Adjective clauses (also known as relative clauses) give information about a noun. They always follow the nouns they describe.
(c) The person **who** plays the piano is a teacher. OR (d) The person **that** plays the piano is a teacher.	Adjective clauses begin with a relative pronoun. To refer to people, you can use the relative pronouns *who* or *that*. *That* is more commonly used in informal conversation than in writing.
(e) Sid loves the person who **plays** the piano. OR (f) Sid loves the person that **plays** the piano.	Every adjective clause contains a verb.
subject (g) **The person** who tells amusing stories is a pilot. *object* (h) Lee loves **the person** who speaks Swahili.	An adjective clause can describe the subject or object of the main clause.

EXERCISE 1

Go back to the clues in the Opening Task on page 349.

(a) Underline every adjective clause you find.

(b) Circle every relative pronoun.

(c) Draw a line to connect the relative pronoun with the noun it describes.

(d) Write "S" if the adjective clause describes the subject of a sentence. Write "O" if it describes the object.

▶ **EXAMPLE:** The pilot loves the person who runs three miles a day.

ANSWER KEY

Exercise 1
Adjective clause is underlined; relative pronoun is italicized and noun it describes is in parentheses.
1. Lee loves the (person) <u>_who_ speaks French</u>. **0**   2. Tracy loves the (person) <u>_who_ tells amusing stories</u>. **0**   3. No adjective clauses. **4**. The pilot loves the (person) <u>_who_ is interested in history</u>. **0**   5. Sid loves the (person) <u>_that_ plays the piano</u>. **0**   6. The (person) <u>_who_ tells amusing stories is a pilot</u>. **S**   7. The (person) <u>_that_ runs three miles a day</u> is a doctor. **S**   8. The (person) <u>_who_ plays the piano</u> is a teacher. **S**   9. The (person) <u>_who_ is interested in history</u> is a doctor. **S**   10. The doctor loves the (person) <u>_who_ tells amusing stories</u>. **O**   11. The (person) <u>_who_ speaks French</u> is a writer. **S**   12. The pilot loves the (person) <u>_who_ runs three miles a day</u>. **0**

EXERCISE 2

Get together with a partner and look over the information in the chart below. The owners of the houses on this block of Upham Street are all women.

House	Habits	Likes	Dislikes	Place of birth	Occupation
1	swims three times a week	dogs	TV	Manchester	lawyer
2	eats out every night	fast cars	baseball	Madrid	marketing manager
3	lifts weights	music	politics	Miami	marketing manager
4	drinks five cups of coffee a day	cats	ballet	Mexico City	lawyer
5	sings in the shower	art	baseball	Montreal	marketing manager
6	walks to work	movies	basketball	Moscow	lawyer

Use the information in the chart to make as many true statements as you can about the owners of these houses, using adjective clauses. We have started the first ones for you.

1. The woman who _likes dogs_____ lives next to the woman who _____ .

2. The lawyer that _dislikes ballet_____ lives between the marketing manager who _____ and the marketing manager who _____ .

3. The marketing manager who _____ lives between the lawyer that _____ and the marketing manager who _____ .

4. The woman _____
_____

SUGGESTION

1. Copy this exercise onto an overhead transparency.
2. Model the activity by doing the first two together.
3. When pairs are finished, have them compare answers with another pair.

Answers will vary.

Workbook Ex. 1, pp. 176–177.
Answers: TE p. 502.

ANSWER KEY

Exercise 2
Answers will vary

5. The lawyer _____

_____

6. The marketing manager _____

_____

7. _____

_____

8. _____

_____

9. _____

_____

10. _____

_____

Look back at the sentences you have written. Underline the adjective clauses, circle the relative pronouns, and draw arrows to the appropriate nouns (as you did in Exercise 1).

FOCUS **2**

Which and *That*

EXAMPLES	EXPLANATIONS
(a) I bought a book **which** I really wanted to read. OR	To refer to things in adjective clauses, you can use *which* or *that*. *That* is more common in informal conversation than in writing.
(b) I bought a book **that** I really wanted to read.	
(c) The book **which** he wrote is excellent. OR	
(d) The book **that** he wrote is excellent.	

FOCUS 2

Point out that, as with Focus 1, these adjective clauses can be in the subject or object position of the sentences.

S U G G E S T I O N S

1. To create examples of subject and object adjective clauses, put a map of the world on the board or copy one onto an overhead transparency.
2. Be sure Ss are close enough to see the map and that they are familiar with the points on the compass.
3. Tell Ss that they should guess which country you are talking about based on your description of the country.
4. For each country make a statement such as:
   I am looking at the country <u>which is east of the Czech Republic.</u>
   The country <u>that is south of India</u> is an island.

5. After Ss guess correctly, write each of your examples on the board.

EXERCISE 3

Do this exercise with a group of five or six classmates. Make a chart like the one in Exercise 2, only instead of the "house" category, use "student." Decide on who will be Student #1, then use your positions in the group seating arrangement to finish writing your names in the chart.

Student	Habits	Likes	Dislikes	Place of Birth	Occupation or Desired Occupation
1					
2					
3					
4					
5					
6					

STEP 1 Interview each other to fill in the blanks on the chart. Ask each other questions using adjective clauses whenever possible. For example: *What does the student who comes from Beijing like to do?* Feel free to make up your answers, just for fun.

STEP 2 When you have filled in your charts, report to the class. Using adjective clauses in your statements, tell each other what you have found about your classmates.

Exercise 3

Refer Ss back to Exercise 2 (p. 351) for the format of this chart.

VARIATION

Ss can complete Step 2 as written homework.

Exercise 4

1. If possible, copy this exercise on an overhead transparency.
2. Model this exercise with statements about yourself. Have Ss choose the relative pronoun for you.
3. While Ss are completing Step 1, circulate around the room to see if they need any help.

Workbook Ex. 2, pp. 177-178.
Answers: TE p. 502.

Exercise 5

SUGGESTION

1. In class, have pairs—preferably of different language backgrounds—work without dictionaries.
2. Instruct them to read through the text first, helping each other with unfamiliar vocabulary.
3. After pairs edit the passage, review the exercise on an overhead transparency, or have pairs compare their answers with another pair, only discussing as a class their disagreements.

EXERCISE 4

STEP 1 Complete the following to make true statements about yourself. Try to describe both people and things in your statements. Circle the appropriate relative pronouns. (More than one relative pronoun may be possible.)

1. I am bored by people that _____ which / who _____.

2. I am interested in _____ which / that / who _____ _____.

3. I am frightened of _____ which / that / who _____ _____.

4. _____ which / that / who _____ are really annoying.

5. _____ which / that / who _____ is/are often interesting.

STEP 2 Get together with a partner and compare your statements. Be ready to share the most interesting or surprising statements with the rest of the class.

EXERCISE 5

Edit the following story. Use relative pronouns whenever possible to avoid repeating words, as in the example. After you have finished editing the passage, compare your suggestions for changes with a classmate's. (There is sometimes more than one way to make improvements and avoid repetition.)

1. It's interesting talking with women. ~~These women~~ *who* have had experiences. ~~Their~~ ~~experiences~~ *which* are similar to mine. There are a lot of things to talk about.
2. For example, *balance* is a topic. Most of my women friends are interested in this topic.
3. Achieving balance is a challenge for many women. Many women have jobs and family responsibilities.
4. Some women don't have jobs outside their homes. These women sometimes feel criticized. They feel criticized by other people.
5. These people think that women should have careers. This is an attitude. More and more people share this attitude.

6. Some women work at jobs and have young children. These women also feel criticized. They feel criticized by other people.

7. Other people think that all women should stay at home with their children. They should never be sent to a day care center. Day care is a business, not a loving home. This is a belief. This belief makes some women feel a lack of balance in their lives.

8. Some women never have children. These women may feel pressure from their own parents. Their own parents worry that their children won't provide them with grandchildren.

9. These are examples. These examples show how it can be difficult for women to feel sure they are doing the right thing for themselves and for their children.

FOCUS **3**

▶ **Participles as Adjectives**

EXAMPLES	EXPLANATIONS
(a) People who have traveled to many different countries are often very **interesting.** **(b)** We were very **amused** by the jokes that Bruce told us.	*Interesting* and *amused* are participles formed by adding *-ing/-ed* to a verb. These participles act like adjectives when they modify nouns.
(c) Professor Rand is very knowledgeable, but his lectures are **boring.** **(d)** Many students were **bored** during Professor Rand's lecture.	Adjectives that end with *-ing* usually describe the source (the thing or person that makes us feel a certain way). Adjectives that end with *-ed* usually describe the emotion (how we feel about something).

(Source/Boring)   (Emotion/Bored)

Adjective Clauses and Participles as Adjectives | **355**

FOCUS 3

Grammar Notes
The difference between these forms often causes trouble for Ss. Comparing these adjective forms with their verb counterparts can be a helpful illustration. For example:

Active present progressive → present participle:
Martin is interesting his classmates with stories of his trip to Belgium.
→ Martin is interesting.

Passive → past participle:
Boukar was confused by the lecturer's use of technical terms.
→ Boukar was confused.

Exercise 5
There may be some variety in how this passage is rewritten. The following is one way:

It's interesting talking with women who have had experiences which are similar to mine since there are a lot of things to talk about. For example, *balance* is a topic which most of my women friends are interested in, since achieving balance is a challenge for many women who have jobs and family responsibilities.

Women who don't have jobs outside of their homes sometimes feel criticized by other people who think that women should have careers. This is an attitude which more and more people share.

Women who work at jobs and have young children also feel criticized by other people who think that all women should stay at home with their children. Some people believe that children should never be sent to a day care center, which is a business, not a loving home.

This is a belief which makes some women feel a lack of balance in their lives.

Women who never have children may feel pressure from their own parents, who worry that their children won't provide them with grandchildren. These are examples that show how it can be difficult for women to feel sure they are doing the right thing for themselves and for their children.

Exercise 6

SUGGESTION

Have Ss complete this exercise for homework. In class, they can review their answers in groups.

EXERCISE 6

STEP 1 In the pictures below, draw arrows that start at the source (the reason for the feeling) and that point to the emotion (the way the person feels).

STEP 2 Then use the word (on the right) to label the pictures with *-ing* adjectives (which describe the source) and *-ed* adjectives (which describe the emotion). The first one has been done for you.

excite

excited   exciting

embarrass

disgust

surprise

shock

confuse

stimulate

interest

amuse

inspire

ANSWER KEY

Exercise 6
Order of answers: Left to right, down the page.
exciting TV show, excited man, embarrassing rip, embarrassed man; rip ◆ man   disgusting eating habits, disgusted woman; man ◆ woman surprised woman, surprising gift; woman ◆ flowers   shocked man, shocking haircut; man

◆ woman   confusing map, confused man; map ◆ man   stimulating conversation/ discussion, stimulated woman; discussion ◆ woman   interested woman, interesting flower arranging; woman ◆ flower arranging amusing comics, amused man; comics ◆ man inspired man, inspiring view; man ◆ view

EXERCISE 7

Choose the correct adjective for each of the following sentences.

1. Melanie likes the family in the apartment above her, but sometimes she feels that their teenage boy is annoying/annoyed, especially when he plays his stereo too loudly.

2. However, she usually finds their presence upstairs very comforting/comforted.

3. Once she heard a frightening/frightened noise outside. She thought it was a prowler, so she called up her neighbors.

4. They invited her to their apartment for a relaxing/relaxed cup of tea and a soothing/soothed conversation.

5. This helped her to calm down until she was no longer frightening/frightened.

6. Melanie especially likes Jane, the mother. Jane tells Melanie amusing/amused stories about herself and her family members' daily life.

7. Jane's husband Bob is a shoe salesperson. Even though this may sound like a boring/bored job, it's not.

8. Lots of surprising/surprised things happen to shoe salespeople. Just last week, for example, a real prince came into the store with his bodyguards and bought twenty pairs of Italian leather shoes.

9. The prince thought Bob was such a polite and amusing/amused person that he gave him a fifty-dollar tip.

10. Of course, Bob thought that this was very exciting/excited, and he took Jane and the family out to dinner that night.

11. Jane works part-time in a pet store as a dog groomer. She says that some of the customers never give their dogs baths. These dogs are sometimes so dirty and uncomfortable that it is shocking/shocked.

12. Jane's stories are so entertaining/entertained that Melanie usually doesn't mind the noise that Jane's teenage son makes.

13. In fact, Melanie was very disappointing/disappointed when she heard that Jane and her family might move.

Exercise 7

Do the first one or two sentences as a class; then have Ss work independently or in pairs.

Workbook Exs. 3 & 4, pp. 179–180.
Answers: TE p. 502.

ANSWER KEY

Exercise 7
1. annoying 2. comforting 3. frightening
4. relaxing/soothing 5. frightened

6. amusing 7. boring 8. surprising
9. amusing 10. exciting 11. shocking
12. entertaining 13. disappointed

Exercise 8

Start this exercise as a class, looking at the first sentence for possible errors. If you run out of time in class, this exercise can be done for homework.

VARIATION

1. Bring to class enough transparency pens and copies of the passage on overhead transparencies for each pair.
2. Distribute one pen and transparency to each pair, and have them complete the exercise on the transparency itself.
3. Call on different pairs to come to the front of the class and review two or three of their sentences at a time, working through the text. Three or four pairs will be needed to complete the whole text.
4. As one pair discusses their answers, the other Ss use their answers to determine if the sentences are correct or not.

UNIT GOAL OVERVIEW

Remind Ss of the unit goals on p. 348. Can they use the relative pronouns correctly? What is the difference between *-ed* and *-ing* forms of adjectives?

EXERCISE 8

Circle all the *-ed* and *-ing* adjectives in the following passage. Then decide whether the correct form has been used. In other words, are there cases where the *-ing* adjective is used when the *-ed* adjective should be used (or vice versa)?

SHELLEY'S ANCESTORS

Shelley had an interested day yesterday. Three of her favorite cousins dropped in for an unexpected visit, and they had a very stimulating conversation. They told each other surprised stories about some of their relatives. Shelley was shocked by some of these stories. For example, when their great aunt—their grandmother's sister—was quite young, she traveled around the world, fell in love with a Dutch sailor, and had a baby but did not get married. Her embarrassing parents disowned her, but many years later they helped her raise the child. Another distant member of the family was a drug addict in New York in the thirties, and according to Shelley's cousins' mother, he was quite a rude and disgusting fellow. This man's brother was a horse of a different color, though. Apparently he was an inspired and talented artist, who also created amused illustrations for children's books. After hearing all of these stories, Shelley realized that her family history was certainly not bored!

Exercise 8
interested should be ***interesting***
unexpected, stimulating—OK
surprised should be ***surprising***
shocked—OK

embarrassing should be ***embarrassed***
disgusting—OK
inspired, talented—OK; *amused* should be ***amusing***
bored should be ***boring***

Use Your English

ACTIVITY 1: SPEAKING/LISTENING/WRITING

CAN YOU TOP THAT?

STEP 1 Look at the list of adjectives below and choose one that describes an experience you have had (for example, an embarrassing moment, a boring day, an exciting date). Try to remember how you felt as a result.

embarrassing	disgusting	frightening	boring
horrifying	rewarding	exciting	entertaining
disappointing	surprising	relaxing	shocking
annoying	amusing	exhausting	inspring

STEP 2 Circulate for fifteen minutes and exchange experiences with classmates to find out if they have had an experience that "tops" yours—that is, an experience that is even more embarrassing, more boring, or more exciting than yours.

STEP 3 Report to the rest of the class on what you found. Vote on who has had the most embarrassing, boring, exciting (etc.) experience.

STEP 4 Choose two of the experiences that your classmates told you about and describe them in writing.

STEP 5 When you finish writing, read your work and circle any participles used as adjectives. Underline any adjective clauses that you used.

USE YOUR ENGLISH

To give Ss more communicative fluency practice, allow them to work without being immediately corrected. Instead of direct correction, note their errors for later discussion, or use their errors to return to one of the focus boxes to review.

Activity 1
SUGGESTIONS

1. In order to make the stories more interesting, give Ss time to think up their story. Set Step 1 as homework or review the directions in a previous class.

2. To focus on the structure covered in this unit, separate your writing feedback into two sections. In one section, only provide specific correction and feedback on errors made on this unit's structures. Other repeated errors can be commented on in a "general feedback" section or paragraph.

Activity 2

VARIATION

Have Ss post their sentences on an e-mail discussion list.

1. A student posts his/her sentences.
2. Tell Ss that in order to post their own sentences, they must first guess about what the first person is thinking about. The first person who guesses correctly then posts his/her sentences.
3. If people are having trouble guessing correctly, the first person can provide hints in the form of other sentences (following the same structure).
4. While Ss are working, don't participate in the discussion. Instead, save errors for class-time discussion.

Activity 3

SUGGESTION

If this is done as a speaking activity, have Ss record themselves for later analysis of their use of the targeted adjectives and adjective clauses.

VARIATION

For writing practice, this activity can be done as a short essay for homework.

Activity 4

Play textbook audio. The tapescript for this listening appears on p. 512 of this book.

ACTIVITY 2: WRITING/READING

STEP 1 Think of a person that everyone in your class knows (someone famous or someone in your class!). Or think of a thing or object that is familiar to everyone. Write three statements using adjective clauses that describe this person or thing.

For example,
I'm thinking of something that I drink every day.
It's something that is more expensive now than it used to be.
It's something that helps me feel more awake.
(Answer: coffee)

STEP 2 Read your statements one at a time and have others guess what or who you are describing. Work in pairs or in teams if you prefer.

ACTIVITY 3: SPEAKING

Think of someone that you know. Choose someone who is quite a character. In other words, think of someone who stands out in some way or is easy to remember. Describe this person, using some adjectives clauses and some *-ed* or *-ing* adjectives to describe him or her.

ACTIVITY 4: LISTENING

STEP 1 Make a list of all the characteristics you would like to find in the ideal partner (spouse, girlfriend, boyfriend, companion).

STEP 2 Listen to the tape. You will hear three friends talking about their ideal partners. Take notes on the chart below.

PAT	LEE	CHRIS

STEP 3 Look at the list you made in Step 1 and compare it with the notes you made from the tape. How many differences and similarities can you find?

STEP 4 Listen to the tape again. Write down any examples of adjective clauses and participle adjectives that you hear.

ANSWER KEY

Activity 4
Check tapescript on p. 512 for answers.

ACTIVITY 5 : LISTENING/SPEAKING

STEP 1 First think of as many -*ing* adjectives as possible. Your teacher will write each of these on a separate sheet of paper. As your game goes on, your group may add more to the list as needed.

STEP 2 You will use these words to play Password in teams or in pairs. In this game, one person (or team), the Clue-Giver, looks at the word on the piece of paper without letting the other person (or the other team) see it.

STEP 3 Then the Clue-Giver gives a one-word clue that describes this word to the other person (or the other team), the Clue-Guesser.

STEP 4 The Clue-Giver can continue to give as many clues as needed in order for the word to be guessed. The goal is to have the Clue-Guesser guess the word as soon as possible with as few clues as necessary.

ACTIVITY 6 : SPEAKING

Think of as many -*ed* adjectives as possible. Then "mime" (act out) these words and phrases, which are written on separate sheets of paper. You can use gestures and facial expressions, or you can invent a silent story, but you cannot speak. The goal is to have the other person (or the other team) guess the word or phrase as quickly as possible.

Activity 5
SUGGESTIONS
1. Come to class with a number of pre-cut blank pieces of paper in the shape of playing cards.
2. Be sure Ss understand the rules before beginning the game.
3. Model the game with you as the Clue-Giver and the whole class as Clue-Guessers to ensure they know what to do.
4. If using teams, assign one person on each team to keep score. This will help settle any disputes that may come up.

Activity 6
If you do not precede this activity with Activity 5, be sure you go over the previous activity's directions so Ss are aware of the rules for this game. Be sure to model the activity with you as the Clue-Giver and the class guessing.

The test for this unit can be found on pp. 480–481.
The answers are on p. 482 of this book.

Unit 25

UNIT OVERVIEW

Unit 25 provides practice with future, hypothetical, and factual conditionals.

UNIT GOALS

Review the goals listed on this page to see what students (Ss) should learn by the end of the unit.

OPENING TASK

Note: The purpose of this task is to generate talk that naturally uses conditionals. It focuses attention on meaning—*what they would do if . . .*—rather than on form, which will allow you to see whether Ss are able to understand and produce conditionals like these spontaneously.

SETTING UP THE TASK

Use the task illustration to check whether everyone understands "desert island" and to explain the task situation. Make sure that everyone can identify the objects and emphasize that the woman in the illustration is imagining the situation.

To increase opportunities to talk, Ss can work in pairs or groups of three.

UNIT 25

CONDITIONALS

UNIT GOALS:

- To know when to use hypothetical conditionals
- To form correct conditional sentences for present, past, and future situations
- To know the difference between future conditionals and hypothetical conditionals
- To understand the meaning of *would*, *might*, and *may* in conditionals

▶ OPENING TASK
Desert Island

Imagine you are on a desert island. You have nothing with you except these objects.

STEP 1 Get together with a partner and look at each object very carefully. What would you do with them on your desert island?

If we were on a desert island, we would use this [knife image] to

_____. We would _____ with this [sock image] .

If we had this with us on the island, [fishhook image], we would use it to

_____. With this, [yarn image] , we

_____. And finally, we _____

[plastic bags image]
with this .

STEP 2 Share your ideas with the rest of the class. Vote on the most interesting and creative use for each object.

COMPLETING THE TASK

Step 1

Ss complete the sentences as shown. Answers will vary.

Step 2

After comparing ideas and voting on the most interesting/creative uses, Ss could discuss other objects they would take.

CLOSING THE TASK

You can ask Ss to give their ideas aloud, if you want more practice in speaking. Or you could ask Ss to write their ideas on the board. Make two columns. Column A is "Objects." Under column A, write down the different objects from Step 1—knife, sock, fishhook, etc. Leave lots of room in Column B, "Solutions"—Here Ss put down their answers from Step 1.

You don't need to focus on any errors in form at this point: Exercise 1 gives Ss the opportunity to review what they wrote in Step 2 and focus on accuracy.

1. You can focus on meaning by drawing upon Ss' ideas in the Opening Task to introduce the information in Focus 1.
2. Give Ss the opportunity to come up with examples of how they would answer (a) *Have you ever thought about what you would do if you were on a desert island by yourself?*
3. After Ss have given their answers, and if they have omitted the *If-clause* part of the sentence (which they are likely to do), repeat their answer starting with "If I/you/(students name) were on a desert island by my/your/ him/herself."
4. Emphasize that after the first mention of this phrase, it isn't/wasn't necessary to keep repeating this part because the *context*—the situation—is/was understood.
5. Use the sentences in (b) to demonstrate your point.

Exercise 1

VARIATION

Conduct this exercise as a peer correction exercise, asking Ss to exchange papers and, in effect, edit each other's answers. Common questions should be noted, which you can return to at the relevant focus box (e.g., questions about word order and punctuation in Focus 2).

Note: questions about other kinds of conditionals probably will not come up since the contexts in the Opening Task, Focus 1, and this exercise limit the kinds of conditionals normally used. However, as in any unit you are covering, you will probably want to preview the unit, concentrating on the rules presented in the focus boxes.

FOCUS **1**

Hypothetical Conditionals

EXAMPLES	EXPLANATIONS
(a) **Ty**: Have you ever thought about what **you would do if you were on a desert island by yourself?** (b) **Ann**: Yeah! **I would go** crazy. **Shin**: Really? **I'd try** and survive. **I'd look** for food and water, and then **I'd build** a shelter. **Kat**: Me too. **I'd try** to be very positive about the whole situation. **Tom**: Yeah? **I'd escape** as soon as possible. **Ray**: Not me. **I'd lie** in the sun and relax.	Use hypothetical conditionals to talk about an imaginary situation. This is not a real situation, but you are picturing it in your mind. To express these: use *were* for verbs with *be* and the simple past for other verbs in the *if* clause. Use *would* + base form of the verb in the main clause. Use an *if* clause to introduce the topic. After that, it is not necessary to repeat the *if* clause in every sentence. It sounds very unnatural to keep repeating the *if* clause. *Would* + base form of the verb shows that you are talking about a hypothetical situation that has already been introduced.

EXERCISE 1

STEP 1 Look back at the sentences that you wrote in the Opening Task. Check to see if you used *if* clauses and *would* correctly. If not, rewrite the sentences and check them with your teacher.

STEP 2 If you were on that desert island and you could choose three things (*any* three things—not just the ones in the picture) to bring with you, what three things would you choose and why?

_____

_____

_____

Share your ideas with a partner and then with the rest of the class.

ANSWER KEY

Exercise 1
Step 1: Answers will depend on what students wrote in the opening task.
Step 2: Answers will vary.

EXERCISE 2

Get together with a partner and look at the pictures. What would you do if you were in these situations? Which situation would you prefer to be in and why? Share your ideas with the rest of the class.

EXERCISE 3

STEP 1 Choose one of your classmates to be the "leader" for this exercise.

STEP 2 The leader will finish this sentence:

If I were a millionaire, ...

For example: *If I were a millionaire, I would buy a big house in the country and retire.*

            (IF clause)   (Main clause)

STEP 3 The next person will change the main clause into an *if* clause and add a new main clause. For example: *If I bought a big house in the country and retired, I would write poetry all day long.*

STEP 4 Go around the room so that everyone has a chance to add to the "chain" of events.

Exercise 2
SUGGESTIONS

1. Before starting, make sure the contexts of each picture are clear. Ask a student to describe what's happening in the picture to the rest of the class (or you can do this) . Example, picture 1: *There's a man all alone on a really small desert island. It looks like the island is out in the middle of nowhere. There doesn't seem to be any food on the island, but. . . .*Let other Ss add information if you feel that the descriptions were incomplete.

2. We find that it's fun to review this orally as a class, since the ideas can vary widely (and wildly!). If you feel that Ss need more practice with writing, ask them to write a few sentences that answer the questions. They can then read these aloud if you think this would be useful. The rest of the class can listen for accuracy, pointing out any errors in form.

Exercise 3

Usually Ss catch on to this "chain" after one or two "turns" (i.e., after Step 3).

VARIATION

Tape record the answers, handing the tape recorder (if portable) from speaker to speaker. Here or after Focus 2, listen to the sentences for accuracy in form.

ANSWER KEY

Exercise 2
Answers will vary. Main clauses should all use *would*.

Exercise 3
Answers will vary, but main clauses should all use *would*. *If-clauses* should be based on the previous main clause.

FOCUS 2

SUGGESTION

If you tape recorded Ss doing Exercise 3 aloud, then use these sentences to demonstrate the explanation in (a). Whenever the *If* clause came first (and probably it always did if the directions in Exercise 3 were followed), have Ss write the sentence down (on the board or in their notebooks), using appropriate punctuation.

Exercise 4

VARIATION

If you and your class enjoy competitive activities, have Ss work in small teams of four or five rather than in partners. They then follow the instructions, writing as many hypothetical conditionals that they can about the story.

When some teams finish or start to slow down, have them stop. The team with the most sentences, or a representative from each team, can write down their hypothetical conditionals on the board or on an overhead transparency. The team with the most *accurate* hypothetical conditionals—accurate in terms of meaning and form—wins. Or you can score each sentence, awarding one point for accuracy in form, one point for accuracy in meaning. Let the class be the judges!

FOCUS **2**

Word Order in Conditionals

EXAMPLES	EXPLANATIONS
(a) If we were on a desert island, we would use string to make a fishing line. OR We would use string to make a fishing line if we were on a desert island.	Differences in word order do not change the meaning.
(b) If we knew how to build a boat, we would escape. OR We would escape if we knew how to build a boat.	Use a comma after the *if* clause when it comes first.

EXERCISE 4

Read the following:

Ilene hates parties, so just over ten years ago, she was surprised to receive an invitation to a New Year's party from somebody that she didn't know very well. She didn't really want to go by herself, so she asked her friend Diana to go with her. Before the party, Ilene and Diana had a nice dinner together at Diana's house. It was a cold, snowy night and when it was time to leave for the party, all Ilene wanted to do was stay home and watch a video. Diana persuaded her to change her mind, however, and after they had driven all the way across town, Ilene realized that she had left the party invitation at home. Diana wanted to go back and get it, but Ilene thought she could remember the address. They found the right street, but Ilene wasn't sure about the number of the house, so they drove around until they came to a house where there was a party going on. They decided this was the right place. They didn't recognize anybody there and Ilene wanted to leave right away. However, Diana, who wasn't as shy as Ilene, persuaded her to stay. Feeling very uncomfortable, Ilene stood in a corner by herself, watching Diana have a good time. After about an hour, she decided to go home. As she was leaving, she tripped and fell down some icy steps outside the house. Luckily just at that moment, somebody was coming up the steps on his way to the party and he caught her in his arms. And that's how Ilene met her husband . . .

Ilene and Jeff have now been together for ten years, and they are still amazed at the way they met. For a start, Ilene had gone to the wrong party. The one she had been invited to was a couple of blocks away. And then it

---

ANSWER KEY

Exercise 4

Answers are likely to include the following, but Ss may find even more than these:

Examples: If Ilene hadn't received a party invitation, she wouldn't have gone out on New Year's Eve. If Jeff had been gay, he wouldn't have been interested in Ilene. If Diana hadn't persuaded Ilene to change her mind, she wouldn't have gone to the party. If Ilene hadn't left the party invitation at home, she wouldn't have ended up at the party where she met Jeff. If Ilene had remembered the right address, she wouldn't have ended up at the party where she met Jeff. If Diana hadn't persuaded Ilene to stay at the party, she might have left before she met Jeff. If Ilene hadn't tripped down the steps, she wouldn't have been caught in Jeff's arms. If Jeff hadn't been visiting his sister next door, he wouldn't have gone next door to the party at all. If Jeff hadn't gone next door to tell people to turn the music down, he wouldn't have met Ilene. If there hadn't been a terrible snowstorm that night, he would have been in West Africa. If Jeff had stayed in West Africa longer, he might have forgotten about Ilene.

turned out that Jeff hadn't been invited to that party either. In fact, he was only in town because his sister was very sick and he had flown in from out of state to visit her. His sister lived next door, and when he ran into Ilene, he was on his way to ask the neighbors if they could turn the music down. Jeff, who is an anthropologist, was supposed to leave the next day to spend two years in West Africa, but that night, there was a terrible snowstorm and the airport was closed for three days. It was during those three days that Jeff and Ilene first got to know each other. But that's not all; when Jeff got to West Africa, there was a great deal of political unrest in the region where he was working. After two months, he was forced to abandon his research project. The first thing he did when he got back to the United States was call Ilene.

Now, every New Year's Eve, Jeff and Ilene laugh about how they almost never met. "What if. . . . ?" Jeff always asks. "Don't even think about it," Ilene always replies.

Get together with a partner and think about how Jeff and Ilene met (and how they almost didn't meet). How many statements containing hypothetical conditionals can you make about their story? For example: *If Ilene hadn't received a party invitation, she wouldn't have gone out on New Year's Eve. If Jeff had been gay, he wouldn't have been so interested in Ilene.*

Share your statements with the rest of the class. Who was able to make the most?

FOCUS **3**

▶ **P**ast Hypothetical Conditionals

EXAMPLES	EXPLANATIONS
past perfect **(a)** **If you had called** me last night, I *would + have + past participle* **would have come** to see you. **(b)** If we **had known** it was Marianne's birthday, **we would have had** a surprise party for her. **(c)** If Bonnie **hadn't robbed** a bank, she **wouldn't have gone** to jail.	Past hypothetical conditionals talk about imagined situations in the past. It is not possible for these situations to happen because they refer to the past. To express these situations, use past perfect in the *if* clause and *would + have + past participle* in the main clause. We know that it is impossible to change the past, but we often think about how things might have been different in the past. In (a), I *didn't* come to see you because you *didn't* call me. In (c), Bonnie *did* go to jail because she *did* rob a bank.

Conditionals | **367**

FOCUS 3

Ss who have studied conditionals might have questions about terminology, since there are different names for the different kinds of conditionals.

SUGGESTION

You can use this opportunity to emphasize *meaning*, and to show how the grammatical term we use here links directly with meaning:
(1) The term "hypothetical" is used because we are talking about "imagined" situations when we use this kind of conditional.
(2) The term "past" is used with hypothetical—*past hypothetical*—because they are about imagined situations in the past.

You can explain that in a sense, we're answering the question: *What might have been different (in the past)*? To elaborate, you might want to make up a few more of these sentences that are meaningful to you, or have Ss provide you with some (or you can wait until Exercise 6, where they do this). *Example: If I hadn't returned to graduate school and gotten my Master's degree, I probably wouldn't be teaching this class. If I hadn't met my partner, I would still be looking for the "right woman".* and so on.

Workbook Ex. 4, pp. 184–185.
Answers: TE pp. 502–503.

EXAMPLES	EXPLANATIONS
past perfect **(d)** If John Kennedy **had lived,** he *would + base verb* **would be** an old man now. **(e)** If Pia **had been born** in Egypt, she **would speak** fluent Arabic by now. *past perfect* **(f)** If we **had won** last week's lottery, we *would + be + verb + -ing* **would be lying** on a beach in the South of France today.	Some hypothetical conditionals make a connection between the past and the present. They show an imagined change in a present situation, caused by an imagined change in a past situation. These are untrue situations because it is impossible to change the past. You usually use past perfect in the *if* clause and *would* + base form of the verb or *would* + *be* + verb+ *-ing* in the main clause.

Exercise 5
VARIATIONS

1. Do this exercise as a guessing game. Collect Ss' written papers and read them aloud, letting Ss guess the identity of the writer. This also allows the opportunity for more practice with writing. If Ss first work individually (or if you have assigned this exercise as homework), circulate to see if Ss' *If-clauses* are satisfactory to them: Does it say what the student wants it to say? If not, help them to re-phrase this statement, since it is the topic that they will develop.

2. To focus on accuracy, have Ss review their work, either individually or exchanging their papers with a partner. They can then rewrite sentences that are inaccurate in form.

EXERCISE 5

How would **your** life be different now if things had been different in the past? Think of a topic and then make a list of as many differences as possible related to that topic. For example: TOPIC: *If I had been born in the United States, I wouldn't be studying English now. I would have gone to school in the United States so I would speak English perfectly, but I probably wouldn't be able to speak any other languages. . . .*

Some other ideas for topics: *If I had been born male/female, . . . If I had never gone to school, . . . If my parents had never met, ...*

When you have made your list, get together with another student and tell him or her about your topic and how your life would be different now. Then tell the rest of the class about your partner's topic and how his or her life would be different now.

ANSWER KEY

Exercise 5
Answers will vary. Some Ss may start out with answers similar to the model/example.

EXERCISE 6

For each situation, complete the following hypothetical conditionals, using the given verb in your answers.

Situation A

▷ **EXAMPLE:** **1.** Eloise's husband has always been a thin man in good physical condition. If he suddenly _____ (become) fat, Eloise _____ (be) shocked.

This is a hypothetical situation which will probably **not** happen because Eloise's husband has always been a thin man.

Answer: Eloise's husband has always been a thin man in good physical condition. If he suddenly ____*became*____ (become) fat, Eloise ___*would be*___ (be) shocked.

2. Eloise started seeing a doctor about her cholesterol problem three years ago. If she _____ (knew) about her problem earlier, she _____ (change) her diet years earlier.

Situation B

3. Ali's doctor says that one of the reasons Ali has high blood pressure is that he never expresses his anger. His doctor says that it is not healthy to "bottle it up." He says that if Ali _____ (get) angry once in a while, his blood pressure _____ (not + be) so high.

4. Ali never gets angry with his family. His children _____ (run away) from him if he ever _____ (yell) at them.

Situation C

5. Dan, who doesn't earn very high wages, has been shopping at discount stores for years. Even if he _____ (have) a lot of money to shop with, he _____ (buy) from discount stores.

6. When Dan graduated from college, his father gave him a used truck. Together they worked on the truck until it was in excellent condition. If Dan _____ (not + learn) how to repair trucks, he _____ (be) more enthusiastic about new trucks.

Conditionals | **369**

Exercise 6

Explain that the sentence after Example 1 is the reasoning for choosing *became* and *would be* as the answers for the blanks.

S U G G E S T I O N

If you decide to do this exercise orally, as a class, Ss can use the sentence after Example 1 as a model to say why they chose their answers—why they considered their answer a hypothetical past conditional or a hypothetical conditional.

A N S W E R   K E Y

Exercise 6
2. knew/had known; would have changed
3. got; would not be   4. would run away; yelled   5. had; would buy   6. had not learned; would have been   7. had not rained; would have remembered   8. would be able; rained

Step 2 can become a bit outrageous. You could encourage your Ss to think of a context where the read-aloud sentence *does* make sense.

Step 4 isn't necessarily redundant, since there may me more than one "match."

Situation D

7. People who live in this area have forgotten how to conserve water. If it _____ (not + rain) so much last year, people _____ (remember) water conservation practices.

8. People _____ (be able) to water their lawns every day if it _____ (rain) more this summer. However, the forecast is that this area is going to experience a drought this summer.

EXERCISE 7

STEP 1 On one sheet of paper, write the following words and complete the hypothetical *if* clause.

If I were _____ .

Now, on another sheet of paper complete the main clauses.

I would _____ .

STEP 2 Your teacher will collect and scramble your *if* clauses and your main clauses, and then you will take one of each. Read your sentence aloud to the rest of the class. Does it make sense?

STEP 3 After hearing everyone read their sentences, find the person who has the main clause that matches the *if* clause you have now.

STEP 4 Now find the person who has the *if* clause that matches your main clause.

ANSWER KEY

Exercise 7
Answers will vary, and will depend entirely on what Ss wrote in Step 1.

▶ **Future Conditionals**

EXAMPLES	EXPLANATIONS
simple present 　　　｜　*will/be going to* + base verb 　　　｜　　　　　　　　｜ **(a)** If you **study** hard, you **will get** a good grade. **(b)** If it **rains** tomorrow, I'm **going to bring** my umbrella. **(c)** Steve **will give** you a ride if you **ask** him.	Future conditionals make predictions about what will happen in the future. You usually use simple present in the *if* clause and *will be* or *be going to* + base form of the verb in the main clause.

EXERCISE 8

Most countries have superstitions. Here's a common North American superstition: If a black cat crosses your path, you will have bad luck.

Match A and B below to create some other common North American superstitions. Check your answers with other students and with your teacher.

A	B
1. If you break a mirror,	**(a)** if you knock on wood.
2. If you find a four-leaf clover,	**(b)** you will bring bad luck to all the people in the house.
3. You will have bad luck	**(c)** you will have seven years of bad luck.
4. You will prevent something bad from happening	**(d)** if you carry one in your pocket.
5. If you open an umbrella indoors,	**(e)** you will be the next person to get married.
6. A rabbit's paw will bring good luck	**(f)** if you walk under a ladder.
7. If you catch the bride's bouquet at a wedding.	**(g)** you will be vey lucky.

Do you have any of these superstitions in your country? Do any of these superstitions have a different meaning in your country? (For example, in Great Britain, if a black cat crosses your path, you will have **good** luck.) Think of some common superstitions from your country and tell them to the rest of your class. How many people in your class believe in these superstitions?

Conditionals | **371**

FOCUS 4

Student questions may center around the contrasts between future conditionals and hypothetical conditionals. Focus 5 addresses the contrasts in meaning, so it might be helpful for you to preview this.

SUGGESTIONS

1. Elicit the differences in form, or present these yourself: For future conditionals, (1) In the *if-clause* the simple present is used instead of the simple past (in hypothetical conditionals) or the past perfect (in hypothetical past conditionals). (2) In the main clauses, usually *will* or *be going to* is used instead of *would* (in hypothetical conditionals) or *would* + *have* + *past participle* (in hypothetical past conditionals).

2. If you feel that these differences are challenging for Ss, continue to demonstrate the differences by using student examples from Exercise 5 and 7 (hypothetical conditionals and hypothetical past conditional) and from the two Exercises that follow, Exercise 8 and 9 (future conditionals).

Exercise 8
SUGGESTIONS

1. If you have a multicultural/multilingual class, you should allow enough time for the second part of this exercise—where Ss think of common superstitions from their own languages/cultures.

2. Afterwards, be sure to point out the variety of things/objects that are the source of luck or lack of luck/"unluckiness."

3. Analyze (or have Ss analyze) the sentences. Note the use of *will* rather than *be going to* in the main clause, since *will* is used for predictions. Also note (or have Ss point out) the verb that is used in *if clause*—simple present.

Exercise 9

It's fun to review this exercise aloud. Have different Ss each read a different answer.

VARIATION

Have Ss mime/act out the different answers. The rest of the class guesses what the sentence is (as in "Charades").

EXERCISE 9

Go around the room and ask the other students the following questions. Change partners after every question. Write the answers you receive in the chart below.

When your chart is complete, compare your answers with your classmates'. In your opinion, what was the most interesting or surprising answer to each question? Write it in the chart.

▶ **EXAMPLE:** *Question:* What will you do if you get an A in this class?

Answer: I'll hug my teacher and say, "Thank you! Thank you!"

WHAT WILL YOU DO . . .

Question	Answer	Most interesting answer
1. . . . . if you get an A in this class?		
2. . . . . if your pants rip in tomorrow's class?		
3. . . . . if I give you $10 right now?		
4. . . . . if there is a fire drill?		
5. . . . . if you don't see me tomorrow?		
6. . . . . if our teacher is sick tomorrow?		
7. . . . . if it's raining when class is over?		
8. . . . . if you lose this book?		

ANSWER KEY

Exercise 9

Answers will vary, depending on Ss' creativity (and/or energy level that day!).

FOCUS **5**

Future Conditionals or Hypothetical Conditions?

EXAMPLES	EXPLANATIONS
Future Conditional: (a) If Colin Powell **runs** for president of the United States one day, a lot of different people **will support** him.	Future conditionals talk about possible situations and show what you think will happen in those situations.
Hypothetical Conditionals: (b) If I **ran** for president, nobody **would vote** for me. (c) If Elvis **had run** for president, a lot of his fans **would have voted** for him. (d) If Ross Perot **had become** president in 1992, American politics **would be** quite different today.	Hypothetical conditionals talk about improbable situations: situations that probably will not happen (b), or impossible situations (c and d).

EXERCISE 10

Say whether the situations in the *if* clauses are future (possible) or hypothetical (improbable). Compare your answers with a partner's.

1. If it rains, I will not have to water the garden.
2. If it rained, I would be very happy.
3. Marcy would quit her job if she got pregnant.
4. If I won the lottery, I would travel around the world.
5. Aunt Shira will give us a wedding shower if we decide on a wedding date.
6. If Laurel gets hurt again, her father will make her quit the girl's soccer team.
7. If the baby slept through the night without waking up, his parents would finally get a good night's sleep.
8. Jasmine would buy a big house if she were rich.

FOCUS 5

SUGGESTION
You might need to explain that there can be differences of opinion about whether something is possible and whether something is hypothetical. It's exciting for Ss to realize that this attitude is revealed in the type of conditional used. If speakers or writers use *will* or *be going to* in the main clause and the simple present in the *if-clause*, then it is clear that they think this is a possible situation—it could/might happen.

Similarly, when the form of the conditional is hypothetical, as in (b)–(d), we know that the speaker or writer thinks that the situation is either improbable—it will probably not happen, impossible—it can't happen. This point can serve as a bridge to Exercise 11.

Exercise 10
SUGGESTIONS
1. To elaborate further on the instructions, you can use item 1 as an example, asking: *Does the writer/speaker think that this situation (1) will or might happen?* (= possible = future conditional) or (2) *probably won't happen?* (= improbable = hypothetical conditional).
2. To give Ss more time to come up with and discuss their answers, it makes sense to do this exercise in small groups or pairs. When you re-group as a class, if there are differences of opinion for particular items, discuss answers, asking Ss to defend their answers in terms of likelihood/ probability. Why do they think the situation will or might happen, or probably won't happen?

Exercise 11

SUGGESTIONS

1. Like Exercise 6, each pair of items in this exercise talks about one story, so if your Ss are first working in pairs or small groups, you can ask them to focus on one story (for example, one pair/group looks at 1 and 2; another looks at 3 and 4, another at 5 and 6, another at 7 and 8).

2. If you think it will be useful to continue to focus on meaning—and to give Ss practice in talking "about" grammar, ask Ss to defend their answers in terms of likelihood/probability. Is the situation likely to happen? Is it improbable/not likely to happen? Or is it impossible?—it can't happen because the situation is in the past, which cannot be changed.

EXERCISE 11

Work with a partner to complete the following. In each sentence, decide if the situation is possible or hypothetical and write an appropriate form of the verb.

Situation A

▶ **EXAMPLE:** Gao is a doctor, but if he __were__ (be) a truck driver, he __would have__ (have) very different skills. (This situation is hypothetical because Gao is not a truck driver.)

2. Gao's wife is a doctor, too, but she is planning to change her career. If she _____ (change) her career, she _____ (study) to become a lawyer.

Situation B

3. Antonieta is Brazilian, but she has lived in the United States and New Zealand, so she speaks excellent English. If she _____ (stay) in Brazil, her English _____ (not) (be) so good.

4. However, Antonieta _____ (speak) French too if she _____ (move) to France next year.

Situation C

5. Mary's car is old. If it _____ (break down), she _____ (buy) a new one.

6. Because Mary has a car, she has driven to school every day this term. But if she _____ (not) (have) a car, she _____ (take) the bus.

Situation D

7. Marcia has applied to graduate school. She _____ (start) school next fall if she _____ (get) accepted.

8. When Marcia was twenty-one, she quit school for several years to get married and raise a family. If she _____ (continue) her studies instead of raising a family, she _____ (begin) graduate school a long time ago.

ANSWER KEY

Exercise 11

2. changes; will study (possible; she is planning to change her career)   **3.** had stayed; would not be (hypothetical; she did not stay in Brazil—past fact that can't be changed)   **4.** will speak / moves (or would speak / moved) (possible; it is likely that living in France will enable Antonia to learn French. However, we could say it is hypothetical because we don't have clear evidence that Antonia will move to France)   **5.** breaks down; will buy (possible; the car is old and could break down)   **6.** did not have; would take (hypothetical; she does in fact have a car)   **7.** will start; gets accepted (possible; she applied and could be accepted)   **8.** had continued; would have begun (hypothetical; she didn't continue her studies—past fact that cannot be changed)

Factual Conditionals

EXAMPLES	EXPLANATIONS
simple present *simple present* **(a)** If you **leave** milk in the sun, it **turns** sour. **(b)** I **eat** yogurt and fruit for breakfast if I **have** time.	Factual conditionals talk about what usually happens in certain situations. You really expect these things to happen. Use simple present in the *if* clause and simple present in the main clause.
(c) **When** you leave milk in the sun, it turns sour. **(d)** I eat yogurt and fruit for breakfast **whenever** I have time.	Because you expect these situations to happen, you can use *when* or *whenever* (every time that) instead of *if*. The meaning does not change.

EXERCISE 12

Get together with a partner and complete the following statements to make factual conditionals with *if, when,* and *whenever*. Check your answers with your classmates and your teacher.

1. Cats purr if _____.
2. Water boils if you _____.
3. An ice cube melts whenever _____.
4. Red wine stains when _____.
5. Rain changes to snow if _____.
6. If you push the "Power" button on a computer, _____.
7. Wool shrinks _____.
8. In the theater, people applaud _____.

Many of your Ss may already be familiar with factual conditionals, since for many, it is the first type of conditional learned/taught in English. Emphasize that this is the simplest form, since simple present verbs are usually used in both the main clause and the *if-clause*.

However, the information in (c) and (d) may be new to many of your Ss since they might have learned that only sentences with *if* are "real" conditionals. Reassure them that the meaning is the same whether or not *when, whenever,* or *if* are used in the *If-clause* "slot." Practice rephrasing all the sentences in (a) through (d) replacing *if* with *when* or *whenever,* and vice versa.

Exercise 12

This exercise is usually fairly straightforward and goes quickly.

SUGGESTIONS

1. Point out that *if, when,* and *whenever* can usually replace each other with little or no change in meaning (as in Focus 6).
2. Point out that the word order is flexible: it doesn't matter which comes first—the main clause or the *if*-clause (as in Focus 2)

ANSWER KEY

Exercise 12
You might get slightly different answers, but they are likely to be the following.
1. if you pet them 2. if you heat it

3. whenever it is warm 4. when you spill it
5. if the temperature is below 0° Celsius/32° Fahrenheit 6. it will turn on 7. if you heat it
8. if they like the play

In one sense this is a review of all the conditionals covered in this chapter but factual conditionals.

S U G G E S T I O N

1. Read one sentence from (a) to (g) at random, aloud for Ss (with books closed) or write it on the board. Elicit from them what the meaning is—Is the situation likely to happen? Not likely to happen? Impossible?, and what type of conditional it is—Hypothetical? Past hypothetical? Future?

2. Emphasize how, with conditionals, the meaning is reflected in the form.

3. The new information here is the use of modals *might* and *may*. If you think it is helpful, you can review Units 5 and 10, which treat the relative "strength" of the prediction—how likely the situation is and how certain the speaker/writer is of the result.

FOCUS **7**

Would, Might, May, and *Will* in Conditionals

EXAMPLES	EXPLANATIONS
Hypothetical Conditions:	
(a) If I were on that desert island, I **would** definitely try to get away as soon as possible.	Use *would* in the main clause to show the most probable result of the *if* clause.
(b) If I were on that desert island, I **might** try to get away or I **might** wait for someone to rescue me.	Use *might* in the main clause to show other possible results of the *if* clause. When you use *might*, you are less certain of the result.
(c) If Americans got more exercise, they **might** be healthier.	
Past Hypothetical Conditionals:	
(d) If John Lennon hadn't died, the Beatles **might have** reunited. OR If John Lennon hadn't died, the Beatles **may have** reunited.	In past hypothetical conditionals, you can use *might have* + past participle or *may have* + past participle. The meaning does not change.
(e) If we had arrived at the airport ten minutes earlier, we **might have** caught the plane. OR If we had arrived at the airport ten minutes earlier, we **may have** caught the plane.	
Future Conditionals:	
(f) If it rains tomorrow, we **will** stay home.	In future conditionals, use *will* in the main clause to show that you strongly expect this result to happen.
(g) If it rains tomorrow, we **might** stay home or we **might** go to the movies. OR If it rains tomorrow, we **may** stay home or we **may** go to the movies.	Use *might* or *may* in the main clause to show that this result is possible, but you are not so certain that it will happen.

EXERCISE 13

Complete the following conversations with *will, would, may, might, would have, might have,* or *may have.*

Conversation A

Abel: Have you and Ken decided what you're going to do over Labor Day weekend?

Miles: Not really. It all depends on the weather. If it's nice, we
(1) _____ (go) camping, that's for sure. But if it rains, we
(2) _____ (visit) my folks in Oakland or we (3) _____ (stay) here and catch up on our reading. I'm really not sure yet. I guess we'll just wait and see.

Conversation B

Mother: Don't drop that glass!

Three-year-old Child: Why not?

Mother: If you drop something made of glass, it (4) _____ (break).

Child: Oh.

Mother: Watch out! Don't turn it upside down.

Child: Why not?

Mother: Because if you do that, it (5) _____ (spill).

Conversation C

Janette: Did you hear about the guy who found an old Lotto ticket in a trash can?

Dean: Yeah, the guy who won eight million dollars? The guy with four grown kids and a bunch of grandchildren?

Janette: Yeah. He bought the ticket six months ago and he found it just two days before it was due to expire.

Dean: If he had found it two days later, he (6) _____ (not) (win) the eight million dollars.

Janette: Yeah, and his children (7) _____ (not) (be) rich now.

Dean: And his grandchildren (8) _____ (not) (have) college funds.

Janette: And the eight million dollars (9) _____ (go back) into the next Lotto!

Dean: And *we* (10) _____ (win) it!

Conditionals | **377**

Exercise 13

It's fun for Ss to do this orally, as "real," natural-sounding dialogues or mini-dramas.

SUGGESTION

If you choose to do this exercise orally,
1. Give Ss a few minutes to work with a partner, and check to make sure they have answers for each blank, ensuring that the class is not waiting for the speakers to search for answers
2. Give Ss a few more minutes to rehearse. Remind them before they start to link words together smoothly, to use reduced forms/contractions when appropriate, and to use intonation effectively—falling intonation at the end of a statement, rising intonation at the end of a yes-no question, and louder volume, higher pitch for important or surprising information.
3. Demonstrate if you feel this would be helpful.

UNIT GOAL REVIEW

Ask Ss to look at the goals on the opening page of the unit again. Assist them in understanding how much they have learned. One way is to present the items in the focus boxes as a checklist, having Ss give examples for each.

USE YOUR ENGLISH

Activity 1

VARIATION

Make this activity into a competitive game by awarding points for correct matches of guesses and answers. For a little extra pressure, points can be deducted for incorrect use of conditionals.

SUGGESTION

Ss can redraw this chart on a larger piece of paper so that there is more room.

Use Your English

ACTIVITY 1: SPEAKING

STEP 1 Work in groups of four.

STEP 2 Read the following questions. Without showing anyone else your paper, write down what you think you would be and what each person in your group would be in the following situations:

(a) If you were an animal, what would you be?

(b) If you were a color, what would you be?

(c) If you were food, what would you be?

▶ **EXAMPLE:** *If I were an animal, I would be a cat. If Terri were an animal, she would be a deer. I also think that Rachel would be a mouse, and Peter would be a flamingo.*

STEP 3 When you have all finished, share your ideas and compare what **you** think your group members would be with what **they** think they would be.

	(a) Animal	(b) Color	(c) Food
You			
Name:			
Name:			
Name:			

Remember that it is not necessary to repeat the *if* clause in every sentence.

ACTIVITY 2: WRITING

In a paragraph or two, describe the most interesting results about **yourself** from Activity 1. First tell why you described yourself the way you did. Then tell why you think your group members described you the way they did.

For example, if you said "If I were a color, I would be purple," but everyone else said you would be yellow, give us the possible reasons for these opinions.

Remember that it isn't necessary to repeat the *if* clause in every sentence.

ACTIVITY 3: WRITING

Form teams. Together write an imaginary situation or a predicament on a piece of paper. For example, *What would happen if* . . . everyone in the world were ten feet taller? *What would you do if* . . . you found somebody's purse with two hundred dollars in it and no identification? *What would happen if* . . . there were suddenly a huge earthquake?

After you write down one predicament, work together to solve the problem or describe the results. Then your team will tell some of your solutions to the other teams. They will try to guess the situation and tell what the *if* clause is. The team that guesses the situation most often wins.

ACTIVITY 4: LISTENING

You have all heard of the Beatles. Find people who are familiar with the words to their songs and complete the following lyrics:

• If I fell in love with you, would you promise to be true . . . .
• What would you do if I sang out of tune, would you . . . .

Peter, Paul, and Mary were a popular folk-singing group in the sixties. Find people who are familiar with Peter, Paul, and Mary lyrics, and see if they can help you finish this sentence:

• If I had a hammer . . . .

What are the other *if* clauses in this song?

Carousel is a famous Rodgers and Hammerstein musical. Find people who can help you complete the *if* clause in the following song:

• If I loved you . . . .

Activity 2
EXPANSION

If you feel Ss could benefit from more practice in writing, assign this activity as homework or allow them plenty of class time to do this. You can use this as a basis for a peer-editing activity: Ss exchange descriptions, first
(1) making sure the meaning is clear and asking for clarification or elaboration if necessary, and then
(2) looking for errors in form. They should concentrate on errors in the conditional (if any), but if you'd like to open this analysis up to look for other types of errors, feel free.

Activity 3

To get Ss started on this activity, it's helpful to brainstorm together as a class some possible predicaments and the results—what they would do.

VARIATION

If you want to do this activity more spontaneously and are comfortable with games/competitive activities, first make sure that you have generated a large number of predicaments in your brainstorming session (described above). Then

1. Write down each predicament on a separate slip of paper.
2. Hand out one slip of paper to a team.
3. Let the team confer. Time them (one or two minutes) if you think this extra element (time pressure) will enhance the activity.
4. Ask team members to list as many results as they could come up with. Each result that makes sense (!) and is properly formed is awarded a point (or two points—1 for meaning, 1 for form). The team with the most points wins.

Activity 4
SUGGESTIONS

You'll need a pool of "Westerners" born in the 50s or 60s, probably, for this activity to be successful. Or, if there are people proficient in English who lived overseas during the Beatles, Peter,Paul, and Mary, or Rodgers and Hammerstein "eras," these are also good interviewee sources. Finally, if you know someone who is a music collector or your Ss have access to a good music library, great.

Activity 5

You might need to elaborate a bit on the concept of "time capsule." If you have ideas on what you would put in a time capsule, present these ideas to your Ss as examples.

VARIATION

Use this activity as the source for a writing activity. Ss describe each of the items they would put in a time capsule and defend their choice. In other words, this can be an exercise in argumentation. Effective argumentation leaves the reader convinced of the writer's opinion. Thus, as you read these paragraphs/short essays (or if you are doing peer work—as Ss read each others'), ask: Am I convinced that these are good/the best items for the time capsule?

Activity 6
VARIATION

If you don't have access to a pool of Americans/native speakers, have Ss interview each other or people outside of the classroom who are proficient in English, asking about American culture or about the speaker's native culture (or the country you are in).

EXPANSION

Take Step 2 a bit further and do a more general analysis of the taped talk. You can open up a discussion with: *What else do you notice about how the speakers said things? Is there anything about the talk that surprised you, or was hard to understand?* (Likely answers: *They speak so quickly. Their words "run together." They always use contractions. Sometimes you can't hear certain syllables or words/they always use reductions.* and so on.) You can talk a little about what you know about natural, "fast" speech: that words in "native speaker" or "fluent" English are linked together smoothly, and that "shorter is better," i.e., reduced forms and contractions and ellipses are common.

ACTIVITY 5: LISTENING/SPEAKING

Your school is about to build a new library. The president of the student union wants to celebrate the event by placing a time capsule inside the walls of the new building. (A time capsule is a box containing a number of objects that represent the culture of a community at that point in time. You put into the time capsule objects that you feel reflect the ideas, culture, and values of the community. If people find the time capsule one hundred years from now, they will have an idea of what life was like in the past.)

If the president asked you about what to put in the time capsule, what would you say? Get together with two or three other students and decide on a list of five objects that you would put in the time capsule because you believe they represent American culture now. Share your ideas with the rest of the class and explain why you chose these objects. When you have heard everybody's ideas, vote on the five objects that you, as a class, would put in a time capsule to represent current American culture.

ACTIVITY 6: RESEARCH/LISTENING

The purpose of this activity is to find out what Americans would put in a time capsule like the one in Activity 5.

STEP 1 Interview three different native speakers of English by asking the question: If you had to put three things in a time capsule to reflect American culture right now, what would you choose and why? Tape your interviews.

STEP 2 Lisen to your tape and report your findings to the rest of your class. As a class, make a list of the objects that everyone interviewed would put in the time capsule. What does this tell you about American culture today? Compare this list with the one that your class made in Activity 5. How many differences and similarities are there in these lists? Do your ideas about what represents American culture differ from Americans' ideas?

STEP 3 Listen to your tape again. How many times do the speakers use *would/'d*? Write down any sentences conaining *would/'d*. How many times do the speakers use full *if* clauses? Why do you think this is so? Write down any sentences containing *if* clauses. What does this tell you about the use of *if* clauses in real conversations?

ACTIVITY 7: LISTENING

Listen to the tape of three different Americans talking about what they would put in a time capsule.

STEP 1 What would they put in the capsule? List the objects.

STEP 2 Listen to your tape again. How many times do the speakers use *would/'d*? Write down any sentences containing *would/'d*. How many times do the speakers use full *if* clauses? Why do you think this so? Write down any sentences containing *if* clauses. What does this tell you about the use of *if* clauses in real conversations?

ACTIVITY 8: SPEAKING/LISTENING OR WRITING/READING

If you had to put five objects representing **your** culure into a time capsule, what would you choose and why? Make a report (eihter written or oral) on your choices. If you make a written report, read your or another student's work carefully and check to see if you or s/he were able to use any of the language from this unit. If you choose an oral report, tape yourself as you make the report. Listen to your tape and write down any sentences containing language from this unit.

Activity 7

Play textbook audio. The tapescript for this listening appears on p. 513 of this book.

Activity 8
SUGGESTION

If you adapted Activity 5 to serve as a written activity, you can focus here on spontaneous speech. In this case, allow Ss to make notes but not full sentences so that they don't read their report but "say it" more ad lib, referring to notes if necessary.

The test for this unit can be found on pp. 483–484 of this book. The answers are on p. 485.

TOEFL Test Preparation Exercises for Units 22–25 can be found on pp. 194–196 of the Workbook.
The answers are on p. 503 of this book.

ANSWER KEY

Activity 7
See tapescript (p. 513). Step 1: The man would include a copy of *The New York Times,* a laptop computer, an autographed major league baseball. The woman would include Levi's jeans, a Big mac, and a copy of *TV Guide.*

Appendices

Appendix 1A   **Simple Present (verb/verb + –s)**

Statement	Negative	Question	Short Answers
I You We They } work. He She } works. It	I You We They } do not/ don't work. He She } does not/ It } doesn't work.	Do } I you we they } work? Does } he she it } work?	Yes, } I you we they } do. Yes, } he she it } does. No, } I you we they } don't. No, } he she it } doesn't.

Statement	Negative	Question	Short Answers
I am (I'm) working.	I am not (I'm not) working.	Am I working?	Yes, I am. No, I'm not.
You are (you're) working	You are not (aren't) working.	Are you working?	Yes, you are. No, you aren't. **OR** You're not.
She/He/It is (She's/He's/It's) working.	She/He/It is not (isn't) working.	Is she/he/it working?	Yes, she/he/it is. No, she/he/it isn't. **OR** She's/He's/It's not.
We are (We're) working.	We are not (aren't) working.	Are we working?	Yes, we are. No, we aren't. **OR** We're not.
They are (They're) working.	They are not (aren't) working.	Are they working?	Yes, they are. No, they aren't. **OR** They're not.

Appendix 1C Simple Past (verb + –ed or irregular form)

Statement	Negative	Question	Short Answers
I You We They He She It } worked.	I You We They He She It } did not/ didn't work.	Did { I you we they he she it } work?	Yes, { I you we they did. he she it } No, { I you we they didn't he she it }

Appendix 1D Past Progressive (was/were + verb + –ing)

Statement	Negative	Question	Short Answers
I She } was He } sleeping. It	I She } was not He } sleeping. It (wasn't)	Was { I she sleeping? he it	Yes, { I she } was. he it
We You } were They } sleeping.	We You } were not They } sleeping. (weren't)	Were { we You sleeping? they	No, { we you } weren't. they

Appendix 1E Present Perfect (*has/have* + verb + past participle)

Statement	Negative	Question	Short Answers
I You We They } have gone. ('ve) She He It } has gone. ('s)	I You We They } have not gone. (haven't) She He It } has not gone. (hasn't)	Have { I you we they } gone? Has { she he it } gone?	Yes, { I you we they } have. Yes, { he she it } has. No, { I you we they } haven't. No, { he she it } hasn't.

Appendix 1F Present Perfect Progressive (*has/have* + been + verb + *–ing*)

Statement	Negative	Question	Short Answers
I You We They } have ('ve) been sleeping. She He It } has ('s) been sleeping	I You We They } have not been (haven't) sleeping. She He It } has not been (hasn't) sleeping.	Have { I you we they } been sleeping? Has { she he it } been sleeping?	Yes, { I you we they } have been. Yes, { he she it } has been. No, { I you we they } haven't been. No, { he she it } hasn't been.

Appendix 1G   Past Perfect (*had* + verb + past participle)

Statement	Negative	Question	Short Answers
I You We They } had ('d) She arrived. He It	I You We They } had not She (hadn't) He arrived. It	Had { I you we they } arrived? she he it	Yes, { I you we they } had. he she it No, { I you we they } hadn't. he she it

Appendix 1H   Future: *will* (*will* + verb)

Statement	Negative	Question	Short Answers
I You We They } will leave. She ('ll) He It	I You We They } will not/ She (won't) He leave. It	Will { I you we they } leave? she he it	Yes, { I you we they } will. he she it No, { I you we they } won't. he she it

Appendix 1I   **Future:** *be going to (am/is/are + verb)*

Statement	Negative	Question	Short Answers
I am going to leave. ('m)	I am not going to leave. ('m)	Am I going to leave?	Yes, I am.
You, We, They } are going ('re) to leave.	You, We, They } are not going (aren't) to leave.	Are you, we, they } going to leave?	Yes, you, we, they } are.
She, He, It } is going ('s) to leave.	She, He, It } is not going (isn't) to leave.	Is she, he, it	Yes, he, she, it } is.
			No, I am not. ('m not.)
			No, you, we, they } are not. (aren't)
			No, he, she, it } is not. (isn't)

Appendix 2A   The *Be* Passive

To form the passive, use the appropriate tense of *be*, followed by the past participle (pp).

		Tense	Form of *Be*
(a)	Wool **is produced** here.	Simple Present	*am/is/are* +pp
(b)	Wool **is being produced** here right now.	Present Progressive	*am/is/are being* +pp
(c)	Wool **was produced** here.	Simple Past	*was/were* +pp
(d)	Wool **was being produced** here ten years ago.	Past Progressive	*was/were being* +pp
(e)	Wool **has been produced** here since 1900.	Present Perfect	*have/has been* +pp
(f)	Wool **had been produced** here when the island was discovered.	Past Perfect	*had been* +pp
(g)	Wool **will be produced** here next year.	Future *(will)*	*will be* +pp
(h)	Wool **is going to be produced** here.	Future *(be going to)*	*am/is/are going to be* +pp
(i)	Wool **will have been produced** here by the year 2010.	Future Perfect	*will have been* +pp

Appendix 2B   The *Get* Passive

		Tense	Form of *Get*
(a)	Her cookies always **get eaten.**	Simple Present	*get/gets* +pp
(b)	Her cookies **are getting eaten.**	Present Progressive	*am/is/are getting* +pp
(c)	Her cookies **got eaten.**	Simple Past	*got* +pp
(d)	Her cookies **were getting eaten.**	Past Progressive	*was/were getting* +pp
(e)	Her cookies **have gotten eaten.**	Present Perfect	*have/has gotten* +pp
(f)	Her cookies **had gotten eaten.**	Past Perfect	*had gotten* +pp
(g)	Her cookies **will be eaten.**	Future *(will)*	*will get* +pp
(h)	Her cookies **are going to get eaten.**	Future *(be going to)*	*am/is/are going to get* +pp
(i)	Her cookies **will have gotten eaten** by the time we get home.	Future Perfect	*will have gotten* +pp

Appendix 3A   Factual Conditionals

If Clause [*If* + simple present]	Main Clause [simple present]
If you heat water,	it boils.

Appendix 3B   Future Conditionals

If Clause [*If* + simple present]	Main Clause [*will/be going to* + base verb]
If you study hard,	you will get a good grade.

Appendix 3C   Hypothetical Conditionals

If Clause [*If* + simple past]	Main Clause [*would* ('*d*) + base verb]
(a) If we had lots of money,	we'd travel around the world.
[*If* + B*e* verb → subjunctive *were*]	[*would* + base verb]
(b) If I were rich,	I'd travel around the world.

Appendix 3D   Past Hypothetical Conditionals

If Clause [*If* + past perfect]	Main Clause [*would* + *have* ('*ve*) + *verb* + past participle]
If you had called me,	I would have come to see you.

Appendix 4A   Probability and Possibility (Unit 5)

	Possible (less than 50% certain)	Probable (about 90% certain)	Certain (100% certain)
Present Forms	**less certain** 　He *could* play golf. 　He *might* play golf. 　He *may* play golf. **more certain**	He *must* play golf.	He plays golf.
	less certain 　She *could* be a doctor. 　She *might* be a doctor. 　She *may* be a doctor. **more certain**	She *must* be a doctor.	She is a doctor.
Question Forms	**less certain** 　*Could* he play golf? 　*Might* he play golf? **more certain**	—	*Does* he play golf?
	less certain 　*Could* she be a doctor? 　*Might* she be a doctor? **more certain**	—	*Is* she a doctor?
Negative Forms	**less certain** 　He *might* not play golf. 　He *may not* play golf. 　He *couldn't* play golf. **more certain**	He *must not* play golf.	He *does not/doesn't* play golf.
	less certain 　She *might not* be a doctor. 　She *may not* be a doctor. 　She *couldn't/can't* be a doctor. **more certain**	She *must not* be a doctor.	She *is not/isn't* a doctor.

	Possible (less than 50% certain)	Probable (about 90% certain)	Certain (100% certain)
Past Forms — less certain ↕ more certain	He *could have* played golf. He *might have* played golf. He *may have* played golf.	He *must have* played golf.	He *played* golf.
	She *could have* been a doctor. She *might have* been a doctor. She *may have* been a doctor.	She *must have* been a doctor.	She *was* a doctor.
	Could he *have* played golf? *Might* he *have* played golf?	—	*Did* he play golf?
	Could she *have* been a doctor? *Might* she *have* been a doctor?	—	*Was* she a doctor?
Progressive Forms — less certain ↕ more certain	He *could be* playing golf. He *might be* playing golf. He *may be* playing golf.	He *must be* playing golf.	He *is* playing golf.
	He *could have been* playing golf. He *might have been* playing golf. He *may have been* playing golf.	He *must have been* playing golf.	He *was* playing golf./ He *has been* playing golf.

Possible (less than 50% certain)	Probable (about 90% certain)	Certain (100% certain)
less certain It *could* rain tomorrow. It *may (not)* rain tomorrow. It *might (not)* rain tomorrow. **more certain**	It *will probably* rain tomorrow. It *probably won't* rain tomorrow.	It *will/will/not/won't* rain tomorrow.

(Future Forms — arrow from *less certain* to *more certain*)

Appendix 4B   Giving Advice and Expressing Opinions (Unit 10)

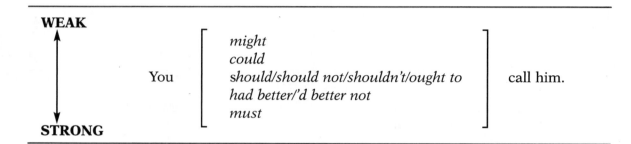

WEAK

You [*might* / *could* / *should/should not/shouldn't/ought to* / *had better/'d better not* / *must*] call him.

STRONG

Appendix 4C   Necessity and Obligation (Unit 11)

Present	Past	Future
Necessary and Obligatory		
She *must* go.	—	She *must* go.
She's/*has got to* go.	—	She's/*has got to* go.
She *has to* go.	She *had to* go.	She *has to* go./
		She'*ll/will have to* go.
Not Necessary and not Obligatory		
She *doesn't/does not have to* go.	She *didn't/did not have to* go.	She *doesn't/does not have to* go.
		She *won't/will not have to* go.

Appendix 4D   Prohibition and Permission (Unit 11)

Present	Past	Future
Prohibited and not Permitted		
We *can't/cannot* smoke in here.	We *couldn't/could not* smoke in here.	We *will not/won't be able to* smoke in here.
We *mustn't/must not* smoke in here.	—	
Permitted.		
We *can* smoke in here.	We *could* smoke in here.	We *will be able to* smoke in here.

Base Form	Past-Tense Form	Past Participle	Base Form	Past-Tense Form	Past Participle
be	was	been	leave	left	left
become	became	become	lend	lent	lent
begin	began	begun	let	let	let
bend	bent	bent	lose	lost	lost
bite	bit	bitten	make	made	made
blow	blew	blown	meet	met	met
break	broke	broken	pay	paid	paid
bring	brought	brought	put	put	put
build	built	built	quit	quit	quit
buy	bought	bought	read	read*	read
catch	caught	caught	ride	rode	ridden
choose	chose	chosen	ring	rang	rung
come	came	come	run	ran	run
cost	cost	cost	say	said	said
cut	cut	cut	see	saw	seen
dig	dug	dug	sell	sold	sold
do	did	done	send	sent	sent
draw	drew	drawn	shake	shook	shaken
drink	drank	drunk	shoot	shot	shot
drive	drove	driven	shut	shut	shut
eat	ate	eaten	sing	sang	sung
fall	fell	fallen	sit	sat	sat
feed	fed	fed	sleep	slept	slept
feel	felt	felt	speak	spoke	spoken
fight	fought	fought	spend	spent	spent
find	found	found	stand	stood	stood
fly	flew	flown	steal	stole	stolen
forget	forgot	forgotten	swim	swam	swum
get	got	gotten	take	took	taken
give	gave	given	teach	taught	taught
go	went	gone	tear	tore	torn
grow	grew	grown	tell	told	told
hang	hung	hung	think	thought	thought
have	had	had	throw	threw	thrown
hear	heard	heard	understand	understood	understood
hide	hid	hidden	wake	woke	woken
hit	hit	hit	wear	wore	worn
hold	held	held	win	won	won
hurt	hurt	hurt	write	wrote	written
keep	kept	kept			
know	knew	known			
led	led	led			

* Pronounce the base form: /rid/; pronounce the past-tense form: /red/.

Answer Key (for puzzles and problems only)

Answers to Exercise 8 (page 11)

- Horses sleep standing up.
- Bats use their ears to "see."
- Scorpions have twelve eyes.
- Elephants sometimes go for four days without water.
- Swans stay with the same mates all their lives.
- Antelopes run at 70 miles per hour.
- Bears sleep during the winter months.
- Spiders live for about two years.

A-14

Answer to Opening Task (page 19)

Answers to Exercise 5 (page 25)

1. I love you.
2. I see you.
3. I hate you.
4. I hear you.
5. He knows you.
6. Are you 21?
7. I see you are too wise for me.
8. I think you are great.

UNIT 4

Answers to Exercise 10 (page 62)

1.	A	5.	M	9.	E	13.	O	17.	K
2.	P	6.	R	10.	B	14.	F	18.	D
3.	G	7.	Q	11.	I	15.	C	19.	S
4.	J	8.	N	12.	L	16.	H		

UNIT 5

"Official" Answers to Activity 1 (page 84)

1. A giraffe passing a window.
2. A pencil seen from the end.
3. A cat climbing a tree.

UNIT 6

Solution to the Opening Task (pages 88–89)

Mrs. Meyer killed her husband. She entered the bathroom while he was brushing his teeth, and she hit him over the head with the bathroom scale. Then she turned on the shower and put the soap on the floor.

How do we know this?
- From the toothbrush: He was brushing his teeth, not walking out of the shower.
- From the soap: It was not possible to slip in this position.
- From the bathroom scale: The scale does not indicate zero.

UNIT 7

Solution to the Opening Task (pages 104–105)

LINDA	BOB	GEORGE
SUSAN	DIANA	FRANK
	CARLA	

UNIT 10

Solution to Exercise 7 (page 159)

First, the woman should take the mouse to the car, leaving the cat with the cheese. Next, she should return and pick up the cat and take it to the car. As soon as she gets to the car with the cat, she should remove the mouse and take it with her, leaving the cat in the car. When she gets back to the shopping area, she should pick up the cheese and leave the mouse. Then she should take the cheese to the car and leave it there with the cat. Finally, she should return to collect the mouse and bring it with her to the car.

UNIT 22

Solution to Exercise 4 (page 317)

Picture B

Solution to Opening Task (pages 328–329)

Solution to the Opening Task (page 349)

Lee loves Sid.
Kit loves Tracy.

Credits

Text Credits

p. 88: From *Crime and Puzzlement* by Lawrence Treat. Reprinted by permission of David R. Godine, Publisher, Inc. Illustration Copyright © 1981 by Leslie Carbarga.

p. 146: Idea from Wendy Asplin, University of Washington.

p. 176: "How not to collide with local road laws." Adapted from The European (Magazine Section), June 9, 1985.

pp. 286, 287, 291–293: Focus Boxes 1, 2, 5, 6, and 7: Ideas from *Systems in English Grammar* by Peter Master. Reprinted by permission of Prentice Hall, 1995. Ideas also from Master, P. (1990). "Teaching the English articles as a binary system." TESOL *Quarterly*, 3, pp. 461–478. Copyright © 1990 by Teachers of English to Speakers of Other Languages, Inc. Excerpt used with permission.

p. 295: Focus Box 8: Idea from "Rearticulating the articles" by Roger Berry, from ELT Journal 45, 3, 1990. Reprinted by permission of Oxford University Press: pages 252–299.

p. 306: Adapted from *Burma; A Travel Survival Kit,* by Tony Wheeler. Lonely Planet Publications, 1982.

p. 308: Adapted from *San Francisco TESOL Convention* 1990, Leslie Reichert.

p. 328: "Calvin and Hobbes." Copyright Universal Press Syndicate. Reprinted with permission.

p. 365: Idea from Betsy Branch, Melissa Anne Povey Rowden, and Gabrielle Nicas, English 575 project, University of Washington.

C-1

Photo Credits

Page 1: The Stock Market/Tom & Deeann McCarthy. Page 5: Upper left, © Corbis/Kevin R. Morris; lower left, © Corbis/Michael Pole; lower right, © Corbis/Bob Rowan.

Page 10: Photo by Jonathan Stark, property of Heinle & Heinle.

Page 29: Photo by Jonathan Stark, property of Heinle & Heinle.

Page 48: Photo by Jonathan Stark, property of Heinle & Heinle.

Page 59: Photo by Jonathan Stark, property of Heinle & Heinle.

Page 70: © Corbis/Gail Mooney.

Page 71: Photo by Jonathan Stark, property of Heinle & Heinle.

Page 85: Photos by Jonathan Stark, property of Heinle & Heinle.

Page 96: © Corbis/Bettmann.

Page 120: © Corbis/Todd Gipstein. Page 136 © Corbis/Ellen Frank; middle left, © Corbis/Carl Corey; middle right, © Corbis/Michelle Garrett, far right, © Corbis/Richard Fukuhara.

Page 196: © Corbis/Warren Moran.

Page 226: Photo by Jonathan Stark, property of Heinle & Heinle.

Page 248: Photo by Jonathan Stark, property of Heinle & Heinle.

Page 262: Upper left, © Corbis/AFP; upper middle, © Corbis/Neal Preston; upper right, © Corbis/Neal Preston; lower left, © Corbis; lower middle, © Corbis/Neal Preston; lower right, © Corbis/Neal Preston.

Page 263: Michael Jackson, UPI/Bettmann. All other photos on this page are from *Yearbook, The Most Star-studded Graduating Class* by the Editors of *Memories Magazine*, © 1990 by Diamandix Communications, Inc. Used by permission of Doubleday, a division of Bantam Doubleday Dell Publishing Group, Inc.

Page 284: © Corbis/Joel W. Rogers.

Page 297: © Corbis/Raymond Gehman.

Page 314: Photo by Jonathan Stark, property of Heinle & Heinle.

Page 340: Photo by Jonathan Stark, property of Heinle & Heinle.

Page 348: Photo by Jonathan Stark, property of Heinle & Heinle.

Index

measure words, 120–135
- containers for food, 122
- count nouns and, 125–128
- food described using, 120–125
- measurements of quantity, 123
- noncount nouns and, 125–128
- portions of food, 123
- shapes and states of food, 124
- singular vs. plural nouns and, 126

might, 72, 74, 77, 81
- advice expressed using, 157–160
- conditionals using, 376–377

modal auxiliaries, *should/ought to* as, 152

modals (*See also* phrasal modals)
- affirmative statements using, 74, 77
- *be* used with, 74, 77
- certainty about a situation expressed using, 72–73
- future tense, probability and possibility, 81–83
- guessing or drawing a conclusion using, 79
- *have to/has to* as phrasal modals, 169–171
- *must* as, 169–171
- necessity expressed using, 166–183
- negative statements (*not*) using, 74, 77
- past tense, probability and possibility, 77–78
- permission expressed using, 168
- phrasal modals, 169–171
- probability and possibility expressed using, 70–87
- progressive tense and, probability and possibility, 79–80
- prohibition expressed using, 166–183
- questions using, 74, 77
- short answers using, 74, 77
- *wh*-questions using, 52
- *yes/no* questions using, 51

most, *129*

much, *129*

must not/mustn't used to express prohibition, 168, 173–177

must, 72, 74, 77, 81
- expressed using, 160
- future tense and, 178–180
- modal use of, 169–171
- necessity expressed using, 168, 175–177, 175
- present tense and, 178–180
- *should* and *ought to* vs., 154

nearly, 108

necessity
- *do not have to* used to express lack of, 175–177
- *have to/have got to* to express, 168, 172–173, 175–177
- modals to express, 166–183
- *must* used to express, 168, 175–177

need to used to express advice, 153, 160

need, 26

negatives
- *anymore* used in, 265
- *had better* and, 155–157

ought to used with, 152
- passive verbs used in, 320
- *used to* in, 265

neither do I to express similarity in likes and dislikes, 188–189

neither used to express similarity in likes and dislikes, 186–187

never, 4, 7, 268
- in questions, 217

no article (∅), 284–301
- general statements expressed using, 292–293
- place names using, 304–308

no thanks/no thank you, 242–244

no, *130*

noncount nouns
- articles used with, 286–287, 289
- degree complements using, 142
- measure words and, 125–128
- *some* used with, 286, 290
- *the* used with, 291–292

none, *130*

nonprogressive or stative verbs, 26
- actions described using, 28
- emotions and feelings described using, 26
- *have* used with, 28
- knowledge, opinions, or beliefs described using, 26
- sensory events described using, 26
- states described using, 28

not as...as to express similarity or difference, 107–109

not nearly, 108

not quite/not quite as, 113

noun clauses, *as....as* and *not as...as* used with, 110

nouns
- articles used with, 286–287, 289, 291–292
- *as...as* and *not as...as* used with, 110
- comparatives and superlatives with, 106
- *some* used with, 290

nowhere near, 108

object pronouns, *as...as* and *not as...as* used with, 110

obligation
- *have to/have got to* to express, 172–173

off, *330*

offering, 238–247
- accepting offers in, 242–244
- *do you want* used in, 238–247
- refusing offers in, 242–244
- *would you like* used in, 238–247

often, *4*

on, *330*

only, *295*

opinion and beliefs (*See also* likes and dislikes), 150–165
- nonprogressive or stative verbs to describe, 26
- *ought to* used to express, 161
- *should not* used to express, 161
- *should* used to express, 161

TESTS AND ANSWERS

Grammar Dimensions Book 2

Name _____

Unit 1 Simple Present: Habits, Routines, and Facts

Score _____
100

A. Circle the letter of the *incorrect* underlined word or phrase.

1. Allison (A) <u>plays</u> the violin in an orchestra and (B) <u>sometimes</u> (C) <u>give</u> private lessons.

2. She (A) <u>hardly never</u> (B) <u>works</u> in the morning and she (C) <u>enjoys</u> sleeping late.

3. She (A) <u>usually</u> (B) <u>wears</u> a black dress for concerts but she (C) <u>don't wear</u> a uniform.

4. She (A) <u>drinks</u> some coffee and (B) <u>she always eat</u> a sandwich before the concert (C) <u>begins.</u>

5. (A) <u>Sometimes she walks</u> home, but she (B) <u>rides usually</u> the bus. She (C) <u>doesn't ever take</u> taxis.

B. Philip is a high school English teacher. He's talking to his friend Ann about how he spends his lunch period at school. Complete what he says using verbs that will complete the meaning. Sometimes more than one answer is possible.

Ann: What (6) _____ (you usually) for lunch?

Philip: We (7) _____ (not) much time to eat and I (8) _____

(not) to spend much money on lunch, so I usually (9) _____

sandwiches from home.

Ann: (10) _____ you ever _____ lunch in the school

cafeteria?

Philip: No, I hardly ever (11) _____ there, but my friend Tom always

(12) _____ his lunch there and he (13) _____ the food is

pretty good.

Ann: (14) _____ all of the students _____ in the

cafeteria?

Philip No. A lot of them (15) _____ lunch outdoors.

C. **Complete the sentence with one of these frequency adverbs (*always, usually, sometimes, never*) to make the sentence true. Sometimes more than one answer is possible.**

16. Cats and dogs _____ don't get along with each other.

17. Animals _____ escape from zoos.

18. The sun _____ rises in the west.

19. It _____ sets in the west.

20. Bears _____ sleep a lot in the winter.

D. **Write a sentence about something you usually do on your birthday.**

21. _____.

Write a sentence about something you never do in your English class.

22. _____.

Choose an animal and write two sentences about its habits.

23. _____.

24. _____.

Write a sentence about something that a lot of people do in hot weather.

25. _____.

UNIT 1 ANSWERS

A. 1. C
2. A
3. C
4. B
5. B

B. 6. do . . . have/eat
7. don't have
8. don't like
9. bring
10. Do . . . have/eat
11. eat
12. has/eats
13. says
14. Do . . . eat
15. have/eat

C. 16. usually
17. sometimes
18. never
19. always
20. always/usually

D. 21.–25. Sentences will vary.

Grammar Dimensions Book 2

Name _____

Unit 2 Present Progressive and Simple Present:

Score _____
                        100

   Actions and States

A. Look around you in the classroom. Write two sentences about what's happening right now.

   1. _____.

   2. _____.

Think of some people (friends or family members) who are not in your English class. What are they probably doing at the moment? Write two sentences.

   3. _____.

   4. _____.

What are you wearing today? Write a complete sentence.

   5. _____.

B. Check the sentence a) or b) that is closest in meaning to the first statement or pair of statements.

   6. A: John's eating a lot these days.
      B: I know. He's getting ready to run the marathon.
      a) He doesn't usually eat so much.   b) John always has a big appetite.

   7. My parents are staying in a hotel.
      a) They live in a hotel.   b) They plan to leave in a few days.

   8. Isabel teaches history at the community college.
      a) She's in class right now.   b) She has a job at the community college.

   9. Great! We're going out for dinner tonight!
      a) We go out for dinner every night.   b) We seldom go out for dinner.

   10. Andrew's really tired this semester. He's driving a taxi.
      a) His last job was easier.   b) He's working right now.

C. Complete the following using either the simple present or the present progressive. Use the words in parentheses.

A: Where (11) _____ you _____ (go) in this awful weather?

B: To class. The teacher (12) _____ (give) a review for next week's test.

C: Where's Kim?

D: He (13) _____ (take) a nap on the porch right now. He

(14) _____ (not sleep + usually) very well at night.

E: Most of my friends (15) _____ (study) in the library, but I

(16) _____ (study + always) better at home.

F: Not me. My brother and sister (17) _____ (make) too much noise.

G: There's Meredith. See? She (18) _____ (eat) soup and

(19) _____ (read) the newspaper.

H: She (20) _____ (read) everywhere. How can she concentrate?

D. Complete the following with the simple present or the present progressive, using the words in parentheses.

Marjorie (21) _____ (not like + usually) detective stories, but she

(22) _____ (love) the one she (23) _____ (read) now. With

most books, she (24) _____ (know) who's guilty after the first few

chapters, but this time she (25) _____ (have) trouble solving the mystery.

UNIT 2 ANSWERS

A. 1. –5. Students' own sentences.

B. 6. a

7. b

8. b

9. b

10. a

C. 11. are . . . going

12. is giving

13. is taking

14. doesn't usually sleep

15. study

16. always study

17. make

18. is eating

19. reading

20. reads

D. 21. doesn't usually like

22. loves

23. is reading

24. knows

25. is having

A. **You visit a fortune teller. He predicts some good things about your future, and some things that don't make you very happy. Match the two parts of his predictions by writing the correct letter in the space after each number. Don't use any part more than once.**

1. You will have

2. You're going to

3. You won't

4. You'll learn to

5. You're not going

A. to live to be 100 years old.

B. have more than two children.

C. an interesting life.

D. make a lot of money.

E. speak English perfectly.

B. **Complete these sentences with *will* or *be going to*. Sometimes both forms are possible.**

A: The weather report says it (6) _____ snow.

B: Cool! Do you think they (7) _____ close the schools?

A: Do you think people (8) _____ carry passports fifty years from now?

B: I don't know, but I think it (9) _____ be easier to travel from one country to another.

A: So, Doctor, what (10) _____ happen if I don't take this medicine?

B: Your condition (11) _____ get much worse.

A: What's all that lumber doing in your garage? What (12) (you) build?

B: I (13) _____ make some shelves for my son's room.

I don't believe it! That guy (14) _____ take that parking space, and I was here first!

I (15) _____ be exactly twice your age in five more years.

C. Use *will* or *be going to*.

Write two predictions about a friend's future.

16. _____.

17. _____.

Write two sentences about things you intend to do this weekend.

18. _____.

19. _____.

Write a sentence about something you don't intend to do this weekend.

20. _____.

D. Complete the following sentences using *be going to, will* or *'ll* as appropriate.

A: It's freezing in here!

B: Hold on! I (21) _____ close the window.

I (22) _____ make coffee. Do you want a cup?

What time (23) _____ (you) leave for the airport?

I (24) _____ be glad to help you if you have any questions.

May I borrow this book? I promise I (25) _____ bring it back next week.

UNIT 3 ANSWERS

A. 1. C
   2. D (B) (E)
   3. B (D) (E)
   4. E
   5. A

B. 6. is going to
   7. will
   8. will
   9. will
   10. will/is going to
   11. will/is going to
   12. are you going to
   13. 'm going to
   14. is going to
   15. 'll

C. 16.–20. Students' own sentences.

D. 21. 'll
   22. 'm going to
   23. are you going to
   24. 'll
   25. 'll

Grammar Dimensions Book 2

Name _____

Unit 4 Asking Questions: *Yes/No, Wh-,*

Score _____
100

Tag Questions, Choice Questions

A. Write an appropriate question word in the space provided.

1. A: _____ cut your hair?

    B: Why? Don't you like it?

2. A: _____ do your exams begin?

    B: In about three weeks.

3. A: _____ of these coats is yours?

    B: Neither.

4. A: _____ has everybody gone?

    B: Don't ask me. I just got here myself.

5. A: _____ didn't you take the bus?

    B: I forgot my pass.

B. Put the words in the correct order to form the appropriate questions.

6. A: (start/skiing/did/when/you) _____?

    B: I was so young that I can't remember.

7. A: (did/how long/you/it take/learn/to) _____?

    B: It didn't take me long at all.

8. A: (you/bones/have/ever/any/broken) _____?

    B: Just this one.

9. A: (to/ski/have/favorite/you/place/do/a) _____?

    B: Wherever there's snow.

10. A: (teach/could/me/to/you/ski) _____?

    B: Sure, but it will take some time.

C. In the blank below, write the question that would give you the following answers.

A: We had such a great weekend. We visited friends who have a farm about two hundred miles from here.

B: 11. _____?

A: By train. We were going to drive there, but we were both too tired on Friday afternoon. Our friends picked us up at a little station about ten miles from their farm.

B: 12. _____?

A: Oh, they only grow enough vegetables to feed themselves. It's a pretty small place.

B: 13. _____?

A: I don't know. Probably not more than ten acres, but it's beautiful and very quiet.

B: 14. _____?

A: We got back late Sunday night, and we were so glad we didn't have to fight traffic!

B: 15. _____?

A: They're coming to see us at Thanksgiving.

D. Complete the following statements with an appropriate question tag.

16. You both liked the restaurant, _____?

17. He'll be thirty next month, _____?

18. The test was awful, _____?

19. They speak French in Haiti, _____?

20. Chickens can't fly, _____?

21. You haven't seen Gabriel today, _____?

22. Lisa can use a computer, _____?

23. They weren't late to class, _____?

24. Rain smells great, _____?

25. He won't be here tomorrow, _____?

UNIT 4 ANSWERS

A.   1. Who
    2. When
    3. Which
    4. Where
    5. Why

B.   6. When did you start skiing?
    7. How long did it take you to learn?
    8. Have you ever broken any bones?
    9. Do you have a favorite place to ski?
  10. Could you teach me to ski?

C. 11. How did you get there?
  12. What do they grow on the farm?
  13. How big is it?/How big is the farm?
  14. When did you get back?
  15. When are they coming to visit you?/When are you going to see them again?

D. 16. didn't you
  17. won't he
  18. wasn't it
  19. don't they
  20. can they
  21. have you
  22. can't she
  23. were they
  24. doesn't it
  25. will he

A. Fill in the blank with the simple form of the verb in parentheses or with *could, might, must,* or *may* and the verb.

A: Does John speak Vietnamese? I know he was born in the U.S.

B: His last name is Nguyen, so he (1) _____ (speak) it.

C: Not necessarily, but I know that his grandmother (2) _____ (not understand) much English, and he's very close to her. So, he (3) _____ (speak) it.

D: I have no idea what to get Suzy for her birthday.

E: You (4) _____ (give) her a house plant.

D: No, I don't think I've ever seen a plant in her apartment. She

(5) _____ (have) some kind of allergy or she

(6) _____ (not like) them.

F: You teach math at Central High? So does my brother!

G: Well, I (7) _____ (know) him then.

H: Whose book is this? It was left in the school cafeteria.

I: It (8) _____ (belong) to anyone.

H: Well, not any of the kids, but it (9) _____ belong to a teacher or one of the office staff.

I: Wait, it has Muriel's initials in it and I know she loves this author. It

(10) _____ be hers.

B. Check the statement that best describes the situation.

11. The bumper sticker on the car in front of you says, "I brake for animals."
    a. Someone who uses the car must be a veterinarian.
    b. Someone who uses the car could be a veterinarian.
    c. Someone who uses the car is a veterinarian.

12. George always stops for a few drinks after work and often gets into fights. Sometimes at the office his breath smells of alcohol. The police stopped him last week for drunk driving and took away his license.
   a. George might have a drinking problem.   b. George must have a drinking problem.
   c. George has a drinking problem.

13. You know that Walter takes singing lessons every week and practices every day. He sings in a church choir on Sunday and in a choral group on Wednesdays. You've never heard him sing.
   a. Walter may sing very well.   b. Walter must sing very well.
   c. Walter sings very well.

14. Alex and Carol were robbed three times last year, so they've decided to sell their house. They spend very little time at home now, and they've started looking at apartments.
   a. They may want to move.   b. They must want to move.
   c. They want to move.

15. Mike always turns down invitations to go to the beach. If he's near a pool, he's always fully dressed and usually says he's getting a cold and can't go in the water.
   a. He may not know how to swim.   b. He must not know how to swim.
   c. He doesn't know how to swim.

C. You find a small black bag on the ground. Write five thoughts you have about the person who lost it, based on the items you find in the bag. Use *could, might, may,* or *must* to show how certain you feel.

16. a pack of cigarettes, matches, and some breath mints _____.

17. a business card that reads, "Miguel Guerra, insurance broker." _____.

18. a tape measure _____.

19. a computer diskette _____.

20. a tiny pair of scissors _____.

D. Fill in the blanks with *could have, might have, must have,* or *may have*.

21. David was out late last night and he's not in class today. He _____ overslept again.

22. I walked home alone at two o'clock in the morning.
   Are you crazy? You _____ been killed.

23. What's Steve's degree in? Steve _____ studied economics; I'm not sure.

24. I really put my foot in my mouth. You _____ told me that Ben and Yoko had broken up.

25. Who ate the last of the cheesecake? It _____ been your brother. He's got a key to this apartment.

UNIT 5 ANSWERS

A.
1. must/may
2. doesn't understand
3. may/must
4. could
5. may/might
6. might/may
7. must
8. could
9. may/might
10. must

B.
11. b
12. c
13. b
14. c
15. a

C.
16. He must be a smoker./He must smoke.
17. He might/may be Miguel Guerra or he might/may know someone named Miguel Guerra.
18. He could be a tailor or a carpenter. (or students' own ideas)
19. He must use a computer.
20. He may use them to cut his nails./They might be for cutting out newspaper articles. (or students' own ideas)

D.
21. may have
22. could have
23. might have
24. could have/might have
25. must have

Grammar Dimensions Book 2

Name _____

Unit 6 Progressive and Simple Past with Time Clauses:

Score _____
100

When, While, and *As Soon As*

A. Match the parts of these sentences by writing the correct letter in the space after the number.

1. When I was studying last night

A. I was still trying to catch the cat.

2. My cat was sitting in my lap while

B. the firefighters turned off the alarm.

3. As soon as the alarm rang

C. the fire alarm went off.

4. When the fire truck arrived

D. I was working on a math problem.

5. I was carrying him out of the building when

E. he ran under the bed.

B. Check the sentence (a) or (b) closest in meaning to the statement.

6. The alarm rang at the fire station while the firefighters were playing cards.
   (a) The firefighters finished their game before the alarm rang.
   (b) The firefighters started playing cards before the alarm rang.

7. As soon as the alarm sounded, some of them started putting on their gear.
   (a) They put on their gear after the alarm sounded.
   (b) The alarm sounded after they started putting on their gear.

8. The captain was shouting instructions while they were getting into the truck.
   (a) He was shouting and the firefighters were getting into the truck at the same time.
   (b) After the firefighters got into the truck, the captain began to shout.

9. When the fire truck arrived, people were running out of the building.
   (a) People ran out after the fire truck arrived.
   (b) People started to run out before the fire truck arrived.

10. As soon as they put out the fire, the firefighters turned off the alarm.
    (a) The alarm was ringing when they put the fire out.
    (b) The alarm stopped ringing before they put the fire out.

C. **Janet and Fred were out walking the dog when the alarm went off, so they missed the excitement. They're talking to one of their neighbors outside their apartment building. Use the simple past or past progressive to fill in the blanks.**

Steve: It was so stupid. I (11) _____ (heat) a pizza in the oven. It's all my

fault.

Fred: What (12) _____ (you) (do) when you (13) _____

(hear) the alarm? (14) _____ (you) (sleep)?

Steve: No, I (15) _____ (watch) T.V. and I (16) _____

(think) the noise was part of the program.

Janet: What (17) _____ (you) (do) when you (18) _____

(realize) it was the fire alarm?

Steve: As soon as I (19) _____ (smell) the smoke, I (20) _____

(run) into the kitchen.

D. **Some other people are standing in front of the building, too. Write sentences using the simple past and the past progressive to describe what they were doing and what they did when the alarm went off.**

(A man holding a crying baby and the baby's bottle)

21. _____ when _____ .

22. As soon as _____ , _____ .

(A man with paint on his hands and clothes, with a woman holding a book and a pair of glasses)

23. _____ while _____ .

(A woman with wet hair wearing a bathrobe and holding a cat)

24. _____ when _____ .

25. _____ as soon as _____ .

UNIT 6 ANSWERS

A. 1. C
2. D
3. E
4. A
5. B

B. 6. b
7. a
8. a
9. b
10. a

C. 11. was heating
12. were you doing
13. heard
14. were you sleeping
15. was watching
16. thought
17. did you do
18. realized
19. smelled
20. ran

D. 21. He was feeding the baby when the alarm went off.
22. As soon as the alarm went off, he ran out of his apartment.
23. He was painting while she was reading. / The alarm went off while he was painting and she was reading.
24. She was washing her hair when the alarm went off.
25. She got out of the shower and got her cat as soon as she heard the alarm.

Grammar Dimensions Book 2

Unit 7 Similarities and Differences: Comparatives,

Superlatives, *As . . . As, Not As . . . As*

Name _____

Score _____
          100

A. **There are five children in the Smith family. Their ages and heights are as follows:**

Albert	Paula	Stephanie	Anthony	Virginia
23	21	21	18	16
5'10"	5'8"	5'8"	6'0"	5'11"

Complete the following sentences with a comparative, a superlative, or an expression of similarity or difference.

1. Anthony is six feet tall. He's _____ of the five children.

2. The twins, Paula and Stephanie, are not _____ Virginia, who's 5'11".

3. Virginia is 16 years old. She's the _____.

4. Paula was born before Stephanie. She's two minutes _____ her twin.

5. Albert is two inches _____ Anthony.

6. Paula and Stephanie are the _____ of the five children.

7. Albert is the _____ child.

8. Anthony is three years _____ the twins.

B. **Correct the mistake in each of the following statements.**

9. All the Smith children are just active and intelligent as their parents.

10. Stephanie is probably the more outgoing member of the family.

11. Paula is anywhere near as friendly as her sister.

12. The twins don't study as much as their brothers, but they make the best grades than the boys.

13. Virginia is very athletic. She plays a lot more sports than her sisters are.

14. Anthony is a little shy. He doesn't have as many friends like Stephanie.

15. Stephanie can sing, but she can't play a musical instrument. She's probably the less musical of the Smith children.

C. Write sentences in which you compare yourself to a member of your family, a friend, or a famous person. Use *as . . . as* and *not as . . . as* one time each.

16. _____ (tall)

17. _____ (old)

18. _____ (smart)

19. _____ (athletic)

20. _____ (creative)

D. Rewrite the following sentences so that they are less direct and more tactful.

21. Anthony is stupider than his brother._____.

22. Albert is shorter than Anthony._____.

23. Paula and Stephanie work hard. Virginia works less than her sisters._____.

24. Albert is the ugliest of the Smith children._____.

25. Virginia is poorer than her brothers and sisters._____.

UNIT 7 ANSWERS

A.
1. the tallest
2. as tall as
3. youngest
4. older than
5. shorter than
6. shortest
7. oldest
8. younger than

B.
9. . . . are just <u>as</u> active and intelligent
10. . . . the <u>most</u> outgoing member
11. Paula is <u>not</u> anywhere near
12. . . . they make <u>better</u> grades than
13. . . . than her sisters <u>do</u>.
14. . . . as many friends <u>as</u> Stephanie
15. . . . the <u>least</u> musical

C. 16.–20. Students' own sentences.

D.
21. Anthony is not as intelligent as his brother.
22. Albert is not as tall as Anthony.
23. Virginia doesn't work as hard as her sisters.
24. Albert isn't as good looking as his brothers and sisters.
25. Virginia doesn't have as much money as her brothers and sisters.

A. You need to go grocery shopping. The only food items you have in your kitchen are the following. What quantity do you have of each? Write a measure word or expression in the space next to the number. Also, circle C (count noun) or NC (noncount noun) next to each food item as appropriate.

1. _____ mayonnaise   C   NC

2. _____ apples   C   NC

3. _____ crackers   C   NC

4. _____ milk   C   NC

5. _____ coffee   C   NC

B. You feel like making and eating a big breakfast. Write the names of the foods you buy. Example: a box of <u>pancake mix</u>.

6. a carton of _____

7. a box of _____

8. a jar of _____

9. a loaf of _____

10. a pound of _____

C. Rewrite each of these sentences to have the same general meaning, using one of the following words or phrases: *most, a few, none, a little, a lot of.*

11. Every friend I have hates lima beans. _____.

12. There are dozens of peaches here. Five or six are green. _____.

13. I have twelve brothers and sisters. Eleven are allergic to chocolate.

    _____.

14. They spent $1000 last month, $300 last week, and $400 this week at the

    supermarket. _____.

15. She can count to 100, say "hello," "please," and "thank you," ask for

    directions, and order a meal in Greek. _____.

D. Fill in the blank with the letter of the most suitable word or phrase.

16. I don't like to go shopping when there are _____ people in the supermarket.
    a. most   b. a lot   c. many

17. I prefer to go very early on Saturday morning, when _____ the produce is really fresh.
    a. some   b. all   c. a great deal

18. _____ shoppers are very aggressive, and move through the aisles very quickly.
    a. few of   b. several of   c. some

19. If you have very _____ items—no more than ten—you can go to the express checkout lane.
    a. many   b. few   c. several

20. My neighborhood supermarket doesn't carry _____ exotic food products.
    a. all of   b. much of   c. a lot of

21. There are _____ smaller grocery stores near my house, too.
    a. a little   b. a couple   c. several

22. _____ the small stores stay open very late.
    a. All   b. Several   c. None

23. Since I have so _____ money, I avoid the small, expensive shops.
    a. much   b. little   c. few

24. There's a health food store around the corner, but it carries _____ foods that I really like.
    a. little   b. some   c. few

25. _____ children enjoy a trip to the supermarket more than their parents.
    a. Most   b. All of   c. More

UNIT 8 ANSWERS

A. 1. a jar of (NC)
2. some/a kilo of/a bag of (C)
3. a box of (C)
4. a carton of/a bottle of (NC)
5. a jar of/a can of (NC)

B. Some answers may vary. Some possibilities:
6. eggs/milk/orange juice
7. cereal
8. jam, jelly, etc.
9. bread
10. butter

C. 11. None of my friends like lima beans.
12. A few of these peaches are green.
13. Most of my brothers and sisters are allergic to chocolate.
14. They spend a lot of money at the supermarket.
15. She speaks a little Greek.

D. 16. c
17. b
18. c
19. b
20. c
21. c
22. a
23. b
24. c
25. a

Grammar Dimensions Book 2

Unit 9 Degree Complements:

Too, Enough, **and** *Very*

Name _____

Score _____

100

A. Complete the following using *too* or *enough* and any words in parentheses.

1. A: That waiter is always rude to me.

   B: Maybe you never leave a_____ tip. (big)

2. A: Aren't you going to finish your dessert?

   B: I can't. It's _____ (rich). It must have a pound of butter in it.

3. A: I can hear everything the people at the next table are saying.

   B: So can I. The tables here are _____ (close together).

4. A: At least the portions are big. I've eaten _____ for three people!

5. A: Me too. But I don't think I'll come back. The service is _____ (slow).

B. Rewrite the following sentences using *too few* or *too little*.

6. We don't have enough eggs to make an omelette.

   _____.

7. There wasn't enough room in that apartment for a family of five.

   _____.

8. There aren't enough police on the streets.

   _____.

9. Not everyone can have a cookie. There aren't enough to go around.

   _____.

10. I haven't enough time to get to the grocery store.

    _____.

C. Complete the following with *enough, not enough, too much/many/little/few, too + to,* or *very* as appropriate.

I must admit I'm not a (11) _____ good traveler. First of all, I either pack

(12) _____ clothes and make my bag (13) _____ heavy carry,

or I take (14) _____ things and don't have (15) _____

to wear. I like to get to the airport (16) _____ early, but then I find I have

(17) _____ time to kill. I really hate flying. Everyone carries on

(18) _____ luggage and there's never (19) _____ room for it.

I can't relax (20) _____ to sleep, there are (21) _____

bathrooms for the number of passengers, and I always seem to sit next to someone

who talks (22) _____. The attendants have (23) _____ time

to serve drinks, show a movie, and feed everyone, so they're usually

(24) _____ busy answer any questions. And the food is never

(25) _____ appetizing, but at least it helps pass the time.

UNIT 9 ANSWERS

A.
1. big enough
2. too rich
3. too close together.
4. enough
5. too slow

B.
6. We have too few eggs to make an omelette.
7. There was too little room in that apartment for a family of five.
8. There are too few police on the streets.
9. There are too few cookies to go around.
10. I've had too little time to get to the grocery store.

C.
11. very
12. too many
13. too . . . to
14. too few
15. enough
16. very
17. too much
18. too much
19. enough
20. enough
21. too few
22. too much
23. too little
24. too . . . to
25. very

Grammar Dimensions Book 2

Name _____

Unit 10 Giving Advice and Expressing Opinions:

Score _____

100

Should, Ought To, Need To, Must, Had Better,

Could, and *Might*

A. Write sentences with *should, ought to,* and *shouldn't* that you might find in these self-help books.

Write three pieces of advice from *Healthy Cats, Happy Owners.*

1. (feed) _____

2. (play) _____

3. (hit) _____

Write two pieces of advice from *Ten Steps to Better Grades.*

4. (television) _____

5. (before an exam) _____

B. Fill in the blanks with *should, shouldn't, must,* or *must not.* Sometimes more than one modal is possible. Try to use each of them at least once.

6. You _____ have a license to drive a car.

7. You _____ keep your car clean and waxed.

8. You _____ leave children or pets alone in your car.

9. You _____ exceed the posted speed limit.

10. You _____ pick up hitchhikers.

C. Complete these sentences with *should, ought to, need to,* or *shouldn't.* (Do not use *should* more than twice.)

11. Hurry up! Your train leaves in ten minutes. You _____ find a taxi now!

12. Nutritionists say you _____ eat five servings of fruits and vegetables a day.

13. You _____ go swimming after a big, heavy meal.

14. You _____ put some ice on your ankle; it's starting to swell.

15. I ought to exercise more often, and you _____, too.

D. Circle your choice in each of the following sentences.

16. In most cities you (shouldn't, must not) eat or drink when you ride the subway.

17. You (must, should) read the want-ads in the Sunday paper if you want to find a job.

18. It looks like someone broke down your front door. We (had better/should) call the police.

19. You (ought to/must) be 21 to enter the casino.

20. Carolyn (should/must) get out of the house more often. She studies too much.

21. If you feel like taking a break, you (could/had better) rent a car and drive out to the coast.

22. Children under ten years old on this bus (must/should) be accompanied by an adult.

23. You (had better not/should not) miss any more of my lectures if you want to pass this course, Mr. Wilson.

24. If you can't sleep at night, you (might/must) try drinking some hot milk before you go to bed.

25. They (should/had better) try that restaurant if they like Mexican food.

UNIT 10 ANSWERS

A. **1.–5.** Students' own sentences

B. **6.** must
  7. should/ought to
  8. shouldn't
  9. mustn't
  10. shouldn't

C. **11.** need to
  12. should/ought to
  13. shouldn't
  14. should/ought to
  15. should/ought to

D. **16.** must not
  17. should
  18. had better
  19. must
  20. should
  21. could
  22. must
  23. had better not
  24. might
  25. should

Grammar Dimensions Book 2

Name _____

Unit 11 Modals of Necessity and Prohibition: *Have To,*

Score _____
100

Do Not Have To, Must/Must Not

A. Circle your choice in each of the following sentences.

1. In public places, you (can/must) keep your dog on a leash.

2. You have a serious drug problem, Cindy. You (should/have got to) get some professional help.

3. See that sign? You (can/should) only park on the right side of this street.

4. You (have got to/should) pay your electricity bill as soon as it arrives.

5. You (cannot/should not) wash clothes in public fountains.

B. Use each of the following only once to complete the text: *can/have to/don't have to/must/must not*

Everyone knows that you (6) _____ be Italian to love pizza. If you want

to make it at home, you (7) _____ have a good but simple recipe for the

crust. For best results, you (8) _____ use only the freshest ingredients,

and you (9) _____ reduce the amount of cheese you use if you're worried

about fat. If you really want to enjoy this American favorite, you

(10) _____ eat pizza with a knife and fork, only with your hands.

C. You and your friends have formed an English conversation club. Write some of its rules below, using the words in parentheses.

11. _____
(have to/an English name)

12. _____
(must/only English)

13. _____
(not have to/perfect English)

14. _____
(must not/dictionary)

15. _____
(have got to/five cents/foreign word)

D. Fill in the blanks in the text using the following: *can/cannot/have to/ don't have to/must/must not/should*

Like all amusement parks, Disneyland was designed for people to have fun in. You can have a really good time if you follow some suggestions and obey certain regulations.

16. You _____ speak English to enjoy yourself in Disneyland.

17. You _____ wear comfortable, casual clothes.

18. You _____ bring small children into the park.

19. You _____ bring animals into the park.

20. You _____ enter the park without shoes.

21. You _____ remain fully dressed at all times.

22. You _____ buy or consume alcohol in Disneyland.

23. Sometimes you _____ wait in line for the more popular attractions.

24. You pay one price at the entrance; you _____ pay for individual rides.

25. For certain rides, you _____ meet a minimum height requirement.

UNIT 11 ANSWERS

A. 1. must
2. have got to
3. can
4. should
5. cannot

B. 6. don't have to
7. have to/must
8. must/have to
9. can
10. must not

C. Suggested sentences:
11. You have to use an English name at club meetings.
12. You must speak only English during meetings.
13. You don't have to speak perfect English.
14. You must not bring a dictionary to meetings.
15. Club members have got to pay five cents for every foreign word they use during meetings.

D. 16. don't have to
17. should
18. can
19. must not
20. must not
21. must
22. cannot
23. have to
24. don't have to
25. must

A. Complete these sentences with *either, neither, so,* and *too*.

21. I like spicy food and _____ does Nacib.

2. He doesn't smoke and _____ do I.

3. I can't drink coffee at night and he can't _____.

4. He loves mint tea and I do _____.

5. He never skips a meal and _____ do I.

B. Fill in the blanks with an auxiliary verb or the appropriate form of the verb *to be* to make the second statement agree with the first.

6. Rehana made a good score on her TOEFL. So _____ Olga.

7. Fatima and Ali won't be here tomorrow. Neither _____ we.

8. You haven't changed a bit! Neither _____ you.

9. The service was terrible. The food _____ too.

10. My mother has studied Spanish for years. So _____ mine.

C. Mitsuki needs a roommate. She's talking to Ada to see if they might be compatible. Write the women's responses to each other's underlined comments in the blanks, using the language covered in this unit.

Mitsuki: I'm asthmatic, so <u>I can't stand any form of smoke</u>—cigarettes, pipes, whatever.

Ada: (11) _____, so that won't be a problem.

Mitsuki: I'll have a glass of wine now and then, but <u>I've never done drugs or given wild parties.</u>

Ada: (12) _____ Gosh! We sound equally boring.

Mitsuki: Yes, don't we? Let's see . . . What else? I mostly listen to classical music and jazz. <u>Do you like jazz?</u>

Ada: Well, (13) _____. I mean, I can take it or leave it. Actually, <u>I watched a good documentary on Ella Fitzgerald last night.</u>

Mitsuki: You did? (14) _____. Didn't you love her?

Ada: Still do, always will. Well, it's late. <u>I should get going.</u>

Mitsuki: (15) _____ I'll give you a call tomorrow.

D. Circle your choice in the following statements.

16. I (enjoy/like) to watch old movies.

17. (To sing/singing) in my college chorus is my favorite pasttime.

18. Martha has been to China and (Bruce has been/so has Bruce).

19. Her parents come from California but his (aren't/don't).

20. He studies at night but (she doesn't/so does she).

E. Put these short phrases in the correct order.

21. I/neither/do _____

22. too/have/I _____

23. they/so/do _____

24. can't/either/he _____

25. so/mine/are _____

UNIT 12 ANSWERS

A. 1. so
2. neither
3. either
4. too
5. neither

B. 6. did
7. will
8. have
9. was
10. has

C. 11. Neither can I
12. Neither have I
13. Sort of/Kind of
14. So did I
15. So should I

D. 16. like
17. Singing
18. so has Bruce
19. don't
20. she doesn't

E. 21. Neither do I.
22. I have too.
23. So do they.
24. He can't either.
25. So are mine.

A. Mr. Scott is interviewing Mei Chang for a job in his record store. Write the questions he asked her in order to get these responses:

1. _____.

Yes, I do. I work in a drugstore after school.

2. _____.

I started working there during my first year in high school.

3. _____.

I've worked there for two years now.

4. _____.

Yes, I do. I play the clarinet.

5. _____.

I've taken lessons since I was ten years old.

B. Write *For* or *Since* in the space before each time phrase.

6. _____ as long as I can remember

7. _____ the past few weeks

8. _____ the snowstorm

9. _____ he moved to Mexico

10. _____ most of her life

C. Indicate whether these sentences have the same or different meanings by circling S or D.

11. A: He has worked there two years.

    B: He has worked there for two years.   S   D

22. A: She played basketball for three years.

    B: She has played basketball for three years.   S   D

13. A: She stopped working out for a long time.

    B: She hasn't worked out for a long time.   S   D

14. A: He has worn glasses for a long time.

    B: He started wearing glasses a long time ago.   S   D

15. A: (It's Friday. They got married on Saturday.)

    A: They've been married since Saturday.

    B: They've been married for almost a week.   S   D

D. Fill in the blanks with *since* or *for* or the appropriate form of the verb in parentheses.

I (16) _____ (know) Audrey for a couple of years. A few weeks ago I

(17) _____ (ask) her, "How long (18) _____ (wear) your hair

in a braid?" "(19) _____ I was in college," she said. "I

(20) _____ (not cut) it (21) _____ at least five years." Last

Saturday she (22) _____ (decide) to cut her hair very short and

(23) _____ (go) straight to the hairdresser's. I (24) _____

(not see) her (25) _____ she made the big decision.

UNIT 13 ANSWERS

A. 1. Do you work? / Do you have a job now?
2. When did you start working there?
3. How long have you worked there?
4. Do you play a musical instrument?
5. How long have you taken lessons?

B. 6. For
7. For
8. Since
9. Since
10. For

C. 11. S
12. D
13. D
14. S
15. S

D. 16. have known
17. asked
18. have you worn
19. Since
20. haven't cut
21. for
22. decided
23. went
24. haven't seen
25. since

Grammar Dimensions Book 2

Unit 14 Present Perfect and Simple Past:

Ever and *Never, Already* and *Yet*

Name _____

Score _____
100

A. Put the verb in parentheses in the simple past or the present perfect to complete the following sentences.

1. Anna's a good student. She _____ (think) a lot about where she wants to study.

2. She _____ (apply) to five colleges that are not too far from her hometown.

3. Last week she _____ (receive) acceptance notices from three of them.

4. Some of Anna's friends _____ (take) the college entrance exams more than once.

5. Mary and Wilton _____ (take) them twice in their junior year and again last month.

B. Complete the conversations, using the present perfect or the simple past of the verb in parentheses. The first one has been done for you.

1. A. Have you ever tasted octopus salad before? (you/taste/ever)

   B. Octopus salad? Yes, I (6) _____ (taste) it. In fact I (7) _____ (eat) it lots of times.

   A. Where (8) _____ (you/try) it for the first time?

   B. I first (9) _____ (have) it in Portugal, in a little town called Sintra.

2. A. (10) _____ (you/be/ever) to England?

   B. As a matter of fact, I (11) _____ (be) there several times.

   A. When (12) _____ (go) there for the first time?

   B. About ten years ago, right after I (13) _____ (graduate) from college.

   A. (14) _____ (drive) when you were there?

   B. Are you kidding?! I (15) _____ (drive/never) on the left side of the road in my life, and I hope I never have to!

C. Put the letter of the right word or words in the space to complete the following.

16. Wake up! The alarm clock _____ twice.
    (a) went off already   (b) has already gone off   (c) has gone off yet

17. George _____ worked a day in his life.
    (a) has already   (b) has never   (c) has yet

18. _____ worked as a babysitter?
    (a) Have you ever   (b) Did you already   (c) Do you ever

19. She _____ nothing about her problem to me.
    (a) hasn't said   (b) has never said   (c) has said

20. Have you _____?
    (a) had dinner ever   (b) had already dinner   (c) had dinner yet

D. Write questions that correspond to the following answers.

21. _____?

"The Wizard of Oz"? Yes, I have. In fact, I've seen it dozens of times.

22. _____?

Oh, the first time I saw it was when I was about eight years old.

23. _____?

Today's newspaper? No, I haven't read it yet.

24. _____?

I'm afraid <u>I have</u> had lunch already. I couldn't wait for you.

25. _____?

No, Mom, I haven't taken the garbage out yet, but I'm just about to.

UNIT 14 ANSWERS

A.
1. has thought
2. has applied
3. received
4. have taken
5. took

B.
6. have tasted
7. have eaten
8. did you try
9. had
10. Have you ever been
11. have been
12. did you go
13. graduated
14. Did you drive
15. have never driven

C.
16. b
17. b
18. a
19. c
20. c

D.
21. Have you ever seen "The Wizard of Oz"?
22. When was the first time you saw it?/When did you first see it?
23. Have you read today's newspaper yet?
24. Have you already had lunch?
25. Have you taken out the garbage yet?

A. Your cousin is visiting you for a week. When you get home in the evening you can see how he's been spending his time. Write a sentence for each of your discoveries.

1. The TV is on. Your cousin is asleep on the sofa and the remote control is still in his hand.

   _____.

2. Every pot and pan in the kitchen is dirty.

   _____.

3. There was a lot of beer in the refrigerator last night. Now several cans are gone.

   _____.

4. Your diary is open on your bed.

   _____.

5. The ashtray on the coffee table is full and the living room smells of cigarette smoke.

   _____.

B. Complete the following dialogues.

Example:
a. Have you talked to your mother this week?

b. No, she's been spending all her time with her new boyfriend. (spend)

6. Gas station attendant: Can I help you folks?

   Andrew: I hope so. We _____ around for half an hour and we can't find this address. (drive)

7. Kate: Has your sister found a job yet?

   Sam: No, but she _____ for very long. (not look)

8. John: Are Fran and Paula getting ready for their trip?

   Paul: I guess so. They _____ a lot of maps and travel guides recently. (study)

9. Edith: I'm so tired I can't keep my eyes open.

    Chris: _____ a lot at night? (cry/the baby)

10. Marian: I _____ in that flower bed since eight o'clock. (work)

    Ed: Well, sit down and have some lemonade.

C. Read each situation and circle the letter of the statement that best describes it.

11. Terry started taking piano lessons when she was seven and stopped a few years later.
    a. Terry has been taking piano lessons.
    b. Terry has taken piano lessons since she was seven.
    c. Terry has taken piano lessons.

12. It's 6:30. Dinner is almost over and the children's hands and faces are all greasy. There are only two pieces of fried chicken left on the platter.
    a. They've eaten fried chicken.
    b. They've been eating fried chicken for a long time.
    c. They've been eating fried chicken.

13. Virginia knitted a sweater for me two years ago. She started knitting another one for me a month ago, but she's only finished the back. Her needles and the wool are on her chair now.
    a. Virginia has been knitting me sweaters for two years.
    b. Virginia has been knitting me a sweater.
    c. Virginia has knitted me two sweaters.

14. Bill made a short film when he was in college and he made another short film two years later.
    a. Bill's been making films for several years.
    b. Bill's been making films since college.
    c. Bill's made two films.

15. Rosemary went to France for two weeks last year. She also went in 1993 and 1995.
    a. She's been going to France since 1993.
    b. She's been to France three times.
    c. She's gone to France for two weeks.

D. Complete the dialogue using the present perfect progressive, the present perfect, or the simple past tense.

Allison: Where (16) _____ (you/be)? I (17) _____ (drive)

around the block for twenty minutes.

Tom: I (18) _____ (talk) to my math teacher. I (19) _____

(not do) all of the homework assignments this term and I

(20) _____ (fail) the last test,

so . . .

Allison: But you (21) _____ (study) nothing but math for weeks.

Tom: I know, but I (22) _____ (not take) my math courses last year, so

this one (23) _____ (be) a lot harder. And the teacher

(24) _____ (go) really fast recently.

Allison: Well, let's get something to eat. I (25) _____

(have/just) an apple, but I'm still hungry.

UNIT 15 ANSWERS

A.
1. He's been watching TV.
2. He's been cooking.
3. He's been drinking beer.
4. He's been reading my diary.
5. He's been smoking.

B.
6. have been driving
7. hasn't been looking
8. have been studying
9. Has the baby been crying
10. have been working

C.
11. c
12. c
13. b
14. c
15. b

D.
16. have you been
17. have been driving
18. have been talking
19. haven't done
20. failed
21. have been studying
22. didn't take
23. has been
24. has been going
25. have just had

A. **You've invited your future in-laws for dinner. It's the first time you've met them and they seem very formal. Change the following suggestions into polite offers using *Would you like . . . ?***

1. Another drink? _____

2. Wash your hands? _____

3. Let me get you some more bread. _____

4. Some more soup? _____

5. You don't look well. Let me call a doctor for you. _____

B. **Write the letter of the appropriate response in the space before each offer.**

6. Would you like Mark to help you?   **a.** Thank you, I'd love to.

7. Do you want another cup of coffee?   **b.** Not yet. He's in a bad mood.

8. Do you want me to tell Dad about the car?   **c.** Yes, please. They're delicious.

9. Would you like to see the garden?   **d.** Are you going to have one?

10. Would you like another brownie?   **e.** Thanks, but I can manage.

C. **Write the letter of the correct phrase in the space.**

11. My TV is broken. _____ some music?
    a. Would you like to listen   b. Would you like to hear   c. Do you want me

12. You look tired, honey. _____ to make you some coffee?
    a. Do you like me   b. Do you want   c. Would you like me

13. _____ and tell me all your troubles, son.
    a. Do you want to sit down   b. Sit down   c. Would you like to sit down

14. Excuse me. _____ a clean spoon, pelase?
    a. Do you want me to bring you   b. Would you bring me   c. Do you want to bring

15. Quiet down there! We're trying to sleep! _____ to call the police?
    a. Do you want   b. Would you like   c. Do you want us

D. You're in a clothing store. Complete the salesperson's remarks by filling in the blanks with an appropriate word or words.

Please come in. Let me know if I can help you with anything. Would you

(16) _____ see a particular color? Would you like (17) _____ get you a larger

size? These have just come in. (18) _____ to try one on? The woman who does our

alterations is here today. Would you like (19) _____ make this shorter for you? Do

(20) _____ put that in a box or on a hanger for you?

E. Write offers that correspond to these responses.

21. _____.

Thanks very much, but I'll have to say no. I'm driving.

22. _____.

No, please don't get up. I'll close it.

23. _____.

Sure, why not? Are you going to have more, too?

24. _____.

Thank you. Ordinarily I'd love to stay, but I've already had dinner.

25. _____.

That's okay. I'll wash them. You did them last night.

UNIT 16 ANSWERS

A. 1. Would you like another drink?
    2. Would you like to wash your hands?
    3. Would you like me to get you some more bread?
    4. Would you like some more soup?
    5. Would you like me to call a doctor for you?

B. 6. e
    7. d
    8. b
    9. a
   10. c

C. 11. b
   12. c
   13. b
   14. b
   15. c

D. 16. like to
   17. me to
   18. Would you like
   19. her to
   20. you want me to

E. 21. Would you like another drink?
   22. Do you want/Would you like me to close the window?
   23. Would you like some more cake?
   24. Would you like to stay for dinner?
   25. Do you want/Would you like me to do the dishes/

Grammar Dimensions Book 2

Unit 17 Requests and Permission:

Can/Could/Will/Would/May

Name _____

Score _____
100

A. Rewrite the incorrect requests and make the others more polite by using the words provided.

1. Do you mind to give me a hand with these bags? (would)

_____.

2. Tell me when those books come in, okay? (will)

_____.

3. Hold that door for me! (could)

_____.

4. Please you turn down your radio. (would)

_____.

5. I've missed my bus, dad. Drive me to school. (can)

_____.

B. Write a polite request for each situation using one of the following: *will, can, mind, may, could*

6. The people behind you at the movie keep talking. You finally turn around and say politely:

_____?

7. You ask someone for directions to the library. He speaks so fast that you don' understand the directions at all. You say:

_____?

8. You're holding a baby, a shopping bag, and the Sunday paper. Your hands are full and you need to use the phone. Ask your friend for help:

_____?

9. You're at the dinner table. You can't reach the salt, but you think your sister can. Ask her to pass it to you.

_____?

10. A friendly looking stranger is walking a tiny new puppy in the park. You don't want to touch the dog without the owner's permission, so you say:

_____?

C. Write the letter of the appropriate response in the space by each number.

11. Could you lend me fifty dollars?

    My electricity bill is due. _____

12. Would you mind very much driving me

    to the post office? _____

13. Will you see who's at the door? _____

14. Make sure you water my plants

    while I'm gone. _____

15. You're going to the store? Can you

    pick up some ice cream? _____

a. Sure. Just a second.

b. I could, but why don't you just come with me?

c. Are you asking or telling me to?

d. Not at all. I'd be happy to.

e. Sorry. I'd like to help you, but I can't.

D. Fill in the blanks with the missing word or words.

A. Dad, (16) _____ the car tonight? I'm going over to Stephanie's to study.

B. Sorry, I'm (17) _____ I need it. Why don't you ask her to come here for dinner?

A. (18) _____ I? Thanks (19) _____ make us one of your incredible pizzas?

B. (20) _____. (21) _____ running out to the store for some olive oil?

A. (22) _____ glad to. Now (23) _____ the keys to the car?

B. Of course, but (24) _____ taking your brothers with you?

A. Not (25) _____.

UNIT 17 ANSWERS

A. 1. Would you mind giving me a hand with these bags?

2. Will you tell me when those books come in (please)?

3. Could you (please) hold that door for me?

4. Would you (please) turn down your radio?

5. Can you (please) drive me to school?

B. 6. Would you mind not talking?

7. Could you speak more slowly (please)?

8. Will you hold the baby for me (please)?

9. Can you pass me the salt (please)?

10. May I pet your dog?

C. 11. e

12. d

13. a

14. c

15. b

D. 16. Can/could I borrow/use

17. afraid

18. Can

19. Will/Would you

20. Sure./Certainly.

21. Would you mind

22. I'd be

23. may I have

24. would you mind

25. at all

A. Put the verbs in parentheses in the correct form (the simple past, the present tense, *used to,* or *didn't use to*).

Ten years ago, Philip and Ann (1) _____ (move) to the country because

they (2) _____ (want) to write a book. They (3) _____

(give) away their TV and Philip (4) _____ (stop) shaving. Last year

they (5) _____ (rent) a house in a big city and (6) _____

(get) nine-to-five jobs in offices. They always (7) _____ (sleep) late in

the country, but these days they (8) _____ (get up) at seven o'clock.

Philip (9) _____ (shave) every morning now, but he

(10) _____ (not shave) in the country.

B. Write sentences about Philip and Ann's life in the country using *used to* and *didn't use to* with he words provided.

11. (grow their own vegetables) _____.

12. (watch TV) _____.

13. (wear jeans everyday) _____.

14. (Philip/a beard) _____.

15. (get up early) _____.

C. Complete the following with *still* or *anymore*.

16. They love fresh bread, but they don't bake their own _____.

17. Turn that music down! People are _____ sleeping.

18. Is there someone else? Don't you love me _____?

19. Some people _____ don't believe that man has walked on the moon.

20. I love my computer; I hardly ever use my typewriter _____.

D. Circle the letter that indicates where the frequency adverb should be placed in each sentence.

21. She (a) used (b) to (c) smoke cigars, but she does (d) now. (never)

22. (a) We (b) have (c) any news from our cousins (d) in Canada. (seldom)

23. (a) Mike and Steve (b) don't (c) go (d) to the movies on weeknights. (usually)

24. He (a) has (b) wanted (c) to (d) go back to school. (always)

25. (a) He (b) was (c) sick (d) as a child. (often)

UNIT 18 ANSWERS

A.   1. moved
     2. wanted
     3. gave
     4. stopped
     5. rented
     6. got
     7. used to
     8. get up
     9. shaves
   10. didn't use to

B. 11. They used to grow their own vegetables.
   12. They didn't use to watch TV.
   13. They used to wear jeans every day.
   14. Philip used to have a beard.
   15. They didn't use to get up early.

C. 16. anymore
   17. still
   18. anymore
   19. still
   20. anymore

D. 21. a
   22. b
   23. c
   24. b
   25. c

A. Put the verbs in parentheses in the simple past or past perfect tense.

1. By the time Mozart _____ (be) eight years old,

   he _____ (compose) a lot of music.

2. When I _____ (get) home the next day, I could see that my room-

   mates _____ (have) a party.

3. The exam _____ (already + begin) by the time I

   _____ (find) the right classroom.

4. We _____ (just + sit) down at the dinner table when the door-

   bell _____ (ring).

5. When your grandparents _____ (b) children, television

   _____ (not be) invented.

B. Join the two sentences to make one sentence, using *because* or *by the time*.

6. The ice cream melted. We got home from the supermarket.

   _____.

7. Her car ran out of gas. She asked to use our telephone.

   _____.

8. The rain stopped. We arrived at the station.

   _____.

9. Bill was angry. His computer crashed.

   _____.

10. Karen couldn't walk. She broke her ankle.

   _____.

C. There is a mistake in each of the following sentences. Circle it and write your correction in the space provided. Use the simple past or past perfect tense.

11. Kevin is happy because his favorite soccer team had won the

    game _____.

12. Mark was upset because Kate has forgotten his birthday _____.

13. Lisa and Gabriel have lived in Texas for years, but they have never been to

    Mexico until last week _____.

14. Margie doesn't want to go out for pizza because she had had it for dinner last

    night _____.

15. Susan and Russell are tired because they had worked twelve hours that

    day _____.

D. Put the verb in parentheses in the appropriate tense. Use the simple past, the past progressive, the present perfect, or the past perfect tense.

Nita and Paul (16) _____ (be) engaged for three years now. They first

(17) _____ (meet) when they (18) _____ (study) English

at the community college. By the time the course (19) _____ (end)

they (20) _____ (decide) to get married. A few months ago, Paul's

company (21) _____ (transfer) him to San Francisco. Nita

(22) _____ (go) to visit him last week, and since she

(23) _____ (be/never) to California before, it was a really exciting trip.

She (24) _____ (get back) on Sunday and is full of their wedding

plans. Her friends (25) _____ (see/never) her look happier than she

does these days.

UNIT 19 ANSWERS

A.
   1. was; had composed
   2. got; had had
   3. had already begun; found
   4. had just sat; rang
   5. were; hadn't been

B.
   6. By the time we got home from the supermarket, the ice cream had melted.
   7. She asked to use our telephone because her car had run out of gas.
   8. By the time we arrived at the station, the rain had stopped.
   9. Bill was angry because his computer had crashed.
  10. Karen couldn't walk because she had broken her ankle.

C.
  11. Kevin <u>was</u> happy . . .
  12. . . . <u>had</u> forgotten
  13. they <u>had</u> never been
  14. she <u>had</u> it for dinner
  15. <u>were</u> tired

D.
  16. have been
  17. met
  18. were studying
  19. ended
  20. had decided
  21. transferred
  22. went
  23. had never been
  24. got back
  25. have never seen

A. Fill in the blanks with *a/an/some/the/* or Ø.

1. When I was _____ child, my family used to spend

   _____ week every summer in Maine.

2. _____ friends of my parents had a cabin there, and they would give

   us _____ keys.

3. The cabin was on _____ lake, at the top of a steep hill that was

   covered in _____ pine trees.

4. There was _____ large fireplace in _____ living room

   of the cabin and the living room was two stories high.

5. Needless to say, the cabin almost never got warm, and _____

   mornings we would stand in front of the fireplace and pull on

   _____ jeans and sweaters as quickly as we could.

6. The cabin had no bathroom, but there was _____ outhouse which

   seemed to a child (but wasn't) very far from the cabin, hidden

   among _____ trees.

7. I remember having wonderful breakfasts of _____ pancakes made

   on _____ pot-bellied stove in the kitchen.

8. I had never seen _____ pot-bellied stove anywhere else, and I was

   fascinated. My mother would get _____ wood from outside and let

   me put it in the stove.

9. When the sun had warmed _____ hillside a bit, we would climb slowly

   down the hill in our bathing suits to go swimming in _____ icy lake.

10. The cabin in Maine wasn't _____ especially comfortable place, but

    I spent _____ of the happiest days of my life there.

B. Fill in the blanks with *the* or Ø.

11. Your plants are all dying. They need _____ sun.

12. This jacket is made of wool, but _____ lining is made of silk.

13. Money can't buy _____ happiness.

14. Home is where _____ heart is.

15. The road to hell is paved with _____ good intentions.

C. Find the mistake in each sentence and correct it. Use the space provided if necessary.

16. Americans drink gallons of the coffee every day. _____.

17. I bought some interesting book. _____.

18. Sam listens to radio all day, every day. _____.

19. He has a old used car that needs painting. _____.

20. Children in that family are very bright. _____.

D. Write your answers to the following questions in complete sentences.

21. What kind of winter coat do you need?

_____.

22. Which restaurant in this area do you like best?

_____.

23. If you flew to another city and the airline lost your luggage, what would you need to buy?

_____.

24. What did you eat and drink between 5 P.M. and midnight yesterday?

_____.

25. What do you want for your birthday?

_____.

UNIT 20 ANSWERS

Each answer in numbers 1–10 counts two points.

A.
  1. a; a
  2. Some/∅; the
  3. a; ∅
  4. a; the
  5. some; ∅
  6. an; the
  7. ∅; the
  8. a; some/∅
  9. the; the
  10. an; some

B.
  11. ∅
  12. the
  13. ∅
  14. the
  15. ∅

C.
  16. . . . gallons of (∅) coffee
  17. . . . <u>an</u> interesting / . . . interesting <u>books</u>
  18. . . . <u>the</u> radio
  19. . . . <u>an</u> old
  20. <u>The</u> children . . .

D. 21.–25. Students' own sentences.

A. Fill in the blanks with *the* or Ø.

The historic and commercial center of Philadelphia is located between

(1) _____ Delaware and Schuylkill Rivers. A statue of its founder,

William Penn, watches over the city from the top of (2) _____ City

Hall. Once the capital of (3) _____ United States, Philadelphia is

visited year round by tourists who line up to see such attractions as

(4) _____ Liberty Bell in (5) _____ Independence

National Park and the home of Betsy Ross, the woman credited with sewing the

first American flag. The city is also home to a number of educational and cultural

institutions including (6) _____ University of Pennsylvania,

(7) _____ Temple University, and (8) _____ Philadelphia

Museum of Art. On weekends, students from (9) _____ Penn, as the

locals call the university, head for the clubs and restaurants of

(10) _____ South Street, the heart of the city's nightlife.

B. Write a sentence about each of the following (the first one has been done for you):

(a city you would like to visit)
I'd like to see Paris from the top of the Eiffel Tower.

11. (a school or institute you have attended)

_____.

12. (a river near where you live)

_____.

13. (a country you would like to visit)

_____.

14. (a museum you have visited)

_____.

15. (a monument you have seen or would like to see)

_____.

C. Write the or Ø in the spaces.

16. When most people think of New York, they think of _____ island of Manhattan.

17. Did you know that millions of New Yorkers have never visited _____ Statue of Liberty?

18. Is _____ Martha's Vineyard an island?

19. Of course. And so is _____ Nantucket.

20. People in _____ South have a reputation for being very friendly.

21. He learned to swim in _____ Lake Michigan, but he said he's never liked it much.

22. Imagine how easy it must be to swim in _____ Red Sea, with all that salt to hold you up.

23. I'd love to ride on an old steamboat down _____ Mississippi River.

24. I'd rather cross the U.S. by car and drive from New York to Los Angeles on _____ Route 66.

25. Naturally, I'd stop at _____ Grand Canyon on the way.

UNIT 21 ANSWERS

A.
1. the
2. ∅
3. the
4. the
5. ∅
6. the
7. ∅
8. the
9. ∅
10. ∅

B. 11.–15. Student's own sentences.

C.
16. the
17. the
18. ∅
19. ∅
20. the
21. ∅
22. the
23. the
24. ∅
25. the

A. Match each situation with one of the previous events.

1. _____ That's not what your mother told me, young man.

2. _____ Please clean out your desk and turn in your key to the office.

3. _____ Quick! Grab the food and bring it inside!

4. _____ I'd like to call my lawyer.

5. _____ I didn't know it had just come out of the oven.

6. _____ Great, but now I'll have to rent a tuxedo.

7. _____ You mean, the land we bought is worthless?

8. _____ Sorry we're late. You know how rush hour is.

a. She got burned.

b. He got caught in a lie.

c. They got ripped off.

d. She got fired.

e. They got held up in traffic.

f. He got invited to a black-tie dinner.

g. The picnic got rained out.

h. He got arrested.

B. Complete the following in the passive voice, using the appropriate tenses.

No one knows exactly how many movies (9) _____ (make) in the

United States since the art form was invented. Many of the first films

(10) _____ (shoot) in and around New York City, but the industry

soon moved west. By the 1920s, Hollywood, an undistinguished tract of land in

Southern California, (11) _____ (transform) into what

(12) _____ (call, sometimes) the Dream Factory. In the early years,

movies (13) _____ (produce) in a matter of days or weeks by

relatively small crews, and elaborate sets (14) _____ (build) on huge

sound stages to represent exotic places. Modern movies, of course, take much longer to make. Hundreds of people may (15) _____ (involve) in their

production, and most movies (16) _____ (film) on location. Up until

perhaps the end of the 1950s, movie studios had tremendous power over the stars

they created. Actors (17) _____ (tell) exactly what films they would

make, and many facets of their personal lives (18) _____ (arrange)

for them. But the so-called star system died out, and the whole industry

(19) _____ (change) by the advent of television. Going to the pictures

is no longer considered an exciting event but, thanks to the video cassette

recorder, more movies (20) _____ (see) than ever before.

C. Rewrite the following statements in the passive voice, including the agent where necessary.

21. Archaeologists have recently discovered mummies in Peru.

   _____.

22. The Incas buried them about 500 years ago.

   _____.

23. The mechanic is repairing my car today.

   _____.

24. They will hold the meeting in the school auditorium at 8 o'clock on Tuesday.

   _____.

25. A ten-year-old Romanian girl did all of these oil paintings.

   _____.

UNIT 22 ANSWERS

A. 1. b
2. d
3. g
4. h
5. a
6. f
7. c
8. e

B. 9. have been made
10. were shot
11. had been transformed
12. is sometimes called
13. were produced
14. were built
15. be involved
16. are filmed
17. were told
18. were arranged
19. was changed
20. are seen

C. 21. Mummies, have been discovered in Peru.
22. They were buried by the Incas about 500 years ago.
23. My car is being repaired today.
24. The meeting will be held in the school auditorium at 8 o'clock on Tuesday.
25. All of these oil paintings were done by a ten-year-old Romanian girl.

A. Fill in the blanks with the correct particle. Use *back, down, out,* or *to*.

1. As soon as you come _____ from the store, we can start making dinner.

2. When Joan's father passed _____ on the sidewalk, she thought he was dead.

3. After he came _____ in the hospital, the doctor told him he needed surgery.

4. She was offered a small role in a movie, but she turned it _____.

5. The pen I just bought doesn't write, so I'll have to take it _____ to the store.

B. Replace the underlined words in each sentence with a phrasal verb.

6. They <u>postponed</u> the party because of the snowstorm. _____.

7. He <u>distributed</u> the tests and told us to begin. _____.

8. Has your car ever <u>stopped working</u> in the middle of the freeway? _____.

9. He has to <u>collect</u> his children after school. _____.

10. Let's <u>telephone</u> Angela and Hugo and see if they want to go out for pizza. _____.

11. They never <u>go to restaurants</u> now because they're saving for a trip. _____.

12. How did she <u>discover</u> that we were planning a surprise party for her? _____.

13. I <u>encountered</u> an old friend on my way to work today. _____.

14. Please <u>remove</u> your coat and stay a while. _____.

15. When you <u>board</u> the bus, ask the driver if he stops at 16th Street. _____.

C. Use a phrasal verb in an appropriate statement, suggestion, or polite request for each of the following:

16. A friend asks you what a certain word means. You're not sure yourself and there's a dictionary at hand, so you say: _____.

17. Your uncle's garage is filled with stacks of old newspapers. He says he has no use for them, so you suggest: _____.

18. You need to leave the house for about 20 minutes. You don't want to take your baby, who has a bad cold, but you can't leave him alone, either. Your neighbor drops in for a cup of coffee, so you ask: _____.

19. Your brother is leaving the house to meet some friends for dinner at an elegant restaurant. He's wearing shorts and a T-shirt, so you say:

.

20. You're watching a cooking program on TV. The dish the chef is making looks delicious. You know you'll never remember the recipe, so you grab a pen and paper and say: _____.

D. In the following sentences, cross out the word that is in the wrong place and indicate its correct position in the sentence. Then substitute a pronoun for the object and write the verb + object phrase in the space.

Example: She pointed out a big mistake in the third paragraph. <u>pointed it out.</u>

21. He put his shoes, clothes, books, and all his sports equipment away.

_____.

22. You should start studying for exams now. If you put studying until the last minute off, you won't do well.

_____.

23. How can you buy shoes from a catalogue? Don't you want to try the shoes first on?

_____.

24. He didn't understand the homework, so we went again over the homework.

_____.

25. Margie wants to talk her plans with a good lawyer over.

_____.

UNIT 23 ANSWERS

A.
  1. back
  2. out
  3. to
  4. down
  5. back

B.
  6. put off
  7. handed out
  8. broken down
  9. pick up
 10. call up
 11. eat out
 12. find out
 13. ran into
 14. take off
 15. get on

C. Answers may vary. Some possibilities include:
 16. Let's look it up.
 17. Why don't you throw them out?
 18. Could you look after the baby for half an hour?
 19. Why don't you put on a jacket and tie?
 20. I'd better write this down.

D.
 21. He put away his shoes . . ./He put them away.
 22. If you put off studying . . ./If you put it off . . .
 23. Don't you want to try on the shoes first?/try them on
 24. . . . so we went over the homework again./went over it again
 25. Margie wants to talk over her plans with a good lawyer./talk them over

Name _____

Score _____
100

A. Combine each pair of sentences using adjective clauses.

1. A boy lives next door to me. He studies physics.

   _____.

2. Some students speak Italian. They love to watch Fellini movies.

   _____.

3. I don't like some people. They ask to copy my homework.

   _____.

4. The teacher helps some students. They've worked hard.

   _____.

5. Some students didn't study. They failed the exam.

   _____.

B. Put the words in the correct order to make sentences.

6. man/television/Apartment 4C/the/in/who/all/day/watches/lives

   _____.

7. I/just/Christmas/for/read/me/the/gave/book/that/you

   _____.

8. call/cousins/in/live/never/New Jersey/our/us/who

   _____.

9. the/which/all/illegible/notes/are/lent/he/me

   _____.

10. downstairs/supermarket/woman/saw/lives/he/the/who /at/the

   _____.

C. Complete the following to make true statements. Choose the appropriate relative pronoun.

11. I don't eat _____ (that/which/who) _____ .

12. _____ (that/which/who) _____ are crazy.

13. I like _____ (that/which/who) _____ .

14. _____ (that/which/who) _____ is very expensive.

15. This school needs _____ (that/which/who) _____ .

D. Choose the correct adjectives in the following sentences.

16. I asked George if he wanted to go on the picnic with us, but he just said he was busy. I don't think he found the plan particularly (exciting/excited).

17. I also invited Brian, who's traveled all over the world and has such great stories to tell. He's a much more (interesting/interested) person than George.

18. I was (fascinating/fascinated) by Brian's account of his trip to Turkey.

19. He seemed very (disappointing/disappointed) that he didn't have more time to spend there.

20. I don't think the American consulate was very (amused/amusing) by Brian's losing his passport.

21. They must find all those tourists with their little problems very (annoying/annoyed).

22. Brian said his flight was cheap. I was (tempting/tempted) to ask how much it cost, but I didn't.

23. He and I both love London. The last time I was there I was really (mystifying/mystified) by a language I heard some people speaking. It turned out to be English, and the speakers were from my hometown.

24. Brian and I agreed that prices in London are really (shocking/shocked).

25. We were (relieving/relieved) to get back home before our money ran out.

UNIT 24 ANSWERS

A.
1. The boy who lives next door to me studies physics.
2. The students who speak Italian love to watch Fellini movies.
3. I don't like people who ask to copy my homework.
4. The teacher helps students who have worked hard.
5. The students who didn't study failed the exam.

B.
6. The man who lives in Apartment 4C watches television all day.
7. I just read the book that you gave me for Christmas.
8. Our cousins who live in New Jersey never call us.
9. All the notes which he lent me are illegible.
10. He saw the woman who lives downstairs at the supermarket.

C. 11.–15. Student's own sentences.

D.
16. exciting
17. interesting
18. fascinated
19. disappointed
20. amused
21. annoying
22. tempted
23. mystified
24. shocking
25. relieved

A. Write the letter of the possible result in the space next to the appropriate *if* clause.

1. _____ If I don't take my umbrella,　a) I won't graduate.

2. _____ If I get wet,　b) I won't make good grades.

3. _____ If I'm in bed for a week,　c) it will probably rain.

4. _____ If I get behind in my studies,　d) my parents will be really upset.

5. _____ If I do really badly,　e) I may catch cold.

6. _____ If I have to repeat this year,　f) I'll miss school.

B. Answer the questions in complete sentences.

7. If a fire broke out in your house, what would you do first?

_____.

8. If you had time, what personal possessions would you try to save from the fire?

_____.

9. If you were confined to your house, what would you do?

_____.

10. If you could talk to anyone in history, who would it be?

_____.

11. If you could have any job you wanted (and the skills to do it), what would you choose?

_____.

C. Fill in the blank with the correct form of the verb in parentheses.

12. A: I just heard that you were in the hospital for a month. If I _____
(know) you were sick, I _____ (visit) you. What was wrong?

B: I lost control of my bike on a curve and fell down a hill. Luckily, I had on a helmet.

13. A: Wow. I wonder what _____ (happen) if you _____ (not have on) a helmet. How was your stay in the hospital?

14. B: Let's just say that if I never _____ (eat) hospital food again for the rest of my life, I _____ (be) very happy.

15. A: You poor thing! If my refrigerator _____ (not be) empty at the moment, I _____ (invite) you over for dinner tonight. How about this weekend?

16. If you _____ (tell) me what you'd like, I _____ (cook) it for you on Saturday.

17. A: Maria is so lucky. Her mother is Cuban and her father is from Beijing. When she _____ (finish) her degree, she _____ (be able) to teach three languages: English, Spanish, and Chinese.

18. B: If I _____ (speak) all those languages, I _____ (want) to work as an interpreter.

19. A: When you _____ (get) to the top of the hill, you _____ (see) a small church. Walk past it and turn left, and the hotel is right there.

20. B: Thanks. I _____ (be) back for more help if I _____ (not find) it.
    A: You'll find it.

D. Complete these conversations with *will*, *would*, *may*, *might*, *would have*, *might have*, or *may have* and the correct form of the verb in parentheses.

21. A: If I take that job, I _____ (need) to buy a car, I don't know.

22. B: Well, I hope not. You don't know how to take care of one. Remember the last car you had? If you'd had an accident in that, you _____ (be) killed.

23. A. Oh, probably not. If I decide to get a car, _____ (help/you) me pick it out?

24. A. If I'd known you were coming, I _____ (go) to the station to meet you.

25. B. I'm glad you didn't. There were so many people that I _____ (not see) you.

UNIT 25 ANSWERS

A. 1. c
2. e
3. f
4. b
5. a
6. d

B. 7.–11. Students' own sentences.

C. 12. had known, would have visited
13. would have happened, hadn't had on
14. eat, will be
15. weren't, would invite
16. tell, will cook
17. finishes, will be able
18. spoke, would want
19. get, will see
20. will be, don't find

D. 21. may need
22. would have been
23. will you help
24. would have gone
25. might not have seen

WORKBOOK ANSWER KEY

Unit 1

Simple Present: Habits, Routines, and Facts

EXERCISE 1

like; study; listen; raise; have; try; helps; rewrite; ask; helps

doesn't participate; interrupts; whispers; eats; drinks; pays attention; does

EXERCISE 2

Sentences will vary.
1. A good student works hard to improve his/her writing.
2. He/she studies hard. 3. She/he listens carefully to the directions. 4. He/she raises his/her hand when he/she has a question. 5. She/he tries to encourage other students.
6. A poor student doesn't participate in class. 7. He/she interrupts the teacher. 8. She/he whispers to other students.
9. He/she never pays attention. 10. She/he hardly ever does her/his assignments.

EXERCISE 3

2. Suzette and Raul write . . . 3. Yaniv and Valentina don't read . . . 4. Yaniv doesn't discuss . . . 5. Yaniv doesn't watch . . . 6. Jean Marc and Wan-Yin speak . . . 7. Su-Ling goes . . . 8. Roberto practices . . . 9. Mohammed watches . . . 10. Wan-Yin doesn't listen . . .

EXERCISE 4

Add "Do you . . ." to make questions with the ideas from Exercise 3. Answers will be "Yes, I do./No, I don't." Record of answers: "Yes, he/she does./No, he/she doesn't."

EXERCISE 5

2. changes 3. lives 4. swims 5. eats 6. builds 7. flies 8. washes 9. catches 10. breathes 11. sits

EXERCISE 6

Answers will vary.

EXERCISE 7

Answers will vary. Possible answers:
1. I sometimes . . . 2. I never . . . 3. I always . . .
4. I hardly ever . . . 5. I usually . . . 6. I seldom . . .
7. I rarely . . . 8. I often . . . 9. I sometimes . . .
10. I usually . . .

Unit 2

Present Progressive and Simple Present: Actions and States

EXERCISE 1

is acting; these days; isn't smiling; today; isn't eating; 's not smoking today.
now; 's fasting; This month; isn't eating, drinking, smoking; 's trying

EXERCISE 2

1. Is; typing; is 2. is using/'s using; is 3. are you filing; 'm not/am not; is 4. is dying/'s dying; am/'m watering 5. Are you checking; are you checking; am/'m checking 6. are they standing; are/'re punching 7. are they filling 8. are you wearing; 'm wearing 9. is he taking 10. is he quitting

EXERCISE 3

(1) is running   (2) competes   (3) has
(4) is training   (5) swims   (6) runs
(7) is swimming   (8) is running   (9) works
(10) is lifting   (11) is bicycling   (12) is
(13) eats   (14) is making   (15) eats/is eating
(16) is trying   (17) is   (18) is

EXERCISE 4

This exercise requires students to listen very carefully if all of their photographs are similar in theme. You may wish to have them all bring in pictures of two women, two men, two children, two people on the telephone, or two people playing a sport.

EXERCISE 5

(1) is   (2) are   (3) travel
(4) are staying   (5) have   (6) think
(7) is   (8) don't own   (9) are taking
(10) isn't/is not   (11) is   (12) is
(13) tries   (14) thinks
(15) doesn't understand   (16) knows

(17) are trying   (18) are treating
(19) take   (20) play   (21) doesn't know
(22) is training   (23) is learning   (24) is beginning
(25) are looking   (26) love   (27) seems
(28) belongs   (29) loves

EXERCISE 6

S = State/Quality   A = Action/Experience
1. S   2. S   3. A   4. S   5. A   6. S   7. A   8. S   9. A
10. A   11. S   12. S   13. A   14. S   15. A

EXERCISE 7

ACROSS
2. ensemble   8. opera   10. or   12. baaa   13. be   14. GE
15. SOS   16. echo   19. tete   20. torn   21. beta   22. HRS
23. nor   24. ED   25. cana   29. MC   30. finito   32. teachers
DOWN
1. together   3. SOB   4. EPA   5. mea   6. bra   7. la
9. research   11. record   13. bottom   15. seen   17. HRS
18. on   19. TB   25. CIA   26. ANC   27. NIH   28. ate
30. fe   31. or

Unit 3

Talking About the Future: *Be Going to* and *Will*

EXERCISE 1

Nancy's mother: We're going to go shopping this weekend; you'll look
Nancy: I'm not going to spend; I'll never wear
Nancy's mother: Your father and I will pay
Nancy: I'm going to wear
Tim: I'm going to wear
Nancy's mother: We're going to have
Nancy: Will you and Dad have
Nancy's mother: it'll be; I'll ask; tonight

EXERCISE 2

Questions and answers will vary.

EXERCISE 3

(1) will   (2) will   (3) won't/will not   (4) will   (5) will
(6) won't/will not   (7) will   (8) won't/will not want   (9) 'm going to/am going to   (10) 'm going to/am going to   (11) 'm going to /am going to   (12) 'm going to/am going to   (13) 'm going to/am going to/will   (14) will   (15) are going to/'re going to   (16) 'm going to/am going to

EXERCISE 4

Answers will vary.

EXERCISE 5

1. I'll get it right away.   2. I'll be on time from now on./It won't happen again.   3. I'm going to go in July.   4. I'll help you.
5. I'll call her as soon as I can.   6. I won't tell anyone.   7. It'll be better next year.   8. It won't happen again.

EXERCISE 6

ACROSS
1. fortune   6. Al   7. ok   9. AC   11. do   13. in   14. oh
15. saw   17. pie   18. spend   19. shelf   20. never
24. sweet   27. dad   28. ICU   29. rr   30. tu   31. ad
33. or   34. men   35. mom   37. sadness
DOWN
1. fa   2. old   3. non   4. EK   5. Cassandra   8. the future   10. cap   12. odd   13. its   14. oil   16. we
17. PE   21. ear   22. VD   23. round   24. Shame   25. El
26. eco   30. tea   32. dos   34. MS   36. Ms

Exercises for the TOEFL® Test

Units 1–3 Answer Key

1. B	4. C	7. B	10. D	13. D	16. B	19. D	22. D	25. A	28. A
2. B	5. B	8. C	11. A	14. A	17. B	20. C	23. A or B	26. A	29. C
3. A	6. A	9. B	12. C	15. B	18. A	21. C	24. A	27. C	30. B

Unit 4

Asking Questions: *Yes/No, Wh-,* Tag, Choice Questions

EXERCISE 1

2. Do; study   3. Is; living   4. Will; study   5. Would; eat
6. Is   7. Are; working   8. Am   9. Were; working   10. Was
11. Did; take   12. Do; sing

EXERCISE 2

Questions and answers will vary.

EXERCISE 3

2. You usually study on Saturday?   3. Your mother is living in the United States right now?   4. You'll study English next year?
5. You would eat meat?   6. English is a difficult language for you?   7. You're working right now?   8. I'm taller than you?
9. You were working last night?   10. Mathematics was your favorite subject in elementary school?   11. You took a vacation last summer?   12. You sometimes sing in the shower?

EXERCISE 4

Questions will vary.

EXERCISE 5

Questions may vary.
What do you think your strong points are?   Are you looking for a full-time or part-time position?   Where do you come from?
When did you leave your last job?   Why did you leave it?   What kind of computers do you know how to use?   When will you be available to work?   How will you get to work?   When can you start working?   How much do you expect to earn?

EXERCISE 6

Questions will vary.

EXERCISE 7

2. Who is the oldest? Ken . . .   3. Who played basketball in high school? Ken . . .   4. Who visited Korea last year? Joy . . .
5. Who will start college next year? Bill is entering . . .   6. Who is the youngest? Bill . . .   7. Who likes Chinese food? Joy . . .
8. Who has children? Ken . . .   9. Who likes sports? Ken . . .
10. Who is the middle child? Joy . . .   11. Who is married? Ken . . .   12. Who is single? Joy and Bill are . . .   13. Who is a pilot? Ken . . .   14. Who is artistic? Bill . . .   15. Who sings? Bill . . .

EXERCISE 8

3. When will he start . . .   4. What will he start in two months?   5. Who went with his uncle . . .   6. Who(m) did he go with . . .   7. Who found a nice apartment?   8. What did they find near the university?   9. Who needs a roommate?   10. What does Glenn need?   11. Who called several friends?   12. Who(m) did Glenn call?   13. Who else needs a roommate?   14. What does Sean need?
15. Who will share his apartment with Sean?   16. Who(m) will Glenn share his apartment with?

EXERCISE 9

Oral practice; intonation.

EXERCISE 10

Jim: I am
Catherine: isn't she?   Jim: she is
Catherine: don't you?   Jim: we do.
Catherine: won't you?   Jim: I will/we will.
Catherine: aren't you?   Jim: I am.
Guillermo: do you?   Chris: I don't; are you?
Chris: did you?   Guillermo: isn't it?
Chris: it is.   Guillermo: shouldn't it?

EXERCISE 11

Oral practice; intonation.

Unit 5

Modals of Probability and Possibility

1. is   2. must be   3. must work   4. could be   5. must use
6. could be; might be (or vice versa)   7. may/must/could;
may/could   8. doesn't have; could have   9. must not/;must
10. could might/must; could/might/must

1. She must like chocolate.   2. She might be a nurse.   3. He
must ride a motorcycle.   4. They must be related.   5. Natalya
couldn't be Oleg's mother.   6. It might not because Lin is sick.
7. He may not know that's rude.   8. She must be engaged.
9. She might not know how to drive.   10. She could be in the
wrong class.

2. They must be drug dealers.   3. They could/might/may have
inherited the money,   4. or they could/might/may have won the
car in a contest.   5. There must have been a dozen wine bottles.
6. They must be alcoholics.   7. Kathy and Tim
could/might/may have had a party,   8. or they
could/might/may have invited friends over for dinner.   9. Kathy
must have gone to one of those AA meetings.   10. She

could/might/may have been at a store near the church.
11. Tim must have gotten drunk and hit him.   12. Gladys, the
boy could/might/may have fallen off his bike.   13. Gladys, you
must be crazy.   14. You could/may/might be right.

1. could/may/might be taking a nap./could/may/might be
sleeping.
2. must not/couldn't be taking a nap./must not/couldn't be
sleeping.
3. must be grocery shopping.
4. must not/couldn't be grocery shopping.
5. must be walking the dog.
6. must have been drinking coffee.
7. may/might/could have been playing chess.
8. may/might/could have been reading.
9. may/might/could have been roller-blading.
10. must have been smoking.

1. B   2. B   3. B   4. B   5. B   6. A   7. C   8. C   9. B
10. C

Unit 6

Past Progressive and Simple Past with Time Clauses: *When, While,* and *As Soon As*

Answers will vary slightly, according to students' interpretations of
the pictures.

Case 1:   2. He was short and thin. He had curly/wavy hair and a
mustache.   3. I ran after him./I followed him./I chased him.

Case 2:   4. I was on Rodeo Drive (and I was) shopping.
5. Yes, he was average height. He was wearing a hat, sunglasses,
and a tie.   6. No, he didn't./No, he didn't have a mustache.
7. I shouted/yelled/screamed.

Case 3:   8. We were playing cards.   9. He was tall and thin.
He had a beard.   10. He was wearing a suit/tuxedo.   11. No,
he didn't./Yes, he did.   12. We shouted for/yelled for/called the
manager.

Answers will vary slightly.
1. A man with a beard was talking on the telephone.   2. A/The
security guard was watering the plants.   3. There was a line of
customers/people waiting./A lot of people/Six people were waiting
in line.   4. Two tellers were taking care of/waiting on
customers./There were two tellers taking . . .   5. A woman
wearing slippers and carrying a little dog in her purse was standing in
line./There was a woman . . .   6. A young couple was holding
hands and kissing (in the line)./There was a young couple . . .
7. A bald man with glasses and a mustache was reading the
newspaper (in line)./There was a bald man . . .   8. A young
woman was writing a check/signing something/filling out
something./There was a young woman . . .   9. A young mother
with a baby carriage was holding her baby./There was a young

mother . . . **10.** Just outside the door, a man was smoking./Just outside the door, there was . . . **11.** Another man was outside washing/cleaning the windows./There was another man . . .

Answers will vary slightly.
1. He was (sitting) at his desk (and he was) talking on the telephone. **2.** Yes, he was. He was watering the plants. **3.** Yes, there were. Another teller was talking to/taking care of/waiting on a customer./A man/An employee was outside cleaning/washing the windows./There was a man/an employee outside . . . **4.** Yes. (A lot of/Six customers were standing in line.) **5.** It was a woman. She was wearing slippers and carrying a little dog in her purse. She had long hair (she wore it up and in a bun). She was wearing a short-sleeved polka-dot dress and a scarf. **6.** It was a young mother. She had medium-length wavy/curly hair. She was pushing a baby carriage and holding her baby. She was wearing a dress/skirt. **7.** Yes, the man at the door was just standing there. He was smoking. **8.** It was 10:30/ten-thirty/half past ten. **9.** He was wearing a tank top/sleeveless shirt and bell-bottoms/bell-bottom pants. I think he was wearing a hat. Maybe it was a helmet. **10.** I was talking to/taking care of/waiting on a customer.

1. False—Veronica Rio ran after the thief when he stole her jewels. **2.** False—Ms. Rio was having a drink when the thief took her jewels./Ms. Rio ran after the thief as he took her jewels.

3. True **4.** False—While Eva Galor was shopping, the thief took her jewels. **5.** True **6.** False—As soon as/When the thief took her jewels, Eva said/shouted, "Stop! Thief!" **7.** True **8.** False—As soon as/When the Gentleman Jewel Thief took their jewels, the women shouted for/yelled for/called the manager./When the Gentleman Jewel Thief took their jewels, the women were playing cards. **9.** True **10.** False—When/While the Gentleman Jewel Thief was committing his crimes, he was polite/not rude to his victims.

1. When the thief stole her jewels, Veronica Rio ran after him. **2.** When the thief took her jewels, Ms. Rio was having a drink. When the thief took her jewels, Ms. Rio ran after him. **3.** The Gentlemen Jewel Thief began to talk to Veronica while she was having a drink. **4.** The thief took Eva Galor's jewels while she was shopping. **5.** When the second robbery took place, the thief was wearing sunglasses, a hat, and a tie. **6.** Eva shouted, "Stop! Thief!" as soon as/when the thief took her jewels. **7.** When the third crime took place, Mrs. Rox and her friends were playing cards. **8.** The women shouted for/yelled for/called the manager as soon as/when the Gentlemen Jewel Thief took their jewels./The women were playing cards when the Gentleman Jewel Thief took their jewels. **9.** When the thief committed these crimes, he was probably wearing a disguise. **10.** The Gentleman Jewel Thief was polite/not rude to his victims when/while he was committing his crimes.

Exercises for the TOEFL® Test

Units 4–6 Answer Key

1. D	**3.** A	**5.** A	**7.** D	**9.** A	**11.** B	**13.** B	**15.** B	**17.** C	**19.** C
2. D	**4.** C	**6.** C	**8.** B	**10.** B	**12.** C	**14.** D	**16.** C	**18.** D	**20.** A

Unit 7

Similarities and Differences: Comparatives, Superlatives, As . . . As, As, Not As . . . As

2. more; than **3.** more; than **4.** most **5.** neater; than **6.** more than **7.** more; than **8.** more; than **9.** less; than **10.** more; than **11.** more than **12.** most

Answers will vary.

1. the most; the least **2.** longer than **3.** thicker than **4.** wider than **5.** the biggest **6.** the tightest **7.** curlier than **8.** more carefully than **9.** less popular than **10.** more friends than

1. T **2.** F **3.** F **4.** T **5.** F **6.** T **7.** T **8.** T **9.** F **10.** F **11.** F **12.** T

1. less; than   **2.** as; as   **3.** as many; does/takes   **4.** as; as
5. the most; the least   **6.** as; as   **7.** as many; as   **8.** as; as;
does   **9.** as; as; does/talks   **10.** more than; does

1. Mr. and Mrs. Callahan, Johnny is not doing as well . . .
2. Johnny doesn't seem . . .   **3.** Johnny doesn't concentrate . . .
4. Johnny's spelling isn't . . .   **5.** When learning new lessons,
Johnny isn't . . .   **6.** Johnny isn't quite as . . .   **7.** Johnny
doesn't read . . .   **8.** Johnny isn't as . . .   **9.** In music class,
Johnny doesn't . . .   **10.** All in all, Johnny isn't . . .

Unit 8

Measure Words and Quantifiers

2. a loaf   **3.** a carton of/a dozen   **4.** a head   **5.** a jar
6. a can/a bag   **7.** a box   **8.** a bunch   **9.** a bottle
10. a carton/a pint/a quart

Sentences will vary.

1. bananas C   **2.** bread NC   **3.** eggs C   **4.** lettuce NC
5. mayonnaise NC   **6.** dog food NC   **7.** cereal NC   **8.**
radishes C   **9.** white wine NC   **10.** ice cream NC

Avocado Ice Cream
2 cups of milk
1/2 cup of granulated sugar
1/4 teaspoon of salt
2 eggs
1 cup of heavy cream

2 teaspoons of lemon extract
1 cup of mashed avocado

Cheese Enchiladas
1 dozen corn tortillas
1 pint of heated enchilada sauce
1 tablespoon of chopped onion
1 pound of shredded cheddar cheese
8 ounces of sour cream

2. There is some/a little juice . . .   **3.** There is some/a little
juice . . .   **4.** There is some/a little juice . . .   **5.** through
8. There is a lot of/lots of/a great deal of juice in the glass.

Sentences may vary.

1. All of the children are in the swimming pool.   **2.** Most of/a
lot of/the children are in the swimming pool.   **3.** A few children
are diving into the pool.   **4.** There are a lot of/lots of children in
the pool.   **5.** Several/Some children are lying next to the pool.
6. Most of/a lot of the children are out of the pool.   **7.** There are
a few children in the pool.   **8.** There are a couple of children in
the pool.   **9.** There are no children in the pool.

Unit 9

Degree Complements: *Too, Enough,* and *Very*

1. too   **2.** not enough   **3.** not; enough.   **4.** too   **5.** enough
6. enough   **7.** enough.   **8.** enough.   **9.** enough.   **10.**
enough.   **11.** too   **12.** too   **13.** too

Answers will vary greatly.

At the caterer's
  1. No, ice cream isn't sophisticated enough, and it has too
many calories.
  2. No, it's too rich and not unusual enough.
  3. No, they're too heavy for dessert.

At the department store
  4. No, it's too tight.
  5. No, it's too long, and I couldn't move easily enough.
  6. Definitely not, it's too sexy and has too many spots.

7. Yes, it's perfect. It's not too short, and it's loose enough to be comfortable.

Auditioning musicians

8. No, they play too wildly, and there's not enough space for their equipment.

9. No, they play too quietly and seriously.

10. No, they sing too loudly, and they're not sophisticated enough.

11. Perfect. They play softly enough, and the room isn't too small for four musicians.

(1) too many   (2) too few   (3) too much   (4) too much
(5) too little   (6) too little   (7) too many.   (8) too much
(9) too much   (10) too few

Sentences will vary.

Exercises for the TOEFL® Test

Units 7–9 Answer Key

1. C	4. C	7. A	10. C	13. A
2. D	5. B	8. C	11. D	14. B
3. D	6. B	9. D	12. B	15. D

16. C	19. C	22. D	25. D	28. C
17. D	20. B	23. C	26. C	29. B
18. B	21. D	24. A	27. D	30. C

Unit 10

Giving Advice and Expressing Opinions: *Should, Ought To, Need To, Must, Had Better, Could,* and *Might*

EXERCISE 1

Sentences will vary.

2. You should explain that your heritage is important to you.

3. You should take her to a game with you.   4. You shouldn't do things just "to be like the other kids."

1. You should sit down with your husband and tell him what's on your mind.   2. If you both have jobs, he ought to do half of the housework.   3. You should take turns making dinner and washing the dishes.   4. You shouldn't pick up or wash his clothes if he drops them on the floor.

1. First of all, you shouldn't listen to your friends but should decide what's important to you.   2. You ought to talk to someone at your local community college about careers in nursing

3. You should try to talk to a nurse about his or her work.

4. You should definitely change jobs if you're very dissatisfied.

EXERCISE 2

Sentences will vary.

1. He ought to look for a job with a band.   2. He shouldn't expect to become famous overnight.   3. He needs to pay the ticket immediately.   4. He should drive more carefully.   5. She ought to try to replace it.   6. She doesn't need to tell him she lost it.   7. She needs to get a really big key ring that's easy to

find.   8. She should always put her car keys in the same place.

9. He needs to call a plumber.   10. He shouldn't try to fix the pipes himself.

EXERCISE 3

1. must   2. should   3. must   4. should   5. should
6. must not   7. should   8. must   9. must   10. must not

EXERCISE 4

Answers may vary.

1. had better/should   2. had better
2. shouldn't   4. should/ought to
5. had better not   6. had better
7. should/ought to   8. had better
9. ought to/should   10. had better not

Sentences with *should, ought to, had better,* or their negative forms will vary. Suggestions are

1. You should be more careful with your allowance. I can't give you more money every time you need some.   2. Do you think I ought to major in chemistry?   3. You had better quit smoking if you want to live much longer.   4. You shouldn't drive this care on the freeway. It's too old to go that fast.

EXERCISE 5

Migalie: should; could Victoria: could Migalie: could Victoria: could Migalie: should; should; Victoria: should; might Migalie: might Victoria: should Migalie: should

EXERCISE 6

Sentences will vary greatly.
1. He must bring a . . . to the Bureau of Motor Vehicles. *Explanation:* Identification is required. "Must" implies that it is absolutely necessary. **2.** He might fail the . . . if he doesn't learn all the rules of the road. *Explanation:* It's a real possibility but not a certainty. **3.** He shouldn't be nervous if he's studied enough for the test. *Explanation:* It's normal to be nervous before a test, but if he feels prepared for it, it will probably go well. A simple modal verb is used. **4.** He ought to . . . before the test. *Explanation:* It's a good idea to practice parallel parking. This is simple, friendly advice. **5.** Angelica must get . . . *Explanation:* This is required for registration. **6.** She ought to . . . *Explanation:* It's a good idea to register early so she can get the classes she wants. **7.** She should find . . . *Explanation:* It's not necessary, but it's a good idea. **8.** She needs to buy . . . *Explanation:* This may be a matter of some urgency if the books are likely to sell out quickly. "Need" is slightly stronger than "should." **9.** I must remember to buy her . . . *Explanation:* It's not obligatory, and I am free to do what I choose, but I will feel terrible if I don't, so a strong modal is used. **10.** I could bake . . . *Explanation:* It's a possibility or option. **11.** I'd better remind my father about it. *Explanation:* My mother would be seriously hurt if he forgot about it, so it's very important that I remind him. **12.** They ought to start . . . *Explanation:* It's always a good idea. **13.** They mustn't turn . . . *Explanation:* They are required to turn it in on time or take a lower grade. **14.** They must type . . . *Explanation:* It's obligatory. The teacher will not accept handwritten papers. **15.** They need to go . . . *Explanation:* They can't do research without consulting reference materials. This is not just a good idea, but a necessity. **16.** Diego ought to call . . . *Explanation:* It's a good idea, especially if he's not sure what's wrong. **17.** He should go . . . *Explanation:* It's a good idea. **18.** He could take . . . if he has a headache or fever. *Explanation:* It's one possibility or option.

EXERCISE 7

Answers will vary.

EXERCISE 8

Discussions will vary.

EXERCISE 9

Sentences will vary.
1. . . . should work outside the home if they want to.
2. Men should wash clothes as often as women do.
3. Boys ought to learn . . .
4. Girls ought to learn . . .
5. Boys and girls should go
6. Women should participate . .
7. Women should become . . .
8. Teenagers shouldn't be able . . .
9. Students shouldn't study . . .

Unit 11

Modals of Necessity and Prohibition: *Have To, Do Not Have To, Must/Must Not*

EXERCISE 1

True sentences: 1, 2, 6, 8, 9, and 11.

EXERCISE 2

2. you do   3. Does she have to   4. she doesn't have to   5. Do we have to   6. must   7. do we have to   8. mustn't/must not
9. have to   10. Do we have to   11. mustn't/must not
12. have to   13. must   14. have to

EXERCISE 3

2. have to   3. have to   4. does Irene have to; has to   5. have to   6. has to   7. has to   8. have to   9. have to   10. have to

EXERCISE 4

2. You mustn't drive . . .   3. You mustn't go in . . .   4. You mustn't take . . .   5. You mustn't push.   6. You mustn't bring/have . . .   7. You mustn't break . . .   8. You mustn't have/bring pets/that dog here.   9. You mustn't eat or drink . . .
10. You mustn't hit . . .

EXERCISE 5

2. must not/ mustn't   3. have to; must not/mustn't
4. doesn't have to   5. don't have to   6. have to
7. mustn't/must not   8. has to   9. doesn't have to
10. have to/must

EXERCISE 6

Answers will vary.

EXERCISE 7

(1) didn't have to   (2) have to/must   (3) had to   (4) did you have to   (5) had to   (6) had to   (7) didn't have to

(8) did you have to   (9) had to   (10) have to/must   (11) must/have to   (12) mustn't/must not   (13) do I have to/must I   (14) have to/must

EXERCISE 8

Answers will vary.

Unit 12

Expressing Likes and Dislikes

EXERCISE 1

1. does too   2. don't either   3. doesn't either   4. do too   5. do too   6. doesn't either   7. do too   8. don't either   9. do too   10. doesn't either

EXERCISE 2

1. Ramon studies Spanish, and so does . . .   2. I don't understand Greek, and neither do my friends.   3. Ann doesn't like liver, and neither does . . .   4. Cheryl loves animals, and so do . . .   5. Elizabeth loves the English language, and so do . . .   6. Maria doesn't like to write in English, and neither does Dora.   7. Gennadiy listens to classical music, and so do I.   8. She doesn't listen to rock and roll, and neither do I. 9. I like the teacher's new haircut, and so do . . . 10. Roberto doesn't like it, and neither does David.

EXERCISE 3

Errors are indicated in parentheses, corrections follow the word in italics.
1. . . . and so (is) does Debbie.   2. . . . and my brother doesn't (neither) either.   3. . . . and neither (Fathi can) can Fathi. 4. . . . and Alonzo (didn't) did too.   5. . . . and (either) neither did Irene.   6. . . . and Sato (isn't) hasn't either.   7. . . . and you (was) were too.   8. . . . and (neither) so was Sheila.   9. . . . and (either) neither will Ed.   10. . . . and so (has) does Patty.

EXERCISE 4

2. G   3. C   4. E   5. D   6. J   7. K   8. A   9. F   10. H 11. I

EXERCISE 5

1. sort of/kind of   3. Brian: I did too./So did I. Daniel: I don't either./Neither do I.   4. Brian: I am too./So am I. Daniel: Sort of./Kind of.   5. Brian: I don't either/Neither do I.   6. Brian: So am I./I am too.   8. Brian: So am I!/I am too!   10. Brian: Sort of./Kind of. Daniel: Kind of./Sort of.

EXERCISE 6

Answers will vary. The gerunds to be circled are
LEFT-BRAIN: doing, sewing, working, writing, doing, meeting, buying, speaking, competing
RIGHT-BRAIN: swimming, skiing, bicycling, thinking, dancing, making, fishing, running, meeting, shopping, rearranging, decorating
The infinitives to be underlined are
LEFT-BRAIN: to plan, (to) arrange, to collect, to read
RIGHT-BRAIN: to relax, (to) do, to paint, (to) sketch, to sing
Gerunds to be circled: 21; infinitives to be underlined: 9

EXERCISE 7

Answers will vary.
1. gerund   2. gerund and gerund   3. gerund or infinitive 4. gerund or infinitive   5. gerund   6. gerund   7. gerund or infinitive   8. gerund   9. gerund   10. gerund and gerund

EXERCISE 8

Group activity.

Exercises for the TOEFL® Test

Units 10–12 Answer Key

1. A	4. C	7. C	10. C	13. B	16. D	19. A	22. D	25. C	28. D
2. C	5. C	8. C	11. C	14. C	17. A	20. B	23. A	26. B	29. C
3. D	6. B	9. C	12. A	15. D	18. A	21. D	24. D	27. A	30. D

Unit 13

Present Perfect: *Since* and *For*

EXERCISE 1

Past: **1.** She wanted to be . . . when she was a child.
2. She moved . . .   **3.** She began . . .

Present: **1.** She is studying . . .   **2.** She wants . . .
3. She is volunteering . . .

Began in the past and continues now: **2.** She has studied . . .
3. She has wanted . . .

EXERCISE 2

Sentences will vary.

EXERCISE 3

Donor: haven't eaten
Donor: have given
Donor: haven't donated
Donor: haven't had
Donor: haven't been
Donor: have been; have lived

Interviewer: Have you given
Interviewer: has it been
Interviewer: Have you had
Interviewer: Have you been
Interviewer: Have you traveled

EXERCISE 4

Answers will vary.

EXERCISE 5

Count Dracula: since
Stoker: for; since
Count Dracula: since; since
Stoker: since
Count Dracula: since
Stoker: since; for

EXERCISE 6

Sentences may vary.
1. Dr. Moreau has worked at Mercy Hospital for _____ years.
2. Dr. Jekyll has worked at the hospital since 1978.   **3.** Dr. Zhivago and Nurse Nightengale have worked at the hospital for _____ years.
4. Dr. Faust has worked at the hospital for _____ years.   **5.** Nurse Ratchet has worked at the hospital for _____ years.   **6.** Dr. Doolittle has worked at the hospital since 1973.   **7.** Dr. Spock has worked at the hospital for _____ years.   **8.** Nurse Candystripe has worked at the hospital for _____ years.   **9.** Nurse Shark has worked at the hospital since 1984.   **10.** Dr. Livingston has worked at the hospital since 1969.   **11.** Dr. Freud and Dr. Spock have worked at the hospital since 1988.

EXERCISE 7

1. Lisa has taken that medicine since 1997.   **2.** Have you wanted to be a surgeon since . . .   **3.** Larry has been . . . since 1989.   **4.** My stomach hasn't hurt since . . .
5. Joe has delivered flowers to the hospital for two years.
6. Sylvia has known my doctor since they met . . .   **7.** It hasn't rained since 5:00.   **8.** The doctor has been in the room with Doug for thirty minutes.   **9.** Medical technology has been improving since the last century.   **10.** She hasn't taken any X-rays since 1995.

Unit 14

Present Perfect and Simple Past: *Ever* and *Never, Already* and *Yet*

EXERCISE 1

(1) began   **(2)** flew   **(3)** told   **(4)** has flown   **(5)** has met   **(6)** has seen   **(7)** went   **(8)** saw   **(9)** has done
(10) jumped   **(11)** rode   **(12)** hasn't been   **(13)** crashed   **(14)** had   **(15)** had   **(16)** fought   **(17)** won   **(18)** has been   **(19)** have

Answers will vary.
1. Have you ever found . . .   2. Have you ever flown . . .
3. Have you ever fought . . .   4. Have you ever broken . . .
5. Have you ever given . . .   6. Have you ever met . . .
7. Have you ever had a . . .   8. Have you ever worn . . .
9. Have you ever ridden . . .   10. Have you ever seen . . .

EXERCISE 3

Answers will vary.

EXERCISE 4

1. Have you called/telephoned your travel agent yet?   2. Have you already bought your (air)plane ticket?   3. Have you ever lost a plane/an airplane ticket on a trip?   4. Have you already made your hotel reservations?   5. Have you packed your suitcase yet?
6. Have you found a pet/cat sitter yet?   7. Have you already gotten your passport?   8. Have you already applied for a visa?
9. Have you changed your money yet?   10. Have you read any travel books yet?   11. Have you ever missed a flight/plane?
12. Have you ever taken someone else's suitcase/bag at the airport?

Unit 15

Present Perfect Progressive

EXERCISE 1

2. He has been sleeping.   3. He has been dreaming.
4. He has been lifting boxes.   5. She has been unpacking dishes.   6. They have been moving furniture.   7. They have been moving into a new house.   8. They have been sitting in the sun.   9. They have been swimming.   10. They have been looking for shells.

EXERCISE 2

Questions and answers will vary.
1. How long has he been sleeping?/He's been sleeping for a couple of hours.   2. What has he been dreaming about?/He's been dreaming about his final exams.   3. Why has he been having a nightmare?/Because he's been studying all week.
4. What have they been doing?/They've been moving into a new house.   5. How long have they been moving furniture./They've been moving furniture all day.   6. Who has been lifting heavy boxes?/The man has been lifting heavy boxes.   7. What has the woman been doing?/She's been unpacking dishes.   8. How long have they been sitting in the sun?/They've been sitting in the sun for three hours.   9. What have they been doing at the beach?/They've been swimming.
10. What have they been looking for?/They've been looking for shells.

EXERCISE 3

Answers will vary. The pattern will follow "Have you been speaking only English/talking to your classmates?" and so on. The answers will include "Yes, I've been speaking . . ./She's been speaking . . ." and so on.

EXERCISE 4

Sentences will vary.

EXERCISE 5

Jimmy: haven't been sleeping
Joel: Have you been feeling
Jimmy: haven't been feeling; have been bothering
Joel: Has something been happening; has been worrying
Jimmy: have been thinking; 've been studying
Joel: Have you been studying; asking
Jimmy: have been memorizing; have been trying

EXERCISE 6

(1) have been reading   (2) have been reading   (3) have; realized   (4) has been   (5) have been collecting   (6) has been waking up   (7) has had   (8) has been   (9) has been working   (10) has been setting up

Exercises for the TOEFL® Test

Units 13–15 Answer Key

1. C	5. C	9. C	13. B	17. D	21. D	25. B	29. A
2. D	6. A	10. A	14. C	18. D	22. A	26. C	30. D
3. A	7. B	11. D	15. B	19. D	23. D	27. B	31. C
4. B	8. D	12. B	16. C	20. B	24. B	28. A	32. A

Unit 16

Making Offers with *Would You Like*

EXERCISE 1

Would you like a table by the window?   Would you like some coffee?   Would you like sugar or cream in your coffee?   Would you like to order now?   What would you like?   How would you like your eggs?   Would you like me to tell the cook to make them over easy?   Would you like eggs, too?   Would you like anything else?

EXERCISE 2

Sentences will vary.

First Date   2. Yes, thank you. I'd like that very much.   3. What kind of restaurant would you like to go to?   4. I prefer French or Italian restaurants.   5. What movie would you like to see?
6. I'd really like to see _____.

One Year Later   7. Want to stay home and watch the football game?   8. I'd really rather go country-western dancing.
9. Want to order out for pizza?   10. No, I'd rather have Chinese food.   11. Well, do you want to go bowling and eat at the bowling alley instead?   12. Sure.

EXERCISE 3

Sentences will vary.
1. No, thank you, but I would like something to drink.
2. Want me to help you with your homework, son? Yeah, that would be great. *Explanation:* Both the offer and acceptance are quite informal because the speakers are father and son.
3. Would you like me to wash your windshield? Thanks.

Explanation: The gas station attendant is doing his job. The exchange might be fairly formal if the two people don't know each other.   4. Would you like me to help you with those packages? Yes, please. That's very kind of you. *Explanation:* This is a polite, formal exchange between strangers.
5. Would you like me to phone someone for you? No, thank you. I'm waiting for my son. He'll be here soon. *Explanation:* The man offering help is concerned for the older man and speaks to him respectfully.   6. Want some lemonade? Sure. Thanks. *Explanation:* This is a very informal exchange between friends.
7. This is a great city. Let me show you around. That would be great, but I'm going to be tied up in this meeting all day. *Explanation:* This is a polite, fairly informal exchange between two people who don't know each other well.   8. Want an aspirin? Yes, please. *Explanation:* This an informal exchange between husband and wife.

EXERCISE 4

Sentences will vary.
1. Would you like me to call a doctor for you? No, thanks. I think I'll be OK.   2. Would you like me to show you around? Thanks, but I think I can manage.   3. Would you like some more coffee? No, thank you. We'd like the check, please.
4. Would you like me to see if we have your size in the back? Yes, please. That's very kind of you.   5. Do you want another hot dog? Sure. Thanks.   6. Would you like to see our video of the Greek islands? Yes, thanks. That would be great.

Unit 17

Requests and Permission: *Can, Could, Will, Would, May*

EXERCISE 1

Sentences will vary.
1. Would you please tell me which bus goes to the beach?
2. Could you tell me how often the bus stops here?
3. Would you mind opening the door for me? I've got my hands full here.   4. Will you please wake me up half an hour early.
5. Could you please show us where our seats are.   6. Will you please pick up some milk on your way home.   7. Can you lend me some eggs? I've run out, and I'm making a cake.   8. Could you please tell me where the immigration building is?   9. Would

you mind handing me that box of cake mix on the top shelf, please?   10. Will you please sing my favorite song?

EXERCISE 2

Answers may vary.
1. I'd like to, but I don't understand it myself.   2. I'm sorry, but I don't have any money with me.   3. I'm sorry, but I can't help you. I'm scared of heights.   4. I'm sorry, but I've never changed a tire, and I'm not very good with tools.   5. I'm sorry but we're all out of orange juice.   6. I'd like to, but I have to finish this report.
7. I'm sorry, but my care is in the garage, too.   8. I'd like to, but

I have to be downtown in ten minutes.   9. I'm sorry, but I don't know how this copier works.

Answers will vary.
1. Sure, I'd be glad to.   2. Yes, I will.   3. Of course, I'd be happy to.   4. Certainly, no problem.   5. Yes, I will.   6. I'd be happy to.   7. Sure, why not?   8. Yes, I will.   9. I'd be glad to.
10. Yeah, I guess so.

EXERCISE 4

Questions will vary.
1. May I spend the night at Suzy's?   2. Would you excuse me for a moment?   3. Do you mind if I smoke?   4. Would you

mind if I brought a friend to class?   5. May I put one of these posters in your window, please?   6. Do you mind if I leave work early today?   7. May I open the window a little, please?
8. May I check this out?   9. May I park here?   10. May I please visit my counselor?

EXERCISE 5

1. I'm sorry, but you can't sleep at Suzy's on a school night.
2. Certainly.   3. I'm sorry, but I'm allergic to cigarette smoke.
4. Certainly. I'd like to meet your friend.   5. Sure, go right ahead.   6. I'm sorry, but I need you to finish this project today.
7. Yes, you may.   8. I'm afraid not. Magazines may only be read in the library.   9. Sorry, but there's no parking on this block.
10. Yes, you may.

Unit 18

Used to with *Still* and *Anymore*

EXERCISE 1

1. T   2. T   3. F   4. F   5. T   6. T   7. F   8. T   9. F
10. T

EXERCISE 2

Answers will vary, but all will include *used to/didn't used to* + verb. Questions are
1. Where did you used to live?   2. . . . what did you used to play?   3. . . . what did you used to do after school?
4. . . . did your parents used to read to you?   5. . . . did you used to have?   6. What did you used to look like?   7. Who used to be . . .   8. Did you used to live . . .   9. Where did you used to . . .   10. Did you used to wear glasses?

EXERCISE 3

(1) used to	(2) used to	(3) anymore
(4) used to	(5) anymore	(6) anymore
(7) anymore	(8) used to	(9) anymore
(10) used to	(11) anymore	(12) used to
(13) anymore	(14) used to	(15) anymore
(16) used to	(17) anymore	

EXERCISE 4

1. T   2. T   3. F   4. T   5. F   6. F   7. F   8. T   9. T
10. F

EXERCISE 5

Greta: isn't anymore; still is
Holly: Does he still wear; Does he still play
Greta: doesn't play rock and roll anymore
Holly: Does she still look
Greta: doesn't have long brown hair anymore; is still; still has; still does; still does

EXERCISE 6

1. She always used to go dancing on weekends.   2. No, she does not read novels anymore.   3. Yes, she sometimes helps them/the kids with their homework.   4. She used to travel often.   5. No, she seldom/hardly ever used to cook and clean.
6. Yes, she often cooks and cleans now.   7. No, she never goes dancing anymore.   8. Yes, she still goes to the beach.   9. No, she seldom/hardly ever goes out to eat anymore.   10. She usually does the laundry every day.

Exercises for the TOEFL® Test
Units 16–18 Answer Key

1. C	4. A	7. C	10. A	13. C	16. B	19. B
2. B	5. C	8. C	11. C	14. B	17. D	20. A
3. D	6. B	9. D	12. B	15. A	18. D	

Unit 19
Past Perfect: *Before* and *After*

EXERCISE 1

BEFORE ACCIDENT: 2. He had never seen so many doctors.
3. He had never felt so much pain. 4. He had played tennis.
5. He had sailed. 6. He had had a dog. 7. He had been engaged to Debbie.

AFTER ACCIDENT: 2. He had a lot of operations. 3. He had to learn to get around in a wheelchair. 4. He needed a specially trained dog. 5. He got Connie.

NOW: 2. He's learning to play table tennis. 3. He sails.
4. He competes in races. 5. He's engaged to Patty.

EXERCISE 2

1. How many times had you been in the hospital before the accident? Never./I had never been in the hospital. 2. What sports had you played before the accident? I had played tennis and (I had) sailed. 3. Had you run in races? No, I hadn't. 4. Before Connie, had you had a dog? Yes, I had. 5. Had you been engaged to Patty? No, I hadn't./I'd been engaged to Debbie.

EXERCISE 3

2. He slept late because nobody had . . ./Because nobody had set the alarm, he . . . 3. Nobody had done the laundry, so Allen didn't have . . . 4. There wasn't any coffee because nobody had gone . . ./Because nobody had gone grocery shopping, there . . . 5. There wasn't any gas in the car because Allen had forgotten to . . ./Because Allen had forgotten to go to the gas station, there . . . 6. His boss had told him not to be late anymore, so he was . . . 7. While he was driving, he looked in the mirror and saw that he hadn't combed . . . 8. He realized that he hadn't cashed his paycheck when he got . . ./When he got to the gas station, he realized that he hadn't cashed . . . 9. As soon as he got to work, Allen found that he had . . ./Allen found that he had left his wallet at the gas station as soon as . . . 10. When he noticed there were no cars in the parking lot, he realized that he had forgotten . . ./He realized that he had forgotten it was Saturday when he noticed there were . . .

EXERCISE 4

The number in bold before the verb is the correct choice.
2. He 1/locked the doors, 2/turned off the lights, and 3/went upstairs.

3. When he 2/got upstairs, he 3/realized that he had 1/forgotten to take out the garbage.
4. He 1/went back downstairs and 2/took out the garbage.
5. When he 1/went upstairs to brush his teeth, he 2/heard a noise.
6. By the time he 2/got to the door, the noise 1/had stopped.
7. Mr. Wilson 1/went back upstairs and 2/heard the noise again. It 3/sounded like someone crying.
8. He 1/went back downstairs, and again, by the time he 3/reached the door, the noise had 2/stopped.
9. By that time, Mr. Wilson had 1/gone up and down the stairs so many times that he 2/was dizzy. He 3/went to bed.
10. The next morning when Mr. Wilson 2/went outside to get the newspaper, he 3/saw what had 1/caused the noise the night before.
11. He 2/was surprised to see that the cat 1/had had kittens. These sentences should be checked: 3, 6, 8, 9, 10, 11.

EXERCISE 5

2. He had walked the dog and let the cat out. 3. He was going upstairs to brush his teeth. 4. He went (back) downstairs (when he heard the noise). 5. To take out the garbage./He first went back downstairs to take out the garbage. 6. After he went upstairs./He heard the noise after he went upstairs. 7. He felt dizzy because he had gone up and down the stairs so many times. 8. He had walked up the stairs four times. 9. The/His cat had./The/His cat had caused the noise.

EXERCISE 6

(2) went	(3) went	(4) had never worn
(5) (had) been	(6) has learned	(7) has also learned
(8) visited	(9) was	(10) had ever seen
(11) was	(12) was	(13) stayed
(14) fished/had fished		(15) grew
(16) fell	(17) got	(18) is
(19) is	(20) has	(21) has
(22) is teaching	(23) is learning	(24) isn't
(25) has written		

Unit 20

Articles: *The, A/An,* and *Some* Ø

EXERCISE 1

I/Indian; Prize; D/Indians
D/book; D/customs; D/ceremonies; D/Indians; I/girl;
I/plantation; D/beans; D/plants
D/story; D/army; D/Indians; I/property; I/soldiers
D/violence; I/peace; D/Indians

EXERCISE 2

(1) a (2) the (3) the (4) the (5) a (6) the
(7) the (8) the (9) a (10) the (11) the (12) the
(13) the (14) the (15) the (16) a (17) the
(18) The

EXERCISE 3

1. a 2. A 3. Ø 4. an 5. a 6. a 7. An 8. Ø 9. an
10. Ø 11. a 12. a 13. Ø 14. Ø 15. Ø 16. Ø

EXERCISE 4

(1) a (2) some (3) the (4) the (5) a (6) The
(7) the (8) an (9) an (10) the (11) the
(12) The (13) some (14) some (15) the (16) the
(17) the

EXERCISE 5

(1) the (2) Ø (3) Ø (4) Ø (5) the (6) The (7) Ø
(8) The/Ø (9) the (10) Ø (11) Ø (12) Ø (13) Ø
(14) Ø (15) Ø (16) Ø (17) Ø

EXERCISE 6

(1) The (2) the (3) the (4) the (5) the (6) A
(7) the (8) An (9) a (10) a (11) the (12) the
(13) the (14) The (15) the (16) The (17) The
(18) an

Unit 21

Articles with Names of Places

EXERCISE 1

Words to be circled are in parentheses; names that take articles are underlined.

(North America); (Canada); the United States; the Arctic Ocean; the Atlantic Ocean; the Pacific Ocean; (Alaska); (Canada); (Quebec); (Prince Edward Island); (Canada); (Montreal); (Toronto); (Canada); (Mount Logan); (Mount St. Elias); (Canada); Rocky Mountains. The Great Lakes; (Lake Huron); (Canada); the St. Lawrence River; the Mackenzie River

EXERCISE 2

Individual writing practice.

EXERCISE 3

Answers will vary.

EXERCISE 4

(1) Ø (2) the (3) Ø (4) Ø (5) Ø (6) Ø (7) Ø
(8) the (9) Ø (10) Ø (11) Ø (12) the (13) the
(14) the

Exercises for the TOEFL® Test
Units 19–21 Answer Key

1. D	4. B	7. A	10. C	13. A	16. A	19. A	22. C	25. D	28. A
2. A	5. D	8. D	11. B	14. B	17. D	20. D	23. C	26. A	29. B
3. B	6. D	9. B	12. B	15. C	18. A	21. D	24. A	27. A	30. A

Unit 22

The Passive Voice

(1) was made   (2) was bought   (3) (was) moved   (4) were drawn up   (5) was limited   (6) was designed   (7) was built   (8) was covered   (9) were cut   (10) were visited   (11) was named   (12) was called   (13) was nicknamed   (14) was named   (15) was finished   (16) wasn't painted   (17) was/had been sent   (18) were moved   (19) were seen   (20) has been sold   (21) have been notified   (22) had just been promoted   (23) are both going to be employed/will both be employed   (24) will be allowed/are going to be allowed   (25) haven't been bothered/weren't bothered

2. The boy's father, Donald Derby . . .   3. Derby had run . . .   4. The boy was thrown . . .   5. Derby's daughter, Debbie, 3, was also in the car, but she was not . . .   6. The father was taken . . .   7. The driver of the bus . . .   8. He was taken to . . .   9. The Derbys were not . . .   10. Derby will be charged . . .

2. The meals get cooked.   3. The dishes get done.   4. Parks are getting designed.   5. Historic buildings are getting renovated.   6. Housing for poor people is getting built.   7. Classrooms got painted.   8. Trees got planted.   9. The cafeteria got remodeled.   10. Salaries will get cut./Salaries are going to get cut.   11. Employees will get laid off./Employees are going to get laid off.   12. New employees will not get hired./New employees are not going to get hired.

(1) got laid off   (2) got poisoned/was poisoned   (3) was served   (4) did not get delivered/were not delivered   (5) got lost/had gotten lost   (6) got confused   (7) got torn/was torn   (8) was interrupted/got interrupted   (9) got scared   (10) was going to be held/was held   (11) got put/was put

These are the phrases that should be crossed out.
Paragraph 1: by the turtles
Paragraph 2: by them; by the people; by the people
Paragraph 3: by them
Paragraph 4: by officials, by someone, by the government, by them

Unit 23

Phrasal Verbs

Answers may vary.
(1) didn't put on   (3) sat down   (4) put down   (5) cleans up   (6) picks up   (7) writes out   (8) turns out/turns off

1. put off   2. look up   3. write up   4. put on   5. help out   6. find out about   7. hand in   8. met up with   9. go out   10. woke up   11. got out

2. cleans up; takes out   3. turn down; music   4. turns off; turns on; television   5. set up; put off; meeting   6. call off; meeting; set up

2. . . . cleans her room up and takes the trash out   3. . . . turn that music down!   4. . . . turns the radio off and turns the TV on.   5. . . . set a meeting up . . . put the meeting off . . .   6. call the meeting off . . . set another meeting up

1. . . . to cheer her up.   2. I called her up . . .   3. . . . turned it on . . .   4. . . . take it back . . .   5. . . . get by with it.   6. No change possible.   7. . . . went over it . . .   8. . . . to throw it out.   9. He found it out.   10. . . . came across it

Answers will vary.
1. They forgot to turn them off.   2. . . . turn off all the electrical appliances before . . .   3. I called my family up on Sunday.

4. I called them up.   5. He quickly got off the horse.   6. He quickly got off it.   7. I took off my wet . . .   8. I took my shoes off.   9. I looked it up in the phone book.   10. I looked up the new address of the movie theater in the phone book.   11. She ran into her parents at the movies.   12. She ran into them at the movies.

Unit 24

Adjective Clauses and Participles as Adjectives

EXERCISE 1

1. . . . is a person who likes to talk about other people.
2. . . . are young people who are between the ages of thirteen and nineteen.   3. . . . are thieves who steal money from your pocket or purse . . .   4. . . . are people who think they're better than everyone else.   5. . . . is someone who doesn't drink alcohol.
6. . . . is someone who think(s) he knows everything.   7. . . . is a soldier who has the lowest rank in the army.   8. . . . is an individual who spends a lot of time watching TV.   9. . . . are people who are elderly.   10. . . . is a guy who's a lazy good-for-nothing.

EXERCISE 2

2. Dogs are pets that we call . . .   3. Piranhas are fish that people are . . . / . . . we see in hot . . .   4. The monkey is a wild animal that we see in the jungle . . .   5. The parrot is a colorful bird that we see in hot . . .   6. The polar bear is a big wild animal that we see living in ice . . . / . . . people are afraid of.   7. Cockroaches are insects that exterminators . . .
8. Dogs are domestic animals that scientists classify . . .
9. Piranhas are fish that we call carnivores . . .   10. The

monkey is a primate that scientists have . . .   11. The parrot is a multicolored bird that we find inhabiting tropical . . .
12. The polar bear is a mammal that we find inhabiting that arctic . . .

Conversational definitions: shorter than the written definitions; vocabulary is easier

Written definitions: longer than the conversational definitions; vocabulary is more difficult/scientific

EXERCISE 3

(1) experienced	(2) obsessed	(3) disciplined
(4) disappointed	(5) surprising	(6) covered
(7) shocked	(8) frustrated	(9) annoying
(10) exhausted	(11) worried	(12) relieved

EXERCISE 4

Answers will vary, with the following -ed/-ing forms for each verb.
1. surprised	2. frustrating	3. confused
4. exciting	5. worried	6. frightening
7. fascinating	8. embarrassed	9. annoyed
10. relieved		

Unit 25

Conditionals

EXERCISE 1

1. were; wouldn't have   2. would live/would be living; didn't have   3. would have; lived/were living   4. knew; would work/would be working; wouldn't work/wouldn't be working
5. went; would learn; (It's understood that he doesn't go to school.)   6. would live/would be living; had   7. would be; didn't have   8. were; would bring/could bring   9. would be; brought/could bring   10. were; would have

EXERCISE 2

Answers will vary.

EXERCISE 3

Answers will vary.

EXERCISE 4

In all of these answers, the main clause can come first, followed by the *if* clause (comma deleted). The following contractions are used: *would've (would have), hadn't (had not),* and *wouldn't (would not).*

1. If Mary hadn't met Gordon, she would've married . . .
2. If Gordon hadn't gone to medical school, he would've gone . . .
3. If Gordon hadn't become a doctor, he would've . . .
4. If Claudia hadn't had Mr. Stack for algebra, she wouldn't

have . . . **5.** If Mr. Stack hadn't been Claudia's teacher, Claudia would've . . . **6.** If Barb hadn't married Tom, she wouldn't have . . . **7.** If Barb hadn't know how to speak French and Spanish, she wouldn't have gotten . . . **8.** If Jan hadn't gotten pneumonia, she wouldn't have . . . **9.** If Jan hadn't moved to Arizona, she wouldn't have . . . **10.** If there had been birth control years ago, my grandmother wouldn't have had . . . **11–13.** Answers will vary.

EXERCISE 5

In all of these answers, the main clause can come first, followed by the *if* clause (no comma). The same contractions as those in Exercise 4 are used in these answers, plus *'d (would & had)*.

1. If I had seen her, I would've given . . . **2.** If I'd had some money, I would've gone . . . **3.** If I had known you were in the hospital, I would've visited . . . **4.** If we hadn't broken the law, we wouldn't have gotten . . . **5.** If I had known we were going to be so late, I would've called . . . **6.** If the cookies hadn't been there, I wouldn't have eaten . . . **7.** If you had been careful, you wouldn't have made . . . **8.** If Lexi had been at the meeting, we would've been . . . **9.** If I had had a car, I wouldn't have taken . . . **10.** If you hadn't told me the news, I wouldn't have known.

EXERCISE 6

In all of these answers, the main clause (with the name Eva) can come first, followed by the *if* clause (comma deleted).

1. If Eva moves to Tokyo, she'll . . . **2.** If Eva learns Japanese, she'll . . . **3.** If Eva marries Mack, she'll . . . **4.** If she lives in Fremont, she won't . . . **5.** If she doesn't leave Fremont, her life won't . . . **6.** If Eva marries Travis, she'll . . . **7.** If she lives in a mansion, she'll . . . **8.** If she doesn't feel like herself, she'll . . . **9.** If she marries Sato or Travis, her life will . . . **10.** If she doesn't get married, she won't . . .

EXERCISE 7

Answers will vary. The possible verb forms/tenses are indicated.
1. *will/be going to/can/might/may* + verb **2.** simple present tense **3.** *will/be going to/can/might/may* + verb

4. simple present tense **5.** *will/be going to/can/might/may* + verb **6.** simple present tense **7.** *will/be going to/can/might/may* + verb **8.** *will/be going to/can/might/may* + verb **9.** *will/be going to/can/might/may* + verb **10.** simple present tense

EXERCISE 8

ACROSS:
1. lightning **9.** FAA **10.** uno **12.** ow **14.** shins **15.** PR **16.** mew **18.** lei **19.** Eden **21.** sued **22.** bad **23.** hike **25.** okay **27.** INS **30.** yet **31.** N.C. **32.** spill **33.** RH **34.** tie **36.** horseshoe

DOWN:
2. if **3.** gas **4.** haha **5.** nuns **6.** INS **7.** No **8.** something **11.** Friday the **13.** wed **15.** pee **17.** weeks **18.** lucky **20.** cat **24.** Inc. **26.** aer **28.** apes **29.** ales **32.** sir **34 & 35.** to

EXERCISE 9

1, 3, 5, 6, and 10

EXERCISE 10

1. make a reservation **2.** don't eat your food in the restaurant **3.** order another round **4.** want more coffee **5.** order an appetizer **6.** like it cooked very little **7.** ask for the check **8.** ask for a doggy bag **9.** the service is all right **10.** ask for the manager

EXERCISE 11

1. G **2.** E **3.** H **4.** C **5.** F **6.** D **7.** A **8.** B

EXERCISE 12

1. I felt a lump . . . **2.** he might have died. **3.** I see anything . . . **4.** I call . . . **5.** I hadn't quit . . . **6.** I might have . . . **7.** I had the flu. **8.** you have . . . **9.** the doctors hadn't . . .

Exercises for the TOEFL® Test
Units 22–25 Answer Key

1. A	**4.** C	**7.** B	**10.** D	**13.** D	**16.** C	**19.** C	**22.** C	**25.** C	**28.** B
2. A	**5.** C	**8.** C	**11.** A	**14.** A	**17.** D	**20.** B	**23.** B	**26.** D	**29.** C
3. B	**6.** B	**9.** B	**12.** D	**15.** B	**18.** A	**21.** D	**24.** B	**27.** C	

TAPESCRIPT

Unit 1 (Activity 3)

Speaker 1 (man): Tell me what happens on this holiday where you live.

Speaker 2 (man): Well, I live near New York City, and in midtown Manhattan, I think it's on Fifth Avenue, there is a huge parade on this day in New York, and you don't have to be Irish to celebrate in this parade. Most people wear green and they're in a very festive mood, and it's a huge deal in New York.

Speaker 1: Uh-huh. Any kind of special food eaten on this day?

Speaker 2: Yes. As a matter of fact, if you're Irish, especially, people like to eat—oh, what is it?—not sauerbraten, that's German . . .

Speaker 1: Corned beef and cabbage.

Speaker 2: Thank you, corned beef and cabbage. I don't usually do it myself, but if you go in restaurants or homes of Irish families, certainly for dinner or maybe even for lunch, you would have corned beef and cabbage.

Speaker 1: Sounds great. Now, for our next holiday, is there any special food eaten on this holiday?

Speaker 3 (woman): Oh, yeah. Food is the most important thing about this holiday.

Speaker 1: Is it?

Speaker 3: Oh, yeah. You eat a big turkey, you eat a lot of potatoes, yams, yams are always eaten, you eat a lot of vegetables, and you eat a big pie, usually pumpkin pie.

Speaker 1: Is this the holiday with cranberry sauce?

Speaker 3: Oh, that's right, cranberry sauce. I forgot about cranberry sauce. You have to eat that, too.

Speaker 1: Mmm, sounds great.

Speaker 3: Yeah, it's delicious.

Speaker 1: What about customs on a day like this?

Speaker 3: Um, customs. Well, it's really important that you get together with family and friends and people you care about and that you give thanks for everything that you have.

Speaker 1: Is this an official holiday? Do people get the day off from work and all of that?

Speaker 3: Oh, it's an important holiday. Yeah, usually you do get the day off from work and school, and it's a public holiday.

Speaker 1: That sounds warm and wonderful. A real family get-together. OK. Now, for this next holiday, is it true that the kids love it especially?

Speaker 4: (woman): It's a great time for kids, Kids dress up, parents make costumes, kids go trick-or-treating.

Speaker 1: Well, these costumes are kind of interesting, aren't they?

Speaker 4: Yes, kids are witches, kids dress up as princesses, princes, swordsmen, um, whatever you want to be.

Speaker 1: Oh, that's wonderful, that's terrific. This happens once a year?

Speaker 4: This happens once a year, right.

Speaker 1: Fascinating.

Speaker 4: Yeah.

Unit 2 (Activity 1)

Man: Every year around this time, middle of the summer season, people all over North America go to country fairs. This week, as part of our series on life in small-town America, Marcia Chandler is traveling around country fairs and telling us about the sights and sounds. Today she is in Petaluma, a small town in northern California. Marcia?

(*background sound of fair/crowds*)

Marcia: Petaluma holds its country fair every June, and every June farmers from all over the county bring their finest animals: cows, bulls, pigs, horses, even llamas, to compete in the show. But that's not all that happens here. Right now I'm standing by the fruit and produce hall. Oh, what a display? Magnificent piles of fruit and vegetables. The judges are looking at the tomatoes and are trying to decide which one to award First Prize to. Bill Andretti right here beside me is looking anxiously at his tomatoes. He brings vegetables to the show every year and usually wins several prizes, so he's hoping for another one today. Good luck, Mr. Andretti.

OK, let's move outside. Let's see what's going on. Oh, some musicians right over here are under the trees, and they're just starting to play. Oh, yes, there's quite a crowd. People are gathering around, clapping their hands, having fun. Ah, yes, and there are a few people who are dancing. That looks like so much fun.

OK, ah, what else? Over here to my left, oh, the baked goods! I'm getting hungry here. Cakes, cookies, oh, bread, freshly baked bread. Oooh, what's this? Someone's giving me a slice of cake. Oh, thank you. Mmm. Oh, chocolate cake, oh, mmm, this is wonderful, delicious. Mrs. Jill Anderson's secret recipe. Thank you, Mrs. Anderson.

OK, and over here right in front of me there are some—oh, wow, here's a cowboy, a real cowboy! He's riding past. (fade out) Oh, well, let's follow him and see where he's going. Oh, oh, he's going right over to this corral. There's going to be a western show. Let's follow.

Unit 3 (Activity 4)

Speaker 1: Do you have any plans for the future?

Speaker 2: Oh sure. Once I graduate from college, I'm going to take a trip to Europe.

Speaker 1: Any country in particular?

Speaker 2: Well, I was thinking of going to Prague maybe in Czechoslovakia. I'm going to stay for awhile. And I'll write to my friends back home. And I thought while I was there from Prague I'm going to get one of those train tickets, I'm going to get a Eurail Pass.

Speaker 1: Mm-hmm, a Eurail.

Speaker 2: Uh-huh, and in order to make it affordable I'm going to try to get a job.

Speaker 1: Oh, that's great. Any idea of uh, what kind of job you might be looking for?

Speaker 2: Well, I was an English major, I was thinking maybe I'd get a job teaching English.

Speaker 1: Great. That's nice. Thank you; thanks. Now my next student is a high school graduate and I'd like to ask her if she has any special plans following her graduation.

Speaker 3: Yes I do; I have lots of plans. But I can also tell you one thing I won't do—I won't stay home this summer. I'm not going to study or work this summer either.

Speaker 1: Well, do you have any idea what you do, want to do this summer?

Speaker 3: Yes, I'm going to go to summer camp. Yeah, I'm going to relax a lot. It's really great because I go back every summer. I've gone to the same camp for like 10–12 years and, all my friends are there and it's great because you get to be outside all the time and play sports, I really like to play sports. And it's also very social because it's a coed camp. It's really, really fun. It's going to be terrific.

Speaker 1: That's a great way to spend the summer. Have you had any thought in terms of what you're going to do about your career?

Speaker 3: When September comes next year I'll go back to school and I'll probably study liberal arts in college because I'm not sure exactly what it is I want to do and I think liberal arts is a great overall education.

Speaker 1: Yes, that will give you a good overview. OK, well thank you, that's very good. Thanks for sharing those thoughts about college, and liberal arts, and your future. Now my next guest here is a young fellow and I'd like to ask him what his plans are for his education, college and career.

Speaker 4: I'll probably be a lawyer. I'll get married, have a couple kids, a girl and a boy. And we'll have a good life together. I'm not going to make any decisions for my kids. They're going to make all their own decisions.

Speaker 1 (man): Well, that's great. I think they'll really appreciate that. Thank you very much!

Unit 4 (Activity 6)

Lisa: Hello?

(*pause*)

Lisa: Yes, this is she.

(*pause*)

Lisa: Oh, hi.

(*pause*)

Lisa: Yeah, I speak three, actually: Spanish, German and Italian.

(*pause*)

Lisa: Yes, that's right. I'm currently teaching English for international business here at Perry College.

(*pause*)

Lisa: Ah, from Asia, mostly. Most of them come from Japan and Taiwan.

(*pause*)

Lisa: Ah, well, they usually stay between three and six months.

(*pause*)

Lisa: Before this job? I taught English in a private language school in Italy, in Milan.

(pause)

Lisa: No, I didn't teach any business classes there. Mostly conversation classes and classes in American culture.

(pause)

Lisa: Um, that was from 1991 to 1993.

(with Gary's conversation)

Lisa: Hello?

Gary: Yes, hello. Is this Lisa Hartman?

Lisa: Yes, this is she.

Gary: Hi, Lisa, this is Gary Berman with Riga Language Academy calling about the job you applied for.

Lisa: Oh, hi.

Gary: Hi. Lisa, as you know, we'd like a little more information about your background and experience—questions we ask everybody. OK. First of all, do you speak any foreign languages?

Lisa: Yeah, I speak three, actually: Spanish, German and Italian.

Gary: Oh, great. And right now you're teaching at Perry College, aren't you?

Lisa: Yes, that's right. I'm currently teaching English for international business here at Perry College.

Gary: Mm-hmm, interesting. Where do your students come from?

Lisa: Ah, from Asia, mostly. Most of them come from Japan and Taiwan.

Gary: Mm-hmm. And how long do they stay?

Lisa: Ah, well, they usually stay between three and six months.

Gary: And what did you do before this job?

Lisa: Before this job? I taught English in a private language school in Italy, in Milan.

Gary: Oh. So did you teach business English there, too?

Lisa: No, I didn't teach any business classes there. Mostly conversation classes and classes in American culture.

Gary: Mm-hmm. And when was this, when did you work there?

Lisa: Um, that was from 1991 to 1993.

Unit 5 (Activity 5)

Speaker 1 (woman): Well, this woman might be looking out her window. There might be blinds. And that might be her boyfriend pulling up and getting out of his car in the parking lot. It appears that it might be her boyfriend walking up a set of circular stairs, and I think it might be the boyfriend falling down the stairs on what looks like what could be a skateboard. And then I think the woman probably heard the noise and ran out her front door which was left ajar.

Speaker 2 (man): I think what is here is a little girl that is looking out a window. And here we see someone running very quickly up a set of stairs. Now here this looks like someone's hand over the top of the stairs and maybe he's falling and his hand is sticking up as he tries to steady himself. And here we have someone getting out of a car. I think he might be coming to visit the girl that we saw going up the stairs. This appears to be a door. Maybe this is the door to the apartment where the girl lives. I think this might be a story about a little girl and her uncle coming to visit her in her apartment.

Unit 6 (Activity 5)

Speaker 1 (woman): What were you doing when you heard the news of President Kennedy's death?

Speaker 2 (woman): I was ironing my husband's pants, and I couldn't believe it. I thought it was a joke. It just devastated me. All I remember is that I was ironing pants. I think it was a Friday afternoon. I was a Cal graduate and living in Los Angeles at the time, and I sat down and cried. I couldn't believe I was crying. And then when my husband came, I mean, because I had three little kids, I went to church.

Speaker 1: These stories, they're just so moving to hear all the different stories. Do you remember what you were doing when you heard the news of President Kennedy's death?

Speaker 3 (man): I was living in England. I was very young.

Speaker 1: Uh-huh.

Speaker 3: I remember it was the middle of the afternoon and I heard it on the radio, and I was standing by a fish tank with tropical fish in it. And I remember I ran and told my father.

Speaker 1: What were you doing when you heard the news of President Kennedy's death?

Speaker 4 (man): Well, I remember that day very well. I was working at an advertising agency in Phoenix, Arizona. And a sales rep came into the office and told me that Kennedy was dead. I remember thinking that it couldn't be true. I didn't believe him. And it was only after that, as we turned on the radio and got the news, that little by little we absorbed the truth, that he was actually, had actually been shot and was dead. It was a horrible afternoon.

Unit 7 (Activity 4)

Speaker 1 (woman): OK. So how many differences between a pizza and a hot dog did you find?

Speaker 2 (man): I didn't count them, but there are lots of differences.

Speaker 1: There's about 20, I think. We got here.

Speaker 2: At least.

Speaker 3 (woman): Uh-huh.

Speaker 2: Yeah.

Speaker 1: What are some of them?

Speaker 3: Well, first of all, a hot dog is longer.

Speaker 1: Uh-huh.

Speaker 3: Pizza's rounder.

Speaker 2: Right. And a pizza has more variety, you know, you have a lot of different toppings on a pizza.

Speaker 3: Yeah, pizza has more bread, more toppings, it's healthier than hot dogs.

Speaker 2: I guess less fattening.

Speaker 3: Yeah, well, no, I think it's more fattening.

Speaker 2: More fattening?

Speaker 3: I think it is. But it's better for parties.

Speaker 2: Sure. A hot dog is great if you're at a ball game and you don't have much time.

Speaker 3: Yeah.

Speaker 2: And you can eat it standing up.

Speaker 3: Yeah, and you can eat a hot dog in fewer bites than you can eat a piece of pizza.

Speaker 2: And if you're going somewhere, you're walking along

Speaker 3: Yeah, it's easier to eat.

Speaker 2: Going to a shop or job or something.

Speaker 3: Yeah, yeah.

Speaker 2: You can eat a hot dog easily.

Speaker 3: But you can't flip a hot dog.

Speaker 2: You can't flip it, no.

Speaker 1: No, no.

Speaker 2: Pizza is kind of better to look at, more interesting to look at, I think, with all those different toppings.

Speaker 3: Yeah, you get more to choose from.

Speaker 1: Uh-huh.

Speaker 2: Vegetables and things.

Speaker 3: And it's cheesier.

Unit 8 (Activity 5)

Jeff: Hello.

Eliza: Hi, Jeff?

Jeff: Yeah.

Eliza: It's Eliza.

Jeff: Hi, how are you?

Eliza: Hi, I need your help desperately.

Jeff: What's the matter?

Eliza: Well, I'm cooking Thanksgiving dinner for the first time for my entire family, and I don't know how to make stuffing, and I know that you make a great stuffing.

Jeff: Oh, yeah. Let me—it's really easy.

Eliza: OK.

Jeff: First, in as little oil as possible, like a tablespoon, saute a pepper, an onion, and about a pound of diced mushrooms.

Eliza: OK

Jeff: Let them reduce. Throw in a tablespoon of tarragon and some ground black pepper.

Eliza: Uh-huh.

Jeff: Then when it cools throw it in a bowl with your cubed bread, the stuffing.

Eliza: Right.

Jeff: Um, then add one beaten egg.

Eliza: Mm-hmm.

Jeff: And a little bit of ground parmesan cheese.

Eliza: Oh, sounds delicious.

Jeff: It's really good, and it's fat-free except for the oil.

Eliza: Wow, great!

Jeff: Good luck!

Eliza: Thank you.

Jeff: Let me know.

Eliza: OK.

Jeff: OK.

Unit 9 (Activity 6)

Speaker 1 (man): I think the whole thing, the whole overpopulation issue it's really a myth, and I think the dangers are very greatly exaggerated.

Speaker 2 (woman): I actually don't agree with you on this one at all because I really think that it's the most serious problem that we have to solve for the 21st century.

Speaker 1: Really?

Speaker 2: Yeah! I mean, I think that we really, we really have to do something about it. It's too important an issue to ignore. People are just having too many children, and some people don't even have enough money to raise a big family!

Speaker 1: Well, I do think that we can grow enough food for everybody if we just try. You see, people are too pessimistic. Take the media, they just give too much publicity to all this stuff about global warming and not enough resources. No wonder everybody, everybody is upset because they just believe everything they read in the papers and see on TV.

Speaker 2: Well, I don't know, I mean I think you may be a little too hopeful. I mean I think there really are too many people in urban areas and I think that if you look at pollution; look at how many cars there are; the air we breathe; it's just not healthy.

Speaker 1: You see, I think you're being very pessimistic. I just feel that the world probably regenerates itself better than we think and that the world is very big and its resources are great and very powerful.

Speaker 2: I do think that the world's resources are great, but I think that we need to take better care of them.

Speaker 1 (man): OK.

Unit 10 (Activity 7)

Man: So you think that smoking should be banned in all public places?

Woman: Yes, that's right, all public places. That means restaurants, places of business, public bathrooms. I just feel that people need to feel that they can enjoy a meal in surroundings where people are not likely to smoke.

Man: You think that restaurants ought to be smoke-free?

Woman: That's right, restaurants definitely should be smoke-free.

Man: And people need to feel that they can have an enjoyable meal where there's no smoking?

Woman: That's exactly what I feel. And I also feel that drug stores and restaurants shouldn't sell cigarettes and that there should be special stores where cigarettes are sold and that way they can be strictly controlled.

Man: You mean like the government should set up a special group of stores, chain of stores, which are controlled by the government.

Woman: That's right, I think the government should do that.

Man: What about education, do we need to educate young people about the dangers of smoking?

Woman: Oh, absolutely we need to educate young people about the dangers of smoking, particularly I think it's the parents' responsibility, not the schools' and teachers'. They shouldn't do this. The parents should teach their children that smoking is dangerous.

Man: So you believe that the school and the teacher shouldn't do this, but the parents should?

Woman: That's what I believe. I think it starts in the home.

Man: What about advertising? Do you think that cigarette companies should be able to, you know, advertise or should not be able to advertise?

Woman: Oh, absolutely. I think it's very important that cigarette companies shouldn't sponsor any kind of sporting event. I think this is particularly bad for young people.

Man: So there should be a law, in your opinion, that cigarette companies should not be able to sponsor sporting events?

Woman: Yes, I think you could go that far. The government should get involved.

Man: Mm-hmm. What about medical research, should there be more medical research on the dangers of smoking?

Woman: Yes, once again, I think the government ought to spend more money on helping people to stop smoking, and that means they should do much more medical research and they need to research particularly I think the addiction and how people become addicted to smoking. I think banning smoking is not enough. I think we need to think about how to treat the problem.

Man: So, in your opinion, we need to understand how to help people learn how to fight this addiction . . . and banning smoking isn't enough.

Unit 11 (Activity 4)

Man: Oh, well, I don't know a lot about it, but I think one way is simply if you're born here in this country, your parents don't have to be from here. They don't have to have been born here. But if you are, then you automatically are a citizen.

Woman: Uh-huh.

Man: Another way is you have to get a green card, and I think after a certain amount of time having a green card, you have to take a test.

Woman: Mm-hmm.

Man: The test covers I think language skills and the American Constitution, perhaps history, and then I think you have to go to a special ceremony and probably do the Pledge of Allegiance.

Woman: Mm-hmm.

Man: Yeah, those are the only ways I know of.

Unit 12 (Activity 5)

Speaker 2 (woman): I love to go to baseball games.

Speaker 1 (man): Oh yeah, I do too. You know, I get so hungry I always eat about three hot dogs when I go to a ball game.

Speaker 2: So do I. Ketchup, mustard...

Speaker 3: Three hot dogs! Wow! You guys!

Speaker 2: But you know what, I have to say, I don't like to watch football on TV.

Speaker 3: Oh, I don't either.

Speaker 2: Why not?

Speaker 3: It's so boring! Oh it takes forever! I don't even understand first and ten, all these downs.

Speaker 2: I know; I don't get that either. I don't understand that at all.

Speaker 3: No, it's silly.

Speaker 2: Well, do you play any sports? Like do you play baseball?

Speaker 3: No, I've never played baseball.

Speaker 2: Neither do I.

Speaker 3: Huh.

Speaker 2: Oh! You know, do you like watching soccer on TV?
Speaker 1: Well, kind of. But I'd rather watch a football game. American football, that is. Not soccer.
Speaker 2: Bill, do you like jogging?

Speaker 1: Well, sort of.. I'd rather play tennis, at least you get to hit a ball back and forth.
Speaker 2: Yeah, that's fun; I like that too!

Unit 13 (Activity 4)

Interviewer: How long have you worked as a word processor?
Patrick: I've been at Smithton and Banks' firm for seven years now. Wow, it's hard to believe since 1989. And during that time in my role as office manager, office manager is really not an appropriate role, I've done a lot more than just manage the office. I've overhauled the whole systems management, I've reorganized the EDS, electronic document storage system, and I've also implemented new, more efficient software.

Interviewer: OK. What software have you implemented?
Patrick: They were using something else, and I've switched us over to Microsoft Word.
Interviewer: What were you using previously?
Patrick: Syntrex, which was getting pretty dated.
Interviewer: Mm-hmm.

Unit 14 (Activity 8)

Speaker 1 (woman): So it sounds like you've traveled a lot. Where, France—
Speaker 2 (man): I've traveled mostly in Europe, western Europe.
Speaker 1: Wow!
Speaker 2: France, Italy, Spain. And where have you traveled?
Speaker 1: I've traveled a lot in Italy and a little bit in France and a lot of, you know, backpacking and that kind of thing. That's how I traveled.
Speaker 2: When? In the summer, fall, winter—
Speaker 1: Well, mostly in the spring and summer when I was in my 20s, you know, late 20s.
Speaker 2: And as far as transportation, did you ever use a train or plane or was it always on foot?
Speaker 1: No, I'd fly over there. I certainly couldn't walk.
Speaker 2: You couldn't swim the Atlantic, no.
Speaker 1: But I, yeah, mostly backpacking but, you know, I'd take the train, sure. You, what did you do? How did you travel?
Speaker 2: Well, I'm a lazy guy, and I drove when I was out in the countryside, and of course I flew over to Europe, but then I would taxi in the big cities and get a car and drive where I wanted to go.
Speaker 1: How much time did you spend in these countries?

Speaker 2: I would try to get at least three weeks so I didn't feel rushed.
Speaker 1: Oh, that's great.
Speaker 2: I like to do it sort of on the spur of the moment. Did you stay in hostels—
Speaker 1: Yeah, and sometimes just, you know, under the stars. And you?
Speaker 2: So in good weather you'd actually camp out and sleep out in some farmer's field?
Speaker 1: Yeah. That's right, in a barn somewhere, we'd knock on the door and ask if that was OK. You know, in Europe they're pretty hospitable too—
Speaker 2: Yeah, they understand that, that they're welcoming to the backpacker and—
Speaker 1: Yeah, they're pretty used to us. And you, where did you stay? Did you ever—I bet you never backpacked?
Speaker 2: Oh, no, no, no, no. I love my comfort.
Speaker 1: So have you ever stayed in a hostel or inexpensive hotel?
Speaker 2: No, I never have.
Speaker 1: Wow.

Unit 15 (Activity 4)

Man: Amy, it is so good to see you. I can't believe we haven't run into each other before.
Woman: I know. How long have you lived here?
Man: Six years.
Woman: My God.
Man: Yeah, since 1990 I moved here.
Woman: I've been here for about five years.
Man: That's amazing. And you work just around the block?
Woman: Yes, I do.
Man: Wow. What have you been doing?
Woman: Well, I work as an editor.

Man: Uh-huh.
Woman: So, that's really been going really well.
Man: Good.
Woman: It's a lot of long hours. I've also been on—I took sailing lessons.
Man: Oh, terrific. Good, good, good. . . , Are you still mountain climbing, too?
Woman: I am, I do mountain climb.
Man: That's great, oh, that's terrific. How's Eddy?
Woman: Eddy is great. Eddy is really terrific.
Man: Good. What's he up to?

Woman: He is working in a law firm, he works really, really long hours, and we have a daughter.

Man: Oh, congratulations! I had no idea.

Woman: Thank you.

Man: How old is she now?

Woman: Her name is Sarah, she's five, and she's beautiful.

Man: Oh, gosh, I haven't seen you for so long.

Woman: I know. What are you doing?

Man: Well, I have two children.

Woman: You do? Oh, that's great!

Man: I've been busy being a dad, yes, when I'm not you know, doing the dry cleaning thing.

Woman: So, are you still doing the dry cleaning thing?

Man: Yeah, I'm up to four stores now. We just opened one in Somerville.

Woman: Is your wife working with you?

Man: Yeah, yeah, when she can, you know, when she's not with the kids.

Woman: Oh, I know—

Man: Yeah, Michael and Katie. Michael's four and Katie's about to turn one.

Woman: Oh, that's great. Well, I'm literally running to a PTA meeting, so—

Man: Great to see you. I know where you work now, I'll call you.

Woman: OK, great.

Man: Good to see you. Bye.

Woman: Bye.

Unit 16 (Activity 3)

Woman: Hi.

Man: Hi; thanks for coming early and helping me set up.

Woman: No problem.

Man: I really want this to be a good party.

Woman: Oh, don't worry, it will be.

Man: Well, I'm kind of nervous about it. Can I ask your advice?

Woman: Sure.

Man: What should I do if I run out of coffee?

Woman: Oh, well why don't you say, "Would you like some tea instead? We have plenty."

Man: What should I do if I run out of food?

Woman: Well, you could say, "Would you like me to order pizza? It's no trouble."

Man: Thank you; those are good ideas.

Woman: Sure! Is there anything else I can help you with?

Man: You know what I have a problem with sometimes? Getting people to get up to dance. They just sit there. What can I do if no one dances?

Woman: Well, you know a lot of times the problem is the music. You could just say, "Do you want me to change the music? What would you like to hear?"

Man: Oh, that's a great idea. Hey, what can I do if Jim starts playing the piano?

Woman: Oh, Jim! Well, you can ask people, "Would you like Jim to stop playing?"

Man: An, good thinking. Thanks!

Woman: You're welcome! Now relax; let's just enjoy the party!

Unit 17 (Activity 6)

Man: Question No. 1: Agnes, you are in the book store with a friend standing in line to buy a text book that you need for class later that day. You realize that you've left your wallet at home and you want your friend to lend you $20 to pay for the book. What do you do?

Agnes: Oh, I would say, "Oh, my God, I left my wallet home. Please give me some money."

Man: Eliza, same question.

Eliza: I would say, "I left my wallet at home. Would you be able to lend me some money?"

Man: Great. Question No. 2: Agnes, you've just heard about a new teaching assistanceship in your field and you feel that you're qualified. You need to ask your teacher for a letter of recommendation. How do you do that?

Agnes: I would say, "I heard there's a teaching assistantship in the next district and I really would like this job. I'm qualified.

Could you please write me a letter of recommendation? I need one."

Man: Good. Eliza, same question.

Eliza: I think I would do the same thing. I'd explain how much I wanted the teaching assistanceship, and then I would ask him or her if they would be so kind as to write me a recommendation.

Man: Good. Question No. 6 Eliza, you are visiting a close friend's elderly mother. She has made a peach pie, and you'd love to have a second piece. Your friend has told you that her mother loves to feed people, so you know that it wouldn't be rude to ask for another piece. What do you do?

Eliza: I would say, "This is the best peach pie I have ever eaten. Could I have a second piece?"

Man: Flatter her into a second piece. Larry, same question.

Larry: Oh, I love peach pie, and knowing she loves to feed people, I wouldn't hesitate to ask for a second piece.

Unit 18 (Activity 5)

Speaker 1 (man): Since you have decades more experience of the world than I have, can you tell me in your lifetime what changes have you seen?

Speaker 2 (man): Well, I think the computer has changed things more since I was a young man than anything else. It's amazing how fast you can get information. You go to the doctor's office and they press a couple of buttons and they find out when you were last there and what medication you're on and stuff like that.

Speaker 3 (woman): When I first got married, using the telephone was too expensive. I used to write my family.

Speaker 1: Really?

Speaker 3: Yes, of course. Absolutely.

Speaker 1: Do you think people don't write letters anymore?

Speaker 3: Ah, no, but I believe that it's probably sent by, you know, what is that called?

Speaker 1: Email?

Speaker 3: Yes, electronic mail.

Speaker 1: Well, it's the computer again.

Speaker 3: Yes, yes.

Speaker 1: What other changes?

Speaker 2: Well, I think things have sped up kind of generally, like isn't there an airplane that can fly you from New York City to London in like three hours?

Speaker 3: Oh, yes.

Speaker 1: That's the Concorde.

Speaker 2: The Concorde, that's it.

Speaker 3: And even everyday things, you know, like going shopping. I didn't go shopping in big supermarkets. I went from store to store. I went to the butcher and the produce man and the butter and egg man.

Speaker 2: And there's less use of cash these days, you know, you give them a credit card and push it through a slot—

Speaker 3: Absolutely.

Speaker 2: And they know what your account balance is.

Speaker 3: Right. And I had a running bill at my grocer's. Really, I mean—

Speaker 1: You mean you bought groceries on credit?

Speaker 3: Oh, absolutely. He knew everyone in the neighborhood.

Unit 19 (Activity 5)

Man: So Harriet, tell me about your life.

Harriet: Oh, gosh. Well, my mother was always sick when I was little. By the time I was in the third grade, my mother had died.

Man: Oh, so young.

Harriet: Yeah, I think it was in 1941 when she passed away. And then I finished high school in 1950.

Man: Was high school a very important part of your life?

Harriet: Well, you know, I was still getting over my mother's death actually. It was rough. But, then after I finished high school, Ralph and I got married. That was a very special time in my life, and that was in 1952.

Man: So you got married just two years out of high school.

Harriet: Right, right, Ralph wanted to go to college, so I got a job in an office and then I worked and he went to college.

Man: So you supported him throughout that time.

Harriet: I sure did, I did indeed and by the time he finished college, I was 25 years old. Yes and you know, by then, I was ready to have children. Yes, so we did. Our first child, little Annie, was born in 1955. By the time she was two years old, we had a second child. Little Richard-he's a doll! He was born in 1956. And then Ralph got a new job in 1958. And actually that wasn't such a good thing because he started working day and night.

Man: So you didn't see very much of him.

Harriet: Not at all. The kids were asleep by the time he got home at night. And so they never saw him and I never saw him either. And we got a divorce in 1960. And you know at that time, divorces were not as common as they are now.

Man: Oh, I know, that's true.

Unit 20 (Activity 6)

Man: So Amy, what was one of your favorite toys growing up?

Woman: Well, I liked dolls. I had some dolls.

Man: Which ones?

Woman: I had a Barbie doll that I really loved. [yeah, you know] I think that was my favorite toy. I have to say it was hard to give up playing with it [you know] when I knew it was time to stop playing with my dolls.

Man: Did you have a Ken Doll, too?

Woman: Yes, I did. You know what else? I also had the Barbie Dollhouse. I would make up stories about Barbie and Ken. I loved playing with my dolls; it was great. Did you, did you have a favorite toy?

Man: I loved playing with trucks. Did you like trucks?

Woman: No, but I'll tell you something. My brother had some trucks and I remember now—he had this big red truck and he used to give my dolls rides in it.

Man: I had trucks under my bed, trucks in the closet, trucks all over the place. They were my favorite toys.

Woman: Did you have the Hess truck—you know, the truck they advertised on TV every Christmas?

Man: I know the one you mean. No, no, but I did have a Jeep. It was an orange Jeep. It was my favorite toy. I still have it. Wow! It's funny what you remember!

Woman: Yes, it is, isn't it?

Unit 21 (Activity 4)

Man: Maria, where are you living these days?

Woman: I've been in South America for three years. I live in Rio De Janeiro.

Man: No kidding! Do you like living in Rio?

Woman: Sure! The people are so nice and there's so much to see!

Man: I've always heard it's beautiful there. Can you tell us about some of the places you really love?

Woman: There are a lot of places. Well, there's City Park. It's on Santa Marinha Street.

Man: What's special about City Park?

Woman: It has a beautiful view of Leblon Beach. You can also visit the City Historic Museum in City Park.

Man: What else is there to see?

Woman: Let me see. Everyone wants to go to Sugar Loaf Mountain. There's a beautiful view of the city from there, too.

Man: Sugar Loaf Mountain. That's the mountain with the cross on top.

Woman: Yes, exactly. How did you know?

Man: Oh, I've seen pictures. What's your favorite beach?

Woman: Well, I love swimming at Ipanema Beach. I think it's the most beautiful beach on the Atlantic Ocean.

Unit 22 (Activity 5)

Woman: So Larry, Paul told me you got ripped off a couple of weeks ago. What happened?

Larry: You won't believe this. I was actually in a bank making out a deposit slip, and I had a briefcase between my legs on the floor, and I was concentrating on what I was doing, right? And I felt something moving against my, my pants, and I wasn't terribly aware, until I looked down and my briefcase was gone.

Woman: Wow, that's terrible!

Larry: Which contained important papers, it contained my cell phone, and I looked around . . .

Woman: So that was all taken?

Larry: It was entirely taken. I looked around and the thief had left. I don't know whether this person was hiding somewhere in the bank or handed off the briefcase to somebody that left out on the street, but I was absolutely panic-stricken.

Woman: Sure.

Larry: And important things were taken. And . . .

Woman: So what did you do?

Larry: Well, first I went to the bank guard who hadn't seen anything. Then I went to the bank manager, I filed a report, and then I had to go back to work.

Woman: Well, Larry, the reason I'm asking you about this is because my house was broken into last week.

Larry: I heard about that.

Woman: Oh, it was . . .

Larry: What got taken?

Woman: Everything got taken. I mean, everything. We were gone maybe—

Larry: Nothing got left? I mean, all the valuables got taken?

Woman: Television, stereo, jewelry, money, you know, just everything was taken.

Larry: Was the back door broken into or . . .

Woman: No, I think they got in through a fire escape in the window, and we were only gone, I don't know, an hour and a half, and in that time they took everything.

Unit 23 (Activity 3)

Woman: So Jeff, what's your morning routine? What do you do from the moment you wake up?

Jeff: Um, I usually wake up around the same time every morning, around 5:30, and I turn on the radio and listen to the news for a bit and then I get up. And I usually put on an old pair of sweats and a tee shirt, sweatshirt and I go out and run.

Woman: Oh.

Jeff: I leave the house around 6:00, so I get back around 6:30 or so, and then I put on some real loud music. I turn it up really loud.

Woman: Oh.

Jeff: Well, I don't have any neighbors close by so it doesn't matter.

Take off my running clothes and jump in the shower and sing along with the music.

Woman: Oh, that must be pretty.

Jeff: Like I said, there are no neighbors. And after my shower I get dressed and I go into the kitchen and make breakfast. I always make myself a pot of tea and then have a bowl of cereal and some fruit and when my tea is ready I sit down and I read the paper for about ten minutes. And then I put all the breakfast stuff away and I go and brush my teeth, make sure that I've turned off all the lights, and put on my coat and walk to the station.

Woman: Well, that's a pretty full morning. What about you, Agnes, what do you do?

Agnes: Well, I set my alarm for 7:00. I don't like it, but I do. And as soon as it goes off, I usually turn over and go right back to sleep for another 20 minutes or so.

Woman: That's just like me.

Agnes: Oh, really, I hate to actually get out of bed, and I put it off until the last minute. But I usually get up around 7:30, sometimes even later. So the first thing I do is go into the kitchen and make myself a cup of coffee, and then I turn on the TV. I watch the news or a breakfast show for a few minutes. And then I take a shower, very quick one, and then I get dressed, I put on my make-up, do my hair, and if I have time I grab something to eat, but usually I don't. (fade out) I'm just running around too much because I have to get to the bus stop and get on the bus at 8:15.

Unit 24 (Activity 4)

Lee: Oh, here's a good one. Pat, what would you say your ideal partner would be like?

Pat: Hmmm, oh, God. Well, let me see. My ideal partner would be someone who is amusing, definitely amusing. I mean, he has to be someone who would be funny. That's important for me. That's the most important thing. I mean, not that, you know, I don't want him to be ugly, but . . .

Lee: Right.

Pat: But he should be someone who has a sense of humor, who likes to laugh, who likes to be silly. Someone who's silly. What about you?

Lee: My ideal partner? Just like me. No, I'm kidding. No, I think someone who is pretty attractive, I mean, I have to admit it, it sounds shallow, but looks are important to me. But I think intelligent and a sense of humor and a real dedication to the relationship I think is important, but yeah, humor helps get through a relationship.

Pat: Oh, yeah.

Lee: Yeah, so that's my story and I'm sticking to it. What about you, Chris?

Chris: My ideal mate would have to be a person that is taller than I am, and when you're six-one that's not easy, and he'd have to be dark, I don't want a person who's blond or a red-head. I just don't find them attractive. And someone who makes me laugh. That's the most important.

Pat: That's the key.

Chris: Yeah, a commonality.

Unit 25 (Activity 7)

Speaker 1 (woman): If you had to choose three objects to represent American culture at the end of the twentieth century, which ones would you choose?

Speaker 2 (man): Well, I think I'd choose a copy of the New York Times and a laptop computer, and I think an autographed major league baseball.

Speaker 1: Why would you choose the baseball?

Speaker 2: Well, baseball is the American national game, it's played everywhere.

Speaker 1: Right, right.

Speaker 2: And the baseball is the symbol, and I'd have some famous baseball players autograph it, sign it.

Speaker 1: Well, if you had to choose one, of all three, which one would you choose if you had to make a decision?

Speaker 2: Oh, I'd have to choose I think a copy of the New York Times, the most read paper, in terms of importance, in the country.

Speaker 1: Mm-hmm.

Speaker 2: Definitely include that.

Speaker 1: Good. What would you choose to represent American culture at the end of the twentieth century if you had to choose three objects?

Speaker 3 (woman): I guess I'd choose a pair of jeans, Levi's, a Big Mac, and a copy of the TV Guide.

Speaker 1: And which do you think is like the most important if you had to choose?

Speaker 3: I guess the TV Guide would give the most information. So I guess if I could only put one object in the time capsule I would choose that.

Speaker 1: Yeah, that sounds good. I agree.